PENGUIN BOOKS

THE PENGUIN COMPANION TO TROLLOPE

Dr Richard Mullen's *Anthony Trollope: A Victorian in His World* (1990) won widespread critical acclaim and was awarded the *Yorkshire Post* Book of the Year Award. He has edited several works by Anthony Trollope and his mother, Fanny, and has written many programmes for the BBC including four on the Trollope family. He is presently completing a biography of W. M. Thackeray and is the editor of *Contemporary Review*, established in 1866.

After reading and then teaching history at Oxford, Dr James Munson now devotes his time to writing. He has written over thirty-five programmes for the BBC and his research has been published in both popular publications and learned journals like *Historical Journal* and *Church History*. He has specialized in nineteenth-century religious history and in 1991 published *The Nonconformists*. In 1987 James Munson and Richard Mullen wrote *Victoria: Portrait of a Queen*, based on the BBC series.

Praise for *Anthony Trollope: A Victorian in His World*

'This is a great literary biography, one of the best to appear in recent times. It is unlikely ever to be superseded'
– Lord Blake in the *Financial Times*

'Richard Mullen brings to this task a knowledge of the period which is rivalled only by his understanding of Trollope's own work'
– Peter Ackroyd in *The Times*

'[Richard Mullen's biography] will delight those who love Trollope and may introduce others to the delights of reading him'
– Allan Massie in the *Sunday Telegraph*

RICHARD MULLEN
WITH JAMES MUNSON

THE PENGUIN COMPANION TO
TROLLOPE

PENGUIN BOOKS

PENGUIN BOOKS

Published by the Penguin Group
Penguin Books Ltd, 27 Wrights Lane, London w8 5tz, England
Penguin Books USA Inc., 375 Hudson Street, New York, New York 10014, USA
Penguin Books Australia Ltd, Ringwood, Victoria, Australia
Penguin Books Canada Ltd, 10 Alcorn Avenue, Toronto, Ontario, Canada m4v 3b2
Penguin Books (NZ) Ltd, 182–190 Wairau Road, Auckland 10, New Zealand

Penguin Books Ltd, Registered Offices: Harmondsworth, Middlesex, England

First published 1996
1 3 5 7 9 10 8 6 4 2

Printed in England by Clays Ltd, St Ives plc

To
the Memory of
COLIN HAYCRAFT (1929–1994)
who preserved the civilities of Victorian publishing
and of
BETTY ABEL (1916–1996)
who preserved the traditions of Anthony Trollope's
Fortnightly Review through her editorship of *Contemporary Review*

CONTENTS

PREFACE

'Nor you nor I have written so many novels as that damned man,' wrote Hugh Walpole to his fellow novelist, Arnold Bennett, in 1927. Walpole was understandably tired after reading so many of Anthony Trollope's forty-seven novels in such a short space as he struggled to complete his book about his great predecessor. Only those who have followed in Walpole's weary footsteps can completely understand the enormity of the task he faced as well as appreciate the final judgement he reached a few days later: 'It is wonderful how well the old boy lasts. Even now after all this reading I'm not tired of him.'

In the last decade there has been an explosion of interest in Anthony Trollope throughout what he called 'the English world'. There are now at least five publishers in Great Britain and the United States who are bringing out complete sets of his forty-seven novels. Penguin has published not only its own complete paperback edition but has brought out Trollope's forty-two short stories. The interest has also extended far beyond the English-speaking or English-reading world: in 1990 a Russian translation of *Barchester Towers* sold several hundred thousand copies within a few months of appearing.

Anyone who appreciates the works of Anthony Trollope must be grateful, as I am, for the research and insights of other biographers and scholars. Two works in particular are invaluable: the late Michael Sadleir's *Bibliography* and N. John Hall's *Letters of Anthony Trollope*.

In the years since the publication of my biography, *Anthony Trollope: A Victorian in His World*, I have spoken to numerous readers. They told me that what they needed was a book to which they could constantly refer. They wanted something which would help them to understand Trollope and his world so that their enjoyment of his fiction could be both deepened and broadened. This *Companion* is designed to meet that need.

The *Companion* describes all Trollope's novels, short stories, non-fiction books and some shorter works. It shows how each fits into the totality of his writing and how each reflects not only his own life but the spirit of the Victorian age which he so magnificently portrayed and embodied. Trollope was a consummate literary businessman and his work was greatly affected by the magazines, newspapers, editors and publishers for whom he wrote. That is why these subjects are also included, as well those members of his family, important contemporaries and fellow writers who influenced his work. The *Companion* also lists important characters who play considerable roles in more than one novel. In a few cases a character who is confined to one novel, such as the Reverend Obadiah Slope, is listed because he or she is frequently cited when people speak about Trollope or because the character has tremendous significance for Trollope's writing. Important characters in individual novels will be found in the entries for those novels.

As I was planning this book I came across a comment by the distinguished American critic, Paul Elmer More, when he was reading one of Trollope's lesser-known novels, *John Caldigate*: 'When I get into Trollope's England I know that my home is there, and I have a kind of shuddering horror of days not so far in the future when we shall no longer be able to comprehend and enjoy the stability and the character of the society he depicts – stability and character and magnificent stolidity.' If More's thoughts applied in 1907 – twenty-five years after Trollope's death – how much more do they apply today. Thus I decided that this *Companion* must explain aspects of Victorian life that Trollope took for granted, such as servants, carriages, money, entail, or popular expressions that have either vanished or changed beyond recognition since he wrote. To give but one example: it is amazing how frequently he refers to hearth-rugs in his novels. Once a reader understands the significance of a place on the hearth-rug to a Victorian, the struggles of various characters 'to get onto the rug' at the Bishop of Barchester's Palace make sense. Such understanding also allows the full impact of Trollope's humour to come across.

This *Companion* also tries to show how Trollope treated topics like marriage, the role of women, emigration, or the nature of being a gentleman, because such explanations should help readers to enjoy Trollope all the more. The *Companion* is not a Concordance: it does not attempt to record every reference by Trollope to any one particular topic but only those which illustrate the topic being discussed. Thus an alert reader will find many more references to rugs than those given here. Nor does the *Companion* cover every allusion made by Trollope: it is not an attempt to provide footnotes for all his works. Professor Edgar Harden and a team of scholars have recently done just this for Trollope's friend, Thackeray, and their splendid *Annotations for the Selected Works of William Makepeace Thackeray* fills two volumes and almost 1500 pages. Since Trollope wrote so much more than his friend, any attempt to do this with his works would amount to two or three times that size.

As I worked on the *Companion* I became aware that it was a task too large for one person to finish and I was fortunate to be able to persuade Dr James Munson, with whom I had collaborated on a biography of Queen Victoria, to help me. He brought to the task not only several decades of devotion to the works of Anthony Trollope, but a vast knowledge of Victorian religious history and Victorian publishing. Religion was central to much of Trollope's writing, but this fact is often obscured unless the reader knows how it permeated all the byways of Victorian life. Only an historian like James Munson could see the significance of Trollope's choice of language in his frequent allusions to religious topics.

I have no doubt that there are other topics in Trollope's writings that are not covered here, but I take consolation in what Trollope himself said as he was packing up his vast library of books to move to his final home: 'Life is limited . . . there are some branches of human knowledge which must be renounced by anyone who values his brain.' However, if readers of Trollope find that the *Companion* assists them in enjoying this most companionable of novelists, my original intention will have been fulfilled. Like Hugh Walpole I may say, 'I'm not tired of him.'

RICHARD MULLEN
Oxford,
15 January 1996

USING THE COMPANION

As well as discussing all of Trollope's forty-seven novels, forty-two short stories, five travel books and important non-fictional works published in his lifetime, this *Companion* also includes the two collections of his occasional journalism published after his death. Titles of novels and other books are italicized (*The Warden*). Trollope's short stories are within inverted commas ('The Spotted Dog').

Basic information about the writing of a work and its publication is given in the opening paragraph of the relevant entry. The numbering of the novels is by order of publication, with the exception of his two final novels, *An Old Man's Love* and *The Land-Leaguers*, which are numbered in the order in which Trollope wrote them. Although he left *The Land-Leaguers* incomplete at his death, it was published before its predecessor, *An Old Man's Love*. It seems pedantic not to call *The Land-Leaguers* his forty-seventh and final novel.

The *Companion* only deals with topics that occur in more than one of Trollope's works. Significant characters who appear in more than one novel are also included. Some of these are gathered under family groups such as the Grantlys or the Pallisers. In these cases members of the family are given in their order of importance. The use of an arrow followed by a separate entry means that a reader will find further useful information under that entry [➤ *The Warden*].

Chapter numbers of the novels are given in square brackets and take no account of volumes. Therefore readers do not need a particular edition to find references. The only novel in which there may be a problem is *The Three Clerks* and this is explained in its entry. A complete list of Trollope's novels, other books and collections of short stories can be found on pages xvi–xviii and there is a Chronology of the important events in his life on pages xiii–xv. A List of General Entries is given on pages xix–xxii so that readers may find their way rapidly to those topics that will help them understand Trollope's writing and the world in which he wrote. This list does not therefore include Trollope's works or his major characters.

References are occasionally given to Richard Mullen's biography of Anthony Trollope to enable the interested reader to find out more about a particular topic. Thus, in the entry on *The American Senator*, one has [Mullen, 608–9] which means that further information may be found on these pages of *Anthony Trollope: A Victorian in His World* (London: Duckworth, 1990 and Savannah, Georgia: Frederic Beil, 1992).

CHRONOLOGY OF TROLLOPE
AND HIS TIMES

Titles in square brackets indicate those works which were influenced by the events listed

1815 Anthony Trollope born on 24 April in Keppel Street, London.
Wellington defeats Napoleon at Waterloo.
The Trollopes move to their Harrow farm.

1823 Trollope starts as a day boy at Harrow School.

1825 Trollope sent to a small private school in Sunbury.

1827 Trollope enters Winchester College.
Fanny Trollope embarks on a long trip to America.

1831 Trollope sent back to Harrow School.

1832 Fanny Trollope's *Domestic Manners of the Americans* published, followed by her first novel, *The Refugee in America*.
The First Reform Act begins era of reforms. [*Lady Anna*]

1833 John Keble preaches Assize Sermon, later regarded as the beginning of the Oxford Movement. [*The Bertrams*]

1834 The Trollope family flees to Belgium.
Anthony Trollope appointed clerk in the Post Office. [*Marion Fay*; *The Three Clerks*]

1837 Reign of Queen Victoria begins.
Dickens's *Pickwick Papers* popularizes part issues.

1840 Penny post established.

1841 Sir Robert Peel Tory Prime Minister (1841–6).
Trollope sent to Ireland by Post Office.

1842 Mudie's Circulating Library founded.

1844 Trollope marries Rose Heseltine.

1845 Irish potato famine begins. [*Castle Richmond*; *Examiner* letters]
Newman converts to the Roman Catholic Church.

1847 Trollope's first novel, *The Macdermots of Ballycloran*, published.
Publication of *Vanity Fair* by Thackeray, *Jane Eyre* by Charlotte Brontë and *Wuthering Heights* by Emily Brontë.

1848 Year of revolutions in Europe. [*La Vendée*]

1851 The Great Exhibition opens.
Trollope sent to lay out postal routes in the West Country; he has the idea for Barsetshire and also for the pillar-box.

1852 Thackeray's *Henry Esmond* published.

1853 Northcote–Trevelyan Report calls for reform of Civil Service. [*The Three Clerks*]

1854 Crimean War (1854–6). [*The New Zealander*]
Dickens's *Hard Times* published.
Trollope appointed Surveyor of Northern District of Ireland.

1855 Trollope's fourth novel, *The Warden*, begins Barsetshire series and has some success.

1856 Fanny Trollope's last novel, *Fashionable Life: or Paris and London*, published.

1857 Trollope's fifth novel, *Barchester Towers*, published.
George Eliot's *Scenes of Clerical Life* published.
Flaubert's *Madame Bovary* published.

1858 Trollope sent on postal mission to Egypt and visits the Holy Land. [*The Bertrams*]
Trollope sent on postal mission to the West Indies and begins writing travel books. [*The West Indies and the Spanish Main*]

1859 Trollope makes first visit to America and starts writing short stories.
Lord Palmerston Liberal Prime Minister (1859–65). [*Lord Palmerston*]
Charles Darwin's *Origin of Species* published.
Trollope leaves Ireland to become Surveyor of Eastern District of England and settles in Waltham Cross in Hertfordshire. [*Castle Richmond*]

1860 Trollope's *Framley Parsonage* appears in Thackeray's *Cornhill Magazine*: his serialized first novel. Its success places him in front rank of novelists.
Wilkie Collins's *The Woman in White* published.
Essays and Reviews published.

1861 American Civil War (1861–5) [*North America*; 'The Two Generals'; 'The Widow's Mite'; lecture on the War]
Trollope begins a long visit to America to write *North America*.
Orley Farm published. First Trollope novel to appear in part issues.
Dickens's *Great Expectations* published.

1862 Trollope's *The Small House at Allington* becomes very popular in the *Cornhill Magazine*.

1863 Death of Trollope's mother in Florence.
Death of W. M. Thackeray.

1864 Trollope's first Palliser novel, *Can You Forgive Her?*, begins in part issues.

1865 Trollope's second son, Frederic, goes to Australia. [*Harry Heathcote of Gangoil*]
Trollope's connection with the *Fortnightly Review* and the *Pall Mall Gazette* shows his increasing interest in political questions.
Tolstoy's *War and Peace* (1865–72) begins publication.

1866 Publication of *Nina Balatka* – his eighteenth novel – begins an attempt by Trollope to establish a new career as author of short, anonymous novels.
The Last Chronicle of Barset, the final Barsetshire novel, begins serialization.

1867 Trollope resigns from the Post Office.
Saint Pauls Magazine begins under Trollope's editorship. [*An Editor's Tales*]

1868   Trollope visits America on a postal mission and tries to negotiate copyright treaty with US.

Trollope defeated when he stands in Beverley as Liberal candidate in general election. [*Ralph the Heir*]

Disraeli is Conservative Prime Minister from February to December, when Gladstone becomes Liberal Prime Minister (1868–74)

1870   Trollope retires from editorship of *Saint Pauls*.

Franco-Prussian War. [*The Golden Lion of Granpère*]

1871   Trollope and his wife give up their Waltham Cross house and embark on a long visit to Australia and New Zealand (1871–2). [*John Caldigate*; 'Catherine Carmichael']

1872   Thomas Hardy's first novel, *Under the Greenwood Tree*, published.

1873   Trollope's *Australia and New Zealand* published.

The Trollopes settle in Montagu Square, London.

Mark Twain's *The Gilded Age* published.

1874   Trollope's thirty-second novel, *The Way We Live Now*, begins publication in same month in which Disraeli defeats Gladstone to become Conservative Prime Minister (1874–80).

1875   Trollope's second visit to Australia. [*The Tireless Traveler*]

Trollope starts his *Autobiography* on ship returning from his fifth and last visit to America.

Tolstoy's *Anna Karenina* published.

1876   Trollope upset by adverse critical reaction to *The Prime Minister*.

Trollope completes his *Autobiography* (published 1883).

Trollope finishes the last Palliser novel, *The Duke's Children*, his thirty-ninth novel.

Mark Twain's *The Adventures of Tom Sawyer* published.

Henry James's first novel, *Roderick Hudson*, published.

1877   Trollope visits South Africa to write travel book. [*South Africa*]

1878   Trollope visits Iceland and writes his fifth and final travel book. [*How the 'Mastiffs' Went to Iceland*]

1879   Trollope writes *Thackeray*.

1880   Trollope and his wife move from London to Harting in Sussex.

1881   Trollope's last continental trip. [*Mr Scarborough's Family*]

Henry James's *The Portrait of a Lady* published.

1882   Trollope visits Ireland for material for his forty-seventh and final novel, *The Land-Leaguers*.

Trollope suffers stroke on 3 November; he dies on 6 December in London and is buried at Kensal Green Cemetery.

BOOKS BY TROLLOPE

*The books are listed in chronological order of publication, giving the original
publisher and price, and details of any serialization.*

Novels

The Macdermots of Ballycloran (1847) 3 vols. Newby. 31*s.* 6*d.*

The Kellys and the O'Kellys (1848) 3 vols. Colburn. 31*s.* 6*d.*

La Vendée (1850) 3 vols. Colburn. 31*s.* 6*d.*

The Warden (1855) 1 vol. Longman. 10*s.* 6*d. Barset I*

Barchester Towers (1857) 3 vols. Longman. 31*s.* 6*d. Barset II*

The Three Clerks (1858) 3 vols. Bentley. 31*s.* 6*d.*

Doctor Thorne (1858) 3 vols. Chapman & Hall. 31*s.* 6*d. Barset III*

The Bertrams (1859) 3 vols. Chapman & Hall. 31*s.* 6*d.*

Castle Richmond (1860) 3 vols. Chapman & Hall. 31*s.* 6*d.*

Framley Parsonage (1861) 3 vols. Smith, Elder. 21*s.*
   (serialized: *Cornhill Magazine,* Jan. 1860–June 1861) *Barset IV*

Orley Farm (1862) 2 vols. Chapman & Hall. 22*s.*
   (20 monthly part issues, Mar. 1861–Oct. 1862, at 1*s.*)

The Struggles of Brown, Jones, and Robinson (1870) 1 vol. Smith, Elder. 5*s.*
   (serialized: *Cornhill Magazine,* Aug. 1861–Mar. 1862)

Rachel Ray (1863) 2 vols. Chapman & Hall. 21*s.*

The Small House at Allington (1864) 2 vols. Smith, Elder. 26*s.*
   (serialized: *Cornhill Magazine* Sept. 1862–Apr. 1864) *Barset V*

Can You Forgive Her? (1864–5) 2 vols. Chapman & Hall. 22*s.*
   (20 monthly part issues, Jan. 1864–Aug. 1865, at 1*s.*) *Palliser I*

Miss Mackenzie (1865) 2 vols. Chapman & Hall. 21*s.*

The Belton Estate (1866) 3 vols. Chapman & Hall. 31*s.* 6*d.*
   (serialized: *Fortnightly Review* May 1865–Jan. 1866)

Nina Balatka (1867) 2 vols. Blackwood. 10*s.* 6*d.*
   (serialized: *Blackwood's Magazine* July 1866–Jan. 1867; serial and book were
   anonymous)

The Last Chronicle of Barset (1867) 2 vols. Smith, Elder. 20*s.*
   (32 weekly part issues, Dec. 1866–July 1867, at 6*d.*) *Barset VI*

The Claverings (1867) 2 vols. Smith, Elder. 26*s.*
   (serialized: *Cornhill Magazine* Feb. 1866–May 1867)

Linda Tressel (1868) 2 vols. Blackwood. 12*s.*
(serialized: *Blackwood's Magazine* Oct. 1867–May 1868; serial and book were anonymous)
Phineas Finn (1869) 2 vols. Virtue. 25*s.*
(serialized: *Saint Pauls Magazine* Oct. 1867–May 1869) *Palliser II*
He Knew He Was Right (1869) 2 vols. Strahan. 21*s.*
(32 weekly part issues, Oct. 1868–May 1869, at 6*d.*)
The Vicar of Bullhampton (1870) 1 vol. Bradbury, Evans. 14*s.*
(11 monthly part issues, July 1869–May 1870, at 1*s.* except final double issue at 2*s.* 6*d.*)
Sir Harry Hotspur of Humblethwaite (1871) 1 vol. Hurst & Blackett. 10*s.* 6*d.*
(serialized: *Macmillan's Magazine* May–Dec. 1870)
Ralph the Heir (1871) 3 vols. Hurst & Blackett. 31*s.* 6*d.*
(19 monthly part issues, Jan. 1870–July 1871, at 6*d.* and separately as a supplement to *Saint Pauls Magazine*, Jan. 1870–July 1871)
The Golden Lion of Granpère (1872) 1 vol. Tinsley. 12*s.*
(serialized: *Good Words* Jan.–Aug. 1872)
The Eustace Diamonds (1873) 3 vols. Chapman & Hall. 31*s.* 6*d.*
(serialized: *Fortnightly Review* July 1871–Feb. 1873) *Palliser III*
Phineas Redux (1874) 2 vols. Chapman & Hall. 24*s.*
(serialized: *Graphic* July 1873–Jan. 1874) *Palliser IV*
Lady Anna (1874) 2 vols. Chapman & Hall. 14*s.*
(serialized: *Fortnightly Review* Apr. 1873–Apr. 1874)
Harry Heathcote of Gangoil (1874) 1 vol. Sampson Low. 10*s.* 6*d.*
(*Graphic* Christmas issue, 1873)
The Way We Live Now (1875) 2 vols. Chapman & Hall. 21*s.*
(20 monthly part issues, Feb. 1874–Sept. 1875, at 1*s.*)
The Prime Minister (1876) 4 vols. Chapman & Hall. 36*s.*
(8 monthly part issues, Nov. 1875–June 1876, at 5*s.*) *Palliser V*
The American Senator (1877) 3 vols. Chapman & Hall. 31*s.* 6*d.*
(serialized: *Temple Bar* May 1876–July 1877)
Is He Popenjoy? (1878) 3 vols. Chapman & Hall. 31*s.* 6*d.*
(serialized: *All the Year Round* Oct. 1877–July 1878)
An Eye for an Eye (1879) 2 vols. Chapman & Hall. 12*s.*
(serialized: *Whitehall Review* Aug. 1878–Feb. 1879)
John Caldigate (1879) 3 vols. Chapman & Hall. 31*s.* 6*d.*
(serialized: *Blackwood's Magazine* Apr. 1878–June 1879)
Cousin Henry (1879) 2 vols. Chapman & Hall. 12*s.*
(serialized: *Manchester Weekly Times* Mar.–May 1879, simultaneously in *North British Weekly Mail*)
The Duke's Children (1880) 3 vols. Chapman & Hall. 31*s.* 6*d.*
(serialized: *All the Year Round* Oct. 1879–July 1880) *Palliser VI*
Dr Wortle's School (1881) 2 vols. Chapman & Hall. 12*s.*
(serialized: *Blackwood's Magazine* May–Dec. 1880)
Ayala's Angel (1881) 3 vols. Chapman & Hall. 31*s.* 6*d.*

The Fixed Period (1882) 2 vols. Blackwood. 12*s.*
  (serialized: *Blackwood's Magazine* Oct. 1881–Mar. 1882)
Marion Fay (1882) 3 vols. Chapman & Hall. 31*s.* 6*d.*
  (serialized: *Graphic* Dec. 1881–June 1882)
Kept in the Dark (1882) 2 vols. Chatto & Windus. 12*s.*
  (serialized: *Good Words* May–Dec. 1882)
Mr Scarborough's Family (1883) 3 vols. Chatto & Windus. 31*s.* 6*d.*
  (serialized: *All the Year Round* May 1882–June 1883)
The Land-Leaguers (1883) 3 vols. [incomplete] Chatto & Windus. 31*s.* 6*d.*
  (serialized: *Life* Nov. 1882–Oct. 1883)
An Old Man's Love (1884) 2 vols. Blackwood. 12*s.*

Collections of short stories

Tales of All Countries (1861) Chapman & Hall. 10*s.* 6*d.*
Tales of All Countries. Second Series (1863) Chapman & Hall. 10*s.* 6*d.*
Lotta Schmidt and Other Stories (1867) Strahan. 10*s.* 6*d.*
An Editor's Tales (1870) Strahan. 12*s.*
Why Frau Frohmann Raised Her Prices and Other Stories (1882) Isbister. 12*s.*

Travels

The West Indies and the Spanish Main (1859) 1 vol. Chapman & Hall. 15*s.*
North America (1862) 2 vols. Chapman & Hall. 34*s.*
Australia and New Zealand (1873) 2 vols. Chapman & Hall. 36*s.*
South Africa (1878) 2 vols. Chapman & Hall. 30*s.*
How the 'Mastiffs' Went to Iceland (1878) 1 vol. Virtue. Privately printed

Other books

Hunting Sketches (1865) 1 vol. Chapman & Hall. 3*s.* 6*d.*
Travelling Sketches (1866) 1 vol. Chapman & Hall. 3*s.* 6*d.*
Clergymen of the Church of England (1866) 1 vol. Chapman & Hall. 3*s.* 6*d.*
British Sports and Pastimes, edited by Anthony Trollope (1868) 1 vol. Virtue.
  10*s.* 6*d.* (Trollope wrote only the preface and the essay 'On Hunting')
The Commentaries of Caesar (1870) 1 vol. Blackwood. 2*s.* 6*d.*
Thackeray (1879) 1 vol. Macmillan. 2*s.* 6*d.*
The Life of Cicero (1880) 2 vols. Chapman & Hall. 24*s.*
Lord Palmerston (1882) 1 vol. Isbister. 2*s.* 6*d.*
An Autobiography (1883) 2 vols. Blackwood. 21*s.*

Since Trollope's death, four important works have been published:
London Tradesmen, edited by Michael Sadleir (1927)
The Tireless Traveler, edited by Bradford Booth (1941)
The New Zealander, edited by N. John Hall (1972)
The Letters of Anthony Trollope, edited by N. John Hall with the assistance
  of Nina Burgis (1983, Stanford, California, 2 vols.)

LIST OF GENERAL ENTRIES

A

'Aaron Trow'. This short story was written between 3 and 12 February 1861, when Trollope was writing *Orley Farm*. It is set in Bermuda, which he visited in May 1859 towards the end of his Post Office trip to the West Indies; he described this visit in his book *The West Indies and the Spanish Main*. The story was one of eight he sold to the *London Review* but after the hostile reception to the first two, 'A Ride across Palestine' and 'Mrs General Talboys', the magazine would publish only one more, 'The Parson's Daughter of Oxney Colne'. 'Aaron Trow' is one of the five remaining that were sold to *Public Opinion*, in which it was published on 14 and 21 December 1861. It was then included in the second collection of his short stories, *Tales of All Countries* (Second Series), in 1863. Trollope received £50.

The story is about the escape of three prisoners from Bermuda's 'convict establishment', one of whom is Aaron Trow. Among the white residents of the island are a timber dealer named Mr Bergen and his daughter, Anastasia; she is engaged to the local Presbyterian minister, Caleb Morton. When she is left alone one night Trow comes to the cottage and attacks her with a knife. Here we have the best example of Trollope's habit of refusing to keep a 'secret' from his readers. In the midst of an exciting account of Anas-

tasia's struggle, he ruins the suspense by letting us know that she survived. Her fiancé leads a search party to find Trow, who is eventually killed. Later it was said that his ghost (a very rare item in Trollope) haunted the area.

This was one of Trollope's few 'murder mysteries' with shades of Wilkie Collins and Dickens.

[➤ Dissenters.]

'The Adventures of Fred Pickering'. This short story was written between April and August 1866, while Trollope was writing *The Last Chronicle of Barset*, as part of an agreement with Alexander Strahan to provide four stories for the *Argosy*, of which three were published. (The other two were 'Lotta Schmidt' and 'Father Giles of Ballymoy'.) This story was published in September 1866 under the title 'The Misfortunes of Frederick Pickering' and was included, with 'Adventures' substituted for 'Misfortunes', in Trollope's third collection of short stories, *Lotta Schmidt and Other Stories*, published in the following year. Trollope received £60.

Fred Pickering throws in his work at a Manchester solicitor's, marries without a regular income, is disowned by his father and leaves for London with grand schemes to become a writer. He settles down to study Milton's *Paradise Lost* but gets nowhere. He then finds work on the *Morning Comet*, a daily penny paper. To improve his chances he pays £20 for a short-hand-writing course in order to become a reporter like Dickens. Unfortunately he loses his position at the *Comet* and finds he cannot learn shorthand. There is salvation of sorts when a friend establishes a new newspaper in Salford and asks Pickering to write a weekly letter from London. (Most provincial papers had their own London correspondent.) The letters are a failure because Fred is too didactic, political and reforming: the editor wants social gossip. He gets a reader's ticket to the British Museum Reading Room with the help of a literary giant who befriends him, and he returns to Milton. Eventually he is offered work as an indexer at £10 an index (as was Julius Mackenzie in 'The Spotted Dog') but he fails at this as well. A baby is born and starvation is looming, when the man who had written the book for which the rejected index was intended visits him and forces £10 on him. His wife, now ill, threatens to write to his father but he does so instead. His father demands he return to Manchester and gets the solicitor to agree to take him back, not as an articled apprentice but as a clerk. An allowance of 30*s*. a week will be paid until he has his own income.

This short story is one of Trollope's best accounts of a failed writer and much of it is remarkably similar to the 'Grub Street' world described by George Gissing. The plight of unsuccessful writers in London's literary world is one Trollope knew through *Saint Pauls*, the Royal Literary Fund and his own early fantasies about writing great histories of literature and editing powerful newspapers.

[➤ 'The Spotted Dog'; 'Josephine de Montmorenci'; 'Mary Gresley'.] Two Trollopian messages are delivered by the man who rejected Fred's index. He tells him that writers must serve apprenticeships as in any other work, that a few may rise to greatness but not the majority. Fred asks him, 'You mean that a man must be either a genius or a journeyman.' 'Yes, Mr Pickering; that, or something like it, is what I mean.' The second message is that writing, like any other profession, requires hard work, a knowledge of the market for which the goods are intended, and an acceptance of the purchaser's right to define the nature of the goods he buys. Both of these messages are repeated throughout Trollope's *Autobiography*. Frederic was the name of Trollope's younger son.

Advertising. Trollope had a deep distrust of advertising, which he feared was leading to a decline in the national sense of honesty. Like Carlyle, he was horrified at the exuberance of Victorian advertising techniques and in *The New Zealander* he denounced 'that plague of the nineteenth century . . . that disease in which are combined the two most pernicious evils with which man can be afflicted, falsehood and self-praise'. *The Struggles of Brown, Jones, and Robinson* is a sustained attack on advertising, although he assured one publisher that it did not include literary advertising. The practice was also attacked in 'The Panjandrum'. He has a hit at the most noticeable type of Victorian advertising, for patent medicine, in *Doctor Thorne*, in the person of Martha Dunstable and the fortune she makes from the 'Ointment of Lebanon'. Advertising was also attacked in his *Pall Mall Gazette* essays on London Tradesmen and he particularly singled out the new practice of coal merchants sending circulars to potential customers.

Age. As Trollope almost always indicates the age of his major characters shortly after they are introduced, it is helpful to understand his attitude towards age. This is particularly important in two areas that frequently occur in his fiction: marriage and old age. Trollope married when he was 29, three years later than the average age for men according to the 1851 Census. His wife, Rose, was 21 when they were engaged and 23 when they were married. Generally in the novels a girl who is in her mid-twenties and unmarried is regarded, particularly by herself, as being almost too old to marry. In the Victorian age, average life expectancy was much lower than today and the difficulties surrounding childbirth meant that marriage for women should take place early in life. Young men could wait till their late twenties because they needed to be able to provide for a wife. If men remained unmarried after that, they could become a menace. Thus in *Can You Forgive Her?* Lady Glencora Palliser's behaviour is somewhat more excusable when we remember she is still under 21. Her cousin Alice Vavasor's view that at 24 she is too old to marry is also more understandable. Likewise, the roué Burgo Fitzgerald is all the more contemptible to Trollope because he is over 30.

Of course some 'older' women do make happy marriages, most notably Madame Max Goesler to Phineas Finn and Martha Dunstable to Doctor Thorne, but both ladies are somewhat exceptional. When it comes to ageing,

Trollope saw this as generally setting in in one's forties, and many people who at first appear elderly – such as the widowed Mrs Ray in *Rachel Ray* – would not be so regarded today. Many of Trollope's characters appear to be older than they are: Mr Harding at his first appearance in *The Warden* is in his late fifties, but he always behaves as if he were much older. Trollope himself, in spite of his vigour, had a tendency to valetudinarianism and exaggerated his maladies. His weak vision, for example, became 'blindness'. He also added a few years to his age when writing about himself, although much less than Thackeray was inclined to do. The character of the greatest age in Trollope must be Bunce in the Barsetshire novels: by the time of his death in *The Last Chronicle of Barset* he must have been well into his nineties.

Trollope tackled the whole question of old age and euthanasia in *The Fixed Period*.

'Alice Dugdale'. This short story was written in 1878. Trollope agreed on 12 May to write a story 'to the length of 20,000 words' for William Isbister and promised it for early July, but in the event he sent it on 10 June. The story appeared in the Christmas issue of *Good Words* (which was called *Good Cheer*), although it is not a Christmas story. It was later included in Trollope's fifth collection of stories, *Why Frau Frohmann Raised Her Prices* (1882). Trollope received £135.

The story is similar in plot to 'The Lady of Launay' and to *The Belton Estate*, and is another of Trollope's stories of star-crossed lovers. Alice Dugdale, in her mid-twenties, lives with her father and stepmother in the large village of Beetham and looks after her seven stepbrothers and stepsisters and has an admirer, Major John Rossiter, the vicar's son, with an income of at least £1,500 a year [➤ Military]. Mrs Rossiter thinks John could do better than marry a village doctor's daughter. Like most of Trollope's heroines, Alice is independent of mind and dislikes talk of her chances of marriage; she also hides her true feelings by raillery at Major Rossiter after he visits the country-house of Sir Walter Wanless. Lady Wanless is keen for him to marry her daughter, Georgiana, who has nothing more than her looks to recommend her. He wonders if Alice is not too much of a home-body to fit into his London life even though he loves her. Alice realizes her error in playing hard to get and in the end they are married.

Trollope has great sport with the Wanless family and Sir Walter Wanless is one of his best baronets. He 'was one of those great men who never do anything great, but achieve their greatness partly by their tailors, partly by a breadth of eyebrow and carriage of the body, – what we may call deportment, – and partly by the outside gifts of fortune'. Trollope here employs one of his favourite criticisms of pretentious people: they serve cheap wine. With little money and five daughters the Wanlesses find it 'hard to maintain a family prestige'. The author also exercises his penchant for funny names. In addition to the Wanless family there are the Owless family, Mr Cobble, the Duchess of Ditchwater, Mrs Bakewell the baker and Lady Deepwell. Of Lady Deepwell he wrote, 'Her title went for something; but her husband had been only a Civil Service Knight, who had deserved well of his country by a merit-

orious longevity. She lived in a pretty little cottage ... which was just large enough to enable her to talk of her grounds.' (Trollope, like his brother-in-law and old friend, Sir John Tilley, had been civil servants, so this might have been a private joke.) Finally, Trollope gives Alice Dugdale a 'brown complexion' [➤ Women], or what we might call suntanned, as he gave Lucy Graham in 'The Telegraph Girl' and Ophelia Gledd in 'Miss Ophelia Gledd': it indicated not only health and the benefits of a rural life but also a certain independence.

All the Year Round (1859–95). This weekly magazine, which cost only 2d., was founded by Charles Dickens after he broke with his printers, Bradbury & Evans; it was designed to continue *Household Words*, which he had established in 1850. The magazine was mainly a vehicle for Dickens's own works and he was the editor, but it also published novels by Bulwer-Lytton, Mrs Gaskell, Charles Reade and Wilkie Collins. Tom Trollope wrote some articles on Italy for the magazine. Circulation in Dickens's time was normally 120,000 a week, much higher than that enjoyed by its predecessor. The magazine's connection with Trollope began after its heyday: in 1877, when it belonged to Dickens's son, Charles Dickens, Jnr. Trollope sold the serialization rights to *Is He Popenjoy?* to the magazine and in the following year, 1878, he sold similar rights to *The Duke's Children*. In 1881 Trollope offered Dickens the serial rights to either *Dr Wortle's School* or the longer *Mr Scarborough's Family*. Dickens preferred the longer novel. In all three cases he paid Trollope £400. *Mr Scar-*

borough's Family was still being serialized when Trollope died.

Alpine Club. See Clubs.

Ambition. For Trollope ambition was a great virtue, an essential part of being 'manly'. The role of ambition is important in his writing. To deny it under a façade of humility was a sham; he expressed his view in 'Mrs General Talboys': 'As to ambition, generally as the world agrees with Mark Antony in stigmatizing it as a grievous fault, I am myself clear that it is a virtue.' Provided its excesses were restrained by morality and manners, Trollope believed it was almost always good. Trollope himself was highly ambitious, although not in his troubled youth. His *Autobiography* is really an account of how he learned to be ambitious and then realized his ambitions: he became a respected civil servant, a successful writer, and a man popular with his many friends. The book also recounts the one great ambition he failed to achieve: entry into the House of Commons. In most of his novels, men without ambition, such as Maurice Maule in *Phineas Redux*, are quite contemptible or at least worthy of little respect. [Civil Service.]

Lack of ambition, or at least driving ambition, is often associated with elderly and titled men, particularly baronets. Septimus Harding in *The Warden* and *The Last Chronicle of Barset* is a rare example of a man who lacks ambition yet wins the respect of Trollope himself, but then Mr Harding is a veritable saint. The Barsetshire novels may be seen as presenting different levels of ambition, ranging from Mr Harding at one extreme to the excessive ambitions of Mr Slope and Mrs Proudie at the other. In between are the more restrained ambitions of the Reverend Mark Robarts in *Framley Parsonage* and Archdeacon Grantly throughout the series. Particularly noteworthy is the way in which Trollope depicts the conflict between worldly ambition and genuine religious feeling in the opening scene of *Barchester Towers*, in which the Archdeacon is at his father's deathbed.

There were few ambitions for women in Trollope's times and only four receive any wide coverage. The most frequent is the ambition to find a husband (normally a good ambition for Trollope, but one that occasionally turns into intrigue, as with Arabella Trefoil in *The American Senator*). He insisted that a woman's ambition to get married should be openly admitted, though he was criticized for this [➤ *Saturday Review*]. The second ambition for some women is to control their husbands (this can be either good, as with Mrs Grantly, or bad, as with Mrs Proudie). The third ambition is to play an influential role in religion (Mrs Winterfield in *The Belton Estate*) or in political society (Lady Glencora Palliser throughout the Palliser novels). The fourth ambition, for a few women, is to become a writer. [➤ 'Josephine de Montmorenci'; 'Mary Gresley'; 'Mrs Brumby'.]

America. Trollope visited the United States five times, in 1859, 1861–2, 1868, 1872 and 1875. No major English writer of his time was as knowledgeable about the country. He was among the first to go there to arrange to write directly for the American market. The United States had played an important role in his youth, as his mother and sisters were there between 1827 and

1831. Fanny Trollope earned fame for her controversial book on American life, *Domestic Manners of the Americans* (1832), which founded the literary fortunes of the Trollope family. Trollope wrote about his first visit in his *West Indies and the Spanish Main* and this visit led to his career as a writer of short stories, three of which are set in America: 'The Courtship of Susan Bell', 'Miss Ophelia Gledd' and 'The Two Generals'.

Trollope's second visit was the basis for his *North America* as well for a lecture on the Civil War. His third visit was to negotiate a postal treaty and to try to do something about the question of an international copyright agreement with America; the lack of this was a source of great annoyance and injustice to British authors. This visit led to some articles for the *Pall Mall Gazette*. His fourth visit was made when he was returning home from a tour of Australia and New Zealand. *En route* he stopped in Hawaii and California, which he described in articles for various UK newspapers. [➤ *The Tireless Traveler*.] He then crossed America and stopped to meet 'the great polygamist' Brigham Young. His fifth trip was made on his way home from a second visit to Australia.

Trollope generally had a very favourable view of America and once told Kate Field, perhaps with tongue in cheek, 'I was thinking today that nature intended me for an American rather than an Englishman. I think I should have made a better American.' Like his mother, he was interested in the American character. Unlike her, he was more sympathetic and objective and saw much she had missed. He mixed mainly with the cultured classes and described one lasting trait in their character through Ophelia Gledd: 'You English people are certainly wanting in intelligence, or you would read in the anxiety of all we say about England how much we all think of you. What will England say of us? what will England think of us? ... is of importance to us. We abuse you, and admire you. You abuse us, and despise us. That is the difference.'

Trollope had many American friends. He took great pride in 'those wondrous children of English civilization' and believed that 'they have all our virtues; and their vices are our own too'. In his novels, stupid people often denounce America: the best example is the letter from a stupid squire, who has never been there, warning his nephew about what he might find on a transatlantic visit [➤ *Mr Scarborough's Family*, 48]. Trollope was particularly fond of Boston, where he mixed with some of the country's greatest writers and where he was fêted. He was ignorant about the South and rather critical of the West. During the Civil War his sympathies were with the Northern side: the conflict is portrayed in 'The Two Generals' and referred to in 'The Journey to Panama' and 'The Widow's Mite'. His political views, particularly his increasing concern for popular education, were heavily influenced by his American travels. During his later visits he disliked the growing dishonesty which followed the Northern victory – as did American writers such as Mark Twain and Henry Adams – and this is reflected in *The Way We Live Now*, which has several American characters. His views on America were more complex in his final years: in *The American Senator* he uses Senator Gotobed simply to comment on

English society. However, in the last novel he wrote, *The Land-Leaguers*, the Irish-American, Gerald O'Mahony, not only comments on the English but comes to encourage Irish terrorists, thereby introducing a new and dangerous strain in Anglo-American relations. *Dr Wortle's School* is the only novel to have scenes actually set in America.

Trollope's novels were very popular in America and no praise pleased him as much as Nathaniel Hawthorne's. Beginning with *Barchester Towers* his novels were regularly re-published there, sometimes in pirated editions. He read widely in American authors such as Cooper and entertained American writers, among them Twain and Howells. At his death *Harper's Weekly* commented, 'The name of no English writer is so honored by American readers.' This has continued and much of the scholarly work on him has been done in the United States.

[➤ American Characters; Anglo-American Marriages; Canada; Copyright; English World.]

American Characters. There are over thirty important American characters in Trollope's fiction. As with his English and Irish characters, they represent a wide range of types and it is foolish to generalize about his attitudes towards America if the generalization is based on only one or two characters. Americans began to appear in Trollope's fiction in the 1860s in his short stories, which were written for Harpers in New York. The American girls who give their names to 'The Courtship of Susan Bell' and 'Miss Ophelia Gledd' are sympathetically portrayed. Beginning with 'Miss

Ophelia Gledd' Trollope made a regular practice of showing that American young ladies behaved differently from British ones. They were allowed more freedom and were more outspoken [➤ Women]. This provided him with a good theme to use when American characters began to appear regularly in his novels in the 1870s. Trollope liked the vivacity of the American girls he had met, like Mary Knower and more especially his close friend, Kate Field. He used some of her characteristics, notably in Ophelia Gledd. In general, American women come out better than American men, who – like Jefferson Ingram in 'An Unprotected Female at the Pyramids', Frederic F. Frew in 'The Widow's Mite', Senator Gotobed in *The American Senator*, the diplomat Jonas Spaulding in *He Knew He Was Right* and Gerald O'Mahony in *The Land-Leaguers* – have a tendency to boast about their country's greatness and to lecture others. Trollope did point out that this 'vice' was one that America had inherited from the mother country.

American women are often employed by Trollope to disturb the regularity of English social life. This is the case with Mrs Hurtle in *The Way We Live Now* and with Isabel Boncassen who marries the heir to a dukedom in *The Duke's Children*. The fact that American women characters' backgrounds were not always easily ascertainable gave them an air of mystery and provided good plots and sub-plots for novels; a notable example is Ella Peacocke in *Dr Wortle's School*. Trollope argued in *North America* that Americans approached topics differently from Englishmen and he tries to demonstrate this in the character of

Frederic F. Frew in 'The Widow's Mite'. He gives him his middle initial because 'To an American it is always a point of honour that, at any rate, the initial of his second Christian name should be remembered by all men'.

[➤ Anglo-American Marriages; English World.]

The American Senator. Trollope's thirty-fourth novel was written between 4 June and 24 September 1875 while he was in Australia (his second visit) and America (his fifth visit). It was serialized in the monthly magazine *Temple Bar* in fifteen instalments between May 1876 and July 1877, and published in three volumes by Chapman & Hall in July 1877. Trollope received £1,800.

In spite of the title, this is not a novel about American politics. The publisher had tried to persuade Trollope to give the book a different title but he was rather sensitive about his books' titles. However, in the last chapter he admits that it might have been better to have called the book 'The Chronicle of a Winter at Dillsborough'; this is the title used for the Dutch translation. Dillsborough is a town with a population of about 3,000 in the county of Rufford, on the border with the larger, more industrialized county of Ufford. Trollope chose the name Ufford as a private connotation: Ufford Hall belonged to his cousin, Sir John Trollope, Bt.

The local squire, John Morton, returns home with three troublesome guests: his fiancée, Arabella Trefoil (the surname he had once used for the Dean of Barchester in *Barchester Towers*), her mother, Lady Augusta Trefoil, and the 'most distinguished American of the day', Senator Elias Gotobed. Arabella is in search of a rich husband and soon drops Morton to pursue the vastly wealthy Lord Rufford. She is a fascinating and well-drawn character and one of the few that Trollope ever discussed in his correspondence: 'I swear I have known the woman, – not one special woman . . . but all the traits, all the cleverness, all the patience, all the courage, all the self-abnegation and all the failure.' Her disputes with her mother provide a great deal of comedy and she ends up losing Morton through death, and Lord Rufford because he never loved her. There is also another love plot between two daughters of a local solicitor, Mary and Kate Masters. Larry Twentyman, the 'hero' of the novel, is loved by Kate but loves Mary. When Mary chooses John Morton's cousin, Reginald Morton, Larry transfers his affections to Kate and marries her. Mary Masters also suffers from a difficult stepmother.

In Twentyman we are given a marvellous portrait of a rising class in the Victorian countryside, the yeoman-farmer who has made himself into a gentleman-farmer. (By denigrating Twentyman's education at Cheltenham, Trollope takes the opportunity to fire a final shot in his private war with that Evangelical town.) Senator Gotobed, a Republican politician from the mythical western state of Mikewa, has come to England to learn about English 'institutions'. He does to England what Trollope himself and his mother Fanny had done to America: he visits and comments on a country that was of the greatest importance to his own [➤ *North America*]. Trollope points out that the numerous similarities between the two great English-speaking peoples only make travellers more apt to criticize when they find something that is different [77]. In one of his delightful letters to another American politician, Senator Gotobed says: 'When a Britisher over in the States says what he thinks about us, we are apt to be a little rough with him ... Here there is no danger of that kind' [28].

The English reviewers were almost unanimous in their dislike of the senator: to *The Times* he was 'an excrescence on the work to which he gives his name'. Perhaps if Trollope had adhered to his original plan of having the Senator accompanied by his wife, he would have emerged as a more rounded character. As it is, Gotobed is on the attack almost from the moment he leaves the carriage at Bragton Hall, the Mortons' house: 'Quite a pile ... I guess it's damp?' The explanations given to the senator about English society provide a good introduction to present-day readers who are anxious to know more about the Victorian world and such subjects as primogeniture [➤ Entail] and clerical livings [➤ Church of England].

At the end of the novel, the senator delivers a lecture at St James Hall in London where he attacks many features of English life. (A few months later, on 8 December 1876, Trollope himself was to speak at a rally in this hall for which Queen Victoria thought he and his fellow speakers should be prosecuted [Mullen, 608–9]. It is not easy to decide when Trollope agrees with the senator's views and when he does not. He certainly agreed with the senator's criticisms of the great inequality in the payment of clergymen. Although Trollope knew the old system was 'picturesque' and a key ingredient in so many of his plots in the Barsetshire novels, he had also been outspoken in his own attacks on it [➤ *Pall Mall Gazette*].

Trollope certainly did not agree with the senator's attacks on fox-hunting. This novel has some of the best fox-hunting scenes in Trollope's fiction and that is saying quite a lot. The accusation that Dan Goarly has used poison to stop fox-hunting is an adaptation of an actual incident in Trollope's own Essex Hunt six years earlier. The novel also has the novelist's most outspoken attack on the 'trash of the philoanimalists' who attacked fox-hunting. They were 'a knot of self-anxious people who think they possess among them all the bowels of the world' [73]. Incidentally, the use of the antiquated term 'bowels' in its older sense of pity or compassion is a good example of the way in which Trollope laid himself open to attacks on his 'vulgarity'.

Several of the characters from this novel, particularly Twentyman and Captain Glomax, the MFH, reappear in *Ayala's Angel*, which Trollope wrote three years later. Senator Gotobed reappears in *The Duke's Children* as the United States' minister in London. One almost wonders whether this 'chronicle of Dillsborough' in the county of Ufford was intended as a possible start for another series similar to the Barsetshire novels, particularly as the Palliser series was drawing to an end. Lord Drummond, a character from that series, appears at the end of this novel to take the chair at the Senator's lecture.

In many ways *The American Senator* seems a novel at war with itself: the book has some of Trollope's most glowing descriptions of the pleasures of English country life, but it also contains some of the most telling attacks upon the injustices of the time. The key to this contradiction is the fact that Trollope wrote the novel during a long absence from England. Such trips made him nostalgic for the joys of his normal life, hence the many references to wine and to fox-hunting. (He even alluded to his old career as a Post Office surveyor by praising these officials as the 'trusty guardians of our correspondence' [34].) However, lengthy trips abroad also led the liberal side of Trollope's mind to question aspects of English society. On his first long journey in 1858, he had begun *The Bertrams* with a strange attack on the Victorian idea of 'success'; in 1862, when completing *North America*, he was horrified at the sight of beggars when his ship put in at its first UK port; and in 1873 he returned from Australia and New Zealand to write a powerful attack on contemporary society in *The Way We Live Now*. Thus the senator's criticisms of British life come not only from a fictional American politician but from a real English novelist who found that ordinary people often fared far better in the colonies and who wanted to know why this was so.

While *The American Senator* was appearing in *Temple Bar*, Trollope wrote to a friend that he thought the character of Senator Gotobed would be popular in America 'as he is a thoroughly honest man wishing to do good, and is not himself half so absurd as the things which he criticizes'. But one American reader, the diplomat and historian J. L. Motley, who lived in England, was bemused by Gotobed. When inviting Trollope to visit him in Dorset, Motley told him, probably in jest, that he had 'no visitor but the American senator whom we are expecting again with much anxiety'.

A careful comparison of the manuscript of this novel and the first edition of the book was made by the manuscript's owner and the great Trollope collector, Robert Taylor, and this showed that Trollope had changed the names of some of the characters after starting the novel. There were other discrepancies. The printers, quite understandably, had misread some of the author's handwriting. Thus one family takes tea 'at six o'clock one November morning' which sounds somewhat strange. Trollope had scrawled 'one November evening'.

The American Senator remains a delightful novel, particularly for readers who admire the Barsetshire books and who like stories of Victorian country life.

[➤ American Characters; English World; Names, Silly.]

Anglo-American Marriages. Such marriages occur frequently in Trollope's fiction and he, rather than Henry James, should be given credit as their literary inventor. His first such marriage occurs in 'An Unprotected Female at the Pyramids' which he wrote in 1859 within months of his first trip to America. Here Miss Damer marries Mr Jefferson Ingram. (Trollope's mother Fanny had used 'Jefferson' for her American character in her 1836 novel, *The Life and Adventures of Jonathan Jefferson Whitlaw*.) There were such marriages in two other short stories: 'The Widow's Mite' and 'Miss Ophelia Gledd'. It is interesting that Anglo-American marriages do not occur in those stories first published in America: interest was greater in England. They also feature in *The*

Duke's Children, He Knew He Was Right, Dr Wortle's School, The Way We Live Now and *The Land-Leaguers*. In writing about such marriages, especially among the aristocracy, he was again reflecting current trends. (The most famous such marriage was between Lord Randolph Churchill and Jenny Jerome, parents of Sir Winston Churchill.) In *The Eustace Diamonds* the marriage between Lucinda Roanoke and Sir Griffin Tewett does not come off, and in *The Way We Live Now* that between Mrs Hurtle and Paul Montague also fails.

Normally it is an American woman who marries an English man. In 'The Widow's Mite' and 'An Unprotected Female ...' it is the other way round. The usual difficulty is that the American woman is more outspoken and less reserved than her English counterpart and she often wonders if she will be 'received' in English society. Trollope posed the question in 'Miss Ophelia Gledd' which he wrote after his stay in Boston: 'An Englishman ... is often at a loss to judge of the "ladyship" of a foreigner, unless he has really lived in foreign cities; ... but I do not know that he is ever so much puzzled in this matter by any nationality as he is by the American ... the words, and habits, and social carriage, of an American woman, of the best class, too often offend the taste of an Englishman ...' It is interesting that in *The Fixed Period* he asks the same question about the proposed marriage between an Englishman and a woman from the make-believe colony of 'Britannula' which was based on New Zealand. The difficulty was, apparently, England versus the rest of what Trollope called 'the English world'.

[➤ Women.]

Anglo-Saxon v. Norman. In Victorian England there was a continuous and serious historical debate about the relative merits and contributions of the Anglo-Saxons and the eleventh-century Norman invaders. Trollope had some mild fun with this in *Barchester Towers* by contrasting two families, the stolid Thornes of Ullathorne, who traced their descent from the Anglo-Saxons, and the arrogant De Courcys, who pretended to Norman origins. Ironically Trollope and his brothers, when at public school, claimed that their name was Norman and that their ancestor Tallyhosier, when hunting with William the Conqueror, had killed three wolves; since this was *trois loups* in French, the name eventually became Trollope [Mullen, 2]. The mature Trollope would have laughed at such a fable and as a fox-hunter would have enjoyed the name *tally-ho-sier*. He poked gentle fun at such pretensions in his account of the Norman ancestry of the Palliser family in *Can You Forgive Her?* and at the end of *The Duke's Children* when the Duke has a mild laugh at his own Norman name of Plantagenet. [➤ Names, Origin of.]

Anonymous Novels. As early as 1858, on the publication of *Doctor Thorne*, there was criticism that Trollope was writing too much. He thought one way to cope with this was to publish some novels anonymously, and in the mid-1860s he persuaded *Blackwood's Magazine* to accept two anonymous novels, *Nina Balatka* and *Linda Tressel*: their serialization in the magazine would be anonymous, as usual, but so would their publication as books. As both were short works set on the continent, Trollope hoped this would disguise their authorship. Perceptive readers, one of them the principal critic of the *Spectator*, spotted the author at once. Even though the experiment did not work with *Nina Balatka* he had good reasons for persevering. He had finished two large and important novels, *The Last Chronicle of Barset* and *Phineas Finn*. With the Barsetshire series complete and the Palliser series now at a halt, it was useful to have short novels with single plots. Also, Trollope had decided to give up his Post Office career. He would therefore need extra money to make up for his lost income, without having to face renewed criticism about writing too much. In addition, he was curious to know whether his popularity and high fees came mainly from his name. A further factor could have been the possibility of writing some novels with his son Henry: this is based on a piece of literary gossip recorded by Henry James. However, Blackwood urged Trollope to drop the idea, and the third novel he had planned for anonymous publication, *The Golden Lion of Granpère*, was eventually issued under his own name. In *The Claverings* [14] Trollope defended the right of a person to lie when questioned about the authorship of an anonymous book.

Anticant, Dr Pessimist. See Carlyle, Thomas.

Arabin, Eleanor. See Bold [née Harding], Eleanor.

Arabin, The Very Rev. Francis. Arabin first appears in *Barchester Towers* [20], where he receives one of the longest and most detailed accounts that Trollope gives of any character.

In his early youth Arabin has several similarities to his creator: they were at the same school and each failed to win a scholarship to Oxford. Arabin, unlike Trollope, eventually gets to Oxford, where he becomes a clergyman and a devoted disciple of John Henry Newman, so much so that he almost becomes a Roman Catholic. Arabin eventually becomes Professor of Poetry (as was that great leader of the Oxford Movement, John Keble). At the age of forty he is brought into the Diocese of Barchester by Archdeacon Grantly to wage war on the Proudies and Mr Slope. Arabin discards his celibacy (a practice which Trollope found absurd) to become a suitor for the hand of Mr Harding's daughter, Eleanor. His successful wooing of her forms the main love plot of *Barchester Towers*, and at the end Mr Harding even obtains the prestigious and prosperous post of Dean of Barchester for him. Arabin appears in several of the later Barsetshire novels mainly because of his friendship with the poor clergyman, Josiah Crawley. Somehow his character never really develops after he settles into a peaceful life at the Barchester Deanery.

[➤ Church of England; Universities.]

Archdeacon. For Archdeacon Theophilus Grantly of the Barsetshire novels, see the Grantly Family. For the office of archdeacon, see Church of England.

Architecture. Trollope set out his views on architecture in his unpublished book *The New Zealander*, in the chapter on art [12]. There he is mainly concerned with the philosophy of art and with painting, but he includes a defence of Britain's architectural heritage and gives his approval to some of the new buildings being built in London and Dublin: the Treasury and the Bank of Ireland buildings, St Martin-le-Grand, the new Houses of Parliament, and churches like All Saints, Margaret Street. He attacks, as elsewhere, those who know more of the architecture of foreign countries than of England, and singles out Ruskin. He also mentions his love of the country houses of the sixteenth century. In his later fiction he often provides brief asides about his architectural tastes, particularly about the churches and country houses that occur so frequently in his fiction. He always regarded the country houses of the sixteenth century as particularly English and preferred them to the straight lines and balance of Georgian houses [*Barchester Towers*, 22]. He claimed that Baroque architecture was 'generally odious to an Englishman's eye' [*The West Indies and the Spanish Main*]. [➤ 'Christmas Day at Kirkby Cottage.']

The Argosy (1865–1901). This 6*d.* monthly magazine was originally the creation of the publisher Sampson Low, but before publication it was taken over by Alexander Strahan. He tired of the controversy surrounding its opening serialization, that of Charles Reade's *Griffith Gaunt*: it was a short story about bigamy. Strahan thought of re-launching the magazine and approached Trollope in 1866 for a three-volume novel to be serialized, but in the end Trollope only contributed three short stories: 'Father Giles of Ballymoy', 'Lotta Schmidt', and 'The Misfortunes of Frederick Picker-

ing' later changed to 'The Adventures of Fred Pickering' when it was published in his third collection of short stories. When it became known that Strahan wished to sell the magazine, James Virtue thought of buying it and of making Trollope the new editor, but instead he launched the new *Saint Pauls* under Trollope's editorship. In the end Strahan sold the magazine to the novelist Mrs Henry Wood, and she re-designed it round her own fiction.

Aristocracy. Many of Trollope's novels provide a superb fictional portrayal of the Victorian aristocracy, or what he calls 'the upper ten thousand of this our English world' [*Can You Forgive Her?*, 1]. Trollope was a firm believer in the benefits of an aristocracy and he based his use of the term on his knowledge of the classics. For him, as for Aristotle, *aristokratia* meant 'rule by the best'. [For rules governing titles and succession, ➤ Peerage.] The 'aristocracy' for Trollope consisted of titled people, such as the Duke of Omnium; squires and gentry; the well-born and wealthy; and those who had raised themselves by the exercise of superior talents, like Dean Lovelace in *Is He Popenjoy?*

Trollope disliked what he called 'the tyranny of democracy'. Even in the middle of the Crimean War, when writers like Thackeray and Dickens were attacking aristocratic government, Trollope defended it: 'the main duty of all aristocrats, and we may say their only duty, is to govern' [*The New Zealander*]. It is significant that his political novels revolve round a ducal family, the Pallisers. In his *Autobiography* Trollope tried to reconcile two of his political convictions: social distinctions should be lessened so long as there would always be an element of inequality in society.

It is easy to pick a statement or a character in almost any novel and present him or her as the embodiment of Trollope's definitive view on this complex question. It is only by looking at his work as a whole that his basic belief in the rightness of an aristocracy emerges clearly. The point of the Palliser novels is to show that the benefits of an hereditary aristocracy outweigh its disadvantages. In many novels Trollope is anxious to contrast good aristocrats who perform useful functions in their neighbourhood with selfish and useless ones. Thus in the Barsetshire novels the Luftons embody many aristocratic virtues while the De Courcys and the dissolute landowner Sowerby embody its vices.

As early as his second novel, *The Kellys and the O'Kellys* [11] Trollope showed his ability to describe aristocratic characters with enough humour to make them human, but not so much as to make them absurd. His aristocratic portraits lack the bias of Dickens and the bitterness of Thackeray. No other group in Trollope's novels – not even clergymen – get so many memorable portraits. It is often the younger sons like Undy Scott in *The Three Clerks* who exhibit the worst aspects of aristocracy. While he was quite capable of making fun of aristocratic names [➤Names, Silly], inflated family histories and crass snobbery, his humour is normally a gentle one.

Trollope often observes that it is pleasant to have acquaintances among the great aristocrats: 'there are men who have the most lively gratification in calling lords and marquises their friends'. He regarded this as a very minor fault, 'a gentle insanity which prevails in the outer courts of every aristocracy' [*The Small House at Allington*, 59]. He criticized Thackeray for going too far in his *Book of Snobs* in attacking the English love of having titled acquaintances [*Thackeray*, 2].

Trollope also knew that aristocracy in England benefited from the way in which it constantly recruited new members to its ranks: it was a class of people, not a caste. Several novels, notably *Framley Parsonage*, deal with a middle-class girl who marries a peer, while *The Duke's Children* reflected the growing trend for aristocrats to marry wealthy American girls [➤Anglo-American Marriages]. *The Duke's Children* and *Marion Fay* also have the opposite dilemma: in the first, Lady Mary Palliser wishes to marry a commoner, while in the latter, the heir to a marquisate and his sister both wish to marry commoners. Late in his career he discussed the tensions caused by this 'recruitment' in several other novels, including *An Eye for an Eye, Is He Popenjoy?* and *Lady Anna*. [➤Palliser Novels.]

Several novels, especially *The Claverings*, show the misery that normally results from a woman marrying a peer for position, wealth and title.

One American visitor observed Trollope's own behaviour in the presence of aristocrats and said he was free from 'the toadyism of middle-class Englishmen ... always willing to yield to others the place that the accidents of society entitled them to, but he was never subservient' [Mullen, 407]. This could well stand as a summation of the general treatment of the aristocracy in his fiction.

Army. See Military.

Art. Trollope had a deep and genuine love of art which had been encouraged in his boyhood by his mother, who arranged for her children to be taught drawing by a professional artist. Although Trollope had no talent himself, he came to have an intense interest in art. In his fiction he features artists in several novels but generally avoids discussion of art itself. There are occasional exceptions, such as his attack on the Pre-Raphaelites in *The Warden*. Sometimes he compared the difficulties of portraying human behaviour in novels with the work of different artists. (For a good example, see *The Eustace Diamonds*, 35.)

As a young Post Office clerk in London he frequently visited the National Gallery in its first home in Pall Mall. He may well have accompanied his mother's brother, Henry Milton, himself a writer on art. Trollope was also interested in the philosophical aspect of art and studied Edmund Burke's *Philosophical Enquiry into the Sublime and Beautiful*. In his unpublished analysis of British life, *The New Zealander*, written in 1855–6, he devoted an entire chapter to art. Here he supported the building up of a great national collection and praised British architecture and painting. His love of visiting art galleries remained with him throughout his life, and in 1865 he included a delightful essay on 'The Art Tourist' in his *Travelling Sketches* for the *Pall Mall Gazette*. Some of his own recollections of early visits to the National Gallery are recalled in another essay he wrote for the *St James Magazine* in 1861. When he visited his brother Tom in Florence they spent much time in the Pitti Palace, where both could enjoy the vast treasure of paintings. (His brother was well known as a writer on Renaissance artists and had an impressive collection of their works.) Trollope had little use for theories about art: 'God has given us eyes, and we must use them, as we do upon a landscape. But we must use them with patience.'

Trollope followed his mother in revering Titian, but he disliked Michelangelo and Raphael and hated Guercino. He liked the Dutch school, especially Rembrandt's 'The Night Watch'. In his travels round Europe he resembled the hero of 'The Art Tourist' who had 'that laborious perseverance which distinguishes the true Briton as much in his amusement as in his work'. When he visited galleries abroad he often carried a chair with him in order to study the paintings at leisure. He was a regular visitor to the Royal Academy's exhibitions and it was rare for him to visit a foreign city without hurrying to see 'the pictures'. [➤ *Ralph the Heir*.] He knew artists like Holman Hunt and Leighton through his membership of the Moray Minstrels and was a particular friend of Sir John Millais, whom he met at the first *Cornhill* dinner in 1860. (This friendship may have influenced him in his contempt for Ruskin.) Millais's illustrations appeared in his novels and were much valued by Trollope.

Trollope was also friendly with William Frith, who made the novelist a central figure in his painting, 'The Private View of the Royal Academy, 1881'. Frith gave the vast canvas two focal points: Trollope and Oscar Wilde. Trollope, shown carefully studying the paintings round him, represented the solid values of the mid-Victorians. Surrounding him are great figures like W. E. Gladstone, Robert Browning and the then Archbishop of York. Wilde, seen caught up in a rapturous gaze in some artistic elysium, represents the 'art for art's sake' of the end of the century which saw art and literature as a private preserve of the illuminati.

Few aspects of Trollope's life have been as neglected as his interest in art.

Artists. Artists feature in several novels and and short stories. Trollope's first real artist is the feckless Ethelbert (Bertie) Stanhope in *Barchester Towers*. He is a painter who later tries sculpting. He is talented but dishonest. In the short story 'Mrs General Talboys' (1861), Trollope portrayed a set of 'rum characters' living in Rome, among whom was Charles O'Brien, an Irish sculptor who has left his wife in Ireland and who has a 'fling' with Mrs Talboys. In *The Last Chronicle of Barset* (1866–7), Conway Dalrymple is a successful but adventurous Society artist of low morals. His painting of 'Jael and Sisera' forms one of the sub-plots of the novel. He flirts with a married woman and then falls in love with Clara Van Siever, whom he marries. Dalrymple's character represents a seedy aspect of London life which is in juxtaposition to Barchester's quieter ways. In *Ayala's Angel* (1881), the Dormer household is something of an artistic colony: Egbert Dormer, Ayala's father, is keen on 'art for art's sake' while Isadore Hamel, in love with Ayala's sister Lucy, is a young English sculptor of more common sense. Unlike either O'Brien or Dalrymple, Hamel is respectable enough and his work as an artist is secondary. The difficulty lies with his father, who is also an artist living in Rome and who has a disreputable reputation which in the end is redeemed by the son.

Trollope made the acquaintance in Florence of the American sculptor Hiram Powers, who was an old friend of his mother and who may have given Trollope the idea of making the characters Bertie Stanhope, O'Brien and Hamel sculptors. He mentioned Powers by name in *The Warden* when he described an 'admirable bust' of Sir Robert Peel, said to be by 'Power' [Powers], in Tom Towers's office [14]. Trollope was also a friend of Millais, Frith, Holman Hunt and Leighton.

[➤ Art; Illustrations.]

Athenaeum. See Clubs.

Attorneys. See Lawyers.

Auld Reekie, Marquis of. The Marquis appears in both the Barsetshire (*The Small House at Allington*) and Palliser series (*Can You Forgive Her?*) and makes several appearances in *The Way We Live Now* when his son, Lord Nidderdale, seems about to marry Marie, the daughter of the great financier and swindler Melmotte. This Scottish peer is the uncle and guardian of Lady Glencora MacCluskie, who becomes Lady Glencora Palliser. The Marchioness of Auld Reekie also appears in *Can You Forgive Her?* and *The Way We Live Now*. 'Auld Reekie' was a nickname given to Edinburgh for its smoky atmosphere. [➤ Entails.]

Aunts. See Nieces.

Austen, Jane (1775–1817). Trollope was considerably influenced by Jane Austen, whose novels he read carefully throughout his life. Not only do some of his best-known novels have similar settings, but his comic sense was enriched by her example [➤ Comedy]. As a young man he was convinced that *Pride and Prejudice* was the 'best novel in the English language' although he later came to prefer Thackeray's *Henry Esmond*. Even so, as late as 1869 Trollope referred to Jane Austen as 'my chief favourite among novelists'. His admiration was not an uncritical one, as he made plain in some notes he wrote after re-reading *Emma* when he was preparing to write a history of fiction. He criticized her for 'timidity in dealing with the most touching scenes' and for 'not allowing the final part to be told in dialogue'. Trollope's set of her works is now in the Taylor Collection at Princeton University. Since Trollope's novels had considerable similarities to Jane Austen's, several of his contemporaries contrasted the two novelists, most notably R. H. Hutton in 'From Miss Austen to Mr Trollope' in the *Spectator* (16 December 1882).

Australia. There are many references to Australia in Trollope's fiction, normally as a place free of the English class system to which people may flee to start a new life, and in which they may prosper if they work hard. In his unpublished book, *The New Zealander* (1855–6) he, like most people, saw Australia as the natural destination for excess population from the United Kingdom. When discussing education he asked rhetorically, 'But who would not sooner look forward to seeing his son a shoemaker at Melbourne, if as such he could be educated as becomes a gentleman, than contemplate his living as a gentleman in London with no better education than that be-

coming among shoemakers?' In his fiction it sometimes served as a refuge for those who could no longer live in England: in *The Three Clerks* Alaric Tudor emigrates with his wife and children after release from gaol, and in *Orley Farm* Lucius Mason emigrates to start a new life after the scandal of his mother's forgery. This theme is most pronounced in *Lady Anna* in which the radical tailor and his aristocratic bride emigrate to get away from the publicity concerning their marriage. (Trollope contemplated a new series, like the Barsetshire and Palliser novels, based on their adventures in Australia.)

Trollope had two family connections with Australia. Recent research has shown that by the 1860s Rose Trollope's elder sister, Ellen Heseltine Davitt, had emigrated to Australia, where she became a writer and artist. There is, however, no record of Trollope's reaction to this. In 1865 his younger son Frederic, then eighteen, emigrated to Australia. As agreed with his parents, he returned home after a few years before making up his mind about his future. In 1869 he returned to Australia and set up a sheep station in New South Wales. Trollope, accompanied by his wife, made his first trip there in 1871–2 at a time when public interest in the Empire was quickening. Out of this visit came his book *Australia and New Zealand*. He liked the country and her people and predicted not only a federation of the colonies, achieved in 1901, but independence from the Crown. Australia featured next in his 1873 Christmas story, 'Harry Heathcote of Gangoil', later published as a novel. This he based on his son's life on a sheep station. Six years later he set part of *John*

Caldigate in Australia; here a 'frontier' existence was contrasted with the more controlled life in England. (The American South and West served the same purpose in *Dr Wortle's School.*) In 1875 he made a return visit by himself and while there wrote twenty 'letters' for a variety of British newspapers: letters seven to sixteen concern Australia. [➤ *The Tireless Traveler.*]

Trollope thought that life was better for ordinary people in Australia than it was in England. 'Work is more plentiful. Wages are higher. Food is cheaper.' He also spoke highly of some Australian wine and lavished praise on Sydney as 'one of those places which, when a man leaves it knowing he will never return, he cannot leave without a pang and a tear. Such is its loveliness.' Many Australians were delighted to see a man whose novels had helped to keep them in touch with 'home'. Three thousand people attended his lecture on fiction in Melbourne and a few years later he told a commission on copyright that more books were published in Melbourne *per capita* than in any other city in the world.

Australia and New Zealand. Trollope's third travel book was written between 23 October 1871 and 15 January 1873. It was based on his first visit to Australasia, which took place between 24 May 1871 and 3 October 1872. The book was published in two volumes by Chapman & Hall in February 1873. In the same year it was published in Australia and in 1874 it was published in four parts (New Zealand, Victoria and Tasmania, New South Wales and Queensland, South Australia and Western Australia) as a guide for emigrants from the United Kingdom. Trollope received £1,300, the same amount he was paid for his *North America*.

Trollope had two reasons for visiting Australia. The first was to see his younger son Frederic, who had emigrated there in 1865. 'I went to Australia chiefly,' he wrote in his *Autobiography*, 'in order that I might see my son among his sheep.' The second was to continue his career as a travel writer who visited all parts of the English-speaking world: 'I had, however, the further intention of writing a book about the entire group of Australasian Colonies.' He visited all six colonies, still independent of each other, as well as New Zealand and the tour took eighteen months. Aboard the *Great Britain* en route for Australia Trollope wrote *Lady Anna*, in which the heroine and her tailor husband emigrate to Australia.

Trollope rated *Australia and New Zealand* below his book on the West Indies but above that on America. 'I spared myself no trouble in inquiry, no trouble in seeing, and no trouble in listening. I thoroughly imbued my mind with the subject.' It was, he wrote, 'a thoroughly honest book' but he later thought it 'dull and long' and one cannot but agree. The two volumes sometimes read like a Post Office surveyor's report. It surprised him that they sold so well. This was because he wrote at the right time: interest in the expanding Empire was increasing, as was emigration, and Englishmen wanted to know more about Australasia.

The book is burdened with too much information just mastered. Even before he left England he began research. (This included buying some tinned Australian meat which his servants refused to eat.) While in

Australia he continued his reading and also met G. W. Rusden, Clerk of the Legislative Council of Victoria. Rusden, who was to become a close friend, dedicated a tract on Port Philip to Trollope and this encouraged him to amass information about the history of each Australian colony. All this he incorporated into the 1,049 pages of the book, along with statistical information from government officials. The book is fairer than his two earlier travel books but much less enjoyable. One of the reasons for writing it was to enhance his reputation as a 'serious' writer rather than as simply a novelist.

Trollope genuinely liked Australia and Australians, and took pride in their achievements; but the book betrays his occasional boredom, as well as a feeling that he is straining to finish the work. While he took great pride in English colonization he had no doubt that in time the colonies would become independent of the mother country, as the United States had done. After a year and two days in Australia he and Rose went on to New Zealand, where they stayed for two months, afterwards returning to England via America. [➤ English World.]

Austria. Austria and the Austro-Hungarian Empire provided scenes for several novels and short stories. *Nina Balatka* is set in Prague, then part of the Empire, while other novels have short scenes set in Austria, such as *The Duke's Children* in which one chapter has as its setting the resort of Bad Ischl, even though this chapter has little local colour. Several short stories have an Austrian background: 'Lotta Schmidt' is set in Vienna, 'Why Frau Frohmann Raised Her Prices' in the

Tyrol, and 'The Last Austrian Who Left Venice' is the love story of an Austrian officer during the 1866 war between Austria and Italy. The early lives of two important characters in the Palliser novels, the Reverend Joseph Emilius and Madame Max Goesler, are shrouded in mysteries set in the Austrian Empire.

In the 1830s Trollope nearly accepted a commission in the Austrian cavalry, but for most of his life he had the usual mild hostility of a Victorian Liberal towards the Hapsburg monarchy, as can be seen in comments in his *North America*. He took a more favourable view after some of his European travels took him to Austria, and in *Lord Palmerston* he correctly describes the Austrian emperor as a man who has 'reigned, through many troubles, with good sense and moderation'. He and his wife Rose were particularly fond of the Tyrol and she spent much of her widowhood there. He said in *The Bertrams* that Innsbruck occupied the most picturesque site of any city in Europe.

'Authorial Intrusion'. Trollope followed the practice of many Victorian novelists in which the writer interrupts his narration to speak directly to his readers, sometimes in the first person. The *Saturday Review* denounced him as one of the 'conversational school who address their readers from first to last in a tone of raillery'. The fact that novels were so often read aloud seems to have encouraged this habit. Trollope adopted the practice in his first novel, *The Macdermots of Ballycloran*, in which, in an early chapter [II], he makes three different personal comments: 'I may as well now make his character no longer doubtful' he says of one man; next, he gives his view of secret informers in what 'I must call a most iniquitous system'; finally he introduces an anecdote with, 'A very few years since I was walking down the street of a small town...'. Often Trollope pops up in the middle of a story to tell the 'gentle-hearted reader' not to worry because some dreaded outcome will not really occur. In the well-known account of the wooing of Eleanor Bold in *Barchester Towers*, he announces that 'it is not destined' for Eleanor to marry Mr Slope or Bertie Stanhope. Sometimes this lessens the dramatic impact of the story or chapter, as in 'Aaron Trow'. Trollope justified the practice in *Barchester Towers*: 'Our doctrine is that the author and the reader should move along with full confidence with each other' [15]. Likewise the practice fitted in with his strong dislike of 'mystery' in fiction. This aspect of Trollope's writing particularly infuriated Henry James, who regarded it as 'suicidal' to let readers know that the author could control events. However, the constant presence of Trollope at the reader's side is one of the great delights of his novels. [For one of his most important 'intrusions', ➤ *The Eustace Diamonds*.]

An Autobiography. Trollope started his memoirs sometime between 20 and 30 October 1875, when he was aboard ship on his way home after his last visit to America. He arrived in Liverpool on 30 October, having written thirty-three pages, and did not resume writing until 2 January 1876. He finished on 11 April, although the manuscript shows that he altered it, inserted new material, and later removed certain passages. On 30 April 1876 he gave the manuscript to his elder son,

Henry, to be published after his father's death. Henry arranged publication in two volumes by Blackwood in October 1883, ten months after Trollope's death. Trollope once told Henry he thought it would fetch £1,800 but in the event Henry had to settle for £1,000. For many years the manuscript has been on display in the British Museum.

Among English memoirs, Trollope's *Autobiography* is famous for its honesty and straightforwardness. He wrote it when he was sixty, six and a half years before his death. The book does not appear to have been influenced by other autobiographies but by an awareness that age was creeping up on him: two years earlier he had lost the hearing in one ear. There is a certain elegiac tone throughout the book, partly due to his having had to give up fox-hunting at this time and partly due, perhaps, to his having said so many farewells to his American friends. Because of his religious belief, he knew he would have to give a reckoning of his life to his Maker; he had told his fellow members on the Copyright Commission that 'an author... has it upon his conscience to use his life for doing good work for the world around him'. The *Autobiography* is that reckoning, that apologia not so much for his life but for his work. It was through his work that he had made something of himself and it was by that he would be judged.

The purpose of the book is not to impress readers with his greatness or with the number of great people he had known, or could claim to have known. It is, simply, to record his life and achievements in a detached and remarkably objective manner and to analyse some of those whose lives touched his own, especially his parents. He ranked the novelists and the ten greatest living writers. He examined his own works and gave frank opinions as to whether they were good or bad. He also hoped the book would, like his other works, help young people. He went into such detail about his manner of work and the financial rewards he earned because he was justly proud of his achievements and because he wanted to teach and inspire younger writers. He included chapters on how to write, on criticism, and on the financial rewards that one could reap.

His theme is a straightforward one not unusual in memoirs: how a miserable, undervalued 'hobbledehoy' rose through work and self-discipline to greatness. Like most Victorian autobiographies by men there are references to his numerous floggings at public school. (His brother Tom devoted even more space to this topic in his memoirs.) Victorian autobiographers tended either to idealize their childhood or to exaggerate its miseries; Trollope chose the second option. [➤ Public Schools.] As he wrote, memories flooded back, a train of thought was created and exaggeration ensued. At one stage he describes himself as 'reeking from a dunghill' and disgracing the 'curled darlings' of Harrow. He simplified the story of his father's financial collapse and made Lord Northwick out to be far worse than he was.

As well as the tendency towards exaggeration, there are occasional errors based on faulty memory, especially when writing about his 'miserable' youth. (His brother Tom disliked some of this and felt, wrongly, that Trollope had made his mother too

Radical in politics before her trip to America.) He does not discuss his early childhood but jumps from his birth to his schooldays: nor does he mention his brother Arthur, who died as a youth. He gives the impression he had only two brothers. He also exaggerated his time as a Post Office clerk when he talked of his youthful 'dissipation': this has led some writers to provide the missing details from their own imaginations. Some stories are embellished, like that of his 'murder' of Mrs Proudie at the Athenaeum [Mullen, 458–60], or of Edward Chapman's holding a poker to defend himself as Trollope obliges him to accept the manuscript of *Doctor Thorne* [Mullen, 319]. Sometimes his penchant for understatement harmed his reputation, as when he says of the Barsetshire series that 'no one at their commencement could have had less reason than myself to presume himself to be able to write about clergymen' [5]. He makes it perfectly clear, unlike most writers of modern memoirs, that he will not tell all: 'That I, or any man, should tell everything of himself, I hold to be impossible.' He tells us, for example, very little of his wife and sons.

To help him with his writing, his wife wrote out a seventeen-page chronology, probably based on her own diary. Occasionally she inserted little reminders like: 'Conductor takes us for discharged prisoners' or 'Row with driver when we start'. In addition she made transcripts of documents for him to use, like the 1859 letter from Thackeray asking him to contribute more than novels to the new *Cornhill.* He also had his own journals on which to draw.

The *Autobiography* contained twenty

chapters. They were, on the whole, chronological and the first five took him up to 1849: 'My Education, 1815–1834'; 'My Mother'; 'The General Post Office, 1834–1841'; 'Ireland – My First Two Novels, 1841–1848' and 'My First Success, 1849–1855'. Subsequent chapter titles were of those books published in the period covered, such as Chapter 11, ' "The Claverings", the "Pall Mall Gazette", "Nina Balatka", and "Linda Tressel".' There are four exceptions: Chapter 13, 'English Novelists of the Present Day'; Chapter 14, 'Criticism'; Chapter 17, 'The American Postal Treaty – the Question of Copyright with America – Four More Novels'; and Chapter 12, 'Novels and the Art of Writing Them'. It was this chapter, with its description of his early-morning writing and his work sheets, that made him appear to be a 'mechanical' writer. Needless to say he did not go into details which might throw light on his inspiration and creative genius; the picture in the *Autobiography* is therefore incomplete. (For a full picture, one also needs to read 'A Walk in a Wood', *The Life of Cicero* and 'The Panjandrum'.)

He went over what he had written carefully; even after it was finished he returned to it to insert new material, such as his work on the Copyright Commission in Chapter 17, or the footnote in Chapter 20 regarding the hostile review he received on the publication of *The Prime Minister*, a review which claimed his powers as a novelist were failing. At the end of the last chapter Trollope included a list of his earnings up to the publication of *South Africa*. He then added in the £1,800 he received for *John Caldigate* so that the total up to then amounted to £68,959. 17*s.* 5*d.* (This included £7,800 for 'sun-

dries'.) More sensitive literary souls were horrified at this open confession of his pride in the money he had earned, but by including the list he gave us a true picture of the man who had written the memoir. Few other autobiographies can make such a claim.

As editor, Henry made few changes, although he did remove a passage about W. H. Russell's indolence which might have given offence. Mudie took 1,000 copies, which would have pleased the author. Reviews were mixed: some, like those in the *Spectator*, the *Daily Telegraph* and the *Pall Mall Gazette*, praised it, while the *Cornhill*, and years later *The Times*, wondered if his description of his methods of work and his profits might not harm his reputation. In 1909 Arnold Bennett wrote of this: 'People who chatter about the necessity of awaiting inspirational hypersthenia don't know what the business of being an artist is.'

The Reverend W. Lucas Collins, the first person outside the family to read the manuscript, wrote to Henry: 'Every word reveals to me the man himself, his warm heart, sterling honesty, abhorrence of meanness and injustice and even his prejudices.' It was a fitting and accurate summary.

[➤ Field, Kate.]

Autocratic Women. See Women.

Ayala's Angel. Trollope's fortieth novel was written between 25 April and 24 September 1878, during which time he travelled to Iceland (about which he wrote *How the 'Mastiffs' Went to Iceland*) and to Switzerland and Germany. Trollope first sent it to *Blackwood's Magazine*, which rejected it, as did *Macmillan's Magazine*. He then sent it to Alexander Ireland, publisher-manager of the *Manchester Examiner and Times*, for serialization but was again unsuccessful. In November 1880 he sold the serial rights to the National Press Agency for £200, but no serialization appeared in Britain. The novel was actually first published in America serially in the *Cincinnati Commercial* between 6 November 1880 and 23 July 1881. He arranged this through his American friend, George Smalley. (Cincinnati was a somewhat odd place to publish a book by Fanny Trollope's son.) He sold the book rights to Chapman & Hall, who paid him £750 and published it as a three-volume novel in May 1881. His difficulty in finding a publisher was probably because the number of novelists was increasing and serialization was therefore becoming more difficult. *Ayala's Angel* was one of only four of his novels written since he had come to fame with *Framley Parsonage* that did not have some type of serialization in Britain. Trollope received £1,050 in total.

Trollope began writing *Ayala's Angel* the day after his sixty-third birthday, yet its style and tone read more like something written ten or fifteen years earlier. Like *The Small House at Allington*, the novel is centred on the loves of two sisters, Ayala and Lucy Dormer. (Trollope, who was devoted to champagne, probably took Ayala's unusual name from the well-known champagne house established in France in 1860 by the son of a Colombian diplomat.) The novel is set in London and the countryside and there are short forays to the Continent. It opens with the death of Egbert Dormer, an improvident artist. Ayala and Lucy, his daughters, are each sent to live with an uncle [➤ Nieces], one of whom, Sir Thomas Tringle, is wealthy while the other, Reginald Dosett, is not. Like Eleanor Bold in *Barchester Towers*, Ayala is pursued by three suitors, a favourite device of Trollope [➤ *The Claverings*; *Miss Mackenzie*]. She finally chooses the solid though shy and ugly Jonathan Stubbs, who is that rather rare character in a Trollope novel, a serving military officer. Trollope, who was not very knowledgeable about military life, tells us that Colonel Stubbs was engaged in 'the ordinary pursuits of Aldershot'. Lucy is in love with the sculptor Isadore Hamel, but because of his father's reputation she faces obstacles. In the end love conquers all.

Trollope was increasingly preoccupied with the question of whether to leave money to his own niece, Florence Bland, and in this novel he has Ayala's rich uncle leave money to her in his will. Trollope would only solve his own dilemma about how much money to leave Florence, and how it should be left, while writing his next novel, *Cousin Henry*. *Ayala's Angel* contains more love plots and marriages than almost any other Trollope novel. Indeed it is in this book that he states his view that marriage is almost the only good ending for a novel [64]. Many aspects of Trollope's past are reflected here. Reginald Dosett is a Civil Service clerk at the Admiralty: his salary of £900 a year is close to what Trollope was earning when he retired from the Post Office ten years earlier. (When Trollope states that a 'youth of nineteen' would think this a 'pecuniary paradise' [2], he is of course thinking back to his own entry into the Civil Service.) Uncle Dosett was using almost one fifth of his income to pay for two insurance policies, and the ways in which his wife keeps down expenditure reveal a great deal about Victorian domestic life. We see the opposite side of the Victorian world in the other uncle, the vastly wealthy banker Sir Thomas Tringle, perhaps the author's most favourable picture of a City figure.

This novel, like so many, shows the dangers of basing life upon theories or dreams. Normally when Trollope sets out to assault utopian notions, as in *Orley Farm*, or Byronic romanticism, as in *The Eustace Diamonds*, his attack can be quite fierce. However, in *Ayala's Angel* he is more gentle: Ayala's dream of a perfect man, an 'Angel of Light' is shown to be ridiculous and even she comes to realize it. Of course, her artistic background is partly to blame and we are led to see this by observing the many artists in this book. As well as recalling some of Ayala's father's silly conversations, Trollope introduces other artists into the novel, including Isadore Hamel's father, also a sculptor.

The characters of the artists in the book allowed Trollope to attack the increasingly fashionable theories of 'art for art's sake'. Behind all the lightness and love-making of *Ayala's Angel*, the novelist had a serious purpose: to attack the latest versions of his old foe, excessive Romanticism, which was threatening a new revival in its attempt at undermining British society. It is worth noting that in the first pages of the novel, Trollope refers to an artist showing off his blue china; he may well have had in mind the remark, attributed to Oscar Wilde, about the difficulty of living up to one's blue china. This fatuous remark was apparently making the rounds of Society two years before Trollope

began the book. Such an attitude was completely at variance with Trollope's own concepts of both art and life.

In this novel Trollope made use of several characters, most notably Larry Twentyman, who had appeared in *The American Senator*. These characters are involved in the inevitable fox-hunting scene: by the time Trollope was writing *Ayala's Angel* he had given up the sport. The novel makes an even greater use of letters than one normally finds in his fiction. There are also more personal allusions, often through 'authorial intrusions', than is normal: he tells us that Château Leoville, 1864 was 'the most divine of nectars' [➤ Wine]. There are the usual silly names, like Septimus Traffick, the bald and boring son of Lord Boardotrade. The sections on Rome and a comment that an English artist should live in England may well have been stimulated by a visit his brother Tom made to him from Rome while he was writing the book; they are also reminiscent of his short story, 'Mrs General Talboys'. The portrayal of London, particularly the descriptions of riding and walking in Hyde Park, reflects his life in the 1870s. Even a small tribute to the safety of Cunard ships was a compliment to the chairman of that line, who had taken Trollope on his yacht to Iceland. The frequent use of a metaphor concerning a Newfoundland dog has echoes of his childhood.

Ayala's Angel has several interesting asides about novel-writing. He pokes fun at the sensational novels of his day by showing the farcical results of attempts at a duel and an elopement. There are also numerous references to the importance of Mudie's Library for Victorian readers and writers. By the time the book was published in 1881, he had to put in a footnote explaining that an allusion to the Russians and Afghanistan was no longer accurate [61].

Trollope had allowed one of the longest gaps in his writing of novels before he began work on *Ayala's Angel*: nine months had elapsed since he had finished *John Caldigate*, although in the meantime he had visited South Africa and had been writing a travel book about it. However, all this travelling was not the main reason why he picked a long sea voyage as a cure for one of Ayala's disappointed suitors; in selecting this cure, he was only endorsing a popular Victorian remedy. Only a few years earlier he had sent his elder son, Henry, on just such a trip to prevent him from making an unsuitable marriage.

He wrote a great deal of *Ayala's Angel* while on holiday in the Swiss Alps and the Black Forest. He told George Eliot that he was writing for four hours a day, and when he finished the novel he wrote to a friend in Aus-tralia that he had just completed his eightieth work of fiction: while this was his fortieth novel, he had also written about the same number of short stories. Occasionally one senses a slight tiredness with the constant grind of writing and he refers in passing to his 'tally of pages' [4].

In general the book received only mild praise from the reviewers, although the normally hostile *Saturday Review* lauded the 'extraordinarily life-like' dialogue and compared the portrayal of Colonel Jonathan Stubbs to Thackeray's achievement in the character of William Dobbin in *Vanity Fair*. *Ayala's Angel* has never been one of the most popular of Trollope's novels, but it can be warmly recommended to those who have read his best-known novels and who are anxious for an enjoyable book to read. Perhaps the fact that a 1993 issue of *Private Eye* could carry a 'personal' advertisement reading: 'Jonathan Stubbs seeks Ayala. Box 8819' may point to a growth in its popularity.

B

Bachelors. Since so many of Trollope's novels are centred on marriage, there are numerous young bachelors in his writing and naturally he drew on recollections of his own bachelor ways. A bachelor is usually portrayed as having 'no fixed hour for his meals, no fixed place for his books, no fixed wardrobe for his clothes' [*Doctor Thorne*, 3]. In almost all cases, marriage is the ideal solution for bachelors, especially if they are no longer young. Middle-aged bachelors can be stable men, like the Reverend Francis Arabin in *Barchester Towers*, Dr Thorne himself, John Pryor in 'Miss Ophelia Gledd' or Herr Crippel in 'Lotta Schmidt', and these are thought preferable to young 'curled darlings' as good husbands. In some cases – for instance, Peter Prosper in *Mr Scarborough's Family* – they are silly, especially when they attempt marriage. Middle-aged bachelors can also become suspect as 'wolves' and, as in the case of Colonel Osborne in *He Knew He Was Right*, acquire a reputation as a roué.

Baker, Mary. Mary Baker was the niece by marriage of George Bertram, the wealthy City merchant in *The Bertrams*. Miss Baker visits the Holy Land with her friend, Miss Todd. Both ladies live in the Evangelical town of Littlebath (Cheltenham) and both reappear in *Miss Mackenzie*. Miss Baker is the guardian of Caroline Waddington, the heroine of *The Bertrams*. [➤ Spinsters.]

Baldness. 'There is a baldness that is handsome and noble, and a baldness that is peculiarly mean and despicable,' said Trollope, who became quite bald in his forties [*Ralph the Heir*, 22]. One finds examples of both in his fiction: Neefit the tailor, referred to in this passage, has a 'despicable' baldness. John Ball in *Miss Mackenzie*, Herr Crippel in 'Lotta Schmidt' and Mr Pryor in 'Miss Ophelia Gledd' benefited from a 'handsome' baldness. Trollope presumably identified with 'noble' baldness and it is amusing to see, particularly in the short stories, that balding men triumph at the expense of younger 'curled darlings'.

Bankruptcy. The total financial collapse of a man and his family was a fearful thing for any Victorian as there was no 'welfare state' to provide for basic needs. Although bankruptcy was not an uncommon occurrence, it still brought disgrace and often exile. With clergymen the penalty was even harsher: a bankrupt parish priest could have his ecclesiastical income seized by his bishop to pay the debt. [➤ *Framley Parsonage*.]

Trollope had painful memories of his father's financial collapse and these affected his fiction, not only in his realization of the importance of money but in the misery endured, particularly by wives, when families faced bankruptcy. Throughout his boyhood his father's debts caused great worry, and in 1834 the family, including the nineteen-year-old Trollope, fled to Belgium so that his father could escape from bankruptcy and possible arrest for his debts. In his first novel, *The Macdermots of Ballycloran*, he portrays a family that faces financial and social ruin through the foreclosing of a mortgage. He is not interested in the legal mechanics of bankruptcy, but in the victim's reaction to the prospect of it. In *Framley Parsonage* [44] he uses one of his 'authorial intrusions' to speak directly to his female readers when a young clergyman's debts cause his creditors to take action: 'O ladies, who have drawing rooms, in which things are pretty ... think of what it would be to have two bailiffs rummaging among them with pen and ink-horn.' His accounts of other characters who face similar disasters are less emotional, particularly if the offender has met his fate through vast spending to keep up an inflated position. The bankrupt MP in *Framley Parsonage* gets less sympathy than the foolish clergyman he has led astray, and there is little sympathy for the bankrupt Melmotte in *The Way We Live Now*. Suicide is the fate of many of Trollope's bankrupts, such as Melmotte, Dobbs Broughton in *The Last Chronicle of Barset*, Sir Henry Harcourt in *The Bertrams* and Ferdinand Lopez in *The Prime Minister*. Trollope's mercy is usually bestowed on their widows and enough money is usually found to support them. For the details he needed he could turn to his oldest friend, John Merivale, who was a Bankruptcy Commissioner.

Banks and Bankers. These were difficult subjects for Trollope because of a family scandal. His father-in-law, Edward Heseltine, was the manager of the Sheffield and Rotherham Bank in Rotherham. In 1854, shortly after his retirement, bank officials discovered that £4,000 was missing; Heseltine refused to return to Rotherham to answer questions. He fled to France, where he died in 1855. The scandal never became public knowledge. [For details, see Mullen, 130–31, 292–3.] As Trollope wrote in *Doctor Thorne* almost three years later: 'You will see men labouring night and day to become bank directors; and even a bank direction may be the road to ruin' [18]. Bankers and City financiers occur in many novels, often in an unfavourable light as in *The Way We Live Now*. Glimpses of provincial banking appear in the Barsetshire novels, but not in any great detail. Bankers and their families play important roles in *He Knew He Was Right*, *Ayala's Angel* and *John Caldigate*. The most developed portrait of a banker in the novels is that of the kindly and generous Sir Thomas Tringle, a former Governor of the Bank of England, in *Ayala's Angel*.

Bankers also appear in several of the short stories ('The Mistletoe Bough', and 'The House of Heine Brothers in Munich' in which Trollope probably drew on his brother Henry's luckless attempt to become a banker in Paris). One of his last published pieces of fiction, 'The Two Heroines of Plumplington', is set in part in a Barsetshire banker's house. Here Trollope drew on recollections of his wife's early home life above her father's bank. Like many Victorian novelists, Trollope made great use in his plots of the difficulties that could arise from borrowing.

Trollope's sole legacy from his mother was shares in a bank and he made profitable investments in buying more of the same. He had his own current account at the Union Bank, Prince's Street, London.
[➤ Bankruptcy; Bills; Debt.]

Barchester. The principal city in the county of Barsetshire and the cathedral city for the Diocese of Barchester. [➤ Barsetshire Novels for those cities on which it was based.]

Barchester Towers. This was Trollope's fifth novel and the second in the Barsetshire series. He appears to have started it in January 1855 and by 17 February he had finished about a third of the text, only to drop it in order to write *The New Zealander*. He did not resume work on it until 12 May 1856 and he finished the book on 9 November. During this period he reached the peak of his Post Office career in Ireland, and at this time he also moved from Belfast to Dublin. Longman published the book in May 1857 as a three-volume novel. Trollope was offered £100 advance and received half profits. Eventually he received £707. 7s. 6d. [➤ Publishers and Publishing.]

Trollope's fourth novel, *The Warden*, was the first which he felt to be moderately successful. Even before its publication and favourable reception, he decided to continue the story of Barsetshire. *Barchester Towers* is really a sequel to *The Warden* and the books should be read in the proper order, even though Trollope makes some at-

tempt in *Barchester Towers* to give readers brief summaries of characters or events from the earlier novel.

Barchester Towers records the battles between clergymen and their families when the new bishop, Thomas Proudie, succeeds old Bishop Grantly. Bishop Proudie's formidable wife and his oleaginous chaplain, Obadiah Slope, struggle first with the Grantly faction and then with one another to gain control of the diocese. A form of this battle was occurring in virtually every diocese of the Church of England in Trollope's time and informed contemporary readers understood his allusions. The Grantlys, led by the old bishop's son, Archdeacon Theophilus Grantly, stand for the old-fashioned clergy, gentlemen of moderate High Church, Tory views, while the Proudies adhere to the Evangelical party. Since Proudie gained his bishopric through the favour of a Liberal prime minister, the Proudies are supporters of Church reform. The novel was set in the decade in which it was written and as Trollope adhered to his normal practice of leaving the last digit in the year blank we only know that the novel begins in the 1850s. Liberal politicians were in the ascendant in the 1850s, but there were two brief interludes of Conservative rule; it is Archdeacon Grantly's misfortune that his father's death coincides with the death of a Tory ministry, thus depriving him of his hoped-for bishopric.

The Grantly party includes not only the Archdeacon and his wise wife, Susan, but her father, Septimus Harding, who had resigned as Warden of Hiram's Hospital in the previous novel. They acquire a clever new recruit from Oxford, Francis Arabin, a more advanced High Churchman, influenced by Newman and the Oxford Movement. Arabin receives one of the longest and most carefully drawn background portraits in all of Trollope's writings, one that reveals much about the author's own religious position [20]. Much of the action centres on the attempts of the Proudies to promote Evangelical and Sabbatarian ideas in a conservative diocese and there is a great struggle as to whether Mr Harding or Mrs Proudie's candidate, Mr Quiverful, shall occupy the vacant wardenship of the almshouses. Mr Harding's younger daughter, Eleanor Bold, a wealthy widow, is the focus of the novel's love plot when she is pursued by three suitors. Trollope is rather fond of the idea of a woman being pursued by three suitors, of whom at least one is slightly farcical [➤ *Ayala's Angel*; *The Claverings*; *Miss Mackenzie*].

With *Barchester Towers* Trollope entered into his maturity as a novelist after almost thirteen years of effort. The book opens with a death scene: Archdeacon Grantly is at his father's deathbed and the son's ambition, which depends on a quick death, battles with his genuine religious belief and a son's natural love for his father. It is one of the finest moments in all Trollope's writing. Because Trollope is restrained and because he does not wallow in emotion, this scene does not repel modern readers who often find fictional accounts of Victorian death, as in the novels of Dickens, too sentimental. (Aspects of this scene have a parallel in the final Barsetshire novel, *The Last Chronicle of Barset* [81], when the archdeacon witnesses Mr Harding's death.)

Not only did Trollope display a

mastery over such an intimate episode, but, like a great film director, showed an equal mastery over the large 'crowd scene' at the *fête-champêtre* at Ullathorne, when he assembled most of Barsetshire society. Here we are introduced to the subtle gradations of rural life and the difficulty of deciding who shall sit among 'the quality'. 'It is in such definitions,' Trollope says with a mixture of mild sarcasm and genuine seriousness, 'that the whole difficulty of society consists.' Much of his later writing career would be devoted to establishing those 'definitions'. This party, one of the longest in fiction, occupies eight chapters, yet the reader never tires because the details, narration and dialogue move about among different characters and different parts of the house and grounds. There is a genuine sense of being at a party, far more so than when Trollope describes the Duke of Omnium's party in one and a half chapters in *Phineas Finn*. The country house, Ullathorne, is based on Montacute in Somerset, and the medieval games reflect the fad for medievalism inspired by men like Pugin, Kenelm Digby and Tennyson, as well as the Eglinton tournaments. [➤ 'The Gentle Euphemia'.]

Another sign of Trollope's maturity as a novelist is the contrast that can be made between the clumsy and envious parodies of Carlyle and Dickens in *The Warden* and the gentle mockery of the silly Ullathorne games or the splendid portrait of the Stanhope family. In describing this quintet of Italianized Englishmen, Trollope could draw on people he had met and conversations he had heard during his two recent trips to Italy to visit his mother and his brother Tom at their villa in

Florence [➤ 'Mrs General Talboys']. The three Stanhope children may lack that greatest of Trollopian virtues, honesty, but they are the life of Mrs Proudie's reception at the Palace. This is Trollope's most celebrated comic writing and rightly so. The details are arranged with infinite care and we have one of the first appearances of a favourite Trollopian device to make the reader dislike a character: the Proudies exult in Slope's achievement in buying cheap wine. Trollope uses such details, including Mrs Proudie's earlier chatter about her carriage and horses, to illustrate the pretensions of some characters. In this case we also get a glimpse of Mrs Proudie's snobbishness and insecurity.

When Italian servants enter bearing Madeline Stanhope − or to give her her acquired name, La Signora Madeline Vesey Neroni − on a litter, Trollope manages to bring the cosmopolitan and tantalizing world of Italy into the provincial sitting-rooms of Barchester's clergy. In this scene there is an amusing example of the way in which Trollope paid tribute to the two women who had so influenced his life, his mother and his wife, Rose. La Signora is described as wearing a headband 'on the centre of which shone a magnificent Cupid in mosaic'. This jewel is almost exactly like the one that Princess Metternich had given to Fanny Trollope on her visit to Vienna in the 1830s and she had given it to Rose Trollope when they visited her in Florence [Mullen, 299]. This is typical of the way in which Trollope inserted private jokes, in this case designed for his wife, the only person allowed to read and criticize his MSS. before he sent them to his publishers. (The jewel was used again in *The Claverings*, 41.)

Rose's interest in fashion and hair styles, and her skill in needlework, contributed especially to descriptions of women's clothes in this novel.

Trollope's family was not his only source for this picture of English society. To consider only one chapter [3]: he refers to a trio of real clergymen, Sydney Smith, Bishop Hampden of Hereford and Archbishop Whately of Dublin. According to Escott, Trollope had known Smith; he had written some of *The Warden* in Hampden's diocese in which one of his own distant cousins was a canon of the cathedral with the 'sweet close'; Whately was Trollope's own bishop in Dublin. A few paragraphs later he refers to three ecclesiastical subjects then causing much agitation in Ireland: the Presbyterian Synod of Ulster, the *Regium Donum* or royal grant to Presbyterian ministers, and the Maynooth grant to the Catholic Seminary there. These passing references − although the liberal Hampden would pop up again as an old foe of Archdeacon Grantly − provided a buttress of topical allusions for contemporary readers. As in *The Warden*, Trollope also drew on his careful reading of *The Times*, which he caricatures as the *Jupiter*. Thus the conversation between Bishop Proudie and the archdeacon about university reform shows that Trollope had read the evidence of the Commission considering the topic; he also appears to have read Canon Edward Pusey's criticisms of it.

In *The Warden* Trollope's mind often seems divided between the need for Church reform and a sympathy for those, like Mr Harding, who were swept aside by the reforming spirit of the age. In *Barchester Towers*, the novelist seems more content with himself.

The uncertainties caused by British incompetence in the Crimean War, for which see *The New Zealander*, were laid aside as the country resumed its progressive march forward. His conservative side – what might be called his Grantly side – is almost totally in the ascendant in this novel. Here is the Trollope whose own quiet devotion to the Church of England allowed him to portray most of its clergy with sympathy, the writer whose family background [➤ Baronets] led him to admire gentry families like the Thornes. When he has finished describing the Thornes with all their quixotic charm, he says, 'Such, we believe, are the inhabitants of many an English country home. May it be long before their number diminishes' [22].

Women play a crucial role in the novel, but this is rarely noted. Since Mrs Proudie – probably Trollope's best-known character in his own day, at least according to Henry James – makes her first appearance in this book, it is easy to allow her to overwhelm the other female characters. Yet throughout the novel men are constantly being guided by strong women: Mrs Quiverful fights the battle for her weak husband; Mrs Grantly imposes a sensible restraint on her impetuous husband, the archdeacon; Eleanor Bold defeats Mr Slope and undermines Mr Arabin's celibacy; Monica Thorne, in her own scatty way, leads her brother, Wilfred; Charlotte Stanhope rules her father and her brother; and even in the novel's brief glimpse of Shakespearian 'low life', the 'dames' in farming families like the Lookalofts determine social behaviour. *Barchester Towers* is as much a portrait of powerful women in the Victorian world as it is of combative clergymen. The

difference between all these women and Mrs Proudie is that while they exercise their influence and power in private, Mrs Proudie hectors and humiliates her spouse in public, an unforgivable sin to her creator. [For the way in which Mrs Proudie exemplifies the Victorian comic idea of a shrewish woman, ➤ Cradell, Joseph.]

This novel shows Trollope's ability to sum up minor characters in a few pithy words. The dean's daughter, Miss Trefoil, is 'a gaunt spinster ... very learned in stones, ferns, plants, and vermin, and ... [she] had written a book about petals' [10]. Here we can see Trollope's literary descent from Jane Austen and his central role in a tradition of gentle English comedy that reaches down to Barbara Pym in our own time. Dickens would have struck poor Miss Trefoil such a blow that she and her ferns would have disappeared. The humour extends to Miss Trefoil's name, an example of the fun Trollope had in choosing names: a trefoil is, of course, a medieval design of three parts, like a leaf, and was often used for windows of churches [➤ Names, Origin of]. One must also add that *Barchester Towers* is not without its faults: as Hugh Walpole observed, the most noticeable is the lack of any real description of Barchester Cathedral.

Barchester Towers marks a crucial step in Trollope's development as a professional writer. He began a practice that he would follow in all other novels. He began to keep a daily schedule of his writing on work sheets: thus we know that he wrote eight pages on 12 May 1855, the day he resumed the writing of this novel. He could write portions of his manuscript in pencil while travelling for his wife to copy for the publishers, thus giving her an increasing influence in his writing.

Trollope had difficulty with Longmans, who had published *The Warden*. Their reader thought the manuscript inferior to its predecessor and found the Signora 'the great blot on the work'. He wanted the book shortened by removing Mrs Proudie's reception. Although Longmans rejected these absurd recommendations, it was only with reluctance that they agreed to pay Trollope an advance of £100, the first substantial sum he made from writing. They also insisted he remove language such as 'foul breathing' and alter 'fat stomach' for which he substituted 'deep chest'. Nor was Longman himself happy with Trollope for retaining a scene where a clergyman kisses a woman. Longman would not be the last person to condemn parts of Trollope's writing as vulgar.

However, the reception of this novel made Trollope's reputation: *The Warden* had brought him to the attention of readers. Now he began to attract the plaudits of critics. George Meredith, just beginning his own career as a novelist, praised the book as a novel which, 'without resorting to politics' or social reform, could be enjoyed by men. Almost a decade later another beginner, Thomas Hardy, said it was Trollope's best. One of Trollope's greatest admirers was John Henry Newman who is called 'the great Newman' in Chapter 20 and is often referred to in the novel. The novel attracted even more eminent readers than Newman: Prince Albert read it, as well as Queen Victoria. At first she found it 'very amusing' but then decided it did not have enough 'Romance'. Her eldest daughter dared

to disagree and said it made 'one laugh till one cries', while the Queen's half-sister replied in words echoed by many subsequent readers: 'It is very clever and well written and the characters admirably drawn after life. I read it slowly – *pour fait durer la plaisir*' [Mullen, 305–6]. It also remained close to its author's heart. A quarter of a century later he wrote to a young relative: 'There is not a passage in it I do not remember. I always have to pretend to forget when people talk to me about my own old books. It looks modest; – and to do the other things looks the reverse. But the writer never forgets.'

In the Second World War, Somerset Maugham was asked to draw up a list of books which would help Americans to understand the British character: *Barchester Towers* was the first novel on his list. It ranks high among Trollope's achievements, and while it may not be his greatest novel, no other contains so many humorous and enjoyable scenes.

Baronets. Baronets are often portrayed as either humorous or sinister figures in much nineteenth-century fiction because of their history and their uneasy position halfway between commoners and peers. Baronets occur frequently in Trollope's fiction, and unlike most of his fellow novelists he painted them in a variety of colours. A baronet is a man who holds a hereditary knighthood. James I created baronets in 1611 to raise funds and sold them at first for £1,095. A baronet is addressed as 'Sir', with the abbreviation Bt. or Bart. following his name. The title is inherited by his eldest son or closest surviving legitimate male relative. The wives of baronets have the title 'Lady'. Baronets are not peers, and when Francesca Altifiorla hopes to marry one so that she will be within 'the bounds of an English peerage' Trollope's informed readers saw yet another absurd aspect of her character [*Kept in the Dark*, 18]. Although baronets do not have the right to sit in the House of Lords, the title conveys considerable social prestige and rank.

Trollope himself was the descendant of a Lincolnshire family that had acquired a baronetcy in 1642. Trollope's grandfather was a younger son of the fourth baronet: like a baronet in *The Prime Minister*, the novelist could claim that his 'forefathers had been baronets since baronets were first created' [13]. He was expressing a traditional view when he said that 'a man who gets himself to be made a baronet cleanses himself from the stains of trade'. Against this view he argued in the same novel that a man who could claim he was a cousin to a baronet with an *old* title 'had reason to be proud of his blood' [*Miss Mackenzie*, 1]. To modern readers there may be a touch of humour in this, but it reflected the author's own sentiments and those of his age. Trollope was 'proud of his blood' and used the family crest on his notepaper and the coat of arms on his bookplates. He often stayed with his distant cousin, Sir John Trollope, Bt. (1800–1874), a Tory politician who was eventually ennobled as Lord Kesteven. No doubt his advice to his younger son, Frederic, in Australia, to preserve his sons' birth certificates was motivated at least in part by the distant prospect that one of them might inherit the baronetcy. Eventually the senior Trollope baronetcy did pass to Anthony Trollope's descendants in Australia. (A second Trollope baronetcy was created for another younger son who was a celebrated admiral, and the novelist Joanna Trollope is descended from this branch of the family.)

Trollope's baronets, like almost every other group he portrayed, are a mixture. Often they are old-fashioned landowners, living far from London and faithful to older notions of honour and honesty. They may have their foibles, but a man like Sir Alured Wharton in *The Prime Minister* is 'a pure-minded, simple gentleman, who could not tell a lie, and who could not do a wrong' [13]. The same would apply to Sir Harry Hotspur in *Sir Harry Hotspur of Humblethwaite* and Sir Peregrine Orme in *Orley Farm*. One of his best depictions of a silly baronet is Sir Walter Wanless, 'the best dressed old baronet in England', in 'Alice Dugdale', while Sir Anthony Aylmer is a henpecked baronet in *The Belton Estate*. Trollope also portrayed newer types of baronets, men who were given their title because of wealth derived from new sources, such as the vulgar Sir Roger Scatcherd in *Doctor Thorne*, who made a fortune from building railways, or the genial and generous City banker Sir Thomas Tringle in *Ayala's Angel*.

On the other hand, baronets like Sir Felix Carbury in *The Way We Live Now*, Sir Hugh Clavering in *The Claverings*, or Sir Florian Eustace in *The Eustace Diamonds*, can be thoroughly disreputable, or at least not admirable, men.

Barristers. See Lawyers.

Barsetshire Novels. There are six novels in the Barsetshire series and from their publication they have usually been the most popular of

Trollope's forty-seven novels. The six, with their dates of publication, are: *The Warden* (1855); *Barchester Towers* (1857); *Doctor Thorne* (1858); *Framley Parsonage* (1861); *The Small House at Allington* (1864); and *The Last Chronicle of Barset* (1867). *Framley Parsonage* was the first to be serialized. In 1878, after much negotiation over copyright, a collected edition in eight volumes, *The Chronicles of Barsetshire*, was issued by Chapman & Hall with a short introduction by Trollope. Trollope did not wish to include *The Small House at Allington* as most of the novel does not take place in Barsetshire but in the next county. However, because this novel contains several characters from the first four novels and introduces others who would feature in the last one, popular opinion had always rightly insisted that it should be included and Trollope yielded.

In 1851, Trollope was asked by the Post Office to improve rural deliveries in the West of England. He spent much of the next two years visiting villages and hamlets. He rode an average of forty miles a day and often walked the round a letter-carrier would follow to see that the 'walk' did not exceed sixteen miles. Trollope's duties also required him to question local people about postal deliveries. The best sources were clergymen and the gentry. All this gave Trollope an unrivalled knowledge of real life in mid-Victorian rural England. The basic theme lying behind much of the Barsetshire stories is the conflict between this seemingly unchanging England and the newer forces associated with political and church reforms, railways, the rise of industrial wealth and the ever-increasing influence of London and newspapers. He later wrote that the 'English character, with its faults and virtues, its prejudices and steadfastness, can be better studied in the mansions of noblemen, in country houses, in parsonages, in farms, and small meaningless towns, than in the great cities' [*Australia*].

Trollope offers a lyrical description of Barsetshire at the beginning of *Doctor Thorne*. 'Barset' – as the county name is often abbreviated – is 'purely agricultural' and has no cities of any size. Barchester, the county town, is only called a 'city' because it is the seat of the Bishop of Barchester. The Reform Bill of 1832 divided Barsetshire (as it did some of the larger, real counties) into two parliamentary divisions, in this case East and West. East Barsetshire is even more Conservative than West as the latter contains the residences of two great Whig magnates, Earl De Courcy at Courcy Castle and the old Duke of Omnium at Gatherum Castle. Trollope made a rough sketch-map of Barsetshire so that his characters' movements would be correct.

In the last weeks of his life, Trollope paid one final visit to the West Country where he assured the historian E. A. Freeman that Barsetshire was based on Somerset but that Barchester itself was based on Winchester, where he had been at school [Mullen, 651–2]. To create Barsetshire, Trollope added to Somerset some aspects of Dorset and of his favourite county, Devon. He may well have taken some aspects of Salisbury, Exeter and Hereford for Barchester.

The Barsetshire novels portray the aristocracy (the families of peers like Omnium, De Courcy, De Guest and Lufton), the gentry (the Greshams, the Thornes and the Sowerbys) and the clergy (the Grantly and Proudie families as well as Mr Harding and his successor, Quiverful, Canon Stanhope and the bishop's chaplain, Slope), and the 'new money' like the Scatcherds. Anyone who knows the novels will realize that this list of characters, admittedly incomplete, contains a mixture of both good and bad, town and country. As well as these traditional figures in society, the Barsetshire novels offer numerous portraits of the professional classes: lawyers such as Gazebee, and doctors, the most notable being Dr Thorne himself. Tradesmen, farmers and servants appear in the books, but are rarely developed as characters.

The novels describe contemporary events and cover about fifteen to eighteen years: the Reverend Septimus Harding, the central character, is 'verging on sixty years' when *The Warden* begins and is seventy-eight when *The Last Chronicle of Barset* ends. Unlike the later Palliser series, politics play a minor role and feature mainly in the occasional parliamentary election, in the appointment of bishops or other high-ranking clerical figures, or in the animosity between an old Tory family like the Luftons and the Whig Duke of Omnium in *Framley Parsonage*. The Barsetshire novels were written and set in the 1850s and early 1860s when British politics were dominated by Liberal governments, by that patriotic moderate Liberalism associated with Lord Palmerston with which Trollope had broad sympathy. Although the clergy do not dominate every novel in the series – they are not of great importance in *Doctor Thorne* and *The Small House at Allington* – they are the most memorable characters. The saintly Mr Harding, his combative son-in-law Archdeacon Grantly, the pusillanimous Bishop Proudie and the fierce 'priestess', Mrs Proudie, the oleaginous Mr Slope, the bishop's chaplain, – these are probably the best-known and most often cited of all Trollope's characters.

Many reviewers and readers implored Trollope to continue the series after he proclaimed that *The Last Chronicle of Barset* meant exactly what it said in its title, but he refused. Not only had *The Last Chronicle* ended with the deaths of two of the essential characters, Mr Harding and Mrs Proudie, but the world that Barsetshire embodied was changing. Those forces for change and 'progress', mentioned above, could no longer be kept outside Barsetshire by the late 1860s. Likewise the Church of England had changed and the battles between High and Low, Conservative and Liberal, had grown more intense. A few of the characters, notably Plantagenet Palliser, reappear in the Palliser series of novels. Silverbridge, the second most important town in Barsetshire, is also mentioned frequently in the Palliser books, usually as the scene of an election. In the last year of his life, Trollope made one slight, feeble attempt to return to the 'dear county' with a short story, 'The Two Heroines of Plumplington'. *The Claverings*, too, may be set in Barset because the rector's bishop is Bishop Proudie, although the county is not mentioned. In his short story 'Mrs Brumby', Trollope makes a passing reference to the *West Barsetshire Gazette*.

The Barsetshire novels are the best starting point for anyone to begin reading Trollope and the true Trollopian will return to the novels time and time again, always to find something new because of the author's outstanding ability to paint scenes and to portray characters. Clergymen have always been among Trollope's most devoted readers and they have kept the fame of their fictional prototypes alive. In the final paragraph of *The Last Chronicle of Barset*, Trollope wrote: 'To me Barset has been a real county, and its city a real city.' He was therefore able to make it real for his readers; this, more than anything else, makes him the great novelist he is.

Beards. In *Barchester Towers*, written between January 1855 and early November 1856, one feature of Bertie Stanhope's 'most singular' appearance when he returns to provincial Barchester from Italy is his 'patriarchal' beard, something so unusual on an English gentleman as to require comment. The fashion for beards was growing in Victorian society as Trollope was writing. It is often said to have started when officers came back from the Crimean War, during which conditions had made shaving difficult. Before that time beards were rarely worn by gentlemen, who regarded them as a sign of foreigners and revolutionaries. In his book on Palmerston, Trollope quotes that Liberal politician's description of the 1848 Chartists as 'whiskered and bearded rioters'.

From 1858 onwards most of the men in Trollope's novels are described, or pictured in the illustrations, as having beards or at least facial whiskers. This probably follows Trollope's own growth of a beard which may date from his long Post Office visit to the Middle East between January and May 1858. By November it was so well established that the Spanish official who validated his passport when he wished to travel to Cuba described him as having a *poblada* or thick beard. By 1860 Elizabeth Barrett Browning, writing of course as an expatriate, described his beard as 'extraordinary', a judgement confirmed by the first extant photograph of Trollope which was taken that year.

In *Doctor Thorne*, completed during the Egyptian trip, young Frank Gresham also returns from a trip to Egypt with a long beard. Unlike Bertie Stanhope's his is not part of its owner's strange appearance but very fashionable: its 'silken sheen' fascinates young women and even his old-fashioned father is proud of this 'patriarchal adornment', although he wonders how his son manages to drink soup. In *The Bertrams*, which Trollope started the day after he finished *Doctor Thorne*, beards are now a standard part of manly appearance: the leading character is criticized for not wearing 'the slightest apology of a whisker'[1]. Beards must not just be worn but worn long. In 'La Mère Bauche', written in 1859, the hero, Adolphe Bauche, naturally not only has a beard but a long beard.

By the 1860s Trollope felt that beards gave character to the face [*Can You Forgive Her?*, 22]. Men who are 'manly', like John Eames or Phineas Finn, have beards, while a 'curled darling' like Burgo Fitzgerald refuses to disguise 'his almost godlike face' with a beard [*Can You Forgive Her?*, 29]. The absence of a beard is often an indication that a man is not to be trusted. Older men, normally described as being either clean-shaven or having only whiskers, are excused, and here Trollope as usual is reflecting Victorian custom.

Beauty. See Women.

Beeswax, Sir Timothy. A Tory politician in the Palliser novels. In *The Prime Minister* he becomes particularly hostile to Plantagenet Palliser, by now Duke of Omnium, and therefore incurs the great enmity of his wife, Glencora, Duchess of Omnium. Beeswax is a lawyer with few political principles but is anxious not to be limited to the legal offices of government. In *The Duke's Children* [21] he becomes the leader of the House of Commons under Lord Drummond's Tory administration.

Belgium. In 1834, when Trollope was nineteen, his family fled to Belgium so that his father could escape his debts. Anthony lived in Bruges, and his father and brother Henry died and were buried there. Trollope had only just begun to teach in an English school in Brussels when he accepted a position in the Post Office in London. He recalled Antwerp in his first published short story, 'Relics of General Chassé', which is set in that city. Much later, in *Mr Scarborough's Family*, he recalled Brussels as a place where Englishmen could find cheap education. He also wrote in that novel that the best Belgians looked like Englishmen – although he said roughly the same thing about Dutchmen in an article on his tour in Holland for the *Cornhill Magazine*. Ostend is the place where a farcical elopement ends in *Ayala's Angel*, and Bruges is near the spot where Lord Chiltern and Phineas Finn fight their duel in *Phineas Finn*.

The Belton Estate. Trollope's seventeenth novel was written between 30 January and 4 September 1865. Its serialization began in the first issue of the *Fortnightly Review* on 15 May 1865 and ran until 1 January 1866. It was published in three volumes by Chapman & Hall in December 1865, but dated 1866. Trollope received £1,757.

This novel has been given short shrift by many people, including Trollope himself. In his *Autobiography* he wrote: 'It is readable, and contains scenes which are true to life; but it has no peculiar merits, and will add nothing to my reputation as a novelist. I have not looked at it since it was published; and now turning back to it in my memory, I seem to remember almost less of it than of any book that I have written.' This disclaimer may have been made partly because he wrote it to order for the first issue of the *Fortnightly Review* when his own view, as chairman of the magazine's board, was that the magazine did not need a serialized novel. The other men involved in the new magazine knew that a novel by Trollope would help to secure an audience. Secondly, this novel was only one of the twenty books (fourteen novels, three collections of short stories, two volumes of occasional essays and his *North America*) that he published in that decade. Among the books were *Framley Parsonage*, *Orley Farm*, *The Small House at Allington*, *The Last Chronicle of Barset* and *Phineas Finn*: it is no wonder that Trollope discounted this novel.

The story centres on Clara Amedroz, the 25-year-old only daughter of the owner of Belton Castle in Somerset. Because her only brother had committed suicide, the heir to her father's distressed estate was, under entail, her cousin, Will Belton. [For another estate whose heir was a daughter, ➤ *Sir Harry Hotspur of Humblethwaite*.] Clara regularly visits her aunt, Mrs Winterfield, one of Trollope's formidable Evangelical ladies whose expression 'seemed ever to be telling of her own sorrows in this world and of the sorrows of others in the world to come'. She is not as nasty as some of Trollope's other Evangelical lady-tyrants, such as Mrs Proudie, Mrs Bolton in *John Caldigate*, or the continental version in *Linda Tressel* [➤ Women]. Clara falls in love with Mrs Winterfield's nephew, Captain Frederic Folliott Aylmer, MP, the younger son of a baronet; he is the heir to his aunt. After Mrs Winterfield's death the couple become engaged but Clara, headstrong and sharp of tongue, breaks it off when she thinks he has only asked her because his aunt requested it on her deathbed. Later the engagement is renewed. While this is going on a more distant cousin, Will Belton, a Norfolk farmer, falls in love with Clara. This provides one of Trollope's favourite situations: two men in love with the same woman – the dilemma that dominates *The Small House at Allington*. While Belton is exuberant and manly, Aylmer is cold and cautious. The novel describes Clara's disenchantment with Aylmer, heightened by a visit to his ancestral home in Yorkshire where his formidable mother opposes the match (not unusual in Trollope's fiction) and demands that Clara disown her friend and neighbour, Mrs Askerton, who had once 'lived in sin' with her present husband. In the end Clara refuses, drops Aylmer and marries Will Belton.

While the novel might seem another 'will she – won't she' story, the characterization and the moral problems that permeate it make this far from being the case. The story is largely one of people at sixes and sevens, each one frustrated in getting what he or she wants out of others or out of life. Clara's situation is that faced by thousands of Victorian women. She is hemmed in by convention and lacks the education and training needed to earn her livelihood. Her spirit and sharpness in questioning accepted standards bring her to life. When told by a man that something would be 'settled' about her future she retorts, 'Oh what a weary word that is ... at least, for a woman's ears! It sounds of poverty and dependence, and endless trouble given to others, and all the miseries of female dependence. If I were a young man I should be allowed to settle for myself.' [For a similar view by another frustrated female character, ➤ *The Bertrams*.] Will Belton is Trollopian in his manly self-confidence and exuberance. Frederic Aylmer's father, Sir Anthony, is cynical and his observations on marriage [27] add to the novel's sharpness, already evident in Clara and Mrs Askerton's dialogue.

In the plight of Colonel and Mrs Askerton, Trollope tackles Victorian moral codes and examines the nature of Christian compassion, as he did in *Sir Harry Hotspur of Humblethwaite* and *The Vicar of Bullhampton*. The Askertons, with whom he clearly wishes us to sympathize, have taken a house on the Belton estate. In his treatment of them Trollope shows a liberal attitude towards divorce. Mrs Askerton had been married to a brutal man whom she left with the aid of Colonel Askerton. She then lived with the colonel for three years and married him after her husband had died. While Clara refuses to disown the Askertons, she admits that if she had known their story beforehand she would have conformed to the world's standards and would not have befriended Mrs Askerton. But she did not know. She asks herself: 'Was it now needful – did her own feminine purity demand – that she should throw her friend over because in past years her life had been tainted by misconduct.' Will Belton, while never actually condoning the Askertons' past, accepts them at face value and implicitly accepts their past as irrelevant. The message is clear: 'Judge not that ye be not judged.' This sub-plot would be welcome to the liberal intellectual readers of the *Fortnightly Review*. Its editor at the time was Trollope's close friend G. H. Lewes, whose long-time relationship with George Eliot was known to Trollope.

Several essential Trollopian themes occur throughout the novel: the slightly sympathetic reference to duels; an excellent discussion on the nature of an English gentleman [24]; the pleasures and responsibilities of owning a landed estate; the boredom that often marked country-house life; the risks of self-deprecation; the love of possessing a grievance. The novel also gives modern readers a good insight into Victorian travel beyond railways. In Chapters 28 and 32 Trollope, presumably through an error, gives the same surname to two minor characters: Will Belton's 'man' in Norfolk is named Bunce, as is the old woman left in charge of Belton Castle after the death of Clara's father.

In much of its tone, the novel has similarities with the Barsetshire books, which is only to be expected since Somerset, where much of it is set, was

the model for Barsetshire. By the time Trollope was writing *The Belton Estate*, it was more than a decade since he had laid out the postal routes in Somerset; his current work for the Post Office covered eastern England, where Will Belton's own land lay. Belton is one of those practical men with a real knowledge of agriculture that Trollope liked to portray.

The 21-year-old Henry James, reviewing the book, found it 'a very pleasing tale' but ultimately one lacking any serious purpose: 'we seemed to be reading a work written for children'. James, who was still in America, did not perhaps realize that divorce and entail were two legal problems that greatly interested serious English readers. There is, however, a point in the *Spectator*'s criticism that the novel would be better if there were more characters in it, allowing Trollope to create more amusing scenes. Michael Sadleir believed that 'in no other novel is the essence of Trollope so concentrated' [➤ *Essays and Reviews*].

Richard Bentley & Son (1829–98). A leading nineteenth-century publishing house that was instrumental in establishing both the 'three-decker' novel and the idea of a relatively cheap reprint which followed it. The firm was established by Richard Bentley, a printer, and for a short period it was allied with Henry Colburn. In 1837 Bentley began *Bentley's Miscellany*, which in 1868 was absorbed in the firm's new magazine, *Temple Bar*. Richard Bentley was succeeded by his son, George. The *Miscellany* published Dickens's *Oliver Twist* and the firm went on to publish many other famous writers, including Wilkie Collins,

'Ouida', Marie Corelli and Charles Reade. In 1898, three years after George Bentley's death, the firm was bought out by Macmillan.

The Trollope family's connection with Richard Bentley began when he published Fanny Trollope's novel *Tremordyn Cliff* in 1835. After that he published nine of her books. Trollope's connection also began in 1835 when the twenty-year-old Post Office clerk took round proofs of *Tremordyn Cliff*. He asked if Bentley could advise where he should try to place articles; Bentley's response is not known. Trollope next approached Bentley in 1847 about publishing *The Kellys and the O'Kellys* but he rejected it on the terms Trollope demanded. Ten years later he took the manuscript of *The Three Clerks* to Bentley. Richard Bentley agreed to publish it. The next year, 1858, Trollope offered *Doctor Thorne* to Bentley for £400, but as Bentley could only offer £300 Trollope took it to Chapman & Hall, thereby beginning his long relationship with his principal publisher. After that, Trollope had no further dealings with the firm although he was involved with George Bentley in the serialization of *The American Senator* in *Temple Bar*.

Bermuda. Trollope visited the island during his trip for the Post Office in May 1849. He described it in *The West Indies and the Spanish Main* as beautiful but 'triste' because people seemed content to accept their poverty. He used the island as the setting for his short story 'Aaron Trow', and he referred to it in *John Caldigate*.

The Bertrams. Trollope's eighth novel was written between 1 April 1858 and 17 January 1859, a period in which

he travelled on Post Office business to Egypt, the Holy Land, Scotland, the North of England and the West Indies. Trollope began it in Egypt, the day after he finished *Doctor Thorne*. The book was published in March 1859 as a 'three-decker' by Chapman & Hall. Trollope received £400.

The Bertrams has never been one of Trollope's popular novels. In his *Autobiography* he was very critical: 'I do not know that I have ever heard it well spoken of even by my friends.' The characters were not memorable and the plot, he said, was 'more than ordinarily bad; and as the book was relieved by no special character, it failed. Its failure never surprised me ... the love-scenes ... are not good.' The circumstances of its composition give it its weaknesses, but they also provide its strength. At the top of the work sheet he kept for this novel he records: 'The Bertrams begun in Egypt, and written on the Mediterranean – in Malta, Gibraltar, England, Ireland, Scotland and finished in the West Indies.' He finished the novel about ten months later, in January 1859. Few facts give a better indication of the hectic pace at which Trollope lived.

Trollope had been two months in Egypt on his first foreign assignment for the Post Office when he started work. The reason for such speed was financial. His going rate for a novel had reached £400, about half his annual salary. If he could produce three novels every two years he could have an income large enough to support his family in comfort, educate two sons, and pay for his fox-hunting.

The plot is one of the great weaknesses in *The Bertrams* and the devising of plots was perhaps causing him trouble; in the novel he had just finished he had drawn on his brother Tom for the plot. Probably the speed at which he was writing did not help. For *The Bertrams* he took several elements from his previous novel, *The Three Clerks*: both follow the careers of three young men. Another similarity in *The Bertrams* is that two of the young men are cousins: Arthur Wilkinson and George Bertram spent some of their early life together at the vicarage where Wilkinson's father was the vicar. Both lads were, like Trollope, sent to Winchester [➤ Public Schools]. Both went on to Oxford where they became friends with Henry Harcourt who became a successful barrister [➤ Universities].

This novel has the strangest opening of any of Trollope's works: a long address on the Victorian idea of success. He himself was unquestionably now a 'success'; he was considered the leading postal official in Ireland and was being sent on an important semi-diplomatic mission abroad. Here we have the successful but far from self-satisfied Trollope in his mid-forties reflecting on life and ambition. (In the novel he refers to those who, like himself, had been born during 'the consulship' of Lord Liverpool, prime minister from 1812 to 1827.) The nineteenth century may be 'the age of humanity', but there is little sympathy for the man who falls by the wayside, whose talents are not appreciated. For an example of such a man Trollope only had to recall his father, who like George Bertram achieved great success at Winchester and Oxford but who, after being disappointed as Bertram is by not inheriting an uncle's fortune, sank into a morose and purposeless existence. Trollope also had a personal interest in showing that early

academic success does not guarantee later achievements. His own life showed that a youth who was undistinguished at school could carve out a responsible place for himself in the world. (One of his favourite sayings was that the best fruit ripens slowly.) Yet the novel also stresses the difficulty of getting on in life if a character does not get on to the right path early.

Again like *The Three Clerks, The Bertrams* was set in the previous decade when Trollope was coming to the end of his days as a young clerk in London. He had spent much of the 1850s in Ireland, so he had to be careful not to make mistakes about such a rapidly changing world as early Victorian England. The 1840s were in many ways a more exciting decade than the 1850s, with great political debates and religious controversies surrounding the High Church revival and John Henry Newman.

In his writing in the 1850s Trollope was preoccupied with the question of honesty, and in this novel each young man as he chooses a profession faces a struggle to square his early idealism with the practical and often dishonest demands of mature life. Harcourt becomes a successful politician and a follower of Sir Robert Peel, for whom Trollope entertained an extraordinary detestation [➤ *The Three Clerks*]. His life ends – quite literally – in dishonesty. Although Arthur Wilkinson seems to disappear for large parts of the book he eventually emerges as the most successful, if success is counted in happiness and satisfaction. Bertram is the central character of the book, but unlike Trollope's other young men – Johnnie Eames in *The Small House at Allington*, for instance, or Charley

Tudor in *The Three Clerks* – he does not arouse the sympathy of most readers. This is also the case with the two principal women in the book. When Trollope introduces Wilkinson's beloved Adela Gauntlet he flings a gauntlet of his own in the face of fictional conventions. He refuses to describe her: 'For once I will venture to have a heroine without describing her. Let each reader make what he will of her.'

The main female character is Caroline Waddington, with whom both her cousin Bertram and Harcourt are in love. Hugh Walpole, writing in the 1920s, found her 'bitter', but many modern readers might find her realistic. She makes one of the most telling comments of any woman in Trollope's fiction regarding the position of women in Victorian society: 'It is useless for a woman to think of her future; she can do so little towards planning it' [10]. [For a similar comment, ➤ *The Belton Estate*.] In Caroline, Trollope confronts something that would perplex him later with Lily Dale, Emily Wharton in *The Prime Minister* and Emily Hotspur in *Sir Harry Hotspur of Humblethwaite*: can a woman love twice? Her plight allows him to portray the misery a woman endures in an unhappy marriage. Two other women are quite memorable: Miss Todd and Miss Baker. They and the Wilkinsons would reappear in *Miss Mackenzie* five years later. Sally Todd was one of those jolly spinsters that Trollope delighted in portraying and she adds a much-needed touch of humour to this rather sombre novel. One character from the Barsetshire books makes a professional appearance here: Sir Omicron Pie, 'the great physician'.

Yet Trollope fails to develop several characters who could have added interest to the book. Pritchett, the man of business to Bertram's miserly uncle, would have been made into a much fuller character by Dickens, who would have shown us Pritchett's home life. Certainly Dickens or Balzac would have made more of the rich old miser. Thackeray would have made John the footman, who spies on Caroline for Harcourt, a figure of interest in his own right [➤ Servants]. However, one can see how much Trollope was influenced by Thackeray in his portrayal of Sir Lionel Bertram, the elderly roué.

This is the most intellectual of Trollope's novels. No doubt his long absence from home meant that he had no opportunity to discuss the meaning of life, success, money, marriage and the role of religion with his wife or with any close friend. Thus this novel contains more of his reflections on these topics than almost any other. His visit to the Holy Land naturally caused him to think deeply about his own religious views and no other novel is so full of discussion of the Bible and of religious doubt. Trollope was of course writing for readers alive to the use of religious language. When Bertram enters a church Trollope uses the phrase, 'in sundry places to acknowledge and confess his sins'. Readers would have recognized the words from the call to confession in the service of Morning Prayer in the Prayer Book. They also would have seen that some of Trollope's usages indicated a sympathy with aspects of the High Church movement. Both Newman and 'poor Froude' are referred to by name and with sympathy. This is one of the few novels in which

Trollope does use religious language: the visit to the Holy Land naturally leads to allusions to 'our Saviour'. Here also is his fullest discussion of religious doubt: he did not believe that a man should try to spread religious doubts and he denounces those who make money by 'infidelity'. There are also many reflections on the writing of a novel.

It is difficult to think of many other novels in which Trollope drew as widely on his own life for detail. The Wilkinson vicarage is set in the area – on the Berkshire–Hampshire border – in which Trollope's grandfather was a clergyman. (He was to use the area again in *Ralph the Heir*.) Young Wilkinson is forced to visit the Lake District, an area Trollope knew from his mother having lived there in the 1830s. Before that she had lived in Hadley, near Barnet, and Trollope had spent months there as a young postal clerk. This novel contains two of the most personal 'authorial intrusions' in all Trollope's writing and each records one of the most emotional events in his life. In Chapter 30, while describing the Harcourt wedding at Hadley, he says, 'I have stood in that green churchyard when earth has been laid to earth, ashes to ashes, dust to dust – the ashes and the dust that were loved so well.' Here he is remembering the burial of his younger sister, Emily, who died there in 1836 and whose grave can still be seen in the churchyard, immediately behind the east end of the church. The second 'intrusion' comes at the end of the novel, when Bertram is debating a date for his wedding. He finally chooses 11 June. 'Let us trust that the day may always be regarded as propitious,' wrote Trollope [43] – a refer-

ence to his own marriage, which took place on 11 June 1844.

Writing at the speed he did, he naturally sought to use his own travels to good purpose. The descriptions of Egypt and the Holy Land with 'their soupçon of danger' would have appealed to many readers. [For Trollope's use of these locations elsewhere, ➤ Holy Land.] Not all the reviewers liked the travel scenes and the *Athenaeum* complained about being 'taken to the east twice in one novel'. Trollope claimed that the love scenes were not good because they were written in the evening after he had come back from a busy day arranging postal services in Scotland.

The reaction of reviewers to the novel was mixed, but many pointed out that Trollope was writing too quickly. However, two notable readers, both fellow novelists, commented on it. John Henry Newman was naturally interested in a novel with such religious overtones and wrote, 'It is decidedly the most powerful thing of his that I have read – tragic, instructive, humiliating.' He came to feel that there was too much scepticism in it, while the end was disappointing, 'a dreadful fall off'. Tolstoy read *The Bertrams* a few years later while writing *War and Peace* and noted: 'Read Trollope. If only there was not the diffuseness. Excellent. Trollope captivates me with his mastery' [Mullen, 325–6].

Trollope wished that 'a serene gratification might flow from my pages' [13]. While *The Bertrams* is far from 'serene gratification' it remains essential reading for any reader of Trollope who wants to understand the ideas that motivated the author.

[➤ Dogs; Novel, The; Picnics; Suicide.]

Beverley. Trollope created a fictional Bishop of Beverley when writing *The Warden* [5] in 1853–4 but his real connection with the Yorkshire borough came in 1868. This market town was famous not only for its splendid Minster but for the political corruption involved in the return of its two MPs. When Trollope was chosen as one of the town's two Liberal candidates he spent £400 in a vain effort to get elected: he came bottom of the poll. He hated the canvassing involved in elections. He would make use of his experiences in *Ralph the Heir* [23] in which Beverley would become Percycross (a name inspired by the famous Percy monument in the Minster) and in *The Duke's Children* [5]; he even alluded to the canvassing when writing his *Life of Cicero*. Trollope campaigned for the disestablishment of the Church of Ireland and for more state involvement in improving education for working-class children. The Tories circulated an amusing piece of doggerel [Mullen, 519] which ends:

Say no to him sweetly without any fighting
Friend Anthony Trollope is wanted for writing.

The clergy at the notoriously low-church Minster attacked the Liberal candidates – the other Liberal was a Catholic – over Irish Disestablishment and Trollope's agent said it would be better if he did not attend services at the Minster. Trollope was furious. When local politicians tried a deal, frequent at the time, whereby each side removed one candidate thus securing for each party one MP, the town's working men refused to agree because it meant sacrificing Trollope, whose support for popular education delighted them. After the Tory victory the Liberals petitioned because of the bribery. A Royal Commission was set up to investigate and the borough was one of two disenfranchised. Trollope, who appeared as a witness, was exonerated along with the other Liberal candidate. He used aspects of this bribery investigation in *Phineas Redux* [44]. The story of his one attempt at entering the House of Commons is well told in his *Autobiography*.

Bible. Trollope acquired a knowledge of the Bible, including the Apocrypha, in part through attending school chapel at Harrow and Winchester and, while at Winchester, through regular attendance at Winchester Cathedral. His writing is laced with quotations from and paraphrases of the Scriptures, the full import of which he assumed his readers would immediately understand. Even chapter titles and one peer's title, Lord Boanerges, are taken from the Bible. He refers to biblical stories in at least twenty passages in his novels. Two of his favourite phrases are biblical: 'His lines had fallen in pleasant places' and a warning that a person cannot touch pitch and remain undefiled.

Sometimes Trollope erred in saying that a quotation is biblical when it is not. In *Rachel Ray* he wrongly writes that the phrase 'charity begins at home' is biblical, and in *The Last Chronicle of Barset* [50, 61] he has Mr Crawley incorrectly say, 'We must bear it . . . We are told that He tempers the wind to the shorn lamb.' Most biblical quotations are used by characters in dialogue and not by Trollope as narrator. His characters tend to quote with reverence, whereas when he quotes he does so in an offhand manner, perhaps to distinguish himself from Evangelicals or to remind readers that he did not think it was the novelist's task to prattle on about religion. Normally the Bible is quoted from memory, with inevitable distortions. About half the quotations and use of biblical phrases appear in *Barchester Towers*. He also quoted from the Vulgate on four occasions, though perhaps without knowing the origin of the quotes. Some have argued that his quotations and paraphrases show he heard the texts during church services, rather than reading them in the Bible. However, the phrase 'His lines had fallen in pleasant places' is from the Authorized Version of the Psalms, whereas the Prayer Book uses the Coverdale translation: 'The lot is fallen unto me in a fair ground ...' This may imply more personal reading of the Bible by Trollope, or the discovery of the quotation from a secondary source.

The nineteenth century saw a fierce debate over the Bible because of new geological evidence, Darwin's writings and the 'Higher Criticism' from Germany. Trollope wrote in one of his articles for the *Pall Mall Gazette*, later published in *Clergymen of the Church of England*, of the loss of old certainties: 'If one could really believe that the old shore is best, who would leave it? ... Who would not stay behind if it were possible to him?' In *The Bertrams* [26] Trollope gives an insight into his own debates over the Bible in the discussion between Arthur Wilkinson and George Bertram.

In *The Way We Live Now* [78] Trollope has great sport when Lady Pomona Longstaffe discovers that her daughter, Georgiana, wants to marry a Jew: 'This is dreadful ... It's unnatural ... I'm sure there's something in the Bible against it. You never would read your Bible, or you wouldn't be going to do this.' Normally, however, ignorance of the Bible, as when Mountjoy Scarborough says, 'Somebody says somewhere that nobody can live upon bread alone' [37], is a good sign of a character's low moral state. In *The Small House at Allington* the village postmistress likes reading those parts of the Bible that she does not understand.

Bigamy features in several Trollope novels although it is more often suspected than committed. In *Castle Richmond*, published in 1860, a charge of bigamy forms the basis for blackmail which lies at the heart of the novel. This novel preceded the wave of interest in bigamy by many novelists in the 1860s. In 1861, serialization of Mary Braddon's *Lady Audley's Secret* began and it caused a literary sensation. In addition there was a celebrated trial for bigamy, the Yelverton case, which reached the House of Lords in 1864. (Trollope may well have heard details of this from his friend Lord Houghton, who was fascinated by the case.) Although Trollope disliked 'sensational' novels, he returned to the subject of bigamy in the 1870s. His most important bigamist was the Reverend Joseph Emilius: his bigamy is only proved when Madame Max Goesler goes to Bohemia to search for evidence. Generally bigamy in Trollope has some connection with the Continent: the marquis in *Is He Popenjoy?* is suspected of some form of bigamous marriage in Italy. In *Lady Anna* the question of the wicked old earl's bigamous marriage, also in Italy, is crucial to the plot and Trollope sought advice from a lawyer before writing. In *John Caldigate* his hero is convicted of bigamy only because witnesses commit perjury. His handling of the topic in this novel equals in excitement his first treatment of it in *Castle Richmond*. [➤ Divorce.]

Bills. A Victorian means of borrowing money from private money-lenders which arose because of banks' reluctance to lend without security. An individual would give a bill to a money-lender for a specified sum of money to be handed over on an agreed date minus the lender's discount, or profit, either to himself or to a third party. The borrower would then get someone to 'accept' the bill, that is, to act as collateral. Every time the bill was 'rolled over' the indebtedness soared because bills were normally for short periods and the discount or rate of interest was enormous. There was a considerable trade in buying bills from other lenders because purchasers knew that if they could not get the money owed they would have no trouble in having the bailiffs sent in (as happened with Mark Robarts in *Framley Parsonage*).

Trollope had had personal experience of this in his own youth. He asked his tailor to accept a bill for £12 to settle his account. By the time it was finally paid off, Trollope had to pay over £200. (In this case it was the tailor who sold Trollope's indebtedness to the money-lender in exchange for payment; the bill was in Trollope's name.) When Lord Lufton tells Mark Robarts in *Framley Parsonage* that 'Bills are like dram-drinking ... when one once begins, it is very hard to leave off' [44], he is right.

The sordid world of Victorian bills is crucial to the plot of *Framley Parsonage*, in which Mark Robarts 'accepted' a bill for £400 to be given by Nath-aniel Sowerby and signed by him. When the bill came due and Sowerby could not pay, Mark Robarts signed a new bill for £500 without asking for the old one. This meant that his indebtedness rose to £900. Bills were normally taken by young men like Mark Robarts: Charley Tudor in *The Three Clerks*, George Vavasor in *Can You Forgive Her?*, Ferdinand Lopez in *The Prime Minister*, Phineas Finn in *Phineas Finn*, and poor Bertie Stanhope in *Barchester Towers* where the £150 he had actually received from the 'Jew discounter' became a debt of £700 [19]. Jews were often lenders or 'discounters' but the term 'Jew' when used for a money-lender does not always literally mean someone who is Jewish.

Another form of bill was called a 'post-obit', which meant that payment of the debt would become due when the borrower succeeded to the family estate. Captain Mountjoy Scarborough's problems in *Mr Scarborough's Family* flow from his father's schemes to defeat the money-lenders who hold numerous bills and post-obits from his son. In Trollope's novels an older person often settles a bill for an improvident young man.

[➤ Bankruptcy; Debt.]

Bishops. No other novelist is as well known for his portrayal of bishops as Trollope. Yet most readers would be hard pressed to remember any bishop other than old Bishop Grantly and his successor, Bishop Proudie, in the Barsetshire novels. However, bishops occur in several other novels although none has such a memorable personality as these two. In *Dr Wortle's School* Dr Wortle comes into conflict with his bishop, as does Mr Clavering with his

(Bishop Proudie, no less) in *The Claverings*. *The Eustace Diamonds* and *The Way We Live Now* also have bishops. Bishop Yeld in the latter novel is, at least partly, modelled on a real prelate: Trollope's notes show he based Yeld on 'old Longley'. (Charles Longley was Archbishop of Canterbury from 1862 to 1868 but Trollope remembered him from Harrow, where he had been Headmaster from 1829 to 1836.) Archbishops, while referred to, do not really occur as characters in any real sense, although Mrs Arabin, a High Churchwoman, 'assumes a smile of gentle ridicule when the Archbishop of Canterbury is named' [*Barchester Towers*, 53]. In *Barchester Towers*, one of Obadiah Slope's many faults as an extreme Evangelical is that he has no time for the Church's teaching about the need for bishops to be in apostolic succession. In his *Clergymen of the Church of England*, Trollope described and in part decried the changes he had seen in his lifetime as bishops became less wealthy and less grand and were replaced by committee men: the Grantlys gave way to the Proudies. In *The Vicar of Bullhampton* the vicar, Frank Fenwick, perhaps has this type of man in mind when discussing a character who is most adroit at pouring oil on troubled waters and at getting himself liked by everyone. Fenwick, who exemplifies many Trollopian attitudes, comments, 'He can be everything to everybody, and would make an excellent bishop' [72]. In *La Vendée* there is a Catholic bishop.

[➤ Catholicism; Church of England; Clergymen; Religion.]

Blackwood & Son; *Blackwood's Magazine* (1817–1980). This publishing house brought out six of Trollope's books, the second largest number published by any one firm; Chapman & Hall published thirty-two. The firm began as Edinburgh printers in 1804 under William Blackwood. In 1845 his son, John Blackwood, took over. The head of the London office was Joseph Langford who became a friend of Trollope. The firm was best known for publishing George Eliot, Edward Bulwer-Lytton, Charles Lever and Margaret Oliphant. The first Trollope novel it published as a book was *Nina Balatka* (1867). The other five were *Linda Tressel*, *The Fixed Period*, *The Commentaries of Caesar* and, after Trollope's death, *An Old Man's Love* and *An Autobiography*.

Like many publishers it established its own journal, *Blackwood's Magazine*, which was a conservative publication to counter the influence of the Whig *Edinburgh Review*. (It was, strictly speaking, *Blackwood's Edinburgh Magazine*.) Within four years it began serializing fiction; it was very successful and was known among contributors as 'Maga'. The first Trollope novel it serialized was *Nina Balatka* (July 1866 – January 1867). After that came four other novels: *Linda Tressel* (October 1867 – May 1868); *John Caldigate* (April 1878 – June 1879); *Dr Wortle's School* (May – December 1880); *The Fixed Period* (October 1881 – March 1882). With the appearance of the *Cornhill Magazine* in 1860, its circulation fell.

Blackwood, John (1818–79). Trollope's friend, publisher and editor, John Blackwood studied at Edinburgh University and entered his father's firm, William Blackwood & Sons, in 1839. From 1840 to 1845 he was head of the London branch and in 1845 he succeeded his older brother, Alexander, as editor of *Blackwood's Magazine*. Seven years later, on the death of another brother, he became head of the company. Under his direction *Blackwood's Magazine* became a major force in British literary life and published the work of many of the great Victorian writers. Blackwood, a strong Tory, disliked Dickens just as his father and brother had earlier disliked the 'Cockney School' of poets and writers (Charles Lamb, Leigh Hunt, Shelley and Hazlitt). His friendship with Trollope began with the serialization of *Nina Balatka* in the magazine. The following year it also serialized *Linda Tressel*. Their growing friendship was not damaged when Trollope demanded that the two works' subsequent publication as books should be anonymous, with the consequent loss in revenue to the firm [➤ Anonymous Novels].

The Trollopes paid many visits to Strathtyrum, the Blackwoods' country home near St Andrews in Scotland. They played golf together and Trollope teased Blackwood for his Tory views. The friends also disagreed over the American Civil War, as Blackwood supported the Confederacy. They were both members of the Cosmopolitan Club. Blackwood asked his London manager, Joseph Langford, to help Trollope when he wanted to establish Henry Trollope as a publisher. Trollope 'puffed' Blackwood's 'Ancient Classics for English Readers' series in *Saint Pauls* and Blackwood then asked him to undertake the translation of Caesar's *Commentaries*. Trollope gave Blackwood the copyright of his translation as a birthday present. Blackwood appeared before the Royal Commission on Copyright and was questioned by Trollope, a member. On that occasion Blackwood attacked the domination of the circulating libraries. Unusually for Victorian publishers, Blackwood went over Trollope's manuscripts carefully and suggested changes [➤ *The Fixed Period*]. Blackwood's nephew, William, who succeeded him, brought out the *Autobiography*. Through Blackwood, Trollope also met the Reverend W. Lucas Collins, who became a close friend. [➤ Classics.]

Bland, Florence (1855–1907). Trollope's niece, Florence Bland, was the daughter of Rose Trollope's sister Isabella, who had married the head clerk of her father's bank in Yorkshire. (In 'The Two Heroines of Plumplington' the bank manager's daughter marries a cashier in her father's bank.) When both her parents died, she was adopted by Anthony and Rose in 1863. He was very fond of her and sent her to be educated at Aix-la-Chapelle. (In the novel he started writing that same year, *Can You Forgive Her?* [1], Alice Vavasor is also sent to Aix.) Since Trollope never had a daughter he gained many of his much admired insights into 'the English girl' from observing his niece, and nieces also began to play an important role in his fiction. In the 1870s, when he began to suffer increasingly from 'writer's cramp', 'Flo' became his amanuensis and the manuscripts of many of his later novels show that large portions of them were dictated to her. Several of his books have characters named Florence. She also wrote many of his letters for him and usually accompanied him on his daily ride in Hyde Park. In his last years he worried about leaving her enough money and no doubt enjoyed one of his private jokes as he dictated

Cousin Henry. In the first chapter an uncle leaves £4,000 to his niece, Isabel; Trollope was in fact doing the same thing at that time – he signed a will leaving Florence £4,000 three days after starting the novel. Although he regarded her as 'clever' she was never allowed to make suggestions while he was dictating. Florence was said to 'adore' her uncle [Mullen, 612, 654]. She accompanied him on his last two trips to Ireland when he was gathering material for *The Land-Leaguers*. After his death she became the companion of his widow.

[➤ Florence; Milton, John.]

Boanerges, Lord. A character in several novels written in the late 1850s and early 1860s. The word Boanerges, used to describe a loud-voiced orator, comes through the Greek from the Hebrew *b'ney regesh*, which means 'sons of thunder'. In the Bible (Mark 3:17) Christ used the description when speaking of James and John: 'He surnamed them Boanerges, which is, The sons of thunder.' Lord Boanerges is an elderly peer 'who would have his way in all things' and appears first in *The Bertrams*, then in *Framley Parsonage*. In *Orley Farm*, he is President of the International Legal Congress at Birmingham. Boanerges shares several traits, such as a love of statistics and support for congresses, with the real Lord Brougham (1778–1868), whose *Memoirs* Trollope later took a hand in editing. Brougham was a great force in legal and educational reform. In *Orley Farm* [17] Trollope has one of his private jokes when he refers to the obvious similarities between Boanerges and Brougham: after writing of Boanerges attending a conference, Trollope adds, 'Vox et praeterea nihil.' Brougham's

full title was Baron Brougham and Vaux and it was a frequent – though unfair – Victorian quip that he was 'Vox and praeterea nihil'. Trollope, who had considerable respect for the real peer, well knew he was not 'voice and nothing else'. The name derived from 'son of thunder' may also recall the fact that at one time Brougham had had a close connection with *The Times*, which was often called 'The Thunderer'. [➤ Copyright.]

Board Wages. See Servants.

Bold, Eleanor. See Harding, Eleanor.

Bold, Mary. The close friend of Eleanor Harding in the Barchester series. She becomes Eleanor's sister-in-law when her brother John, the reforming doctor, marries Eleanor in *The Warden*. By *Barchester Towers* Mary and the widowed Eleanor are living together. Mary Bold is one of those independent spinsters that Trollope liked and excelled in creating. Although Miss Bold is comfortably off, she is not sufficiently grand to be invited to Society events such as the party at Ullathorne in *Barchester Towers*. She is an amused spectator of Mr Slope's antics and Eleanor's reactions to them in that novel.

Bonteen, J. A politician who holds posts in various Liberal governments in the Palliser novels. At the beginning he is a junior Lord of the Admiralty in *Phineas Finn*; by *Phineas Redux* he has become President of the Board of Trade, though without a seat in the Cabinet. He is a type of professional politician that was becoming more common in the second half of the Victorian era. Trollope describes him as 'an ass' [*Phineas Redux*, 40]. He is a great enemy of Phineas Finn and when he is murdered after leaving the Universe Club in *Phineas Redux*, Finn is suspected. His wife, the gossipy Mrs Bonteen, is an even greater enemy of Phineas Finn. Both the Bonteens are also in *The Eustace Diamonds*. There is some confusion about his Christian name: in *Phineas Redux* [34–5] Finn writes to him as Thomas Bonteen, but he signs his reply 'J. Bonteen'.

Boyce, The Rev. Mr. The Vicar of Allington in *The Small House at Allington* and *The Last Chronicle of Barset*. He and his wife are friends of Lily Dale. He has a large family and is sometimes known to fall asleep during his own services.

Bradbury, Evans. The partnership of William Bradbury and Frederick Evans began, like so many London publishing houses, when the two were printers in 1830. In 1844 they began publishing Dickens after he left Chapman & Hall, for whom they worked. When Dickens broke with them they started, in 1859, *Once A Week*, a magazine which soon became a leading publisher of serialized fiction. (They also published *Punch* and the *Gentleman's Magazine*.) They published many of Thackeray's works and also brought out Surtees and Charles Reade. Trollope's connection with them began in 1868 when they agreed to publish *The Vicar of Bullhampton* in *Once A Week*. [For the difficulties and delays Trollope encountered, ➤ *The Vicar of Bullhampton*.] Frederick Evans was, like Trollope, a member of the Garrick Club. [➤ Publishers and Publishing.]

Breast-Feeding. See *He Knew He Was Right*; *Is He Popenjoy?*; Women.

Brentford, Earl of. A Whig politician whose family name is Standish and who is related to many of the other great Whig aristocrats in the Palliser series [➤ St Bungay, Duke of]. He is a widower and two of his children, Lady Laura (who marries Robert Kennedy) and Lord Chiltern, are prominent in *Phineas Finn*, in which he first enters the Cabinet, and in *Phineas Redux*. (A second daughter lives abroad.) He has a town house in Portman Square and a country house called Saulsby. The earl controls a pocket borough, Loughton, and he arranges for Phineas Finn to be elected MP for that seat. The earl is constantly quarrelling with his son, Chiltern. [➤ Aristocracy; Peerage; Politics.]

Brewers. Brewers occur in several of Trollope's novels and short stories. They normally live in provincial towns and, while respectable, are often not gentlemen. The names Trollope chose for breweries allowed him great scope for humour and were normally puns on various aspects of brewing. In *Rachel Ray* (1863) the brewer, Luke Rowan (of Bungall and Tappitt), is the hero. His social standing is helped by the fact that he had been articled to a solicitor in London before entering his uncle's brewery. He saw being a brewer as a 'trade' and himself as a 'tradesman', although his mother considered him a gentleman [11]. In no other novel by Trollope are brewers major characters. In *The American Senator* (1876–7) Ned and Frank Botsey, brewers from Norrington, hunt with the Ufford and Rufford United Hunt Club. They are decent enough men and if they complain of making bets 'with a man who was not a gentleman', meaning an innkeeper, he in his turn could sneer at them for their trade [11]. In *Mr Scarborough's Family* the brewer's lot has improved, for a rector's daughter is engaged to a son of a brewer, who also rides to hounds. She becomes Mrs Joshua Thoroughbung. Joshua's aunt, Miss Matilda Thoroughbung, is said to be worth £25,000: as Trollope had written in *Rachel Ray*, 'There is something in the very name of beer that makes money'[3]. His last brewer occurs in his amusing short story, 'The Two Heroines of Plumplington', in which provincial Barsetshire town action is divided between the Peppercorn and Greenmantle households. 'It cannot be said that Mr Hickory Peppercorn had ever been put on a par with Mr Greenmantle.' Peppercorn was a brewer while Greenmantle was a bank manager, and while Mr Greenmantle was a gentleman, Mr Peppercorn was 'a kind of top sawyer in the brewery establishment of Messrs du Boung and Co.'.

Britannula The imaginary country used as the setting for *The Fixed Period*. It is based on New Zealand.

British Sports and Pastimes. A collection of eight essays, all first published in *Saint Pauls*. It was edited by Trollope and published by Virtue & Co. in November 1868. Trollope wrote the preface and one essay. The essays with their writers and date(s) of publication – some were published in two parts – are: 'On Horse Racing' (Hon. Francis Lawley, October 1867, April 1868); 'On Hunting' (Anthony Trollope, November 1867, March 1868); 'On Shooting' (Hon. Francis Lawley, February 1868); 'On Fishing' (Dr Bertram, June 1868); 'On Yachting' (Edward Pigott, May 1868); 'On Rowing' (Leslie Stephen, December 1867); 'On Alpine Climbing' (Leslie Stephen, January 1868); 'On Cricket' (Charles Merewether, August 1868). Trollope's essay on fox-hunting is his best account of his beloved sport. His comparison of fox-hunting with other sports is also discussed in *Marion Fay* [2], where he singled out shooting for his special ire. There are no records of what Trollope received from Virtue. [For Charles Merewether, ➤ *The Eustace Diamonds*.]

Brougham, Lord. See Boanerges, Lord. For the carriage named after Brougham, see Carriages.

Brown Complexion. See Women.

Bruges. See Belgium.

Buffle, Sir Raffle. Sir Raffle first appears in *The Small House at Allington* in which he is First Commissioner at the Income Tax Office with a salary of £2,000 a year. John Eames becomes his Private Secretary. Buffle, 'a great bully', is a comical figure, always boasting of his friendship with Earl De Guest. He also appears in *The Last Chronicle of Barset*. Trollope was accused of portraying a particular Civil Servant but in his *Autobiography* he said, 'Sir Raffle was intended to represent a type, not a man ... I have never seen the gentleman with whom I am supposed to have taken the liberty.' Trollope was friendly with one of the Commissioners of Inland Revenue, Alfred Montgomery, a rich source of political gossip [Mullen, 487].

Bunce. Trollope was fond of this surname, which he used for several working-class characters. The most memorable is John Bunce, the head bedesman of Hiram's Hospital and devoted friend of Mr Harding in *The Warden*. He is proud that he can read and refuses to join the other bedesmen in the petition demanding more money. Bunce is over eighty when the Barsetshire novels begin, but survives to appear in *Barchester Towers* and, though blind, to be at Mr Harding's funeral in *The Last Chronicle of Barset* [81]. In the Palliser novels the name is used again for Phineas Finn's landlord: Jacob Bunce works for a legal stationer and is a supporter of radical reform. He does not look kindly on Finn's friendship with various aristocratic ladies. His wife, Jane, is devoted to the handsome Finn. Both Jacob and Jane support Finn in *Phineas Redux*, when he is charged with murder. In *The Belton Estate* the name is used for two separate servants: a man in Norfolk and a woman in Somerset, and in *An Eye for an Eye* Mrs Bunce is the domineering housekeeper at Scroope Manor. Thackeray also had a fondness for the name Bunce, and it occurs in several of his works including *Doctor Birch and His Young Friends*, *Pendennis* and *The Newcomes* in which a character named Bunce is an MP. [➤ Names, Origin of; Servants.]

Butterwell, Mr. A civil servant at the General Committee Office in the Barsetshire novels, whose promotion from the secretaryship of that body to be the junior member of the Board opens up a place for Adolphus Crosbie in *The Small House at Allington*.

He reappears in *The Last Chronicle of Barset*.

Byron, Lord (1788–1824). Trollope's connection with the poet began in his childhood. His mother, Fanny, was a staunch defender of Byron against the Evangelical Vicar of Harrow, who refused to bury the poet's illegitimate daughter unless the burial was in an unmarked grave. When Byron died Trollope was at Harrow School and he was taken with the other boys to the parish church to hear this same vicar denounce Byron's abuse of 'natural gifts'. As a grown man Trollope came to dislike Byron, not for his verse, which he grudgingly admired, but for his influence. He frequently denounces emotional excesses and self-indulgence under the term 'Byronic'. Luke Rowan was criticized in *Rachel Ray* in these terms [4]: 'It may be that he was not altogether devoid of that Byronic weakness which was so much more prevalent among young men twenty years since than it is now ... he dabbled in romance, and probably wrote poetry in his bedroom.' 'Byronic' denotes the opposite to 'manly' uprightness which demanded that 'you should carry your outer self, that the eyes of those around you should see nothing of the sorrow within' [*The Vicar of Bullhampton*, 68]. Those men who read Byron were normally weak characters and, sometimes, bad. The same applied to women: Lizzie Eustace in *The Eustace Diamonds* constantly reads Byron, has visions of a Byronic lover and refers to one suitor as a 'corsair'.

C

Caesar. See *The Commentaries of Caesar.*

Canada. Trollope visited Canada at least twice: in 1859 he paid a brief visit which he described at the end of *The West Indies and the Spanish Main.* He went to see Niagara Falls, which he regarded as the greatest sight in all his travels. He returned in the autumn of 1861 and visited the Falls again as well as Quebec, and Montreal. He liked Canada but did not feel it was equalling the progress of its southern neighbour. He describes his reactions in *North America,* in which he advocates a Canadian federation (achieved in 1867) as he would later advocate for Australia. Unlike most Englishmen of his time, he did not think that America could successfully annex Canada, and he expected that Canada would eventually become independent from Britain. He may have made a third brief visit to the Falls in 1872.

Canada does not play as important a role as Australia in his fiction. In *Phineas Finn,* Finn assists Lord Cantrip in devising legislation to help Canada, and in *The American Senator* a minor character is married to a Canadian. Trollope's works were popular in Canada, but when he was the driving force on the Royal Commission on Copyright (1876) he complained that Canadians bought pirated American editions of his novels because they were much cheaper.

[➤ English World.]

Cantrip, Lord. A hard-working Liberal politician in the Palliser novels. In *Phineas Finn* he is the Colonial Secretary and Finn serves under him as Under-Secretary. Cantrip is a good example of the type of aristocrat that Trollope respected because he does his public duty. Cantrip and his wife are close friends of the Pallisers, and they also appear in *Phineas Redux, The Prime Minister* and *The Duke's Children.*

Can You Forgive Her?. Trollope's fifteenth novel was written between 16 August 1863 and 28 April 1864. It was published by Chapman & Hall and issued first in parts, which began on 1 January 1864 and ended in August 1865. [➤ Publishers and Publishing.] Trollope was still writing as the novel was appearing. Chapman & Hall then published it in two volumes: the first in September 1864, the second in July 1865. It is the first novel in the Palliser series. Trollope received £3,000. The novel was illustrated.

It was just over three years since *Framley Parsonage* brought Trollope great fame as a novelist and he could count payments in thousands rather than hundreds. His last major novel, *The Small House at Allington,* was still being serialized in the *Cornhill.* He had spent much of the spring and early summer finishing *Rachel Ray*, which was about to be published. He could, of course, have continued the Barsetshire series and developed some of the uncompleted stories in *The Small House at Allington*, yet Trollope often showed a reluctance to return to Barsetshire after completing each novel in the series. He could write another short novel like *Rachel Ray*, but of course that did not pay as well as a full-scale work and both were open to the growing charge that he was writing too quickly. As he complained to a friend shortly after starting *Can You Forgive Her?*: 'It is awfully hard work spinning continual novels.'

Trollope started writing *Can You Forgive Her?* the day after he returned from a lengthy holiday in Switzerland. He liked to fashion plots for new novels while walking in the clear air and no doubt he had given much thought to his next novel on holiday. He based the plot on *The Noble Jilt*, the unsuccessful play he had written about a dozen years before about a girl who rejects her lover because he is too perfect. Certainly this must have been one of the hardest novels for Trollope for not only was he writing one of his longest but he was setting out on a new series and he was peopling it with a vast array of characters. In his *Autobiography* he claimed that he had thought these out from the beginning. The two most important had already been introduced to readers: Plantagenet Palliser and his future wife, Lady Glencora, in *The Small House at Allington*. It would be wise to read Chapters 23 and 55 of that novel before starting *Can You Forgive Her?* as these form a prelude to the whole

Palliser series. It is easy enough to imagine that the *Her* of the title is Lady Glencora. It is not. Far from being about one of Trollope best-known heroines, the novel concerns one of his least remembered: Alice Vavasor. Henry James reviewed the novel when he was a young and over-critical writer, and sneered: 'Can we forgive her? Of course we can, and forget her, too.' Looking back, Trollope himself believed that Alice was not an 'attractive' character. Yet she improves with each re-reading.

In *Can You Forgive Her?* there are three contrasting women, each of whom is involved with two men. Alice seems to be in a constant process of jilting one of her suitors, John Grey, 'the worthy man', or her cousin George Vavasor, 'the wild man'. As well as Alice there is her comic Aunt Greenow who is being sought by two equally comical suitors. Finally there is Lady Glencora MacCluskie, the 'great heiress of the day', who is forced to marry Plantagenet Palliser, MP, the heir to a mighty dukedom. However, Glencora's disappointed suitor, Burgo Fitzgerald, a handsome scamp, hopes that he may be able to persuade her to flee abroad with him. Yet almost every woman in the book is in need of forgiveness for some departure from the Victorian code of behaviour: Alice for her continual jiltings; Lady Glencora for contemplating adultery; Aunt Greenow for slipping into vulgarity; Kate Vavasor for constant dishonesty in the service of her brother, George; Lady Monk, for abetting her nephew Burgo's schemes; and Lady Glencora's aunts for forcing her into a loveless marriage. Even the two minor characters who make a brief but moving appearance, the prostitute [29] and George Vavasor's discarded mistress, Jane [71], are in need of forgiveness. Yet with all of them – save Lady Monk and Glencora's aunts – Trollope is using his vast canvas to preach Christian forgiveness, a forgiveness encouraged by showing how each woman has been led into her behaviour by others, usually by men. (This question of forgiveness also permeates *The Small House at Allington* and *Sir Harry Hotspur of Humblethwaite*.)

The idea that someone of the rank of Lady Glencora would even contemplate adultery was horrifying to many readers. In his *Autobiography* Trollope mentions a letter from an unnamed clerical dignitary protesting at such an episode. The clergyman forbade his daughters to read any more of the novel aloud to him. Trollope replied, saying that just as the clergyman rightly denounced adultery from his pulpit, the novelist rightly ventured on to this 'ticklish ground' to warn not only of the dangers of adultery, especially with beautiful young men like Fitzgerald, but also of the immorality of forcing a girl to marry someone she does not love. *Can You Forgive Her?* contains powerful 'sermons' against the fate that could befall a young woman: the poverty and starvation facing the prostitute and the discarded mistress were stark warnings.

The idea of Lady Glencora Palliser abandoning her husband and the prospect of a duchess's coronet to run off with Burgo may seem improbable behaviour for a Victorian lady. However, there had been a very similar scandal about ten years before, when Lady Lincoln, wife of the heir to the Duke of Newcastle, ran off to Italy with her lover, Lord Walpole. In one of the most ludicrous episodes in Victorian history, Lincoln's friend William Gladstone followed the lovers and even climbed the wall of their villa disguised as a guitarist, only to see a heavily pregnant and veiled Lady Lincoln being helped into a carriage. Gladstone gave evidence so that Lincoln could obtain a divorce. Many contemporary readers would have recalled that episode when reading of Burgo's schemes. Trollope greatly admired the Duke of Newcastle (as Lord Lincoln had become in 1851). 'We can conceive nothing nobler than a man working as he worked . . . for the sake of his country' [*The New Zealander, 5*]. Newcastle and Palliser have much in common.

Can You Forgive Her? is a superb introduction to the 'Upper Ten Thousand of this our English world', particularly the highest level of the 'Upper Ten Hundred' on whom much of the novel concentrates [1]. Every subtle gradation of the Victorian upper classes is displayed here. At the bottom is Squire Vavasor who lives a very straitened existence in Westmorland on £1,000 a year. He is probably the poorest squire in all Trollope's novels and is barely able to keep up his status with a superannuated butler, a boy-of-all-work, a maid and a cook. The novel is also good at showing how the relations of grand people lived on the fringes of Society. Lady Macleod saves £50 a year to be able to leave Cheltenham for a month in London for the Season so that she may bask in the glow of titled people. John Vavasor, the idle barrister, bemoans his fate of having an income of £800 a year for which he is forced to sign some papers three times a week. Jeffrey Palliser, Plantagenet's cousin and possible heir to the dukedom, is 'poor' with £600 a year because he insists on living among those with ten times as much. From Jeffrey we get an idea of what those people on the aristocratic fringes regarded as necessary in order to live comfortably. He tells Alice that if he could marry a girl with a 'fortune' of £10,000 – exactly what she has – that would add £400 a year to his own £600 and they 'might be able to live – in some second-rate French town perhaps' [25]. There is, indeed, no better novel in which to observe the way of life of the Victorian upper classes. Observe, for instance, the constant attention given to carriages and all the etiquette involved with them.

In the novel most characters are introduced with an account of their 'fortune' or income. Some might think this materialistic or vulgar. Trollope had no time for such a view and he summoned Plantagenet Palliser to enunciate one of his own basic principles, echoes of which are heard in almost all his works: 'Civilization comes from what men call greed. Let your mercenary tendencies be combined with honesty and they cannot take you astray' [25]. This novel also reminds readers how important a factor age was in Trollope's world: Burgo's behaviour is more reprehensible because he is thirty and, by Victorian standards, no longer a young man; Lady Glencora, on the other hand, is under twenty-one and therefore not skilled in the ways of the world; her cousin, Alice Vavasor, at twenty-four is getting rather too old to engage in such indecisive behaviour as to whom she should marry.

Palliser himself is, of course, a complete contrast to Burgo. They share only two features: aristocratic birth and the lack of a beard. Yet where

Burgo is all that is bad in an aristocracy, Palliser embodies all that is good. His passion for public service and unremitting hard work is constantly emphasized by Trollope. He emerges as someone with deep feelings beneath all his restraint, as we see when Glencora tells him that she does not love him. The sensitivity with which he treats her and the way in which he treats the impoverished Burgo in Baden gives some hint of the way he would behave in the final Palliser novel, *The Duke's Children*.

The alert reader who knows his Trollope will spot several dangerous signs when Burgo is described as a man 'with dark hair and blue eyes – who wear[s] no beard ... certainly among the handsomest of all God's creatures' [18]. The fact that Burgo is not a young man makes his idleness and his fortune-hunting all the more contemptible in Trollope's eyes; but faithful to his creator's view that no character is all bad, Burgo behaves with great kindness when he encounters a starving prostitute.

We have a rare glimpse of what was on Trollope's mind as he wrote this novel from the diary of an American friend whom he entertained several times during these months. William Glenn was taken hunting by Trollope and was surprised at the 'heartlessness' with which Trollope and the other members of the hunt ignored men who tumbled off their horses. He recounts a story about Trollope's delight when another rider knocked off the top rail of a fence, making it easier for the American and his host to leap over it. A version of this episode turns up in the chapter Trollope was writing at about this time. Here we are told about a 'sporting literary gentleman ...

who weighed fifteen stone' and who did not like to jump high fences. Trollope had noted down the real incident in the notebook he carried, put it in his current novel and added a private joke by portraying himself as fifteen stone as his weight about this time. It is also likely that Glenn, who was shocked at the rampant prostitution in London, may have discussed it with his host and this may have contributed to the episode in which Burgo helps the prostitute. [Mullen, 181–2, 447–8.]

The novel has more episodes involving travel than almost any other by Trollope. 'Travel' still inferred Europe and the traditional 'Grand Tour' cities of France and Italy, while Switzerland was also becoming very popular. Trollope comments that as he had just returned from a Swiss tour it would have been convenient for him to describe it, but he accepted that readers no longer wanted such things in novels [5]. However, he did make good use of a visit to Baden. It may be remembered that at the end of *The Small House at Allington*, Countess De Courcy and her daughter Lady Alexandrina Crosbie went to Baden to escape from their husbands. The German spa had a reputation as a place where 'rum' Englishmen wasted away their lives. This had been well sketched by Fanny Trollope in her travel book on Germany, as well as by Thackeray and Charles Lever. However, Burgo Fitzgerald was seeing the gambling spa in its last days. Within a few years a newly-united Germany would close down the gambling casinos and the gamblers would move on to a new mecca, Monte Carlo. This Trollope would record in one of his last novels, *Mr Scarborough's Family*.

Two deaths affected Trollope in the midst of writing *Can You Forgive Her?* He hurried to Florence to see his mother in September 1863, a month before she died. He was so upset that his work sheet shows that he wrote nothing while he was staying there. The character of Aunt Greenow bears more than a passing resemblance to Fanny Trollope's best-known fictional character, Widow Barnaby, and perhaps Trollope intended this as a tribute. He also put a tribute in the novel to Thackeray, who died in December 1863. He had used the name Cinquebars for a nobleman mentioned in passing and he added a footnote saying that he had borrowed this from 'my friend' [16]. Lord Cinqbars (as Thackeray spelt it) appeared in *The Book of Snobs*, *The Shabby Genteel Story*, *The Virginians* and several other of his works. Trollope also has his usual number of private jokes: Mudie's Library, the ultimate source of so much of his wealth, occasions a gentle laugh and Alice Vavasor's education at Aix-la-Chapelle [1] recalls the fact that Trollope would send his niece, Florence Bland, to a girls' school there. The reference to 'our excellent American friend and critic, Mr Hawthorne' who described some English ladies as 'beefy' [33] reminds us that Trollope carried about with him Nathaniel Hawthorne's comment praising Trollope's novels for being 'as English as a beefsteak'. [Mullen, 383–4.]

Trollope was not happy with the illustrations by H. K. Browne, better known as 'Phiz', who was famous for his work in Dickens's novels. 'Phiz' makes Trollope's characters look like visitors from Dickens. Trollope had 'Phiz' replaced by an unknown woman, 'a Miss Taylor of St Leonards', who received five guineas per drawing [➤ Money]. One drawing, 'Great Jove', shows a man wearing a top hat, asleep, or at least pretending to be asleep, on the government front bench in the House of Commons. Any contemporary would have immediately spotted this as a portrait of Lord Palmerston, then prime minister, in his well-known pose. No doubt this gave many people at the time the idea – the erroneous idea – that Trollope was portraying real figures in his fictional politicians.

Can You Forgive Her? is one of Trollope's longest novels – a recent recording of the whole text takes more than twenty-eight hours to read – and one of the most complex. Although the *Saturday Review* claimed that it had no plot, most readers today would agree with the *Spectator* that this is among Trollope's best novels.

Captain Bold of Halifax. Captain Bold was the villain who seduced young Miss Bailey in the old song, 'Miss Bailey's Ghost', one of the songs sung to the young Trollope children by their mother, Fanny. Trollope's brother Tom recalled that they did not have 'the faintest notion of the nature of the evil which was inflicted on the poor girl and led to her suicide'. Captain Bold makes numerous appearances in Trollope's fiction. In his short story 'Relics of General Chassé', he referred to 'a well-known gallant captain' who had a conversation with 'the posthumous appearance of Miss Bailey'. In *He Knew He Was Right* (1868–9) he describes an old rogue who tries to seduce the heroine as a 'Captain Bold of Halifax' [10]. To Victorian critics of Trollope, such references were probably another sign of his vulgarity.

Carlyle, Thomas (1795–1881). Trollope may be said to have had a love–hate relationship with the famous Scottish philosopher and historian whose books and pamphlets were such a dominant force in Victorian Britain. As a young man Trollope bought his works, among which was the *Latter Day Pamphlets* (1850). He was very disappointed: 'I look on him as a man who was always in danger of going mad in literature, and who has now done so. I used to swear by some of his earlier works.' While Trollope admired Carlyle's trenchant and uncompromising insights, he lamented his pessimism and caricatured him in *The Warden* as Dr Pessimist Anticant, a Scotsman addicted to German thought [15]. However, if imitation is the sincerest form of flattery then Trollope often flattered Carlyle by adopting his style of addressing readers in *The New Zealander* and in occasional novels. *The New Zealander* tackled the same subject, private and public dishonesty, which Trollope had felt Carlyle 'harped on' in the *Latter Day Pamphlets*. The Longman's reader of the manuscript of *The New Zealander* said, 'both in style and matter, [it] is a most feeble imitation'. It was not accepted. When Trollope helped to establish a library for Post Office clerks in London he donated many copies of Carlyle's works.

One must not think Trollope's generosity to the clerks' library was merely a way to get rid of unwanted books. By the 1870s his library had fifty-four volumes of Carlyle's works. For his part Carlyle dismissed Trollope's novels as 'alum'. He did, however, very much like *The West Indies and the Spanish Main* because it supported his own work, *The Nigger*

Question. Two years after Trollope's book appeared, his friend G. H. Lewes arranged for him to meet Carlyle. Lewes told Tom Trollope that 'the two got on very well together; both Carlyle and Mrs Carlyle liking Anthony – and I supposed it was reciprocal, though I didn't see him afterwards to hear what he thought'.

Trollope's view of Carlyle softened somewhat. In *The Small House at Allington* he includes Carlyle's *French Revolution* as one of the improving books that Lily Dale had been advised to read by Adolphus Crosbie; she sets herself to read it after she has been jilted by Crosbie [44]. In 1865 Trollope reviewed Ruskin's *Sesame and Lilies* for the *Fortnightly Review* and said of Carlyle: 'We are ready to pardon the abuse he showers on us, on account of the good that we know he has done us.' In private he told Lewes, regarding Carlyle's strictures, that one feels 'they are all struck in the dark, & may probably, after all, not be deserved'. In one of his last novels, *Marion Fay*, he has a character quote approvingly from *Sartor Resartus* in support of an attack on shooting as a sport.

Carlyle for his part resumed his old view and in a letter to his wife referred to Trollope as 'a little pug ... irredeemably embedded in commonplace, and grown fat upon it, and prosperous to an unwholesome degree ... nasty gritty creature'. Warfare continued at the public dinner to honour Dickens before his departure for America in 1867. There Trollope defended fiction against Carlyle's latest attack about the 'cousinship it has with lying'. Perhaps Trollope understood the reason for so much of Carlyle's ill humour, because in *The Claverings* (1866–7) he has a Polish count declare: 'Your Carlyle must have the worst digestion in the world, because he never says any good of anything' [14].

In 1875, however, Trollope subscribed a guinea towards the cost of a medallion to be given to Carlyle on his eightieth birthday. Trollope had the last laugh, and one Carlyle would have envied, when Chapman & Hall, of which he was a director, advertised three editions of Carlyle's works within days of his death. As Trollope told his son Henry, 'We have sold a *lot*.' For his part, Henry called Carlyle 'the Chelsea lunatic' [Mullen, 658].

Carriages. To Victorians, carriages were a sign of status as well as a means of transport and Trollope assumed his readers would understand this. The Victorian world was divided into two vastly unequal portions: 'carriage folk' and the rest. In 1856, just over 200,000 people owned carriages. (In 1861 the population of the United Kingdom would have been just under 29,000,000.) The vast majority walked, took public transport, or hired a vehicle or horse. Trollope was himself born into the 'carriage folk' and as a boy in Harrow was taken about by his father in the family gig, which he also learnt to drive. When he started at the Post Office its famous coaches were the principal means of carrying the mail, although Trollope is almost always critical of them [➤ *The Kellys and the O'Kellys*, 28]. However, he does speak highly of the large French carriages or 'diligences' used for long European journeys. These are described in *He Knew He Was Right*.

While in his early Irish novels he is more interested in describing public transport, by the late 1850s he uses the types of carriage to convey to readers both a character's wealth and personality, much as a present-day novelist can describe characters in terms of the motor-car they own. (This may have reflected his own increasing prosperity.) The two most common carriages mentioned in Trollope's novels are gigs (a relatively cheap, two-seater and two-wheeled open carriage with one horse, usually driven by the owner) and broughams, in which two people could sit in a closed carriage driven by a coachman. Owning a carriage was a sign of greater wealth and position than having servants. This is well expressed in the comment of Trollope's son Henry after the publication of the *Autobiography* when some critics complained that Trollope had been too concerned with money: 'Is a man wanting in ideal notions because he wants to give a horse and carriage to his wife?' [Mullen, 657]. In *John Caldigate* old Mr Bolton, the banker, does not keep his own carriage, but it is a sign of the family's rising position that each of his sons has his own. Another wealthy character, Mrs Winterfield, went about Perivale in a 'low, four-wheeled, one-horsed phaeton ... driven by the most solemn of stable-boys, dressed up in a great white coat, the most priggish of hats, and white cotton gloves' [*The Belton Estate*, 1].

In the Barsetshire novels we are usually told what type of carriage is used by clergymen or doctors. Most doctors used gigs but the fashionable Dr Fillgrave normally used a brougham; when speed was required he went in a post-chaise, which had more horses. In these novels most 'carriage folk' assume that one possesses a carriage. Therefore Mrs Proudie is shown to be pretentious in her first appearance in

Barchester Towers [5] by her constant boasting about her carriage. In the same novel Archdeacon Grantly makes quiet use of several of his own carriages (he has at least three) and maintains a separate pair of carriage horses for his wife's exclusive use. When he has matters of business, he uses his brougham or his gig, but for family trips he uses the family carriage which only has room for four so the archdeacon has to get up on the box with the driver. At the end of *Barchester Towers* he celebrates his sister-in-law's marriage to Mr Arabin by giving her a small pony-carriage. The chapters on the party at Ullathorne in this novel are enriched by many details about the etiquette connected with carriages – for instance, the concern about who would 'hand' a lady into a carriage. The place of pre-eminence was the back seat, facing the direction in which the carriage was travelling. (This etiquette is still followed in royal carriages.)

Carriages occur in almost all Trollope's novels, but they are best observed in *The Small House at Allington* and *Can You Forgive Her?*. In the first novel, Lady Alexandrina De Courcy's main worry on her approaching marriage to Adolphus Crosbie is that they cannot afford a carriage and that she will have to make her calls in a hired one. Trollope is also showing the De Courcys' niggardliness when they arrange for Crosbie, having been accepted as a son-in-law, to be taken from the Castle in a hired dog-cart [25]. (A dog-cart, which was originally used to transport hunting dogs, was an open carriage for three or four people.) As a wife, Lady Alexandrina wants her hired carriage to look like a private one and greatly resents her husband's insistence that he can only afford to hire a 'fly' or type of cab. She refuses to go about in an ordinary cab. After the collapse of their marriage the novel ends with her being seen 'in the one-horse carriage with her mother at Baden-Baden'.

In *Can You Forgive Her?* we see how people immediately establish their social position after leaving a train. When ordinary people arrive at Yarmouth station they get into a large public omnibus (usually a two-horse vehicle carrying about sixteen people) to take them to their hotels. Mrs Greenow, anxious to impress, makes a great point of hiring a 'fly' to take her to the hotel. Even so, the landlady wonders why such a rich widow did not come in her own private carriage [7]. When Alice Vavasor arrives at the station near the Pallisers' country house she also sees an omnibus 'intended for people who had not grown upwards as had been her lot'. A delegation of footmen, porters and the stationmaster conduct her to a 'light stylish-looking cart which she would have called a Whitechapel if she had been properly instructed in such matters'. Lady Glencora Palliser was driving this carriage herself with her two horses, Dandy and Flirt. A footman sat on the back of the carriage. Alice's bags and maid are put in another carriage by another footman in what Lady Glencora calls a dog-cart. Trollope adds, 'it wasn't a dog-cart, but Lady Glencora knew no better' [22]. At Alice's grandfather's there was no such luxury: this small squire used the same horse to pull a manure cart one day and a lady's carriage the next. This novel also alludes to the difficulties ladies could face in London: many husbands did not like their carriage horses to be out in the evening, but it was improper for a lady to go about in a cab at night. During the day a lady would use her carriage not just to maintain her social status but to avoid walking along pavements on which prostitutes plied their trade. Carriage rides were in themselves regarded as a form of 'exercise' by ladies because they allowed them to get some fresh air; Mrs Winterfield found, like Queen Victoria, that being driven round at five miles an hour was 'the amusement of life' [*The Belton Estate*, 1].

There was a tax on carriages, but the main expense, particularly in London, was the horses. A fellow novelist, Mrs Oliphant, admitted that 'I envy and admire' the fact that Trollope kept his own 'homely brougham' in London in the 1870s. This would have cost him about £200 a year. (The rich old Duke of Omnium went about London on his 'private' calls in a green brougham with, significantly, no ducal coronet on the door.) Many people who could not afford their own carriages rented them from livery stables which could 'job out' carriages and horses at a monthly fee for the London Season. Mrs Proudie 'jobbed about the streets of London' before her husband became a bishop. Sometimes people more fortunate than Lady Alexandrina Crosbie could rent a carriage that looked like a private one with its 'agreeable air of proprietorship', while lesser folk went in cabs [*The Three Clerks*, 25].

At the time Trollope was writing his novels, a system of public transport was being rapidly built up in towns, in which most people now lived, while railways had replaced coaches for journeys between towns. Carriages were mainly used for relatively short journeys like social calls, business errands, shopping, or getting to the station. However, when he set *Lady Anna* in the 1830s, he mentioned that travellers had to have a series of hired horses to 'post' on a long journey in the pre-railway age. Trollope himself, from his postal and private travels, understood the costs of renting carriages for short journeys in country towns. His own correspondence as well as the novels are often full of instructions about ordering a hired carriage to be ready at a station. (The best descriptions of the difficulties of arranging this type of transport are in *The Belton Estate.*) At times this could be expensive, as Mark Robarts learned when he thought of paying £1 to hire a gig with a pair of horses to get him about a dozen miles from Barchester in time to preach a sermon [*Framley Parsonage*, 7].

As an external key to character and as a way of observing how well informed he was about his own world, there are few better subjects than carriages in Trollope's fiction.

Carruthers, Lord George de Bruce. A disreputable Scottish adventurer who plays an important role in *The Eustace Diamonds*. Although he begins life apprenticed to an attorney, a series of deaths brings his elder brother the title of Marquis of Killiecrankie and George emerges with the courtesy title of Lord George. He has no regular income and is a strong Radical in politics. At the end of *Phineas Redux* he is about to marry Lady Eustace.

Cassell's Illustrated Family Newspaper (1853–1932). This weekly penny magazine was begun by John Cassell (1817–65) and was aimed principally at the higher level of the expanding working-class audience. Cassell himself was born in Manchester's slums and rose through his preaching of working-class self-education, his teetotalism, the sale of tea and a good marriage. He was famous for his *Popular Educator* series of self-instruction booklets. In 1855 he was 'rescued' by his printers and the firm became Cassell, Petter and Galpin. By 1859 his personal involvement with the paper had ended. Trollope's connection with the magazine began in 1860 when he sold it four short stories at £40 each: 'An Unprotected Female at the Pyramids'; 'The Château of Prince Polignac'; 'Miss Sarah Jack of Spanish Town, Jamaica'; and 'John Bull on the Guadalquivir'. The foreign settings of the stories, based on his travels, would have appealed to the magazine's audience. For the magazine to have got Trollope to write for them was a distinct *coup*.

Castle Richmond. Trollope began writing *Castle Richmond*, his ninth novel, on 4 August 1859. Chapman & Hall bought the rights to the manuscript but generously agreed to allow Trollope to offer it to the new *Cornhill Magazine.* However, the *Cornhill* wanted a 'classical novel', not an Irish one, and Trollope dropped *Castle Richmond* to begin *Framley Parsonage.* He returned to it on 2 January and finished it on 31 March 1860. It was published by Chapman & Hall in three volumes on 10 May 1860. Trollope received £600.

A month before Trollope began writing, in July 1859, he returned from his long Post Office mission to the West Indies to find that *The Times* of 23 May 1859 had carried an article by

E. S. Dallas, one of the best critics of the age, saying that he wrote 'faster than we can read' and that he had become 'the most fertile, the most popular, the most successful author ... of the circulating library sort'. Fortified by this welcome praise he was able to demand his largest payment to date when he signed the contract for *Castle Richmond* on 2 August 1859. The £600 marked an increase of £200 over his previous novel, *The Bertrams*. This was an important day for Trollope for other reasons: he wrote to his wife, Rose, that he had found a large house for them near London as he was about to take up an important position in the Post Office. That same summer he had also arranged to begin contributing short stories to the most important magazine in America [➤ Harper & Brothers].

As Trollope began to write this novel he knew he was at a crossroads in his life, both as a postal official and as an author. To return to England as the head of an important postal district was to reach a long-desired position. But it also meant leaving Ireland, a country he had come to love and which had been his home since 1841. *Castle Richmond* was his emotional farewell to Ireland. No other novel is so closely connected with his own feelings at the moment he began it. He went back further into the past than was customary in his fiction: only *Lady Anna* and, of course, *La Vendée* exceed *Castle Richmond* in this regard.

Throughout his writing career, Trollope showed a reluctance to accept the fact that the reading public did not care for Irish novels. Because of his own great knowledge of and love for Ireland and Irishmen, he was anxious to set novels in a country which had

some similarities but more dissimilarities to England. While the failure of his first two Irish novels had happened more than ten years earlier it had not been forgotten when he started *Castle Richmond*. Perhaps the introduction of more English characters as well as of scenes in London was an attempt to make this Irish novel more popular than its two predecessors.

Castle Richmond actually opens with a complaint about the unpopularity of Irish novels and Trollope then takes the opportunity to praise his Irish friends and servants and to testify to the far greater honesty he had found in Ireland than in England. Yet, fair as always, he mixes criticism with praise and says that it is difficult to get Irish workers, however honest, to be punctual or regular [18]. Of course here he is drawing on his own experience of managing Irish postmen. The habit of observing human behaviour that added so much richness to his fiction had been perfected in Ireland. He was always observing even the smallest action: thus he notes that if an English workman stopped to chat he would set down his wheelbarrow, but an Irish workman, thinking that to be 'low economy', holds the load while talking.

Trollope's Irish years helped him in another way: he listened carefully to the nuances of speech and noted colourful dialogue which he employed not to raise a condescending smile, but to add authenticity to his fiction. Phrases like 'may the heavens be your bed, for it's you is the frind to a poor man' [25] or 'God bless his sweet face' [42] abound in the novel. *Castle Richmond* depicts, as does Trollope's other Irish fiction, that exotic blend of feudal devotion and resentment that made up Ireland and he has sympathy with both. Thus he tells his English readers – and the novel always assumes that the readers are English – that 'the love which a poor Irishman feels for the gentlemen whom he regards as his master – "his masther" ... is astonishing to an Englishman'. Yet Trollope does not think this 'altogether good' because 'love should come of love'. He follows this with a judgement that expresses an attitude that is found throughout his fiction: 'Unbounded respect for human grandeur cannot be altogether good; for human greatness, if the greatness be properly sifted, it may be so' [25].

Unlike his first two Irish novels *Castle Richmond*'s plot is centred on the Protestant land-owning class. As so often, Trollope denies that the novel has a 'hero' in the conventional sense, but if there is one, he says, it is Herbert Fitzgerald, the son of a baronet. Sir Thomas and his English wife, Lady Fitzgerald, once known as 'the Dorsetshire Venus', live at Castle Richmond. (There is no connection between these Fitzgeralds and the Palliser novels' Burgo Fitzgerald, as he comes from the 'Worcestershire Fitzgeralds'. Trollope would have known that Fitzgerald was the family name of Ireland's sole duke, Leinster.) Herbert, the heir to a £12,000-a-year estate, is a Protestant although his silly aunt, Miss Letty Fitzgerald, is afraid that he has been corrupted at Oxford by the High Church Puseyites. She knew that the Pope had 'a sort of second head-quarters' at Oxford [5]. As usual, Trollope allows attacks on the High Church and Catholicism to appear ridiculous by putting them into the mouths of stupid people.

Suddenly the comfortable life of the Fitzgeralds is disturbed when a disreputable father and son, the Molletts, appear from England. Here we get Trollope's first depiction of bigamy, a subject he would return to in later novels. Old Mollett had been married to Lady Fitzgerald who had assumed he was dead before she married Sir Thomas. This upsetting news virtually kills Sir Thomas as he realizes that his own marriage is non-existent. He also realizes that Herbert is illegitimate and unable to succeed to either the title or the property because the law of entail – another topic that would play a large role in Trollope's fiction – required heirs to be legitimate.

The new heir is Herbert's cousin and neighbour, Owen Fitzgerald, a small landowner with an income of £800 a year. (Trollope received £700 a year, plus generous expenses, from the Post Office.) They are already rivals in love. There is also an old, aristocratic family living in the area, the Desmonds. Although their title is an ancient one, and one of those rare titles that could be inherited by a woman, they are not well off. The widowed Countess of Desmond, a woman of almost forty, had married an impoverished earl to get a title, as Julia Brabazon would do in *The Claverings*. As ever, Trollope is anxious to show that such mercenary marriages will, in the end, bring an awful punishment. The countess has two children, the young earl, a sixteen-year-old schoolboy, and Lady Clara.

Owen Fitzgerald's involvement with the Desmonds sounds more like a modern than a Victorian novel. Not only is he in love with Lady Clara, but he is loved by the widowed countess and the young earl. A few years before, Thackeray had shown the complications of a young man involved with both a mother and a daughter as well as being idealized by the young titled son in *Henry Esmond*, which was Trollope's favourite novel. This may have influenced Trollope in a subtle way, but the account of the Desmonds is all Trollope's own. The plight of the countess, with her passionate love for Owen, is well done and is a prelude to the description of Lady Laura Kennedy's passion for another handsome Irishman, Phineas Finn, in *Phineas Finn* and *Phineas Redux*. The countess has to try to balance her own desire for Owen with an equally strong desire to find a rich and titled husband for her daughter.

Castle Richmond is the only novel in which Trollope gives sustained attention to a romantic attachment between a youth and an older man. This was a frequent occurrence in Victorian society although it never appears to have occurred in Trollope's own life. Yet he handles it with a surprising sensitivity. Patrick, the young earl, looks upon Owen with 'strong boyish love,' though Trollope has already reassured us that the young earl is 'manly' as is the dashing Owen. Almost nowhere else in Trollope's fiction does such a young character play such a large and complicated part as the young earl. (In Trollope's last novel, *The Land-Leaguers*, an even younger Irish boy would play a different and sinister role.) Owen's other passion, fox-hunting, allows Trollope to make many comments about his favourite sport which he had taken up in his early years in Ireland; he tells us that one reason he enjoyed it so much was that it gave men a chance to appear in colourful dress [23].

The miserable prospects of Herbert and his mother are resolved when their English solicitor discovers that Mollett was already married when he married Lady Fitzgerald. This means his marriage to her was never valid and that hers to Sir Thomas was. Herbert is the rightful baronet. Both Herbert and Owen had behaved honourably throughout these difficult days and Sir Herbert now marries the faithful Lady Clara Desmond while the unhappy Owen goes off on a long trip with the devoted young Patrick.

While many of the characters are well drawn, they fade in one's memory when compared with his description of the Famine, which permeates the novel. In many ways it is an historical novel, not because it is set more than a decade before it was written but because it is a blend of fact and fiction. Trollope recounts what he saw during the Irish famine. The novel opens in 1846 or 1847, when he was stationed in County Cork, the scene of some of the worst suffering, and he placed 'Castle Richmond' itself near the small town of Mallow to which he moved in 1848. The Famine is a constant presence in the novel, but he gives his most detailed account of it in Chapter 7, which opens with an attack on those extreme Evangelicals who saw the Famine as God's curse upon Ireland. Sometimes Trollope personally recalls aspects of the Famine that he saw or stories that he heard. At other times he refers to something seen by 'a certain public officer'. Few people probably saw as much of the Famine as he did: his travel journals show that he rarely spent a night in his own house in the summer of 1846 as he constantly moved about the south of Ireland. (Keeping the postal deliveries safe and efficient during this time was of crucial importance to the efforts to help people as money poured in from England and America.)

The true horror of the famine is best shown in the pathetic scene in which Herbert Fitzgerald enters a poor cabin to see a mother with a dying child in her arms and a dead child lying on the floor [33]. It is his most moving death scene and there are few paragraphs that are better written or more tragic in all Trollope's writings. It is highly likely he was recalling something he had seen himself. When the novel ends the Famine is at its height, but in the final chapter Trollope insists that ultimately it proved a 'blessing' because Ireland became more prosperous as agriculture improved when the land was no longer divided into so many small plots. This seems a very harsh and heartless conclusion, yet he always insisted that it was so. Much statistical evidence bears him out: for instance, average wages increased in Ireland by about one-third in the twelve years between the end of the period in which the novel is set and the time Trollope began writing it. In the areas he knew, he had seen the meagre wages of agricultural labourers doubled. Trollope's portrayal of the Famine is different from so many of the simplistic accounts that pass for history and that still nourish nationalistic nonsense. He shows how both English and Irish, Catholic and Protestant, rich and poor struggled to help the starving. Throughout, his sympathy is clearly with the suffering, as can be seen in his description of the grief caused by emigration as people leave for America [32].

In spite of the misery that is constantly present, there is much humour in *Castle Richmond*. Trollope displays this in his handling of clergymen: the Catholic priest, Father Barney; the Protestant rector, the Reverend Aeneas Townsend; a visiting High Church clergyman, Mr Carter. All three are anxious to help famine victims but they are suspicious of the others' motives; eventually they come to work together. Here Trollope is anxious to display his own ecumenical attitudes as he had done in *The Kellys and the O'Kellys*. Often he puts his own views about religion into Herbert's dialogue, in which he points out that the two Churches share 'belief in Christ, belief in the Bible, belief in the doctrine of a Saviour's atonement'. The bigoted Aunt Letty will have none of this and proclaims that she would 'sooner be a Mohammedan than a Papist'. Herbert has a ready retort for the old spinster: 'You would alter your opinion after the first week in a harem' [12].

One social difference between England and Ireland that is seen in *Castle Richmond* is the way in which servants constantly wander in and out of rooms and conversations. This does not happen in his English novels. People at all levels were 'more intimate' in Ireland than in England. [➤ 'The O'Conors of Castle Conor', *The Land-Leaguers* and 'Father Giles of Bally-moy'.] The conversation between Mr Townsend's wife – an Irish version of Mrs Proudie in many ways – and Richard, the Catholic servant of the Fitzgeralds, would have been inconceivable in an English novel. The rector's wife offers the Catholic servant a glass of whiskey, but he proudly tells her that he is a teetotaller thanks to the great 'apostle of temperance Father Mathew' (1790–1856).

The novel abounds with 'authorial intrusions' and private jokes. The amusing anecdote about the English witness in an Irish courtroom stems from Trollope's own appearance as a witness in a trial [35]. The frequent descriptions of hotels and means of travel recall his own years of travelling about Ireland. His feelings on leaving his Irish house and garden come out plainly when the Fitzgeralds are leaving their home [32]. Here Trollope speaks of the things that played such a role in his life: his house, his flowers, his servants, his children and his place in church. By the time he wrote that passage he had already settled in England.

The critics were not, in general, hostile and several were complimentary. One fell back on that oft-repeated jibe of a jaded and vapid reviewer: the writing was 'slovenly'. The *Saturday Review* had a little laugh at the fact that Trollope, already the father of an 'enormous family' of novels, was now producing 'twins'. (This referred to the fact that *Framley Parsonage* was only in its fifth month of serialization when *Castle Richmond* was published.) It did not enjoy the popularity with circulating-library readers that some of his other novels did, for within a few months Mudie was selling surplus library copies at nine shillings, less than a third of the novel's original price. From the historical point of view and for anyone interested in Trollope and his times, especially in that still reverberating horror, the Irish Famine, *Castle Richmond* is an important novel. For those who just wish to read for the laudable purpose of amusement it will not command as much attention as some other novels, yet its plot still makes it an enjoyable book.

'Catherine Carmichael; or Three Years Running'. This short story was written in 1878. The editor of the *Masonic Magazine* asked Trollope for a Christmas story in September 1878. He told the editor that he could write nothing less than 10,000 words, for which he charged £100; he would, if required, write a shorter story but would still charge £100. On 2 October they reached agreement and he submitted the story twelve days later. He used the interval between finishing *Ayala's Angel* and starting *Cousin Henry* to write the story. It was published in the 1878 Christmas number. It was not included in his fifth collection of stories, *Why Frau Frohmann Raised Her Prices*. The story is the only fiction he set in New Zealand, having rejected the idea of setting a novel there.

This story, the tale of a woman's vulnerability due to poverty and a loveless marriage, is divided into three parts: Christmas Days Nos. 1, 2 and 3 – a good example of how Trollope could adapt a story for Christmas. Catherine Baird is a young woman whose mother has died, leaving her to look after the family; her father is a gold-miner. (Trollope tended to have a low opinion of mining.) She falls in love with another miner named John Carmichael. Then her father dies and John's hard-hearted but wealthy older cousin arrives to sort out matters. He arranges a marriage between himself and Catherine. They are married on the first of the three Christmas days, *en route* to his sheep-station. Her husband treats her like a servant and she begins to hate him; her only friend is a Maori servant. Christmas Day No. 2 starts with the announcement that John Carmichael is to come back to work at the station. Catherine opposes this for fear her love might show itself. She confesses her innocent love for John to her husband and orders him to send John away. Christmas Day No. 3 opens with her learning that she has become a widow. The story ends happily with Catherine finding her true love. She is, like Lucy Graham in 'The Telegraph Girl', one of Trollope's working-class women who, though they lack the opportunities that money and position bring, are nevertheless proud, honest and resourceful.

Like 'The Telegraph Girl', this story shows Trollope's ability to describe the lives of the working classes, which he rarely did in his novels. He drew on his son Frederic's life on an Australian sheep-station for background. In the 1870s there was a growing interest in the Empire and parents like the Trollopes, whose children were living in 'the English world', wanted to know something of their lives, particularly at Christmas. Trollope had described an Australian Christmas in *Harry Heathcote of Gangoil* a few years before.

Catholicism. For a Victorian Liberal, Trollope had a surprisingly friendly attitude towards Catholics and Catholicism. Yet as with so many of his beliefs there were two sides to this. His reservations were best expressed when he wrote about French Canadians in *North America*: 'A Roman Catholic population can never hold its ground against one that is Protestant, and yet', he went on, 'I love their religion. There is something beautiful and almost divine in the faith and obedience of a true son of the Holy Mother. I sometimes fancy that I would fain be a Roman Catholic, – if I could; as also I would often wish to be still a child, if

that were possible.' Catholicism's 'faults' could be corrected 'by the force of the human nature of its adherents', whereas with extreme Evangelicals 'the austerity of self-punishment' was at war with human nature [*Linda Tressel*, 14].

He had enjoyed his time in Ireland and had made many Catholic friends there. He preferred to live in Catholic Dublin rather than in Protestant Belfast. In his first novel, *The Macdermots of Ballycloran*, the central family were Catholics and the hero was a Catholic priest. He particularly enjoyed travelling in Catholic countries, especially Italy, France and the Austrian Empire. His love of art and architecture led him to an appreciation of Catholic liturgy and his own High Church views made him sympathetic to much in Catholic sacramental teaching. Trollope had been at Harrow with Cardinal Manning and they remained friendly after Manning left the Church of England [➤ *Thackeray*]. The cardinal told Trollope that his readers should give him 'signal honour', while the even more eminent Catholic prelate, Cardinal Newman, was one of Trollope's greatest admirers.

As the High Church movement developed in the Church of England, and as the Roman Catholic Church changed with the advent of papal infallibility and younger priests became more 'Roman' than in Trollope's youth, hostilities between English Catholics and Anglicans grew more bitter. This change was reflected in Trollope's own life when he befriended a Catholic convert clergyman who abused Trollope's church in a vain attempt to convert him to Catholicism while being entertained in Trollope's house. This man, Father

George Bampfield, became the basis for the unpleasant proselytizer, Father Barham, in *The Way We Live Now.*

For Roman Catholic priests he had on the whole a great respect born of his time in Ireland. He told one Catholic lady: 'I have lived much with clergymen of your church and have endeavoured to draw them in their colours as I saw them. But, because they were the priests of a church which was not my church, I have never drawn one as bad, or hypocritical, or unfaithful.' More than a dozen Catholic priests play substantive roles in Trollope's fiction, of whom nine are Irish, two are French, one is Austrian, one is Czech and only one is English. In his first novel, *The Macdermots of Ballycloran*, Father John is the hero and in his third novel, *La Vendée*, Father Jerome is an important and admirable figure. In 'Father Giles of Ballymoy', Father Giles, the model for whom became a friend of Trollope, is a thoroughly lovable character. In *Nina Balatka*, Father Jerome is a good priest. In *An Eye for an Eye*, Father Marty, a central figure, is treated with great respect, while his character is developed enough for him to have mixed motives. In the last novel Trollope wrote, *The Land-Leaguers*, his sympathetic view gave way somewhat in the light of some priests' support for Irish terrorism. There are three priests in the novel: one is admirable, one neutral and one, the youngest, a supporter of terrorism.

Nuns are only rarely referred to in his novels, and usually, as in *John Caldigate*, to show that fanatical Protestant ladies are far more austere. However, when Phineas Finn, the only Catholic layman of importance in Trollope's English fiction, returns to London he asks after his old friend, the Honourable Augusta Boreham. Her mother, Lady Baldock, laments, 'She is lost to us for ever ... and calls herself Sister Veronica John' [*Phineas Redux*, 2]. In this brief exchange Trollope follows his normal method of making anti-Catholicism ridiculous. [➤ *Castle Richmond.*] This is done most conspicuously in *The Warden* when there is a debate in the Commons about 'the bodily searching of nuns for Jesuitical symbols', and here Trollope ridicules a real proposal to inspect Catholic convents. As early as *The Kellys and the O'Kellys* one Protestant clergyman says, 'I'd sooner be half be a Roman myself, than think so badly of my neighbours' [38]. This was Trollope's own view. [➤ Religion.]

Celibacy. See Church of England.

Ceylon. Trollope visited Ceylon in 1875 when he was making his second trip to Australia. He described the island in four of the 'letters' he sent back to the United Kingdom for publication in various newspapers. He was pleased to see progress, racial harmony and prosperity 'due to the gentleness of the present British rule'. His old Irish friend, Sir William Gregory, was the governor. Trollope was particularly impressed with the coffee plantations; coffee was then the island's main crop. [➤ English World; *The Tireless Traveler.*]

Chadwick, John. A solicitor who appears in many of the Barsetshire novels. He is the steward of the Bishop of Barchester's estates and, like his father and grandfather, manages both the bishop's lands and diocesan property such as Hiram's Hospital. As such he is greatly involved in the legal dispute in *The Warden*. He reappears in *Barchester Towers*, *Framley Parsonage* and *The Last Chronicle of Barset*. He is best described in the last novel as 'a man of prudence and sagacity' who, from his long connection with clergymen, appeared to be half a cleric himself [34]. Rachel Ray's father is described in similar terms in *Rachel Ray* [1].

Chaffanbrass, Mr. Of Mr Chaffanbrass, Trollope's most famous barrister, his creator rightly boasted, 'I do not think I have cause to be ashamed of him' [*Autobiography*, 6]. This formidable figure first appears in *The Three Clerks*, then in *Orley Farm*, where he defends Lady Mason, and finally in *Phineas Redux*. Trollope told Escott, his first biographer, that Chaffanbrass had the same trick of dropping his voice and constantly rearranging his wig as the real barrister, Edwin James, whom Dickens portrays in *A Tale of Two Cities* [9]. (By the time Trollope said this, James had been disbarred and had become an actor in America.) In *Orley Farm* Chaffanbrass is introduced as 'my old friend Mr Chaffanbrass' whose peculiar talent is 'the brow-beating of witnesses' [10]. In the same novel Trollope says that he reminded him of an assassin he had once met in Ireland [10]. Chaffanbrass has no social graces and is remarkably dirty in his person. [➤ Trials.]

Chapman & Hall (1830–1938). The firm, founded by two London booksellers, Edward Chapman (1804–80) and William Hall, published thirty-two books by Trollope, about half his total output. Their success began with the publication of *The Pickwick Papers* by Dickens in 1836 and the firm became

his main publishers. They established the monthly issue of illustrated novels selling at a shilling, and also published Mrs Gaskell, Charles Kingsley, W. M. Thackeray and Thomas Carlyle. In 1847 Hall died, and in 1858 the firm began a long relationship with Trollope with the publication of *Doctor Thorne*. Six years later Edward Chapman was replaced by his cousin, Frederic Chapman (1823–95). In 1865 Frederic helped Trollope and others to establish the *Fortnightly Review*. Trollope bought a large number of shares in Chapman & Hall and became a director; he also arranged for his son Henry to become a partner in 1869 by investing £10,000, an enormous sum, in the firm. In 1871, Trollope told one correspondent that 'Chapman & Hall are in truth Chapman & Trollope', and that 'the Trollope is my son'. In 1873 Henry gave up his active partnership and the money was re-invested for him by Trollope. In 1878 the firm brought out the first collected edition of the Barsetshire novels, *The Chronicles of Barsetshire*, in eight volumes. In 1880 it became a limited company, with Trollope as one of the three directors. Shares were also owned by many of the Trollopes: Rose, Henry, Tom and his wife, Frances Eleanor. Chapman & Hall published several books on Italian history by Trollope's brother, Tom, and his first wife. As a director Trollope received £500 a year and spent about ten hours a week in the office. He hated the work and did not trust Frederic Chapman's business sense. Although the house had been successful in pioneering cheap reprints and part issues and had had many famous authors it was increasingly unsuccessful financially; in 1938 it was bought by Methuen.

By Trollope's death the firm had published all four of his large travel books (*The West Indies and the Spanish Main, North America, Australia and New Zealand* and *South Africa*); two of his five collections of short stories (*Tales of All Countries* and *Tales of All Countries,* Second Series); twenty-two of his novels (*Doctor Thorne, The Bertrams, Castle Richmond, Orley Farm, Rachel Ray, Can You Forgive Her?, Miss Mackenzie, The Belton Estate, The Eustace Diamonds, Phineas Redux, Lady Anna, The Way We Live Now, The Prime Minister, The American Senator, Is He Popenjoy?, An Eye for an Eye, John Caldigate, Cousin Henry, The Duke's Children, Dr Wortle's School, Ayala's Angel* and *Marion Fay*); three collections of articles (*Hunting Sketches, Travelling Sketches,* and *Clergymen of the Church of England*); and *The Life of Cicero.*

[➤ Publishers and Publishing; Serialization.]

'The Château of Prince Polignac'. This is one of the five short stories written during Trollope's holiday in the French Pyrenees with his wife Rose, his brother Tom, and his brother-in-law John Tilley in September–October 1859. It was published in *Cassell's Illustrated Family Paper* on 20 and 27 October 1860 and was included in his first collection of short stories, *Tales of All Countries* (1861). In his *Autobiography* Trollope wrote that the stories included in that collection 'have, most of them, some foundation in such occurrences', that is, in 'true tales of my adventures'. Trollope received £40.

The story is set in the town of Le Puy, which the Trollope party visited. Like many nineteenth-century travel stories, it makes use of the *table d'hôte* in an hotel as the means for characters to meet. The story centres on a young widow, Frances Thompson. Another guest, M. Lacordaire, falls in love with her and invites her and her daughter to visit the ruins of the château of Prince Polignac, outside Le Puy. Here the Frenchman proposes in suitably melodramatic manner. Mrs Thompson is at first put off by his trade – *un tailleur* – but then accepts him; Trollope sees no reason why she should not marry a tailor.

Trollope contrasts the Frenchman's 'sugar of romance' with the Englishwoman's common sense and propriety to good effect. He also shows his interest in the details of women's dress, and comments regarding Mrs Thompson: 'She was good-looking, lady-like, and considering that she was an English-woman, fairly well dressed.' Trollope named his tailor Lacordaire; the French Dominican, Henri Dominique Lacordaire (1802–61), was much in the French and even English news in the 1840s and 1850s as a popular preacher. He was the man responsible for re-establishing the Dominican Order in France. Like Miss Mackenzie in the novel of that name, Lady Frances Trafford in *Marion Fay* or, more famously, Lady Anna Lovel in *Lady Anna*, the story deals with a lady's marriage to someone beneath her socially. Prince Polignac was the well-known French premier whose reactionary policies caused the downfall of Charles X in 1830. Fanny Trollope, who gives her name to the heroine of the story, refers to his imprisonment in her *Paris and the Parisians* (1836). [➤ Names, Origin of.]

Chatto & Windus (1855–). Although this publishing house was started in the mid-century it became important in the 1870s under Andrew Chatto, originally a junior partner. Chatto, who had travelled in America, introduced Mark Twain to Britain and bought copyrights, including some of Trollope's novels, lying unused in the hands of older publishers like Chapman & Hall. Chatto then reissued these in cheap editions at 3s. 6d. and then in 2s. 'yellow backs'. They had money and engaged in what Michael Sadleir called 'ostentatious advertisement'. The firm was one of the 'new breed' of publishers who promoted the overthrow of the three-decker system of publishing. In 1882 Chatto established direct links with Trollope by publishing *Kept in the Dark* in book form. They also published two of his final novels, *Mr Scarborough's Family* and *The Land-Leaguers*. It is a sign of Chatto's good sense and of Trollope's continuing appeal and vibrancy as a writer that they were negotiating in the year of his death.

Cheltenham. Often called 'Littlebath' in Trollope's fiction, Cheltenham is singled out for attack when it has that name. To Trollope it was the capital of sham religion – the Evangelicals – and sham gentility. If Bath was built in stone, Littlebath was built in stucco. His onslaughts were usually accompanied by an attack on Evangelicals for good measure. These can sometimes be very bitter. In *The Bertrams* he denounces the 'pious set' as 'a strong, unctuous, moral, uncharitable people. The men never cease making money for themselves, nor the women making slippers for their clergymen' [13]. In *Miss Mackenzie* the heroine settles in Littlebath on the advice of her London clergyman and associates herself with the same set one met in *The*

Bertrams. He singles out the Reverend Mr Stumfold, whom he describes as a 'shining light ... the man of men, if he was not something more than mere man, in the eyes of the devout inhabitants of that town' [2]. There are also little barbs, as in *Framley Parsonage*. There Olivia Proudie wrote her anonymous letter warning Mrs Grantly that her daughter was to be jilted, and had it posted, appropriately, from Littlebath. Mrs Grantly referred to the act as 'a part of the new Christianity' [45]. In *The American Senator* Trollope had a swipe not specifically at Cheltenham, where Mary Masters went to think over her future, but at Cheltenham College, which he blamed for the hero's less than perfect grammar. Normally, however, when he levels attacks, it is at Littlebath; when he merely sets an ordinary scene there, he calls it Cheltenham, as in *Mr Scarborough's Family* or *Can You Forgive Her?*.

Nowhere else in his fiction is a dislike so vitriolic and it must have been based on personal experience. He and Rose had lived in Cheltenham for several months in 1852 and 1853 when he was doing his special Post Office work in the West of England. They lived at No. 5, Paragon Buildings, the same terrace in which Margaret Mackenzie takes a house and Harry Annesley proposes to Florence Mountjoy in *Mr Scarborough's Family*. The Paragon, we are told in *Miss Mackenzie*, 'is the nucleus of all that is pleasant and fashionable at Littlebath'. In *Can You Forgive Her?*, Alice Vavasor stays with Lady Macleod at No. 3, Paramount Crescent, the Paragon Buildings under a different name. (In *The Vicar of Bullhampton* Trollope mentions a Paragon Crescent but sets it in the fictional town of Loring.)

The Trollopes were in Cheltenham when the Reverend Francis Close was Rector of Cheltenham (1826–56). To *The Times* he was, simply, 'the Pope of Cheltenham'. His power was enormous and helped to make the town the centre for Evangelicals, many of whom were ex-Indian Army officers. In commenting on *The American Senator* in a letter of 27 December 1876, Trollope speaks of his 'long-ago-entertained dislike of Dean Close and Cheltenham School'. The fact that Trollope's dislike was so intense and so long-lasting probably indicates that Close had insulted either Trollope or his wife and sons in some way, although he would also have disliked his frequent ranting against Catholicism. When the pious ladies of Littlebath knit slippers for their clergy in *The Bertrams*, Trollope was having a private joke at Close's expense, as he was said, according to one authority, to have received 1,500 slippers in his clerical career. In *Miss Mackenzie*, Trollope refers to a Dr Snort by whom he probably meant Close. Trollope must also have known that Lord Northwick, regarded by the Trollope brothers as the author of their father's financial ruin, was a prominent figure in the nineteenth-century development of Cheltenham as a spa town. The population of Cheltenham had reached 39,693 by 1861.

Children. Children play only a small role in Trollope's fiction: in the Barsetshire series the number of Mr Quiverful's children actually varies from chapter to chapter. Babies get even less attention. Trollope referred to 'baby worship' as a pleasure confined normally to women, but did give a description of Johnny Bold as an example of 'baby perfection' [*Barchester Towers*, 16, 2]. Perhaps his most important babies occur in *The Claverings* and *He Knew He Was Right*. In the first, the baby son and heir of the hard-hearted baronet, Sir Hugh Clavering, dies and the chapter devoted to his death is poignantly written. In the second, the tragic plot's intensity is heightened by Louis Trevelyan's kidnapping of his infant son.

Appearances by children normally heighten the sense of happiness and wellbeing, for instance when Mr Harding is shown with his granddaughter, Posy Arabin, in *The Last Chronicle of Barset*, or Mary Lowther plays with the vicarage children in *The Vicar of Bullhampton*. Sometimes they are merely adjuncts to the main plot, like Mabel Lownd in 'Christmas Day at Kirkby Cottage'. Archdeacon Grantly's three sons in *The Warden* are used as representations of three bishops in the Church of England. In *Phineas Finn*, Lady Glencora takes her young son to the Duke of Omnium as a warning not to marry Madame Max Goesler and breed another heir. Parents who have an enormous number of children, such as the Quiverfuls, are often comic figures or at least mildly ludicrous.

There are three novels in which children play more substantial roles. In *The Claverings* Harry Clavering visits the Burton family where the children are used to reinforce the contrast of a happy home life with Lady Ongar's world. In *Castle Richmond* the young Earl of Desmond has a schoolboy's 'crush' on Owen Fitzgerald. In *The Land-Leaguers* Trollope gives a ten-year-old boy a vital part. Florian Jones is important because his unlikely 'conversion' to Roman

Catholicism means he is unwilling to testify against fellow religionists who flood his father's best land in an act of terrorism. The main plot centres on getting him to testify. Even here, however, Trollope admits his limitations when introducing Florian: 'What can be said of a boy who is only ten which shall be descriptive and also interesting? He was small of his age, but clever and sharp ... He was beautiful to look at ... but the neighbours declared that his education had been much neglected' [1].

Trollope was himself a devoted father to his two sons, Henry and Frederic, but he had a typically Victorian view of children, as expressed in *North America*: 'The uncontrolled energies of twenty children round one's legs do not convey comfort or happiness ... I must protest that American babies are an unhappy race. They eat and drink just as they please; they are never punished; they are never banished, snubbed, and kept in the back ground as children are kept with us ... Can it be, I wonder, that children are happier when they are made to obey orders and are sent to bed at six o'clock, than when allowed to regulate their own conduct; that bread and milk is more favourable to laughter and soft childish ways than beef-steaks and pickles three times a day ... ?'[10].

[➤ Daughters; Fathers and Sons; Mothers and Daughters.]

Chiltern Hundreds. Since the mid-eighteenth century the normal way for an MP to resign his seat in the House of Commons has been to apply for and 'accept' the sinecure office of Steward of the Chiltern Hundreds. Trollope made mild fun of this 'grand bulwark of the British constitution' in *The Three Clerks* [24] when one corrupt MP uses it to avoid expulsion from the Commons. Later in the novel an even more corrupt MP is denied the office and instead is expelled from the house. Other MPs in Trollope's fiction follow the normal procedure and apply for the Chiltern Hundreds, although there is some debate as to whether Phineas Finn should be allowed this dignified way of resigning when he is accused of murder [*Phineas Redux*, 71].

Chiltern, Lady. An important character in the Palliser novels. She appears first in *Phineas Finn* as the rich young orphan, Violet Effingham, and is a close friend of Lady Laura Standish [Kennedy] who hopes that she will marry her brother, Lord Chiltern. Although supervised by her aunt, Lady Baldock, she is pursued by several men anxious to win her for her beauty and wealth. Among these are Phineas Finn, Lord Chiltern and Lord Fawn. She chooses Chiltern in the hope that she can reform him. Her success in this is seen in all the subsequent Palliser novels where she appears. She also makes a brief appearance in *The American Senator* [36–40].

Chiltern, (Oswald) Lord. A major character in several of the Palliser novels, he first appears in *Phineas Finn* and reappears in all the subsequent novels. He is the son and heir of the Earl of Brentford with whom he is in constant conflict although without the viciousness seen in the De Courcy family. [➤ Fathers and Sons.] Although Lord Chiltern causes several upsets, he is not really a scoundrel. This volatile red-faced young lord is one of

Trollope's many young men who are having trouble as hobbledehoys. His devoted sister, Lady Laura Kennedy, sacrifices her own fortune to pay off his debts. Chiltern wants no part of politics and devotes himself passionately to fox-hunting; he eventually finds a sort of salvation as a model MFH. His wife says he 'has taken up hunting as his duty in life' [*The Duke's Children*, 62]. Although he is often in rivalry with Phineas Finn to the point of fighting a duel, they become close friends in the end. Chiltern defeats Finn by marrying Violet Effingham and making her Lady Chiltern. He is the opposite of Plantagenet Palliser, as he himself admits [*Phineas Redux*, 14]. There is no ground for accepting Escott's absurd suggestion that Trollope took Chiltern as a 'snapshot' of the prominent politician, Lord Hartington, later the eighth Duke of Devonshire [Mullen, 485].

Christmas and Christmas Stories. Christmas to Trollope was an occasion not only of feasting but of profound religious importance. This is demonstrated in *Orley Farm*, in which he attacks the sensual Moulder, and in the short story 'Not If I Know It', in which he shows the effect of the Christmas Day Eucharist. *Orley Farm* features his longest piece of writing on the holiday and a nephew said that the Christmas described in Chapter 22 was based on Trollope's own. Trollope described an ideal Christmas in some of those short stories written for the occasion. It consisted of church, with the celebration of Holy Communion, followed by a three o'clock dinner with 'a sirloin of beef a foot-and-a-half broad, a turkey as big as an ostrich, a plum-pudding bigger than the

turkey, and two or three dozen mince-pies' ['Christmas at Thompson Hall'], followed by the Loyal Toast and games ['Christmas Day at Kirkby Cottage']. Occasionally a short description of some Christmas custom would be inserted in a novel, as when Lily Dale decorates the church with holly [*The Last Chronicle of Barset*, 16].

However much Trollope enjoyed traditional Christmas festivities, he thoroughly disliked writing Christmas stories. In his *Autobiography* he wrote: 'Nothing can be more distasteful to me than to have to give a relish of Christmas to what I write. I feel the humbug implied by the nature of the order. A Christmas story, in the proper sense, should be the ebullition of some mind anxious to instil others with a desire for Christmas religious thought, or Christmas festivities, – or, better still, with Christmas charity.' When he wrote this he was under contract to provide just such a story – 'Christmas at Thompson Hall' – and added that he was 'cudgelling my brain for the last month'.

Despite his personal view, the Christmas story was an accepted part of the new Victorian Christmas, like trees, crackers, puddings and Christmas cards, and he ended up writing eight Christmas stories in addition to 'Christmas at Thompson Hall': 'Catherine Carmichael', 'Christmas Day at Kirkby Cottage', 'Harry Heathcote of Gangoil', 'Not If I Know It', 'The Mistletoe Bough', 'The Two Generals', 'The Two Heroines of Plumplington' and 'The Widow's Mite'. In at least four other cases ('Alice Dugdale', 'George Walker at Suez', 'Josephine de Montmorenci' and 'The Telegraph Girl') stories not designed for Christmas were published over the holidays. The only Christmas story Trollope mentions in his *Autobiography* is 'Harry Heathcote of Gangoil', which describes Australian life, including Christmas. It was later published as a short novel.

'Christmas at Thompson Hall'. This short story was written in 1876. Trollope never liked writing Christmas stories and when writing his *Autobiography* he moaned, 'Alas! at this very moment I have one to write, which I have promised to supply within three weeks of this time [April 1876] ... as to which I have in vain been cudgelling my brain for the last month.' The request was from *The Graphic* to write a second Christmas story. (The first had been 'Harry Heathcote of Gangoil' in 1873.) 'Christmas at Thompson Hall' was published on 25 December 1876 and Trollope facetiously told a friend, Mrs Bronson, that 'It is a tragedy, and will harrow up her [Mrs Bronson's daughter's] young heart in quite the proper style.' It caused Trollope further trouble in 1879 when he wanted to include it in a fifth collection of stories. (He needed the magazine's consent as he had sold it the copyright.) The publishers wanted, in exchange, another story from Trollope. He agreed this and three years later his last collection of stories, *Why Frau Frohmann Raised Her Prices and Other Stories*, was finally published with this story included. There is, however, no record that Trollope sent the promised story to the magazine. Even after his death there were problems. Was it a story or a novel? It had been published as a novel in America in 1877 by Harpers. Trollope inscribed a copy of the American edition to his wife: 'This is, I imagine, the only copy of this

book in England 7 June 1877.' (This copy is now in the Taylor Collection in Princeton.) Trollope received £150 which, according to extant records, is the largest sum he was ever paid for a short story.

This humorous story starts in a Paris hotel two days before Christmas. Mr and Mrs Brown, who normally spend their winters in the South of France, are *en route* for the family seat in Essex to celebrate her sister's engagement. The husband complains of a sore throat and asks his wife to go down in her dressing-gown to the restaurant and steal some mustard for a mustard-plaster. She returns and puts the mustard-plaster on the man's neck, only to discover that she is in the wrong room. She is afraid to remove the plaster for fear of waking the stranger but she dare not leave it on too long. She takes flight. Next morning, on their way out of the hotel the porter hands her her handkerchief, which she had left in the wrong room: it has her name stitched on it. The porter says that 'something very bad indeed' was done to the man in whose room the handkerchief was found. Mr Brown is furious, goes to see the injured man and apologizes. Once in England the Browns discover that the man is Mrs Brown's sister's fiancé. On Christmas Day the large family gathering goes to church and enjoys a Trollopian feast. Mrs Brown confesses and her sister's fiancé forgives her. This is one of Trollope's most enjoyable short stories.

'Christmas Day at Kirkby Cottage'. This Christmas story, probably written between 3 and 10 June 1870 while Trollope was writing *The Eustace Diamonds*, was published in *Routledge's*

Christmas Annual for 1870 and took pride of place as the first story. It was never reprinted in any of Trollope's five collections. Its publishing history gives an interesting insight into Trollope's honesty and business habits. In April 1869 the publisher Edmund Routledge (who had unsuccessfully approached Trollope in 1867) asked him to write a story for his *Christmas Annual* and to name his price. He told Routledge that his novels worked out at six guineas a page and that he would have to charge that. However, with novels came a copyright in the story but with short stories Trollope usually retained the copyright. In other words, Routledge would not be getting fair value for his money; if he insisted, Trollope would demand £100. Nothing came of this until April 1870 when negotiations were re-opened but this time Routledge got the copyright and Trollope got £100. This may explain why the story was not reprinted by Trollope.

This is a love story set at Christmas. Like 'The Parson's Daughter of Oxney Colne', *Dr Wortle's School*, *Framley Parsonage*, 'The Widow's Mite' and *The Vicar of Bullhampton*, it is set in a parsonage, in this case the rectory of Kirkby Cliffe, in Yorkshire. A guest in the house is Maurice Archer, a recent Oxford graduate and local landowner. Maurice, who is in love with the rector's daughter, Isabel Lownd, is 'bored' with Christmas – it is nothing but over-eating – and refuses to help her decorate the church. Isabel is put off by his cynicism. She accuses him of finding tedious those things that provide 'unusual enjoyment to poor people, who very seldom have any pleasure'. On Christmas Day Maurice proposes and asks forgiveness for his

apparent cynicism, but she refuses for reasons she cannot understand. Maurice now thinks he will sell up and emigrate to Africa. When visiting the poor after church, Isabel finds that in spite of his offhand comments Maurice has sent round beef to his tenants. Later, while Christmas parlour-games (similar to those in *Orley Farm* and in Trollope's own home) are going on, Maurice renews his offer and Isabel accepts.

Trollope take the opportunity of a scene in the parish church to denounce the Victorian passion for church restoration, which he calls a 'kind of destruction', and to praise the old eighteenth-century three-decker pulpit. He did admit that this attitude was 'offensive to many'. [➤ Architecture; Church of England; Religion.]

The Chronicles of Barsetshire. The title given to the collection of Trollope's six Barsetshire novels prepared under his supervision and issued by his own firm of Chapman & Hall in 1878. At first he had not planned to include *The Small House at Allington*. Difficulties arose in making up the collection because of complications over copyright, which was held by several different publishers and, in some cases, by Trollope himself. The set was issued in eight volumes and contains a short but important introduction by Trollope as well as a few footnotes by him.

Church of England. No other novelist is so closely identified in the public mind with the Church of England as Anthony Trollope. Since clergymen and talk about the Church enter into almost all of his novels, it is essential to have an understanding of the Church as Trollope saw it. As George Eliot said, her friend Trollope was 'a Church of England man'.

After Trollope's death his rector wrote that he had been 'an alert and reverent and audible worshipper, and a steady communicant'. Throughout his life he was a devout but moderate High Churchman with a liberal attitude towards doctrine and scripture. In 1862 he wrote, 'It has been hard to steer between idolatry and irreverence, between too much ceremony and too little. We, with our much maligned church in England, may perhaps boast we have done so.' His grandfathers were both parish priests, he went to public schools imbued with a strong Church atmosphere and his masters were clergymen. There appears to have been some idea by his parents that he might become a clergyman himself.

Trollope was brought up in the old High Church tradition. His first biographer, Escott, the son of a clergyman who was a schoolmate of Trollope, wrote that Trollope's 'sympathies were... inclined towards the moderate, lettered, and generally accomplished members of the High Church party'. The term 'high' was a common Victorian use, meaning a serious view of a subject and was used, for example, with reference to farming. (Trollope even refers to 'high cooking', by which he meant what we would call gourmet cooking.) In church terms it meant regarding the Church of England as part of the universal catholic Church and not merely as an established national 'institution'. This view went hand in hand with a decidedly 'Protestant' rejection of papal supremacy.

Trollope's High Church tradition was often caricatured as 'high and dry' and this annoyed him. It placed great emphasis on the Sacraments and in his last short story, 'Not If I Know It', he refers to 'the Sacrament, more powerful with its thoughts than its words'; this was High Church language. The tradition also emphasized the Church's Catholic legacy and was devoted to the Prayer Book, if not, in Trollope's case, to its compiler, Cranmer. In *Barchester Towers* Trollope dismissed Cranmer as 'a time-serving priest, willing to go any length to keep his place' and Elizabeth I as 'in heart a papist, with this sole proviso, that she should be her own pope' [22]. Because the old High Church tradition eschewed enthusiasm and practised a restrained style of worship, it was labelled 'dry' by the new generation of High Churchmen beginning in the 1830s. Septimus Harding and Archdeacon Grantly are examples of 'high and dry' clergymen.

Trollope's High Church beliefs must not be confused with the later stages of the Oxford Movement from the 1860s onwards, whose supporters were sometimes called Puseyites after the Oxford High Church leader, Canon Edward Pusey (1800–1882). To Trollope they over-emphasized liturgical worship, dress and church design. He disliked this because he saw in it 'the huge evil of unreality'. In his *Pall Mall Gazette* articles on the Church he praised the High Church movement, but dismissed the liturgical 'excesses' or what he called the 'wiggeries' as 'the dross which has come from their fused gold'. He often had sport with the pietistic excesses of High Church ladies like the Germain sisters in *Is He Popenjoy?* and was 'mainly indifferent to the vestment' worn by the clergy; elsewhere he referred to 'a passion for ribbons', by which he meant stoles bearing the colour of the liturgical season. Even so, he constantly refers to altars and not communion tables, to altar cloths and to Sacraments. [➤ 'The Two Heroines of Plumplington'.] He had no time for clerical celibacy and celibate clergymen, such as Mr Arabin or Caleb Oriel, usually come to their senses before the end of a Trollope novel.

Trollope always supported the early work of the Oxford Movement and in 1859 he praised it in *The West Indies and the Spanish Main* by recalling 'the sleeping, droning, somnolent service ... so common in England twenty years since; but which are common no longer, thanks to certain much-abused clerical gentlemen'. In *Barchester Towers* [20] he wrote, 'How great an amount of good ... has followed that movement in the Church of England which commenced with the publication of Froude's *Remains*!' (Hurrell Froude's (1803-36) High Church reflections, posthumously published by J. H. Newman and mainly drawn from his diaries, were, among other things, an outspoken assault on the Reformation.) Trollope frequently attacked those who denounced the High Church revival or Oxford Movement and 'live in daily fear of the scarlet lady' [*Doctor Thorne*, 32]. He also had great fun with the 'Convent Custody Bill' in *The Warden* [7].

Like most High Churchmen, Trollope supported the establishment of the Church and recognized that English history and the Church were inextricably bound together. 'For myself,' he wrote, 'I love the name of State and Church, and believe that much of our

English well-being has depended on it. I have made up my mind to think that union good ...' Although he advocated disestablishment of the Church of Ireland when he stood as a candidate at Beverley, he was a firm supporter of the continued establishment of the Church of England. In *Phineas Redux* the main political action is centred on an attempt, happily unsuccessful, to disestablish the Church of England. His general Church views meant that he always felt friendly towards Catholicism, but disliked Evangelicals and Low Churchmen in his own Church and Dissenters outside it. His best discussion of the Church's relations with Dissenters occurs in *The Vicar of Bullhampton*.

He grew up knowing a great deal about the Church, despite disclaimers in his *Autobiography*, and this interest continued throughout his life. Both of his parents were deeply interested in ecclesiastical topics and both wrote about them. Few schoolboys, even in the 1820s, could name all the bishops, but young Trollope could. This knowledge was reflected in his Barsetshire novels. He was also keenly aware of the problems of the Church and had strong views about them, especially the vast inequality of payment among clergymen. [➤ *Framley Parsonage*, 14.]

It may be helpful to have some basic idea of the Church's structure in Trollope's time. In the 1850s, when he started the Barsetshire series, the Church of England was divided into two provinces, Canterbury and York, each headed by an archbishop. There were twenty-seven dioceses in the two provinces and each diocese was under a bishop who took his title from the principal seat of his diocese, like the Bishop of Barchester. Bishops' residences were normally styled 'palaces'. (By the year of Trollope's death the number of bishops had increased to thirty-one.) Each diocese was divided into parishes which numbered some 11,077 in 1831, a number which had changed little in over 600 years. Bishops were appointed by the Crown. The prime minister was always concerned with the political affiliations because they had a seat in the House of Lords. That is why Archdeacon Grantly's hopes of becoming a bishop in *Barchester Towers* depends on the Tories remaining in office. Each cathedral was administered by a dean and several canons or prebendaries (the differences are not important in Trollope's fiction) who also owed their appointments to the Crown. Bishops appointed one or more archdeacons to assist them in the administration of the diocese. Archdeacons were considerable figures and examined men coming forward for ordination. Bishops normally received £5,000 a year, deans £1,500, while archdeacons were also well paid and many of them lived in great comfort. Most of these important clergymen were connected to prominent families. In *Barchester Towers* Bishop Proudie and Canon Stanhope were related to peers; Archdeacon Grantly was the son of the Bishop of Barchester. Such men were considered part of 'county society' and looked down, like Henry Clavering, on rural clergymen not connected, as he was, to the 'squirearchy'. Mr Clavering's nephew was a baronet [*The Claverings*, 33]. In his later novels Trollope shows the growing trend for men without family connections to rise to high positions, such as Dean Lovelace of Brotherton in *Is He Popenjoy?* and Canon William Owen in *Cousin Henry*.

A complicated structure had developed to provide parish priests: the 'patron' was the person or body which had the 'advowson' or the legal right to select a man to present to the 'living' or 'benefice', that is, the possession of a particular parish. Because most of the income for a living came from tithes it was possible to give relatively precise figures for what each living was worth. A priest had full legal right to hold his living for the rest of his life and this independence allowed for the development of colourful personalities such as Trollope depicts. The power of bishops to govern their clergy was quite limited, as Dr Wortle demonstrated in *Dr Wortle's School*. The best livings often went to family members: a younger brother holds the living in *Lady Anna*, Squire Prosper's brother-in-law holds the living of Buston in *Mr Scarborough's Family*, while Gregory Newton holds the 'family living' in *Ralph the Heir*. A priest could hold more than one living (pluralism) and could then pay a curate to do his work in the parish where he did not live. (Canon Vesey Stanhope is the most notorious example of this in Trollope's fiction.)

The income of curates varied as much as that of the higher clergy. Mr Slope was offered the place of curate at Puddingdale at £50 and in *An Old Man's Love* the vicar goes off to the Riviera to die and makes the Reverend Montagu Blake his curate at £120 a year, a relatively comfortable sum. As income was tied to livings the only way to get money was to keep livings and contract out the work to curates at less than the full income. There were strange anomalies such as the 'perpetual curate' who was not 'inducted' but only 'licensed'. Some people looked down on them as second-class priests; Trollope put this to good use in *The Last Chronicle of Barset* when he makes Josiah Crawley perpetual curate of Hogglestock on £130 a year.

In *The Claverings* a well-off clergyman with 'nearly £800 a year' could hire a curate like Mr Saul for £70 a year to be his assistant. Normally the parish priest was either a rector or a vicar and for the purposes of Trollope's fiction the distinction is of little importance. Clergymen's income varied from parish to parish: Mark Robarts had £900 a year in *Framley Parsonage*, while in *Barchester Towers* Mr Quiverful at Puddingdale had £50. The incomes depended on rents or crops from Church-owned lands ('glebe lands'), from ancient endowments, from fees and from tithes or from payments in kind [➤ *The Vicar of Bullhampton*]. By Trollope's time tithes had become payable in money. With the living came, normally, a vicarage, sometimes called a parsonage, which the priest had to maintain.

Trollope's novels reflect the central role of the Church of England in Victorian society. Almost all his English characters appear to be members of it. Even people like Abel Wharton, QC in *The Prime Minister*, who are less than regular in their church attendance, regard themselves as active members. (Ferdinand Lopez in the same novel claims to be a member though he is often denounced as 'a Portuguese Jew'.) To dissent from Anglicanism was, in some sense, to dissent from respectable society, at least that which Trollope knew. That is why he constantly emphasizes that a clergyman must be a 'gentleman'. It can be as-sumed that almost all Trollope's clerical characters would have been educated at Oxford or Cambridge, though in one novel there are unfriendly references to the growth of other places of clerical education [*Miss Mackenzie*, 4]. In Trollope's time the Church of England saw many battles between High and Low – the Grantlys versus the Proudies – and between liberals like the Reverend Mr Jobbles (based on the real Benjamin Jowett) in *The Three Clerks* [11] or John Bold in *The Warden* and traditionalists like Septimus Harding. There were attempts by Parliament on several occasions to control the High Church revival. The seemingly farcical Bill to inspect nuns for Jesuitical symbols in *The Warden* is based on a real attempt at such legislation: 'The Recovery of Personal Liberty in Certain Cases Bill' of 1853 wanted government agents to inspect convents to free 'any female . . . detained . . . against her will'.

As the population grew there were increasing attempts by all parts of the Church to work in the slums of rapidly expanding cities, like that undertaken by the Reverend Oliphant Outhouse in *He Knew He Was Right*. The number of curates also grew. For novelists, this juxtaposition of younger, more enthusiastic and often poorer and socially inferior curates into a parish created a host of dramatic possibilities. This figured in Trollope's novels, most notably in *The Claverings* and *The American Senator*. Trollope's treatment of religion, especially in connection with his own Church, is very subtle and repays the close attention of any reader. For his portrayal of clergymen fashioned after his own tastes, see *The Vicar of Bullhampton* and *Is He Popenjoy?*.

[➤ Bible; Churches; Clergymen; *Clergymen of the Church of England*; Colenso; *Essays and Reviews*; Evangelicals; Prayer Book; Religion; Sermons.]

Churches. Trollope's views on churches roughly followed those on country houses, with a preference for older styles and a dislike of the eighteenth century. He had mixed views on the Victorians' passion for 'restoring' churches and for copying medieval patterns in building new ones. He expressed this in *The Small House at Allington* when describing Allington's medieval church. He attacked the eighteenth-century interior with its 'ugly useless' pulpit, 'high-backed ugly pews': 'upon the whole things there were not quite as I would have had them'. Instead of going on to praise those Victorian restorers who got rid of the last century's works, he continued, 'But, nevertheless, the place looked like a church, and I can hardly say so much for all the modern edifices which have been built in my days towards the glory of God.' In this case, the church's history was evident from its floor brasses [1]. An indication of his taste in Victorian church architecture comes in *The New Zealander*, written in the 1850s, in which he praised the polychromic exuberance of the interior of William Butterfield's All Saints Church in Margaret Street, London: 'Had such a gem been constructed five centuries since on the other side of the Alps, thousands of English tourists would yearly make pilgrimages to the shrine ... and coloured bricks would now be as natural to the eye as painted glass.' (While the present interior, especially the chancel, is not exactly as in Trollope's time, the overall structure is.)

There was a continuous debate over wholesale 'restoration' of churches and Trollope expressed different views at different times. In *The West Indies and the Spanish Main* (1859) he alluded to worn-out seventeenth- and eighteenth-century English church interiors with their 'rickety pews, and creaking doors, and wretched seats made purposely so as to render genuflexion [kneeling] impossible'. Eleven years later, in his 1870 short story, 'Christmas Day at Kirkby Cottage', he referred to 'that kind of destruction which is called restoration'.

It is rare for Trollope to set scenes within churches. He did so in *Barchester Towers*, when he described Mr Slope's sermon; in *The Bertrams*, when he discussed the obnoxious behaviour of British tourists in European cathedrals and the unpleasant experience of getting into and out of the Christian shrines in Jerusalem; in *The Small House at Allington* and 'Christmas Day at Kirkby Cottage', when the parish church is decorated for Christmas; and in his last short story, 'Not If I Know It', where the plot turns on the Christmas Day Eucharist. [➤ *Barchester Towers* for Hugh Walpole's comment about Trollope and Barchester Cathedral.]

Cicero. See *The Life of Cicero*.

Cinquebar, Lord. See *Can You Forgive Her?*; Thackeray, W. M.

Cities. Although Trollope believed that 'the battle of the world has to be fought in the cities' [*North America*] the only large British city to play an important role in his fiction is London. He had little knowledge of and less liking for England's 'manufacturing leviathans', the great industrial cities that were changing England. Occasionally, as in *Orley Farm*, some characters visit cities like Birmingham or Leeds while others use Liverpool as a port [*The Way We Live Now*]. Sometimes the short stories feature people from cities like Manchester but they are mentioned only as places which people like Fred Pickering leave in order to find literary fame in London [➤ 'The Adventures of Fred Pickering']. Even Dublin, which he knew well, plays only a minor role in his Irish fiction, as in *The Kellys and the O'Kellys*. Trollope utilizes London, the countryside, smaller towns, or cathedral cities like Exeter or the fictional Barchester.

City of London. Trollope's interest in the City, as opposed to London generally, was a longstanding one. Normally in his fiction City men are 'hard men' for, as a woman says in 'The Journey to Panama', 'men become hard when they deal in money'. In *The Three Clerks*, the first novel really to deal with the City, it is described as 'the weary city' where 'every heart is eaten up by an accursed famishing after gold' [36]. Yet the City is also a place where great fortunes are made, as with old Bertram in *The Bertrams*. It is in the novels of the 1870s that the City begins to feature strongly as this was the decade when City men started to play a central role in social and political life [➤ *The Way We Live Now*]. Trollope in his fiction is not normally interested in the world of sensible investment. In his own life, however, he was increasingly involved in investments, mostly of a sensible and highly profitable type. His fiction is best known for its portrayal of dishonest

speculators such as Melmotte in *The Way We Live Now* and Ferdinand Lopez in *The Prime Minister*. In *Ayala's Angel* he gives his most favourable portrait of a City man in Sir Thomas Tringle. [➤ Banks and Bankers; Bills; Honesty; Money-Lenders.]

Civil Service. Trollope took great pride in being part of the Civil Service and spent considerable time in thinking about the expanding role of the 'profession'. He wrote in his *Autobiography* about his modest hopes for his future when entering the Post Office in 1834: 'I did not know then how very much good work may be done by a member of the Civil Service who will show himself capable of doing it.' When he entered the Service it numbered about 21,000; by the time he retired it had grown to above 50,000. In *The New Zealander* he devoted a chapter to the Civil Service but removed this when re-writing the book in 1855–6. In 1855 he published an article with the title 'The Civil Service' in the October issue of the *Dublin University Magazine* and this could have been the chapter he removed. In 1858 he brought out *The Three Clerks* and included in it a chapter on the Civil Service. This, too, may have been based on the first version of *The New Zealander*. *The Three Clerks* certainly offended his superiors in the Post Office.

In *The New Zealander* he refuted the old charge that the Civil Service was where politicians found 'jobs' for their friends: 'Happily it requires no argument to convince men at all conversant with public affairs that such practices do not, and cannot, now exist ... Even from the highest of our civil servants work is exacted for wages paid.' Five years later he admitted to a Commons committee that MPs did still influence Post Office appointments, and he used his own influence to get G. H. Lewes's son into the Post Office although he still had to pass the examination (see below).

Remembering that it was influence that got him his position in the Post Office, he agreed in an 1861 lecture on 'The Civil Service as a Profession' (in a series of lectures he had designed to help Post Office clerks in London) that 'men do not go into the Civil Service with ambitious views ... The profession is generally chosen for them ... because an early income is desirable.' (This lecture got him into trouble: he abridged it for an article under the same title in the March 1861 issue of the *Cornhill*. Rowland Hill, his superior, protested that this was 'unwise and indiscreet'. Trollope reacted by having the entire lecture printed privately to enable him to give copies to friends.) The lack of ambition to which he referred was a serious fault to Trollope but he had no doubt that 'there is no profession by which a man can earn his bread in these realms, admitting of a brighter honesty, or a nobler purpose, or of an action more manly and independent' than employment in the service of the Crown.

Although one old-fashioned lady in *The Vicar of Bullhampton* [9] doubted whether a civil servant could be considered 'a gentleman', Trollope himself had no doubt. In *Marion Fay* a clerk on £170 a year was deemed a gentleman but in the same novel he alluded more than once to the view that those in the Post Office could not be considered equal to those in the Foreign Office [45, 64]. While the Post Office did not

have the prestige that attached to the Foreign Office or the War Office, it was still the most rapidly expanding of all government departments and the most efficient. Trollope therefore resented attacks on the Service, whether they were on the government's handling of the Irish Famine or caricatures by writers like Dickens who in *Little Dorrit* created the Circumlocution Office. Trollope wrote an unpublished article attacking Dickens and he never forgot Dickens's sneers. In *Marion Fay* he included a dialogue between a clerk in the City and a Post Office clerk which debated the issues at stake: '"Ten till four, with one hour for the newspapers and another for lunch ... I never knew a young man yet from a public office who understood the meaning of a day's work." "I think that is a little hard," said Roden. "If a man really works, six hours continuously is as much as he can do with any good to his employers or himself"' [29]. ('Fashionable' branches of the Service worked from noon till six.)

Trollope was never uncritical of the Civil Service. He agreed that promotion by 'merit' should be abolished because it led to favouritism. Regarding competitive examinations, worshipped by Victorian reformers, he doubted 'whether more harm has not been done than good'. He mocked them in *The Three Clerks* and also in *Framley Parsonage* when talking of Mark Robarts's brother John who was a clerk in the Petty Bag Office. He had been well educated, 'for in these days, a young man cannot get into the Petty Bag Office without knowing at least three modern languages; and he must be well up in trigonometry too, in Bible theology, or in one dead language – at his option' [10]. He told Lewes, when helping his son to get a place in the Post Office, that 'For myself I should not dream of passing. I sd. break down in figures & spelling too, not to talk of handwriting.' Examinations, he argued, were certainly not required for every position, for example, for postmen, where their introduction had caused no improvement. Trollope also argued that all civil servants should be allowed the vote, a right they acquired only after he retired. [➤ Politics.]

Trollope made use of his Civil Service experiences and connections by creating characters who are civil servants in one short story, 'The Telegraph Girl', and in several novels in addition to *Marion Fay*. These include *The Small House at Allington* [46], *Miss Mackenzie* [1], *Framley Parsonage* [10–11, 18, 32] and *Ayala's Angel* [1], but his most complete portrayal of them is in *The Three Clerks* and *Marion Fay*. In neither novel does he give the reader that same high opinion of the Service that he himself had. The portraits of men like Major Fiasco and Sir Raffle Buffle, Mr Jerningham and Sir Boreas Bodkin in *Marion Fay*, or John Vavasor (who gets £800 a year for attending an office three time a week and signing his name) in *Can You Forgive Her?* is as harsh as anything that Dickens or Thackeray said about those who worked in the Service. Much as Trollope admired Thackeray, he attacked his friend's attempts to use political influence to gain a lucrative position in the Civil Service – in the Post Office, no less [➤ *Thackeray*].

Trollope became sensitive to talk that his fox-hunting along with his literary work meant he had not given 'to the public much more than I took in the shape of salary'. (Many Victorian writers were also civil servants, although Trollope is the best remembered.) He admitted when writing his *Autobiography* years after retiring that 'I am still a little sore on the subject.' His ambition was always 'to be a thoroughly good servant to the public'. This, and his pride in his work, were reflected in his decision to include in his *Autobiography* the official letter of commendation written by his brother-in-law, John Tilley, the Post Office Secretary, on his retirement.

Classics. Trollope, like all boys at public school in the nineteenth century, had an education based almost exclusively on learning Greek and Latin and on mastering, or at least memorizing, a body of classical prose and poetry. This was true at both his schools, Harrow and Winchester. However, his first lessons started before he went to school when his father, who had a passion for classical education, taught him Latin grammar and the Greek alphabet while shaving at six in the morning. The character which makes most of his classical learning is the Reverend Josiah Crawley in *The Last Chronicle of Barset*. It is not by accident that he has so many characteristics of Trollope's father. Like him, his lines had not fallen in pleasant places. Just as Trollope Senior had taught his son Greek, so Crawley teaches his daughter the same language. Trollope later admitted that while his schools had not given him a devotion to the classics, they had given him 'that groundwork of the language which will in the process of years make its way slowly, even through the skin'.

His schoolboy interest was revived in 1851 when he reviewed the first two volumes of the Reverend Charles Merivale's *History of the Romans under the Empire* for the *Dublin University Magazine*. (He reviewed volumes three to five in the same magazine in 1856.) To write his review he read extensively on Caesar and developed an interest in 'the character of probably the greatest man who ever lived'. It is typical of Trollope that his revived interest centred on an individual and not on historical trends or periods. The research he did also created 'a taste generally for Latin literature, which has been one of the chief delights of my later life'. Among the many books in his library was the *Bibliothèque Latine-Française*, a collection of Latin texts with French translations published between 1825 and 1828; these he read carefully and annotated extensively. To Caesar he added Cicero and Horace as favourite authors and personalities. (These are also the favourite authors of the main character in *An Old Man's Love*.) He threw himself into the two books that drew on his classical education, *The Commentaries of Caesar* in 1870 and *The Life of Cicero* in 1880. He told one friend that he was prouder of the *Cicero* than of any other book. In 1879 he also hinted to John Blackwood that he would be interested in producing a book on Quintillian, whose works he was reading, for the series in which his translation of Caesar had been published. Blackwood did not take up his offer.

Trollope was proud of his classical learning and saw those books and articles that drew on it as a way of showing the world that he was a serious writer as well as a popular novelist. He was, not surprisingly, very sensitive to criticism and therefore bitterly resented an attack by the Dean of Canterbury, Henry Alford, in reference to his essays, *Clergymen of the Church of England*. Alford specifically criticized his command of Greek. In his *Autobiography* he referred to the incident. 'The critic told me that I did not understand Greek. That charge has been made not unfrequently [*sic*] by those who have felt themselves strong in that pride-producing language. It is much to read Greek with ease, but it is not disgraceful to be unable to do so. To pretend to be able to read it without being able, – that is disgraceful.' [For Trollope's final word on Alford, ➤ *Clergymen of the Church of England.*]

Classical allusions occur frequently in Trollope's novels and sometimes he overdoes it. In *Framley Parsonage* he gets rather caught up in a series of comparisons of Victorian politicians with ancient gods and goddesses. In *The Warden*, written after the revival of his interest in the classics, there are at least fourteen allusions including one quote from Horace. Indeed, Horace provides over half of all the Latin quotations in his novels, although his favourite Latin tag comes from Virgil: *Facilis descensus Averni*, or 'Easy is the descent to Hell'. Horace was a general favourite of the Victorians. Trollope's classical allusions often consist of just one word, such as calling most doctors 'Galen' [➤ *Nina Balatka*]. Trollope's final classical reference occurred in his last novel, *The Land-Leaguers*, in which someone carrying a letter is referred to as a 'mercury'. As a general rule there were fewer classical references in his short stories. He often used Latin sayings for chapter titles; for example Livy's *Vae victis* ('Woe to the vanquished') is used both in *The Bertrams* and in *The Small House at Allington*.

The Claverings. Although this, Trollope's twentieth novel, was written between 24 August and 31 December 1864, before *The Belton Estate*, it appeared after it, when it was serialized in the *Cornhill* in sixteen monthly instalments between February 1866 and May 1867. It was one of his most quickly written novels. Not only that, it was one of three novels finished in one year (1864) along with *Can You Forgive Her?* and *Miss Mackenzie.* It was published by Smith, Elder in two volumes on 20 April 1867. Trollope received £3,000 which, he later noted in his *Autobiography*, was 'the highest rate of pay that was ever accorded to me'. (That is, while he got more for some novels, he never got more for the amount he had written.) It was the last novel he wrote for the *Cornhill.*

The Claverings follows the activities of various members of the Clavering family. From the rectory side of the family come the Reverend Henry Clavering, lazy on £800 a year plus his wife's £1,600; Harry, his son, self-indulgent and untried but not unmanly; Fanny, his younger daughter; Samuel Saul, his zealous but rather embarrassing curate who is slightly reminiscent of Josiah Crawley in *The Last Chronicle of Barset*, which he started writing in 1866. From the nearby estate, Clavering Park, come Sir Hugh, one of Trollope's most unpleasant baronets and the nephew of Mr Clavering; Sir Hugh's unloved wife, Lady Hermione; and his useless brother, Archie.

The story opens with a scene in which Harry is jilted by Julia Brabazon. She prefers to marry the drunkard, Lord Ongar, for his money. He is one of Trollope's middle-aged lovers who is wealthy, bald and wears a wig.

She departs only to return not long after from Italy a widow. In the meantime Harry has given up teaching to study engineering and while doing so becomes engaged to Florence Burton, one of Trollope's 'good girls'. Lady Ongar returns and brings in her train two unsavoury foreign adventurers, Count Pateroff and his sister Sophie Gordaloup, who is thought to be a Russian spy. Harry, who is no 'hero,' befriends Lady Ongar who is shunned by Sir Hugh because of an unjustified reputation. He becomes entrapped, does not tell her he is engaged and almost jilts the gentle Florence. Sir Hugh and Archie go fishing off the coast of Norway and conveniently are drowned, thereby making the rector the new baronet and Harry the new heir.

The secondary plot is the love between Samuel Saul and Fanny Clavering. She grows to love him but her parents are opposed as he has no money. In the end, the rector – now the baronet – gives up his living to move to Clavering Park; Saul becomes the new rector and marries Fanny; Harry and Florence Burton marry and Lady Ongar disappears, having made friends with her Ongar relations. The dowager Lady Clavering retires with her marriage settlement of £800 a year. (This was Trollope's Post Office income and the amount of money he normally gave as an adequately comfortable income, in this case both to Lady Clavering and to the rector.)

In his *Autobiography* Trollope wrote of the novel: 'I consider the story as a whole to be good, though I am not aware that the public has ever corroborated that verdict ... From beginning to end the story is well told. But I doubt now whether any one reads *The*

Claverings.' While he liked Lady Ongar, he felt on looking back that Harry Clavering was too weak to carry out his role as hero. The book's 'chief merit' is in 'the genuine fun of some of the scenes. Humour has not been my forte, but I am inclined to think, that the characters of Captain Boodle, Archie Clavering, and Sophie Gordeloup are humorous.' The comic scenes between Captain Boodle and Archie [17] and between each of them and Sophie Gordeloup are extremely funny. The chapter devoted to the death of the small child who is Sir Hugh's heir [20] is beautifully written, as are the descriptions of Lady Clavering's tragic marriage and of life in a country house. The novel's four deaths, all of which are necessary for the plot's development, are a fairly large number for Trollope. With its rural clerical setting, its two superbly drawn clergymen, its interfering bishop, the tension between curate and incumbent, and the travails of a clergyman in love, it is redolent of the Barsetshire books.

The reflections on being a school usher harken back to Trollope's own time as an usher in Belgium in the 1830s. His reference to a woman's 'majestic bust' [47] was the type of comment that allowed some to criticize Trollope as vulgar. Both the Claverings and the Ongars take their names from Essex villages although there had been a Lady Clavering in Thackeray's *The Newcomes* (1853–5). Fanny Clavering's name may be traced to Trollope's mother, Fanny; likewise Florence Burton's wise sister-in-law, Cecilia, could trace her name to Trollope's own sister, Cecilia.

Trollope digresses on Lord Ongar's baldness to ask 'if to be bald early in life be a misfortune' [3] and also has Count Pateroff give interesting observations on riches [14] and digestion [19]. He attacks two of his greatest hatreds, rigorous mourning [47] and spiritualism [39], and through Count Pateroff has jokes at Milton's and Carlyle's expense [19]. By describing the lives of Captains Boodle and Clavering, Trollope gives a good description of London club life [14,15]. The chapter on Lady Ongar's trip to the Isle of Wight [27] is based on Trollope's visit there with his wife, Rose, in October 1864, some two-and-a-half months after he had begun writing the novel. The Proudies are referred to [2] when Mr Clavering recalls how Bishop Proudie had forbade his riding to hounds ten years earlier. (This means that Clavering is in the Diocese of Barchester if not in the County of Barset.)

When Mrs Clavering sends Florence Burton a jewel, Trollope has one of his private jokes. Mrs Clavering sends 'a Cupid in mosaic surrounded by tiny diamonds' [41]. He is referring to the same jewel that La Signora Vesey Neroni wore at Mrs Proudie's reception [*Barchester Towers*, 10]. In both cases he had in mind a jewel which Princess Metternich had given his mother and which she gave to his wife. When Lady Ongar refers to a 'lady's secret' [43], readers would have spotted the allusion to the best-seller, *Lady Audley's Secret* by Mary E. Braddon, which had been appearing in serial form between 1861 and 1863.

The Claverings was not one of Trollope's popular successes although some critics praised aspects of it. Several singled out the portrait of Lady Ongar. The *Saturday Review* wrote: 'Mr Trollope, as the agent of the Providence of respectable virtue, will see that she is punished just enough, and not more than enough, to vindicate the ways of society to women.' Although *The Claverings* does suffer from a weak 'hero' it is still worth reading for its humorous scenes and the character of Lady Ongar.

The novel shows how life was changing when people accepted that a rector's son, educated at Cambridge, should choose engineering as a profession. Ironically, thirty years after Trollope's death his Australian grandson, Gordon Trollope, an engineer, wrote from his house, named Clavering, to Rose Trollope to tell her that he was engaged to the daughter of the engineer under whom he had studied. He had done exactly what Harry Clavering did fifty years earlier. Fiction had become fact.

[➤ Church of England; Florence; Workhouse.]

Clergymen. Clergymen abound in Trollope's fiction. In one of his self-deprecatory understatements Trollope wrote that before starting the Barsetshire novels he had 'enjoyed no peculiar intimacy with any clergyman' (*Autobiography*). However, from his childhood he had lived in the company of clergymen. Some of his parents' friends were clergymen, as were all his masters at the schools he attended. Both his grandfathers and two of his uncles were clergymen. In his extensive travels round Ireland and England on Post Office work he met hundreds of Anglican priests and visited their parsonages. He took a keen interest in the clergy and clerical issues as he demonstrated in his *Pall Mall Gazette* articles in 1865–6, later published as *Clergymen of the Church of England*. The Victorian usage of the word 'clergymen' was confined to priests of the Church of England and Trollope almost always follows that convention.

Clergymen were the single largest 'professional' group in England in Trollope's day: in the decade when the Barsetshire novels began there were just under 20,000 clergymen, if we include deacons (those men ordained but not yet fully priests), retired priests and priests who worked outside parishes – for example as schoolmasters like Mr Peacocke in *Dr Wortle's School*. The clergy had grown in numbers in the nineteenth century and were much more numerous than barristers, solicitors, doctors, teachers or military officers. They provided a wonderful selection of characters from which novelists could draw. Trollope's ranged from the magnificent Archdeacon Grantly to the saintly Septimus Harding, from the evil Mr Greenwood in *Marion Fay* to the debonair Mark Robarts in *Framley Parsonage*, from the lazy Mr Clavering to the hard-pressed but devout Mr Saul, both in *The Claverings*, from the pompous Mr Stumfold in *Miss Mackenzie* to the lovable Gregory Newton in *Ralph the Heir*, and concluded with the jolly Montagu Blake in *An Old Man's Love*.

Trollope made his popular reputation as a writer with the Barsetshire novels which seem to overflow with clergymen of every rank and type. As George Smith told him in 1859, people had come to expect clergymen in his fiction. There are ninety-seven priests who play substantive roles in his novels and short stories; this number includes those of the Church of Ireland which was united with the

Church of England for most of Trollope's life. Some of his most memorable characters, Obadiah Slope, Theophilus Grantly and Septimus Harding, were clergymen and Mrs Proudie usurped so much of her husband's authority that Trollope called her a 'priestess' – although there were none of those in the Church of England at that time.

In his time Trollope was criticized for being disrespectful to the clergy because he talked about them as men with ambition and love lives. One publisher, William Longman, objected to Trollope's having 'a clergyman kiss a lady whom he proposed to marry'. When he dramatized *The Last Chronicle of Barset* as *Did He Steal It?* he changed the clergymen into schoolteachers lest Victorian propriety be offended. He frequently referred to clergymen as having a 'profession' not because he did not revere their sacramental role but because he observed them as men in the world. He defended himself in *Barchester Towers* [6]: 'In endeavouring to depict the characters ... I am forced to speak of sacred things. I trust, however, that I shall not be thought to scoff at the pulpit, though some may imagine that I do not feel all the reverence that is due to the cloth. I may question the infallibility of the teachers, but I hope that I shall not therefore be accused of doubt as to the thing to be taught.'

England's social order was reflected in the clergy portrayed in Trollope's novels. If Mr Slope was not a gentleman, Archdeacon Grantly certainly was. If Mr Crawley was not well connected, both Bishop Proudie and Canon Stanhope were related to peers while Archdeacon Grantly was the son of a bishop. In *The Claverings* the Reverend Henry Clavering was the uncle of a baronet and not surprisingly looked down on his curate, poor Mr Saul, as well as on those rural priests not connected to the 'squirearchy'. It was possible to become one of these clerical dignitaries without family connections if a young man met the right people: in *Framley Parsonage* Mark Robarts achieves wealth, position and eventually is offered a canonry at Barchester Cathedral through his schoolboy friendship with Lord Lufton. In *Is He Popenjoy?* Dean Lovelace of Brotherton is a man of 'very humble origin' but gets on because he is handsome, marries a wealthy woman whose family buys him a living and then '[preaches] himself into fame'.

Trollope's novels also reflect the growth in the number of clergymen. The rapid increase in numbers in the nineteenth century coincided with the enormous increase in the population. This meant that parish priests needed and could now find assistants or curates to help them in their parish or to substitute for them in a second living. Of the ninety-seven clergymen referred to above, at least thirteen are curates who appear in ten novels.

Clergymen's incomes, like the size of parishes, varied: Mark Robarts had £900 a year in *Framley Parsonage*; in *Barchester Towers*, Mr Quiverful at Puddingdale had £400; and in *The Last Chronicle of Barset* Mr Crawley had £130. The incomes depended ultimately on agriculture: from rents for church-owned lands ('glebe lands') that were let to farmers, from ancient endowments, from fees and from tithes or payments in kind. By Trollope's time tithes had become payable in money. The rate payable was fixed by Parliament and depended on the price of corn. In addition there were church rates set by the parish. With the living came, normally, a vicarage (sometimes called a rectory or parsonage) which the priest had to maintain.

Trollope's personal attitude towards the clergy was expressed in *The Warden* with regard to Archdeacon Grantly: he is 'a man to be furthered and supported, though perhaps also to be controlled' [20]. He insisted that clergymen be gentlemen: in *Rachel Ray* he praised the Reverend Mr Prong as a good, devout man but he was 'deficient in one vital qualification for a clergyman of the Church of England; he was not a gentleman. May I not call it a necessary qualification for a clergyman of any church?' The clergy must not be cut off from the mainstream of life: he had no time for the excessively 'priestly' younger High Church clergy, nor for the Evangelical 'kill-joys'. Clergymen should always remember their position, but never seek to remind others of it [*An Old Man's Love*, 17]. Their power should not be too great: 'The ordinary life of gentlefolk in England does not admit of direct clerical interference' [*John Caldigate*, 32].

Trollope described the work of a parish priest in *Ralph the Heir* [14]. For Evangelical clergymen he had an intense dislike. He depicted the work of the newer 'slum priests' in *He Knew He Was Right* but did not make the priest in the novel an Anglo-Catholic; in this he showed a better understanding of London slum life than many subsequent writers who assumed all slum priests were Anglo-Catholics. In many parishes, both in town and country, the clergy were the only educated men and they organized much of the help given to the poor. In *Castle Richmond*, Trollope emphasizes how much help was given in Ireland during the Famine. In *The Last Chronicle of Barset* there is a good example of the way this was done on a small scale: Archdeacon Grantly sends one of his curates (he has two) to read to a woman who is ill, while Mrs Grantly sends nourishing food. The archdeacon himself calls round 'in his ordinary way of business' to see how the woman is getting on [32].

Titles for clergymen and bishops by Trollope's time had become standardized. The form of address for clergy was The Reverend Mr Smith, and in conversation simply Mr Smith. (The use of 'Reverend Smith' occurred among uneducated Victorians and is an Americanism which has now spread to England.) Archdeacons were The Venerable Theophilus Grantly and were addressed as Archdeacon or Mr, or in this case, Dr Grantly. Deans of cathedral chapters were The Very Reverend Francis Arabin, Dean of Barchester, and were addressed as Dean, Mr Dean or Mr Arabin. Bishops were The Right Reverend Thomas Proudie, Lord Bishop of Barchester and addressed as Bishop or My Lord. Formal letters by Bishop Proudie contain an abbreviation of the Latin rendering of Barchester: Thomas Barnum. Archbishops were His Grace the Most Reverend John Smith, Lord Archbishop of Canterbury, and addressed as Your Grace or Archbishop. In addition, the Archbishop of Canterbury had been given at the Reformation (and still keeps) the power of granting Lambeth degrees and Archdeacon Grantly's doctorate could well have come from the archbishop if not from Oxford.

Most of Trollope's clergymen would have dressed in black; the formal signs of their office would have been a white neckcloth, which later developed into a 'clerical collar' and, sometimes, a high waistcoat and 'shovel hat'. Bishops wore black top-hats with small strands running from near the bottom of the crown to the brim on each side.

Trollope's best-known clergymen are in the Barsetshire novels. The Palliser novels are virtually clergy-free. However, most of his other novels do contain clergymen. Many of these clerical portraits are no more than perfunctory, but some of his most colourful clergymen appear in novels after the Barsetshire series. Among the most interesting are Mr Clavering in *The Claverings*, Dr Wortle in *Dr Wortle's School*, Dean Lovelace in *Is He Popenjoy?* and the Reverend Frank Fenwick in *The Vicar of Bullhampton*; the last novel also has a splendid vignette of a canon of Salisbury, the Reverend Henry Fitzackerley Chamberlaine [24]. In Frank Fenwick Trollope painted his ideal, but not idealized, parish priest. Not surprisingly Fenwick agreed with Trollope's views that the clergy should not overly interfere in people's lives and that God is marked more by mercy and love than by judgemental wrath. Some of Trollope's best portraits of Evangelical clergymen are to be found in *Miss Mackenzie* and *Rachel Ray*.

[➤ *Framley Parsonage* and *The American Senator* for criticism of the inequalities regarding clerical pay; Bible; Catholicism; Colenso; Dissenters; *Essays and Reviews*; Prayer Book; Sermons; Universities.]

Clergymen of the Church of England.
This collection of ten essays by Trollope first appeared in the *Pall Mall Gazette* under the title 'Clerical Sketches' between 20 November 1865 and 25 January 1866. They were then published in one volume by Chapman & Hall on 30 March 1866. The essays with their dates of publication are: 'The Modern English Archbishop' (20 November); 'English Bishops, New and Old' (27 November); 'The Normal Dean of the Present Day' (2 December); 'The Archdeacon' (11 December); 'The Parson of the Parish' (18 December); 'The Town Incumbent' (29 December); 'The College Fellow who has taken Orders' (5 January 1866); 'The Curate in a Populous Parish' (20 January); 'The Irish Beneficed Clergyman' (23 January); 'The Clergyman who Subscribes for Colenso' (25 January).

In his *Autobiography* Trollope wrote that 'in writing about clergymen generally, I had to pick up as I went whatever I might know or pretend to know about them'. This conceals the fact that what he 'picked up' was a great deal, as is evident in these essays. They are a very valuable analysis of the changes taking place in the Victorian Church, whether intellectual, as in the essay on Bishop Colenso and his liberal views on the accuracy of some Old Testament books and on eternal punishment of the damned, or structural, as those on the lives and work of parish priests, archdeacons and bishops. They also show Trollope's divided mind: while he supported reform he also hankered after the certainties and customs of the past.

The essays aroused 'the critical wrath of a great dean of that period', that is, Henry Alford, Dean of Canterbury. In an article in the *Contemporary Review*, of which he was the first editor, Alford said that Trollope was 'almost entirely ignorant' of the clergy and had 'a hair-dresser's estimate of mankind'. Alford, something of a Greek scholar, distrusted Trollope's knowledge of Greek as well as his English grammar. He must have resented Trollope's assertion in his essay on deans that a dean 'has been described as a church dignitary who . . . has little to do and a good deal to get'. (A few years later Alford wrote to the then Archbishop of Canterbury that deans were 'practically useless . . . almost without employment, and absolutely without power'. But this was a criticism within the organization, not from without.) Trollope rightly described the article as 'the most ill-natured review that was ever written upon any work of mine'. He had his revenge in his *Autobiography*: 'The critic, however, had been driven to wrath by my saying that Deans of the Church of England loved to revisit the glimpses of the metropolitan moon.' This cryptic passage is based on Alford's book, *Plea for the Queen's English*, which attacked Americanisms. He was then attacked by an American grammarian, George Washington Moon, in his book *The Dean's English*, in which Moon pointed out mistakes in Alford's grammar. [➤ Classics.]

Trollope was also attacked by *The Guardian*, the leading Church of England newspaper, for his criticisms of the low pay of some curates. This was a topic he took seriously, frequently exposed in various novels, and dealt with even more vigorously in the *Pall Mall Gazette*. Within weeks curates were writing in to show that Trollope had got it right.

Clerks. Whether in business or in the Civil Service, clerks occur frequently in Trollope's fiction. This is hardly surprising as he began his own Post Office career as a clerk. Eventually he supervised many young clerks himself. His best portraits of them occur in *The Three Clerks*, *The Small House at Allington* and *Marion Fay*. In *John Caldigate*, Samuel Bagwax, a Post Office clerk, is instrumental in getting Caldigate released from gaol by using his Post Office knowledge. In *Miss Mackenzie* the heroine's brother is a clerk in Somerset House but conveniently dies, as far as the plot is concerned, on the novel's first page [1]. Although clerks in private businesses do occur in his fiction, their lives, both in the office and outside it, are not normally developed with the detail given to young government clerks. One exception occurs in *Marion Fay*: the honourable but rigid Quaker, Zachary Fay. In the nineteenth century the term 'clerk' covered a wider variety of employment than it does today and included work of some importance like that done by Zachary Fay or by Reginald Dosett in *Ayala's Angel*. At the time of the 1851 Census clerks formed about one per cent of the working population, but their numbers expanded greatly during Trollope's final years. [➤ Civil Service.]

Clubs. Clubs played an important role both in Trollope's life and in his writings. In the 1850s he lacked what he called somewhat wistfully in *The Three Clerks* 'the comforts of a first rate club' [8]. In the early 1860s after his move to England he became a member of the two most important literary clubs of his time. The Garrick, where he played whist, gave him an increasing intimacy with Thackeray. The Athenaeum provided not only a place to write (and, according to the legend, to 'kill' Mrs Proudie) but an open acknowledgement that he belonged to the intellectual élite. Both these clubs satisfied, as he said in his *Autobiography*, the long-held desire to be popular with other men [➤ Friendship]. Most important of all for his writing was the Cosmopolitan Club, which existed to provide a meeting-place for conversation between literary men and public figures such as the Prince of Wales and major politicians. Conversations at the Cosmopolitan provided Trollope with much of the background for the Palliser novels and the club is portrayed as 'the Universe' in *Phineas Redux* [34].

Clubs occur in most of his novels and they are often the setting for humorous episodes. A recurrent theme in many of his novels concerns young men and their somewhat 'fast' clubs. The best example is the Beargarden Club in *The Way We Live Now* and in *The Duke's Children*, when Lord Silverbridge takes his father, the Duke of Omnium, to dine there. They discuss the merits and demerits of club life [16–17]. Clubs provided places for characters to meet [*An Old Man's Love*, 21] or to try to hide from a meeting, as when Adolphus Crosbie hides at his club from the irate Squire Dale [*The Small House at Allington*, 25]. The prospect of being expelled from his club is one of the final humiliations that propels Ferdinand Lopez towards suicide in *The Prime Minister*. Although Trollope was not a member of the Alpine Club, he was a guest at one of their dinners and his publisher, Longman, was a leading member. The 'Alpine Club Man' is one of the topics in his

Travelling Sketches and it is also mentioned in *Can You Forgive Her?* and *Ayala's Angel*.

Clubs in Trollope's fiction are a male preserve in which men, according to Lady Ongar in *The Claverings*, have 'cigars and brandy and water, and billiards, and broiled bones, and oysters, and tankards of beer' [15]. The *Spectator* in its review of *North America* rightly described Trollope, as early as 1862, as a 'club man'.

Coffee. Trollope liked coffee and started the day at dawn with a cup; he also liked exchanging literary gossip with his friend G. H. Lewes 'over a cup of coffee and a cigar'. The 1850s saw a debate in *The Lancet* and *The Times*, and later in the Commons, on the adulteration of drugs and food; coffee was adulterated with chicory, sawdust, horses' livers or other substitutes. Trollope added his denunciation of adulteration first in *The New Zealander* and then in almost all the novels of the late 1850s and early 1860s [Mullen, 314–15]. He saw adulteration as a symbol of the national trend away from public honesty. In the 1870s Trollope visited and described coffee plantations in Ceylon [➤ *The Tireless Traveler*].

Colburn & Co. (1808–53). Henry Colburn's publishing career began in London in 1808 at the British and Foreign Library, a circulating library which he soon took over. As a publisher he specialized in the wealthy 'carriage trade', especially in 'silver fork' fiction, that is, books by aristocrats, about aristocrats and designed for the middle classes. He became one of the principal publishers of 'threedeckers'. His background was dubious as were his business practices, and his exaggerated advertising earned him the title 'Prince of Puffers', from the Victorian expression 'to puff' or promote. He published books by Bulwer-Lytton and Disraeli and helped to establish the highly influential magazine, the *Athenaeum*. He had a short and unhappy partnership with his printer, Bentley, and went into a brief decline only to bounce back. Between 1836 and 1853 he brought out three-deckers especially for Mudie and was Bentley's main rival. Trollope's connection came through his mother in 1840 when Colburn published her novel, *The Widow Married*; in all, he published seventeen of her novels. In 1848 Trollope approached Colburn after Bentley had turned down *The Kellys and the O'Kellys* and he agreed to publish it; he lost £63.10s.1½d. Despite his letter discouraging Trollope from writing further novels he agreed to see the next one, *La Vendée*, which he published in 1850. Trollope's brother Tom acted for the writer and secured a payment of £20, the first money Trollope made from writing. Since Trollope complained in 1851 that Colburn did not give him much encouragement, he must still have looked on him as his publisher at that time. Although he placed his next two novels with Longman he did take *The Three Clerks* to Hurst & Blackett, Colburn's successors, before successfully placing it with Bentley. [➤ Publishers and Publishing.]

Colenso, Rt Rev. John William, Bishop of Natal (1814–83). Bishop Colenso was one of the most famous – to many, infamous – Victorian Liberal churchmen and a hero to Trollope. In *The Belton Estate* [17] he has an 'ignorant' and 'stupid' lady say that the bishop, as well as the liberal *Essays and Reviews*, 'came direct from the Evil One'. In *He Knew He Was Right* Miss Jemima Stanbury regards the bishop as an 'apostate' [7]. (Readers know a character is an adamantine Tory when he or – here – she denounces Colenso; in the Irish novels the same kind of person denounces Pusey and the High Church movement. [➤ *Castle Richmond*.])

Colenso, a Cornishman, was the first Bishop of Natal. In South Africa he was a defender of the native races and soon became anathema to conservative Anglicans. He did not insist that natives who had more than one wife should divorce all but one. He denied eternal punishment of the damned and questioned some sacramental theology in 1861; later he questioned some of the horrific punishments described in the Old Testament, the authorship of some Old Testament books, and stories like that of Noah's ark. He was deposed by his superior, appealed to the Privy Council and won. He was excommunicated and a new Bishop of Natal was appointed. A schism resulted which was not healed until 1911. On 25 January 1866 Trollope published the last of his essays on clergymen for the *Pall Mall Gazette* (later published as *Clergymen of the Church of England*) with the title 'The Clergyman who Subscribes for Colenso'. When he agreed to write a series of articles on the May Meetings later on that year he did so under the guise of a Zulu to honour Colenso. (The bishop's appeal to the Privy Council had been upheld two months before and Trollope had contributed to his costs.) In his writing Trollope shows a familiarity with Colenso's works. When Trollope visited South Africa in 1877 he called on Colenso, who had enjoyed his novels.

[➤ Bible; Church of England; Clergymen; Evangelicals; Grantly, Archdeacon; Harding, Septimus; Prayer Book; Religion.]

Collins, The Rev. W. Lucas (1817–87). Collins played a more active role in Trollope's literary career than any other clergyman. Trollope met him through John Blackwood, who had asked Trollope to provide a translation of Caesar's *Commentaries* for his 'Ancient Classics for English Readers' of which Collins, an adviser to the firm, was editor. They afterwards became close friends, stayed at each other's houses and went on holiday together with their wives. Trollope would have felt comfortable with Collins's old-fashioned High Church views. Collins would lend Trollope his rectory for hunting while he and his wife wintered in the South of France or in Italy. It was while staying at Collins's Northamptonshire rectory at Lowick in April 1879 that Trollope wrote *Dr Wortle's School*, which he set in 'Bowick'. (The actual Dr Wortle's school may be traced to Lowick where Collins tutored young men before they went up to university.)

Collins took Trollope's funeral service at Kensal Green and was the first person outside the family to read his *Autobiography*, which he urged Blackwood to publish. [➤ *The Fixed Period*.]

Collins, Wilkie (1824–89). Although Trollope entertained Collins at his home in Montagu Square more than once he was never a very close friend. Collins, an intimate associate of Dickens, began his career as a novelist in 1850, a few years after Trollope, with his historical novel, *Antonina*. This was the same year in which Trollope published his third novel *La Vendée*. While both books were historical, Collins's launched his career as a writer of what Trollope called the 'sensationalist' style. Trollope praised him in his *Autobiography* and ranked him as number eight in his list of the ten leading Victorian novelists between Charles Reade at number seven and Annie Thackeray at number nine. He added that his and Collins's methods of plot construction were completely opposite because Collins's plots were so carefully constructed that 'I can never lose the taste of the construction ... One is constrained by mysteries and hemmed in by difficulties ... such work gives me no pleasure.' Occasionally Trollope did use sensational scenes reminiscent of Collins: the suicide of Lopez in *The Prime Minister*, the kidnapping in *He Knew He Was Right*, the murders in *The Land-Leaguers* and *An Eye for an Eye*. [➤ Crime; Violence.] He had a gentle joke at the expense of Collins's most celebrated novel, *The Woman in White* (1860), in *The Small House at Allington* [17]. Collins memorably described Trollope's 'immeasurable energies' as 'an incarnate gale of wind' and wrote of him that he was 'as good and staunch a friend as ever lived'.

Comedy. Trollope's one sustained attempt at a comic novel, *The Struggles of Brown, Jones, and Robinson*, was a failure: it was 'a style for which I certainly was not qualified'. However, he was excellent at shorter humorous scenes: Bertie Stanhope's behaviour and conversation at Mrs Proudie's reception in *Barchester Towers*; Johnnie Eames's life in his London lodging-house in

The Small House at Allington; Captain Boodle and the Rag Club in *The Claverings*; the Evangelical tea-party in *Miss Mackenzie*, and life in the Post Office clerks' office in *Marion Fay* and *The Three Clerks*. A strong vein of gentle, sometimes mocking, humour runs throughout most of his narration in the novels. Several of his short stories – 'Father Giles of Ballymoy', 'George Walker at Suez', 'The Turkish Bath', 'Mrs Brumby', 'Christmas at Thompson Hall', 'The Two Heroines of Plumplington' and 'The O'Conors of Castle Conor' – are full of humour. Comedy dates quickly, and stories such as 'The Gentle Euphemia' and 'Relics of General Chassé' are not as amusing to a modern reader as they were to a Victorian.

The Commentaries of Caesar. Trollope worked on his translation between 29 January and 25 April 1870 and it was published by Blackwood in one volume on 1 June in the same year. Trollope received no payment, as he gave the copyright to his friend John Blackwood as a birthday present.

Trollope had used the pages of *Saint Pauls* to 'puff' John Blackwood's new series, 'Ancient Classics for English Readers'. Blackwood then asked him if he would prepare this translation as the fourth in his series for people who did not read Latin or Greek and who had little if any higher education. Each volume sold for half-a-crown. Trollope was happy because it allowed him to apply his interest in the classics; the work fitted in with his longstanding wish to show that he was a 'serious' writer; finally, it allowed him to put into practice his belief that education should be readily available for people who had not been to public

school or university. When making the proposal Blackwood included himself among the potential readers, people who were 'educated up to the muzzle ... [and] other busy men, and ladies or gentlemen who have not had a thorough education'. The series carried a laudatory comment from the *British Quarterly Review*, saying it was for 'unlearned readers'.

Trollope told Blackwood: 'It has been a tough bit of work, but I have enjoyed it amazingly ... It has been a change to the spinning of novels, and has enabled me to surround myself with books and almost to think myself a scholar.' His 'dear little book' is more a paraphrase or re-telling than a translation and it received, in Trollope's words, 'faint praise' from the critics. *Vanity Fair*, for example, wrote: 'We can only say that all admirers of Mr Trollope will find his "Caesar" almost if not quite as attractive as his most popular novel, while they will also find that the exigencies of faithful translation have not been able to subdue the charm of his peculiar style ... the introduction and conclusion are admirably written ...' His fellow novelist, Mrs Oliphant, Blackwood's most constant writer, told her publisher that 'I cannot read [the book] without laughing – it is so like Johnny Eames.'

Trollope sent a copy to the Very Reverend Charles Merivale, brother of his oldest friend, John Merivale, and a classical historian [➤ Classics]. They had crossed swords years before when Merivale complained unjustifiably about postal deliveries in Essex, but Trollope held no grudge and praised Merivale in the book. Later, Trollope remembered Merivale's response when writing his *Autobiography*: he had referred to Trollope's 'comic Caesar'.

Merivale's nephew, who later published the incident, added, 'Trollope wept.' How he was able to eavesdrop on Trollope he did not say. Charles Merivale was probably annoyed at a mere Post Office official, let alone a novelist, intruding into 'his field'. The book fitted the requirement set by Blackwood: 'It was not exactly a school-book that was wanted, but something that would carry the purposes of the school-room into the leisure hours of adult pupils.' It was Trollope, not Merivale, who helped keep classical learning alive in an age which increasingly had little time or use for it.

The work also introduced Trollope to the editor of the series, the Reverend W. Lucas Collins, who became his friend. Trollope told the poet Austen Dobson, 'My Caesar will be a little thing, – but it has been a great delight to me to do it, as giving a break to the constant writing of prose fiction and taking me back to the old books which I read when I was young.' As for Caesar himself, Trollope agreed with Merivale's view that he was 'the greatest name in history', but he loathed what he called 'Caesarism', the exaltation of any man, especially a dishonest one like Caesar. Trollope would have added Napoleon III, himself another translator of Caesar, and Disraeli to the list. [➤ *The Life of Cicero.*]

Commons, House of. See Parliament.

Companions. For the most part, companions have as unhappy a life in Trollope's fiction as most of them must have had in reality. Trollope's best portrayal of a companion's fate is that of Julia Macnulty in *The Eustace Diamonds* [5]. However, Miss Tickle, the

companion to Matilda Thoroughbung in *Mr Scarborough's Family*, is quite contented; indeed the final reason why Matilda decides not to marry Peter Prosper is his refusal to provide a home for her companion of twenty years. Some aristocratic or wealthy men have men who are, in effect, their constant companions, but they are usually shown to be lazy toadies. Good examples are Septimus Jones, the inseparable friend of Augustus Scarborough in *Mr Scarborough's Family*, and Captain Archie Clavering, the brother of Sir Hugh Clavering in *The Claverings*.

Consumption. Tuberculosis or consumption killed two of Trollope's brothers and two of his sisters, and several children of his sister, Cecilia [➤ Trollope Family]. Regarding his brother Henry's death, he later wrote that 'the horrid word, which of all words was, for some years after, the most dreadful to us, had been pronounced. It was no longer a delicate chest . . . but consumption'. Henry's laboured breathing, and the death of his sister Emily, left a deep impression on him, although hers was the only close family death he witnessed. He remembered it when he wrote *The Three Clerks* and described Katie Woodward's illness: unlike Emily, his fictional creation recovers. In *The Eustace Diamonds* Sir Florian Eustace dies of consumption, leaving Lizzie his wealth and troublesome diamonds. In two short stories consumption plays a part: in 'George Walker at Suez' the narrator is sent to Cairo because of 'a slight cough' (as is another character in *The Bertrams*) and in 'Mary Gresley' Mary's fiancé dies from the disease, with disastrous consequences for her novel-writing career. In *Marion Fay* the Quaker heroine, Marion, knows she suffers from the Fay family curse and refuses to marry Lord Hampstead; she later dies a slow death. With the fictional Fays and Eustaces, as with the Trollopes themselves, Trollope could write, 'Consumption had swept a hecatomb of victims' [*The Eustace Diamonds*, 1].

Cophetua, King. Trollope makes frequent allusions to King Cophetua in his fiction. He could have come across the story of this mythical African king in a variety of sources familiar to him. The king lived in Africa and was not interested in women until he came across a beggar-girl with whom he fell in love and whom he later married. He and his queen lived happily ever after. The story occurs in a ballad in Percy's *Reliques*, where the beggar-queen is called Penelophon. Shakespeare used the story in *Love's Labour's Lost* [IV.i] where she becomes Zenelophon. He also referred to the story in *Romeo and Juliet* [II.i] and *Henry IV Part II* [V.iii]. Ben Jonson used the story in his *Every Man in His Humour* and Tennyson refers to it in 'The Beggar Maid'. Trollope refers to the story in 'The Lady of Launay', in *The Duke's Children* [53] and in *He Knew He Was Right* [78]. In *Framley Parsonage* the African king even provides a chapter title [35].

Copyright. At the time Trollope began writing, an author's copyright lasted for forty-two years after the date of publication or for the lifetime of the author plus seven years after his death, whichever was the longer. This was the law between 1842 and 1911. For an author's works to be copyrighted outside the United Kingdom the government had to have an agreement with the relevant country; while Britain had agreements with sixteen European nations, the United States refused to enter into such a treaty. (See below.)

With regard to Trollope's first five novels, he kept the copyright and agreed to take 'half-profits' from the publisher, but in the case of *La Vendée* he agreed a schedule of payments according to numbers of copies sold. Starting with the publication of *The Three Clerks* he followed his mother's custom and normally sold his copyright to the publisher. He wrote in a cancelled passage in his *Autobiography* that 'It is the feeling of disappointment coming from such uncertainty [in the half-profits agreements] which has induced me to part with so many of my copyrights.' Sometimes he sold the copyright for a specific period of time, or for a specific number of copies, after which it reverted to him. He could then sell all or part of the copyright back to the publisher or to another house. Sometimes only part of the copyright reverted to him, while the remainder stayed with the publisher.

In some cases the publisher bought the copyright for both serialization and for publication as a book, and in others the copyright was divided between a magazine and a publisher. Sometimes a second publisher was brought in to publish a cheap edition. Payment was normally an agreed fee, not a percentage royalty, although he did get a royalty for *The Life of Cicero*. On one occasion Trollope gave his copyright away [► *The Commentaries of Caesar*]. By the 1870s he tended to sell the absolute copyright to publishers.

Because different books were owned in differing degrees by different publishers, re-publication could be extremely difficult. This was the case when Trollope wanted to re-publish the Barsetshire books in a new collection, *The Chronicles of Barsetshire*.

Trollope was a very good literary businessman and, given his fame in America, he took a considerable interest in the question of international copyright. The situation in his lifetime was the opposite of what it is today: many more books were published in the United Kingdom than in the United States, and America was heavily dependent on UK authors. American publishers kept their costs down by 'pirating', or publishing without consent, from the part issues or serialization in the UK. This made these editions very cheap because the publishers paid the author nothing. *The Prime Minister* sold in the United States for 5s. 9d., one-sixth of the UK price. This practice also hurt the Canadian book market because Canadians could buy smuggled US editions more cheaply. Not surprisingly, in one letter to William Blackwood Trollope referred to 'the Yankees, – who are dishonest beasts'.

In 1866 Trollope contributed a paper on International Copyright for that year's meeting of the National Association for the Promotion of Social Science. Because of this he was asked to serve on the Royal Commission on Copyright in 1876–7. He was its most active member and asked the most questions [Mullen, 598–9]. In 1878 he supported the Paris International Literary Congress which discussed copyright. British writers or publishers had to negotiate with American publishers on each book and Trollope felt that if he were paid properly in America he should have been able to double his income. British writers could sometimes secure some payment if their British publisher forwarded 'early sheets' of the book to be bound in America, but given the widespread piracy this brought in little. Trollope noted in his *Autobiography* that he got £20 from one publisher for the early sheets of a novel for which he received £1,600 at home.

Sometimes a British writer could reserve US rights to himself, as Trollope did with *North America*: he negotiated an agreement with Lippincott when in America to sell them early sheets. This still could not prevent someone from pirating the book, as Harpers did on this occasion. Trollope wrote a long public letter about copyright to his friend the Boston poet, James Russell Lowell, and sent a copy to the *Athenaeum*. He pleaded for 'honest payment for goods supplied by me to your countrymen ... [and] honest payment of goods supplied by you to my countrymen'. Because of his experience in transatlantic publishing, the Foreign Office asked him to attempt an Anglo-American agreement with Washington when he visited the United States on a Post Office mission in 1868. His mission was a failure due, he felt, to the influence of large publishing houses over the government. (Despite this, his view of American dishonesty was much less hostile than that of Dickens.)

Trollope also wanted writers to be able to copyright their plots and supported those who campaigned for this. He was furious when Charles Reade adapted *Ralph the Heir* as a stage play called *Shilly-Shally* without his permission and without paying any fee. In the event the play failed.

Cornhill Magazine (1860–1975). The magazine was started by George Smith and was intended to be a shilling monthly; it was inspired by New York's *Harper's Magazine.* Smith had wanted the novelist Thomas Hughes, famous for *Tom Brown's Schooldays*, to be the editor but in the end got a much more distinguished novelist, W. M. Thackeray. The magazine was an immediate success and the first issue sold 120,000 copies. Although circulation fell by half within a few years the magazine held its own in a fiercely competitive market. Smith paid extremely well and enlisted some of the most famous names in Victorian fiction, including Thackeray, George Eliot, Mrs Gaskell, Thomas Hardy, Charles Reade and Wilkie Collins. The magazine had illustrations by Millais. Thackeray was only editor from 1860 to 1862; a later editor was Trollope's friend, G. H. Lewes. The title of the magazine came from Thackeray in honour of Smith's London offices and set a trend for magazines to be named after London sites.

Trollope's connection, which provided the basis for his great fame and prosperity, began in 1859 when he wrote to Thackeray from Ireland to offer a series of short stories. Smith replied and offered twice *Harper's* rate of pay, but said he preferred a three-volume novel at £1,000. For the first time Trollope could benefit from serialization so that the earnings from a book would exceed his annual Post Office salary. Trollope first offered the half-completed *Castle Richmond* but Smith preferred a 'clerical' novel and Trollope obliged with *Framley Parson-*

age. When the first number appeared, the first three chapters of Trollope's book were given pride of place and Thackeray's *Lovel the Widower* came later on in the issue. The magazine's fame guaranteed Trollope a readership of not much under 1,000,000. His appearance in the magazine was a turning-point: it brought him wealth, fame and the friendship of both Thackeray and Smith. As he wrote in his *Autobiography*, 'My connection with the *Cornhill* . . . was the means of introducing me very quickly to that literary world from which I had hitherto been severed by the fact of my residence in Ireland.' Of great importance to Trollope were the famous monthly *Cornhill* dinners given by Smith, at which Trollope met Lewes, W. H. Russell, Millais and Thackeray.

In addition to *Framley Parsonage* the magazine published three other novels, *The Struggles of Brown, Jones, and Robinson*, *The Small House at Allington* and *The Claverings*, and three articles, 'My Tour in Holland', 'The Civil Service as a Profession' and 'W. M. Thackeray'. There were also under discussion a novel set in Italy, a travel book on India and a series of articles on America, but the publication of his book on America precluded the last of these ideas. There was a discussion about publishing *Orley Farm* in the magazine but it was issued in twelve monthly parts instead. The magazine rejected two short stories: 'The Banks of the Jordan' ['A Ride Across Palestine'] and 'Mrs General Talboys'. Trollope was also instrumental in getting his brother, Tom, published in the magazine.

Costa Rica. Trollope visited Costa Rica in 1859 during his Post Office trip to the West Indies and his visit is described in *The West Indies and the Spanish Main.* He visited the country to see the volcano of which his friend, the diplomat Sir William Ouseley, had descended into the crater. He wanted to go deeper than Sir William and actually went down into the crater before breakfast one morning. Getting back up proved harder work and once on the top he fell asleep, despite the rain. The country forms the background for a short story, 'Returning Home'.

Country Houses. Throughout Trollope's writings country houses play an important role. The earliest are in his Irish fiction and it was the sight of a ruined country house in Ireland that inspired his first novel, *The Macdermots of Ballycloran.* In *The Kellys and the O'Kellys* we are given a detailed description of Grey Abbey in County Kildare, but this account reads more like the reminiscences of a tourist who has once had a guided tour. Indeed we are told that the house was open to tourists two days a week for a half-crown tip to the housekeeper [11]. Trollope's own familiarity with country houses probably began in Ireland as a result of his postal inspections: he describes one humorous visit to a lonely old gentleman in County Cavan in his *Autobiography.* His newfound passion for fox-hunting brought him into other country houses and he describes the jovial life in one such in 'The O'Conors of Castle Conor'. His friendship with his fellow Harrovian, Sir William Gregory, MP, gave him frequent access to his home, Coole Park. [➤ Ceylon.]

In the 1840s, when his mother lived in the Lake District, Trollope became familiar with English country houses and it is no accident that one of his most lyrical descriptions of any country house is set there in *Sir Harry Hotspur of Humblethwaite* [3]. Here he emphasizes that he loved those houses that reflected all the changes in English history. It must have been during one of these visits in the 1840s that he dined at Eden Hall in Cumberland and drank from the celebrated goblet whose story Longfellow immortalized in 'The Luck of Eden Hall'. He recalled the incident at the start of *The Small House at Allington.*

In the 1850s his Post Office work gave him the opportunity to call at many country houses and observe their inhabitants. In the West Country he developed his strong preference for the Tudor or Jacobean style of country house which he saw as essentially English: their windows were 'of all windows invented the ... sweetest'. [*The Small House at Allington*, 1]. In *The New Zealander* he attacks English travellers who rave about the beauties of Italy, but know nothing of the country houses of Dorset and Somerset, 'quiet gems ... embosomed among the finest trees in Europe'. He was particularly fond of Montacute, then not a particularly well-known house, and admitted that he used it as the model for Ullathorne in *Barchester Towers.*

In his fiction, the most admirable characters, such as the Greshams in the Barsetshire novels or the Hotspurs in *Sir Harry Hotspur of Humblethwaite,* normally dwell in country houses at least two centuries old [➤ Squires]. The Greshams' house also seems to owe something to Montacute. Normally Trollope did not like the vast country houses in the classical style of the eighteenth century and sometimes he liked to make fun of the previous century's fashion: 'The house was Greek in its style of architecture – at least so the owner says' [*Orley Farm*, 7]. Gatherum Castle, the Barsetshire seat of the Duke of Omnium, was ruined by the desire to impress visitors with a magnificent hall which destroyed the comfort of the house [*Doctor Thorne*, 14]. That is why the younger Pallisers prefer their Yorkshire residence, Matching. Longroyston, the seat of the Duke of St Bungay, is also uncomfortable.

Trollope often reveals how life in a country house reflects its owners' personalities. In *Framley Parsonage* we are shown contrasting lives at two country houses: the Duke of Omnium entertains in cold magnificence at Gatherum Castle, while Lady Lufton presides over quiet domestic pleasure at Framley Court. In *The Belton Estate* Trollope depicts two gloomy houses: Belton Castle in Somerset, 'an ugly residence, three stories high built in the time of George II' [1] and Aylmer Park, yet another eighteenth-century house in Yorkshire. The family at Aylmer are slowly being ruined by the vast expense of keeping up the house and especially all the servants. Aylmer is Trollope's best description of the boredom of life in some Victorian country houses where people 'neither read, nor flirt, nor gamble, nor smoke', although the women do spend much time 'putting on bonnets' [17, 26].

Country houses were changing and becoming more luxurious in Trollope's lifetime. People with money from trade were acquiring old estates: Miss Dunstable buys Chaldicotes in *Framley Parsonage*. Trollope disliked the growing trend to isolate the country house in a large park, away from the village [*The Small House at Allington*, 1]. The desire for privacy was already forcing one earl and his countess to hide themselves on the day that tourists were shown round their house [*He Knew He Was Right*, 96].

After his early novels, Trollope rarely depicts the interior of a country house in great detail, but provides just enough of a description to give a flavour of the place. Sometimes he concentrates on describing one room, as he does with the library in *Mr Scarborough's Family* [53].

As he became a well-known author Trollope was invited to various country houses, although there appears to be no indication that he stayed in any of the most famous ones. He and his wife Rose visited Fryston in Yorkshire, the seat of his friend Lord Houghton, but we do not know if Houghton unlocked his celebrated collection of pornography for his friend. He enjoyed the hospitality of Baron Rothschild at one of his country houses and in the late 1870s he often went to Lord Carnarvon's house, Highclere, where the hospitable Tory Colonial Secretary who had admired Trollope's *South Africa* liked to assemble literary celebrities. There, in the peer's library, Trollope enjoyed exchanging classical quotations with Browning. Trollope also spent much time at the ancestral seat of his family, Casewick House in Lincolnshire, where he visited his cousin Sir John Trollope, later Lord Kesteven. He frequently went there for fox-hunting and it was also there that he seems to have written those passages in the *Autobiography* defending the role of an hereditary class of gentlemen.

Trollope's writing about country houses often demonstrates his

conservative side, a side well illustrated by his remarks about the
Thornes of Ullathorne: 'Such ... are
the inhabitants of many an English
country home. May it be long before
their number diminishes' [*Barchester
Towers*, 22].

[➤ Architecture; Aristocracy; Gentry; Landed Estates.]

'The Courtship of Susan Bell'. This
short story is one of two Trollope
wrote on his return from his first visit
to America at the end of his trip to the
West Indies and Central America (16
November 1858 to 3 July 1859). It was
also one of the first short stories he
wrote. When in New York he called in
to the offices of Harper Brothers to
see if they were interested and once
back in England he sent them this
story and 'The Relics of General
Chassé'. The story was published in
Harper's New Monthly Magazine in
August 1860 and later included in his
first collection of short stories, *Tales of
All Countries* (1861). In his *Autobiography*
Trollope wrote that the stories included in that collection 'have, most
of them, some foundation in such occurrences', that is, in 'true tales of my
adventures'. Trollope received $100
(£20).

Susan Bell lives in Saratoga Springs,
New York – a famous spa which Trollope visited in 1859 – with her widowed mother and elder sister, Hetta.
Aaron Dunn takes rooms in the Bell
household. While the Bells are Baptists, Dunn is an Episcopalian. Hetta,
something of a religious fanatic, is
keen on the Reverend Phineas Beck-
ard, their minister. The mother is timorous and Hetta is opposed to the
developing friendship between Susan
and Aaron. Dunn is finally successful

despite their opposition, but the marriage is delayed until he has shown
them he has steady employment.

Trollope understood American language and social customs: he has Dunn,
when reading aloud to the ladies, read
Longfellow along with Shakespeare
and Byron. He refers to the Baptists'
church service as a 'meeting' and to
the chapel as the 'meeting-house': the
term 'chapel' was not used in America.
He is far more generous to the Baptist
minister – as he was to Caleb Morton,
the Presbyterian minister in Bermuda
in 'Aaron Trow' – than he was to Dissenting ministers in England, recognizing the difference made by the lack
of an established church in America.
He makes use of the American reputation for immediately placing a monetary value on an object (in this case
as a reason to refuse a gift). He rather
overdoes the use of 'I guess', seen in
the nineteenth century as the quintessential American phrase.

The setting and the characterization of a widow and daughter may
have been suggested by Trollope's
meeting an American widow and her
daughter (Mrs Harriet Knower and
Mary Knower) aboard the ship
bringing him back to England in 1859.
They were from Albany, New York,
where the Bells had lived before Mrs
Bell was widowed and moved to Saratoga. Mary Knower was about the
same age as Susan Bell and Mrs
Knower was, like Mrs Bell, a young
widow. The story shows that Trollope
was aware of the religious debates that
raged in America. It also shows how
he made literary use of his fascination
with young women in the years between the end of girlhood and the beginning of married life. The plot of a
love-story set against the background

of a timorous mother and a religious elder sister was used again in *Rachel Ray*.

Cousin Henry. Trollope's thirty-eighth novel was written between 26 October and 8 December 1878. First publication was a weekly serialization in the *North British Weekly Mail* and the *Manchester Weekly Times* between 8 March and 24 May 1879. It was published in two volumes by Chapman & Hall in October 1879. Trollope received £400.

Like many of Trollope's later novels, *Cousin Henry* is concerned with property and inheritance. He had originally considered calling the book 'Getting at a Secret', but his wife Rose, with her usual forthrightness, told him that was 'claptrap'. The plot revolves round the question of whether or not Henry Jones, who lives and works in London, is the true heir to his uncle's estate in Wales. The inheritance of Squire Indefer Jones's estate was no longer governed by the law of entail, but for him 'it was a religion ... that a landed estate in Britain should go from father to eldest son, and in default of a son to the first male heir'. He was torn because he was also deeply attached to his niece, Isabel Broderick, who had looked after him for many years. The old squire, like several other landowners in Trollope's fiction, had tried to promote a marriage between the cousins, but had failed. He made a series of wills but on his death the only will found is the one leaving the estate to Henry. Isabel leaves the house and Henry, knowing that a later will gave the estate to Isabel, takes possession. He puts the will back in its hiding-place. Rumours start concerning the will and articles appear in a local newspaper. The trusted family lawyer demands that Henry should sue the paper, really to force him to tell the truth about the inheritance. At this point the will is found, Henry leaves, Isabel marries her lover and takes the name of Jones.

In old Squire Jones we get a good portrait of a conservative elderly man. Trollope is particularly adept at describing lonely old squires whose limited minds are focused on only one topic. We are given an account of his reading: a daily newspaper, naturally a very conservative one, 'read carefully from beginning to end'; an hour devoted daily to the Bible; and a weekly reading of the *Guardian*, an excellent High Church newspaper devoted to religious and some secular topics. (The *Guardian* would carry one of the most important obituaries of Trollope with a statement about the novelist's attitude towards religion.) Jones, like the old squires in *Ralph the Heir*, *Sir Harry Hotspur of Humblethwaite* and *The Belton Estate*, is torn between his duty to hand down a landed estate to the next male heir and his desire to provide for another member of his family whom he loves.

Henry Jones is an interesting psychological portrait, but we are not given enough of his background to see him quite clearly. We know he had abandoned the 'church and her services' and lacked both 'fear' and 'love' of God. However, he still retained a vague belief in eternal damnation although he knew that 'many of the wise ones of the earth' thought it an 'old woman's tale'. [For Trollope's own view on this, ➤ Colenso; 'The Spotted Dog'; Religion.] As almost always in Trollope, a villain – which is really too strong a term for Henry Jones – is not without some spark of conscience.

'We are apt to forget,' says Trollope, 'when we think of the sins and faults of men how keen may be their conscience in spite of their sins' [17]. Because of this, Jones is unable to destroy the will that will cost him his estate. (The fact that in our own time we have seen examples of men who did not destroy printed or taped documents that could cause them considerable harm may give the novel added interest for us.)

Henry Jones is a man who lacks any capacity to win people to him and he is despised by his servants and tenants. As so often in Trollope, Jones's disorderly ways as a bachelor, particularly regarding his meals, gives an indication of his moral failings [21]. There is another touch frequently seen in Trollope's fiction: when Jones is defeated and leaves Wales, he does not go away empty-handed. Trollope normally provides some small amount of money to cushion the fall of most of his flawed characters, such as Lady Mason in *Orley Farm* or Burgo Fitzgerald in *Can You Forgive Her?*. Isabel's lover is the Reverend William Owen, a minor canon of Hereford Cathedral. This allowed Trollope to provide one of the clergymen that his readers liked and expected, though he never really develops the character of Owen. (Trollope had a distant cousin who was a canon of Hereford.)

Trollope dictated large parts of *Cousin Henry* to his niece, Florence Bland, and he used the novel to have a private joke with her. For years he had worried about providing for her after his death. Like the old squire, he was conscious of his obligation to provide not only for those who bore his name but for those whom he loved and who had helped him. He was perplexed

about whether or not it was unfair to his two sons to leave some of their potential inheritance to his niece. On 29 October 1878, three days after starting the novel, he went to his solicitor's office to sign his will in which he left Florence £4,000. This is the same sum that Uncle Indefer leaves in one of his wills to Isabel. (Isabella was also the name of Florence Bland's dead mother.)

When the book was published Trollope autographed a copy for Florence but he added a note in pencil, which was later erased by someone. However, all but one word can be made out: 'From the Author to the writer. From the uncle to his own –?– niece' [Mullen, 612–13]. No doubt the hiding of the will in a book of Jeremy Taylor's *Sermons* in the library was something of another joke with Florence, for she assisted Trollope in the arranging and annual dusting of his large library. Taylor's *Sermons* had also played a part in a sub-plot of *He Knew He Was Right* [51].

Although this is the only Trollope novel set in Wales there is little sense of local colour other than a sprinkling of Welsh names. Trollope was writing for a new type of market, weekly-newspaper readers, and he was conscious of the need to stick closely to his plot as many readers of these newspapers would not be used to complicated plots with numerous diversions. We miss any sense of Trollope's own presence in the book. There are few 'authorial intrusions' offering advice or opinions. The closest we get is the 'sermon' given by the lawyer, Apjohn, at the end of the novel. Apjohn shows that old Squire Jones's mistake was that he allowed himself to be 'induced by a theory' and to forget that he also owed an obligation not just to the Jones name but to all those who lived on the estate [24]. This reflects Trollope's own dislike of Utopian plans and reflects his own conservative view of the role of the squire in rural society. As in so many novels – *The Warden* and *Phineas Redux*, to name but two – a newspaper plays an important role in determining the behaviour of the main character.

In many ways, *Cousin Henry* resembles Trollope's short continental novels such as *The Golden Lion of Granpère* or *Linda Tressel* more than it does his English novels. Most reviewers found it an enjoyable book but almost all agreed that only Trollope could make such a plot interesting, especially as Victorians had rather tired of melodramas about wills by the late 1870s. *Cousin Henry* certainly cannot be seen as a great Trollope novel because it lacks the richness of sub-plots and real character development, but it is still an agreeable short novel.

Cousins. Friendship, romance and sometimes marriage between cousins are relatively frequent in Trollope's writing. In *The Vicar of Bullhampton* Trollope traces this to the restrictions placed on young women: 'It is seldom that a girl can allow herself the full flow of friendship with a man who is not old enough to be her father, unless he is her lover as well as her friend. But cousinhood does allow some escape from the hardship of this rule. Cousins are Tom, and Jack ... Cousins are almost the same as brother, and yet they may be lovers. There is certainly a great relief in cousinhood' [14]. (In *The Vicar of Bullhampton* two second-cousins do marry.) [➤ Names, Use of.] In *The Small House at Allington*

Squire Dale tries to bring about a marriage between two cousins, Bell and Bernard Dale. Dr Crofts, himself anxious to marry Bell, warns that it is not 'a good thing for cousins to marry', but an aristocratic lady replies, 'They do, you know, very often; and it suits some family arrangements' [20]. A similar view to Dr Crofts' is expressed by Sir Thomas Tringle in *Ayala's Angel* and by John Caldigate in *John Caldigate* when his aunt tries to force him to marry his cousin. As in so many other things Trollope reflected his century: Queen Victoria was only one of many women who married a first cousin. Indeed one of Trollope's aunts married a Trollope cousin.

Trollope defended marriages between cousins in *The Bertrams* [13]: 'Miss Caroline Waddington was ... speaking with absolute technical propriety, the first-cousin once removed of her lover ... a degree of relationship which happily admits of love and matrimony.' In 'The Journey to Panama' Miss Viner, while recognizing the views against cousins marrying, still believes that cousins are safe. She is attempting to justify her intention of marrying a man she hardly knows by saying, 'And he also is my cousin, – a distant cousin – you understand that.' Her statement that he is a 'distant' cousin means she shares Dr Croft's fears. Cousins can also provide an introduction for a girl to a prospective husband: it was Bernard Dale who introduced Adolphus Crosbie to his cousin, Lily Dale.

Landed families were often anxious to promote marriages between cousins to increase estates or at least to keep them from being divided. Usually the scheme does not work. This idea often occurs to the heads of families in

Trollope's fiction, especially if a title has become separated from its original landed estate. This happens in *Lady Anna, Can You Forgive Her?* and 'The Lady of Launay'. In *Sir Harry Hotspur of Humblethwaite* a man who would otherwise not be considered as a husband is invited to stay because he is a cousin. *The Belton Estate* and *Miss Mackenzie* are, in addition to *The Vicar of Bullhampton*, two of the few novels in which a cousin does actually marry a cousin; in the case of *Miss Mackenzie*, it is first cousins who marry. In 'Catherine Carmichael' there is a marriage between cousins in New Zealand.

The extended nature of Victorian families not only made cousins available but encouraged them to help one another to gain power or money: Lady Laura Kennedy in *Phineas Finn* stands at the centre of a large Whig 'cousinhood', while John Eames and the solicitor, Mr Toogood, are brought into *The Last Chronicle of Barset* to help Josiah Crawley because they are related. Contrasting the behaviour of cousins could form the background to such novels as *The Kellys and the O'Kellys* or *The Claverings*. Inheritance of titles or money could also promote rivalry or hatred, such as that between the baronet and his cousin in *Kept in the Dark*, or between the two Ralphs who are cousins in *Ralph the Heir*.

Cradell, Joseph. Cradell is a fellow clerk with John Eames at the Income Tax Office in London in *The Small House at Allington*. They both live at Mrs Roper's boarding-house and the somewhat absurd Cradell eventually marries Mrs Roper's flighty daughter, Amelia, after Eames breaks with her. Trollope makes a topical allusion by giving him the nickname 'Caudle':

Douglas Jerrold's delightful *Mrs Caudle's Curtain Lectures* became one of the most celebrated pieces of Victorian humour after its serialization in *Punch* in 1845 and was credited with establishing the popularity of the new magazine. Mrs Caudle subjects her husband to nightly 'lectures' once the bed-curtains are drawn. By the time Cradell makes a brief reappearance in *The Last Chronicle of Barset*, we know he has suffered the same fate.

CRAWLEY FAMILY.
The depiction of the Crawleys is Trollope's best portrayal of a Victorian family which strives to keep up its genteel status on an inadequate income. He shows how difficult it was for such a family to survive unless it had some family money to supplement a clerical living. The description of the Crawleys' life is also one of the best insights into the plight of poorly paid clergymen, a subject dear to Trollope's heart. The principal characters in this fictional family are described below. (Bob and Jane are two younger children but are minor characters and play no significant part.)

Crawley, The Rev. Josiah. Josiah Crawley is one of Trollope's greatest and best-known creations in the Barsetshire novels. In *Barchester Towers* there is an unnamed clergyman in Cornwall who dissuades Francis Arabin from joining the Catholic Church [20]. This is almost certainly Crawley. In *Framley Parsonage* Crawley appears by name when Arabin, by now Dean of Barchester, invites the poor clergyman from Cornwall and makes him perpetual curate of Hogglestock. [For the significance of this title, ➤ Church of England.] At this point Crawley is about forty but his ill-fortune and bitterness make him appear older. His income is £130 a year plus a house, which is not enough to support a gentleman with a large family. Crawley is a 'stern, unpleasant man' but a conscientious clergyman to his poor parishioners. He is fiercely proud of his intellectual abilities, particularly his knowledge of Greek, which he imparts to his daughter Grace. Crawley resents the efforts of the Arabins and Lady Lufton to help his family. Since everyone knows that the Crawleys are always in debt, many believe that he stole a cheque for £20 and this forms the main plot of *The Last Chronicle of Barset*.

Crawley is a magnificent portrait of a man who borders on insanity. Trollope believed that he had a chance of being remembered for three characters in his fiction: the two Pallisers and Crawley [*Autobiography*, 20]. There has always been much speculation as to whether Trollope used his own father, Thomas Anthony Trollope, as a model for Crawley. Crawley and the elder Trollope share some traits: financial ill-luck, pride in their knowledge of the classics, insistence upon their rank as 'gentlemen' and a staggering inability to get on with others and even with their own family. It is highly unlikely that Trollope would have consciously set out to portray his father in fiction, especially as his mother was still alive when *Framley Parsonage* appeared. Years later Trollope told George Eliot how furious he was that Dickens had portrayed his father as Micawber [Mullen, 450–57]. Nevertheless, as Trollope says in his *Autobiography*, he had for many years pondered on how ill-luck can destroy a man of great gifts like his father

and cause upset in a family. It is not unreasonable to assume that this was at the back of his mind as he wrote.

Crawley, Mary (Mrs Josiah Crawley). The long-suffering wife of the Reverend Josiah Crawley who, unlike her husband, has common sense and is grateful for the help of friends. She has a deep insight into her husband's strange mental state. She is a cousin of John Eames, which eventually proves a source of good luck. She appears in *Framley Parsonage*, in which she is nursed back to health after a serious illness by Lucy Robarts, and in *The Last Chronicle of Barset*.

Crawley, Grace. Grace first appears as the clever and favourite child of the Reverend Josiah Crawley in *Framley Parsonage*. His only pleasure is in using his great knowledge of the classics to teach her, as Trollope's father had taught his sons. Grace Crawley only comes to prominence in *The Last Chronicle of Barset*, when Archdeacon Grantly's son Henry desires to marry her despite his father's opposition. Her beauty and modesty eventually even win her the support of the archdeacon. Grace Crawley is the best example of one of Trollope's favourite types: a girl who is always a lady in spite of poverty and isolation.

Cresswell, Sir Cresswell. See Divorce.

Crime. There are few greater surprises for anyone first reading Trollope's novels than to discover the amount of crime they contain. Virtually every type of crime, including crimes of violence, occur. [For assaults, beatings, kidnapping, murder and terrorism, ➤ Violence.] Much of the non-violent crime is connected with money: forgery forms the central plot in *Orley Farm*, while yet another attempt to tamper with someone's will takes place in *Cousin Henry*. There is an attempt to cheat a sister out of her inheritance in *The Kellys and the O'Kellys*. Fraud on a colossal scale dominates *The Way We Live Now* and on a lower, though more tragic, level in *The Prime Minister* and *The Three Clerks*. The theft of famous jewels is part of the main plot in *The Eustace Diamonds*. Worries about the theft of jewellery and money while on holiday in Italy form the basis for 'The Man Who Kept His Money in a Box'. Seductions occur in *The Macdermots of Ballycloran*, *The Vicar of Bullhampton* and *An Eye for an Eye*.

Most memorable in Trollope's annals of crime is the poor clergyman, Josiah Crawley, who is accused of stealing a cheque for £20 in *The Last Chronicle of Barset*. Trollope took a very serious view of theft, as one of his principal functions as a Post Office Surveyor was to make certain that postmasters, and in one famous case, postmistresses, did not steal money from letters. His experiences as a witness in the case of an Irish postmistress influenced his handling of trial scenes [Mullen, 229–31]. For an enthusiastic fox-hunter like Trollope, the poisoning of foxes in *The American Senator* was a serious matter, while another notorious sporting crime occurs in *The Duke's Children* when Major Tifto deliberately lames a racing horse.

[➤ Bigamy; Prostitution; Suicide.]

Crofts, Dr James. Dr Crofts, the hard-working local physician in *The Small House at Allington*, marries Isabella ('Bell') Dale. He is about thirty when the novel begins and he reappears in *The Last Chronicle of Barset*. [➤ Cousins; Doctors.]

Crosbie, Adolphus. A major character in *The Small House at Allington*, in which he jilts Lily Dale. Crosbie is one of the most interesting characters in the Barsetshire books. Rather unusually Trollope gives few details of his early life. He is a rising civil servant and his position is superior to that of John Eames. It is no wonder that Lily thinks he is 'an Apollo' or, to Trollope, a 'curled darling'. Trollope shows how Crosbie is so corrupted by his desire to be part of aristocratic society that he jilts Lily and marries Lady Alexandrina De Courcy. When Crosbie is first introduced [2], Trollope says he could not afford 'the comforts of marriage'; this is then followed by 'But –' and the announcement that 'We will not . . . inquire more curiously into the private life . . . of . . . Adolphus Crosbie'. [➤ Women.] This is a good example of the way in which Trollope could convey to sophisticated readers that a man like Crosbie might have an interesting 'private life', in a passage that could be read aloud in a family circle without offending the most straitlaced Victorian. When Crosbie reappears as a widower in *The Last Chronicle of Barset* he is a changed man and is still in love with Lily Dale. Trollope's handling of Crosbie's character and motives is particularly subtle: he is never portrayed as a complete villain. [➤ Rugs.]

Curates. See Church of England.

'Curled Darlings'. This term was

adapted from Shakespeare and was one of Trollope's favourite phrases. His first use seems to have been in his unpublished analysis of English society, *The New Zealander* [10], in which he attacked 'that ingenuous youth, with head stiffly ensconced in a wondrous half monkish coat, with his listless swinging cane, and his lisping cockney twang . . . these wooden specimens of youthful manhood'. In *The Prime Minister* [13], Mr Wharton is amazed that his daughter Emily prefers the suave 'Portuguese Jew', Ferdinand Lopez, a 'curled darling', to a manly Englishman. He quotes Brabantio's speech in *Othello* [I.ii] in which the term is actually used in the opposite sense to his: 'The wealthy curled darlings of our nation' are contrasted with the foreigner, Othello, with his 'sooty bosom'. In Trollope's case the phrase was used to describe young men who were handsome and bordered on being pretty, men who had not been tried by life, who were rather soft and, sometimes, dandies. The classical term, Apollo, was a frequent alternative. To be a 'curled darling' was not necessarily to be a bad character like Lopez or Adolphus Crosbie: the young Lord Lovel in *Lady Anna* was untried by life but not unmanly, while Fritz Planken in 'Lotta Schmidt' was simply immature, as was Peregrine Orme in *Orley Farm* [58]. 'Curled darlings' often competed with middle-aged men (who were frequently bald) for the hand of the beloved. When this was the case Trollope's sympathy was normally with the middle-aged man. 'Curled darlings' are often presented as the type of well-favoured, handsome youth who does well at public school, unlike the more manly 'hob-

bledehoy' – such as John Eames or, of course, Trollope himself – who ripen into maturity later. [➤ Gardens; Manliness.]

Cursing. In Trollope's fiction, cursing was a not infrequent element in his dialogue among men, but its use was governed by strict rules. 'Damn' or 'damned' was the most frequently used curse but normally this was spelt 'D--n' or 'd----d'. He also resorted to euphemisms like 'dashed', taken from the printers' use of dashes in words like d----d for 'damned'. Likewise, it is rare for him to use in narration the word 'devil', as in 'Better the d----- you know than the d---- you don't'. He normally uses old euphemisms such as 'the Evil One' or 'the old gentleman'. Mr Scarborough in the novel bearing his name says 'devil' but then we are told that he was 'a pagan'. [For an example of Trollope's use of 'devil', ➤ *The Eustace Diamonds*.]

Trollope's usage did not just reflect his publishers' censorship, because in general the standard of Victorian spoken English, at least in mixed company and among all but the lowest elements, tended to rely less on profanity, blasphemy and cursing than that of later generations. This view of cursing was expressed in *Marion Fay* [18] when the Marquis and Marchioness of Kingsbury were discussing his domestic chaplain: "D--- Mr Greenwood!" said the Marquis. He certainly did say the word at full length, as far as it can be said to have length . . . He certainly did say it . . . Her ladyship heard the word very plainly, and at once stalked out of the room, thereby showing that her feminine feelings had received a wrench which made it impossible for her any longer to endure the presence of such a foul-mouthed monster.' Trollope went on to refer to the 'vulgarity' of the curse. Often men who curse are not quite gentlemen, like Archie Clavering and Captain Boodle in *The Claverings* [11, 36]. One of his greatest cursers is the drunkard, Sir Louis Scatcherd, in *Doctor Thorne*.

In *The Three Clerks* Captain Cuttwater, a salty old naval officer, frequently breaks into oaths – again disguised by dashes – which are usually followed by 'craving your pardon, ladies'. The problem of a man using an offensive word before ladies occurs elsewhere: in *Ayala's Angel* Tom Tringle uses the word 'devil' before his aunt, and afterwards apologizes [31]. In *The Claverings* young Florence Burton is horrified when her fiancé refers to a 'cursed delay' in their marriage and takes him up for his language [4]. Clergymen especially avoided strong speech although in *Is He Popenjoy?* the combative Dean of Brotherton does use 'd----d', to the horror of his daughter [28].

It is almost unheard of for a lady to use strong language: in *John Caldigate* there is a shipboard exchange between Caldigate and Euphemia Smith, later shown to be an adventuress. She uses the phrase 'go to the devil' [8] thereby giving readers a warning as to her character. In *The Claverings* Sophie Gordeloup says 'damn' and, in French, '*Mon Dieu*' [30, 36]. This is more excusable because she is foreign and a curse or a profanity in French is more acceptable. When Lady Aylmer calls a letter the 'damning proof' Trollope feels compelled to explain that 'there are certain words usually confined to the vocabularies of men' which some women, such as this 'august person', like to use on 'special occasions' [*The Belton Estate*, 17].

Trollope himself was described by a few contemporaries as using quite strong language when annoyed – his brother Tom once described it as 'graphic' – but this would only be in the company of other men; one Scottish minister was horrified by some words Trollope used, while a publisher's clerk recalled him swearing 'like a sergeant-major'.

D

DALE FAMILY.
The Dale family plays a central role in *The Small House at Allington* and some members reappear in *The Last Chronicle of Barset*. The Dales have 'been squires of Allington since squires ... were first known in England'. Allington is a small village in a county that borders on Barsetshire. Trollope had a strong belief in the important role of gentry families like the Dales in English society; he himself was descended from a such a family that had played a similar role in Lincolnshire. [➤ Baronets; Trollope Family.] In *The Small House at Allington* there is a continual contrast between the Dales who, in spite of minor flaws, are basically admirable and the De Courcy family who are selfish and arrogant aristocrats. All the Dales have one consistent trait: it is 'the nature of a Dale to be constant in his likings and his dislikings' [*The Small House at Allington*, 6]. The family is divided between the Great House and the Small House. The principal members of this fictional family are described below.

Dale, Christopher. The unmarried squire of Allington, with an income of about £3,000 a year – not a very large sum for a squire. He lives in the Great House at Allington. The description of him in the first chapter of *The Small House at Allington* is a classic portrait of a Victorian squire. His essentially kind nature is developed in *The Last Chronicle of Barset* [16].

Dale, Mrs Mary. The widow of Christopher Dale's younger brother, Philip. Although she and the squire do not get on, he gives her the free use of the Small House. She has an income of less than £300 a year, which makes her 'poor'. What this highly relative term really means is that she has to be careful and she sacrifices her own pleasures for the happiness of her two daughters, Bell and Lily.

Dale, Isabella (Bell). The elder of two daughters of Mrs Mary Dale of the Small House. She is the especial favourite of her uncle, the squire. He is anxious for her to marry her cousin Bernard, but she remains faithful to her true love, Dr Crofts, from the nearby town of Guestwick.

Dale, Lilian (Lily). Trollope introduces 'dear Lily Dale', the daughter of Mrs Mary Bell, sister of Isabella Dale and niece of Squire Christopher Dale, as a character whom the readers are told to 'love'. Love her they did: she became the most popular of Trollope's much-admired English girls. He spoke of her as 'the heroine I have loved best', although he agreed to write a brief parody of her in *Never, Never*. By the time of his *Autobiography* Trollope appears to have tired of hearing people praise her and came to believe that she was 'somewhat of a female prig'. (Some editions misprint this as a 'French prig'.) Her popularity caused many readers to implore Trollope to continue her adventures beyond *The Last Chronicle of Barset* and allow her to marry John Eames, but Trollope refused. She is nineteen when she first appears. The story of her being jilted by Adolphus Crosbie, and her refusal to accept the love of John Eames because she had already given her love to Crosbie, form the main plot of *The Small House at Allington*. [➤ Women.]

Dale, Bernard. The nephew and heir of Christopher Dale. After Bell Dale refuses to follow her uncle's desire for her to marry her cousin Bernard, he eventually finds a suitable wife in *The Last Chronicle of Barset*. He is a Captain in the Engineers and a man 'who has his feelings under control'. His mother, Lady Fanny Dale, is the sister of Earl De Guest. This connection with the aristocracy gives Captain Dale a rank in society which he neither neglects nor exploits. It is he who brings his friend Adolphus Crosbie on a visit to Allington with tragic results for his cousin, Lily Dale. [➤ Military.]

Daubeny, Mr. A prominent politician in the Palliser novels, as a Tory MP who has been the member for East Barsetshire. He is the leader of the Tory party and at the beginning of *The Prime Minister* is the prime minister. His friends and foes call him 'Dubby' [*Phineas Finn*, 3]. When Trollope says that Daubeny was 'brilliant in mingling a deep philosophy with

the ordinary politics of the day' he did not mean this as a compliment [*Phineas Redux*, 5]. In this latter novel he performs one of his 'conjuring' tricks by proposing the disestablishment of the Church of England. Trollope used some aspects of Disraeli's career in Daubeny's behaviour and even for parts of his personality, but he maintained that in his lifetime all Conservative leaders had been too inclined to abandon principles they had long defended [➤ Peel, Sir Robert]. Daubeny's proposal for disestablishment is not as far-fetched as it might seem. [Mullen, 482–3.]

Daughters. In the vast majority of Trollope's fiction daughters play some part, and they are almost always worrying about marriage. For mothers with daughters, like Mrs Bell in 'The Courtship of Susan Bell', there is the problem of fending off 'wolves' or unsuitable men. One of the greatest concerns of a Victorian lady was to 'bring out' her daughters so that they could find suitable husbands [➤ Season]. Mrs Grantly in *Framley Parsonage* excels at this.

For a Victorian middle- or upper-class father – and these form the bulk of Trollope's fathers – the financial future of his daughters was of prime importance since they could not be expected to earn money. Such fathers had two great duties with regard to a prospective son-in-law: to discover what his resources were and to provide some settlement to supplement those resources. Mr Wharton's failure to do either with his prospective son-in-law Lopez in *The Prime Minister* is a factor in the tragedy of his daughter's marriage. Daughters were a greater expense to a father than sons because money had to be provided either for their marriage settlements or to give them an income to live on. [➤ Fathers and Sons.] In Trollope's fiction this is a particular worry when a landed estate is entailed on a distant male relative. Thus Mr Hall in *An Old Man's Love* tries to save half his yearly income to build up a capital sum to provide for his four daughters, while Sir Harry Hotspur in the novel that bears his name is tempted to consider his debauched nephew George as a possible husband for his daughter simply to keep title and estate together. [➤ also *The Belton Estate*.]

In Victorian times, a lady like Mrs Ray in *Rachel Ray* could live a very retired life in a small town for about £100 a year. Trollope provided £4,000 capital in his will for his niece, Florence Bland, who had become a virtual daughter. This would have given her an income of about £200 a year. (Mrs Marrable, a vicar's widow, 'lived decently' on £300 a year in *The Vicar of Bullhampton*.)

Trollope normally follows the Victorian custom of giving the eldest daughter the title of Miss before her family name while the younger daughters have 'Miss' followed by their Christian names. Thus in *An Old Man's Love*, the squire's eldest daughter is Miss Hall while her younger sisters are Miss Augusta Hall, Miss Evelina Hall, etc.

[➤ Mothers and Daughters; Women.]

Deaths and Death Scenes. There are significant deaths in at least twenty-six of Trollope's novels and eight of his short stories, and their number reflects the frequency of premature death in Victorian England. Given the state of medical knowledge, Victorians did not find it odd that people died unexpectedly or without definite causes. In his first novel, *The Macdermots of Ballycloran*, Feemy Macdermot dies after her brother kills her lover, and in the last novel Trollope wrote, *The Land-Leaguers*, there are two deaths, not counting those numerous people murdered by terrorists. While deaths occur in over half the novels, Trollope does not, like Dickens, squeeze every ounce of emotion from a deathbed scene. In *The Claverings* the description of a baby's death [20] is beautifully written yet it does not actually describe the death but the estranged parents' reaction to it. Likewise in one of his longest death scenes, that of the consumptive Marion Fay in the novel of the same name, the heroine actually dies 'off-stage' despite a long build-up to the event. In *The Land-Leaguers* the death of a ten-year-old boy is dealt with in a short space and with relatively subdued emotion.

There are two main exceptions to Trollope's rule. The first is perhaps his most poignant death scene in a novel. This occurs in *Castle Richmond* [33] and the memory of Ireland's potato famine may have caused him to set aside his normal reticence. The second occurs in the short story, 'Returning Home'. While death is not as frequent in the short stories, here Trollope wrote a scene of death by drowning that could equal Dickens in excitement and pathos.

There are what one might call 'necessary deaths', some of which occur 'off-stage'. They are necessary because without them the plot could not proceed as it does: John Bold's death, announced at the beginning of *Barchester Towers*, occurs because he was no longer needed and his widow must be free to remarry. Mary Finn, the first wife of Phineas in *Phineas Finn*, dies because otherwise Phineas would never be able to return to London. Lady Glencora Palliser, by now Duchess of Omnium, dies before the start of *The Prime Minister*, thereby allowing her husband Plantagenet to emerge as a major character without her overshadowing him. In *Barchester Towers* the death of Dean Trefoil opens up a new story line as to his successor. In *Miss Mackenzie* the death of Margaret Mackenzie's brother gives her the money without which the plot could not develop and in *The Claverings* there are four such deaths – Lord Ongar, Hughie Clavering, Sir Hugh and Archie Clavering. Without these there would be no plot and no happy ending for Harry Clavering. Such 'necessary' deaths also occur in, among others, *The Belton Estate*, *Sir Harry Hotspur of Humblethwaite*, *The Eustace Diamonds*, *Lady Anna* and *Cousin Henry*.

In several novels Trollope begins with a death which opens the main or a subsidiary story line: *Phineas Redux*, *Sir Harry Hotspur of Humblethwaite*, *The Prime Minister*, *Lady Anna*, *Barchester Towers*, *Ayala's Angel*, *Miss Mackenzie* and *The Belton Estate*. In some novels girls who have not got the man they love simply die of a broken heart like Linda Tressel in the novel of that name and Emily Hotspur in *Sir Harry Hotspur of Humblethwaite*.

Perhaps the three most famous deaths are those of Mrs Proudie and of the Reverend Septimus Harding in *The Last Chronicle of Barset*, and of the old Duke of Omnium in *Phineas Redux*. One of the most moving is Bishop Grantly's in *Barchester Towers*. Trollope's handling of the Bishop's son's

emotional conflict during that death is among his greatest pieces of writing.

[➤ Kensal Green Cemetery; Mourning; Suicide; Violence.]

Debt. In Trollope's fiction debt is a constant theme and Trollope himself understood the loaning of money. As a young Post Office clerk he had got into serious trouble over a tailor's bill of £12 and a loan of £4. In time this grew to over £200 [➤ Bills]. Even before that, he had seen how debts forced his father to flee to Belgium. In the 1860s Trollope and Thackeray each loaned a friend, William Synge, £900 and while Trollope records that Thackeray had loaned Synge money in his *Thackeray* he typically omits to mention that he had loaned the same amount. By 1864 Synge had repaid £500 of the £900 loaned him by Trollope.

Because it was relatively easy to find ways of borrowing money if one did not go to a bank, debts were quite common in Victorian times. By allowing credit, tradesmen also tended to allow debts to mount up, but when disaster threatened a family, butchers and grocers would demand payment, as Mr Crawley found in *The Last Chronicle of Barset*. Until 1869 many debtors could be imprisoned, as any reader of Dickens knows.

In Trollope's novels debts tend to be large and of three kinds. The first are personal debts usually incurred by young men like George Hotspur in *Sir Harry Hotspur of Humblethwaite*, Ralph Newton in *Ralph the Heir*, Lord Silverbridge in *The Duke's Children*, John Caldigate in the novel of the same name, Charley Tudor in *The Three Clerks* or Mark Robarts in *Framley Parsonage*. The second are debts that could cripple an estate, like the Greshamsbury estate in *Doctor Thorne*, the Folking estate in *John Caldigate*, Belton Castle in *The Belton Estate* and John Scarborough's Staffordshire estate in *Mr Scarborough's Family*. The third kind are those which cause a man's destruction, such as those which brought down Ferdinand Lopez in *The Prime Minister*, or Augustus Melmotte in *The Way We Live Now*. Occasionally it is a woman who incurs debt, like Julia Brabazon in *The Claverings* or the Countess Lovel in *Lady Anna*.

[➤ Jews; Money-lenders.]

DE COURCY FAMILY.

The De Courcys provide Trollope's most memorable portrait of the worst type of aristocratic family. Members figure in most of the Barsetshire novels and one is also in the Palliser series. The De Courcys, with their Norman French name, have been short-sighted 'for thirty generations'. They are portrayed as essentially false and mean when contrasted with such honest and stalwart English families as the Dales or the Thornes. With this contrast Trollope is exploiting the fashionable 'Norman versus Anglo-Saxon' debate of his day. The De Courcys are connected to the Gresham family who are so prominent in *Doctor Thorne* because Squire Gresham's wife, Lady Arabella, is the sister of Earl De Courcy. The family first appears in *Barchester Towers* [37]. They are also important characters in *The Small House at Allington*. The family name is the same as the title and they live at Courcy Castle in Barsetshire. The heir to the title is the eldest son who uses the courtesy title of Lord Porlock [➤ Peerage]. The principal members of this fictional family are described below.

De Courcy, Earl. The earl is a miserable man who creates much misery around him. He will not allow his eldest son into the castle and he constantly battles about money with the rest of the family, particularly with his wife. He is heavily in debt from gambling and he suffers from gout. In politics he is a Whig and spends much of his time at Court, where he is Grand Master of the Ponies to the Prince of Wales. He is said to curse a great deal, but Trollope does not provide any choice examples. [➤ Fathers and Sons.]

De Courcy, (Rosina) Countess. The countess is the real moving force in the family. She is constantly at war with her husband in her efforts to get money to finance some weeks during the Season at their London house. She has 'a worse time with the earl' than do the children and she fears that he will strike her with his crutch. When her daughter Alexandrina complains that her husband does not talk to her, the countess replies that there are worse faults in a husband.

Porlock, Lord. The eldest son and heir to the title, Lord Porlock is unmarried when he is first mentioned in *The Small House at Allington*. Although he rarely appears in the novel there is much discussion about him. He and his father feud over money and the entail on the family estate. He eventually meets Plantagenet Palliser, another heir to a great title but a man who is his opposite in all things [43]. In due course he marries his mistress. [➤ Peerage.]

De Courcy, The Hon. George. The second son in the De Courcy family, he has married a wealthy coal-merchant's daughter. His father complains that when he sees her he feels he is sitting down to dinner with his housemaid. George De Courcy is very mean and his main hope is that his elder brother, Lord Porlock, will die and allow him to succeed to the title. By *The Last Chronicle of Barset* [8] he is at least living in Courcy Castle and maintaining what is left of the family greatness after his elder brother has become earl.

De Courcy, The Hon. John. The youngest son, who has no real income and is thoroughly idle. It is a sure sign that Trollope does not like him when he is portrayed during a fox-hunt as a man more interested in his dress than in the enthusiastic pursuit of the fox [*Doctor Thorne*, 5].

De Courcy, Lady Margaretta. Lady Margaretta resembles her mother in everything except her mother's beauty. She sides with her mother in all family quarrels.

De Courcy, Lady Rosina. Lady Rosina is extremely religious and has come under the influence of Mrs Proudie. She is one of the characters who connects the Barsetshire books to the Palliser series when she reappears in *The Prime Minister* [20–21]. Here she emerges as a mildly eccentric and impoverished lady who is befriended by the Duke of Omnium when she tells him of the sad fate of the once proud De Courcy family. At this point she is no longer so obsessed with her religious crusades.

De Courcy, Lady Amelia. Lady Amelia, the most sensible of the De Courcy women, is married to Mor-

timer Gazebee, MP for Barchester and a London solicitor who manages all business affairs for the De Courcys. She makes it plain that her husband is beneath her socially.

De Courcy, Lady Alexandrina. Lady Alexandrina is the youngest and most beautiful De Courcy. Adolphus Crosbie jilts Lily Dale to marry her. Trollope picked her name with care. By the time *The Small House at Allington* began to appear in 1863, the name Alexandra was becoming popular in England because of the marriage of the Danish Princess Alexandra to the Prince of Wales in that year. However, Alexandrina was also Queen Victoria's first name, which she discarded when she came to the throne. Alexandrina would have been a perfect choice as a name by such an enthusiastic Court Whig as Earl De Courcy. Lady Alexandrina is a haughty and selfish woman.

De Guest, Lady Julia. The unmarried sister of Earl De Guest. The earl, who is the opposite of Earl De Courcy, becomes the friend and patron of John Eames and leaves him an inheritance. He appears only in *The Small House at Allington* but his sister, who had lived with him, is also prominent in *The Last Chronicle of Barset*. (The Earl's death occurs in the interval between the two novels.) Lady Julia is connected to the Dales because her sister, Lady Fanny, married Squire Dale's brother, Colonel Dale. Lady Julia does everything to help Eames win Lily Dale.

Devonshire. 'Of all counties in England Devonshire is the fairest to the eye' [*Rachel Ray*, 2]. Trollope's mother was proud of her Devonshire blood and Trollope remained friendly with several cousins in the county. Some of his Post Office work in the 1850s was in Devon and he may have used some aspects of the county to create Barsetshire. Exeter is used more frequently than any cathedral city in his fiction. Some of *Framley Parsonage* is set in the county, as is all of *Rachel Ray. He Knew He Was Right* and *Kept in the Dark* have many Devonshire scenes. The isolation of parts of Devonshire, particularly those which skirt Dartmoor, is well portrayed in 'The Parson's Daughter of Oxney Colne'. This short story opens with a tribute to the county: 'The prettiest scenery in all England – and if I am contradicted in that assertion, I will say in all Europe – is in Devonshire...' (The villages in this story were all places for which Trollope had laid out postmen's 'walks'.)

Dickens, Charles (1812–70). As a young man in London Trollope had devoured *Sketches by Boz* and *The Pickwick Papers*, much as Bishop Proudie sat down in his wife's sitting-room with a glass of hot negus to read the last number of 'the "Little Dorrit"' [*Barchester Towers*, 43]. But Trollope always had mixed feelings about England's leading novelist. In his fourth novel, *The Warden*, he attacked Dickens's sentimental optimism and parodied him as 'Mr Popular Sentiment'. In 1856 he had been infuriated by Dickens's attack on the Civil Service through 'The Circumlocution Office' in *Little Dorrit* and wrote an article attacking it. [➤ *The Three Clerks.*]

He often referred to Dickens in his books and short stories, including 'The Adventures of Fred Pickering' and 'Josephine de Montmorenci', and

to his characters: Nicholas Nickleby in *The Macdermots of Ballycloran* [5]; David Copperfield in *The Struggles of Brown, Jones, and Robinson* [8]; Mrs Gamp in *Framley Parsonage*, where hers is the name of a horse; Pecksniff in *The Bertrams* [26]; the 'immortal' lawyers, Dodgson and Fogg, in *The Last Chronicle of Barset.* In *The Three Clerks* he speculates as to why an aristocratic criminal like the Hon. Undecimus Scott, MP, is more wicked than Bill Sykes or 'Sikes' as Trollope consistently misspells the name. (He returns to the subject in *Castle Richmond.*) In *North America* he frequently alludes to *Martin Chuzzlewit.*

When Trollope joined with other postal surveyors to seek an increase in salary from the Postmaster General he cited *Oliver Twist*, which he considered Dickens's best novel. He gave a speech at the farewell dinner for Dickens's last tour of America in 1867 and the following year he arrived in New York on a Post Office mission just as Dickens's ship was about to leave New York harbour. In a typical gesture Trollope arranged to get to the ship just to shake Dickens's hand. Dickens was amazed but delighted.

When Dickens died in 1870 Trollope wrote a tribute in the July issue of *Saint Pauls.* It was fulsome but balanced: 'A great man has gone from us; – such a one that we may surely say of him that we shall not look upon his like again.' He added, however, that his massive popularity lay, as the novelist Charles Lever said, in his ability 'to tap the ever newly-growing mass of readers as it sprang up among the lower classes' throughout the English-speaking world. His characters were 'unnatural' and were either too good or too bad whereas to Trollope people were a curious mixture of both. Even so, Dickens's characters influenced English speech and writing more than those of any other writer save Shakespeare. The older novelist's dislike of politics and government was a drawback, to Trollope's mind: 'To his feelings, all departmental work was the bungled, muddled routine of a Circumlocution Office. State-craft was odious to him … he was a radical at heart.'

When he discussed nineteenth-century novelists five years later in his *Autobiography* he placed Dickens third after Thackeray and George Eliot. His characters were not human beings but 'puppets' who 'walk on stilts', his pathos was 'stagey and melodramatic' and his style was 'jerky, ungrammatical, and created by himself in defiance of rules – almost as completely as that created by Carlyle'. As to his country's politics, Dickens was 'marvellously ignorant', a terrible crime in Trollope's opinion. Trollope also discussed Dickens in his article, 'Novel-Reading: The Works of Charles Dickens, The Works of William Makepeace Thackeray', published in the January 1879 edition of *Nineteenth Century.*

Trollope admired Dickens's abilities and accepted as valid the overwhelming adulation he had received. Considering that as a partner in a publishing house he knew how much more Dickens earned than he himself, his balanced judgement is all the more remarkable. In private he had a mixed attitude towards him as a man. Once within London's literary world Trollope allied with the Thackeray set against the Yates–Dickens set in the aftermath of the Garrick Club quarrels of the 1850s. (Edmund Yates, a minor novelist, had printed gossip

about Thackeray; Trollope and Yates were already rivals in the Post Office.) The public nature of Dickens's separation from his wife would hardly have endeared him to a man like Trollope. When the first volume of Forster's biography appeared he told his friends G. H. Lewes and George Eliot that the book 'is distasteful to me … Dickens was no hero; he was a powerful, clever, humorous, and, in many respects, wise man; – very ignorant, and thick-skinned, who had taught himself to be his own God'. He also disliked Dickens's 'craving for applause'. [➤ Crawley, The Rev. Josiah.]

While Dickens and Trollope never corresponded a great deal they did work together on the campaign for an international copyright agreement. Later, several novels by Trollope were published in *All the Year Round*, edited by Dickens's son. Dickens seems to have respected Trollope as a man, admired his efforts to help poor authors, and described him to Tom Trollope as 'the heartiest and best of fellows' but he found his standing for Parliament at Beverley 'inscrutable'. Tom Trollope's second wife, Fanny, was the sister of Ellen Ternan, whom many thought to be Dickens's mistress. There was a considerable friendship between Tom Trollope and Dickens.

[➤ Dissenters.]

Did He Steal It? A Comedy in Three Acts. This comedy is a dramatized version of *The Last Chronicle of Barset*, the 'he' being the Reverend Josiah Crawley and the 'it' being the cheque for £20. The play was printed by James Virtue [➤ *Saint Pauls*]. In the spring of 1869 Trollope was invited to adapt the main plot of the novel for the theatre, probably by John

Hollingshead, a theatrical manager. He rejected it and Trollope accepted his verdict: 'I have little doubt but that the manager was right. That he intended to express a true opinion, and would have been glad to have taken the piece had he thought it suitable, I am quite sure.' Trollope kept copies of his rejected play in his library and on the title page of the copy he gave to his son Henry he wrote: 'Harry Trollope from the author' and then inserted above a caret before 'author' the word 'unfortunate'.

Trollope had inherited a liking for the theatre from his mother, who had taught her children to enact scenes in French from Molière's plays before her guests. She also wrote little plays for them to act: the most amusing to survive is 'The Righteous Rout', a farce that attacks an Evangelical tea-party [➤ *Miss Mackenzie*]. Finally, Trollope's mother set her children to analyse Shakespearian characters and scenes.

In 1851 Trollope had tried his hand at another comedy, *The Noble Jilt*, but it too was condemned by the experts. It was quite common for novelists to take to the stage. The most famous was, of course, Dickens, but Wilkie Collins, Thackeray, Bulwer-Lytton, Charles Reade and Henry James all tried with varying degrees of success.

For the stage Trollope defrocked his bishops and clergy both out of respect for the Church of England and out of regard for theatrical custom. Crawley becomes a schoolmaster; Bishop Proudie, a magistrate; Major Grantly, Captain Oakley; Mrs Arabin, Mrs Lofty. The other minor characters keep their names and callings.

Diplomats. In Trollope's fiction, diplomats do not appear with any great frequency. In *He Knew He Was Right* the American Minister to Italy, Jonas Spaulding, plays a subsidiary role. Much is made in *Mr Scarborough's Family* of two diplomats in Belgium: Sir Magnus Mountjoy was H.M. Minister and M. Grascour worked in the Belgian Foreign Office. The portrait of the diplomats' work is not a very flattering one. Trollope's implied censures were answered in kind by Walburga, Lady Paget, the wife of a career diplomat, when she referred to Trollope, whom she had met at her husband's Rome Embassy, as 'rough, heavy, persevering and rather vulgar, like his books, but interesting'. In *The American Senator* there are many diplomats, including Mounser Green who is eventually made Ambassador to Patagonia. The fact that John Morton is the Secretary to the British Legation in Washington is the cause of the senator's visiting England. In *The Duke's Children* the senator returns as Minister to the Court of St James in the days before Great Britain and the United States exchanged ambassadors. Eventually the young Lord Gerald Palliser embarks on a diplomatic career.

When sent on his Post Office missions abroad, Trollope often acted in a semi-diplomatic capacity and negotiated treaties. In 1868 he was an informal representative of the Foreign Office when he was in the United States to discuss copyright. In general he was remarkably undiplomatic and had little regard for 'all those little niceties, that smiling and that frowning, that taking off of hats and only half taking them off' in which diplomats engaged [*The American Senator*, 30]. At one point Trollope wished to establish his son Henry in the Foreign Office.

Dirt. In Trollope's fiction, dirt almost always has a moral connotation. A man, or even worse, a woman, whose clothes or house are conspicuously dirty are normally not to be trusted. Good examples of this are in his description of the money-lender, Captain Stubber, in *Sir Harry Hotspur of Humblethwaite* and in that of Sophie Gordeloup in *The Claverings*. Young bachelors are often exempted from this rule. Sometimes Trollope uses dirt as a way to hint at things that were not directly discussed in a Victorian novel. In Madame Gordeloup's case it was her state of personal hygiene.

Disraeli, Benjamin (1804–81). Disraeli was a Tory politician: leader of the Conservative party in the House of Commons 1852–68 and Prime Minister 1868 and 1874–80. He was created Earl of Beaconsfield in 1876. Trollope despised him both as a politician and as a novelist. Disraeli achieved his early fame as a novelist with his best-known works, *Coningsby* (1844) and *Sybil* (1846). They appeared in those years in which Trollope himself was frustrated and anxious to produce his first novel. Perhaps this gave added venom to his dislike. In Trollope's early novels he had a hit at Disraeli by various jibes: he named a money-lender in *Barchester Towers* [4] 'Sidonia' after a Jewish character in *Coningsby* and its sequel, *Tancred*. Trollope believed – as did many Victorians, including many Conservatives – that Disraeli was insincere and was only playing at the serious business of politics. That is why Trollope refers to him sarcastically in *Ralph the Heir* as 'the great reformer of the age'.

Trollope in his attempt at a parliamentary career at Beverley was attacking a Tory party led by Disraeli as Prime Minister. He also believed that he would have been elected if Disraeli's manoeuvres had not delayed the election to 1868. In 1876 Trollope was outspoken in his public attacks on Disraeli for his refusal to aid Christians during the Turkish atrocities in what is now Bulgaria [Mullen, 608–9]. This no doubt encouraged the vituperation in Trollope's attack on Disraeli in the *Autobiography*, written at the time of the 'Bulgarian agitation'. Trollope maintained that his own characters 'have been as real to me as ... the dominion of a party to Mr Disraeli'. He accepted that Disraeli was 'a man of genius' but he believed that his novels were false and misled young readers. They had 'a smell of hair oil'.

Trollope's detestation of Disraeli was no doubt increased by some jealousy at the enormous sums a prime minister could command for a novel. Also many of Trollope's friends, particularly the Liberal writer Abraham Hayward, who like Disraeli came from a Jewish background, despised the Tory leader. Trollope did not attack Disraeli because Disraeli was a Jew (Disraeli was in fact a member of the Church of England) but he was prepared to use that background as an additional club with which to hit an enemy.

Many people have thought that the character of Daubeny in the Palliser novels is based on Disraeli, but Trollope always denied that his characters were portraits of real people. Indeed the fact that Disraeli's own fictional characters were precisely that would have made Trollope all the more likely to avoid such a practice. In the Palliser novels Disraeli and Daubeny certainly share some characteristics, but Daubeny is Trollope's concept of what a Conservative leader of the mid-nineteenth century was like. To him that inevitably meant a 'conjuror' who betrayed old Tory principles to get into office. [➤ Peel, Sir Robert.]

One trait that Disraeli and Daubeny did share was a fierce hatred of those who they thought had sneered at them. Disraeli long remembered Thackeray's sneers and based his character St Barbe in *Endymion* on Thackeray, who had died by the time it was published. Yet Disraeli appears to have shown no resentment of Trollope. According to Trollope's first biographer, Escott, they met at a dinner at the home of a mutual friend, Lord Stanhope, and Disraeli praised Trollope's *The Eustace Diamonds*: 'I have long known, Mr Trollope, your churchmen and churchwomen; may I congratulate you on the same happy lightness of touch in the portrait of your new adventuress.'

Dissenters. Trollope's dislike of Dissenters or Nonconformists was part and parcel of his dislike of Evangelicals. Dissenters, or those Protestant Christians who 'dissented' from the Church of England, basically played little part in Trollope's life or fiction, with one exception: Charles Mudie, a Congregationalist, exercised a strong censorship on the authors admitted to his circulating library and this included Trollope. In effect, however, Dissenters' moral views were basically the same as those of Evangelicals. He told Escott that 'Dickens gibbeted cant in the person of Dissenters, of whom I never knew anything. I have done so in Mr Slope'. The traits Dickens gave to Dissenters Trollope gave to

clergymen like the Reverend Mr Emilius in *The Eustace Diamonds*. Even so, Trollope was much fairer to Dissenters than either Dickens or Thackeray. Ironically Trollope had married a Dissenter, a Unitarian, but in an Anglican church, and his wife then conformed to the Church of England.

In his novels and short stories there are only five Dissenting ministers of any substance: a Wesleyan Methodist in Australia who is referred to in *John Caldigate*; a Canadian Presbyterian in Bermuda; a Baptist in America; and two Methodists in England, one a Primitive and the other a Wesleyan. Trollope's view was essentially that of Matthew Arnold, that Dissenters stood outside the mainstream of English culture, whereas Trollope stood in the very centre of that stream. It is therefore surprising that he knew so much about the inner workings of Dissent. His knowledge probably came from his extensive tours of rural England, and especially the West Country in the 1850s, on behalf of the Post Office. This would have brought him into contact with the new red-brick chapels springing up in villages. In *The New Zealander*, Trollope admitted to a dislike of the ugliness of these chapels filled with 'unwholesome howling', but even so he urged his fellow Anglicans to try to be tolerant.

In *Doctor Thorne*, when Miss Gushing is not chosen by the Reverend Caleb Oriel as his bride she leaves the Church of England, goes to an 'independent' Methodist chapel and marries the minister, the Reverend Mr Rantaway [32]. (Rantaway is a play on the term 'ranter' traditionally applied to Dissenters by their enemies, and the fact that he is an 'independent' Methodist – that is, one of the small sects that broke away from the Wesleyan Methodists – emphasizes her fall in the ecclesiastical scale of things.) In *The Vicar of Bullhampton*, published over ten years later, Trollope gives more attention to Dissent than in any other novel. In it he introduces the Reverend Mr Puddleham, a Primitive Methodist minister, and gives an example of the new ugly chapels he had denounced in *The New Zealander*. (A writer less knowledgeable about English rural life would simply have called him a Methodist, or perhaps a Wesleyan Methodist, but the Primitive Methodists were the most rural and uneducated among Methodists. The choice heightened the dramatic contrast.)

Trollope manifestly dislikes Mr Puddleham and all he represents; he paints him as being far more condemnatory of the village's 'fallen woman' than the vicar. Yet he insists he is 'an earnest man, who, in spite of the intensity of his ignorance, is efficacious among the poor'. Again, lest his Anglican readership should be lulled into a false sense of security, he adds when discussing the chapel: 'It was acknowledged that it was ugly, misplaced, uncomfortable, detestable to the eye, and ear, and general feeling' except, he adds with bitter irony, 'in so far as it might suit the wants of people who were not sufficiently educated to enjoy the higher tone, and more elaborate language of the Church of England services'. He obviously agrees with the words of the Vicar of Bullhampton that Dissenters were 'a great mistake' [1,60]. We see that his dislike is as much because of social attitudes and behaviour as of theological narrowness and hardness. In one of his small errors in writing he makes a builder a Baptist in one chapter [36] and a Wesleyan Methodist in another [55] and gives the Primitive Methodists 'elders'.

As a Liberal he would have been painfully aware of the growing influence of Dissenters within his party and in politics generally. When he wanted to stand for Parliament, he learned that he could not have a safe Essex seat because the party wanted to please the Dissenters in that particular constituency. When he stood at Beverley in 1868 he enjoyed the support of a local Baptist minister, but in *Ralph the Heir*, when discussing the election at 'Percycross' [Beverley], he refers to the candidate's having to meet a Wesleyan Methodist minister who spoke in 'a voice made up of pretence, politeness and saliva' [20]. This was partly because his readership expected such men to talk like that and Trollope was not in the mood to argue. The very fact that the Conservative candidate's agent in Percycross thought it worthwhile for the candidate to meet the Wesleyan minister again shows Trollope's understanding of Dissent: of the five Methodist divisions at the time, Wesleyans were the most likely to vote Conservative.

Much of Trollope's dislike may be traced to social differences. He did not feel comfortable with the new urbanized lower middle classes from which Dissent increasingly drew its strength. He also found that the social divisions were not as strong. He particularly disliked the growing politicization among some Dissenters with their raucous cries for disestablishment, something he strongly rejected. When he was out of England he accepted that Methodists or Baptists were no longer 'dissenters' because there was no established church. Not surprisingly, in Australia or America he wrote of them simply as Christian churches and was impressed at the greater tolerance shown among Christian denominations. In America he visited 'Dissenting' universities and talked to 'Dissenting' writers in Boston, the traditional centre of the English Dissenting settlements. In his short story 'The Courtship of Susan Bell', the Bells are Baptists and if Susan's elder sister is narrow-minded she could just as easily have been an Anglican Evangelical. It is interesting that when he used this plot for *Rachel Ray* he turned the family into Evangelicals. He had an especial dislike of Quakers although in the one novel to feature them, *Marion Fay*, he balanced his strictures with praise for the characters' good points.

[➤ Clergymen; Religion.]

Divorce. Few things mark Trollope's fiction as different from that of later novelists as the almost total lack of divorced people in his books. Until the passage of the Matrimonial Causes Act of 1857, divorce was, for all practical purposes, obtainable only by a private Act of Parliament. The 1857 Act was very controversial and 6,000 Anglican clergymen petitioned against it. Under the Act, divorce could only be obtained by a man who could prove that his wife had committed adultery, whereas a woman had to show that her husband had added cruelty or desertion to his adultery. Bigamy, important in both *Castle Richmond* and *John Caldigate*, was another just cause for divorce. The new divorce court was presided over by Sir Cresswell Cresswell (1794– 1863) and although he sounds like a Trollopian invention, he was a real

judge. Trollope refers to him in *Framley Parsonage*, within two years of the new legislation, when he announces, 'Most marriages are fairly happy, in spite of Sir Cresswell Cresswell' [20]. When Burgo Fitzgerald is plotting to run off with Plantagenet Palliser's wife, he says that Palliser 'would get a divorce' [*Can You Forgive Her?*, 29]. If he had done so, Palliser's political career would have been over as divorced men were not permitted in the Queen's presence. This meant they were excluded from government posts.

Few people were anxious to endure the sordid details that would become public knowledge in a divorce case and divorce remained rare in real life and rarer in fiction. (In the 1860s there was an average of only 148 divorces each year.) Public opinion still regarded anyone involved in divorce as not fit for society although Trollope had several close friends in his London literary and artistic circles, such as G. H. Lewes, who were trapped by the divorce law. Another close friend, Mrs (later Lady) Millais, was able to get an annulment of her marriage to Ruskin because the marriage was never consummated. While Trollope visited George Eliot and her companion G. H. Lewes, it does not appear that his wife, Rose, did so. One factor behind old Squire Jones's dislike of his nephew and heir in *Cousin Henry* is that the young man is the son of a divorced woman.

Divorce was dangerous territory for a writer: Thackeray had rejected 'Mrs General Talboys' because adultery was a part of the story and because Mrs Talboys suggests divorce to the adulterer as a way out: 'Sir Cresswell Cresswell . . . was his refuge.' While we are not meant to like Mrs Talboys we are meant to have sympathy with Mrs Askerton in *The Belton Estate*. She had been married to a brutal man whom she had left with the aid of Colonel Askerton. They had lived together for three years before her husband's death allowed them to marry. Trollope refers to the 'old rigidity' of the pre-1857 situation and, while not condoning the Askertons' action, does not condemn it. (The novel was published in the *Fortnightly* whose editor at the time was G. H. Lewes.)

In Trollopian marriages that break down, separation is the normal solution and Trollope's sympathy is almost always with the woman. Thus in *The Small House at Allington* Countess De Courcy escapes from a brutal husband, while her daughter Lady Alexandrina takes flight from a boring marriage. Both go to Germany, which is also the place of exile for Lady Laura Kennedy when her marriage collapses. If a woman did not go abroad she was still subject to the dictates of her estranged husband, as Emily Trevelyan discovers in *He Knew He Was Right*. However, separation did not occur only among Trollope's upper classes; Mrs Baggett, the housekeeper in *An Old Man's Love*, is separated from her drunken soldier husband although she still helps him.

Divorce was often thought of as peculiarly American and a young girl in *The Way We Live Now* is only expressing a common English attitude when she says of her older rival, the American Mrs Hurtle, 'I believe they get themselves divorced just when they like' [76]. This view is the background to the rumours about Mrs Peacocke's marriage in *Dr Wortle's School*, as she is American. The liberated Mrs Talboys is amazed that the American

'literary lion', Conrad Mackinnon, supports traditional views on marriage and divorce. She attacks him for betraying America's claims to champion freedom: 'You, who have so nobly claimed for mankind the divine attributes of free action!'

Doctors. Other than clergymen and lawyers, doctors provide the largest number of professional characters in Trollope's fiction. He normally distinguishes between surgeons and apothecaries. Doctors are rarely important in their own right as Trollope's fictional characters are abnormally healthy. Often a doctor's appearance allows Trollope a chance for some mild humour, for example in Dr Fillgrave's call on Sir Roger Scatcherd in *Doctor Thorne* [12]. Doctors are normally summoned for older characters, for impending deaths or for those occasions when a young female character is ill as the result of frustrated love. In Trollope's first novel, *The Macdermots of Ballycloran*, a doctor is in attendance at a duel to treat the wounded. Specific illnesses are rarely mentioned although Lily Dale does contract scarlatina from a maid in the house and Mrs Proudie dies from a heart attack.

Trollope had ample opportunity to observe doctors in his youth when so many members of the Trollope family were severely ill. He himself suffered a mysterious illness, partly traceable to asthma, when he was twenty-five. He was treated by Dr John Elliotson, who also played an important role in the lives of Dickens and Thackeray and was famous for his use of mesmerism. In his unpublished analysis of British society, *The New Zealander*, Trollope devoted just over a third of one chapter [4] to 'physic'. In a rather wandering discussion he touched on mesmerism, without rejecting it and without mentioning Elliotson by name, and went on to medical research, public health, spiritualism, quack drugs and the adulteration of medicine. Throughout his adult years Trollope was remarkably healthy and only had a return of bad health in his last years due to a combination of asthma and heart problems.

Most of the memorable doctors occur in the Barsetshire novels. It is a surgeon, John Bold, who sparks the great dispute in *The Warden* from which the series develops. We learn little of Bold's medical work except that it is mainly among the poor. He can afford to practise in this field because he has inherited a comfortable fortune from his father, a rich London physician. When Bold sets up his practice in Barchester there are nine doctors in the cathedral city.

The most important doctor in Trollope's fiction is of course Dr Thorne, who dominates the novel that bears his name. In spite of his connections with the local gentry, Dr Thorne is looked down upon by other medical men because he mixes his own prescriptions (increasingly done by chemists at that time), charges 7s. 6d. per call within a five-mile radius from his home and slightly more beyond instead of a guinea, and worst of all, sends out bills. This arouses a controversy in the medical press [*Doctor Thorne*, 3]. [➤ Money; Newspapers.] The grander doctors with whom he comes into conflict, like Dr Rerechild or Dr Fillgrave, charge more and are apt to arrive in a carriage. (Dr Thorne rides a horse.) Nevertheless Thorne's medical advice is always superior. Fillgrave is often present at other crucial events in the Barsetshire novels, besides Sir Roger Scatcherd's final illness, most notably at the death of Mr Harding when he repeats his standard formula, 'Dear, dear, we are all dust' [*The Last Chronicle of Barset*, 81]. Dr Crofts in *The Small House at Allington* is a relatively important and admirable character who marries Lily Dale's elder sister, Bell.

For the great people in the Barsetshire and other novels, the eminent physician Sir Omicron Pie is sometimes brought from London, occasionally by putting on a 'special' train. Having assisted old Bishop Grantly's and Dean Trefoil's passage out of this life in *Barchester Towers*, he also presides over the final minutes of the old Duke of Omnium in *Phineas Redux*.

A persistent theme in several novels is one heard as much in the twentieth as in the nineteenth century, about 'the young doctors doing all the work and the old doctors taking all the money' [*The Small House at Allington*, 20]. Later in the same novel, when describing Dr Crofts, Trollope comments that village apothecaries are 'generally wronged' when people insist on importing great doctors from the town who only confirm the local man's diagnosis. A young man training to be an apothecary is briefly depicted in *Orley Farm* [57].

The largest fee any medical man receives in Trollope's fiction is the £300 the great surgeon Sir William Broderick receives in *Mr Scarborough's Family*, but he has been brought from London to perform an operation in a Staffordshire country house. Mr Scarborough is quite unusual in undergoing a major operation.

Doctors are also the fathers of two of Trollope's best-known 'heroes',

Phineas Finn and the Reverend Mark Robarts. Dick Shand, an important character in *John Caldigate*, is the son of a doctor who also does a bit of dentistry. Alice Dugdale in the short story that bears her name is the daughter of a country doctor. When describing doctors Trollope often calls them 'Galen' after the famous Greek physician of the second century; it would appear he first used this name in *The New Zealander*. One of the tell-tale signs of Trollope's authorship in the anonymous novel *Nina Balatka* is the description of a doctor as 'a son of Galen'.

Doctor Thorne. Trollope's seventh novel and the third in the Barsetshire series. He began writing on 20 October 1857 and continued after he left London on 30 January 1858 on his first Post Office mission, to Egypt. He finished the novel as his ship crossed the Mediterranean on 31 March 1858. *Doctor Thorne* marks an important stage in Trollope's success as a novelist because he found a publisher with whom he was to be closely connected for the rest of his career. When in London he saw Bentley, who would not pay him the £400 he wanted. He then took his manuscript to Chapman & Hall, who were well known as Dickens's publishers, and secured the £400. [For the reasons for doubting the details of Trollope's version of this story in his *Autobiography*, see Mullen, 319, 699.] It was published by Chapman & Hall in three volumes in May 1858.

When Trollope completed *Barchester Towers* he appeared to have finished with Barsetshire. In the next year, 1857, he wrote *The Three Clerks*, a novel set almost entirely in London, and when he finished that he began work on yet another London novel, *The Struggles of Brown, Jones, and Robinson*, but he made little progress before going on a long autumn holiday to Italy. He must have had time to reflect on his future as a novelist: he was already frustrated with the novel he had begun; he knew that his novels about Ireland had not proved popular, and he felt that the public had enjoyed but wanted no more of his Barchester clergymen. While in Florence, he asked his brother Tom for a plot: this is the only time that Trollope, as he freely admits in his *Autobiography*, used someone else's plot. Tom, who had yet to begin his own career as a novelist, gave his brother one of his best, and certainly one of his most Victorian, plots.

The novel is set in Barsetshire, but rather than concentrating on the life and intrigues of the clergy, Trollope went into the countryside to portray the life of the country house, the gentry and a rural doctor. The book opens with his most lyrical and detailed description of Barsetshire and this shows how vivid the county had become in his imagination: he was still living in Dublin when he began writing. As with so many of Trollope's novels, the action centres on conflict within and between different families, and – fairly rare in a Trollope novel – on families from every social class. *Barchester Towers* had introduced the Thornes of Ullathorne with the old-fashioned squire, Wilfred Thorne and his sister, Monica, two eccentric but admirable examples of an ancient gentry family. Dr Thomas Thorne, 'my hero', is the second cousin of the Thornes of Ullathorne. Although he is estranged from them by a family quarrel, he never forgets that he is connected with the longest-settled landed family in Barsetshire.

Trollope shows his great knowledge of the subtle gradations and snobberies in the world of Victorian doctors by describing the types of carriages they drive and by the nature of their fees. Like Trollope himself, Dr Thorne is conscious of his gentry blood, particularly when he comes into contact with pretentious people. Dr Thorne is the devoted uncle of Mary Thorne, who is one of Trollope's most admired heroines and perhaps one who appeals to many modern readers more than the essentially Victorian Lily Dale.

Mary is the illegitimate daughter of Dr Thorne's brother Henry, who has disgraced his family by drunkenness and by seducing a straw-bonnet maker. Her brother, the drunken stonemason Roger Scatcherd, kills Henry and Dr Thorne adopts Mary. (Those who think the Victorian courts always exacted severe punishments should note that Roger gets only a six-month sentence for manslaughter and Trollope adds, 'our readers will probably think the punishment was too severe'.) This introduces the second family to the story. Roger Scatcherd eventually becomes vastly wealthy through building railways and other enormous projects and is made a baronet. Here Trollope was probably drawing on the career of the great builder, Sir Samuel Morton Peto, and perhaps that of the 'railway king', George Hudson. He also knew that involvement in the topsy-turvy world of railway finance could lead to financial disgrace as well as wealth, for his father-in-law, a banker, had fled abroad after embezzling money. He was, among other things, a railway director [➤ Rose Trol-

lope]. Scatcherd trusts only one man, Dr Thorne. Scatcherd's wife is miserable with her status as Lady Scatcherd and spends her happiest times in the kitchen with her servants. Their son, Louis Philippe Scatcherd, has inherited his father's drunkenness but none of his ability to work hard. The serious moral dilemma of the novel is faced by Doctor Thorne as he strives to reconcile his conscience with his conflicting duties to the local landed family, the Greshams, to the Scatcherds, and to his own niece.

Two upper-class families play prominent roles. Dr Thorne lives in the village of Greshamsbury and becomes a close friend of Francis Gresham, the local squire. Gresham is in financial difficulties because of his debts and has mortgaged part of his estate to Scatcherd. Gresham's son and heir, young Frank, falls in love with Mary (also sought by Louis Philippe Scatcherd) which provides the main love plot, while there is a second, between Gresham's sister Beatrice and the local High Church rector, Caleb Oriel, who is cured of his only fault, celibacy, by his marriage to Beatrice. Trollope has some gentle humour with High Church foibles [32] similar to those he smiles at in *The Warden* [16]. These were drawn from some of the practices of his pious sister Cecilia, who was now dead.

The Greshams are connected with one of the main aristocratic families in Barsetshire, the pompous but impecunious De Courcy family, because Francis Gresham had married Lady Arabella De Courcy. Lady Gresham opposes her son's marriage but eventually gives in after Mary inherits the Scatcherd wealth on the death of Louis Philippe. The descriptions of the De Courcy clan and their antics are among Trollope's finest pieces of humorous writing. *Doctor Thorne* also sees the first appearance of two other characters who play large parts in later novels: Barsetshire's greatest aristocrat, the Duke of Omnium, head of the Palliser family, and Martha Dunstable, the first of a line of remarkable spinsters in Trollope's works, even though she eventually marries in *Framley Parsonage*. She knows that her old-fashioned curls 'always pass muster ... when done up with bank-notes' [16]. Perhaps no other Trollope novel introduces so many memorable characters as *Doctor Thorne*. It also brings back some friends from the two earlier Barsetshire novels. Mr Harding and Archdeacon and Mrs Grantly again play their parts while the most memorable reappearance is that of the formidable Mrs Proudie. Trollope knew she had roused the fascination, if not the affection, of his readers. Her conversation with Miss Dunstable about Rome [16] is quite delightful. He brought these characters back in spite of his comment in his brief introduction to the 1878 collected edition, *The Chronicles of Barsetshire*, that he 'hardly dared' do so. He was uneasy with the idea of a series and therefore wrote this volume 'almost with a hope that the locality' would not be recognized; this 'hope' is somewhat strange, given the lyrical description of Barsetshire in the opening paragraphs.

In *Doctor Thorne* we see the growing involvement of politics in Trollope's novels. We have the first of many election scenes (the election in *The Three Clerks* was not really developed) and here Trollope strikes the conflicting note that was to be heard time and again in his writing: to be elected an MP was a great honour, but the process of getting elected was dreadful and degrading [17]. The speech of the defeated candidate, Moffat, is remarkably similar to the one George Eliot later gave to Mr Brooke in *Middlemarch*, and perhaps partly explains her comment that without Trollope's encouragement she could not have finished that book.

Trollope also included in *Doctor Thorne* what is almost certainly an account of his own proposal to Rose Heseltine in 1842. In the midst of reflecting on Frank Gresham's proposal to Mary Thorne, Trollope inserts an 'authorial intrusion' about an anonymous gentleman and lady which 'did once come to the author's knowledge' [7]. All the circumstances re-told in it, as well as the restrained but still heartfelt emotion in his description of 'the sweetest moment of their lives', point to the near certainty that he is describing his own engagement. The story's inclusion also allowed him to send a message of love to and share a private joke with his wife, who was making a fair copy of this chapter while Trollope was off on his first foreign assignment for the Post Office. Trollope's wish that he might have 'the pen of Molière' [12] to describe the pompous Dr Fillgrave's fury at being snubbed by Sir Roger [12] is another private joke, harking back to Trollope's childhood when the Trollope children enacted Molière plays. [➤ *Did He Steal It?*; France.]

The fact that the book was written while Trollope was *en route* to Egypt no doubt accounts for the references to Egyptian life and history, including that to St Anthony Stylites. Young Scatcherd's Christian names constitute a humorous reference to the late King of the French, Louis Philippe, who had fled Paris in 1848 for safety in England and for whom Trollope had some sympathy. (The King had once given an audience to Trollope's mother, Fanny.) Dr Thorne's Christian name, Thomas, may be a tribute to the plot's originator. If the author were thinking of brothers he might have taken the murdered Henry Scatcherd's name from another brother, the deceased Henry, or from the novelist's elder son who had the same name.) The novel also contains Trollope's first of many favourable references to beards, and it may well be that his own beard dates from this trip.

In his *Autobiography* Trollope said that *Doctor Thorne* was the most popular of all his novels. It was also the first to attract attention and republication in America and to be noticed favourably in France. However, there were stirrings in England of what later became a frequent critical reaction: Trollope was writing too much, too quickly and too carelessly. The novel still ranks high among Trollope's achievements, even if many would not accept Michael Sadleir's belief that it was his greatest.

Dogs. Other than horses, dogs are the only animals that occur with any frequency in Trollope's novels, mainly in connection with fox-hunting. In *The American Senator*, Senator Gotobed's ignorance of rural ways is shown when he refers to the hounds as 'dogs' [9]. Although in *Framley Parsonage* Miss Dunstable has a poodle, the breed normally mentioned was the Newfoundland and the dog's name was often 'Neptune' – the name of Fanny Trollope's dog. She used Neptune in her novel *Uncle Walter* and Trollope did

the same in *Dr Wortle's School* [2]. In *The Bertrams* [9] he compares the damp circle a woman makes from shaking the water off her wet dress to that made by a Newfoundland dog when coming out of the water. In the last novel he wrote, *The Land-Leaguers*, there is his final reference, when he says of one character that he 'had not come back to be constantly on the watch, like a Newfoundland dog' [17]. In his essay 'A Walk in a Wood', Trollope refers to his own love of walking with his dog. He admits that if he really wishes to think on a walk, 'I have found it best even to reject the society of a dog.' The manuscript, now in the Taylor Collection at Princeton University, shows that he had originally written 'hard' – 'I have found it hard even to reject the society of a dog' – and then substituted 'best'.

Double Standard. See Women.

Dowagers. In dowagers Trollope found splendid opportunities for combining sensitive and humorous traits in what are otherwise domineering women. Such portraits sometimes resemble those of his spinsters and widows except that dowagers are widows of husbands who were the owners of large estates and were often titled. Normally the title of dowager is used only when the young heir comes of age and marries; thus Lady Eustace is not depicted as a dowager. Trollope's dowagers are usually too dominant over eldest sons who have succeeded to the family estate and title. They are often resentful of a young woman who succeeds as daughter-in-law to their title and to the position of chatelaine.

Lady Lufton in *Framley Parsonage* is Trollope's best portrayal of a dowager. In the end, her great devotion to her son Lord Lufton forces her to accept that Lucy Robarts will become the new Lady Lufton. Mrs Miles in 'The Lady of Launay' resembles Lady Lufton in her attempt to prevent her son marrying a penniless orphan. Mrs Miles's genuine goodness, like Lady Lufton's, resumes play once she accepts her son's decision.

Dowagers could absorb much of the income from a landed estate and their rights to this income together with a dower house were normally derived from their marriage settlements. Thus Lady Fawn has about half of the £3,000 income that her son gets from his estate in *The Eustace Diamonds* and the Honourable Mrs Morton is a great burden on the family estate in *The American Senator*. If there were no dowager, the dower house could be let or loaned and thus Christopher Dale, the squire of Allington, allows his sister-in-law to occupy the Small House.

Trollope's dowagers often have reputations as busybodies, like the Countess of Millborough in *He Knew He Was Right*, or as manipulative women, like the Countess of Desmond in *Castle Richmond*.

Dowry. See Settlements.

Drinks. Along with food, drinks often provide a key to a character or to a setting. Trollope's Irish fiction is full of 'whiskey punch' – made with Irish whiskey, hot water, sugar and lemons – and this is usually a sign of conviviality with a tinge of vulgarity, for example in the short story, 'Father Giles of Ballymoy'. (In his *Autobiography* Trollope remembers his own first encounter with this drink.) Drinking spirits is, however, rarely a good sign in a Trollope novel set outside Ireland. Ladies often complain of the smell: in *The Three Clerks*, when Captain Cuttwater moves in with the Woodwards the smell of gin disturbs his nieces. Gin is also normally encountered in common pubs such as those frequented by Charley Tudor in the same novel. The drink had not shaken off its seventeenth-century reputation and was not considered a genteel beverage; it was a sign of vulgarity. Not surprisingly the moneylender, Stubber, 'smelt of gin' in *Sir Harry Hotspur of Humblethwaite*. Brandy and water, one of Trollope's favourite drinks, particularly when travelling, was perfectly acceptable, but brandy could be dangerous, especially in excess. Sir Henry Harcourt consumes several glasses before deciding to commit suicide [*The Bertrams*, 46]. Curaçao, and other liqueurs when taken too freely, carried with them implications of weakness and degeneracy. They are the favourite tipple of the roué George Hotspur in *Sir Harry Hotspur of Humblethwaite*, along with brandy and seltzer. Trollope has fun with Devonshire's preference for cider over beer in *Rachel Ray*. Trollope also enjoyed beer and his own favourite appears to have been Bass. [➤ Brewers.]

A good example of the way in which Trollope kept up to date with changing tastes is seen when the Duke of Omnium returns from Windsor Castle and drinks some Apollinaris water in *The Prime Minister* [7]. This had been introduced into England by Trollope's old publisher, George Smith, and *The Times* had begun to carry advertisements for it some months before Trollope wrote that chapter [Mullen, 597]. The drink most frequently mentioned is wine.

[► Coffee; Drunkenness.]

Drought, Sir Orlando. A Tory politician who is a close lieutenant of the Tory leader, Daubeny, when he appears in *Phineas Redux*. In *The Prime Minister* he becomes First Lord of the Admiralty in the coalition government even though Glencora, Duchess of Omnium, dislikes him. His conflict with Plantagenet Palliser, then Prime Minister, about the need to build more battleships sounds similar to the disagreement that would finally force Gladstone to resign as Prime Minister in his last government. However, as this happened twelve years after Trollope's death it is a warning to those who try too hard to connect real historical characters with fictional creations. Sir Orlando is also a minor character in *The Way We Live Now*. (The postal surveyor who was Trollope's first superior in Ireland was named James Drought.)

Drummond, Lord. Lord Drummond appears first in *Phineas Redux* [9] as Secretary for War when he resigns from the Tory Cabinet rather than support Daubeny's measure to disestablish the Church of England. He also features in the remaining Palliser novels. He becomes angry that Plantagenet Palliser does not advise the Queen to give him the Garter, which was then given on the advice of the Prime Minister. By the time of *The Duke's Children* [21–2] he has become Tory Prime Minister. In *The American Senator*, he is Foreign Secretary and takes the chair at Senator Gotobed's controversial lecture.

Drunkenness. In Trollope's novels drunkenness is a common theme and is often the cause of male debauchery. It afflicts young men like Burgo Fitzgerald in *Can You Forgive Her?* and George Hotspur in *Sir Harry Hotspur of Humblethwaite*, middle-aged men like Lord Ongar in *The Claverings* and older men like Captain O'Hara in *An Eye for an Eye*. It affects failures like Julius Mackenzie in 'The Spotted Dog' and successful men like Sir Roger Scatcherd in *Doctor Thorne*. It is often the consequence of a low moral state: a 'red nose' is normally the first sign to readers that something is wrong. 'The first approach of a carbuncle on the nose, about the age of thirty,' Trollope points out, 'has stopped many a man from drinking' [*Can You Forgive Her?*, 29]. Like cursing it normally afflicts men, but there is a female drunk in 'The Spotted Dog' and in this short story Trollope fiercely denounces the 'sin': 'There are vices of which we habitually take altogether different views in accordance with the manner in which they are brought under our notice. This vice of drunkenness is often a joke in the mouths of those to whom the thing itself is a horror. Even before our boys we talk of it as being rather funny, though to see one of them funny himself would almost break our hearts.' Trollope's strongest denunciation of drunkenness comes in *Orley Farm* [57]; his graphic description sounds like a hellfire sermon and even concludes with a prayer: 'May God in his mercy ... protect us' from this state.

Trollope points out the obvious truth that drunkenness can determine whether a man succeeds or fails in life, especially in the colonies: in the gold mines of Australia [*John Caldigate*], or in the diamond mines of South Africa [*An Old Man's Love*]. But when Trollope visited America he saw the effects of Utopian teetotalism put into effect through government-enforced prohibition (the 'Maine Laws') and the hypocrisy which resulted. He attacked them in *North America*, and in his American story 'The Two Generals' he referred to Maine as 'that farthest and most strait-laced State of the Union, in which people bind themselves by law to drink neither beer, wine, nor spirits, and all go to bed at nine o'clock'.

[➤ Drinks.]

Dr Wortle's School. Trollope's fortieth novel was written over twenty-two days in April 1879 for serialization in eight parts in *Blackwood's Magazine* between May and December 1880. It was then published by Chapman & Hall in two volumes in January 1881. Trollope received £500.

Dr Jeffrey Wortle is Rector of Bowick where he has established a school mainly to prepare boys for Eton. His assistant is the Reverend Henry Peacocke, an excellent scholar and teacher who has recently returned from America. Peacocke's American-born wife, Ella, is the school matron. Although the Peacockes are popular, they are reclusive. Their position is undermined by gossip about their marriage by an old foe of Wortle, the Hon. Mrs Staniloup. Peacocke is Ella's second husband and they married believing she was a widow. Then her former brother-in-law appears, to blackmail Peacocke as a bigamist because, he says, Ella's first husband is still alive. Peacocke goes to America to make certain that her first husband has died. In the end Peacocke learns his

wife's first husband was dead when they married. (In *Castle Richmond* Lady Fitzgerald's father went to France to search for evidence that her first husband was dead.) Dr Wortle stands by the Peacockes because of his fierce sense of justice and also because he dislikes outsiders questioning his original selection of Henry Peacocke. There is a conventional love plot between Wortle's daughter Mary and a young nobleman at the school, Lord Carstairs.

The novel was written completely 'on location'. Trollope had been lent the rectory at Lowick in Northamptonshire while the rector, his friend W. Lucas Collins who wrote and edited classical works for John Blackwood, was on holiday. There were severe snowstorms throughout the visit and the Trollopes found it difficult to leave the house. Trollope made good use of his enforced stay by writing the novel. He changed Lowick to Bowick but he borrowed many physical aspects of the place, including the school Collins conducted for young men and the lawn tennis court which both the real and the fictional schools had. Collins's real pupils were, however, older than Wortle's fictional ones. Blackwood's son, and a son of another close friend of Trollope, were among the boys who came to 'read' there. Dr Wortle is in no sense a portrait of Lucas Collins. Since the time of Trollope's first biographer, Escott, it has been traditional to see parallels between Dr Wortle and his creator. 'Dr Wortle has the same reputation as Trollope himself for blustering amiability, an imperious manner and a good heart,' wrote Escott. Certainly Dr Wortle's personality [1] is remarkably similar to Trollope's.

Trollope drew on many recollections of his own life for details. He had been sent to a private preparatory school conducted by a clergyman and had sent his two sons to Bradfield, a school started by a clergyman in Berkshire. Trollope had already alluded to the common practice of clergymen taking in a few pupils to provide extra income: a poor curate does this in *Framley Parsonage* and Arthur Wilkinson planned to do so in *The Bertrams*. There is a scene in which a boy is saved from drowning, as in Trollope's own life, an event included in *The Three Clerks*. The novel has a Newfoundland dog called 'Neptune' and in his youth Fanny Trollope, the novelist's mother, had a dog of the same breed and name. The novel even has a brief reference to Trollope's unresolved debate about the correctness of clergymen joining in a fox-hunt. Dr Wortle, like Trollope's last clergyman in *An Old Man's Love*, may not actually ride to hounds but follows them if they just happen to be near where he is riding.

Dr Wortle expresses Trollope's own view that a man should be paid a just rate for his work, but he must also pay a fair price if he wants to obtain good things [➤ Money]. Dr Wortle's friend, the Reverend Mr Puddicombe, has many characteristics of Trollope's father, and the portrait of the bishop with whom Dr Wortle comes into conflict is a good example of Trollope's ability to draw characters convincingly [II]. For the American scenes, Trollope drew on his five trips to the United States. He had visited Washington College in St Louis, Missouri, where the Peacockes meet. (Trollope's host was T. S. Eliot's grandfather.) His dislike of San Francisco is obvious. He had been one of the few recorded Englishmen to denounce this city as the most uninteresting place he had ever visited. He had visited it in 1875 on his way home from his second Australian trip and he described it in the final 'letter' he sent back to England for newspaper publication [➤ *The Tireless Traveler*]. The American character who attempts to blackmail Peacocke is a rather stereotyped Southern adventurer. Here Trollope uses the American South and West, as he uses South Africa in *An Old Man's Love* and Australia in *John Caldigate*, as places where the settled arrangements of English marriages and life do not always pertain.

Dr Wortle's School appeared at a time when Trollope and Victorians in general were starting to examine the nature of marriage. Six weeks before starting the novel he had finished his biographical study of Thackeray, so he was well aware how miserable a man's life could be made when his spouse was confined in a mental asylum. He had also just written an obituary of another close friend, G. H. Lewes, who could not obtain a divorce from his wife and who lived with George Eliot while unable to marry her. In fact close friends like Trollope treated them as if they were married. Trollope knew the price that George Eliot paid. He probably began the novel with the idea of portraying such a union: the first title was 'Mr and Mrs Peacocke'. As the novel began to evolve the focus shifted to the reactions of Dr Wortle – a man like his creator – to such a situation. This is what makes the book still so interesting: the reaction of one good person to the moral dilemmas of others. Mr Peacocke is prepared to live 'in sin' if his wife's first husband really is alive, while she for her part is prepared to leave him. Newspapers are given short shrift, as in *The Warden* and in so many other novels, for sensationalizing issues.

Critics at the time gave the novel a good reception, although his old foe, the *Saturday Review*, sneered that the author was 'as happy ... as Mr Trollope usually is when he does not meddle with things too high for him'. Blackwood had been 'rather alarmed' that the subject of bigamy might offend readers of his Tory magazine and he was pleased that Trollope revealed the explanation so early in the story. A modern critic, Bradford Booth, concluded: 'I do not know that the history of fiction affords another instance of a novel of real merit, running to 85,000 words, having been written in twenty-two days.' Certainly *Dr Wortle's School* is one of the best introductions to Trollope's work.

Duels. When Trollope inserted a duel in his first novel, *The Macdermots of Ballycloran*, he seems to have shared the overwhelming view in the 1840s – although his sentence is very confused – that duels were an absurd and outdated custom [26]. Some of his later novels, for instance *Phineas Finn* and *Lady Anna*, do contain duels, although in *Lady Anna* the duel is only referred to (it had been fought between old Lord Lovel and the father of a woman whom he tricked into marriage in the first years of the nineteenth century [1]). In *Phineas Finn*, set in the 1860s, Lord Chiltern challenges Finn to a duel over Violet Effingham during which Finn is wounded [38].

Throughout Trollope's youth in the 1820s duels were not uncommon and

even the Prime Minister, the Duke of Wellington, fought one. However, in 1844 Prince Albert became a focus of opposition to duelling, particularly in the military, and the practice died out. Duellists had to go to Europe to fight and in *Phineas Finn* they go to Belgium. Despite the change in public opinion Trollope retained a somewhat nostalgic longing for duels as a device that had solved many difficult arguments, a view shared by several of his characters. In *The Struggles of Brown, Jones, and Robinson*, written between 1857 and 1860, the undersized hero, George Robinson, thinks fondly of duels as a way to make himself equal to his enormous rival in love: 'Big as he is ... pistols would make us equal. But the huge ox has no sense of chivalry' [6]. In the 1860s attitudes began to change. When young women like Lily Dale are jilted, outraged male relatives and friends think back on the time when they could have 'called out' the man who jilts her [*The Small House at Allington*, 27]. Perhaps Trollope's strongest defence of duelling comes in *The Claverings*, written in 1864, the year after he had finished writing *The Small House at Allington*. 'The old way was barbarous certainly, and unreasonable, but there was a satisfaction in it that has been often wanting since the use of pistols went out of fashion among us' [28]. Will Belton in *The Belton Estate*, written in 1865, is furious with a rival and 'thought with an intense regret of the laws of modern society which forbid duelling' [14]. But when Lizzie Eustace tells her cousin in *The Eustace Diamonds*, written between 1869 and 1870, that she has been jilted he can only moan, 'I will not fight him, that is with pistols ... public opinion is now so much opposed to that kind of thing' [23]. By the 1870s duels seemed absurd and one military man in *Ayala's Angel*, written in 1878, refuses even to accept a challenge [35–6].

Englishmen were fascinated that duels survived in America and references are made to this, for instance in 'Miss Ophelia Gledd', set in Boston.

The Duke's Children. Trollope's thirty-ninth novel and the sixth and last in the Palliser series, it was written between 2 May and 29 October 1876. It was first serialized in *All the Year Round* between 4 October 1879 and 14 July 1880 and published by Chapman & Hall in three volumes in May 1880. Trollope received £1,400, but when Chapman & Hall's accountant told him that the company had lost £120 on the book he wrote to them, 'I cannot allow that. It is the first account I have ever seen of one of my own books. I will repay to the Company the amount lost.'

The Prime Minister, the volume preceding it in the Palliser series, had been an essentially conservative book because the new forces threatening traditional society were defeated. *The Duke's Children* takes a view closer to Trollope's own: the traditional aristocratic world of the Pallisers, embodied in the Duke of Omnium, can only be preserved by accepting changes that, because they are not forced, may come slowly and peacefully. Trollope started this novel within a few days of completing his *Autobiography*. Thus the perspective of an older man who watches the world change about him – the perspective of the Duke of Omnium himself – fits in with the author's own mood at the time.

The Duke's Children as published suffered larger cuts than any of Trollope's previous fiction. In the past he had reluctantly removed an unnecessary chapter from *The Three Clerks*, but he rightly resisted the absurd suggestion that he should make massive cuts in *Barchester Towers*. It might be thought odd that almost two decades later he should agree to such a request here. However, Trollope had been shaken by criticism of the book's predecessor, *The Prime Minister* – particularly that in the *Spectator* which pronounced it vulgar and wondered if the writer's skills were fading. This review had appeared while he was in the middle of writing *The Duke's Children* and was probably the underlying reason why he agreed to cut so much: he had intended that this novel should be as long as the earlier one and be published in four volumes. However, it was three years before serialization began, one of the longest delays between writing and publishing experienced by Trollope. (There was a far longer delay with *An Eye for an Eye*, but Trollope rightly did not regard that as a major novel.)

The novel has the simplest plot of all the Palliser books. It describes how the widowed duke deals with his three children and eventually accepts the marriages of two of them. Everything else flows about this central plot. The reader quickly discovers another difference from the previous volumes in the series, for the first chapter bears the title, 'When the Duchess was Dead'. Twice before, the deaths of spouses had occurred between novels so that a new plot could be developed: John Bold expired so that his widow [➤ Harding, Eleanor] could be pursued by a trio of suitors in *Barchester Towers*, and Mary Finn had to die so that Phineas could resume his adventures in *Phineas Redux*. But Mary Finn did not dominate a chapter, let alone a novel, and John Bold, though important, was soon overtaken by events and other characters.

The Duchess of Omnium – the former Lady Glencora Palliser – had dominated most of the previous Palliser books. Shortly before beginning *The Duke's Children* Trollope had written in his *Autobiography* that the duchess was the only one of his female characters who might be remembered in the twentieth century. Trollope knew that the glow from the vibrant duchess often obscured the stolid duke. It is only in his loneliness and isolation that the essential nobility of his character emerges as clearly to the reader as it undoubtedly had already done to Trollope himself. Only a few details of her death emerge in the novel and the event occurs virtually 'off-stage'. This is not as strange as it might appear: Trollope treated death scenes very carefully to avoid wallowing in Dickensian emotion and here he may well have found it too painful to describe. Yet the duchess haunts this book and her unseen presence is symbolized in her burial outside the great house at Matching where so many scenes in the earlier novels had been set. The duke regards her memory as 'holy' and keeps her name to himself, to be pronounced only in private whispers: 'Cora, Cora' [15]. His gift of her ring to his daughter-in-law at the end of the novel allows the duchess to bless the match even from her grave [72].

Trollope had originally planned to call the novel 'The Ex-Prime Minister' to connect it to *The Prime Minister* at the end of which the Duke of Omnium had resigned office. In one sense this title would have been better, for the main character is always the duke himself. His old personality is still present and his shyness, his strong sense of duty and his passion for justice still make him an unhappy man, often at war with himself. Yet now a new aspect of his personality comes to the fore: his love for his children makes him much more demonstrative. When his son takes him to a club, the duke is so overcome with emotion that he longs to kiss him and he does eventually kiss the son's future wife, not only on the forehead but also on the lips. [➤ Fathers and Sons.] His sense of justice does force him to acknowledge that he is wrong in his feud with his wife's old friend, Mrs Finn [Madame Max Goesler]. Because there is relatively little about his political work in this novel, we can see him for the first time as a man rather than as a politician. Anyone who reads *The Duke's Children* carefully will find Palliser a much more engaging character.

The duke's basic problem is that his children are all diverging from his standards, but 'the endeavour to be just was the study of his life' [7]. The antics of his younger son, Lord Gerald, at university (and Trollope is confused about whether he is at Oxford or Cambridge) and his gambling are not really important to the novel, although they provide some amusing dialogue and one marvellous example of a silly young man's letter written in slang [60]. The real focus is the heir, Lord Silverbridge, and his sister, Lady Mary Palliser. Each desires to marry someone the duke does not consider suitable. (Trollope used this plot just over two years after finishing *The Duke's Children* in *Marion Fay*, which he began in 1878.) Silverbridge has already caused his father grief by being sent down from Oxford. A far greater grief was his rejection of the family's traditional Whig allegiance. In his conversion to Conservatism, Silverbridge was only doing what many real Whig aristocrats would do in the next decade. It is not in fact quite clear why Silverbridge does this, though he jokes with his father that as he is a fool he therefore should be a Conservative. However, his talk of the dangers of 'communists', although it may sound absurd, is quite accurate for the term then referred to the horrors of the Paris Commune only a few years earlier. At the end of the book, Silverbridge returns to the family's traditional political allegiance.

With the romance between Lord Silverbridge and the American girl, Isabel Boncassen, Trollope reached the summit of something he had been exploring since the beginning of the 1860s: Anglo-American marriages. Less than six months before he started writing, Trollope had returned from his fifth and final trip to America. He not only knew America extremely well but helped his many American friends who visited London. Trollope was, of course, fashioning a topical plot in having an American marry into the aristocracy; it was only two years since Jenny Jerome from New York had married the son of the Duke of Marlborough. Even so, when Winston Churchill, the son of that marriage, came to read *The Duke's Children* late in his life, he found the duke 'a poop' [Mullen, 481–3].

In the 1870s Americans were flocking to London, and Americans already there, such as Trollope's friend Kate Field, attacked the latest arrivals as 'shoddy' and *nouveaux riches* – people who thought that 'fine feathers make fine birds'. Kate Field's description is echoed in Trollope's phrase about a 'savageness of self-assertion' [33]. This type of American was portrayed in *The Way We Live Now*. The Boncassen family of *The Duke's Children* differs from the Americans Kate Field attacked. Ezekiel Boncassen 'had the reputation of being the most learned man in the States', as did Trollope's American friend, the historian and diplomat J. L. Motley.

Boncassen is a complete contrast to Senator Elias Gotobed in *The American Senator*, a novel finished less than a year before. All the two men share is having as first names those of Old Testament prophets [➤ Names, Origin of]. Where Gotobed had been bumptious and boastful of American 'institutions', Boncassen is quiet and refined, absorbed in his research in the British Museum. The contrast is made plain when Gotobed turns up at lunch at the Boncassens'. Gotobed is now the United States' Minister to the Court of St James – there were no ambassadors until 1893 – and we find him at lunch, still boasting, this time about American tomatoes and squashes, a conversation that harks back to one Trollope had had with James Russell Lowell about the difference between English and American peaches. (Poor Gotobed's political career must have suffered a sudden setback as he has passed from being the most important senator to being a minister in less than a year. Sending Gotobed to London, when his lecture there had caused him to flee for his life, seems somewhat 'undiplomatic'.) Boncassen, unlike Gotobed, is welcomed among the aristocracy and the Duke of Omnium himself admires his American guest.

It was a standard assertion in almost all Victorian writings that Americans' speech had a nasal twang (Americans replied that the English could not pronounce an 'H'). Speech is thus an easy marker to Trollope's attitude towards the Boncassen family: the mother, an amiable but silly woman, has a strong nasal twang; the father has only a slight one; Isabel has none at all. Isabel is remarkable for her beauty, but also for her discretion. She knows that American girls are allowed more freedom than their English sisters, but she is careful to observe English rules. 'When the discrepancies are small, then they have to be attended to' [➤ Women]. When Silverbridge defends the manners of American ladies, his words are quite similar to Trollope's own in 'Miss Ophelia Gledd'. Isabel imitates Lucy Robarts in *Framley Parsonage* by agreeing to marry the young lord only if his stoical parent makes the request. Once the duke does so Isabel is pleased to marry 'among the nobles of the greatest land under the sun' [47].

Silverbridge's sister, Lady Mary, provides a contrast to Isabel. Although both complain about being women, Lady Mary finds her social position a burden and likes to attack the notion of aristocracy. She wants to marry 'beneath' her to a 'nobody', Frank Tregear, the younger son of a Cornish squire. The duchess had encouraged this romance with the remarkably 'handsome and manly' Tregear. For the duke it reawakens dreadful echoes of his wife's infatuation with the 'abnormally handsome' Burgo Fitzgerald. ('Abnormal' is a much stronger epithet than any used about Burgo in *Can You Forgive Her?*, but then memory often

increases rancour.) The duke's opposition to this marriage is far greater than his opposition to Silverbridge's. Yet in spite of it, Lady Mary gets her way in the end. The duke reluctantly accepts Tregear by the 'old-fashioned' gesture of drinking a private toast of wine with him at dinner. This is exactly the gesture that Trollope lovingly described almost two decades earlier as one of his own favourite customs [*Framley Parsonage*, 17].

The duke was in the same position in regard to his daughter's marriage as Archdeacon Grantly was to his son's in *The Last Chronicle of Barset*. In both cases a proud father saw his child about to marry someone from the lowest ranks of their own world. (Trollope used the same basic conflict – a parent or guardian from the nobility or gentry opposing a young person's marriage plans – in *The Small House at Allington, Framley Parsonage, An Eye for an Eye, Lady Anna, The Last Chronicle of Barset, Sir Harry Hotspur of Humblethwaite* and *Marion Fay*.) The duke's attitude is not just snobbery or class prejudice. He is constantly analysing his feelings, which spring from his deep-seated belief that the aristocracy has a duty, a duty to govern. (This was, of course, Trollope's own view.) The duke knows that there are vile and contemptible aristocrats: Earl Grex and his gambler son, Lord Percival, are perfect examples. Even so, he tries to promote a match between Silverbridge and Grex's daughter, Lady Mabel Grex. The hatred between Grex and his son – reminiscent of the De Courcys in the Barsetshire novels – is the exact opposite of the love between the duke and Silverbridge. The *Spectator* was right in its review when it called this novel a 'dramatic essay... upon the aristocratic principle, in its relation to politics, society, and morality'.

However, there is relatively little about politics in this last Palliser novel. The duke is not actively involved until the very end when he agrees to return to the Cabinet as Lord President of the Council. (An example of the way in which Trollope's political touches are often a few decades behind reality: in the early nineteenth century former prime ministers often did return to a Cabinet in an inferior post, but by the 1870s this had stopped, only to be revived again during the First World War.) The duke's concept of politics and of an MP as the 'guardian of [his] fellow-countrymen' is expressed in his moving letter to Silverbridge after he has been elected a Tory MP [16].

Trollope thought a great deal about the writing of his novels and no doubt his recent work on his *Autobiography*, as well as his reading for his unwritten history of English fiction, stimulated these reflections. In *The Duke's Children* he remarks that style for the writer is 'not the wares he has to take to the market, but the vehicle in which they may be carried' [26]. At the start of a chapter called 'In Medias Res', there is an 'authorial intrusion' in a debate on whether a novelist should plunge into a story or first give the reader the basic background, the setting and the characters [9]. Trollope, of course, normally preferred the latter method and returned to this subject in another discussion with the reader at the opening of *Is He Popenjoy?* which he wrote in the following year. *The Duke's Children* is also an excellent example of the way in which he handled what he called 'epistle craft' in his novels; this

book is full of different types of letters, from the Duke's cold reply in the third person to Tregear to Lord Gerald's jaunty letter to his elder brother.

Most of the comedy in *The Duke's Children* centres on Major Tifto, an adventurer who leads Silverbridge into losing the colossal sum of £70,000 on a horse race. (The vastness of this amount is well seen when we remember that it is almost exactly the amount which Trollope records at the end of his *Autobiography* as his total earnings from all his writings, if *The Duke's Children* is added to that total.) Tifto's title of major, we are told, is not a British one but stems from his taking part in the latest Carlist war in Spain: this series of civil wars had been attracting British adventurers for much of Trollope's lifetime. [➤ Military.] Tifto and Silverbridge are both members of the Beargarden Club, which first appeared in *The Way We Live Now*. Many of its delightful 'middle-aged young men' also reappear in their clubhouse, most notably Dolly Longstaffe, who also wants to marry Isabel Boncassen. His pursuit of her reminds one of Bertie Stanhope's pursuit of Eleanor Bold in *Barchester Towers*. Again, if we look at the *Autobiography* we find a key to Dolly's return. Trollope commented in its final pages: 'Dolly Longstaffe is, I think, very good.'

Tifto is an MFH, but just as Trollope contrasts the two types of peers in the duke and Earl Grex, or the two types of Americans in Boncassen and Gotobed, so he brings back his favourite MFH, Lord Chiltern, to contrast him with the rogue, Tifto [➤ Fox-hunting]. Many other characters from the earlier Palliser novels are present, including politicians such as Phineas Finn and Sir Timothy Beeswax. Finn's wife comes into conflict with the duke over Lady Mary's romance, but when all of them meet in Austria the old friendship is restored.

As always, Trollope enjoys various private jokes in this novel although apparently not as many as in some of his earlier books. The brief appearance of an American poet from the far West, Ezekiel Sevenkings, probably recalls Trollope's entertainment of just such a figure, Cincinnatus 'Joaquin' Miller, the so-called 'Oregon Byron', three years before. His own experiences, too, are brought into play. The account of the misery of canvassing in a parliamentary election draws heavily on Trollope's own unhappy experience in Beverley [55]. The comment that nothing requires more justice than the treatment that a father gives a son echoes the novelist's own generosity and deep love for both his sons, Harry and Fred, so evident in the last decade of his life [7].

Since *The Duke's Children* is the last Palliser novel, it naturally invites comparison with *The Last Chronicle of Barset*. The book cannot equal its predecessor in pathos and moving incidents, nor is it as great a novel. Of course it is not obvious, either in the title or in the text, that it marks the end of the series and Trollope could easily have added another volume tracing the Palliser world if he had wished. Yet strangely the two novels do resemble one another in their central characters: the poor clergyman who has little in life and the rich duke who has had too much are constantly at war with themselves in their efforts to find 'justice'. Thus, like so many of Trollope's greatest novels, *The Duke's*

Children portrays the inner torments of the central character. Many readers will echo the comment of the review in the *Nation* published in Isabel Boncassen's native city, New York: 'No one ever, we fancy, read a novel of his without wishing that he might soon write another.'

Dumbello, Lady.
See Grantly Family.

Dumbello, (Gustavus) Lord. Lord Dumbello appears in *Framley Parsonage*, where, as Viscount Dumbello, he eventually marries Griselda Grantly. He comes into a great fortune when he succeeds his father as Marquis of Hartletop. He takes great pride in his possession of a beautiful wife and it is clear that he regards her as just that: a possession. He has no other ambition than 'to be led about as the senior lacquey in his wife's train' [*The Small House at Allington*, 17]. At Courcy Castle, when Lady Dumbello makes her stunning entrance, everyone is in raptures except for Lord Dumbello, although 'a spark of pleasure actually beamed in his eye'. By the time he is mentioned in *The Last Chronicle of Barset* he has become the Marquis of Hartletop and has succeeded to his great estate in Shropshire. Through his mother he is connected to the Pallisers and by his marriage to the Grantlys. [For his wife Griselda ➤ Grantly Family; for his mother, ➤ Hartletop, Marchioness of. ➤ also Aristocracy.]

Dunstable, Martha. One of those outspoken spinsters that Trollope delighted in portraying, Martha Dunstable makes her first appearance in the Barsetshire novels in *Doctor Thorne*. She is about thirty and her curls show that she is not up-to-date in her fashion, but, as she says, 'they'll pass muster when they are done up with bank notes'. She is the great heiress of the 'Oil of Lebanon' fortune, a fact which allows Trollope to criticize popular patent medicine, whose advertisements he especially detested. Martha Dunstable is a woman of great cleverness and is well able to fend off the fortune-hunters who besiege her. She eventually marries Dr Thorne and as Mrs Thorne acquires a famous estate in Barsetshire in *Framley Parsonage*. She reappears in *The Last Chronicle of Barset*.

E

Eames, John. A young civil servant who is in love with Lily Dale in *The Small House at Allington.* Trollope uses many memories of his own youthful days as a Post Office clerk in London in depicting Eames's adventures both in his office and in his boarding-house. Eames is the son of a gentleman ruined by a foolish attempt to become a farmer (as Trollope's father had failed). 'Johnny' Eames is Trollope's most memorable portrayal of how a hobbledehoy turns into a mature man and successful civil servant. Eames is a cousin of Mrs Crawley and this relationship allows him to play a central role in *The Last Chronicle of Barset* when he helps Josiah Crawley. Many contemporary readers implored Trollope to allow Eames to be successful in his desire to marry Lily Dale. Eames has several similarities with an earlier character based partly on Trollope's youthful days in London: Charley Tudor in *The Three Clerks.*

East Anglia. Trollope was appointed Post Office Surveyor for the Eastern District at the end of 1859 and took up residence in Hertfordshire. Almost all of East Anglia was in his district and he acquired a familiarity with it, much as he had come to know the West Country which he used to create Barsetshire. His fox-hunting, particularly with the Essex Hunt, increased his knowledge of the area. Trollope used East Anglian settings for several novels. A small Cambridgeshire squire is well depicted in *Can You Forgive Her?*, and the same novel has a good portrait of a jolly Norfolk farmer as well as of life in the Norfolk seaside town of Yarmouth. *The Belton Estate* combines his knowledge of the West Country with an excellent portrait of a Norfolk farmer. *John Caldigate,* set mainly in Cambridgeshire but with some scenes in Suffolk, makes many allusions to the effect of the landscape on the people. Most of the countryside scenes in *The Way We Live Now* are set in Suffolk, while part of 'Christmas at Thompson Hall' is set in Essex. [For Trollope's use of place-names in the area, ➤ under *The Claverings.*]

Editors. In *The Claverings* Harry Clavering meets an editor and sees such men as 'influential people, who had the world very much under their feet, – being, as he conceived, afraid of no men, while other men are very much afraid of them' [8]. In *Phineas Redux* newspaper editors are portrayed as 'self-willed, arrogant, and stiff-necked' [27]. Editors seldom received favourable treatment in Trollope's fiction in spite of his generally friendly relations with them in his literary career. The editor, Quintus Slide, who appears in many of the Palliser novels, is a thoroughly disreputable demagogue. In *Is He Popenjoy?* there is a low-church paper with an 'elaborate opposition to ritual'; it was edited by the appropriately named Mr Grease, 'a very pious man who had long striven, but hitherto in vain, to get orders' [10]. (In *Miss Mackenzie*, written some eight years before this, an Evangelical curate used a church paper to discredit Miss Mackenzie's family after he had been defeated in his bid for Miss Mackenzie's hand. In that case, however, the editor was not involved.) In *The Way We Live Now* Trollope depicts three editors and their involvement in the political and literary intrigues of the day. However, in *Cousin Henry* (1879) the editor of the local paper plays an important role in bringing to a head the truth about the will. In *Thackeray* Trollope reflected on Thackeray's performance as the first editor of the *Cornhill Magazine* and said he lacked the necessary ingredient of being 'hard-hearted'. Trollope's own performance as editor of *Saint Pauls* was not much better, as may be seen in six short stories published as *An Editor's Tales* in which he describes some of his own experiences. His early desire to be an editor is revealed in 'The Panjandrum'.

[➤ Journalists; Newspapers.]

An Editor's Tales. This, the fourth collection of Trollope's short stories, was published in one volume by Alexander Strahan in June 1870 at 12s. Trollope was pleased with Strahan's work and later referred to it as 'a handsome volume'. The collection's six stories had first been published in *Saint Pauls* magazine. Trollope received £150 for the book and, with the original payment from the magazine, made a total of £378. These stories discussed literary life in London and 'professed to give an editor's experience of his dealings with contributors'. They are among his most autobiographical stories, especially 'The Panjandrum'. In his *Autobiography* he wrote: 'I do not think that there is a single incident in the book which could bring back to any one concerned the memory of a past event. And yet there is not an incident in it the outline of which was not presented to my mind by the remembrance of some fact . . .' The six, with the dates of their original publication, are: 'The Turkish Bath' (October 1869); 'Mary Gresley' (November 1869); 'Josephine de Montmorenci' (December 1869); 'The Panjandrum' (January, February 1870); 'The Spotted Dog' (March, April 1870); and 'Mrs Brumby' (May 1870). The stories are among the best he ever wrote.

Effingham, Violet.
See Chiltern, Lady.

Egypt. Trollope was sent by the Post Office to Egypt in 1858 to negotiate a postal agreement. The country was then part of the Ottoman Empire and was ruled by an hereditary viceroy. Some of Trollope's experiences there are described in his *Autobiography* and Escott, his first biographer, supplements this with additional information from the official who dealt with Trollope. Trollope finished *Doctor Thorne* in Egypt and that novel has several small and amusing allusions to the country. He started *The Bertrams* while he was in Egypt and set some chapters there. He does not portray the country in a favourable light, particularly in his description of the way Englishmen were beset by beggars at the

Pyramids. Two short stories, 'An Un-protected Female at the Pyramids' and 'George Walker at Suez', are also set there and confirm his dislike. He visited Egypt again in 1875 on his second trip to Australia. In one of the travel articles he wrote for syndication in English newspapers he admitted that his earlier opinion, that there would never be a Suez Canal, had been proved wrong. (Work on the canal was finished in 1869.) [➤ *The Tireless Traveler*.] In the last months of his life, Trollope was greatly worried about increasing British involvement in Egypt to secure the Suez Canal, by then vital for British communication with India and Australia.

Elections. In Trollope's time elections were colourful, boisterous and sometimes violent affairs. Balloting could take several days and elections were not held on the same day throughout the country. Men registered their votes by calling out the name of their candidate, often in a public place. As the century wore on some places allowed voting to take place inside special structures or buildings. Because of their dramatic potential, elections occur frequently in Trollope's fiction. Dickens's famous description of the election at Eatanswill in *The Pickwick Papers* gave a highly unfavourable impression of the way in which elections were conducted, and at times Trollope's view of elections seemed almost as critical in spite of his generally favourable view of the House of Commons. Even so, Trollope strongly opposed a secret or written ballot which was only introduced in 1872.

A consistent theme in Trollope's depiction of elections is his distaste for the canvassing which was so much a part of them. This is particularly the case after he experienced it as a parliamentary candidate in Beverley in 1868. His revulsion is best seen in *Ralph the Heir* and *The Duke's Children*. In the latter novel he wrote that there was nothing 'more disagreeable, more squalid, more revolting to the sense' [55]. He had already shown a distaste for the way in which elections were conducted in *Doctor Thorne* and *Can You Forgive Her?* The latter novel shows how important publicans were in elections, while the influence of clergymen in elections is demonstrated in *Rachel Ray* and in *The Duke's Children*. The role of their ecclesiastical rivals, the Dissenters, is seen in *Ralph the Heir*. The bribing of voters was quite common in Victorian elections, but excessive bribery could force a new election, as in *Phineas Redux*.

Great land-owning peers had considerable influence in elections throughout Trollope's lifetime and in *Phineas Finn* the hero is first brought into the Commons through the influence of an Irish peer. He then obtains an English seat through the support of an English earl. Peers, however, had to exercise their influence with some restraint as to use it was technically illegal; in *The Duke's Children* Plantagenet Palliser gives up his electoral control over his 'pocket borough'. Trollope's portrayal of elections was partly coloured by his fury that he could not vote in them because he was a civil servant, but he always took a great interest in them – so much so that on a visit to Chicago in 1861 he was turned out of a polling station with 'some tumult' when he paid too much attention to what was going on.

It is helpful to remember that in Trollope's day, while Parliaments could sit for up to seven years, party control over MPs was much less strong than now and governments could fall much more easily, thereby forcing an election. By-elections were more frequent than at present because an MP had to resign and seek re-election if he accepted a place in the Cabinet or many other positions in government. Also more MPs were sons of peers and when they succeeded to their titles they had to resign, thereby causing yet more by-elections. Although Trollope was a strong Liberal and sometimes assisted friends who were Liberal candidates at elections (including his fellow novelist, Thomas Hughes), the elections in his novels have a reasonable share of Tory victories. [➤ Peerage; Politics.]

Eliot, George [Cross, née Evans, Mary Ann] (1819–80). Trollope met George Eliot through her companion, G. H. Lewes, in 1860. After their first meeting she wrote that Trollope 'made us like him very much by his straightforward, wholesome *Wesen* [personality]'. He became a frequent guest in their home. Through her and Lewes he met the Russian novelist Turgenev, as well as Thomas Carlyle. She was a 'Blackwood writer' and by 1860 she was famous for her *Scenes of Clerical Life* and *Adam Bede*. (He thought this novel her best: it would 'be in the hands of our grandchildren'; there is an amusing reference to it in *The Eustace Diamonds* [34].) In the year of their meeting, *The Mill on the Floss* appeared. Superficially their friendship seems odd, as she is often represented as the pure free-thinking intellectual and Trollope as the boisterous fox-hunter

and loyal Anglican. Much of this is due to caricatures of both writers by their publicists and supporters. Trollope accepted her relationship with Lewes, called her Lewes's 'wife' and referred to her as 'Mrs Lewes' [➤ *The Belton Estate*]. She was pleased with the deep friendship that developed between Lewes and Trollope. His attitude towards their relationship was summed up in a letter to Kate Field when she asked for information about George Eliot after her death for an article she was writing: 'In truth she was one whose private life should be left in privacy – as may be said of all who have achieved fame by literary merits.'

Although George Eliot worried that Trollope's retirement from the Post Office would lead him into 'excessive writing', she admired his work and was influenced by him. She told another novelist, 'I am not at all sure, that, but for Anthony Trollope, I should ever have planned my studies on so extensive a scale for *Middlemarch*, or that I should ... have persevered with it to the close' [➤ *Doctor Thorne*]. She envied Trollope's discipline in writing but was not uncritical. Of Emily Hotspur's love for her wicked cousin in *Sir Harry Hotspur of Humblethwaite*, she wrote: 'Men are fond of that sort of dog-like attachment.' She praised *Rachel Ray* for its 'subtleties of art' and wrote of Trollope's fiction that 'people are breathing good bracing air in reading them ... the books are filled with belief in goodness without the slightest tinge of maudlin. They are like pleasant public gardens, where people go for amusement, & whether they think of it or not, get health as well.'

Trollope wrote of George Eliot,

'You perhaps know how I love and admire her.' He described her as 'among my dearest and most intimate friends'. In his 1869 short story, 'Josephine de Montmorenci', Trollope made several allusions to George Eliot and even referred to her 'feminine metaphysics'. In his *Autobiography* he placed her first among living writers and, in his lifetime, second only to his beloved Thackeray, but he was not uncritical: her defect was that 'she struggles too hard to do work that shall be excellent. She lacks ease.' If in Wilkie Collins's novels there was nothing but plot, in hers 'there is no plot'. He considered this got worse with her later novels. He disliked *Daniel Deronda* as 'trying' and 'all wrong in art'; she was 'striving for effects which she does not produce'. He admitted that there were some passages that he had to read three times to understand. He had told her on the publication of *Romola*, 'Do not fire too much over the heads of your readers.' She was much helped in this novel by Trollope's brother Tom, who was also a close friend of hers.

Emigration. Emigration from the British Isles was one of the main features of nineteenth-century life: between 1815 and 1901, 12,327,000 people left United Kingdom ports for America or the colonies. As a youth Trollope had experienced some of the bitter effects associated with emigration when his mother and sisters suddenly went to America for three years. He was to feel them a second time when his younger son, Frederic, emigrated to Australia. In his wife's family a sister went to Australia, one nephew to the United States and another to Peru. Trollope's travel books, *North America, Australia and New Zealand* and *South Africa*, were intended not only to examine life in these new parts of 'the English world' but to serve as guides for prospective emigrants. He had also witnessed the mass emigration from Ireland during the great famine of the 1840s and movingly described the departure of a train filled with Irish emigrants in *Castle Richmond* [32]. The individual human story is well developed in his short stories, such as 'The Journey to Panama', 'Catherine Carmichael' and 'Returning Home'. Several novels feature characters who emigrate as a means to begin a new life, such as Alaric Tudor in *The Three Clerks*, Lucius Mason in *Orley Farm* and George Vavasor in *Can You Forgive Her?*. This plot line first occurs in *Doctor Thorne* when the unfortunate Mary Scatcherd leaves for America with her hardware dealer to become 'the worthy wife of a good husband, and the happy mother of many children' [*Doctor Thorne*, 2]. Such emigration is most conspicuously the case in *Lady Anna*, in which Lady Anna and her husband go to Australia, but Trollope never carried out his intention to follow their fortunes in a later novel. *John Caldigate*, however, does give a wonderful insight into emigration to Australia and shows what made a successful emigrant, while *Harry Heathcote of Gangoil* describes emigrants' lives in rural Australia. Although Trollope's fiction often shows the sadness involved in emigration, he shared the common Victorian belief that it was a good thing, especially in providing new opportunities for poorer people. 'Emigration, and especially emigration from England,' he wrote in the late 1860s, 'has been God's ordained means of populating the world' [Mullen, 537].

Trollope's library contained dozens of pamphlets about emigration.

[➤ English World; New Zealand.]

Emilius, The Rev. Joseph. Emilius is a Bohemian Jew, born Yosef Mealyus, of mysterious origins who has been converted to Christianity and has become a Church of England clergyman with Evangelical overtones. When he first appears in *The Eustace Diamonds*, some think him the greatest preacher in London. Trollope, with his dislike of sermons, did not mean this as a compliment. 'He was a dark, hookey-nosed, well-made man, with an exuberance of greasy hair ... [with a] squint' [*The Eustace Diamonds*, 73]. (Using a squint to mark a distasteful Evangelical clergyman was a device also used by Trollope in *Miss Mackenzie*, when he describes the Reverend Jeremiah Maguire.) In *Phineas Redux*, Emilius, by then married to Lady Eustace, is shown to be far worse than a fortune-hunter when he murders Mr Bonteen.

In Victorian Britain there were several prominent Jewish converts, like the Reverend Joseph Wolff and the Reverend Ridley Hershell, who had become well-known preachers [Mullen, 485]. Trollope has another Evangelical convert Jewish clergyman, the Reverend Joseph Groschut, in *Is He Popenjoy?*; he also is a disgraceful character who gets into trouble with a farmer's daughter.

Engineers. Engineering was a conspicuous example of one of the new professions Trollope used to provide employment for young men in his novels. Engineers, or civil engineers – the adjective was used to distinguish them from military engineers – were among the most important men in England and were the creators of much of the progress that most Victorians admired. Their handiwork was seen in expanding cities, in industries, public services, buildings, railways and shipping. Some people did not think that engineers could be considered as 'gentlemen' any more than could civil servants. One character sneers: 'Civil engineers were only tradesmen of an upper class, tradesmen with intellects' [*Orley Farm*, 2]. However, in *The Claverings* Trollope has Harry Clavering, who is by birth and education a gentleman, become an engineer and marry an engineer's daughter. The novel also shows how engineers were trained. (Almost half a century later Trollope's grandson wrote from his Australian house, 'Clavering', to tell his widowed grandmother that he was becoming an engineer and was to marry the daughter of the man under whom he had studied.) Trollope illustrates the lives of engineers in the West Indies in 'Aaron Dunn', in America in 'The Courtship of Susan Bell' and in the military through Captain Bernard Dale in *The Small House at Allington* and Jack Neville in *An Eye for an Eye*. In *Castle Richmond*, engineers play a vital role in relief work in the Irish famine. Trollope's work in laying out postal routes and his concern for better transport must have brought him into contact with many engineers in Ireland and England. The use of engineers as characters in his novels provides a good example of how Trollope, in spite of his identification with the older professions such as the clergy and the law, kept up with developments in his own times.

English World. The 'English world'

was the term Trollope used to describe the settled colonies and the United States, 'the greatest British colony of all' [*The Tireless Traveler*]. This 'world', united by race, culture and, most importantly, language, was more important to him than the Empire, united through a common allegiance to the Crown. It was a vehicle for human progress. In *Australia and New Zealand* he wrote: 'We may probably take the language spoken as the truest indication of the influence of nationality and the justest source of national pride. From our little island we have sent forth a people speaking English who are spreading themselves over all the world. It is a much greater boast than that of ruling dependencies on which the sun never sets.' In *The Fixed Period* the Britannulists, who had revolted against the Crown, ask a visiting English peer, '"If we be not foreigners, what are we, my lord?" "Englishmen, of course," said he. "What else? don't you talk English?" "So do the Americans, my lord," ... "Our language is spreading itself over the world, and is no sign of nationality"' [5].

Trollope was never an imperialist in the sense of Rudyard Kipling, for his views had been formed in the 1830s and 1840s, not in the 1870s onwards, and he placed a great value on the Anglo-American bond. In *The West Indies* he wrote, 'We Britishers have a noble mission' which was to spread 'civilization, commerce, and education'. However, Trollope – like other Liberals – found that colonial problems grew in difficulty with the growth in the number of colonies. When in 1877 he was in South Africa he told Sir Theophilus Shepstone, who had recently added the Transvaal to the British

Crown: 'That the thing done has been infinitely for the advantage of the country, – Dutch, English, and native, – there can I think be no doubt. The difficult question is this. If it be our duty to save this or another country from ruin by our money, by our arms, and by our energy, when is that duty to stop? One is tempted to say of every annexation; – that is good; but now let us stop. But when the next case comes we do not stop, and it may be that at last we shall stretch our hands too far.'

In his short story 'Returning Home', Trollope gave a warning that the creation of this 'English world' was not without its drawbacks. He accepted it as a fact of history that as 'it is the destiny of our race to spread itself over the wide face of the globe, it is well that there should be something to gild and paint the outward face of that lot which so many are called upon to choose'. That lot, as portrayed in this story, was tragic and he admitted that living outside England was not a choice he would wish to make: life in England was exciting enough. It is also interesting that the means he chose to overthrow the evil regime of compulsory euthanasia in Britannula was not a popular revolution but the arrival of a Royal Navy gunboat from London.

[► Canada; Emigration; India; *An Old Man's Love*; Patriotism; *The West Indies and the Spanish Main*.]

Entails. In several Trollope novels entails play an important part, especially in *Ralph the Heir* and *Mr Scarborough's Family*. One lady's view of them in the latter novel is that of most people today: 'On the subject of entail her ideas were misty...' [48]. The laws governing them dated from an Act of Parliament in the reign of Edward I and were extremely complicated. Entail ensured that property stayed within a family and descended in a prescribed order. Normally property went to the eldest legitimate male child (primogeniture) and his eldest legitimate male child and so on. Failing a legitimate son the descent was as specified in the entail, normally through other legitimate males, for instance younger brothers, nephews or cousins.

In *The Vicar of Bullhampton*, for example, two male cousins discuss the confusing terms of the entail on a family estate [44]. It was set up by the cousins' grandfather and goes from father to son or, where there is no son living, to brother and then on to his son for three generations only. The third generation male, with whom the entail ended, would, if he married, have to re-start it in his will, if he wanted the entail to continue. If he did not marry and did not give the property away in his will, the provision in the original settlement would apply and the property would go to the nearest relative, regardless of sex.

When an estate was put in entail no part of it could be alienated by gift or sale. Each generation enjoyed a life interest in the property. This practice made it possible for landed families to build up considerable estates to the advantage of the eldest son, while younger sons had to make their own way in life. This prevented reckless men from destroying estates: in *Is He Popenjoy?* a lawyer comments that the deceased Marquis of Brotherton's extraordinary will was 'as bad a will as a man could make; but he couldn't do very much harm. Every acre was entailed' [61]. Entails could be ended

only by agreement between the man holding the property – the 'life tenant' – and his heir, the 'tenant in tail'. This was normally father and son. As Trollope comments in *Ralph the Heir*, the problem is that 'an entail that limits an owner's rights on behalf of an heir who is not loved, who is looked upon as an enemy, is very grievous' [11]. The way round the problem in this novel was for Gregory Newton to buy out the life interest of his heir, who is also his nephew, so that he would be free to leave the property to his illegitimate son. In *The Vicar of Bullhampton* Walter Marrable's debauched father is above him in the line of descent for the entail and the only way to keep the property intact is for the son to buy out his father's rights. This is what is meant when Walter Marrable's father agrees to 'make over his life interest in the property ... on payment of an annuity ... of £200' [71]. The purchase of the heir's life interest by the 'life tenant' also occurs in *John Caldigate*.

The Settled Land Act, passed in the year of Trollope's death, 1882, made it easier to sell land without breaking the entail. Entails dealt only with estates, not titles. (In the late twentieth century landed estates are often kept intact by putting them into a trust.) Debts incurred against the assured income from entailed lands by heirs, repayable on the death of the present owner, were called 'post-obits'. The problem of such a debt besets Mr Scarborough in *Mr Scarborough's Family* and he found an ingenious way round the entail. Indeed, this novel may be called an essay on entails. The opposite of an entailed estate was an estate held in 'fee simple', which meant there were no limitations regarding a particular class of heir, such as a succession limited to the eldest direct legitimate male.

In Trollope's fiction, disputes about entail occur frequently. In the Barsetshire series, one of the main causes of hatred between Earl De Courcy and his heir, Lord Porlock, is over the entail on the estate, while Lord Chiltern and his father have to agree to borrow money against their family estate. (Entails normally specified that both the holder of the estate and the heir had to agree to any borrowing against the estate.) Some properties, like that of the Dales in Allington, had no entail but everyone behaved as if there were one as 'the acres had remained intact' [*The Small House at Allington*, 1].

The lack of an entail could cause as many problems as the presence of one. In *Cousin Henry* the squire cannot decide to whom to leave the property: an entail would have robbed him of his dilemma and Trollope of a plot. Likewise in *Sir Harry Hotspur of Humblethwaite*, Sir Harry's dilemma is based on the lack of an entail. His title must descend to his disreputable nephew but he is free to leave the estate to whom he will. Should he leave it to his disreputable heir to preserve the dignity of the family or follow his natural affections and leave it to his daughter? Should he countenance a marriage between the two cousins to achieve both aims but in doing so marry his daughter to a rake? Sometimes the 'life tenant' of an entailed property could still wield power because he had the right to leave those things outside the entail to whom he wished: this is a threat faced by Augustus Scarborough in *Mr Scarborough's Family* and by Lady Glencora

Palliser when the old Duke of Omnium talks of remarrying. Even if he were too old to produce a more direct heir to supplant Plantagenet Palliser in the entail, he would have someone nearer and dearer to whom to leave his money and jewels. Property other than land could also be entailed: whether jewels were part of the family entail is the main plot in *The Eustace Diamonds*. Because property that lay outside the entail could sometimes be left as the owner desired, Lady Glencora inherited her father's Glasgow property while her uncle got not only her father's title but the family estates through entail.

Erle, Barrington. A Liberal politician who appears throughout the Palliser novels. When the series begins he has already been secretary to the Prime Minister. In *Phineas Finn* Erle helps the young Finn to find a seat in Parliament and in *Phineas Redux* he helps him to return to political life. Erle, a bachelor, is a cousin not only of Lady Laura Kennedy but of almost all the other prominent Whigs in the Palliser novels. Although he does not attain high office he exercises influence behind the scenes. He is not a dishonest man, but his essential belief is that in politics a man must always do as his party leader decides. His letters and gossip often provide Lady Laura with information.

Escott, Thomas Hay Sweets (1850–1924). Escott was Trollope's first biographer. In the 1850s, while doing Post Office work in Devon, Trollope stayed at the house of an old school friend, Escott's father, who was a clergyman. There he first met the young Thomas. Years later he helped him establish himself as a journalist in London where he eventually became editor of the *Fortnightly Review*. Escott interviewed Trollope for an article in a magazine called *Time* in 1879 and said that Trollope had 'nearly the most conspicuous place in the first rank of novelists of the day'. He could also be critical and described Trollope's *Thackeray* as 'hero worship with a vengeance'. Escott planned to become Trollope's biographer and received some help from his subject in his last years. Unfortunately he waited many years before writing *Anthony Trollope: His Public Services, Private Friends, and Literary Originals*. It was published in 1913 but only after the publisher, who rightly found the book rambling and diffuse, was assured that there was still a strong interest in Trollope in America. (It was reprinted there in 1967.) Escott's book is invaluable for all students of Trollope, but it has to be handled with care as sometimes his memory is faulty. His wide acquaintance among the literary, clerical and political world gave him access to much gossip about Trollope. Since Escott became a strong Conservative, he is always apt to play down Trollope's Liberalism. However, he does record several of Trollope's comments on his novels and gives useful information about Trollope's friends. Fortunately the book has that rare item among Victorian biographies, an excellent index.

Essays and Reviews. A controversial collection of articles by leading Liberal Anglicans, published in 1860. The book was written in response to new theological insights and scientific discoveries, symbolized in the 1859 publication of Darwin's *Origin of Species*. It was condemned by the Church of England for having a 'minimalizing' view of orthodox beliefs about the inspiration of the Bible, the accuracy of the Genesis story of creation, and the eternal nature of damnation. (In *The Belton Estate*, written five years after the collection's publication and one year after the Church's condemnation, one lady announces that the book 'came direct from the Evil One' [17]. Significantly, Trollope described her as 'ignorant' and 'stupid'.) Among its contributors were Benjamin Jowett, the inspiration for the Reverend Mr Jobbles in *The Three Clerks*, Mark Pattison, and Frederick Temple, later Archbishop of Canterbury. The collection was denounced by Samuel Wilberforce, Bishop of Oxford. (The deceitful Samuel Grantly, one of Archdeacon Grantly's three sons in *The Warden*, was a caricature of Wilberforce.) It is a further sign of Trollope's liberal views towards Church teaching and biblical inspiration that he had a copy in his library: it was one of the few theological works there. When Lord Carlisle, the Lord Lieutenant of Ireland, asked Trollope about the effect of the book on Barchester society, he replied in an unpublished letter: 'I do not know how the Essays and Reviews may be handled by our hyper protestant pastors and masters in Ireland, but I am afraid that they will be almost too much for the Society of Barchester' [Mullen, 253]. Trollope did not include debates over theological issues in his Barsetshire novels; he preferred debates on internal Church politics, personalities and questions of reforming abuses in the Church. The appearance of books like *Essays and Reviews* shows the changing nature of the Victorian Church and is one reason why Trollope was reluctant to return to Barset when the series ended.

[➤ Bible; Clergymen; *Clergymen of the Church of England*; Colenso; Evangelicals; Prayer Book; Religion.]

Europe. Trollope set three contemporary novels, *Nina Balatka*, *Linda Tressel* and *The Golden Lion of Granpère*, and one historical novel, *La Vendée*, entirely on the Continent. Several of his short stories and occasional chapters in novels were set in different European countries and reflected his extensive travels. In many novels characters go to Europe for lengthy tours of several months, on honeymoon or to recover from upsetting events such as being in prison (*John Caldigate*), or losing the prime ministership (*The Prime Minister*). Sometimes, as in *Sir Harry Hotspur of Humblethwaite*, characters sent to Europe to recover from a disastrous love affair, die there. It is fairly rare for Trollope to give many details of these travels because the growth in tourism had made such descriptions no longer fashionable in fiction. [➤ Austria; Belgium; Exile; Foreigners; France; Germany; Italy; Spain; *Travelling Sketches*.]

The Eustace Diamonds. Trollope's twenty-eighth novel and the third in the Palliser series. It was written between 4 December 1869 and 25 August 1870, during which time he was also working on *The Commentaries of Caesar*. The novel was first serialized in the *Fortnightly Review* over twenty months, between 1 July 1871 and 1 February 1873. (The magazine had become a monthly after November 1866.) It was published by Chapman & Hall in three volumes in December 1873. Trollope received £2,500.

The Eustace Diamonds is generally considered the third in the Palliser series after *Can You Forgive Her?* and *Phineas Finn*, the latter having been published in 1867. Trollope began writing this novel in the same year in which its predecessor was published in book form. He did not consider *The Eustace Diamonds* a part of the Palliser series. [For the debate over whether one should read *The Eustace Diamonds* before *Phineas Redux*, ➤ under the latter novel.]

It is difficult to think of any of Trollope's novels with multiple plots which seems to be so dominated by one character as this is by Lizzie Eustace. The Pallisers themselves are less central to the novel than to any other in the series. Lady Glencora and the old duke find Lizzie's antics amusing and even Plantagenet allows conversation about her to be a brief diversion from his absurd scheme for decimal currency [80]. Of course a close re-reading shows that there are other important characters, yet the impression lingers. When the novel opens, Lizzie Greystock is left an orphan at nineteen and under the care of her 'dreadful old termagant' of an aunt, Lady Linlithgow. Using her stunning beauty, Lizzie soon persuades Sir Florian Eustace, a baronet who is dying of consumption, to marry her.

She is soon a widow with a son and an estate in Scotland and she rents a small house in Mount Street by the month. Her scheming, her marriage and young widowhood are remarkably similar to Julia Brabazon's in *The Claverings*. (Readers with good memories may recall that Sophie Gordeloup in that novel also took lodgings in Mount

Street; so too did Archdeacon Grantly in *Framley Parsonage*.) She has a comfortable annual income of £4,000 [►Money], but finds it difficult to maintain an elegant way of life in London and in the country. For Victorian readers, the obvious parallel to Lizzie was Becky Sharp in *Vanity Fair*, which had appeared almost a quarter of a century earlier. Speaking as 'the historian' Trollope asked readers not to confuse his Lizzie with Thackeray's Becky [3], yet by the time he wrote his *Autobiography* he accepted the comparison of Becky with his 'cunning little woman of pseudo-fashion'. His comment on this throws light on his creation of characters. 'As I wrote the book, the idea constantly presented itself to me that Lizzie Eustace was but a second Becky Sharp; but in planning the character I had not thought of this, and I believe that Lizzie would have been just as she is though Becky Sharp had never been described.' A few years later, in his *Thackeray*, Trollope again reflected on the portrayal of Becky Sharp, which he greatly admired. A close reading of that criticism and a study of Lizzie's character show their essential differences. Trollope stresses Lizzie's dishonesty and duplicity: 'There shall be no whitewashing of Lizzie Eustace. She was abominable' [35].

Lizzie lives in a world of fantasy, one stimulated by her devotion to Byron's poetry. A fascination with Byron is never a good sign in Trollope's characters. Like Ayala Dormer in *Ayala's Angel* she is always dreaming of a Byronic hero, her own 'Corsair'. She thinks she has found him in the penniless though titled rogue, Lord George de Bruce Carruthers, with his radical opinions on the social order

and open denunciation of marriage. These are rare in a Trollopian character.

The portrait of Lady Eustace is subtle compared with that of the popular preacher whom she eventually marries. The Reverend Joseph Emilius was a convert Jew from Bohemia who had become an Anglican clergyman. [For two similar but real clergymen of the time, ►under Emilius, The Rev. Joseph.] Trollope adds a piquant touch by having Emilius ordained by the Bishop of Jerusalem. (This joint Anglican–Lutheran bishopric, which lasted from 1841 to 1886, had infuriated High Churchmen like Newman and Trollope may well have remembered that the first of these bishops was himself a convert Jew.) Even the great Trollope critic, Michael Sadleir, who rated this one of the author's greatest novels, admits that it is hard to see why Lady Eustace eventually marries such a repulsive figure as Emilius. The mistake that she made in this marriage and the ramifications that followed form an important part of *Phineas Redux*.

There is much comedy in this novel, most of which flows round Lord Fawn. He is a minor politician and, as a peer with a small income, he desperately wants a rich wife. He had tried to find one in *Phineas Finn*, but, unsuccessful there, he turns up in this novel as a suitor for Lady Eustace. He would appear again, in a not particularly glorious episode, in *Phineas Redux*. Fawn explains his position to Lizzie: he is 'a poor man – for my rank'. The total income from his Irish estates is only £5,000, but half of that belongs to his mother under the terms of her marriage settlement. Of course he has his salary as a government minister, but only for as long as he and his party cling to office.

There is a more conventional love story between Lucy Morris and Frank Greystock. *The Times* correctly noted how similar this Lucy was to Lucy Robarts in *Framley Parsonage*. Trollope himself also said this in his *Autobiography*. Stories of governesses who make good marriages were popular with Victorian readers. Greystock, a barrister and MP, is advised, like so many of Trollope's young men, not to marry a girl without money. For much of the novel he seems likely to follow that advice. This sub-plot is connected to the main one because Greystock is Lady Eustace's cousin and one of her supporters, while Lucy is governess to the Fawn family. There is a further connection because Frank's father (and, therefore, Lizzie's uncle) is the Dean of Bobsborough. Another clerical link is present in this diocese as the Bishop of Bobsborough is none other than the uncle of the late Sir Florian Eustace. Bringing in a dean and bishop was, Trollope knew, always well received by his readers who still had fond memories of the Barsetshire novels.

The Eustace Diamonds is one of Trollope's best portraits of those who just manage to cling to their positions within aristocratic society. As the dean tells his son, 'You . . . are called upon to live with the rich, but are not rich' and that can only be done by 'wary walking' [35]. Neither Lizzie nor Lord Fawn finds it easy to live on what they regard as poor incomes, although the vast bulk of Victorians would have regarded their incomes as princely. (At the time of writing the novel, Trollope's own income was roughly equal to that of Lord Fawn and Lady Eustace combined.)

The main plot centres on the ownership of a valuable diamond necklace that had long been the property of the Eustace family. Lizzie contends that her husband wanted her to have it but the family lawyer, Mr Camperdown, maintains it is a family heirloom and does not belong to Lizzie herself [➤ Entails]. Trollope was conscious that he had often been attacked for mistakes in legal points in his novels. *Orley Farm* in particular had been subjected to much legalistic nitpicking. In *Phineas Finn* Trollope had asked pity for 'the poor fictionist' for making mistakes about 'those terrible meshes of the Law'. In *The Eustace Diamonds*, in which an issue of law is central to the plot, he took no chances. He asked a barrister friend, Charles Merewether, to write the opinion of the 'learned counsel', Thomas Dove, on the ownership of the necklace [25]. This, Trollope says in his *Autobiography*, is the only time his novels contained anything not written by himself and he also claims that this opinion became recognized as 'the ruling authority on the subject'. Merewether, who later became a Tory MP, had written the essay 'On Cricket' for *Saint Pauls* [➤ British Sports and Pastimes].

The legal battle over ownership was soon overtaken by the theft − or perhaps two thefts − of the jewels. Lady Eustace is not, in the end, punished − at least by the law − for her illegal behaviour, any more than Emilius is punished for murder in *Phineas Redux*. On the other hand, we are led in the final chapter to assume her new married life will not be altogether pleasant. As Trollope had shown in *Orley Farm*, he was reluctant to deliver important characters over to their just fate. Perhaps the execution of his first hero in *The Macdermots of Ballycloran* had convinced him that readers did not like this.

The Eustace Diamonds contains some of Trollope's most important 'authorial intrusions' concerning his view of human nature and the role of the novelist in portraying it. Such reflections were particularly appropriate in a novel that made its debut in an intellectual journal like the *Fortnightly Review*. Trollope was aware that the readers of *The Eustace Diamonds* would be a more analytical audience than those who read *Framley Parsonage* in the *Cornhill*. In the chapter 'Too Bad for Sympathy' [35] he sets out his basic view of the way in which people should be depicted in fiction and this clearly shows how different his approach was from that of writers like Dickens. For him there was little appeal in showing people 'carried away by abnormal appetites . . . and the devil'. He held strongly to the Victorian principle that 'one does not willingly grovel in gutters, or breathe fetid atmospheres, or live upon garbage'. Here, of course, is the crucial difference between Trollope's vision of the novel and that of many modern novelists. Yet he also rejects the idea that a character should be absolutely perfect, an Arthurian figure of knightly splendour. 'In those delineations of life and character which we call novels,' readers seemed to prefer characters who were better than 'our own friends around us'. The novelist should, therefore, show characters becoming 'somewhat better – not by one spring heavenward to perfection, because we cannot so use our legs, – but by slow climbing'. This 'true picture of life as it is' would encourage readers, particularly young readers, to

'rise not indeed to perfection, but one step first, and then another on the ladder'.

Trollope thus saw the novel as a realistic picture whose realism, as in most art, was limited and whose purpose, a basically Christian purpose, was to encourage moral values. He did not always attain his goal, but that is what he sought to do in every novel he wrote. There is always a balance. 'A man is never strong enough to take unmixed delight in good, so may we presume also that he cannot be quite so weak as to find perfect satisfaction in evil' [1]. While he rejects the idea that a human being can be all good, he is scathing in denouncing 'that worst of all disease, – a low idea of humanity' [28]. (This view helped to account for his intense dislike of Evangelicals.) It was, of course, easier to hold this view in the nineteenth century than later.

The Eustace Diamonds is also notable for having the most extensive and best Scottish scenes in Trollope's fiction. Because Lizzie has inherited a castle overlooking the Firth of Clyde, she invites several of her friends to visit Scotland. By the 1860s, excellent railway facilities allowed many people to emulate Queen Victoria's example and take their holiday in 'North Britain'. Trollope had already shown this in *Phineas Finn* when the Scottish laird, Robert Kennedy, entertains his friends and political acquaintances there. However, in *The Eustace Diamonds* we get a better and more varied view of Scottish life, even fox-hunting, and of some of Lizzie Eustace's retainers, such as Andy Gowran [➤ Servants]. Through men like him we are able to observe the strange ways of their southern visitors. Writing about

Scotland not surprisingly brought to mind one of Trollope's favourite novelists, Sir Walter Scott, and two of his novels, *Old Mortality* and *Ivanhoe*. When young he had considered *Ivanhoe* the greatest novel ever written in English [35]. In this same chapter he quotes the verse containing the line, 'It is good to be honest and true', the Scottish song that he quoted in *The New Zealander* and in *Barchester Towers*.

The novel also contains several private jokes reflecting aspects of Trollope's own life. The greatest permanent achievement of his Post Office career is recalled in two allusions to his own creation, the pillar-box. Not only does Frank place his letter to Lucy in a pillar-box, but later Trollope adds two legalistic points about the letter: it became Lucy's property once it was dropped in the box but it could not be delivered on the Sabbath [13, 15]. He also shares a joke with his readers – or at least those who read the book in its serialized form – when Palliser says, 'There's the "Fortnightly Review" comes out but once a month, and I'm told that it does very well' [55]. When he speculates about a character's marrying in the Embassy Chapel in Paris, he was no doubt recalling his brother Tom's wedding there a few years before [54]. The influence of his second trip to America is seen in the naming of one leading character, Lucinda Roanoke: the Roanoke is a river in Virginia. Probably the most bittersweet recollection in the novel occurs when Lady Eustace goes to the Haymarket Theatre to see 'The Noble Jilt' by 'a very eminent' author. Of course, hardly anyone but Trollope and his wife Rose would have known that he had written that play two decades earlier, but had

failed to interest a theatrical manager. Mrs Carbuncle's criticism of the play is quite accurate.

Trollope was pleased with the reaction to *The Eustace Diamonds* and he felt it did much 'to repair ... my reputation' after several novels of the late 1860s had not been as popular as their predecessors. He thought it was his greatest success since *The Small House at Allington*, although he considered *Phineas Finn* and *Nina Balatka* to be better novels. According to Trollope's first biographer, Escott, it gained one unusual admirer. Disraeli and Trollope were guests at a dinner given by Lord Stanhope, a Tory historian and politician. Disraeli said to his fellow novelist: 'I have long known, Mr Trollope, your churchmen and churchwomen; may I congratulate you on the same lightness of touch in the portrait of your new adventuress?' This gracious remark unfortunately did little to mitigate Trollope's detestation of Disraeli.

A very different Victorian, though in his own way as eminent, was Edward FitzGerald, the poet and translator of *Omar Khayyam*. He greatly admired Trollope's novels and wrote in his splendid letters how much he enjoyed having them read to him. While a boy was reading this novel aloud, FitzGerald kept interrupting: 'No, no! She must have known she was lying! He couldn't have been such a fool!' *The Eustace Diamonds* can be read with enjoyment either by those who wish to read the whole Palliser series or by anyone wanting a novel with a delightful blend of satire, comedy, mild crime and a dash of Victorian politics.

Eustace, Lady. The heroine, or rather the central character, of *The Eustace*

Diamonds. As Lizzie Greystock she is left virtually penniless after the death of her father, an admiral. She solves her immediate need for money by a hasty marriage to the dying Sir Florian Eustace, thus giving herself a title and an income. (The same course had been followed by Julia Brabazon when she married Lord Ongar in *The Claverings*, written five years before.) Lizzie Eustace is Trollope's attempt at creating a completely disreputable female character. She also appears in *Phineas Redux* and in *The Prime Minister*.

Evangelicals. Trollope's detestation of Anglican Evangelicals is one of his most consistent themes. He once admitted that he had 'inherited some of my good mother's antipathies towards a certain clerical school'. The dislike was not just theological but social, as his brother Tom recalled: Evangelicalism was 'a sort of thing that might be expected to be met within tradesmen's back parlours ... utterly out of place, among gentlemen'. Trollope disliked the narrow culture of people who made the Church not only the centre but the whole of their lives and used it to control others. This is the world he described in *Miss Mackenzie*.

Trollope's parents, especially his mother, hated the Evangelical Vicar of Harrow, J. W. Cunningham, and she lampooned him for refusing a public burial for Byron's illegitimate daughter. Trollope remembered him as a 'cringing hypocrite and a most confounded liar, who would give [his] eyes to be a bishop'. The presence of Evangelicals is particularly noticeable in those novels written in the 1850s and 1860s, and this was partly based on his personal experience of their increasing importance in the Church. In 1868, when Trollope stood for Parliament in Beverley, he learned he would not be welcome, as a Liberal candidate, to worship in the Minster. It was then under the domination of the Evangelical perpetual curate, the Reverend William Burton Crickmer.

Evangelicals were marked by a passion for long sermons, constant moralizing, an obsession with 'conversions', a false view that life was nothing but a 'vale of tears' to be got through (a view Mrs Proudie frequently expressed), a low regard for the Sacraments and tradition, a fanatical temperament, an inclination to hypocrisy and an anti-Catholicism Trollope found particularly offensive. The extreme Evangelicals shared many characteristics with modern-day fundamentalists. In *Rachel Ray* the Reverend Mr Comfort 'had been regarded as a Calvinist when he was young, as Evangelical in middle life, and was still known as a Low Churchman in his old age' [4]. All three descriptions were distasteful to Trollope and contrasted with his view expressed in *The Belton Estate* when he asked: 'Why has the world been made so pleasant? Why is the fruit of the earth so sweet; and the trees, – why are they so green ... Why are women so lovely? and why is it that the activity of man's mind is the only sure forerunner of man's progress?' [5].

Evangelicals seldom come out well in his fiction. Trollope felt that Evangelical clergymen manipulated women and had little regard for their intelligence. In his article for the *Pall Mall Gazette* called 'The Zulu in London' he endured one of the May Meetings at the Exeter Hall on the

Strand. Here various Evangelical and Dissenting groups met each year. Trollope was miserable, gave up the task and wrote no more articles as a visiting Zulu. In his piece he described how one clergyman patronized his female listeners. His Evangelical ladies, when not being manipulated, are strong-willed, domineering and unpleasant. The most famous is Mrs Proudie but there are many more, including Mrs Bolton in *John Caldigate*, Mrs Miles in 'The Lady of Launay', Mrs Winterfield in *The Belton Estate* and Mrs Prime in *Rachel Ray*. The type is singled out for special attack in *Miss Mackenzie* and *Rachel Ray*.

Evangelical clergymen fare little better and are normally oleaginous, hypocritical, greedy and not gentlemen. Trollope's worst attacks are on Evangelical curates rather than incumbents: as younger men the group's characteristics were perhaps more noticeable. In *The Bertrams* the curate, Mr O'Callaghan, while a severe pastor, 'was known to be condescending and mild under the influence of tea and muffins – sweetly so if the cream be plentiful and the muffins soft with butter'[22]. The most famous is Mr Slope [*Barchester Towers*, 17] but others include: the Reverend Samuel Prong, who drops his H's, in *Rachel Ray*; Mr Maguire, the Apollo with a squint, in *Miss Mackenzie*; Mr Groschut, who disapproves of Dean Lovelace's riding to hounds and smoking, in *Is He Popenjoy?*; and the kill-joy Arthur Donne in 'Mary Gresley', who on his deathbed gets his fiancée to promise to give up writing novels. Quite frequently they end up, like Messrs Slope, Maguire, and Tobias Tickler who marries Olivia Proudie in *Framley Parsonage*,

with livings in London. Some, like Slope and Groschut, get into trouble with women. [For another aspect of Groschut, ➤ Emilius, the Rev. Joseph.]

The Evangelicals' dislike of fiction, treated in 'Mary Gresley', as well as their Sabbatarian dislike of Sunday postal deliveries, treated in *Miss Mackenzie* [14] and *The Last Chronicle of Barset* [17, 73], were two other reasons why Trollope so disliked them. He especially disliked the efforts of some English Evangelicals to claim that the Irish famine was a judgement of God and their attempts at winning converts by promising food in exchange for conversion. He saw that much of their 'self-mortification' was a form of perverted self-indulgence. Significantly, some of his Evangelical clergymen in *Miss Mackenzie* and *The Bertrams* were Irish by birth.

[➤ Church of England; Religion; Sermons.]

Examinations. See Civil Service.

The Examiner. Trollope wrote a series of articles on Ireland for this Liberal weekly newspaper edited by his mother's friend, John Forster (1812–76), who is now best remembered as Dickens's biographer. The articles were an answer to a series published in *The Times* by 'S.G.O.' (the Reverend and Hon. [later Lord] Sidney Godolphin Osborne). Osborne had claimed that the government had done very little to cope with the Irish famine. Nothing annoyed Trollope more than jibes at the expense of the Civil Service and government [➤ Dickens, Charles]. The first 'letter' appeared in August 1849 and five more were published in 1850. They were signed 'A.T.' and described conditions in Ireland as the potato famine came to an end. In general, Trollope defended the efforts of British officials to cope with the disaster. Trollope was not paid for his work and the letters appear to have made little impression at the time.

Exeter. The city was the setting for more scenes in Trollope's fiction than any other, with the exception of London and Cheltenham. Trollope knew and liked the cathedral city from boyhood visits to cousins there, and he increased his knowledge when arranging 'walks' in Devon for the Post Office. *Rachel Ray* and *He Knew He Was Right* have scenes set in Exeter. A recent historian of the city, Bryan Little, was able to identify the original for Jemima Stanbury's house, described in *He Knew He Was Right*. Most of *Kept in the Dark* is set in Exeter. Mark Robarts, of *Framley Parsonage*, is the son of an Exeter doctor. In 1851, about the time of Trollope's postal work, the city's population was 28,000; by 1881, around the time in which *Kept in the Dark* is set, it had grown to 38,000.

Exile. Exile to Europe is a frequent occurrence in Trollope's fiction as it provided a simple way of winding up a character's story. Victorians often went to live abroad for several standard reasons. Some went in search of a better climate for respiratory illnesses; some went because they knew a British income went twice or even three times as far on the Continent; others went because they had fallen into disgrace at home. They usually formed English colonies in places such as Rome and the somewhat racy character of these is depicted in short stories like 'Mrs General Talboys'.

Trollope knew of all three reasons from experiences in his own family. When he was nineteen his parents fled to Belgium to escape their debts. His mother and brother eventually settled in Italy, partly for financial reasons and partly to escape the family curse of consumption. His father-in-law fled to France when he was accused of embezzlement [➤ Trollope, Rose]. All of these motives for 'retiring abroad' occur in his fiction. He gives the least attention to health as a motive: usually it is only a minor character, such as Sir Florian Eustace in *The Eustace Diamonds*, who goes to Italy in pursuit of a warmer climate and health. It rarely seems to do much good for characters in his fiction although some, like Arthur Wilkinson in *The Bertrams*, are restored to health: in his case a trip to Egypt does the trick.

It was quite the custom for people in the early nineteenth century to flee to one of the French ports, where they could remain in touch with England, but be beyond her laws. Perhaps, once Trollope's father-in-law did this, Trollope found it diplomatic to send his fictional exiles farther afield, to Germany or sometimes even beyond. It is more likely that he was influenced by his travels in Europe. Trollope's earliest exiles were Lord Kilcullen and Barry Lynch in his second novel, *The Kellys and the O'Kellys*. Lynch is a true 'exile' as he is forced to take flight to Boulogne because powerful men warn that he will be prosecuted for attempted murder[35]. Two other characters in the Irish novels had profligate husbands living in Paris: Lady Mary Fitzgerald in *Castle Richmond* and Mrs O'Hara in *An Eye for an Eye*. At the end of the latter novel the disgraced Kate O'Hara flees to France where she joins her father in a joint exile. In *The Three Clerks* the corrupt MP Undecimus Scott makes his escape abroad [46]. Betsy Pryor in 'The Lady of Launay' is virtually exiled to Normandy when she seems likely to marry the heir to an estate against his mother's wishes. Henry Grantly threatens to exile himself to Pau when his father, Archdeacon Grantly, opposes his marriage [➤ Grantly Sons].

Frequently characters go abroad or are persuaded to go by friends and family because of the combination of a small income and some impending disgrace. Thus at the end of *Orley Farm* Lady Mason, mortified and impoverished by revelations during legal proceedings, retires to live out her life in Germany. That became a favourite place for Trollope to send his characters. The roué Burgo Fitzgerald in *Can You Forgive Her?* makes his way to Germany and is maintained in Baden-Baden on an income sent by his relatives and Plantagenet Palliser. Lady Alexandrina De Courcy and her mother also find Baden-Baden a comfortable escape from their husbands at the end of *The Small House at Allington*. By moving abroad a wife could escape from the virtually limitless legal power of a husband without the scandal of a divorce: thus Lady Laura Kennedy finds Dresden a safe place to escape her mad husband's legal threats in *Phineas Finn* and *Phineas Redux*.

Some characters are sent further afield. Australia provided a place for characters who were disgraced, like Alaric Tudor in *The Three Clerks*, or who could not prosper in England, like John Caldigate and Dick Shand in *John Caldigate*. When an earl's daughter in *Lady Anna* marries a tailor, they leave England for a new life in Australia. Fallen women, like Mary Thorne's mother, and great rogues, like the ruined MP George Vavasor in *Can You Forgive Her?*, tend to seek refuge in America. [➤ Italy.]

An Eye for an Eye. Trollope's thirty-sixth novel was written between 13 September and 10 October 1870. It was not published until 1878, when serialization began in the *Whitehall Review* on 24 August; it ended on 1 February 1879. It was published as a book by Chapman & Hall in January 1879. According to the *Autobiography*, the long delay in publication was due to Trollope's over-production in the 1870s; when writing the relevant chapter of his memoirs in 1876 he assumed publication would not occur for at least two years. The delay may also have been due to the same lack of interest in stories set in Ireland that had plagued his first three Irish novels (*The Macdermots*, *The Kellys and the O'Kellys* and *Castle Richmond*), or to the controversial nature of the story. Trollope was perfectly aware of the problem, for when discussing publication with Frederic Chapman in 1875 he wrote: 'I think we had better arrange to do nothing ... unless you can refer to me. I should not like it to be placed here or there without my sanction.' Trollope received £425.

The basic plot of this novel would have been familiar to Victorian readers: a wealthy young man, heir to a peerage, seduces a simple peasant girl. It was the stuff of ballets like *Giselle*, 'penny-dreadfuls' and theatrical melodramas. In less capable hands it would have remained melodrama but in Trollope's it became a powerful story of self-discovery and self-destruction among all the leading characters. The plot is also kept from melodrama because – as always with Trollope – no character is totally good or totally bad. Likewise, the reader's emotions alter as the story develops and his outrage or sympathy varies accordingly.

The story, one of only two that uses a flashback, alternates between County Clare on the west coast of Ireland and Scroope Manor in Dorset. The introduction establishes the sense of suspense, mystery and impending doom. It is set in an insane asylum in the west of England in which a woman repeats all day long, 'An eye for an eye and a tooth for a tooth.'

Fred Neville, 'a youth as women love to see about a house', is a lieutenant in the 20th Hussars stationed in County Clare; he is also heir to the Earl of Scroope, a title of great importance and wealth; finally, he is set on an adventure [➤ Military]. Neville is not a stage villain but 'simply a self-indulgent spoiled young man who had realized to himself no idea of duty in life'. As such he resembles Harry Clavering in *The Claverings* and to a lesser degree, George Hotspur in *Sir Harry Hotspur of Humblethwaite*. (His younger brother, Jack, is not only steadfast but ugly.) Neville falls in love with a young and beautiful Irish girl, Kate O'Hara, who lives in seclusion with her mother on the Cliffs of Moher. The local Catholic priest, Father Marty, who is treated with great respect by Trollope, encourages their love affair, again out of mixed motives. He wants the girl to make a good marriage but would also enjoy seeing a poor Irish Catholic girl become the next Countess of Scroope.

Neville seduces Kate and in this the story resembles his first novel, *The Macdermots of Ballycloran,* also set in Ireland, in which seduction by a British officer is accompanied by a promise of marriage. The seduction here is off-stage and secreted in a passage reading, 'Alas, alas! there came a day in which the pricelessness of the girl he loved sank to nothing, vanished away, and was as a thing utterly lost, even in his eyes … To her he was godlike … She gave him all – and her pricelessness in his eyes was gone for ever.' Neville knows that his aunt, the Countess of Scroope, is violently anti-Catholic and anti-Irish and he has sworn to his uncle not to marry an Irish Catholic. He genuinely, at least when in Ireland, wants to marry the girl; he rejects the idea of keeping her as a mistress. He also half-thinks he can marry the girl without giving her the title so that they can live in privacy.

Trollope gives us two Lieutenant Nevilles: the proper one in the safe acres of Dorset and the roguish, immature one in the wilder atmosphere of Ireland. (Trollope would say in *An Old Man's Love* that English life required more proprieties than that in many other parts of the English-speaking world.) Then Kate's drunken father, whom his wife, daughter and Neville had assumed was dead, reappears and justifies the lieutenant in thinking he has been tricked. The widow now sees her daughter's life being ruined, as was hers, by a heartless man and she pushes Neville over a cliff to his death. She loses her mind; Kate's baby dies and she herself goes to France to live with her father in exile.

The novel is a tragedy of youthful love and indiscretion. As always, Trollope preaches that deeds bear consequences. Neville in his own way is like Ayala in *Ayala's Angel*: a young person who allows Utopian dreams to obscure reality. *An Eye for an Eye* also examines the perils of sexual licence, the love of adventure and the nature of duty: the old Earl and Countess of Scroope would not have been seen by Victorians as being as unpleasant in their feeling for preserving a blood line, and for their staunch Protestantism, as they would by twentieth-century readers. Trollope in the speech of the old earl shows his sympathy with English aristocrats who take their heritage, position and responsibilities seriously. Yet in Father Marty he demonstrates both a sympathy for the Irish in their love–hate relationship with the English and a generosity towards Catholicism. It is interesting to note that Father Marty is quite prepared, if Neville marries Kate, for their child to be baptized in the Church of England: the imposition of rigid rules regarding Catholic baptism in the case of mixed marriages had yet to come. [➤ Finn, Phineas.]

As in other novels written in the latter part of his career, Trollope was concerned with inheritance and property and with the continuance of a noble or landed family. This novel also shows the influence of his constant reading of Shakespeare. The title and name of Scroope was obviously derived from three such names in the histories: in *King Richard II* there is Sir Stephen Scroop; in *King Henry IV Part 1* there is the Archbishop of York, Richard Scroop; in *King Henry V* there is Lord Scroop. Likewise the name Neville is the family name of the Earls of Westmoreland who figure so largely in *King Henry IV Part 2*. The role of Father Marty, which is crucial to the story, bears some resemblance to that of Friar Lawrence in *Romeo and Juliet*: a man who acts out of mixed motives and in so doing unleashes forces he cannot control.

It is one of several short novels (*Cousin Henry* and *Dr Wortle's School* are others) that Trollope published in his last few years in which the plot centres on a single moral dilemma. The high degree of tension and suspense bring to mind a comparison with Dickens or Wilkie Collins. As always, Trollope pleads for tolerance and understanding, especially among his women readers who, he writes, are often possessed of a 'hardness of heart' concerning unmarried mothers. 'Fallen women' are also treated in *The Vicar of Bullhampton*.

There is another of Trollope's private jokes in the character of Barney Morony, Fred Neville's manservant: he is 'an idle fellow, but as he has nothing to do he can't help being idle'. His own Irish manservant was named Barney Fitzpatrick [also Smith]. Once again, there is a Mrs Bunce: in this case she is the dominating housekeeper at Scroope Manor. [➤ Bunce.]

When the book was published Trollope told John Blackwood that Chapman 'did very well' with the two-volume edition. Critical reaction was not encouraging and his fear of publishing yet another depressing Irish story was justified. The *Spectator*, however, did praise the book in the issue of 15 February 1879. The story was translated into French as *Oeil pour oeil* and into Magyar as *Szemért-szemért*.

F

Faithfull, Emily (1836–95). Emily Faith-full was the daughter of a clergyman and a leading feminist. She took advantage of new printing methods, which required less physical strength, to establish the Victoria Press 'for the employment of women'. Her aim was to show that women could enter workplaces hitherto confined to men. In 1862 she received royal approval from Queen Victoria when she was made a 'Printer and Publisher in Ordinary to Her Majesty'. In 1861 she produced *Victoria Regia*, a collection of poetry and prose, and in 1863 *A Welcome*, the latter year she also founded the *Victoria Magazine* (1863–80). She approached Trollope with a request for him to contribute free articles for each of her collections, and he sent 'The Journey to Panama' for the first and 'Miss Ophelia Gledd' for the second. In 'The Journey to Panama' Trollope named his heroine Emily, perhaps as a tribute to his friend. Her reputation suffered from her involvement in a divorce case in 1864.

Like Rose Trollope, she was awarded a Civil List pension by the Queen. Trollope, who frequently commented on the narrow range of opportunities open to women, approved of her work [➤ 'Mrs Brumby'] and when travelling in America he distributed her business card in order to promote her work. His warm support

for her, like that for working women in the short story 'The Telegraph Girl', shows that his theoretically conservative view that all women should marry gave way to his liberal desire for women's advancement.

'Fallen Women'. See: Mistresses; Prostitutes; Women.

Family. The Victorian era was primarily an age of family life and Trollope's fiction thoroughly reflected it. Contemporary reviewers often pointed to his novels as providing unrivalled portraits of the family life of his time. Virtually every Trollope novel and short story is concerned with the subject in some way. Trollope also knew that his novels were often read aloud within a family and this imposed restraints upon the way in which he could allude to a difficult subject such as prostitution [➤ Crosbie, Adolphus]. In novels dealing with the aristocracy, gentry, or clergy, the role of family connections in finding a 'place' for a young man is often crucial and there are many examples throughout the Palliser and Barsetshire novels. Most Trollope novels give the family background of the central characters as soon as the story begins, although it is noticeable that many characters come from a family in which either the father or the mother is dead. Among those in this position are: John Eames; Ayala Dormer [*Ayala's Angel*]; Charley Tudor; Clara Amedroz [*The Belton Estate*]; Lily Dale; Frank Jones [*The Land-Leaguers*]; Eleanor Harding; Lady Frances Trafford and Lord Hampstead [*Marion Fay*]. Since Victorian families were larger than today and since young women had fewer opportunities to make friends outside the family circle, cousins often play important roles in his fiction. Trollope's own career as a writer was greatly affected by his own family, particularly by his mother, Frances Trollope.

[➤ Children; Daughters; Fathers and Sons; Marriage; Mothers and Daughters; Settlements; Women.]

Farming. In the 1850s, the decade in which Trollope came to public attention, England became the first country in which the majority of people lived in towns and cities. Nevertheless agriculture and rural life retained a central role in Victorian life and fiction and this is reflected throughout Trollope's work; his novels are filled with landowners, squires and farmers. Trollope was familiar with farming from his earliest days in Harrow. His father, a barrister, spent two decades unhappily trying to make money from farms that he rented. Echoes of his misfortune occur frequently in Trollope's novels when he shows how dangerous it is for 'gentlemen' to take up farming. John Eames's father nearly destroyed his family by such an attempt. As a lawyer says in one of Trollope's last novels, taking up farming without experience makes one 'absolutely throw away' money [*Mr Scarborough's Family*, 62]. As an adult Trollope supervised his large gardens and maintained his own horses, cows and chickens when not living in London, and this kept him in touch with the land.

In the mid-Victorian era there was a growing movement for 'high farming', for farmers and landowners to exploit new methods of drainage, fertilizing and stock breeding. Several of Trollope's characters show interest in this, for instance Lucius Mason in *Orley Farm*, who thought that with 'certain admixtures of ammonia and earths he could produce cereal results hitherto unknown to the farming world' [2]. In 'Malachi's Cove' seaweed is gathered to be used as fertilizer. Guano – made from South American bird droppings – was one of the new discoveries and became a popular fertilizer: Archdeacon Grantly discourses about the quality of a ton and a half of it that he bought for his land [*Barchester Towers*, 23]. (Trollope no doubt would have been pleased to know – if the story is true – that a priest in Connecticut in the 1980s, having read this passage in *Barchester Towers*, was able to repair his church roof from the sale of decades of bird droppings.) The archdeacon was interested in farming because he was a landowner in his own right. However, almost all the clergymen in Trollope's fiction derived their income from the tithes paid on agricultural land. Clergymen in addition often had a small portion of land called a 'glebe', which they normally rented to a neighbouring farmer. [➤ Church of England; *The Vicar of Bullhampton*.]

Most British farming was carried on by tenant farmers who rented their farms from the great landowners. Tenant farmers usually appear in minor roles, such as the Sturts in

Rachel Ray. The actual work on the land was done by agricultural labourers. While Trollope is not normally concerned with their lives in his fiction, he denounced their miserable living conditions in *The New Zealander* and in many of his travel books. One catches a glimpse of the lot of agricultural labourers and life on a large estate when Lady Ongar visits an estate she has just inherited and raises the wages of an old labourer from eight to ten shillings a week [*The Claverings*, 12].

In Trollope's time there was a tendency for some yeoman-farmers to move from their old rank and set themselves up as 'gentlemen-farmers'. Trollope has fun with them in *Barchester Towers*, contrasting traditional tenant farmers, like the Greenacres, with the pretentious Lookaloft family who re-name their farmhouse 'Rosebank' and acquire a 'pianoforte' [35]. On the other hand he presents two memorable portraits of real 'gentlemen-farmers' in the comical Farmer Cheeseacre in *Can You Forgive Her?* and the admirable Larry Twentyman in *The American Senator*. Some of the minor squires are deeply interested in the management of their small estates. Yet a squire who became over-involved, perhaps through not employing a bailiff, could endanger his status as a gentleman. Old Squire Amedroz questions the gentility of his heir, Will Belton, because Will is too closely involved in the farming of his own estate [*The Belton Estate*, 3].

Many of Trollope's upper-class characters, whose wealth came ultimately from agricultural rents, show an interest in farming. Although some peers, including Plantagenet Palliser, take little interest, there are those like Earl De Guest in *The Small House at Allington* who devote a great deal of time and expertise to agriculture, while in *Is He Popenjoy?* Lord Grassangrains is 'that well-known breeder of bullocks' [53].

Most of Trollope's novels were produced in the 'Golden Age' of English agriculture when farmers and landowners prospered. In the 1870s American and German competition, as well as other factors, brought a decline in agricultural income. One catches echoes of this in some of the last novels. Trollope had predicted the vast capacity of American agriculture in his *North America*.

'Father Giles of Ballymoy'. This short story, written in April 1866 for Alexander Strahan as one of four stories for *The Argosy*, was published in May of that year and was included in Trollope's third collection, *Lotta Schmidt and Other Stories* (1867). In his *Autobiography* he wrote about this story and 'The O'Conors of Castle Conor', 'I will not swear to every detail . . . but the main purport of each is true.' Trollope was told to set his own fee and received £60.

This humorous tale is narrated by Archibald Green and set in the west of Ireland in pre-Famine days. Green, who is new to Ireland, arrives after a long trip from London, tired, cross and wet. He is driven to Pat Kirwin's 'hotel'. He undresses and falls asleep in a small bed to be wakened by a man using his clothes-brush. Green assumes the man is about to get into his bed, forgetting that there are two beds in the room, and pushes him out of the door and down the stairs. There are cries of 'Murder!' Green learns that the man is the parish priest who lives in the hotel and who has given permission for the stranger, Green, to sleep in the second bed as there is no other room available. After the uproar, Green is taken to gaol to spend the night. The next morning Father Giles invites him to breakfast and soon Green is forgiven by local residents. Father Giles and he become friends.

Trollope used the story to illustrate the good humour of Irishmen and to laugh at Victorian attitudes to Ireland. Father Giles, in real life and in fiction, was the type of Catholic priest he liked and respected. The story also illustrates how Trollope used incidents in his own life. His friend W. R. Le Fanu recalled the incident as told him by Trollope. Trollope had changed little: the hotel was a small public-house; the priest was dressed in his shirt (which Victorian men often used as nightshirts), not his trousers; Trollope was referred to by the irate Irishmen as a 'b----y sassenach'; Father Giles really was, like Trollope, a guest there. The real Father Giles did become Trollope's 'fast friend' and if he had not come to Trollope's aid, he would, he told Le Fanu, no doubt have been lynched. The fictional Father Giles bears some resemblance to the Very Reverend Peter Daly, a well-known Catholic priest in Galway involved in improving postal services. [➤ *The Macdermots of Ballycloran.*] Trollope has a private joke when Green refers to his 'own room in Keppel Street, Russell Square'.

Fathers and Sons. Trollope had troubled relations with his own father and the relations between fathers and sons fascinated him. They feature frequently in his fiction. He often brooded about his father's ill-luck, ill-health, and abrasive personality which he describes movingly in his *Autobiography*. [➤ Crawley, Josiah.] With his own two sons, Henry and Frederic, Trollope had close and loving relations. He spent a considerable amount of the money he gained from his writing in attempts to set Henry up as a publisher and Fred as a sheep rancher in Australia. Trollope's surviving correspondence with Henry in 1881–2 bears out a remark he had made years earlier in *Phineas Finn* [II] that the 'greatest comfort' a man may have is a son who is his close friend.

Trollope's attitudes towards his sons are best seen through Archdeacon Grantly in *The Last Chronicle of Barset* and through Plantagenet Palliser in *The Duke's Children*. In both cases proud and successful men are annoyed when sons refuse to follow family traditions and make 'unsuitable' marriages. (Henry Trollope himself contemplated a most unsuitable marriage.) In both cases the fathers relent and come to admire their son's choice of a bride. In *Marion Fay* an apparently irreconcilable feud between the Marquis of Kingsbury and his heir over a prospective bride is resolved only when the 'unsuitable' girl dies.

Relations between fathers and sons in Trollope's novels are often complicated by financial considerations, for instance in the difficulties faced by Francis Gresham and his son Frank in *Doctor Thorne*. In the Victorian middle and upper classes a father normally provided his sons with an allowance on which to live or at least to supplement earnings from a profession. Sons expected this almost as a matter of right, particularly if they came from the landed classes. A time could come when a father finally lost patience with a son and refused to give him any more money, as Bertie Stanhope finds in *Barchester Towers* [45]. Sons who finally accept their father's authority can regain their allowance, which is what happens to the failed writer in 'The Adventures of Fred Pickering'.

Matters were further complicated if the son was heir to an estate as he then had certain legal rights under the law of entail. Sometimes this led to outright hatred and warfare, most memorably in the case of Earl De Courcy and his eldest son in *The Small House at Allington*. Such conflicts could sometimes be patched up, like that between Lord Chiltern and his father in *Phineas Finn* or between the old squire and his reformed son in *John Caldigate*. A few selfish fathers show little interest in their sons, for instance Maurice Maule in *Phineas Redux*, while Colonel Marrable's behaviour in *The Vicar of Bullhampton* almost destroys his son's future happiness. In some cases fathers are to blame for their sons' dissolute life because they had not set them better examples [*Doctor Thorne*, 28]. The most complicated of relations between fathers and sons is that between John Scarborough and his two sons in *Mr Scarborough's Family*. Peers or other owners of large estates are often particularly worried about the behaviour of their heirs but are then utterly miserable if the heirs die. Such is the fate of two fathers in *The Belton Estate* and *An Eye for an Eye*.

Trollope believed that it was natural for the father to have greater love for the son than the son had for the father [*Sir Harry Hotspur of Humblethwaite*, 6]. Nevertheless there can be moments of great pathos when a son suddenly realizes how much he loves

his father. The most memorable is, of course, Archdeacon Grantly's prayer by his dying father's bedside at the start of *Barchester Towers*. One also sees glimpses of this in Trollope's first novel, *The Macdermots of Ballycloran*, in which the son is burdened with a near mad father. When a father has lost his son through death or disgrace he seldom recovers, as was the case with Bernard Amedroz in *The Belton Estate*, the Earl of Scroope in *An Eye for an Eye* and Sir Harry Hotspur in *Sir Harry Hotspur of Humblethwaite*.

When there are disputes between fathers and sons, they are normally reconciled. When a son defies his father's advice in Trollope's fiction he usually learns to regret his disobedience. This happens to Mr Whittlestaff in *An Old Man's Love*, to Fred Pickering in 'The Adventures of Fred Pickering', to Quaverdale in *Mr Scarborough's Family* and to Julius Mackenzie in 'The Spotted Dog'. [➤ Entails.]

Fawn, (Frederick) Viscount. A minor politician in the Palliser novels. When he first appears in *Phineas Finn* [41] he is 'an unmarried peer of something over thirty years of age, with an unrivalled pair of whiskers, [and] a small estate'. He lives with his mother and sisters. His lack of money compels him to seek marriage with a woman who is wealthy. Much of *The Eustace Diamonds* is concerned with his search, and it continues in *Phineas Redux*. In spite of his discomfort at the end of the latter novel, he is back in *The Prime Minister* [6], once again as an under-secretary. [➤ Peerage.]

Fellowships. See Universities.

Feminists. Trollope's attacks on the

Victorian 'rights of women' campaign show a strong dislike for feminism. He never forgot the impact of the feminist Fanny Wright (1795–1852) on his boyhood: it was she who enticed Fanny Trollope to America, thereby leaving the young Anthony without a mother for almost four years. As an older man his attitudes were influenced by his visits to America, where young women of the middle and upper classes were less restrained than in England, and by his friendship for the American feminist, Kate Field. His dislike of feminism was part of his hatred for all Utopian schemes. He liked to attack John Stuart Mill for his views [*He Knew He Was Right*, 55]. The earliest example of his dislike of feminists appeared in his 1859 short story, 'An Unprotected Female at the Pyramids', with the character of Miss Dawkins, the 'unprotected female'. His distaste was not for what she believed but for her aggressive manner of expressing it. He later made the same complaint about the 'rights of women' extremists.

As the 'rights of women' movement gathered strength so did his attacks. His first major onslaught came in *He Knew He Was Right*, published in 1868–9, with the feminist poetess, Wallachia Petrie. Kate Field objected to the character as a caricature of herself. Trollope denied this but added, 'I never said you were like W. Petrie. I said that young woman did not entertain a single opinion on public matters which you could repudiate.' Six years later he returned to the subject in *Is He Popenjoy?*, in which he lambasted Baroness Banmann and Olivia Q. Fleabody, Ph.D. and their supporters. It is worth remembering that none of his three leading feminists is English: two

are American and one is German and their attacks on mankind are part of their attacks on England.

Set against his attacks on theoretical feminism is his concern to help women on a practical level. He supported reform of the working conditions of shop girls and constantly helped the feminist printer, Emily Faithfull. He encouraged many women writers, including Kate Field, and in his 1870 story 'Mrs Brumby' he wrote: 'Had she been a man ... she might have been a prime minister ... But she was a woman, – and the ports were not open to her ... fortunately for us and for the world at large ... the port of literature is open to women. It seems to be the only really desirable harbour to which a female captain can steer her vessel with much hope of success.' He treated those women forced to earn a living with great sensitivity, as in his story 'The Telegraph Girl', and he praised the work of women hired by the Post Office in its new telegraph department. [➤ Girls.]

Fiasco, Major. An ineffective civil servant in *The Small House at Allington*. Trollope chose his name from a figure well known in Victorian England. Alessandro Fiasco was a prominent Italian opera impresario who was born in 1792 and died in 1869, seven years after the serialization of *The Small House at Allington* started. By this time the name had become eponymous for a wholesale disaster. He was famous for the accidents, some nearly fatal, that accompanied his opera productions. He came to England where he settled and, to his everlasting credit, helped to popularize the works of Rossini, Donizetti and Bellini. [➤ *Kept in the Dark*; Names, Origin of.]

Field, Kate (1838–96). An American writer, actress and feminist who lectured both in America and England. Trollope first met her at his brother Tom's house in Florence during an 1860 visit. Trollope greatly enjoyed the company of vivacious young American women; the year before, he had met Mary Knower when returning from his first American visit [➤ 'The Courtship of Susan Bell']. Kate Field was the daughter of an American actor and was living in Florence with her mother when they met. As a 'lion hunter' she gravitated to Tom Trollope's literary circle and in time also added Robert Browning and Walter Savage Landor to her circle of famous friends. She gained fame in England in 1878 when she took part in the first telephone call to a royal residence and sang 'Kathleen Mavourneen' and the 'Cuckoo Song' down the line to Queen Victoria at Osborne.

She quickly became a close friend of both Trollope and his wife, Rose, and he undoubtedly had 'heart-flutterings' towards her. He would meet her again when visiting America in 1861–2 and 1868, and during her visits to England in the 1870s as a lecturer. He and his wife both wrote to her. He was anxious that she should settle into one career. Trollope drew on her less inhibited American manners for his various American female characters [➤ Ophelia Gledd] and probably described his fascination with her, with suitable exaggeration, in 'Mary Gresley'. Kate Field was annoyed when she thought Trollope had based his feminist lecturer, Wallachia Petrie, 'the Republican Browning' in *He Knew He Was Right*, on her. Trollope denied this but added that she and Petrie held the same views.

In his *Autobiography* Trollope discussed his friendship with Kate Field and referred to her in a passage that gave rise to some foolish speculation. 'There is a woman . . . In the last fifteen years she has been, out of my own family, my most chosen friend . . . a ray of light.' Originally he had written, 'There is an American woman . . .' because the passage occurred in a section on those Americans he had liked and followed a discussion of the shady business habits of some American publishers: it was a balance to the criticism and he was singling out Kate Field for particular mention among his *American* friends. Unfortunately Henry Trollope deleted the words 'an American' out of deference to Kate and thereby made the passage seem more important than it is. Trollope never used the word 'love' when describing Kate Field in the *Autobiography*, although he did use it with reference to George Eliot, Sir Charles Taylor and the writer Robert Bell.

Fillgrave, Dr. One of the most prominent and prosperous doctors in Barchester. Although he treats most of the wealthy people of Barsetshire, he is not a good doctor. He first appears when treating the dying dean [*Barchester Towers*, 31]. In *Doctor Thorne* he and Thorne are great rivals. In *The Last Chronicle of Barset* he is physician to Mrs Proudie and Mr Harding, and it is said he had no reputation 'for prolonging life, but he was supposed to add a grace to the hour of departure' [81]. Trollope had fun with the names he gave physicians, often relating them, however unfavourably, to their work [➤ Names, Origin of].

Finn, Mrs Mary. The first wife of

Phineas Finn is a sweet but rather colourless Irish girl called Mary Flood Jones, to whom the errant Phineas returns to marry at the end of *Phineas Finn*. By the start of *Phineas Redux* she has died and Finn is free to return to London and eventually to marry again. [➤ Deaths and Death Scenes; Goesler, Madame Max.]

Finn, Phineas. The central character in two of the Palliser novels, *Phineas Finn* and *Phineas Redux*, Finn is twenty-four years old at the start of the first novel. He is an Irishman, the product of a mixed marriage [➤ *An Eye for an Eye*], and while a Catholic himself he seldom discusses religion. (There is a rare allusion to his being at Mass when he is imprisoned in *Phineas Redux*.) He is often called by other characters a 'child of fortune' and has a continuous series of adventures, most of which advance his career as a politician. As a charming and 'very handsome' man he proves remarkably attractive to various Society ladies, notably Lady Laura Kennedy. Although anxious to improve the condition of tenant farmers in Ireland he is no extreme Irish nationalist. He is proud of his connection with England and thinks of himself as a 'Briton'.

In reflecting on Finn in the *Autobiography*, Trollope wrote that he had been mistaken to make him an Irishman as that lessened his popularity with English readers. He had decided to make the central character of the second Palliser novel Irish because he happened to be revisiting Ireland when he created the 'scheme of the book'. Trollope felt that Finn deserved his 'long suffering' because of his vanity but he also deserved his final success because of his 'constant honesty'. Some readers

have felt that Finn is too weak a character on which to base two novels. This is to misunderstand Trollope's idea of the 'hero' in his novels: Finn is no more heroic than John Eames or indeed most of Trollope's young men. Some have also thought that Phineas Finn was based on actual Irish politicians of the time: the two favourite candidates have been Sir John Pope Hennessy (naturally endorsed by his grandson, James Pope Hennessy, in his book on Trollope) and Chichester Fortesque, who, like Finn, married a wealthy widow with Jewish connections. (Naturally Fortesque's wife endorsed her husband's candidature.) However, after spending almost two decades of his life in Ireland, Trollope was fully capable of creating an Irish MP from his imagination [Mullen, 485].

Finney, Mr. Finney first appears as a disreputable lawyer who acts for John Bold in his attack on Mr Harding's income in *The Warden* [2]. He actually incites Bold to act and is a greedy solicitor, always mindful of the six shillings and eightpence he can extort from clients like Bold. (His 6*s.* 8*d.* fee shows he is not an important man, as this was a solicitor's minimum fee.) He reappears briefly under a different spelling – 'Finnie' – at Mrs Proudie's reception in *Barchester Towers* [10]. In *Doctor Thorne* his social progress has continued and he appears as a guest of the Duke of Omnium at Gatherum Castle [19]. His business career has also prospered as he has become the lawyer for the wealthy Sir Louis Scatcherd.

Fish. Certain foods, such as fish, had a symbolic role in the nineteenth century when to serve fish before a meat dish was a sign of regard. In some provincial hotels the landlord would himself serve it before a noteworthy guest [*The Warden*, 16]. When an 'exacting traveller' in *He Knew He Was Right* asked for fish in a country inn he (probably Trollope himself) is told, 'Cock you up with dainties? If you can't eat your victuals without fish, you must go to Exeter. And then you'll get it stinking mayhap' [14]. Johnny Eames knows he has risen in life when, on a visit to his mother's, she serves him 'a little bit of fish' before his leg of mutton [*The Last Chronicle of Barset*, 27]. Trollope's own liking for that Victorian delicacy, turbot, is amusingly recalled in *Castle Richmond* [37].

Fitzgerald, Burgo. Fitzgerald first appears briefly in *The Small House at Allington* [55] when the future Lady Glencora Palliser is shown to be infatuated with a 'terribly handsome man about town ... said to be deep in every vice'. He becomes an important character in *Can You Forgive Her?* in which he attempts to seduce Lady Glencora away from her husband. Trollope, who repeatedly emphasizes Fitzgerald's dazzling good looks, always resented such 'curled darlings' and the fact that Fitzgerald has neither beard nor whiskers is likewise a warning. Yet, faithful to his belief that even villains – and Fitzgerald is a villain – should have some redeeming feature, Burgo shows kindness to a prostitute he meets. In one of the most extraordinary remarks in Trollope's writing, Burgo tells the girl 'we are alike then' [30]. When he is sent into exile, he is at least provided with a small income. Palliser often thinks about him, especially in *The Duke's Children*. Burgo, whose family is

'the Worcestershire Fitzgeralds', appears to have no connection with the Irish Fitzgeralds of *Castle Richmond*.

Fitzhoward Family. See St Bungay, Duke of.

The Fixed Period. Trollope began this, his forty-second novel, on 17 December 1880, two days after finishing *Kept in the Dark*. He finished it on 28 February 1881. It was serialized anonymously in *Blackwood's Magazine* from October 1881 to March 1882, and published in two volumes by Blackwood in March 1882. Trollope received £450.

This is, perhaps, Trollope's most misunderstood book, although William Blackwood found it 'thoroughly fresh and ... very attractive' and felt the author would reap 'fresh honours'. His only 'futuristic' novel, it is set on a fictional island near New Zealand in 1879–80. He had visited New Zealand in 1872 and in his *Australia and New Zealand* warned against the trend towards excessive government. Trollope used the colony's developing welfare state as the base for a extended attack on some of his oldest enemies: radical theorists who preached a Utopian society under an all-powerful state devised along their lines. When writing this novel he was depressed by the weather, advancing age, and, perhaps, by the move from London to the country. His thoughts turned to death. A week into writing he heard that George Eliot had died and two days before finishing he told one correspondent, 'I am now an old man, 66 [he was really sixty-five], and shall soon have come to the end of my tether.' Blackwood asked Trollope to remove some of the religious language used, presumably, by John Neverbend, but a large number of religious references remain.

Trollope probably got his idea – compulsory euthanasia – from Philip Massinger's seventeenth-century play *The Old Law*, which he read on 8 July 1876. A group of New Zealanders, 'the elite', set up a new colony, Britannula, on a nearby island. They gain their independence and adopt compulsory euthanasia: when people turn sixty-seven – the 'Fixed Period' for life – they are to go to a special 'college' to prepare for death which must occur before they reach the age of sixty-eight. The story is told in the first person by John Neverbend, President of Britannula. (The surname, Neverbend, had been used twenty-three years earlier for two Utopian spinsters in *The Three Clerks*.) The first person to be taken away for death is both a friend of Neverbend and in excellent health. Neverbend's son, Jack, is in love with this friend's daughter. Neverbend's wife opposes the 'Fixed Period'. Just as the first victim is being taken away to the special college, a British warship arrives to reassert British rule and abolish the 'Fixed Period'. Neverbend is taken to England and writes his memoirs, unrepentant to the end.

The novel is an attack in the form of satire. Like Swift, who wrote about infanticide as a way to lessen hunger in Ireland, Trollope was thought to accept what he was denouncing. When he told the Reverend Lucas Collins that the story was 'quite true' he meant that its message reflected his own fears, not what he wanted to see. But his worries about senility are reflected in the book and give it, to some, an ambiguous view on euthanasia. The book is also a study in fanaticism. Sir Winston Churchill said that a fanatic was someone who wouldn't change the subject and couldn't change his mind; this is Neverbend. In a telling phrase Neverbend's friend, Gabriel Crasweller, refers to the 'barbarity of your benevolence'. The story has some similarities to George Orwell's *1984*: *The Fixed Period* is set in the future when governments control life and death. As Orwell would do, Trollope names government ministries by their opposite: the Ministry of War is the Ministry of Benevolence. Unlike Orwell, Trollope could not force himself to be vicious enough to be convincing. He also gives the plot away at the beginning by having Neverbend tell the story after he has been ousted from office.

The story has too many silly names for such a serious subject: it was not a topic that could be made lighter by humour. The island's major city is named Gladstonopolis as Gladstone was prime minister when the book was written; there is a Duke of Hatfield (a play on the third Marquis of Salisbury, Foreign Secretary 1878–80), while the civil servant sent to administer the colony is Sir Ferdinando Brown. Trollope names the gunboat that comes to subdue Britannula the *John Bright*, and writes that the name was that of a 'gallant officer, who, in the beginning of the century, had seated himself on a barrel of gunpowder, and had, single-handed, quelled a mutiny'. It was of course a joke against the veteran Quaker Radical, John Bright. Finally, the troops sent out with the gunboat come from the North-north-west Birmingham Regiment: Bright was one of the MPs for Birmingham, a Radical centre. The gunboat's officers include Captain Battleax, Lieutenant Crosstrees and a 'young naval lad', Lord

Alfred Percy, son of the Duke of Northumberland. [➤ Names, Origin of.] Citizens of Britannula include Brittlereed, Tallowax, Puddlebrane and Exorses – all redolent of Trollope's reading in seventeenth-century drama. He used various words associated with cricket in naming the team of visiting English cricketers which included Sir Kennington Oval, Lord Marylebone, Sir Lords Longstop and Mr Stumps. The best private joke is that Trollope was approaching sixty-six when he wrote his novel about automatic death when sixty-seven.

There is an 'authorial intrusion' in the reference to 'the great Banting who has preserved us all so completely from the horrors of obesity'. Trollope himself had tried a Banting diet in the 1860s [➤ Food]. There are other private references. He has Captain Battleax insist on the importance of dressing for dinner, something in which Trollope believed strongly. He recalled his interest in the Alpine Club by predicting 'steel climbing arms' for mountaineers. His decision to have Neverbend exiled to England may have been inspired by Sir Julius Vogel's decision to resign the premiership of New Zealand and go to England as Agent-General in 1876. Vogel (1835–99) was largely responsible for the creation of New Zealand's 'welfare state' and he, like Neverbend, wrote a book, although not his memoirs. [➤ John Caldigate.]

The novel discusses several topics in which Trollope had long been interested. When the English cricket side visits Britannula he asks if ladies from the colonies will be accepted in London Society [➤ Anglo-American Marriages]. The novel touches on the 'English world': the importance of the

language and the question of who is a foreigner [5]. The book reflects Trollope's view that all the colonies would eventually separate from the British Crown. Cremation, still illegal in the United Kingdom, would dispose of those killed in the 'college'. Trollope was a theoretical supporter of cremation in England and while he does not denounce the practice he does not paint it in very attractive colours. He also associates it with the fanatic, Neverbend. There are attacks on European armaments and religious fundamentalists. The Britannulists use decimal coinage, which would have pleased Plantagenet Palliser, and the House of Lords is defended. (Trollope was unaware that he was being considered for a peerage by Liberal leaders in the year in which *The Fixed Period* was published.)

As in any futuristic novel there are references to new inventions: the 'mousometor' and 'melpomeneon' (musical instruments); 'water telegrams' from England to Britannula; wicker helmets, steam-bowlers and new rules for scoring cricket matches; hair telephones; steam curricles and a 'reporting telephone-apparatus'. While the book is neither terribly enjoyable nor one of Trollope's best-written novels, it may have one claim to critical approval: with the continuing growth of governmental power and of demands for euthanasia, it is even more relevant now than in 1881.

Flashback. *An Eye for an Eye* and *The Fixed Period* are the only novels in which the story is told as a flashback, although *The Macdermots of Ballycloran* begins with the narrator viewing the ruined country house and then learning how the family, whose home it once was, had been destroyed.

Florence. A woman's name that Trollope used in his later novels [➤ *Cousin Henry*; *Mr Scarborough's Family*]. His niece, Florence Bland, acted as his secretary and amanuensis for most of his later novels and his use of the name was probably a private joke he shared with her. It appears that the name Florence was unheard of in England until parents began using it for girls born after Florence Nightingale became famous, that is, after 1855. Therefore in *The Claverings* the use of Florence as the Christian name for a main character 'not yet twenty' appears to be an anachronism. As the book was written in the autumn of 1864 the young girl, if nineteen, would have had to have been born in 1845. However, Dickens has a Florence in *Dombey and Son* (1848). [For the city of Florence, ➤ Italy.]

Food. Food is often used to indicate a character's personality in Trollope's fiction. In *The Warden* Archdeacon Grantly's expansive character is seen in his elegant and well-stocked breakfast table [8]. In *The Prime Minister* a brief description of a simple meal indicates the simplicity of Plantagenet Palliser. He returns from Windsor, where he was commissioned by the Queen to form a government, to dine on a steak, a potato and a glass of mineral water [*The Prime Minister*, 7]. Certain foods, like fish, had a symbolic role, and likewise certain ways of serving food [See *service à la Russe*, below]. Mealtimes could also be treacherous, as well as a basis for snobbery, due to the move of the principal meal from the middle of the day or early afternoon to the evening, at least among the middle classes: Mrs Mason puts the lawyer, Dockwrath, in his

place by saying, however ungrammatically, '"If I had known that an early dinner was required, it should have been provided." "I never dine early," replied Dockwrath, thinking that some imputation of a low way of living was conveyed in this supposition that he required a dinner under the pseudonym of a lunch' [*Orley Farm*, 8]. In 'The Two Heroines of Plumplington' the pretentious Mr Greenmantle and his daughter Emily had their 'family meal' at 7.30, not because 'he liked to have his dinner at that hour better than any other, but because it was considered to be fashionable. Old Mr Gresham ... always dined at half-past seven, and Mr Greenmantle rather followed the habits of a county gentleman's life' [3].

The most common use of food is in the portrayal of characters who are either selfish or pretentious. In *Orley Farm* we are given an early warning that we are not going to like the rich Masons when the tight-fisted Mrs Mason serves a guest at their country house a few old bones and a potato [8]. Because Trollope himself enjoyed eating and was a generous host [Mullen, 435–42], it is surprising that there are so few detailed descriptions of pleasurable meals in his fiction. He normally mentions only a few items of food to show joviality and hospitality, but two exceptions – both are descriptions of Christmas feasts – occur in *Orley Farm* and in 'Christmas at Thompson Hall'.

The way in which food was served is very important in Trollope's fiction. In the mid-nineteenth century a new method of dining became increasingly fashionable among the middle classes: *service à la Russe*. This called for more courses with small portions of numerous elaborate – and often foreign – dishes handed round by many servants. The table was highly decorated with massive displays of flowers and silver. Trollope preferred the older, less pretentious English method of setting dishes, such as roasts, on the table for guests to help themselves. His first attack on the new fashion (already attacked by Thackeray) came when he moved back to England and denounced it as 'a vulgar and intolerable nuisance among us second-class gentry with our eight hundred a year' [*Framley Parsonage*, 17]. [➤ Money.] To have a meal in the new fashion meant that those without a lot of servants had to hire outsiders to cook and serve the food. His best account of a pretentious dinner *à la Russe* is in *Miss Mackenzie* in which a hired servant, Grandairs, measures out the champagne and serves little daubs of concoctions that 'could hardly have been intended by Christian cooks as food for men' [8]. It is hardly surprising that the swindler Lopez has a pretentious *service à la Russe* meal prepared by the caterers 'Messrs Stewam and Sugarscraps' [*The Prime Minister*, 48].

On the other hand the knowledgeable reader will know that the solicitor Toogood is going to be trustworthy because, when he first invites John Eames for a meal, he announces that he will not be 'regaled à la Russe'. Instead Eames gets one of Trollope's favourite meals, 'a leg of mutton and trimmings and a glass of port such as you don't get every day of your life' [*The Last Chronicle of Barset*, 40].

Trollope was a firm believer, as he says in *Ayala's Angel*, in the symbolic importance of 'dressing for dinner' and those who neglect such ceremonies as 'a bore' are likely to end up finding that wives, laws and Church are also a bore. He always travelled with the proper clothes for dinner, even on the American frontier. 'Dressing for dinner' could be done fairly quickly, at least by gentlemen, and one lawyer interprets the rule as little more than washing his hands, putting on his slippers, and straightening his tie [*Mr Scarborough's Family*, 17]. At formal dinner parties the guests go into the dining-room in an elaborate order of precedence, mastery of which was essential to a Victorian hostess.

Trollope seems to have had a particular horror, dating from his school days, of greasy, undercooked mutton and it often indicates poverty in his fiction [*The Kellys and the O'Kellys*, 8]. He advises travellers that roast fowl is 'the safest dinner at an English inn' [*An Old Man's Love*, 9]. His detailed knowledge of buying meat and growing vegetables often appears in his travel books or in occasional essays such as those for the *Pall Mall Gazette*. [➤ *London Tradesmen*.] In the mid-1860s he even went on one of the first diets designed by William Banting, hence the reference in *The Fixed Period* to 'the great Banting who has preserved us ... from the horrors of obesity' [9].

[➤ Coffee; Drinks; Wine.]

Foreigners. Foreigners, by which is normally meant Europeans, are not very frequent in Trollope's fiction. The exception are those who appear in those novels and numerous short stories set in Europe, in which they behave in their own countries in much the same way as his British characters. They usually do not play memorable roles in his English fiction and when they do it is almost always a threatening one; for instance Herr Vosner, who defrauds some not very admirable Englishmen at their club in *The Way We Live Now*, the Italian characters in *Lady Anna*, and the 'Franco-Poles', Count Pateroff and Sophie Gordaloup, in *The Claverings*. Foreign servants tend to be either pretentious or troublemakers: the Marquis of Brotherton's Italian servant in *Is He Popenjoy?* and Signora Madeline Neroni's in *Barchester Towers* are good examples.

In *The Three Clerks* Trollope has great sport with a stereotyped Frenchman, Victoire Jaquêtanàpe, who is grinning, swaggering, flamboyant and short, and he has a rather similar character in his short story, 'An Unprotected Female at the Pyramids'. [For how this was connected with Trollope's hatred of Napoleon III, ➤ France.] Many years later a similar character reappears as a French wine merchant in one of his essays for the *Pall Mall Gazette* [➤ *London Tradesmen*]. Sometimes foreigners appear as a form of non-local colour: the best example of this is the German lecturer, Von Bauer, in *Orley Farm* or the Bavarian feminist, Baroness Banmann, in *Is He Popenjoy?* Some rakish noblemen make unsuitable marriages to shady Italians, but the wives are never really developed as characters. [*Lady Anna*; *Is He Popenjoy?*]

Foreigners who are important include the Bohemian bigamist and murderer, the Reverend Joseph Emilius, in *The Eustace Diamonds* and *Phineas Redux*, and the Polish count, Edouard Pateroff, and his sister, Madame Sophie Gordeloup, in *The Claverings*.

There are also some English people who have become almost foreign by their long residence on the Continent: among these the extraordinary Stanhope family in *Barchester Towers* and the admirable Madame Max Goesler in the Palliser novels are the best examples. Some disreputable characters, of whom Melmotte, in *The Way We Live Now*, and Lopez, in *The Prime Minister*, are the most notorious, are of uncertain origin but have some continental connections.

Trollope did not normally regard Americans as foreigners because they were part of the 'English world'.

The Fortnightly Review (1865–1954). In 1865 Trollope became perhaps the most incongruous member of a group behind a new monthly review that he and Frederic Chapman of Chapman & Hall had begun planning the year before. It was to be modelled on the French periodical, *Revue des Deux Mondes*. With him and Chapman were such leading intellectuals as Frederic Harrison, a 'positivist', and G. H. Lewes, a 'free thinker'. The magazine was published from Chapman & Hall's offices. Trollope's involvement was part of his longstanding desire to be regarded as a serious writer and not simply as a novelist. It was also a fulfilment of his youthful involvement in planning an 'abortive periodical which was intended to be the best thing ever done'. (Interestingly, when discussing the planning of the new review in his *Autobiography* in 1875–6 he used terms similar to those he had used in 1869, when writing 'The Panjandrum', his short story about youthful plans to establish a new magazine.)

The review was to be free of 'all restrictions of party and of editorial "consistency"', and was to be based on 'freedom of speech, combined with personal responsibility'. Trollope pledged £1,250 and the company had £8,000 capital. Trollope also became the first chairman of the board. He insisted that articles be signed, which was unusual at the time. Although the original idea was that the magazine was open to all views, Trollope admits in his *Autobiography* that 'our new publication became an organ of liberalism'. Given the growth of agnosticism in liberal intellectual circles, his insistence that 'nothing should appear denying or questioning the divinity of Christ' was in part a reaction to his associates and showed his own discomfort as well as his deep Christian faith. (His continuing unease is seen in the famous interview with John Morley, an agnostic, for the position of editor. Trollope asked, 'Do you believe in the divinity of our blessed Lord and Saviour Jesus Christ?') This drove some supporters away and he later felt the restriction was 'preposterous' in a journal open to all opinions. However, there was 'in truth so little combination of idea among us, that we were not justified in our trust or in our expectations'.

Trollope convinced Lewes that he should become the first editor. Lewes was succeeded by Morley [➤ *Thackeray*] and in 1882 Morley was succeeded by T. H. S. Escott. Trollope alone opposed the idea of serializing novels as this would lessen the high intellectual tone but he was overruled on business grounds so the new magazine started with *The Belton Estate*, which appeared just after Bagehot's first article on 'The English Constitution'. The magazine also serialized *The Eustace Diamonds* and *Lady Anna*.

The magazine's title was Trollope's idea but unfortunately the publication did not prosper, despite the high quality of its articles. A fortnightly distribution was difficult and in November 1866 it became a monthly, like most other reviews; it incongruously kept its title and readers of *The Eustace Diamonds* [55] no doubt smiled when Plantagenet Palliser says: 'There's the Fortnightly Review comes out but once a month and I'm told it does very well.' In fact it did not and in 1871 it was handed over to Chapman & Hall and was worth 'little or nothing'.

For Trollope the *Review* was important because it introduced him to wider intellectual circles, partly through dinners for staff and contributors. It also allowed him to write serious reviews and articles including two on Cicero and one each on the Civil Service, Iceland, and his friend G. H. Lewes after his death. In the May 1866 issue the magazine published his parody of medievalism, 'The Gentle Euphemia'. He used the magazine to wage war against the historian E. A. Freeman, who had written an article attacking fox-hunting. After Trollope's reply Freeman was allowed a rejoinder, but Trollope was not allowed by Morley to reply to this. Despite the fact that Trollope lost money and that by the late 1870s 'there is much in the now established principles of *The Fortnightly* with which I do not myself agree', he was still proud of its high standing. The magazine was incorporated into the *Contemporary Review*, which acknowledges the incorporation by proudly adding, 'founded in 1865 by Anthony Trollope'. The *Contemporary* is still flourishing, the lone survivor of the great Victorian reviews.

Fortune. Trollope usually uses this

term to indicate the money a wife brings to her marriage under her settlement or the money she may eventually inherit from her family. In many novels characters seem exceptionally well informed about women's 'fortunes' although sometimes gossip does inflate the figures, for instance in the case of Eleanor Bold in *Barchester Towers*. Sometimes, as in *The Last Chronicle of Barset* [40], the term can indicate the money both a man and a woman bring to a marriage.

Fothergill, Mr. Fothergill, who manages the properties of the old Duke of Omnium in *Framley Parsonage*, also appears in two other Barsetshire novels, *The Small House at Allington* and *The Last Chronicle of Barset* [8] in which he is a 'sharp man'. In one Palliser novel, *Phineas Redux*, his quarrel about foxhunting with Lord Chiltern causes the new Duke of Omnium to dismiss him. Great ducal estates in the nineteenth century were increasingly managed by a man of business and Fothergill is Trollope's most developed portrayal of the type. 'If one wanted to speak about a woman or a horse or a picture the Duke could, on occasions, be affable enough. But through Mr Fothergill the Duke was approached' [*Framley Parsonage*, 19]. Yates Umbleby, the manager of the Gresham estate in *Doctor Thorne*, is an inferior specimen of the same type, but he is succeeded by Mortimer Gazebee, a man more in the Fothergill mould.

Fox-hunting. Fox-hunting was Trollope's favourite sport and one of his greatest pleasures, although his heavy weight and poor eyesight meant he was not a good horseman. One character in *Is He Popenjoy?* says, 'Hunting is like women. It's a jealous sport' [12]. He admitted in his *Autobiography* that 'I have dragged it into many novels, – into too many no doubt, – but I have always felt myself deprived of a legitimate joy when the nature of the tale has not allowed me a hunting chapter.' He took up riding to hounds shortly after going to Ireland in 1841 and carried it on fervently until the 1876 season, when he gave it up because he felt he was getting too old.

Trollope's passion had several important effects on his writing. One reason he wrote so much was to earn the money to pay for his hunting. He estimated that it cost him £5 a day for each horse for every day that he hunted. This sum did not include the cost for his two sons or for the many guests he invited [*Phineas Redux*, 16]. By the late 1860s he was subscribing about £50 a year to the Essex Hunt, making him almost the largest untitled subscriber. (This sum was, after all, more than a year's wage for one of his letter-carriers.) Trollope spent about £500 in an average year on hunting, a sum equal to the average annual income of more than a dozen postmen.

Trollope liked to hunt on at least two days and often three days a week during the season which lasted from November to March. (He did not approve of cub-hunting in October.) Sometimes he went out even more often: in one seventeen-day period in November 1869 he was out with the hounds on eight days. Hunting for Trollope was not just physical excitement and exercise, though he valued both. Its main benefit was that from the first it was a sign that he was accepted by other people. He portrays the delight he found in Irish hunts in

'The O'Conors of Castle Conor' and in his first fictional fox-hunt in *The Kellys and the O'Kellys*. Significantly his last hunting scene in *The Land-Leaguers* was set in Ireland. While he liked to dress properly, he laughed at those who spent too much time or money on fashionable hunting 'togs'.

When he returned to England in 1859, he used hunting as a means to observe the countryside and county society. The best-informed obituary of him recalled that he carried a note-book in which to record incidents which he could later use [Mullen, 711]. [For examples of this, ➤ *Can You Forgive Her?* and *The American Senator*.] Trollope was quite aware of the growing debate over hunting and the opposition by those he labelled 'philoanimalists'. He discussed the rights and wrongs of hunting in *The American Senator* [10] and in *Marion Fay* he made an enthusiastic defence of hunting both against other sports and against those who attacked it as a 'barbarous' pastime [2, 13]. He engaged in a fierce exchange over it in the *Fortnightly Review* in 1869 with E. A. Freeman, the well-known historian who later became a cherished friend. Ten years later Trollope still remembered his debate with Freeman and when writing his *Life of Cicero* used the book to renew his war with him. He attacked Freeman's daring to use a quote from Cicero to support his arguments against riding to hounds. To Trollope, Freeman's was an argument 'against all out of door sports'. In an article for *Good Words* in February 1879, Trollope claimed that there was no pursuit 'of which people who know nothing know so little as they do of hunting'.

Trollope described different types of hunters in his *Hunting Sketches* and also wrote about the sport in an essay for *Saint Pauls* [➤ *British Sports and Pastimes*]. He reluctantly came to accept that clergymen should not ride to hounds: both the Reverend Henry Clavering in *The Claverings* and Dean Lovelace in *Is He Popenjoy?* exemplified priests for whom the injunction was a heavy burden.

Readers who dislike hunting may generally gallop through those chapters devoted to it and need only pause if an important character is killed during a hunt, as in *Ralph the Heir*. Trollope also used hunting metaphors in many of his writings: in 'Aaron Trow' he compares the feelings of an escaped prisoner to those of a cornered fox.

[➤ Horses; MFH.]

Framley Parsonage. Trollope's tenth novel and the fourth in the Barsetshire series. His work sheet says that he began writing on 2 November 1859 and finished on 27 June 1860 with several interruptions but there is some confusion regarding the date of starting, for which see below. It was serialized in the new *Cornhill* in sixteen monthly parts, beginning in the first issue in January 1860 and ending in April 1861, in which month it was published by Smith, Elder as a three-volume novel. Both the serialization and the book contained illustrations by Millais. Trollope was paid £1,000, almost double his previous payment.

Framley Parsonage was Trollope's most significant novel because it established him as one of the best-known novelists of his day. In the autumn of 1859 he learned that the publisher George Smith was about to start a new monthly magazine to be edited by Thackeray, whom Trollope regarded as the greatest novelist of the day. Because he lived in Ireland, Trollope had few contacts in the London literary world. However, his recent novels had made his name well known: *The Times* hailed him in 1859 as 'the most fertile, the most popular, the most successful author . . . of the circulating library sort' [➤ *Castle Richmond*]. Nevertheless he wrote a 'Dear Sir' letter to Thackeray with a deferential air and offered short stories for the new magazine. He was astounded to receive a letter from Smith as well as a delightful one from Thackeray asking him to provide a novel to begin serialization in the first issue. Trollope was so delighted with this reply that it became one of the few letters that he kept; he included it in his *Autobiography* although Rose Trollope seems to have cut off the signature to add to her autograph collection.

Trollope hurried to London and offered Smith the novel on which he was working, *Castle Richmond*, as Chapman & Hall agreed to release him from their contract. Smith later wrote that 'An Irish novel would not suit my public. His genius shone in delineating clerical life and character and I wanted a clerical novel.' In his *Autobiography* Trollope recalled how 'on my journey back to Ireland, in the railway carriage, I wrote the first few pages'. By the dates given in his memoir this would mean he started on 4 November but his work sheet says he started on 2 November, the day on which he would have left Ireland. Trollope either misdated his work sheet, which seems difficult to believe, or muddled his dates when writing the *Autobiography*. (This would mean he was in London on 1–2 November, not

3–4.) He wrote seven pages in the train and by 5 November he had completed thirty-eight. Within the month the total had grown to 200 – and this was in the midst of moving from Ireland to England and taking up an important new position in the Post Office. The demand for the *Cornhill* was phenomenal and extra printers were hired to produce 120,000 copies. Since many people borrowed these from circulating libraries and read the contents aloud to large families, Trollope's audience was not far short of one million. Probably no other novel by him ever reached such a large audience.

Framley Parsonage also marked several other 'firsts' in Trollope's career: for the first time his work was serialized; for the first time a novel was illustrated; for the first time payment exceeded his official annual income; and for the first time he was paid more than his mother had ever received for a novel. His Post Office salary was about the amount he mentioned in *Framley Parsonage* when he referred to 'us second-class gentry with our eight hundred a year – there or thereabout' [17]. When he added his literary earnings he had already soared far above that level and the success of this novel pointed to yet more money. No wonder Trollope accepted Smith's desire for a clerical novel and said he would produce one with two archbishops if needed.

The action in *Framley Parsonage* begins about six months after the conclusion of *Doctor Thorne* and about four or five years after the Proudies arrived in Barchester [*Barchester Towers*]. As with almost all the other Barsetshire novels, *Framley Parsonage* is centred on a moral quandary confronting one individual. *The Warden* is dominated by Mr Harding's struggle with his conscience, while *Doctor Thorne* is dominated by Thorne's trying to reconcile his conflicting obligations to different people. *The Small House at Allington* is concerned with Lily Dale's stubborn devotion to an unworthy fiancé who jilts her and *The Last Chronicle of Barset* focuses on Mr Crawley's misery when accused of theft. Only *Barchester Towers* is not dominated by any one character, as Mrs Proudie, Mr Slope and Archdeacon Grantly fight for control of the novel as well as of the diocese.

The Reverend Mark Robarts, Vicar of Framley, is the central character – hero would not be the right description – in *Framley Parsonage*. He was the type of boy who was marked for success at Trollope's schools and indeed Robarts and the novelist were both bred up at Harrow. Trollope had worked with tremendous diligence for over a dozen years as a novelist and twice as long in the Post Office to reach the rank he now enjoyed in his two careers. Robarts simply fell into his good fortune because of charm, good looks and good luck. Yet Trollope's account is not spiteful or vindictive, nor does it show any of the sarcasm that had marked *The Warden*. Because of this effortless rise to success Robarts is, not surprisingly, the least memorable of all the major characters in the Barsetshire series. Yet Robarts's story is Trollope's best account of a subject that fascinated him: how a person whose progress through life has been supremely placid reacts to a spell of bad luck that suddenly confronts him, bad luck normally brought on by a minor moral flaw in his character. With Robarts the flaw is the other side of his most obvious characteristic. His 'lines fell into pleasant places' because he had the knack of making himself liked by important people. But he lacked 'the strengthened courage of a man' [42] and in this was similar to many of Trollope's younger men, for example Harry Clavering in *The Claverings*. Robarts attempted to reach too high, into the great world of politics and of Society, the world of the Pallisers, for none of which was he prepared. This new world undermined his judgement, allowed him to trust a man he otherwise would not have trusted, got him into serious trouble with bills, threatened him with disgrace and brought him to the brink of disaster. How he coped and how he was saved at the last moment form the main plot of the novel.

Within the first few pages of *Framley Parsonage* – the pages Trollope wrote on the train leaving London – he gives a description of Robarts's character, which is his general view of human nature: 'He was no born heaven's cherub, neither was he a born fallen devil's spirit. Such as his training made him, such he was. He had large capabilities for good – and aptitudes also for evil, quite enough . . . to make it needful that he should repel temptation as temptation only can be repelled.' Because of his friendship with Lord Lufton, Robarts is offered the living of Framley with £900 a year. For a Devonshire doctor's young son to spring so comfortably high in the clerical world so quickly was a stroke of good fortune, but not one without some parallels in the real world. (Robarts's background and character have many similarities with that of Phineas Finn.)

Robarts's luck finds an exact

opposite in the life of his nearby clerical neighbour, the Reverend Josiah Crawley, who makes his first named appearance in *Framley Parsonage*. Crawley, who is brought into Barsetshire by Dean Arabin, is a man of singular misfortunes, which, Trollope points out, do not make him a saint. Crawley has his own faults – pride and bitterness. By contrasting Robarts and Crawley, Trollope was able to show the glaring inequality of clerical stipends, about which he felt strongly. He knew the old system was 'picturesque' and 'thoroughly English', yet it was wrong and needed reform even though such a reform would destroy most of the situations that made the Barsetshire plots possible.

Fanny Robarts – the vicar's wife – is one of Trollope's best portraits of the ideal Victorian wife. When Lady Lufton, the young Lord Lufton's mother, attacks the vicar for his visit to the Duke of Omnium, Fanny defends him and although her ladyship is furious she eventually says, 'There is no duty which any woman owes to any other human being at all equal to that which she owes to her husband' [5]. Here we have the linchpin of Victorian marriage and this was a view that Trollope was to endorse frequently [➤ *Rachel Ray*]. Yet *Framley Parsonage* also provides one of the best insights into the complicated patterns of married life at the time: how man and wife, though living in separate spheres, could draw together in a time of trouble. Lady Lufton is another of Trollope's forceful older women and his description of her is his finest and most affectionate portrait of a dowager.

It may well be no accident that it was in this novel, the novel that saw

him established as a highly prosperous novelist, that Trollope recalled the most upsetting experience of his early life. The scene in which the bailiffs invade Fanny Robarts's comfortable drawing-room to cart off her possessions to pay for her husband's debts is not a scene that Trollope had to invent. 'O ladies,' he says in one of his direct addresses to his readers, 'think of what it would be to have two bailiffs rummaging' in your rooms [44]. To know what Fanny Robarts was thinking, Trollope had only to recall what Fanny Trollope had felt when the bailiffs rummaged through her drawing-room in 1834 while the nineteen-year-old Anthony smuggled some of her most cherished possessions from their grasp. (His mother was still alive and just capable of reading this episode.) In choosing the name Fanny he may have had this in mind, although it was one of his favourite names for women. He drew upon another disturbing event of his own youth, an involvement with a money-lender, to show how both Lufton and Robarts got caught up in the dreadful world of bills.

While the landed gentry are usually treated with respect by Trollope, Nathaniel Sowerby is his most disreputable representative of an old landed family. He is a man who dishonours all his pledges: he drags Lord Lufton into large debts and by inveigling Robarts into signing a bill he almost ruins him as well. Yet when Lufton denounces him to the vicar as a rogue who has 'pleasure in cheating', Trollope intervenes to say that for all his faults he still could find 'the means of repentance'.

Framley Parsonage has a greater involvement with the sophisticated world of London, particularly the political world, than the previous Barsetshire novels. Cabinet ministers appear and Mark Robarts visits one minister's office in London. Sowerby, who is an MP, even makes an allusion to a well-known saying of Trollope's youth, much heard during the debates on the Reform Bill of 1832, when he says 'the Bill and nothing but the Bill'. The country-house parties that Robarts attends shows the close connection between the world of politics and Society: a connection that Trollope would begin to emphasize in a few years' time with the Palliser novels. Here much of it centres on the head of the Palliser family, the somewhat scandalous old Duke of Omnium. This is also the first of Trollope's novels to give extended attention to the London Season as a stage for husband-hunting. The *Jupiter* continued to carry London's harsh judgements into the quiet vicarages of Barsetshire.

Perhaps because Trollope was settling down to life in England for the first time in two decades, *Framley Parsonage* presents one of his best portraits of English country life. One factor that is constantly present is the overwhelming importance of letters to this world. Trollope lovingly follows the route of one letter and even manages to allude to one of his favourite grievances, the refusal by some people, normally Evangelicals, to receive post on Sunday [5] [➤ Sabbath]. Many of the concerns of the postal surveyor are presented in humorous form: the postman is afraid that if he pauses for hospitality, word will reach his superiors (surveyors like Trollope); a letter-carrier is bribed one shilling by Mrs Robarts when she wants him to wait ten minutes while she finishes an important letter. (One shilling would be close to a tenth of his weekly wage.) We also see the way in which so many people were governed by posting times and the arrival of the postbag at a country house. All of these are superb examples of the ways in which Trollope used his official career to enrich his writing.

As well as telling the story of Mark Robarts, Trollope knew that a love plot was necessary and he provided more than one. The main one centres on Lord Lufton's romance with Mark's sister, Lucy. Few things were more popular with Victorian readers than a middle-class girl being wooed by a rich peer [➤ *The Duke's Children*]. Trollope added another romance, when the stunning though cold beauty Griselda Grantly is pursued by both Lord Lufton and the even greater prize, Lord Dumbello. By developing Griselda's character Trollope was able to bring back from the first two Barsetshire novels the whole Grantly connection and Griselda's grandfather, Mr Harding, in slightly different roles. Mrs Grantly assumes a greater importance as she manages the complicated manoeuvrings involved in finding a titled husband for her daughter. For a third, more mature romance, Trollope brought back characters from the third Barset novel, *Doctor Thorne*. He has the doctor propose to the great heiress, Martha Dunstable, 'the richest woman in England' [39], in one of the most famous letters in Trollope's fiction. *Framley Parsonage* is filled with other familiar characters: the bishop and Mrs Proudie reappear and at first that formidable lady seems almost conciliatory, but she is soon at her old ways again when she takes over a public lecture [6].

Since Thackeray gave *Framley Parsonage* pride of place in the *Cornhill*, it received wide publicity. Mrs Gaskell wrote to Smith: 'I wish Mr Trollope would go on writing *Framley Parsonage* for ever. I don't see any reason why it should come to an end and everyone I know is always dreading the *last* number.' The *Saturday Review* said that the novel 'had been an inmate of the drawing-room, it has travelled with us in the train, it has lain on the breakfast-table' and that 'no London belle dared to pretend to consider herself literary' unless she knew the latest episode. In Florence, it pleased not only Trollope's family but also Elizabeth Barrett Browning: 'Anthony Trollope is really superb.' In France it attracted a major review in the influential *Revue des Deux Mondes* and in America it achieved wide popularity when the *Cornhill* was pirated there, although one senator's wife was slightly annoyed when Dr Thorne's romance threatened to obscure the love matches of the two younger couples [Mullen, 357–8].

The novel also contains attacks on current fashion, like Mrs Proudie's 'conversazione' as opposed to good old-fashioned teas [17]. There is also a reference to the controversial appointment in 1858 of the Whig peer Lord Clanricarde as Lord Privy Seal in Lord Palmerston's administration when Trollope has the *Jupiter* ask if 'vice of every kind was to be considered, in these days of Queen Victoria, as a passport to the Cabinet' [18]. (Clanricarde had been Postmaster General from 1846 to 1852.) Trollope also takes the opportunity to defend himself against charges that he did not write about clergymen's clerical work: 'I could hardly have steered clear of

subjects on which it has not been my intention to pronounce an opinion, and I should either have laden my fiction with sermons or I should have degraded my sermons into fiction' [42].

Framley Parsonage will always be seen as one of Trollope's best novels.

[➤ Cheltenham; Church of England; Music.]

France. Trollope used France as a setting for more of his fiction than any other foreign country. In general, while Trollope agreed that Frenchmen were better at making coffee he disliked French influence on English taste and, stout Englishman that he was, he had a particular horror of flimsy French furniture. Like many Victorians, he had ambivalent feelings about the country. He enjoyed visiting France during his many travels abroad: his first visit appears to have been in the mid-1830s when his mother was writing her *Paris and the Parisians* (1836) and his last was in 1881. In between he made numerous visits to various parts of France. He could read French and was able to speak it to a limited degree. As a child he had acted in several of Molière's plays arranged by his mother for family parties. He retained an interest in the French dramatist which he passed on to his son Henry, who eventually wrote a creditable biography of Molière.

Like many men of his time Trollope had a considerable interest in the French Revolution, which provided the setting of his only historical novel, *La Vendée*, which took a hostile view of it. He had a reasonably favourable view of the moderate king, Louis Philippe [*The Bertrams*, 24], but he developed a deep antipathy to Napoleon

III (ruled 1848–70) whom he considered a tyrant. (This opinion was no doubt strengthened when Trollope and his wife were nearly knocked down by the Emperor's carriage while in Bayonne.) This political hostility influenced his attitude towards France. Napoleon III is ridiculed through the characters of Victoire Jaquêtanàpe in *The Three Clerks* and M. Delabordeau in 'An Unprotected Female at the Pyramids'. The fact that Frenchmen submitted to Napoleon III's rule [➤ *The Commentaries of Caesar*], along with the Emperor's policy towards Italy, made Trollope hostile towards the French government [➤ 'The Gentle Euphemia']. This led to outbursts against the French in his letters and he was probably also influenced by his brother Tom, who was rabidly anti-French. After the fall of Napoleon III, Trollope's dislike lessened. He believed that France would be better under a constitutional monarchy. [➤ *La Vendée*.]

These political feelings rarely enter into his fiction in any sustained manner. This is particularly the case in the short stories set in France, in which French characters are described with great sensitivity and are often introduced by a small sermon in which Trollope advises his readers to remember that the French have a right to their own ways. *La Vendée* is set in western France while his other French novel, *The Golden Lion of Granpère*, is set in the east, on the border of Alsace-Lorraine. His two French short stories, 'La Mère Bauche' and 'The Château of Prince Polignac', reflect his stays in French hotels, the first in the Pyrenees and the other in Le Puy. Two other stories are partly set in France: 'Christmas at Thompson Hall'

(Paris) and 'The Lady of Launay' (Normandy). A few of his novels, such as *Can You Forgive Her?* and *He Knew He Was Right*, have short scenes of travel through France. In *An Eye for an Eye* France is the home of the heroine's disgraced father and serves as her place of exile after her own disgrace.

Trollope's work was known in France and his novels often received long and favourable reviews in the *Revue des Deux Mondes* [➤ *The Fortnightly Review*; *Framley Parsonage*]. Several were translated into French.

French Novels. The use of French novels in Trollope's fiction often denotes an idle and somewhat dissolute man. In Trollope's lifetime French novels were much more 'advanced', especially in sexual matters, than those written in England and America. Lazy men like Maurice Maule in *Phineas Redux* or Burgo Fitzgerald in *Can You Forgive Her?* dawdle over their breakfasts with French novels. In *Sir Harry Hotspur of Humblethwaite*, the villain reads a French novel on his way home from the Prince of Wales's house at Sandringham while his servant reads an English sensational one. In *Mr Scarborough's Family* the wicked paterfamilias reads French novels 'through the hot July days' [1]. In *Phineas Redux* [61] there is an amusing dialogue between an English novelist and a barrister who accuses English novelists of taking their plots from French novels. [For Trollope's fury at Victor Hugo, ➤ *The Vicar of Bullhampton*.]

Friendship. Friendship meant a great deal to Trollope. In his boyhood he had few friends and as he testifies in his *Autobiography* he had a craving to be popular and to have many friends.

This was achieved only when he returned to England from Ireland in 1859 and became a member of several clubs. In these he formed close friendships with many influential men of his time, most notably Thackeray and Millais. Other friendships from fox-hunting circles helped to give him that detailed insight into country life so evident in his fiction. By the end of his life Trollope was known as one of the most popular figures in the literary world and was renowned for his kindness and help to his friends [➤ Eliot, George].

All sorts of friendships between men occur in his fiction. Although Trollope, unlike so many Victorian men, never enjoyed those deep, almost passionate friendships that verged on love affairs, he does portray one such in the relations between Owen Fitzgerald and the young earl in *Castle Richmond*. Trollope was evidently happier with the quiet, 'manly' friendship that he defined best in *The Vicar of Bullhampton* in which there is an almost Wildean aphorism: 'Years are wanted to make a friendship, but days suffice for men and women to get married' [31]. In a later chapter [52] of the same book, he gives his best description of that close male friendship that was such an essential component of Victorian life. It was an 'undemonstrative, unexpressed, almost unconscious affection which, with men, will often make the greatest charm of their lives'.

In his fiction there are fewer close friendships between women and they are not as closely observed. There are,

however, notable exceptions, such as that between Alice Vavasor and Lady Glencora Palliser in the first of the Palliser novels, and that between Lady Glencora's daughter, Lady Mary Palliser, and Mrs Phineas Finn (Madame Max Goesler) in the last. Lily Dale sets out to cultivate female friends in *The Last Chronicle of Barset*. The friendship between the two working girls in 'The Telegraph Girl' is well portrayed. Marriage could often impose a strain between female friends as the two American women discover in *He Knew He Was Right* or as Cecilia Holt finds with her friend Miss Altifiorla in *Kept in the Dark* [➤ American Characters]. In *The Belton Estate* Clara Amedroz's friendship for Mrs Askerton, a woman with a 'past', causes great tension and shows the difficulties a Victorian lady could have over friendships.

Close friendships between men and women in Trollope's fiction are quite uncommon and they always run the risk of being indiscreet or causing gossip, as Phineas Finn and Lord George Germain [➤ *Is He Popenjoy?*] each discover. A friendship between a young married woman and an older man leads to great misery in *He Knew He Was Right*. Male cousins and clergymen were normally exempt from these difficulties.

In Trollope's normal usage 'a particular friend' is even closer than 'an intimate friend' [➤ *The Duke's Children*, 1–4].

Fruit. See Gardens.

G

Gambling. Gambling leads to the ruin of several characters, most notably of Burgo Fitzgerald at the end of *Can You Forgive Her?*, while Mountjoy Scarborough is almost ruined in *Mr Scarborough's Family*. The casino at Baden-Baden, frequented by Burgo, is portrayed in the first novel, while that at Monte Carlo, which became the new gambling mecca after Germany banned such places, is described in *Mr Scarborough's Family* [11]. Indeed, that novel may be seen as one of Trollope's strongest 'sermons to the young' about the evils of gambling. Gambling is often associated with idleness, exemplified by some of the young men in *The Way We Live Now*. Their losses are made all the worse because the debts are allowed to mount up. Like George Hotspur in *Sir Harry Hotspur of Humblethwaite*, notorious gamblers usually unite their passion with other vices. Gambling losses can have a terrible outcome: Charles Amedroz, the heir in *The Belton Estate*, kills himself after he loses a great deal of money at horse-racing [1]. The largest gambling loss is the astronomical sum of £70,000 suffered by Lord Silverbridge in *The Duke's Children*. Luckily his father, the Duke of Omnium, is rich enough to pay it. Many other young aristocrats such as Lord Chiltern have gambling losses in their turbulent youth. Mild gambling at 'penny whist'

– which appears to be the only type of gambling in which Trollope himself regularly indulged – is, not surprisingly, acceptable in his writing [➤ Whist].

Gardens. 'Grounds', 'gardens' or 'lawn' often feature in Trollope's fiction and were important to the expanding Victorian middle classes. In 'Alice Dugdale' Lady Deepbell, the widow of a Civil Service knight, lives in a cottage 'which was just large enough to enable her to talk of her grounds'. From his mother Trollope had acquired an interest in gardens, an interest also shared by his brother Tom, and he had set views: he disliked 'square prim' gardens where there was a 'tree answering to tree' at every corner [*The Belton Estate*, 7]. When living in the country he took a keen interest in his garden, as did his wife. When guests visited him he took them for walks in the garden if weather permitted. When travelling in America and writing *North America*, he thought about his garden at Waltham Cross and listed the staggering amount of vegetables and fruit that he grew. He also argued that English peaches were amongst the finest in the world, to the amusement of his friend Nathaniel Hawthorne. It was said that Trollope's garden at Harting was recalled by the poet Alfred Austin in his book, *The*

Garden that I Love. His garden was also where he, like Dean Lovelace in *Is He Popenjoy?*, was allowed to smoke.

Trollope frequently used gardens as settings, especially as places where lovers could be alone [*The Claverings*; *The Vicar of Bullhampton*; *The Small House at Allington*]. Perhaps the most famous use of a garden for this was at Ullathorne in *Barchester Towers*, where during a *fête champêtre* Eleanor Bold is proposed to by both Obadiah Slope and Bertie Stanhope. Gardens like the one in Allington were also vital if characters were to play the new game of croquet.

Trollope often used a gardening analogy for the growth of character, especially with regard to young men: the fruit that ripens quickest is not the sweetest [*Orley Farm*, 3]. He would also use fruit as a metaphor for the good things in life [*The Claverings*, 36; *The Belton Estate*, 7].

Gardeners are usually depicted as being outspoken and independent men like Hopkins in *The Small House at Allington*. The fact that they lived in cottages by themselves and not as servants in the house made them more likely to claim 'an opinion of their own' [*The Belton Estate*, 7].

[➤ Farming.]

Gatherum Castle. As the seat of the Palliser family in Barset, the castle is mentioned in several novels in the Barsetshire and Palliser series. This mock-gothic pile, with its mock-Latin name, was built by the old Duke of Omnium in the early nineteenth century at the huge cost of about £250,000 [*Can You Forgive Her?*, 18]. (Harlaxton Manor in Lincolnshire, one of the grandest Victorian country houses built in this period, cost about £200,000.) The duke's formal way of entertaining there is well described in *Framley Parsonage* [8]. All three generations of the Pallisers are proud of its magnificence, but find its vast 'barracks' uncomfortable and prefer to live in their other houses such as Matching. 'Gatherum' is also, of course, a pun which drew on the popular Victorian mock-Latin phrase 'Omnium Gatherum', which is used in *Barchester Towers* [11].

Gazebee, Mortimer. Gazebee is a London lawyer who manages the business affairs of the De Courcy family and marries Lady Amelia De Courcy. Gazebee is not dishonest but 'happy in the absolute fact of his connection with an Earl' [*The Small House at Allington*, 55]. He works as constantly for this repulsive family 'as an inferior spider might be supposed to work ... compelled by its instincts to be catching flies always for superior spiders' [*The Last Chronicle of Barset*, 43]. His most conspicuous victim is Adolphus Crosbie. He is also prominent in *Doctor Thorne*. Gazebee becomes MP for Barchester with the clear understanding that while his election reflects credit on the De Courcys, he must pay all the expenses. Gazebee's ruthless subservience to the family shows how Trollope was influenced in his ideas of snobbery by Thackeray, in particular by the latter's *Book of Snobs*. Trollope says in his *Thackeray* that the 'man who allows the manhood within him to be awed by a coronet is a snob'.

'The Gentle Euphemia, or Love Shall Still Be Lord of All'. A short story published in the *Fortnightly Review* on 1 May 1866. In this spoof of Victorian medievalism (popularized by Tennyson, Pugin, Kenelm Digby and the Eglinton tournaments), Trollope was able to exercise his passion for silly names. Euphemia is the daughter of Count Grandnostrel and was taught by Alasco the Wise. She is wooed by the Lord of Mountfidget but prefers Plato's philosophy to talk of love, even though Alasco quotes a variation on one of Trollope's favourite sayings, 'Love will still be lord of all' [➤ *The Struggles of Brown, Jones, and Robinson*]. When Mountfidget comes to woo Euphemia he is repulsed by the count's archers because he arrives without cattle or swine. She falls in love with Mountfidget and escapes her father's castle with Alasco. Mountfidget lies wounded in a cottage as an arrow which struck his neck had been poisoned with strychnine. He is being nursed with 'orange juice mixed with brandy' when a page-boy arrives and collapses at the foot of the bed; he carries a vial marked 'antidote for the oil of strychnine'. The page-boy is really Euphemia who confesses in true Trollopian fashion that 'love is lord of me'. The party returns to the Castle of Grandnostrel and the couple are married.

Part of the humour lies in Trollope's ability to inject contemporary concerns into a medieval setting. (This same device was later used by Mark Twain in *A Connecticut Yankee at the Court of King Arthur* and by F. Carruthers Gould in his mock histories, *Froissart's Modern Chronicles*.) Mountfidget's cattle and swine are depleted by rinderpest and swine-disease and then slaughtered by 'men in authority from the Queen'. (Rinderpest was a great threat to Victorian farmers.) The Lord of Mountfidget has 'ready money in many banks' and threatens Euphemia's father: 'I will set the law-yers at thee, and ruin thee with many costs.' He refers to the 'volunteers' – companies of rifle volunteers were all the rage in the mid-Victorian era for fear of a French invasion under Napoleon III [➤ France]. Strychnine was, of course, the Victorian poisoner's favourite poison. Finally, there are references to tea-parties and billiards. The story's farcical nature is enhanced by having eight small chapters, each beginning with a quotation from Shakespeare, Byron, Milton, Longfellow, Elizabeth Barrett Browning, and others, and each chapter is something of a development of a word or phrase in the quotation. The plot owes much to *Cymbeline* and is another example of Shakespeare's influence. The title Mountfidget is a play on certain Irish peerages like Mountcashell, Mount Charles, Mount Eagle, Mountmorres and Mountgarret [➤Ireland].

Trollope had already privately attempted mock medievalism in his letter of 2 August 1859 to his wife, telling her he had bought Waltham House, their first English home. He began, 'To ye ladie of Waltham House in ye Countie of Herts.'

Gentleman. The identity, role, manners and duties of a gentleman provide some of the most persistent themes in Trollope's writing. He once told an audience that the novelist's moral duty was to teach ladies to be women and men to be gentlemen. Yet for a modern reader it is difficult to grasp exactly what he meant by 'a gentleman'. For Trollope too there was difficulty in defining the term. In *Rachel Ray* [6], when he writes that a 'necessary qualification' for a man to be a clergyman is that he should be a 'gentleman', he goes on, 'I am by no means prepared to define what I do mean, thinking, however, that most men and most women will understand me.' When Lady Mary Palliser tells her father, the Duke of Omnium, that the man she wishes to marry is a gentleman the duke demurs: 'the word is too vague to carry with it any meaning' [*The Duke's Children*, 8; ➤also *John Caldigate*, 7].

Victorian authors often wrote about the 'gentleman', from serious considerations by Cardinal Newman to amusing cartoons in *Punch*. Most would have agreed with Trollope's comment in one of his last short stories that 'the one great line of demarcation' in Victorian society was that which separated gentlemen from nongentlemen. Many would also have been in a similar position to a clergyman in the same story who thinks that line is drawn just below himself ['The Two Heroines of Plumplington']. Though by Trollope's time the word 'gentleman' had ceased to have a precise, legal definition, certain aspects remained: a 'gentleman' who was a witness in a trial could claim more for a day's attendance in court than an artisan.

The word 'gentleman' appears to have been constantly employed in Victorian conversation, as can be seen in Trollope's dialogue throughout his novels and from a letter that he wrote to his son Henry in 1877 from Switzerland in which he described another Englishman he had become friendly with on holiday: 'He is not a bad fellow though not quite a gentleman.'

For Victorians a 'gentleman' could be identified by certain attributes pertaining to behaviour, appearance and background. Acquiring a public school or university education or being a member of certain professions proclaimed that a man was a gentleman. Everyone assumed that clergymen and barristers were gentlemen, as well as all who had degrees from Oxford or Cambridge. Mr Grey reflects on a clergyman in *Mr Scarborough's Family*: 'Mr Matterson was at any rate better than Mr Juniper; that he was by profession a gentleman' [62]. Birth into an aristocratic or a gentry family made a man a 'gentleman' for life. Trollope normally accepts this: thus the De Courcy men remain 'gentlemen' despite their useless lives and boorish manners. Having said that, Trollope, like others of his time, judged a 'gentleman' who did wrong by a harsher standard than he judged an ordinary man. One of the greatest denunciations in his fiction comes in *The Three Clerks* [44], where he says a gentleman criminal deserves greater punishment than an ordinary man.

Which professions made a man a gentleman? Some people did not consider solicitors gentlemen. Thus the Reverend Josiah Crawley, when consulting a relative who is a solicitor and anxious to help the poor clergyman accused of theft, takes comfort in recalling to himself that he had 'rank' and 'precedence' whereas the solicitor is 'a nobody' [*The Last Chronicle of Barset*, 32]. Trollope soon shows in just how gentlemanly a way this solicitor behaves. In the same book Crawley is reconciled to Archdeacon Grantly when that proud and wealthy clergyman says to him, 'We stand on the only perfect level ... We are both gentlemen' [83]. Trollope's own profession of civil servant, like that of engineer, was normally considered to be a gentlemanly one, but not always. In *The Vicar of Bullhampton*, Miss Marrable, one of Trollope's elderly Tory ladies, felt that there 'might also possibly be a doubt about the Civil Service and Civil Engineering' [9]. In *Orley Farm* another character puts engineers on a level with tradesmen, who most definitely could not be considered gentlemen. [For contrasting views, ➤ *The Claverings*.] Certainly Trollope insists that a young Post Office clerk on £170 a year is a gentleman because of his position [*Marion Fay*, 1]. In *Harry Heathcote of Gangoil* he even insists that a sheep farmer in Australia is a gentleman, but here he was influenced by the fact that the farmer on whom the story was based was his son Fred.

Trollope was raised with certain ideas and prejudices about what constituted a gentleman and these affected his behaviour and his writings. Social rank was combined with personal behaviour. Honesty was an essential attribute of the gentleman, but he was frank enough to admit that all gentlemen lie at times [*The Eustace Diamonds*, 29]. Although he was always drawn to the idea that being the son of a gentleman was important, he could suspend this idea both in his life and in his fiction. The Dean of Brotherton, who was not a gentleman by birth, shows himself to be far more of one than the debauched marquis in *Is He Popenjoy?* In his *Autobiography* Trollope said that he believed there were positions that 'can hardly be filled except by "Gentlemen"' although he admitted there should be some exceptions. Ultimately he believed there would always be some barriers, but that 'the gates of one class should be open to the other'.

The idea of the gentleman enters into almost all of Trollope's fiction.

Sometimes a young man like Johnny Eames or Charley Tudor goes through various trials until he assumes the rank of gentleman. Sometimes a young woman like Emily Hotspur in *Sir Harry Hotspur of Humblethwaite*, or Emily Wharton in *The Prime Minister*, worries about whether the man she wishes to marry really is a gentleman. At other times a gentleman like Septimus Harding – perhaps Trollope's finest – comes to see that the rank has duties as well as privileges. There were few things Trollope enjoyed more in fiction than in portraying 'a fine, handsome English gentleman' such as Sir Peregrine Orme in *Orley Farm*, a man who lived by a rigid code of honour [➤Chapter 3 particularly], or Plantagenet Palliser, a 'perfect gentleman' [*Autobiography*]. Some born to the rank of gentleman abandon it: most notably the drunken scholar in 'The Spotted Dog' who says he has sought 'refuge from the conventional thraldom of so-called "gentlemen" amidst the liberty of the lower orders'.

Few tributes would have delighted Trollope more than that contained in his obituary in *Truth* – a Radical publication well known for its revelations of scandals involving gentlemen – which declared: 'He was the perfect gentleman in every fibre of his nature.'

[➤Evangelicals; Lady.]

Gentry. There is no group that comes out so well in Trollope's fiction as England's old landed gentry and Trollope himself was proud of his descent from a long line of Lincolnshire landowners and baronets. It is difficult to define just what the word 'gentry' meant. To the 'lower orders' it could be applied to any well-off person. For Trollope it normally meant someone whose family wealth was derived from the land. However, even if a man or woman had no personal wealth, a connection with the land gives them gentry status. Thus Francis Arabin counts as gentry and moves in 'county society' even before becoming Dean of Barchester because he is 'the younger son of a country gentleman' [*Barchester Towers*, 20]. The gentry can be a trifle silly like Wilfred Thorne or more than a trifle improvident like Squire Gresham but, like Sir Harry Hotspur in *Sir Harry Hotspur of Humblethwaite*, they are normally men of honour. Yet every group in Trollope's fiction, even his own favourites, produces 'rotten apples'. Nathaniel Sowerby in *Framley Parsonage* is the most disreputable representative of a gentry family in all Trollope's writing. [➤ Aristocracy; Squires.]

'George Walker at Suez'. This short story was probably written between 12 and 15 April 1861 when Trollope was working on *Orley Farm* and when he also wrote 'The House of Heine Brothers in Munich'. For his setting Trollope drew on his travels during his Post Office trip to Egypt and the Holy Land (30 January to 10 May 1858). The story was one of the eight he sold to the *London Review* but after the hostile reception of the first two, 'A Ride across Palestine' and 'Mrs General Talboys', they would only publish one more, 'The Parson's Daughter'. This story about Suez is one of the five remaining that were sold to *Public Opinion* in which it was published on 28 December 1861. It was then included in the second collection of his short stories, *Tales of All Countries*, Second Series, in 1863. Trollope received £50.

This humorous story is written in the first person. Walker is a London businessman sent to Egypt for his health. At Shepperd's Hotel (also used in 'A Ride across Palestine', spelt correctly Shepheard's) Walker meets an old London friend, John Robinson. Walker travels with Robinson to Suez. He stays in Suez for a week and languishes in an hotel until approached by an elegant Arab, Mahmoud al Ackbar, who ceremoniously addresses him in French. Through faulty interpretation Walker learns that this man had apparently once been befriended by Walker's father, a Liverpool merchant, that he had learnt of Walker's visit and that he wants to take him across the Red Sea for a picnic at the Well of Moses. Walker rises early and goes to the quayside where he sees a boat lavishly prepared, but no al Ackbar. In the end it turns out that the man had mistaken him for Sir George Walker, a military hero *en route* to take up his new position as Lieutenant-Governor of Pegu (in Burma) and that the 'Arab' was actually an Indian. Walker is no longer a great man in the hotel and resolves on a private trip to the Well of Moses: it costs him £20 and the well turns out to be a 'small dirty pool of salt water'.

Trollope captures the restricted outlook of a London merchant who constantly relates everything abroad to life at home, through comparisons with a business partner named Judkins [➤ *The Struggles of Brown, Jones, and Robinson*]. While he is scathing about Egyptians for their lack of manliness and self-respect, those essential Trollopian virtues, he had obviously carefully observed their social rituals and behaviour. (Mahmoud al Ackbar has many similarities with the Egyptian official, Nubar Pasha, with whom Trollope dealt during his Post Office nego-tiations.) His dislike is also evident in *The Bertrams*, in which Suez comes in for special attack [39].

Germany. Germany is the setting for one of Trollope's anonymous novels, *Linda Tressel*, set in Nuremberg, and for one of his short stories, 'The House of Heine Brothers in Munich'. He also used German settings for scenes in several novels. Trollope was particularly fond of Dresden, the capital of Saxony, and it is there that Lady Laura Kennedy spends her exile from her outraged husband [*Phineas Redux*, 11, 12]. Parts of *Marion Fay* are also set in Saxony. In *Can You Forgive Her?* there are scenes in the gambling casino at Baden-Baden. [For others who go to live in Germany, ➤ Exile.]

In *Barchester Towers* clergymen react with horror to the idea that they could learn anything from 'German profes-sors' [11]. 'German professors' were code words for the 'higher learning' regarding the Scriptures that was being taught in German universi-ties [➤ Religion]. Compared with references to classical or French literature, there are few allusions to German authors in his writings [for one reference to *Faust*, ➤ *Framley Par-sonage*, 9]. Even so, Trollope knew that German ideas were becoming influen-tial in English life. One sees this in *Orley Farm*, published five years after *Barchester Towers*, when young Lucius Mason goes to Germany to study philology. Ironically, two of Trollope's closest friends, George Eliot and G. H. Lewes, were both heavily influenced by 'German thought' as, of course, Carlyle had been, while Thack-eray, whom Trollope venerated, had

spent part of his youth studying in Germany.

Occasionally German characters occur in his fiction, the most notable of whom are two 'lecturers'. Each is a caricature. In *Orley Farm*, the Berlin lawyer von Bauhr gives a three-hour lecture on law that is so brilliant none of the English lawyers understands him. The Millais drawing of this epis-ode portrayed the standard English view of a German of the early nine-teenth century: a dreamy figure suf-fused in clouds of smoke from his pipe. In *Is He Popenjoy?* the Bavarian Baroness Banmann comes to London to lecture on the 'rights of women' [➤ Feminists].

Trollope supported the German side in the Franco-Prussian War of 1870, more from his hatred of Napo-leon III of France than from any love of Prussia. The war led to Prussia uni-fying the various German kingdoms into a united empire whose power loomed ever greater as the century wore on. We find a small echo of this in *The Prime Minister*, in which Bis-marck, the Prussian politician respon-sible for unification, is alluded to [20] and in which a young Tory, Everett Wharton, goes off to Germany to study not philology but social legislation.

Trollope, unlike Thackeray and Lewes, had little knowledge of Ger-many in his early life although he pre-sumably read his mother's *Belgium and Western Germany in 1833*. In the 1850s and 1860s several of his travels were through Germany as he was anxious to see art galleries in Munich and Dresden. In the mid-1870s he began to spend long holidays in the Hollenthal valley near Freiburg. He describes how the Black Forest, where he used to walk, became his favourite place to fashion plots for his novels [➤ 'A Walk in a Wood']. In *North America* Trollope emphasized several times the growing importance of Germans in America, particularly in their support for the Northern war effort. He also used a German character in his Australian novel, *Harry Heathcote of Gangoil.* Many of Trollope's novels were translated into German and, in addition, cheap English language editions of most of them were published by the well-known Leipzig firm of Tauchnitz. [➤ Europe.]

Girls. Trollope defined his use of this word in *Framley Parsonage*: 'Girls are girls from the age of three up to forty-three, if not previously married' [10]. Contemporaries greatly admired his numerous portrayals of girls. Henry James maintained that 'the English girl' was Trollope's natural subject and that he was 'evidently always more or less in love' with whichever one he was describing. [➤ 'The House of Heine Brothers in Munich'; Marriage; Nieces; Spinsters; Women.]

Gladstone, William (1809–98). Gladstone was four times Liberal prime minister. Two of his governments were formed during Trollope's lifetime: his first was from 1868 to 1874 and his second, which began in 1880, was still in office when Trollope died. Gladstone is mentioned by name in *Ralph the Heir* when a Tory candidate denounces 'that fellow Gladstone, who was one thing one day and another thing another day' [25]. In *The Fixed Period*, written during Gladstone's second administration, the principal city of the fictional Britannula is named 'Gladstonopolis'.

Trollope was a great admirer of Gladstone and when he stood as a Liberal candidate in 1868 he pledged himself to give 'active, constant, and unwearied support to Mr Gladstone'. Yet he was not uncritical, as he wrote in *Saint Pauls* in March 1870: Gladstone 'finds it easy to prove anything and is therefore prone to prove too much'. Trollope's last novel, *The Land-Leaguers*, is strongly critical of Gladstone's policy towards Ireland. Though he was critical of Gladstone's policy he would not hear any abuse of Gladstone as a man. Only a few weeks before Trollope's fatal stroke a close friend assured Gladstone that Trollope was still a Liberal. During the previous year members of Gladstone's inner circle had discussed proposing Trollope's name to the Queen for a peerage [Mullen, 643–4]. Trollope's admiration for the Liberal leader was no doubt influenced by his detestation of Gladstone's great rival, Disraeli. Trollope and Gladstone were only acquaintances, although they occasionally spoke at the same meetings.

When reading the Palliser novels many people have assumed that Gresham is based on Gladstone and Daubeny on Disraeli. Although Trollope admitted that some of Gladstone's political views were used in creating Gresham, he denied that he used personal characteristics. To take one example: Gresham springs from an old landed family, whereas Gladstone was well known as the son of a rich Liverpool mercantile family and as a man who always proclaimed his 'middle-class' status.

Gladstone was a great reader of novels, but he preferred those of his youth, particularly Walter Scott, to contemporary ones. However, he does record in his diary that he read Trollope's article on Iceland.

'Gladstone Wine'. This is a phrase that occurs frequently in Trollope's novels. As a result of Richard Cobden's 1860 free trade treaty with France and the Budget introduced that same year by Gladstone as Chancellor of the Exchequer, the cost of French wine fell dramatically. Gladstone's hope was that this would encourage a move towards lighter French wines which would promote temperance by displacing heavier wines like port. As a result, a bottle of claret could be had for 1s. 6d. Gladstone also allowed grocers to sell wine, which led to the growth of 'grocer's claret'. Trollope, in spite of his admiration for Gladstone, often pokes fun at 'Gladstone wine', which he regarded as cheap and not full-bodied. In *The American Senator* a Tory clergyman fulminates against Gladstone and his wine: 'Nothing ... could make such wine as that any cheaper' [12].

Glomax, Captain. Glomax is the MFH in *The American Senator*, in which he is described as 'the greatest man in the county on hunting days'. With several other fox-hunting characters in this novel, he reappears in *Ayala's Angel.*

'God tempers the wind to the shorn lamb'. This phrase, which originally comes from the French, is found in Laurence Sterne's *A Sentimental Journey.* It soon assumed the status of a proverb. Trollope used it extensively. His most successful use of it is in *Orley Farm* [79]; Mr Crawley's use of it sounds almost biblical [*The Last Chronicle of Barset, 50*]. Trollope as a novelist could also temper the wind. In his fic-

tion neither characters nor plots normally go to extremes, especially when punishment for wrongdoing is necessary: a position is found, an accommodation devised, a reasonably comfortable exile is arranged.

Goesler, (Marie) Madame Max. Madame Goesler is one of the most intriguing characters in the Palliser novels. When she first appears in *Phineas Finn* all that is known of her is that she is the rich widow of an elderly Viennese banker. While he was a Jew, no one is sure of her background. Gradually it emerges that she is English by birth, the daughter of a 'small country attorney', and that she has lived part of her youth by the Italian lakes. She is also an important character in *Phineas Redux*, in which she becomes the second Mrs Phineas Finn, and in *The Prime Minister* and *The Duke's Children.* Like Martha Dunstable in the Barsetshire novels, she is not ashamed to administer her own business affairs and is most competent. Every year she disappears to Vienna where she sees to her business interests; her knowledge of the Austrian Empire helps Phineas Finn when she uncovers the background of Joseph Emilius.

One must be careful in reading some of the speculation about her by other characters, as it is often mere gossip or, sometimes, just the jealous thoughts of her rivals [*Phineas Redux, 45*]. Trollope describes her as 'dark, thin, healthy, good-looking, clever, ambitious, rich, unsatisfied, perhaps unscrupulous – but not without a conscience' [*Phineas Redux, 14*]. There was some speculation in London Society that Madame Max was based on the famous hostess, Lady Waldegrave.

There were several reasons for this: Lady Waldegrave was the daughter of a Jewish singer; she was courted by the Duke of Newcastle; she married, as her fourth husband, Chichester Fortesque, whom many people took to be the 'original' of Phineas Finn. Trollope may have heard something of Lady Waldegrave from their mutual friend Abraham Hayward, but Madame Max was his own creation. Incidentally, Lady Waldegrave much admired Trollope's novels and thought they 'will be read for years hence as good pictures of . . . the English in the nineteenth century'.

Because of her exotic connections, Madame Goesler is allowed a greater freedom in action and thought than would have been allowed an ordinary English character. She is the wisest woman – perhaps the wisest person – in all the novels. The *Spectator* (3 January 1874) was right in its opinion that 'Madame Max is one of Mr Trollope's most graceful and carefully studied characters'.

The Golden Lion of Granpère. Trollope's twenty-seventh novel was written between 1 September and 22 October 1867, during which time he resigned his position in the Post Office. He began the story eleven days after returning from a holiday in France and Switzerland. Trollope meant it to be the third of the anonymous or continental novels set in Europe. However, with the failure of the first two, *Nina Balatka* and *Linda Tressel*, he set it aside until 1869 when he proposed it to *Blackwood's Magazine* for serialization. The magazine, which had published the other two, declined the offer even though Trollope withdrew his insistence on anonymity when it was pub-

lished in book form. He then dropped the idea of serialization and offered it to Chapman & Hall as a book but negotiations came to nothing. It was finally serialized in the monthly *Good Words* between January and August 1872. Strahan, who published the magazine, sold the book rights to William Tinsley, who brought it out in one volume in May 1872. Trollope had stipulated to Strahan that if published as a book it must be in one volume to avoid stretching by means of larger print and wider margins, as had been the case with his publication of *Lotta Schmidt and Other Stories.* Trollope received £550.

In the time between the writing of this book in 1867 and its publication in 1872 there was a great change in the area in which the novel is set, Alsace and Lorraine. In 1867 the two provinces, through which Trollope had passed on his way to Switzerland, were part of France. The Franco-Prussian War of 1870–71 resulted in a disastrous defeat for France and they were seized and added to the new German empire. Trollope supported the Prussians in the war and he particularly detested the French Emperor Napoleon III. Nevertheless, when he finally found a publisher he added a few sentences at the beginning of the novel to acknowledge the changes and he even praised the fallen Emperor for improving the quality of the roads in the region.

The story is remarkably simple, and bears some similarity to his earlier short story, 'La Mère Bauche'. It is set in a small hotel, the *Lion d'Or* or 'Golden Lion' of the title. The innkeeper of the Golden Lion is Michel Voss, who has a son, George, by his first wife. Also living at the inn is

Marie Bromar, the niece of his second wife. While Voss is anxious for Marie to marry a Swiss linen merchant, Adrian Urmand, his son is in love with her. While Voss and his son are Protestants, Marie is Catholic and Voss seeks the aid of her priest to persuade her to marry Urmand. (All three of Trollope's continental novels feature some form of religious difficulty.) Voss is not really a tyrant in the manner of Charlotte Staubach in *Linda Tressel*, but he is bull-headed. After many difficulties and heartaches Marie and George are married.

'It is hardly possible to imagine anything slighter' than the events in this story, said a critic in the *Spectator*, and while this is true, Trollope's skill as a storyteller and as a delineator of character bring it to life. He shows the tension between the father and son that must inevitably arise when they share similar personalities, and how this brings them into conflict. Marie herself faces that fairly common dilemma met by young women in Trollope's fiction, be they Lily Dale, Linda Tressel or Violet Effingham (*Phineas Finn*): the need to choose between two suitors.

The readers of *Good Words*, a periodical with a strongly religious readership, would have been pleased to note the kind remarks about the famous Protestant pastor Johann Friedrich Oberlin (1740–1826), whom Trollope praised as this 'wonderful clergyman'. Trollope admired the way in which Protestants and Catholics lived in harmony in Alsace and Lorraine. He makes this particularly clear in the admirable portrait of the Catholic *curé*, Gondin, who was as much respected by the Protestants as by the Catholics [➤ Smoking]. The Protestants respected him because he neither attempted to convert them nor to say behind their backs that they would be 'damned as heretics'. Trollope, normally friendly to Catholics, may be having a hit in a roundabout way at the Catholic priest whom he had befriended and often invited to his home, only to be attacked for his own religious views [➤ *The Way We Live Now*].

When Trollope went to Australia he asked a friend to look after the proofs, and his friend was amazed to find that the manuscript was 'entirely free from alterations'. He thought that it 'seemed to have flowed from his pen like clear liquor from a tap' [Mullen, 533]. When Trollope assessed the novel in his *Autobiography* he thought 'very inferior' to *Nina Balatka* and *Linda Tressel*. In point of characterization or of serious interest to his readers he was right. However, it is far more pleasant than its two continental predecessors and, as befits its origins, it makes perfect holiday reading.

Good Cheer. See *Good Words*.

'Good Time Coming'. A phrase used in numerous Trollope novels, it comes from a popular poem by Charles Mackay that was published in the *Daily News* in 1846 to celebrate the repeal of the Corn Laws. This event was seen as the symbol of a future that promised increasing peace and prosperity, and the poem sold 400,000 copies. It became a favourite of Trollope's mother. In America it was set to music by Stephen Foster. While in many novels it is used as a catch-all phrase, in *Ralph the Heir* [16] it is used in its original connotation to express the hope of Radicals that a better age is dawning [Mullen, 380–81]. In *The*

Prime Minister it provides a handy euphemism for pregnancy.

Good Words (1860–1906). This monthly magazine was published by Alexander Strahan, edited in the 1860s by the Reverend Norman Macleod, and sold for 6*d*. Like *Cassell's Illustrated Family Newspaper*, the magazine aimed at making fiction acceptable to those from Evangelical or Dissenting backgrounds with their traditional suspicion of 'tales'. The publication was the only general magazine to be praised by the Society for Purity in Literature. For thirty years after its founding it was one of the most popular purveyors of fiction in the country: by 1864, circulation – mainly among the lower middle class – had reached 160,000. It published a variety of famous writers, including Mrs Craik, Charles Kingsley, Thomas Hardy, Mrs Henry Wood and George MacDonald. The Christmas issue was called *Good Cheer*. Trollope began his connection with the magazine in 1862 when he was asked for a Christmas story ('The Widow's Mite'). Between then and his death he contributed seven other short stories ('The Two Generals', 'Malachi's Cove', 'The Last Austrian Who Left Venice', 'The Telegraph Girl', 'Why Frau Frohmann Raised Her Prices', 'Alice Dugdale' and 'The Two Heroines of Plumplington'). Of the eight, three ('The Telegraph Girl', 'Alice Dugdale' and 'The Two Heroines of Plumplington') were in *Good Cheer*; the other four were in *Good Words*. Trollope also contributed three articles ('The Young Women at the London Telegraph Office', 'A Walk in a Wood' and 'In the Hunting Field', the latter designed to be the first of four similar articles). The magazine serialized two novels (*The Golden Lion of Granpère* and *Kept in the Dark*). One novel, *Rachel Ray*, was commissioned but rejected by Macleod. [➤ Isbiste, William.]

Gotobed, Senator Elias. Senator Gotobed is the character who gives *The American Senator* its title. He is a Republican senator from the fictional western state of Mikewa. Throughout the novel he is constantly inquiring into and complaining about aspects of British society, and at the end of the book he delivers a long lecture denouncing the British Constitution. Yet Trollope did not disagree with all Gotobed's comments and in a letter to a friend described the senator as 'a thoroughly honest man wishing to do good' and who is 'not himself half so absurd as the things which he criticizes'. Trollope had originally intended to include the senator's wife in the novel but changed his mind. However, when the senator becomes United States Minister in London and appears in *The Duke's Children* he is accompanied by his wife and is still complaining about British institutions. Trollope had met various Republican senators in Washington during his two visits to America in the 1860s and they may have contributed aspects to their fictional colleague [Mullen, 610–11]. The pronunciation of the senator's name is unclear. If one uses Go-to-bed it sounds like one of Trollope's silly names. If one uses go-*to*-bed it is not so. It is actually an English surname and not a contrived word.

GRANTLY FAMILY
This family provides several major characters in the Barsetshire novels and one daughter who features in other novels. The Grantlys, along with

their relatives the Hardings, are one of
the two most important families in
Trollope's fiction. (The other is the
Palliser family.) The Grantlys are a
clerical family, not uncommon in the
Victorian Church of England. One
could cite the Wilberforces or, nearer
to Trollope, the Sewells and the
Drurys. The Grantlys were High Tory
in politics and High Church in ecclesiastical matters. They defend the old
traditions of the Diocese of Barchester
against the new bishop, Proudie, and
his virago of a wife: 'How sharp was
the feud between the Proudies and the
Grantlys down in Barsetshire ... they
headed two different parties in the diocese, which were ... as oil and vinegar'
[*Framley Parsonage*, 17]. The principal
members of this fictional family are
described below.

Grantly, Bishop. Bishop Grantly has
been Bishop of Barchester for many
decades when the *The Warden* begins.
We are told little about his background, but we know he is over seventy and a widower. He is the embodiment of an eighteenth-century type of
bishop who survived into the first half
of the nineteenth century before the
activities of the Oxford Movement,
the Evangelicals and church reform
called for more active, doctrinaire and
businesslike prelates. Trollope has a
considerable affection for this sort of
cleric although he regretfully knew
their day was passing. Old Bishop
Grantly was 'a bland and a kind old
man, opposed by every feeling to
authoritative demonstrations and episcopal ostentation' [*The Warden*, 3]. The
old bishop and Septimus Harding
have been friends for many years. The
bishop receives a large income of
£9,000 a year, which has allowed him

to amass considerable wealth for his
son. The bishop's death is described in
the opening pages of *Barchester Towers*,
but his memory lingers on in the diocese where people recall 'the unspar-
ing, open-handed hospitality of Barchester Palace in the good old days of
Bishop Grantly – God rest his soul!'
[*Framley Parsonage*, 17; *The Last Chronicle of Barset*, 22, 78]. In *Framley Parsonage* [9] Lord Lufton recalls being confirmed by the 'good old man' and still
remembers the pastries that were
served at the Palace. [➤ Fathers and
Sons.]

Grantly, The Rev. Dr Theophilus.
Dr Grantly, Archdeacon of Barchester,
is the only child of Bishop Grantly.
He is the real power in the diocese of
Barchester in his father's lifetime because of his father's unassuming personality and because of his own
position as archdeacon. A Victorian
archdeacon in effect acted as the chief
administrative officer in a diocese and
could exercise much of the bishop's
authority over the parish clergy
[➤ Church of England]. As well as
having a large income as archdeacon,
Dr Grantly is the Rector of Plumstead
Episcopi. (The humorous name shows
it is a rich living in the gift of his
father, the bishop.)

The archdeacon is one of the most
famous and most admired characters
in the Barsetshire novels, indeed in all
Trollope's works. As George Saints-
bury commented, 'There are few men
in fiction I like better and should more
like to have known, than Archdeacon
Grantly.' After he made his final appearance in *The Last Chronicle of Barset*,
the *Spectator* declared, 'What am I to
do without ever meeting Archdeacon
Grantly? He was one of my best and

most intimate friends.' Many readers come to believe after re-reading the Barsetshire books that they actually know him.

When he first appears in *The Warden* he is hectoring his father-in-law, Mr Harding, and then the bedesmen of Hiram's Hospital. This does not make him an attractive figure, particularly to modern readers. However, as we become better acquainted with him in the rest of the Barsetshire novels, he emerges as an admirable man. Trollope's basic view is that he is 'a man doing more good than harm – a man to be furthered and supported, though perhaps also to be controlled' [*The Warden*, 20]. In the penultimate chapter of *The Warden* Trollope emphasizes that this novel had shown the archdeacon's 'foibles' rather than his 'virtues'. For Trollope these virtues were many: he was generous, hospitable and charitable towards the poor, and his religious principles were sincere, but not fanatical. In short, for Trollope the archdeacon was pre-eminently 'a gentleman' and Trollope expresses his genuine regret that the reader had not been able to see all these good aspects.

Most of the remaining Barsetshire novels, particularly *The Last Chronicle of Barset*, allowed the novelist the space to develop the archdeacon's character, which he does with great skill and sympathy. The archdeacon's position in the Church was roughly the same rank as Trollope held in the Post Office, which was the only other national institution of the time. There are many similarities in the character of Trollope and the archdeacon: both are combative men of fierce tempers, modified by sensible wives; both were essentially kind beneath their initial bluster; both fought fiercely for what they believed; both were determined to help their sons; and neither could resist the charms of a young woman in distress. Like his creator, Dr Grantly detests those who prattle on about religion or who try to use the Sabbath to suppress others' pleasures. Trollope also shared the archdeacon's ability to talk on many topics with different men, for instance his conversation with farmers about the use of guano as a fertilizer. The archdeacon expressed one of Trollope's favourite views when he denounces those who want to suspend postal deliveries on Sunday as 'numskulls' [*The Last Chronicle of Barset*, 73].

Trollope does not often portray the archdeacon as a religious figure. However, in *The Last Chronicle of Barset* [33] he shows that Dr Grantly could not allow his anger with his son to continue through evening prayers, any more than he could allow his worldly ambition to overcome his need to pray for his dying father in *Barchester Towers*. [➤ Religion.]

Trollope declares in his *Autobiography* that Dr Grantly, for whom he had 'a parent's fond affection', came forth from his brain without knowledge of any real archdeacons. Yet Trollope did know much about such clergymen from his careful reading of *The Times* and his travels on postal service which took him into countless rectories. Trollope's postal work in the West Country was in the territory of Archdeacon G. A. Denison in Somerset, a controversial High Church figure whose power and influence were similar to the fictional archdeacon's. (At the end of *Barchester Towers*, Mrs Arabin sends a donation to Archdeacon Denison for his trial at Bath.)

Trollope may have taken the idea of a bishop's son as a controversial archdeacon from real events in the diocese of Rochester where the bishop had made his son archdeacon. This was a story that received a great deal of attention in *The Times* [Mullen, 273].

Grantly, Susan. The wife of Theophilus Grantly, the daughter of Mr Harding, the elder sister of Eleanor Harding and thus, later, the sister-in-law of John Bold and eventually of Dean Arabin. She is the mother of Griselda Grantly, later Lady Dumbello. Thus she is connected to many of the central characters in the Barsetshire series. It is easy to neglect Mrs Grantly when first meeting her, but a closer look shows how important and sensible she usually is. She analyses the mistakes that her husband makes in his impetuous and boisterous way and talks to him, in the privacy of their bedroom, about them. She also predicts 'in her own mild seducing way' what will happen as a result of certain actions [➤ *Barchester Towers*, 29; *The Warden*, 8; *The Last Chronicle of Barset*, 5.]

She is about thirty-four when the Barsetshire novels begin and thus ten years older than her sister, Eleanor. The archdeacon and Mrs Grantly have been married for about twelve years. Because of the archdeacon's wealth, she is able to furnish the rectory with expensive objects. Mrs Grantly, like her great enemy, Mrs Proudie, is a powerful wife. There is one great difference: Mrs Grantly lectures her husband in private and seeks to give him a nudge in the right direction. To Victorians, these bedroom lectures were particularly humorous. Douglas Jerrold's book, *Mrs Caudle's*

Curtain Lectures, had been a great success only a few years before Mrs Grantly began her own lectures [➤ *The Small House at Allington*]. However, it was mildly shocking for Trollope to take readers into the marital bedroom of an ecclesiastical dignitary.

In his portrayal of Susan Grantly, Trollope could well have drawn on his own wife, who seems to have had a similar role as the only critic of his writing. The archdeacon was not really a domestic tyrant once he had exploded with his initial outrage, nor was Mrs Grantly the bashful and submissive wife. The complex relationships within a Victorian family among husband, wife and child are beautifully illustrated in the differing reactions of the archdeacon, Mrs Grantly and their son Henry in *The Last Chronicle of Barset* [58]. Although Susan Grantly is a good deal less important than her younger sister Eleanor in *The Warden*, by *Framley Parsonage* she emerges as far more interesting. By *The Last Chronicle of Barset* one can sense that Trollope's initial preference for Eleanor has shifted to her sister.

Grantly Sons. In *The Warden* [8] Trollope introduces three Grantly sons, 'whose characters are taken from three Bishops frequently before the public', according to a review in *The Examiner*. Charles James is the eldest. He is careful, moderate and a promoter of compromise. He is not as talented as his younger brothers. The model for him is Charles James Blomfield (1786–1857) who became Bishop of London in 1828 and exercised great influence.

Henry, the second son, is the archdeacon's favourite. He is brilliant and quarrelsome and in a fight he never gives in. He is also inclined to be a bully. He is modelled on Henry Phillpotts (1778–1869) who became Bishop of Exeter in 1831. Phillpotts was renowned for his High Church views and his combative style. (He is much admired by that old Tory lady, Miss Stanbury, in *He Knew He Was Right* [7].) Although he was a zealous Tory he often caused problems for his party's leaders in the House of Lords. Trollope alludes to this by saying that Henry Grantly was at school in Westminster where 'he would never own himself beat'. Lest any readers be in doubt that Henry Grantly is a miniature version of Henry Phillpotts, Trollope also tells us that young Henry was 'sent on a tour into Devonshire'. Dr Phillpotts is mentioned by name in *The Warden* as there is a bust of him in Archdeacon Grantly's study [12].

Samuel, the youngest Grantly son, is mild, courteous to all and uses his winning ways to gain increasing power, which makes his elder brothers jealous. These characteristics are based on Samuel Wilberforce (1805–73), Bishop of Oxford from 1845. Bishop Wilberforce's nickname of 'Soapy Sam' was widely known and Trollope calls Samuel Grantly 'dear little Soapy'. (Wilberforce was also used as the basis for a bishop by Disraeli in his novel *Lothair*.)

The three boys are not really characters in the full sense in *The Warden*, although all three show their personalities when John Bold makes a visit to Plumstead Episcopi [12]. Henry is the only one who becomes an important character – in *The Last Chronicle of Barset*, by providing the main love interest by falling in love with Grace Crawley. By now Henry is

no longer a caricature of Bishop Phillpotts although he is still combative as becomes a retired officer who has won the VC. (This may well be one of the first appearances in fiction of a VC as the decoration was only created in 1856.)

Although neither Charles James nor Samuel develop into major characters in later novels, Charles James does make brief appearances in other Barsetshire novels. In *Barchester Towers* [53] he is 'great with learning' and by *The Last Chronicle of Barset* he has become a prominent clergyman who has married an earl's daughter and is famous for building churches in London. In these vignettes, Trollope used two traits of Bishop Blomfield: he was a well-known classical scholar, one of the last 'Greek play bishops', and he was said to have built 200 churches in London. In *Barchester Towers* Samuel makes his final appearance in the last chapter when all three Grantly sons are briefly present and Samuel is 'the proudest of the three' [53]. After that he appears to have died, because by *The Last Chronicle of Barset* the archdeacon only has two sons. (However, Trollope is almost certainly making another reference to Bishop Samuel Wilberforce in *Framley Parsonage* [17] when he refers to a 'prelate in the Midlands' who is a friend of Miss Dunstable.)

These portraits show that Trollope had a strong knowledge of Church personalities. He does say in his *Autobiography* that when he left school he knew the names of all the bishops, a fairly unusual feat for a schoolboy, even in that era. He would have come to know more about Blomfield as he lived and worshipped in his diocese for many years, and as for Phillpotts, much of

Trollope's Post Office work when he began *The Warden* was in the diocese of Exeter. Trollope was criticized for his caricature of the three well-known bishops, particularly as these three men did more to strengthen the role of bishops than any other Anglican churchmen of the century. Even some of Trollope's friends were mildly annoyed and he wrote to one unknown correspondent early in 1855, 'I will beg your mother's pardon for the three maligned bishops.' The disappearance of Samuel, the lack of prominence of Charles James and the change in Henry's character indicate that Trollope himself came to dislike the explicit – and what contemporaries would have thought, tasteless – portrayals of real people. This change made him less likely to paint such direct portraits of real people in his later fiction.

Grantly Daughters. In *The Warden* [8] there are two daughters; the elder, Florinda, is also mentioned in *Barchester Towers*, where she has suddenly become the younger sister [20]. She is not in any of the other Barsetshire novels which leaves only the younger daughter, Griselda.

Griselda, when she appears as the youngest Grantly child in *The Warden* [8], is called Grizzel and in *Barchester Towers* [4], Grisel. She appears in several other novels in which her Christian name is Griselda. In *Framley Parsonage* she emerges as an important character when her stunning beauty attracts titled suitors. At first it seems that she will fulfil her mother's hopes and marry Lord Lufton. Instead she marries Viscount Dumbello, the heir to the vast income and title of Marquis of Hartletop. This brings

Griselda within the circle of the Pallisers as her mother-in-law, Lady Hartletop, had been the mistress of the old Duke of Omnium. In *The Small House at Allington* she has an absurd flirtation with Omnium's heir, Plantagenet Palliser. She is a cold beauty with little to say. By *The Last Chronicle of Barset*, her father-in-law's death has made her Marchioness of Hartletop and both of her parents stand in awe of her.

She also plays a part in two of the Palliser novels. In *Can You Forgive Her?* she is described within a few months of becoming a marchioness as 'very beautiful . . . the best dressed woman in London'. She is the exact opposite of Lady Glencora Palliser and it is plain that Trollope detests Griselda as an example of a cold and unemotional Society lady. In *Phineas Finn* [40] she makes a brief reappearance as a guest at a dinner given by Lady Glencora. She is even in *Miss Mackenzie*, in which she is one of the lady patronesses of the Negro Soldiers Orphan Bazaar [27]. Here, as Lady Hartletop, she has her own son and heir, young Lord Dumbello. One reason Trollope may have brought her into this novel is because he had considered using the name 'Griselda' in the title and indeed in this chapter there are several references to that name.

Griselda Grantly, under her various names and titles, appears in more of Trollope's novels than any other character, yet she is never really developed into a sympathetic figure. She remains nothing more than a cold beauty who never makes a mistake and never provokes any strong reaction. It is interesting, however, to observe the change in the relationship between her and her mother until finally Mrs Grantly realizes that in producing a marchioness she has lost a daughter [*The Last Chronicle of Barset*, 2].

The Graphic. This weekly magazine published three Trollope novels and one Christmas story. Trollope's connection with it began during his 1872 tour to Australia and New Zealand when the editor asked him for a Christmas story. The magazine had a large circulation and was the main competitor of the *Illustrated London News*. Instead, Trollope eventually offered them the serial rights to *Phineas Redux* for £1,250 and the novel was published during 1873–4. The magazine then wanted a Christmas story for 1873, to build on the fame earned by publishing a Christmas story by Wilkie Collins, 'Miss or Mrs?', in 1871. Trollope sent them his short novel about Australia, *Harry Heathcote of Gangoil*. He wrote another Christmas story, 'Christmas at Thompson Hall', for their 1876 issue. In 1881–2 they serialized *Marion Fay*. The magazine paid extremely well.

Green, Archibald. Trollope uses this name in his first-person narration in three short stories: 'The O'Conors of Castle Conor', 'Father Giles of Ballymoy' and 'Miss Ophelia Gledd'. He is unmistakably Trollope. In 'Father Giles', Green is even given Trollope's birthplace, Keppel Street, London.

GRESHAM FAMILY

The Greshams are an important Barsetshire gentry family in some of the Barsetshire and Palliser novels. Most unusually, the family is mentioned in 'The Two Heroines of Plumplington'. This is one of the few cases in which there is any connection between the short stories and the novels. Although only a few members of the Gresham family feature in more than one novel, the family is important in county society. The Greshams are a very old family of squires who live at Greshamsbury Park. They are introduced in *Doctor Thorne*, in which Trollope summarizes the career of John Newbold Gresham, Tory MP for Barsetshire and, after 1832, for East Barsetshire. This Gresham died in 1833. (This is an extremely rare example of Trollope's giving actual dates of death for his characters.) He was followed as MP by his son, Francis Newbold Gresham. He and other members of this fictional family are described below.

Gresham, Francis Newbold. Gresham entered the House of Commons as a Tory. However, his marriage to Lady Arabella De Courcy, a member of the great Whig family, made him suspect to many Tories. He did not long retain his seat and several attempts at re-election saddled him with debts. It may seem to some that the £10,000 Gresham spent on just one election is an almost unbelievable sum, but this is well within the range that important families were prepared to spend on county elections, which they saw as symbols of their power in the county. Gresham is always conscious that his family is one of the oldest in Barsetshire, far older than the De Courcys. Gresham's debts and his marriage to an imperious wife make him an unhappy man. He, his wife and family are important characters in *Doctor Thorne*, in which the doctor is his friend and confidant. His concern for his son is a good example of Trollope's perennial interest in the relations between father and son.

Gresham, Lady Arabella. Lady Arabella is the sister of Earl De Courcy and thus the aunt of all the De Courcy children. She is a year or two older than her husband. She is always conscious that she comes from an aristocratic family and resents the fact that her husband does not have a title. Having led him into debt, she is ever anxious to increase it by going to London for the Season. She has ten children, of whom Beatrice marries the Reverend Caleb Oriel while Augusta reappears briefly in *The Small House at Allington*.

Gresham, Francis Newbold. Frank Newbold, as he is usually called to distinguish him from his father, is the handsome heir to the heavily mortgaged estate of Greshamsbury. His family, particularly his De Courcy relatives, are anxious for him to make a wealthy marriage to repair the family's fortunes. He persists in his love for Dr Thorne's illegitimate niece, Mary Thorne, whom he marries. She eventually inherits the Scatcherd fortune which means he can restore the Greshams to their customary position in society. He also features in *Framley Parsonage* and in *The Last Chronicle of Barset*, in which as the 'young squire' he is MFH of the East Barsetshire Hunt. He appears in one Palliser novel, *The Prime Minister*, by which time he is almost forty. He has a son, a daughter who is of marriageable age and, apparently, several other children. Although he dislikes politics, he is an old-fashioned Tory and is forced to use his interest in an election in *The Prime Minister* [34]. In this novel there is an amusing recollection of his youthful exuberance. One can sense Trollope's delight in bringing back a favourite from the Barsetshire novels, particularly one who is an embodiment of old traditional virtues in the midst of all the temporizing politicians. [➤ Beards.]

Gresley. The family name of Trollope's maternal grandmother is used for the heroine as well as in the title of his short story 'Mary Gresley', and for a character, Lord Alfred Gresley, in *Sir Harry Hotspur of Humblethwaite*. Trollope's mother was very proud of this connection with a gentry family. [➤ Names, Origin of.]

Grey, John. In the first of the Palliser novels, *Can You Forgive Her?*, John Grey marries Alice Vavasor. He is a small squire in Cambridgeshire and the title of the chapter in which Trollope introduces him sums him up: 'John Grey, the Worthy Man'. His name is one of those Trollope used to describe a character, for he is very grey [➤ Names, Use of]. As an MP and supporter of Plantagenet Palliser, Grey appears in three more of the Palliser novels. Eventually he is sent on a diplomatic mission to Persia. He should not be confused with John Grey, the solicitor in *Mr Scarborough's Family*.

Grievance. There is nothing, says Trollope, 'as generally consoling to a man as a well-established grievance' [*Orley Farm*, 8]. Trollope's older men in particular often have a pet grievance that they carry about with them. It frequently comes to light when they are angry [*Doctor Thorne*, 12]. This is almost always a male trait and reflects Trollope's own character. His grievances, such as his treatment as a witness in a trial or before a parliamentary committee, or in his various quarrels in the Post Office, appear in his novels. The way in which a man nurses his grievance – such as Dr Wortle's perpetual annoyance with his bishop in *Dr Wortle's School* – is usually portrayed as an endearing aspect of an admirable character; it is only when the grievance comes to dominate a life – for instance, John Scarborough's hatred of entail in *Mr Scarborough's Family* – that it makes the character unpleasant.

Griselda. Trollope used this name for Archdeacon Grantly's daughter [➤ Grantly Family]. He also uses it in referring to certain women like Margaret Mackenzie in *Miss Mackenzie* – indeed, he had originally planned to call that novel 'The Modern Griselda'. Griselda was originally Grissil and the first occurrence of the name is in Boccaccio's *Decameron*. It is used in Chaucer's 'Clerk's Tale' in the *Canterbury Tales*, and then in the early sixteenth century in a comedy entitled 'Patient Grissil' by Thomas Dekker and others, a play which Trollope knew. A shared interest in

The Modern Griselda, a novel by Maria Edgeworth, led to the marriage of Trollope's parents and he had a copy of this novel in his library. Griselda Grantly was Grizzel in *The Warden* and Grisel in *Barchester Towers*. A Griselda was a woman whose fortitude allows her to survive many trials and many of Trollope's women fit this description.

Grogram, Sir Gregory. Sir Gregory is 'the great Whig lawyer' in some of the Palliser novels. As Attorney-General, he conducts the prosecution at Phineas Finn's trial for murder [*Phineas Redux*, 32, 61–7]. He later justifies his action to Finn. In *The Prime Minister* he becomes Lord Chancellor. In choosing Sir Gregory's surname Trollope had in mind not only alliteration but the coarse cloth of silk and mohair, or sometimes wool. In the nineteenth century, gum was sometimes added to stiffen the fabric. In *Lady Anna*, Grogram is used with *lèse-majesté* for the name of the old butler to the reprobate Earl Lovel. [➤ Names, Silly.]

H

Harding, Eleanor. The younger and favourite daughter of the Reverend Septimus Harding in the Barsetshire novels. She lives with him at the start of *The Warden*. John Bold, who precipitates her father's troubles, is in love with her and eventually, in spite of all the upsets, marries her. She is twenty-four when she first appears and is thus ten years younger than her sister, Susan Grantly, wife of the archdeacon with whom Eleanor frequently comes into conflict. By the start of the next novel, *Barchester Towers*, Eleanor Bold is a widow with a child, Johnnie, and a comfortable fortune which makes her a ripe target for fortune-hunters. She eventually marries the Reverend Francis Arabin. She is also in *Doctor Thorne* and *Framley Parsonage*. In *The Last Chronicle of Barset*, she is the innocent cause of Mr Crawley's troubles. Trollope depicts her as being more High Church than her sister [*Barchester Towers*, 53]. Eleanor is remarkably independent for a Victorian young lady: she manages her own fortune both before and after the marriage to Arabin. She is the first of the long series of English girls in Trollope's novels.

Harding, The Rev. Septimus. Mr Harding is probably the most beloved character in all Trollope's fiction. 'He is of that sort that they make angels of,' says the verger of Barchester Cathedral [*The Small House at Allington*, 16]. He is the central character in the Barsetshire novels: his story begins the series in *The Warden* and with his death at the end of *The Last Chronicle of Barset* the series comes to an end. At the start of *The Warden* he is 'verging on sixty years' and he is seventy-eight in *The Last Chronicle of Barset*. As well as appearing in all six Barsetshire novels, Mr Harding's family connections unite the various stories: his elder daughter, Susan, is married to Archdeacon Grantly, which gives Mr Harding links with old Bishop Grantly at the start of the series and with the Grantly children, Griselda and Henry, who play important roles in later novels. His younger daughter, Eleanor, and her marriage to the Radical, John Bold, provide the love plot for the first novel, while her second marriage to Francis Arabin provides that for *Barchester Towers*.

Septimus Harding is a widower and we are told almost nothing of his early life. *The Warden* is the story of how he gave up the comfortable and highly-paid position as warden of an almshouse called Hiram's Hospital. Mr Harding reflects on his resignation and summarizes this episode later in the series when talking to Adolphus Crosbie [*The Small House at Allington*, 16]. His great love is music and he is also precentor at Barchester Cathedral [➤ Church of England]. Mr Harding is an example of the quiet, High Church clergyman formed in the days before the Oxford Movement. Yet he does see that more vigorous methods and church reform are necessary. In Trollope's eyes, Mr Harding's one great fault, idleness, is redeemed by his admission that he has it [*The Last Chronicle of Barset*, 22]. He is also allowed to escape from the criticism Trollope usually directs at men who lack ambition because this lack allows him a 'womanly tenderness'. There is a melancholy side to his beautiful character and this is symbolized by his devotion to his cello; when upset he moves his fingers as if playing the instrument.

The key to his character is found in *Framley Parsonage*, in which he tells his granddaughter: 'Think about the happiness of those around you, and your own will come without thinking' [40]. The archdeacon sums up his father-in-law shortly before his moving death scene: 'He never was wrong. He couldn't go wrong. He lacked guile, and he feared God.' It is notable that Mr Harding's final words to 'my dears' are very similar to the deathbed words of his old friend, Bishop Grantly, in *Barchester Towers* [1].

A careful reading of the Barsetshire books shows how often the true personality of characters appears when they meet Mr Harding: the best aspects of Archdeacon Grantly; the vapidness of his granddaughter, Griselda; the vileness of Mr Slope; the decent side of Adolphus Crosbie. Trollope is inspired to some of his best writing whenever Mr Harding is portrayed, particularly in his later appearances. No other character in his fiction

occasioned so much careful writing with a style that almost verges on the emotional. According to Escott, Trollope's first biographer, he once said that he had taken some of Mr Harding's features from several members of the Sewell family, who played an important role in Oxford and High Church circles.

Harper & Brothers. A New York publishing house famous for its two magazines, *Harper's Weekly* and *Harper's New Monthly Magazine*. Trollope's connection with Harpers began in the summer of 1859 when he called *en route* back to England after his West Indies trip. He talked to Fletcher Harper about their publishing the book on the West Indies which he was finishing and offered them a series of short stories based on his foreign travels at £20 or $100 each. While they did not want the book they were interested in 'tales' or short stories for *Harper's New Monthly Magazine* and, after he returned to Ireland, he sent them four: 'The Courtship of Susan Bell', 'Relics of General Chassé', 'La Mère Bauche' and 'The O'Conors of Castle Conor'. They afterwards changed their minds and did publish *The West Indies and the Spanish Main* along with *The Bertrams* and *Barchester Towers*.

His relations with the firm were not easy: while they published three of his short stories as agreed, they refused to publish 'La Mère Bauche' until 1868. In 1861, during his second visit to the United States, he again met Fletcher Harper and had him agree not to pirate any book which Trollope's United Kingdom publishers had got another United States firm to reprint [➤ Copyright]. The following year, however, Harpers did pirate his *North*

America. Trollope was furious, referred to Fletcher Harper as 'that beast Harper' in a letter to Kate Field, and wrote 'Cheated' in red ink across his tally of earnings beside the entry for *North America.* The incident was the occasion for his long public letter to James Russell Lowell about the treatment of British writers by American 'pirates'. (Trollope's brother Tom called Harper 'the arch-pirate'.)

In 1862 they published *Orley Farm* and *The Struggles of Brown, Jones, and Robinson,* eight years before the first English book edition; in 1866, they republished *The Claverings*; in 1869, *He Knew He Was Right*; in 1871, *Sir Harry Hotspur of Humblethwaite*; in 1876, *The American Senator*; in 1877, they issued his short story 'Christmas at Thompson Hall' as a book; in 1880, they published his *Life of Cicero* and in 1882, *Marion Fay.* However, these arrangements were with his British publishers, not with Trollope himself.

Trollope's justified fury did not preclude further offers of works: in 1875, he offered the *Magazine* an article on Australia for $250 'in gold', but the negotiations came to nothing because the editor insisted that Trollope should provide the illustrations. Escott inserted a long footnote in his biography from information provided by J. Henry Harper about the amount that the firm claimed they had paid to Trollope or his estate between the £25 for *The Bertrams* in 1859 and the £10 for *An Old Man's Love* in 1884. Harper said they had paid him £3,080 of which the highest payment (one-quarter of the total) was for *Sir Harry Hotspur of Humblethwaite.*

Harry Heathcote of Gangoil: A Tale of Australian Bush Life. Trollope's thirty-first novel was written between 1 and 28 June 1873, six months after he returned from his first visit to Australia. It was commissioned by *The Graphic,* for their Christmas 1873 number and was the Christmas story of which he was most proud. The story was to be 38,000 words long and ready by 10 August 1873. The book rights were sold by the paper's publisher to Sampson Low & Co. who published it in one volume in October 1874. Trollope received £450.

This is the first of two novels Trollope based on his time in Australia; the second was *John Caldigate,* published five years later. Trollope wrote to a correspondent three years after this novel appeared in *The Graphic,* 'Harry Heathcote is my boy Frederic, – or very much the same.' The sheep 'run' on which the story is set is based on Frederic Trollope's station in New South Wales. In his *Autobiography* Trollope wrote that he 'was not loth [*sic*] to describe the troubles to which my own son had been subjected, by the mingled accidents of heat and bad neighbours, on his station in the bush.' Trollope also makes Heathcote a magistrate and in July 1872, while in Australia, he used his influence to get Frederic made a JP. He then referred to him as a 'zealous hard-working' man.

Harry Heathcote, although only twenty-four years old (Fred Trollope's age), is self-reliant, somewhat 'imperious' and a successful sheep farmer. He is a 'squatter', a tenant of the Crown who would gain a freehold to his land in due course. Because of his manner he has made many enemies and his great fear is that someone will 'torch' his land, already extremely dry from drought. Among the characters is Giles Medlicot, a neighbour who grows and mills sugar-cane. Medlicot is disliked by Heathcote because he purchased outright some land that had been part of Heathcote's 'run'. Soon a romance begins between Medlicot and Heathcote's sister. On Christmas Eve enemies do start a fire and Heathcote is helped in containing it by Medlicot; in the end harmony reigns and Medlicot becomes engaged to Heathcote's sister.

The story is rich in Australian expressions and Medlicot is one of the earliest of the superior young Englishmen later so prominent in Australian fiction. The story is set in Queensland, although Fred Trollope's station was in New South Wales. Heathcote's house is based on his son's house. Like the Heathcotes, Fred also employed a Chinese cook. In his book on Australia Trollope wrote that life on his son's station was rough and in the story the life is hard, but never primitive. Trollope gave his hero his other son's name, Harry, and also gave him two small children as well as a sister. Much of this short novel is drawn on his experiences of Australian life: the police sergeant, Forrest, an Oxford man who went to the colony to make his fortune, has a ring of truth about him. Trollope exercised his fondness for silly names in the person of Sing-Sing, the disloyal Chinese cook, and Mrs Growler, Heathcote's maid who has a penchant for growling. (A 'growler' was also a four-wheeled cab.) He refers to 'a good time coming', one of his favourite phrases. Trollope shows how English customs and food dominated the Australian Christmas although he thought some of this rather ridiculous, given the differences in climate. But these were the details that other par-

ents with children in Australia wanted to know.

Rather oddly, Trollope refers on several occasions to Heathcote as a 'young aristocrat': this may have resulted from an excess of paternal pride in a character so thoroughly based on his son. He also insisted, not surprisingly, that Harry Heathcote was a gentleman. Trollope had to defend the story's title against the editor of *The Graphic*, who disliked it. Trollope, who always insisted that only an author was fit to choose a title, won. The novel is similar to his continental novels because it is set outside England, is shorter and has only one major plot. The reviewers almost all agreed that the novel was 'slight' but 'pleasant'.

Hartletop, Marchioness of. The elder Marchioness of Hartletop is often talked about in the Barsetshire and Palliser novels, but her actual appearances are rare. In *Framley Parsonage* Mrs Grantly and Lady Lufton discuss the marchioness's scandalous background: as Mrs Grantly says, 'All about Lady Hartletop was known to all the world' [16]. What we learn is that she is married to a 'very feeble' husband who is immensely rich (his Lancashire property alone is worth £200,000 a year). She is 'the intimate friend' of the old Duke of Omnium and probably his mistress. (It is interesting to observe how discreet Trollope is about this, although later Madame Max Goesler is more forthright when she tells the old duke that she would not want anyone to think she would be his new mistress.) The marchioness was the greatest 'potentate' in the world of fashion for twenty years [*The Small House at Allington*, 17] but she is eclipsed by her new daughter-in-law, Lady Dumbello, the former Griselda Grantly.

The marchioness also appears in the Palliser novels, briefly in *Phineas Finn* and in a pathetic scene in *Phineas Redux* [25] when her dying friend, the old duke, refuses to see her. At that point the marchioness, now a dowager, is almost seventy years old.

Hartletop, Marchioness of. For the younger Marchioness, see Grantly, Griselda.

Hartletop, Marquis of. See Dumbello, Lord.

Hawaii. Trollope visited Hawaii, still an independent kingdom, in 1872 and in 1875, on his way back from Australia, and wrote about it briefly in one of his 'letters' published in various United Kingdom newspapers. [➤ *The Tireless Traveler*.]

Hawthorne, Nathaniel (1804–64). This famous American novelist, author of *The House of the Seven Gables* and *The Scarlet Letter*, became an admirer of Trollope's novels during his time as American Consul in Liverpool (1853–7). In February 1860 he wrote to the Boston publisher James T. Fields, praising Trollope's novels as 'solid and substantial, written on the strength of beef and ... ale, and just as real as if some giant had hewn a great lump out of the earth and put it under a glass case'. Trollope was so delighted when this comment was repeated to him that he wrote it down and carried the piece of paper about with him – it still survives in the Taylor Collection in Princeton. Trollope also quoted the comment, from 'a brother novelist

very much greater than myself', in his *Autobiography*. Although he had already read and admired some of Hawthorne's novels, the two novelists only met during his 1861 visit to America. Hawthorne and other New England luminaries were invited to a dinner to meet Trollope, and in spite of a vehement and amusing debate about the merits of English and American fruit and vegetables they became firm friends [➤ Gardens]. A few years after this there is a reference to 'our excellent American friend and critic, Mr Hawthorne' in *Can You Forgive Her?* [33]. In 1879 Trollope wrote one of his best pieces of criticism on 'The Genius of Nathaniel Hawthorne' for the *North American Review*. He praised Hawthorne's fiction, which exemplified what he called the American tendency toward 'speculation'. No doubt thinking of Hawthorne's remark, Trollope added, 'On our side of the water we deal more with beef and ale and less with dreams.' Trollope later entertained Hawthorne's son, Julian (1846–1934), whose own autobiographical books contain some of the most perceptive comments about Trollope, the importance of his wife, Rose, and his position in London's literary society.

Health. In spite of the many doctors in Trollope's fiction, the bulk of his characters appear to be in remarkably good health. This no doubt reflected the fact that, despite a mysterious illness in his youth, Trollope enjoyed good health until his last years. Then he suffered from a loss of hearing in one ear, asthma, heart trouble and, not surprisingly, writer's cramp [➤ Bland, Florence]. Even as a young man he knew that good health 'was meant by

God' to be 'the greatest pleasure that we are capable of enjoying' [Mullen, 71]. He expressed this view in his short story 'The Telegraph Girl': '"It is such a blessing to be strong," said poor Sophy. "Yes; it is a blessing. And I do bless God that He has made me so. It is the one good thing that has been given to me, and it is better, I think, than all the others."'

The most common health problems from which characters suffer come from old age. Mr Harding in *The Last Chronicle of Barset* is the best example of this. Sometimes there are stronger hints of a fatal illness, as with Mrs Winterfield in *The Belton Estate*. John Scarborough in *Mr Scarborough's Family* appears to be suffering from cancer and a surgeon performs an operation at his country house. Normally in the novels sudden death is caused by accidents or violence, although Mrs Proudie dies from a heart attack. Tuberculosis or consumption was a painful subject for Trollope because of the deaths of his sisters and brother and thus such cases are rarer in his fiction than was normal in Victorian writing. The most notable is Marion Fay in the novel named after her. There are a few cases of asthma in his novels [*The American Senator*, 2]. Some characters suffer from mysterious health problems, such as that which caused Madeline Stanhope's lameness in *Barchester Towers* or Gregory Marrable's general ill-health in *The Vicar of Bullhampton*. Josephine de Montmorenci, the reclusive author in the short story bearing her name, suffers from curvature of the spine. On occasion, for instance in the case of Emily Hotspur in *Sir Harry Hotspur of Humblethwaite*, an otherwise healthy girl dies of a broken heart. Trollope's use of the phrase 'brown complexion' normally indicates that a young woman has good health.

Drunkenness is often a fatal disease as it is for the two Scatcherds, father and son, in *Doctor Thorne*, or one that leads to suicide ['The Spotted Dog']. Some characters, particularly dissolute aristocrats such as the Marquis of Brotherton in *Is He Popenjoy?*, may be suffering from venereal disease, but this of course is never made plain. Some old men, for example Sir Anthony Aylmer in *The Belton Estate*, suffer from gout, but that disease is not as common as might be expected. In the same novel Bernard Amedroz is a hypochondriac, for which condition Trollope had no sympathy; he regarded it as 'unmanly' [➤ Manliness].

Victorian doctors often prescribed travel as a cure and this could help a novelist like Trollope to make use of his own extensive travels: the Reverend Arthur Wilkinson is sent away in *The Bertrams*, as is George Walker in 'George Walker at Suez', while in 'The Telegraph Girl' the working-class Sophie Wilson is sent to the seaside at Hastings by the Post Office. Normally characters who are ill are treated at home by doctors. However, when a maid in *The Small House at Allington* comes down with scarlatina, Mrs Dale hires a nurse to care for her. Even so, Lily Dale herself then contracts the disease.

Although Trollope sometimes followed his mother's practice of visiting hospitals and asylums when writing his travel books, he did not seem to have a tremendous interest in medical matters. (He does not mention in his *North America* that he fainted while visiting a hospital in New York.) [➤ Insanity.]

He Knew He Was Right. Trollope's twenty-third novel was written between 13 November 1867 and 12 June 1868, and finished during his third trip to America. The book was first published by James Virtue in thirty-two weekly 6*d.* parts between 17 October 1868 and 22 May 1869, and eight monthly collections at 2*s.* With number thirty, publication was transferred from Virtue, who had overstretched his resources, to Alexander Strahan, who published the novel in two volumes in May 1869. Virtue paid Trollope £3,200, the same as the price for *Phineas Finn*, the highest sums he ever received for any novel.

This is one of Trollope's greatest novels, a superb portrait of the self-destruction of a man's mind. The central plot revolves round Louis Trevelyan, a rich young man who makes what seems an idyllic marriage with Emily Rowley, the daughter of a colonial governor. The well-versed reader of Trollope will spot two danger signals in the first chapter: young Louis is too handsome and he is idle. He is also a man too inclined to govern his life by theories: thus he rejoices that Emily's father is unable to provide her with a dowry because he believes that a woman should not bring any 'fortune' to the marriage [➤ Settlements; Utopian]. This rejection of practical considerations makes Trevelyan all the more likely to allow himself to be dominated by any idea he seizes on. Within a few months of the wedding – and a few pages of the opening of this long novel – trouble arises when Louis becomes jealous of Emily's friendship with an old family friend, Colonel Osborne.

Jealousy – marital jealousy – was one of Trollope's perennial themes. In *Orley Farm* it occurs in a somewhat farcical form when Mrs Furnival becomes jealous of her barrister husband's friendship with a client. Yet in Trollope's fiction, jealousy in its virulent form is primarily a male vice. Lady Laura Kennedy comes to grief because of her husband's jealousy in *Phineas Finn*, the novel that was appearing when Trollope began work on *He Knew He Was Right*. In *Phineas Redux*, written a few years later, Robert Kennedy's jealousy of Phineas Finn would drive him to insanity and attempted murder. Phineas Finn and Colonel Osborne share few common attributes: Finn is a young, handsome, impecunious, Irish Liberal MP, while Osborne is a wealthy, ageing Tory MP with more than a dash of the roué. (Mr Furnival in *Orley Farm* is also an MP: perhaps Trollope was an early observer of the high rate of marital breakdowns among politicians.) Osborne is not really a wicked man but his behaviour leads to evil consequences: the destruction of the Trevelyan marriage.

The cause of the jealousy will seem absurd to most modern readers: Colonel Osborne continues to call Trevelyan's wife by her Christian name. Yet every age places external values on the use or avoidance of certain words. For a Victorian gentleman it was not just impolite to call a married lady by her Christian name but a grievous fault because it implied an intimacy with another man's wife. Trevelyan's reactions to Osborne's behaviour are, of course, absurd even by Victorian standards, but it is important to see that he had at least a right to be annoyed, if not to be insanely outraged. [➤ Names, Use of.]

To appreciate *He Knew He Was Right*

we should remember the circumstances in which it was written. Trollope began it two weeks after his official retirement from the Post Office, and within a few months he was asked to go to America to negotiate a postal treaty and also to see if some agreement could be arranged on the contentious issue of international copyright. Trollope grew increasingly frustrated during his prolonged stay in Washington. He was disturbed by the corruption that had blossomed since his last visit. The American government was thoroughly distracted by the impeachment crisis surrounding President Andrew Johnson and Trollope's impatience was not helped by the sultry heat of a Washington summer. His misery was increased by his desire to return to England as he wanted to stand for Parliament in the coming election [➤ Beverley]. The many American characters, especially Wallachia Petrie and the American diplomat, Jonas Spalding, reflect his frustrations. Although he continued to take a broadly favourable view of America, he saw more faults springing up than he had noted in his book, *North America*. *He Knew He Was Right* is the only Trollope novel of which large portions were written in America and not surprisingly it contains passages examining differences between the two countries [37, 40, 55, 56].

He Knew He Was Right fits into another pattern in Trollope's writing. When he was away from home for long periods, particularly – as in this case – when he was not travelling with his wife, his novels tended to take on a more sombre, a more introspective, indeed a more intellectual character. That was the case ten years before with *The Bertrams*. It would be

repeated in the next decade with *The American Senator*. All these books took a more critical view of Victorian society than novels like *Framley Parsonage* or *Ayala's Angel* (to take but two examples) written when he was contentedly enjoying a normal routine. This novel shares one important characteristic with *Phineas Finn* beyond the theme of jealousy: each portrays popular journalism, which was emerging as an important force in the late 1860s after the passage of the Second Reform Act in 1867. (When Trollope used the phrase 'a leap in the dark' [33] he was quoting the phrase used by Lord Derby, the Prime Minister, in reference to the 1867 Reform Act.) This was mainly the work of Benjamin Disraeli, whom Trollope despised. So, too, did the old-fashioned Tory, Miss Stanbury, when she refers in this novel to 'a certain leading politician of the day ... with the cunning of the devil' [48]. [➤ Editors; Journalists; Newspapers.]

It is difficult to think of any other novel in which Trollope put so many varied aspects of his life as *He Knew He Was Right*. For the scenes in Devonshire he drew upon childhood recollections of his mother's cousin, Fanny Bent, who is said to have been the model for Jemima Stanbury. Trollope also knew Devonshire well from laying out postal 'walks' there in the 1850s, and not surprisingly he introduces two allusions to the Post Office: Miss Stanbury refuses to put her letters in 'an iron stump' as she thinks pillar-boxes are not respectable and a radical innovation [8]. Because Trollope was responsible for the introduction of pillar-boxes he is here enjoying one of his private jokes. Many of Miss Stanbury's traits recall other private jokes in the Trollope family: her devotion to the memory of Lord Eldon (1751–1838) no doubt springs from the vehemence with which Trollope's father denounced the reactionary Tory Lord Chancellor to his sons. The rural postman with the wooden leg is similar in character to many of the letter-carriers Trollope supervised.

In Trollope's portrayal of a mentally unbalanced man, recollections of his own father would have been useful to him. The Italian scenes are, of course, connected with the long residence of Trollope's brother Tom in Florence, which at this point was the capital of the newly-united Italy. Bagna di Lucca was a favourite spot of Trollope's mother, who made an annual migration there to escape the sweltering heat of a Florentine summer. In choosing names like Emily or Jonas, Trollope was following his normal pattern [➤ Names, Origin of]. His choice of Trevelyan had a private meaning for him: in *The Three Clerks* he had portrayed the well-known Civil Service reformer, Sir Charles Trevelyan (1807–86), as Sir Gregory Hardlines. For the colonial governor Sir Marmaduke Rowley, Trollope could draw upon his visits to British colonies in the West Indies and elsewhere. Shakespeare's influence on Trollope is particularly evident in this novel about a husband's all-consuming jealousy. It is hardly suprising that there are numerous allusions to *Othello*, most notably in the Venetian episode. [➤ Captain Bold of Halifax.]

Just as *Orley Farm* rests on the portrayal of Lady Mason or *The Last Chronicle of Barset* on that of the Reverend Josiah Crawley, so *He Knew He Was Right* depends on the portrayal of Louis Trevelyan. One of Trollope's

most remarkable qualities as a writer is his ability to explore the human mind. (Trollope was writing this novel when Freud was a twelve-year-old boy.) Throughout his writing Trollope stresses that almost every character in fiction, as in life, has a mixture of motives. The novel contains one of the best summaries of this view [60]. The author shows how Trevelyan tortures himself by searching through newspapers for accounts of marital infidelity. Here he makes an important psychological observation which shows just how much he had studied human nature: 'They who do not understand that a man may be brought to hope that which of all things is the most grievous to him, have not observed with sufficient closeness the perversity of the human mind.' It was only a few years since Trollope had so memorably portrayed Josiah Crawley in *The Last Chronicle of Barset* as a man on the verge of mental collapse, but his interest in mental instability went back to his first novel, *The Macdermots of Ballycloran*. Yet in *He Knew He Was Right* he made a specific appeal for greater knowledge on 'the line which divides sanity from insanity' [38].

Trollope's sympathy, and that of the reader, is with Emily. Her only real fault is a certain stubborn pride. Indeed the portrayal of the women in this novel is one of its most interesting features. They range from Jemima Stanbury, the stalwart Tory spinster, to Wallachia Petrie, the crusading American feminist we meet in Florence. The women are allowed to make some quite telling – at least by Victorian standards – points against men. These usually occur in dialogue between women, such as that between Nora Rowley and Priscilla Stanbury.

Nora, 'all that an un-married sister should be', is told by Priscilla that there are two things men cannot do: 'They can't suckle babies, and they can't forget themselves' [25]. The suckling of babies by mothers, as opposed to using wet-nurses, was a controversial issue in the nineteenth century and occurs again when Wallachia Petrie tells her protégée, Caroline Spalding, that if she marries a British aristocrat and has a baby, 'I don't suppose you will be allowed to nurse it, because they never do in England. You have read what the Saturday Review says' [81]. During the spring of 1868 the *Review* was carrying a series of articles attacking feminism by the novelist (Eliza) Lynn Linton and in March Mrs Linton had advocated breastfeeding just as Trollope was writing this part of the novel. Although Trollope shows his feeling for many of the women characters, in the end the feminist theories of Wallachia Petrie are defeated when Caroline Spalding does marry her aristocrat [➤ Anglo-American Marriages; *Is He Popenjoy?*].

Caroline's rejection of Wallachia's advice recalls Trollope's constant preaching to Kate Field who complained that Wallachia Petrie had been made to resemble her. Trollope's reply gives another insight into the way in which he could see both sides of a question, in this case the continual boasting about 'democracy' and feminism. 'I never said you were like W. Petrie. I said that that young woman did not entertain a single opinion on public matters which you could repudiate, and that she was only absurd in her mode of expressing them.' (This was also his attitude towards Senator Gotobed's criticisms of English life in *The American Senator*.) The hope

Trollope expressed regarding Wallachia Petrie, that she 'will be cured at last by a husband and half-a-dozen children' [77], is similar to Trollope's half-serious letter to Kate Field written in 1862 in which he recalled a conversation he had had with the Reverend W. G. Eliot: '"Let her marry a husband," said he. "It is the best career for a woman." I agree ... and therefore bid you in his name as well as my own, to go & marry a husband.' But Kate Field was not the only American girl who played some part in the creation of Wallachia Petrie and the other American girls in the novel. Trollope had met another American girl, Constance Beale, during his stay in America and promised to put her in the novel he was writing. It is impossible to say whether this was just polite social chatter on his part or whether he used any aspect of her in one of his characters.

Trollope knew as a result of his Barsetshire series that readers expected a clergyman in his novels. Sometimes he resisted, but in *He Knew He Was Right* he met the demand. Young Gibson, the minor canon at Exeter, does at times seem to be included for no other purpose than to meet this popular desire. However, he does add some humour when the main plot becomes too sombre. (The illustration of Gibson by Marcus Stone shows him in a typical parsonical pose – not at all the way in which one would picture older clergymen like Archdeacon Grantly.) The other clerical character, the Reverend Oliphant Outhouse, is different from Trollope's usual clergymen. He is the rector of a poor parish in the East End. Trollope had some acquaintance with such clergy from his old friendship with the

Reverend William Rogers, a clergyman in a poor London parish. Trollope's portrayal shows a thorough and first-hand knowledge of life in London's poorer inner-city Victorian parishes [29]. We also get a fleeting glimmer of news about an old clerical friend, Bishop Proudie, when we hear that he has been made an Ecclesiastical Commissioner. (In 1948 the title was changed to Church Commissioner.)

He Knew He Was Right contains one of the two most exciting scenes in Trollope's novels: the kidnapping of young Louis. (The other is the suicide of Lopez in *The Prime Minister.*) Likewise, the travel scenes are particularly well done because Trollope used his long experience of visiting Italy to contrast the older methods of coach travel across the Alps with the newer, easier, but less romantic method of going through the mountain by the Mont Cenis railway tunnel which had opened in 1867. When Trollope introduces Samuel Bozzle, the former policeman hired by Trevelyan to spy on his wife, he has a character use the term 'private detective' to describe him [19]. The *Oxford English Dictionary* cites this as the first appearance of the term in print.

Trollope himself was rather scathing about *He Knew He Was Right* in his *Autobiography*: 'I do not know that in any literary effort I ever fell more completely short of my own intention . . . I look upon the story as being nearly altogether bad.' He had intended to create sympathy for Trevelyan, and surely in the end one does feel this for the man even if he is a victim of his own delusions. Contemporaries were far more generous to the novel than Trollope was. Another novelist, Mrs

Oliphant, wrote to tell him that 'hot discussions' were going on among her friends as to what would be Trevelyan's fate. After Trollope's death, Henry James gave high praise to *He Knew He Was Right* because the author had not been afraid of presenting 'a misery which should be too much like life'. It was, said James, worthy of Balzac. Yet one of Trollope's greatest admirers, the poet Edward FitzGerald, was right to complain of the 'longueur' induced by the innumerable sub-plots of the novel. Even so, James's verdict on the greatness of this 'conspicuous intensity of the tragical' should stand. This is a novel for the mature Trollope reader, who wants to see into the inner workings of a Victorian marriage, and indeed into the perversities of the human mind.

High Church.
See Church of England.

Hiram's Hospital. A charitable foundation mentioned frequently in the Barsetshire novels. *The Warden* is dominated by the public dispute about the Reverend Septimus Harding's wardenship of this almshouse for twelve poor old men. In *Barchester Towers*, much of the plot centres on the succession to Mr Harding as warden. The Hospital is mentioned in several of the later Barsetshire novels. In *The Warden* [1] we are told that the Hospital was founded by a wealthy Barchester wool-stapler, John Hiram, in 1434. [For the way in which Trollope used several real debates about charitable foundations to create his almshouse, ➤ *The Warden.*] When *The Warden* was written the term 'hospital' still retained much of its medieval meaning as 'hospice' or charitable foundation.

The term's modern definition developed with the century.

Historical Fiction. While Trollope's third novel, *La Vendée*, is regarded as his one attempt at an 'historical novel', it is not his only work of fiction set in the past. In the 1870s he set *Lady Anna* in the 1830s to allow himself scope to write a new series which he could bring up to date, but this did not materialize. Likewise, his humorous short story 'The Gentle Euphemia' is set in the Middle Ages, and 'The Panjandrum' at the end of the 1830s. His attempt at writing an historical novel was not successful, as he recalled in his *Autobiography*. When writing about *The Three Clerks*, he remembered taking that manuscript to Hurst & Blackett, whose predecessor, Colburn, had published *La Vendée*. The foreman, obviously recalling the failure of *La Vendée*, said, 'I hope it's not historical, Mr Trollope? Whatever you do, don't be historical; your historical novel is not worth a damn.' Trollope himself admitted in the *Autobiography* that 'the facts of the present time came more within the limits of my powers of story-telling than those of past years'.

Hobbledehoy. This is a word that occurs frequently in Trollope's fiction. His briefest definition comes in *Ayala's Angel*: a hobbledehoy is 'one of those overgrown lads who come late to their manhood' [8]. The word dates back to the mid-sixteenth century and was also employed by other Victorian novelists – Thackeray, for instance. Probably no other Victorian writer used the word and described the characteristics as frequently or as lovingly as Trollope. All his hobbledehoys have some similarity with the young Trollope. In his *Autobiography* he describes himself when his family was seeking refuge in Belgium as 'that most hopeless of human beings, a hobbledehoy of nineteen, without any idea of a career'. Charley Tudor and Johnny Eames, two famous hobbledehoys, are particularly based on Trollope. Eames's 'gawky' behaviour draws directly upon his creator's boyish shyness [*The Small House at Allington*, 4]. Trollope's portrayal of hobbledehoys, and occasionally female hobbledehoys or 'hobbledehoyas', is usually followed by a version of one of his favourite sayings to justify delayed maturity, such as the fruit which ripens slowest is the sweetest [*The Duke's Children*, 51]. The hobbledehoy is always ultimately a better man than the 'young Apollo' or the 'curled darling'.

'Hog in Armour'. This phrase is often used by Trollope to refer to an over-dressed man. In *The Three Clerks* he is paying a backhanded compliment to the Frenchman Victoire Jaquêtanàpe, who could get away with overdressing. 'Nothing on earth could be nicer, or sweeter, or finer, than he was. But he did not carry his finery like a hog in armour, as an Englishman so often does when an Englishman stoops to be fine' [25]. The phrase probably dates from the sixteenth century and was used to describe a man who cannot move comfortably because he is so overdressed. The 'hog' is probably a corruption of 'hodge', the condescending term for a farm labourer or rustic. Armour was, of course, worn in the Middle Ages by those of high rank. [➤ France; Manliness.]

Holy Land. Trollope visited the Holy Land, then part of the Ottoman

Empire, in 1858 after finishing a Post Office assignment in Egypt. He recalled his visit in *The Bertrams* [6–11] and in his short story, 'A Ride across Palestine'. While he was deeply moved by his time on the Mount of Olives, in the Garden of Gethsemane and in the area round Jerusalem, he had little time when in Jerusalem for some of the pilgrims from the Eastern Orthodox Churches who came to 'that filthy church of the holy places' [*The Bertrams*, 7]. Here he was probably influenced by the arguments going on after 1849 about the true sites of the Crucifixion and burial of Christ. He had also read Dean Stanley's *Sinai and Palestine* (1856), to which he refers in *The Bertrams* [7]. [➤ Jews; Religion.]

Honesty. For Trollope, honesty was the greatest and most important virtue both for individuals and for nations. One of the vital tasks for fiction was to teach honesty 'in these times, when the desire to be honest is pressed so hard' [*Autobiography*, 12]. In his *Autobiography* he also shows his long-smouldering resentment about an unjust punishment he suffered as a schoolboy because some 'lily-livered curs' did not tell the truth. Contemporary sources almost all emphasize his great personal sense of honesty as a man. While he was quick to demand his just payment from a publisher, he was equally quick to refund any overpayment and to ensure that the publisher got full value [➤ 'Christmas Day at Kirkby Cottage'; *The Duke's Children*].

Personal honesty is a constant theme throughout his writing, although some incorrectly date it from *The Way We Live Now*. The battle between individual honesty and dishonesty occurs in Barry Lynch's behaviour in *The Kellys and the O'Kellys*. Mr Harding's decision to resign his lucrative position in *The Warden* is taken because it would be dishonest to continue to draw a comfortable income for little work. Alaric Tudor's undoing in *The Three Clerks* occurs when he listens to a corrupt MP. Lady Mason forges a will to secure an inheritance for her son in *Orley Farm*. Lizzie Eustace tells so many lies in *The Eustace Diamonds* that she is not herself sure what is true. The Marquis of Brotherton tries to make an illegitimate son the heir to his title and estate in *Is He Popenjoy?*. In *John Caldigate* Euphemia Smith lies and deceives, while Henry Jones's dishonesty over a will in *Cousin Henry* comes in a sin of omission, not commission. In *Mr Scarborough's Family* Mr Scarborough lies to avoid having his estate burdened with his son's post-obits [➤ Bills.] and in *The Land-Leaguers* young Florian Jones takes an oath not to tell the truth.

For Trollope, national honesty was as important a virtue as personal honesty. In *The New Zealander*, which he wrote after *The Warden*, he argued that the only way that Britain could hold off national decline was by adhering to honesty in public life. He chose as the book's motto a line from a Scottish song, 'It's gude to be honest and true', which he used elsewhere in his fiction. He repeated the warning twenty years later: 'Nothing can be so deleterious to a people at large as a lax feeling in regard to general honesty' [*The Tireless Traveler*, letter 15]. He returned to the attack in *The Three Clerks, Framley Parsonage, The Struggles of Brown, Jones, and Robinson, Orley Farm*, and, most memorably, in *The Way We Live Now*. In the novel on which he was working at his death, he attacked what he called government dishonesty over Irish land laws by which rents were fixed by the government and not by a free market [*The Land-Leaguers*, 41]. Ironically, he had always felt that the Irish had a superior sense of honesty to the English. The extraordinary attacks in his fiction on Sir Robert Peel and later on Disraeli came from his belief that their changes in policy undermined the national sense of honesty.

Dishonesty usually brings punishment in the end: Alaric Tudor is sent to gaol; Mr Slope's many lies in *Barchester Towers* eventually cause his downfall; Lady Mason is driven into exile with only a small income; Fred Neville's dishonesty to Kate O'Hara results in his murder and her dishonour in *An Eye for an Eye*; Euphemia Smith's treachery is uncovered and she is imprisoned; Ferdinand Lopez commits suicide in *The Prime Minister*, as does Augustus Melmotte in *The Way We Live Now*; Henry Jones suffers agonies and final humiliation in *Cousin Henry*; Mr Scarborough dies after being deceived by his younger son for whom he contrived so many frauds; Brown, Jones and Robinson collapse in a financial scandal; Sophie Gordeloup's chicanery in *The Claverings* brings about her own undoing and, in the same novel, Julia Brabazon lives without love after the death of Lord Ongar, whom she married purely for money and title; young Florian Jones's lying begins a series of events that lead to his own murder in *The Land-Leaguers*.

Trollope's passionate belief explains his hatred for things as diverse as advertising, the false hair worn by some women and the adulteration of food, especially coffee [➤ *London Tradesmen*].

Horns, The. The villa that belongs to the Duke of Omnium, and the scene of several memorable events in the Palliser novels. It was on the banks of the Thames above Richmond and the old duke gave it as a wedding present to Lady Glencora Palliser. In *Phineas Finn* it is the scene of a memorable party for 500 guests [63–4]. Lady Glencora also uses it for entertaining when her husband is Prime Minister [*The Prime Minister*, 37]. The Horns is 'the sweetest' of all the great villas near London [*The Duke's Children*, 12].

Horses. Horses were such an essential part of Trollope's life and world that they naturally occur in almost all his novels. His brother Tom had taught him to ride as a boy on their farm in Harrow and he rode constantly in the course of his Post Office work as well as when fox-hunting. In the 1870s, when he lived in London, Trollope normally took a daily ride in 'the Park' (Hyde Park's Rotten Row) with his niece, Florence Bland. These rides allowed him to observe how important this parade of fashion was and to use it in his fiction [*Ayala's Angel*, 17]. The great problem in towns was finding stables, which usually either came with a house or were hired. Trollope was able to stable the horses he used for fox-hunting outside London and probably stabled the horses used for riding in the Park or for his carriage in the stables attached to Montagu Square. Although he appears never to have been an elegant rider, he must have been a good one as he once saved a girl – indeed his future daughter-in-law – from death in Rotten Row by stopping her horse which had bolted. It is hardly surprising to learn that he liked to ride fast and in *North America* he describes how he was stopped by military police for galloping through the streets of Washington on his 'nimble trotter'. In this same book he mentions that his wife, Rose, also rode.

Since Trollope was a heavy man he preferred to ride heavy horses, particularly when he was fox-hunting. He appears to have maintained about half-a-dozen horses, of which probably three were for hunting. Two of his best-known ones were Banker, a dark chestnut, and Buff, a blue roan: one fellow hunter recalled that they looked like coach horses. They turn up by name in *Marion Fay* and in *Ralph the Heir*. Other horses are given names in Trollope's fiction: probably the most memorable is Bonebreaker in *Phineas Finn*. In *Framley Parsonage* a horse is named after one of Dickens's best-known characters, Mrs Gamp. Trollope knew that he was writing for readers who understood horses and therefore he took care. He criticized one illustration for *Can You Forgive Her?* because the artist had given the wrong sex to Lady Glencora's horses, Dandy and Flirt.

Owning horses was a sign of considerable wealth, especially in towns. This was not simply because of their initial cost, but the expense of stabling and feeding them. Horses, like motor-cars, were also a principal means to display one's wealth. In *Is He Popenjoy?* Dean Brotherton has only one horse to pull his carriage, while the bishop always has two; but, Trollope adds, 'one horse is enough for town work, and that one horse could lift his legs and make himself conspicuous in a manner of which the Bishop's rather sorry jades knew nothing' [5]. In *The Belton Estate*, Squire Amedroz sadly has to give up his carriage horses and instead use the horses kept for farm work; this had already been a problem for Squire Vavasor in *Can You Forgive Her?*. It was assumed with most of Trollope's 'carriage folk' that they either own or at least can afford to hire carriage horses. Mrs Proudie's frequent boasting about 'my horses' first introduces that formidable lady in *Barchester Towers* [5] and lets us know that we are not going to like her. The haggling over whether Miss Thoroughbung is to have her own ponies in addition to Mr Prosper's carriage horses undoes this middle-aged couple's engagement plans in *Mr Scarborough's Family* [48–9].

Trollope denied that he had much luck in buying horses but when he portrays Mark Robarts doing just that he shows that he had a good idea of what to look for [*Framley Parsonage*, 14]. Like many Victorians he believed that there was 'something in the traffic of horses provocative of deceit and cheating' [➤ 'The Horse Dealer' in his *London Tradesmen*]. Certainly when horses were involved with racing there was likely to be much dishonesty, as with Major Tifto in *The Duke's Children* [6]. In that novel a horse is 'nobbled'.

Trollope frequently alludes to the various questions of etiquette relating to horses. There is the problem of who is to hold the horse's reins when the rider has to go inside a building for a brief while [*The Warden*, 12], and Mark Robarts is often concerned about who will hold his horse when he visits Mr Crawley, who has no horse [*The Last Chronicle of Barset*, 21]. Lord Hampstead has to take his groom with him to hold his horse while he visits his beloved in a London suburb in *Marion Fay*. (Judging by *Harry*

Heathcote of Gangoil, such niceties were not a problem in Australia.) Ladies normally confine their riding either to fox-hunting or, when in London, to rides in 'the Park'. Some husbands, like Jeffrey Houghton in *Is He Popenjoy?,* object to their wives riding to hounds.

Fatal accidents by riders were quite common in Victorian life: Sir Robert Peel and Bishop Wilberforce – to take two men who figure in Trollope's writings – as well as his fellow novelist, George Whyte-Melville, were all killed in riding accidents. Several Trollopian characters, for instance Phineas Finn or Adelaide Houghton [*Is He Popenjoy?,* 8–9], are injured while hunting and Squire Newton in *Ralph the Heir* is killed by a fall from his horse.

A cob is probably the most common type of horse mentioned in his fiction: clergymen often ride these short, strong horses. Archdeacon Grantly presents a cob as a wedding gift to his ally, Francis Arabin [*Barchester Towers,* 53]. Since Trollope had learned much about horses in Ireland, it is not surprising to find his using an Irish term such as 'garron' when referring to horses even in later non-Irish novels like *The Claverings* [19] and *The Prime Minister* [1]. He had admired Irish riders as early as his first novel, *The Macdermots of Ballycloran* [17]. Phrases based on horses, like 'kicking in harness', occur throughout his writing [*Phineas Redux,* 77].

Hotels. Hotels played an important role in Trollope's life and an equally important one in his fiction. Most of his novels have scenes set in hotels and several of the short stories make great use of hotels he visited during his travels. His travel books contain numerous descriptions of hotels, from Cairo in Egypt to Cairo in Illinois, from Turin to New York and Havana (where he had to share a room, something he hated doing).

When Trollope moved to Ireland in 1841, he lived in an hotel for several years and he got to know many other hotels throughout the island because of his Post Office travels. His Irish novels often have portraits of ramshackle hotels and in *The Kellys and the O'Kellys* Mrs Kelly is an innkeeper. The best description of a rundown Irish hotel is that of the Kanturk Hotel in Cork in *Castle Richmond,* with its 'strong smell of hot whiskey and water' [6]. However, in the same novel he praised Irish hotels for their honesty. [1] The joviality Trollope relished in Irish hotels comes out best in 'Father Giles of Ballymoy'.

Once Trollope moved up in the Post Office and began to make money from his books, he made it a rule always to stay in the best hotels. 'You should always live at the hotels as a gentleman,' he advised a young clerk in 1858. 'It will pay best in the long run.' His travels gave him a knowledge in this field rarely equalled by any other Victorian writer. In *North America* he devoted a whole chapter [14] to hotels: America is credited with the creation of the modern hotel with reception rooms, suites, piped water, lifts, bathrooms and toilets on every floor of a large modern building containing a great number of rooms, like the 600 in the Ocean Hotel in Newport, Rhode Island. Trollope did not much like the way of life he saw there, a view echoed by other English visitors. Like them he hated the overheated rooms. He maintained that

Swiss hotels were the best he knew, while German hotels were dirty and French hotels the most expensive. He did not think 'we Englishmen have any great right to be proud' of English inns and believed they were deteriorating. He disliked the railway hotels that were springing up in English cities; they were 'gloomy, desolate ... and almost suicidal'. Another problem with English hotels was that 'the cost is generally too high, and unfortunately grows larger and larger from year to year'.

Despite his general dislike of England's new hotels, Trollope wrote about them in his fiction: he had stayed at some of those he described. Johnny Eames has a 'comfortless' meal in the coffee-room of the Great Western Hotel at Paddington, although Trollope admits it is 'an excellent establishment' [*The Small House at Allington*, 59]. Earlier in the same novel Johnny dines with an earl at a quiet and older type of hotel in Jermyn Street [32]. London hotels often appealed to a specific clientele. Mr Harding, for example, stays at a 'quiet, sombre' hotel near St Paul's [*The Warden*, 16], while his daughter finds a similar hotel in Suffolk Street [*The Last Chronicle of Barset*, 76]. Hers is based on a real hotel called Garlant's at number 14, Suffolk Street, where Trollope spent much time, including most of the last weeks of his life. Garlant's, 'patronized by bishops and deans of the better sort', was where Eames and Mrs Arabin [Eleanor Harding] stayed on their return from Italy [*The Last Chronicle of Barset*, 70]. Some London hotels drew their guests from different parts of the country and Trollope depicts one such which catered for Scotsmen in *Phineas Redux* [23]. In

Is He Popenjoy? a dramatic scene is set in Scumberg's Hotel in London [41]. When Trollope adds that the hotel's real owners, the Tomkins, had 'a German deputy-manager kept to maintain the foreign Scumberg connection' he knew his readers would see his point: the Tomkins were making use of the high reputation of Swiss hoteliers in England.

Trollope rarely gives the price of English hotels, although we are told that one young man in *The Three Clerks* paid 2s. 6d. for a bed in an inn near London. Trollope himself always liked a private sitting-room, for which he says he normally paid an extra 7s. In *The Land-Leaguers*, Rachel O'Mahony and her father have two bedrooms, a sitting-room and a maid's room at Brown's in London for £6. 10s. a week, which they found too expensive [8]. A private sitting-room was virtually essential for a travelling lady so that she could avoid having to dine alone in public. Trollope gives a good account of a lady dining in a private sitting-room at the Great Northern Hotel in *The Belton Estate* [24].

Railway travel brought a demand for modern hotels in London. The Great Northern Railway Hotel had opened in 1854, the same year as the Great Western. In the 1860s hotels began to get grander and more 'American', and Trollope criticized this 'extravagance of architecture' [*Phineas Redux*, 23]. He was probably thinking of the Langham in Portland Place, which was built at the extraordinary cost of £300,000. (One gets some idea of the increasing price of luxury from the fact that it cost £80 million to restore it as an hotel in 1991.) Trollope often made the Langham the base for his American characters, notably in *The Way We Live Now* and *The Duke's Children*. The hotel was managed by a former Confederate colonel who understood American tastes, a fact made plain in *The Duke's Children* in which an American heiress receives a young gentleman there [33]. The German feminist, Baroness Banmann, also 'lodged herself magnificently at the Langham Hotel' [*Is He Popenjoy?*, 60].

Provincial hotels of all types occur throughout Trollope's fiction. In the Barsetshire novels we hear constantly of the Dragon of Wantly owned by Mrs Arabin as part of her inheritance from her first husband. Trollope shows the important role such places played in hiring horses and carriages in *Framley Parsonage* [7] and *The Vicar of Bullhampton* [40]. Hotels like these often took the place of modern committee rooms in elections: the Beverley Arms in Yorkshire's East Riding still boasts in its advertisements that Trollope stayed there in his election campaign in Beverley in 1868. In *Ralph the Heir* it becomes the Percy Standard. Trollope also shows, sometimes with Dickensian humour, the curious (and not always pleasant) ways of the commercial rooms of hotels in the Bull Inn, Leeds, in *Orley Farm* [6] and in its namesake, the Bull at Loring in *The Vicar of Bullhampton* [29]. Trollope naturally knew hotels that catered for fox-hunting. One of these is well described in *Can You Forgive Her?* [16].

The months he had spent working in the West Country in the early 1850s gave him a great familiarity with hotels in towns like Tavistock in Devon, and in *The Three Clerks* he recommends the Bedford Hotel there: 'I beg to assure any travelling readers that they might have drunk tea in a much worse place' [8]. He is also probably remembering one of his postal inspections in Devonshire when he has a woman in a country inn that boasts two 'clean bedrooms' react in fury to a man who asks for fish with his dinner [*He Knew He Was Right*, 14].

Foreign hotels are described in even greater detail in many of his short stories. The careful ways of a French provincial inn are shown in 'La Mère Bauche', while 'Christmas at Thompson Hall' sees its main action in the Grand Hotel on the Boulevard des Italiens in Paris. The bountiful food of a Tyrolean inn is tantalizingly exhibited in 'Why Frau Frohmann Raised Her Prices'. The custom of guests dining at a common table or *table d'hôte* had long been a favourite source of amusement for English novelists (particularly Fanny Trollope) and a convenient means for novelists to have characters meet one another. In *The Bertrams* Trollope assumed that 'all my readers will probably at different times have made part of a table d'hôte' [6], and he used the setting to good effect in 'The Château of Prince Polignac'. The difficulties of coping with luggage in an Italian hotel are amusingly recounted in 'The Man Who Kept His Money in a Box', and in his *Autobiography* there is an entertaining account of an occasion when the well-known Duo Torre hotel in Verona assumed he was visiting royalty because he had reserved his room by telegraph. *The Golden Lion of Granpère* is set in an hotel on the eastern borders of France. The famous Cairo hotel, Shepheard's, makes an early appearance in English fiction in 'An Unprotected Female at the Pyramids' and later in 'George Walker at Suez' (where it is spelled 'Shepperd's'). In 'Relics of General Chassé' the trouser-less clergyman takes refuge in Antwerp's Golden Fleece inn. (Trollope recommends the claret, mutton cutlets and fried potatoes.)

In his colonial travels, Trollope found that the standard of hotels in Australia was often higher than in England. There are amusing anecdotes of his visits to colonial hotels in *Australia and New Zealand*. He describes his stay in a New Zealand hotel made of corrugated iron in which he overheard his host say, 'So this is Mr Anthony Trollope? ... Well he must be a —— [damned] fool to come travelling in this country in such weather as this.' Sometimes in his travel books he would recommend hotels, like the one at Ceres in South Africa, in spite of the fact that the drawing-room had seven dozen canaries [*South Africa*]. He warned readers against Havana's hotels in *The West Indies and the Spanish Main*, and advised visitors to Washington to go to the lodging house kept by Worley, 'a coloured man, in I Street'.

'The House of Heine Brothers in Munich'. This short story was written during the second week of April 1861 when Trollope was also writing *Orley Farm*. The setting for the story is Munich, which Trollope visited in 1855. The story was one of eight he sold to the *London Review*. (After the hostile reception of the first two, 'A Ride across Palestine' and 'Mrs General Talboys', the magazine would only publish one more, 'The Parson's Daughter'.) This story is one of the five remaining that were sold to *Public Opinion*; it was published on 16 and 23 November 1861. It was then included in the second collection of his short stories, *Tales of All Countries*, Second Series, in 1863. Trollope received £50.

Heine Brothers was a small but reputable bank in the Schrannenplatz in Munich. A young Englishman, Herbert Onslow, is a clerk at the bank: he was sent to Munich after he had left Cambridge burdened with debts and without a degree. (Trollope's brother Henry also left Cambridge without taking a degree in the 1830s. In the 1820s he had been sent to Paris to work in a bank.) Herbert falls in love with Isa Heine, a daughter of one of the two partners with whom he boards. He proposes and her family agrees they can marry immediately if his father puts up enough money for him to become a partner in the bank at once and if the other Heine brother agrees to alter the original terms of his employment. Both men say they must stick to the original understanding and this means that the young couple must wait four years. While Isa can bear this, Herbert is distraught and moves out of the house. Isa approaches her uncle, the senior partner, to ask him to relent but he advises her to give up the unofficial engagement. At last, however, both men agree and the couple marry.

Trollope includes a digression on the differences between English and German girls, much as he contrasted English girls with American girls in 'Miss Ophelia Gledd' and *The Duke's Children*, with Austrian girls in 'Lotta Schmidt' and with Spanish girls in 'John Bull on the Guadalquivir' [➤ Banks; Germany; Women].

How the 'Mastiffs' Went to Iceland. Trollope wrote this account of a private visit to Iceland between 22 June and 8 July 1878 for his host John Burns, later Baron Inverclyde, a wealthy industrialist, who had asked him to write it. Trollope arranged for it to be privately printed that year by James Virtue and Burns paid the costs. Copies were given to all members of the party. The sixteen illustrations were provided by Mrs Hugh Blackburn, another passenger, who wrote her own article, 'To Iceland', for *Good Words*. Trollope received twenty-five copies. This was Trollope's last travel book.

The 'Mastiffs' took their name from the name of John Burns's private yacht, which carried them from his home, Castle Wemyss at Wemyss Bay in Scotland, to Iceland. Burns, of the Cunard Steamship Co., had been a friend of Trollope since the 1860s when they were both, along with Norman Macleod, members of the Gaiter Club. Club members undertook walking tours in Scotland, wore gaiters and had an annual dinner. Burns had invited Trollope, with fifteen others, to join him and his wife on the three-week cruise to Iceland. Iceland's fame among Victorians may be said to date from 1856 when Lord Dufferin's highly popular *Letters from High Latitudes* was published. This encouraged that interest in Norse sagas which marked late-Victorian literature and influenced writers like C. S. Lewis and J. R. R. Tolkien in the present century.

Trollope's account is a slight *jeu d'esprit* which recalls amusing incidents during a tour which he thoroughly enjoyed. There was mild adventure and considerable luxury. *En route* to Iceland the yacht visited St Kilda and the Faroe Islands. In Iceland they invited the Governor, the local bishop and other dignitaries to a banquet aboard the yacht and Trollope enjoyed a flirtation with the bishop's daughter, Thora Pjetursson, to whom he referred as 'our particular friend'. Sixty-five ponies were hired to take the party and servants about the island and Trollope, as always, had trouble with mounts. He was, at sixty-five, not only the oldest member of the party but the heaviest, weighing sixteen stone. Servants were sent ahead to their destination so that when the party arrived, tea was ready. Their goal was the island's main attraction, the geysers which Lord Dufferin had made famous. On their way back, the party slept in a church and during the night one lady got up and rang the church bell as a prank. Once awake, Trollope proceeded to make a speech about 'ladies who were very tired, – ladies who would certainly wish to sleep'.

Trollope returned to London with a copy of *Macbeth* in Icelandic and sent a copy of his *Commentaries of Caesar* to a young Icelander he had met.

Trollope also wrote a more serious article on Iceland for the *Fortnightly Review* in which it was published on 1 August 1878. He then had it privately printed as a 28-page pamphlet. This was probably intended for friends but he did send a copy to Mr Gladstone, who was interested in the relations between Iceland and Denmark. (Iceland was still a dependency of Denmark.) Gladstone had wondered if Iceland could serve as a model for Ireland under Home Rule.

Hunting Sketches. These eight essays by Trollope were on different types of riders to hounds. Publication began in the third issue of the new daily newspaper, the *Pall Mall Gazette*, on 9

February 1865; the last essay appeared on 20 March 1865. They were published in one volume by Chapman & Hall on 10 May 1865.

The eight essays, with dates of publication, were: 'The Man who Hunts and Doesn't Like It' (9 February); 'The Man who Hunts and Does Like It' (10 February); 'The Lady who Rides to Hounds' (17 February); 'The Hunting Farmer' (23 February); 'The Man who Hunts and Never Jumps' (7 March); 'The Hunting Parson' (11 March); 'The Master of Hounds' (15 March); 'How to Ride to Hounds' (20 March). For his first year's contributions to the paper Trollope received £234. 17s. 6d., but this amount also included payment for at least one article, the *Travelling Sketches*, and six out of the ten 'clerical sketches' published in 1865 as *Clergymen of the Church of England*. [➤ *British Sports and Pastimes*; Fox-hunting; *Marion Fay* [2], in which Trollope compared riding to hounds with other sports.]

Hurst & Blackett (1853–1926). In 1852 Daniel Hurst and Henry Blackett took over Henry Colburn's publishing firm and carried on his tradition of publishing 'three-deckers' for the circulating libraries [➤ Mudie's Circulating Library]. Their connection with Trollope began in 1857 when he brought the manuscript of *The Three Clerks* to them. He recalled the occasion in his *Autobiography*: after waiting for an hour he was approached by an employee who asked him to leave the manuscript with him. Trollope refused unless the man agreed to buy it on the spot, which he could not do. He had no further connection with the firm until 1870 when Alexander Strahan sold the right to publish a three-volume edition of *Ralph the Heir* to them. That same year Macmillan, who were serializing *Sir Harry Hotspur of Humblethwaite* in their magazine, sold the right to publish that novel in book form to Hurst & Blackett. Both Macmillan and Hurst & Blackett wanted to bring it out in two volumes, but Trollope refused because he felt this would be cheating the public: it had been written as a one-volume novel.

I

Iceland. See *How the 'Mastiffs' Went to Iceland.*

Idleness. In Trollope's fiction idleness is one of the worst vices and the idle usually get into trouble. While there are idle women, like Lady Ongar in *The Claverings*, the vice is usually confined to men. These tend to be contemptible or at least laughable figures like Bernard Amedroz, 'an idle, thriftless man, who, at the age of sixty-seven ... had as yet done no good in the world whatever' [*The Belton Estate*, 1]. Other notably idle men are the Reverend Henry Clavering, a wealthy clergyman 'sunk into idleness' in *The Claverings*, and the selfish idler, Maurice Maule, in *Phineas Redux*. Idleness can lead even a virtuous man like Louis Trevelyan in *He Knew He Was Right* into disaster. Some idle men like the Marquis of Brotherton in *Is He Popenjoy?* easily slide into degeneracy. Young men who are idle, such as those in *The Way We Live Now*, can easily turn to gambling, dishonesty and drunkenness. The surest sign that a young man is improving is when he gives up idleness and takes up a serious purpose, as Everett Wharton does in *The Prime Minister* and Lord Silverbridge in *The Duke's Children*.

Trollope's father had constantly denounced 'idling' in his sons and Anthony followed the parental teaching. As he wrote in a letter in December 1880, 'Nothing really frightens me but the idea of enforced idleness.' However, Tom Trollope thought after Anthony's death that his younger brother might have lived longer if he had possessed 'a very pretty turn for idleness'.

[➤ French Novels; Harding, The Rev. Septimus.]

Illegitimacy. Although illegitimacy was a difficult topic for a Victorian novelist, Trollope used it as an essential element in several novels and one short story. In *Doctor Thorne* it complicates the love story of Mary Thorne and Frank Gresham; in *Ralph the Heir* Gregory Newton's efforts to ensure his landed estate goes to his illegitimate son make up the main plot. In *Mr Scarborough's Family* the plot turns on attempts by a father to make one of his sons appear to be illegitimate to avoid crippling debts on the estate. In all these cases illegitimacy is closely connected to rights to inherit property as well as to social position. In *The Way We Live Now* Augustus Melmotte's daughter, Marie, is illegitimate.

It is rare for Trollope to portray illegitimacy in the working classes yet he gives a careful though brief reference to one such case in the Gubby family in *The Claverings* [12].

Fears of illegitimate births through the seduction of unmarried daughters cause murder in *The Macdermots of Ballycloran*, and in *An Eye for an Eye* Kate O'Hara's illegitimate baby dies at birth. Legitimacy is of particular importance when an aristocratic title is in question and doubts about the legitimacy of an heir's birth are vital in *Is He Popenjoy?* and *Lady Anna*.

Trollope also referred to it in 'Mrs General Talboys' when describing 'rum' expatriates living in Italy. He had great difficulty in getting this story published because one of the characters has illegitimate children.

The Illustrated London News (1842–). This, the most successful Victorian weekly illustrated magazine, began life as Radical in politics; at sixpence an issue it was aimed at the middle classes. It was a pioneer in 'pictorial journalism'. The magazine, which inspired many imitators, concentrated on current affairs and had little serialized fiction until the 1880s, but it did have an annual Christmas supplement and in 1861 it published Trollope's short story 'The Mistletoe Bough', later included in *Tales of All Countries*, Second Series.

Illustrations. Fifteen out of Trollope's forty-seven novels were illustrated. In addition, he had frontispieces drawn for *The Chronicles of Barsetshire*. Several short stories had illustrations in their original periodical publication, but these often disappeared or were cut in number in subsequent book publication. *How the 'Mastiffs' Went to Iceland* had some delightful drawings, several depicting Trollope himself. Trollope's other travel books had folding maps. The first Trollope novel to be il-

lustrated was *Framley Parsonage*, which was also the first to be serialized in a magazine. Illustrations were more common in novels that were either serialized or issued in parts.

Millais, who drew the illustrations for *Framley Parsonage* and several others of Trollope's most successful novels of the 1860s, was Trollope's favourite illustrator. He regarded the Millais drawings for *Orley Farm* as the finest in any Victorian novel. (These also contained a joke in the drawing of 'Sir Peregrine at Mr Round's Office'. In this, the lawyer's metal boxes, which contain clients' papers, lie on top of the bookcase and include one on which is printed 'A. Trollope'.)

Trollope particularly disliked the illustration by 'Phiz' (H. K. Browne) for *Can You Forgive Her?* 'Phiz' was renowned for his illustrations for Dickens, but his style was completely antithetical to Trollope's work. Among Trollope's other illustrators were Mary Ellen Edwards, George Thomas and Marcus Stone.

Trollope took a great interest in the illustrations and made detailed comments about them. His mother believed that her great success had been partly due to the illustrations in both her novels and her travel books by Auguste Hervieu, who had attempted to give the young Anthony some skill in drawing. Frederic Harrison – a friend of Trollope from the *Fortnightly Review* – argued in an introduction to the Barsetshire novels reissued about two decades after Trollope's death that it was a 'fatal mistake to have illustrations to Trollope', particularly those with 'the horrible crinolines'. Yet in recent years there has been a welcome trend towards reissuing the novels with their original illustrations. That, and N. John Hall's *Trollope and His Illustrators* (1980), should make more readers aware of the importance of these illustrations.

'Illustrious Personage'. This was a phrase often used by the Victorians to indicate a member of the Royal Family without naming them. 'Illustrious Personage' up to 1861 normally meant Prince Albert. Trollope uses the phrase several times, for instance in *Framley Parsonage* [23]. The 'Distinguished person' standing on the rug at Windsor Castle who hears a whispered recommendation of Mr Arabin to be appointed the new Dean of Barchester is also intended to be Prince Albert. After the Prince's death, the phrase normally refers to the Prince of Wales, later King Edward VII. Sometimes, as in *Sir Harry Hotspur of Humblethwaite*, Trollope uses 'a distinguished party in Norfolk' [10] to mean the Prince of Wales at Sandringham. The phrase 'Most illustrious personage' refers to Queen Victoria.

Imperialism. See English World.

Income. See Money.

India. India played only a minor role in Trollope's fiction in contrast with that of Thackeray. In the 1860s Trollope was anxious to take up George Smith's idea that he should write a travel book about India, although he admitted that '*per se* going to India is a bore – but it would suit me professionally'. (By 'professionally' he meant in his career as a serious travel writer.) In the event nothing came of the idea. There are a few references to India in his writings: Major Henry Grantly won his military glory there, while Captain Walter Marrable in *The Vicar of Bullhampton* fears

he may have to return to what he calls a 'hell on earth' [29]. In *Phineas Finn* Trollope commented that while India was the most important responsibility of the British Government, no topic bored Parliament more. This certainly was the case when the young MP Frank Greystock tires both sides of the House of Commons with an oration about the Sawab of Mygawb [*The Eustace Diamonds*, 7]. Trollope described Englishmen on their way to India in the 1870s in the travel letters written during his second trip to Australia in 1875 [*The Tireless Traveler*]. He had given a rather unflattering portrait of Anglo-Indians returning home in *The Bertrams*. One of the characters in 'George Walker at Suez' is Indian. His sister-in-law, Theodosia Trollope, was part Indian. [➤ English World.]

Inheritance. The fact that inheritance often provides plots for Trollope's novels is hardly surprising as so many of them deal with landed estates and money. Almost all aspects of inheritance provide subjects for Trollope. Attempts are made to cheat people out of an inheritance in several novels, including *The Kellys and the O'Kellys*, *Orley Farm* and *Cousin Henry*. Many younger people have expectations of an inheritance, as in *The Bertrams*. Women in particular can have problems once they have received their inheritance, for example in *The Eustace Diamonds* and *Miss Mackenzie*. Titles can cause added problems to inheritance especially when the title is to go to a distant relative, as in *An Eye for an Eye* or *Sir Harry Hotspur of Humblethwaite*. Many male characters – like Trollope himself – enjoy reflecting on the inheritance they are building up for a son. Archdeacon Grantly in *The Last*

Chronicle of Barset is the best example of this. This is the 'delight that enables a man to feel, up to the last moment, that the goods of the world are good' [*Ralph the Heir*, II]. However, in that novel the inheritance is complicated by illegitimacy. In *Mr Scarborough's Family* an old man's manoeuvrings over inheritance provide the plot. Sometimes an unexpected inheritance can assist a character like John Eames in *The Small House at Allington*, Phineas Finn in *Phineas Finn*, Jack de Baron in *Is He Popenjoy?*, or Walter Marrable in *The Vicar of Bullhampton*. In *The Struggles of Brown, Jones, and Robinson* inheritance and the lack of a will cause problems for London tradesmen. Lawyers, of course, are usually involved in any discussions about inheritance.

[➤ Entails; Marriage; Settlements; Wills.]

Insanity. The subject of insanity and its consequences occurs in Trollope's first novel, *The Macdermots of Ballycloran*, and in many of its successors. He had a strong interest in the inner workings of the human psyche quite rare in a pre-Freudian novelist and had long observed 'the perversity of the human mind' [*He Knew He Was Right*, 38]. In his second novel, *The Kellys and the O'Kellys*, Barry Lynch tries to force his sister into a mental asylum. In *Phineas Redux* Robert Kennedy becomes mad through jealousy and in *He Knew He Was Right* Louis Trevelyan becomes so obsessively jealous of his wife's imagined infidelity that he too loses his reason. In *The Last Chronicle of Barset* the Reverend Josiah Crawley comes close to madness. *An Eye for an Eye*, which opens with a flashback set in a mental asylum, concerns a woman who has

been judged insane. Trollope particularly excels in describing those who can behave quite normally in many ways, but who at times become completely unbalanced. *Cousin Henry* is a good example of this. In short stories like 'The Spotted Dog' and 'The Turkish Bath' he shows how poverty or drunkenness can lead educated men to madness.

In boyhood, Trollope had ample opportunity to observe his father's slow and painful decline into mental instability and he would draw upon this for aspects of the Reverend Josiah Crawley's character. In his travels he sometimes visited mental asylums and he gives an account of one such visit in New York in his *North America*.

International Copyright.
See Copyright.

Ireland. Ireland played a larger role in Trollope's writing than it did in that of any other major Victorian novelist. He was sent to Ireland in 1841 by the Post Office and though he was often called away for other postal duties the country was his home until 1859. It was there that the 'hobbledehoy' became a man, where he first was recognized as a highly respected civil servant, where he married and settled down to family life, where he wrote his first novel and where he discovered his passion for fox-hunting. All the principal strands of his life were formed in Ireland.

Five of Trollope's novels are set mainly in Ireland: *The Macdermots of Ballycloran*, *The Kellys and the O'Kellys*, *Castle Richmond*, *An Eye for an Eye* and *The Land-Leaguers*. Two of his best short stories, 'Father Giles of Ballymoy' and 'The O'Conors of Castle Conor', are based on his own early days in the country. He often included Irishmen in his English novels, most notably Phineas Finn in the two Palliser novels that bear his name. In Phineas Finn, Trollope does not draw the 'stage Irishman' so often caricatured in *Punch* or in most English writing of that era. Trollope greatly resented the fact that English readers were not particularly interested in Irish fiction, as he made plain in the opening pages of *Castle Richmond*. Throughout his writing career – which began and ended with Irish novels – he made consistent but unsuccessful attempts to write an Irish novel that would equal the appeal of his Barsetshire and other English novels.

To understand Trollope's Irish fiction it is essential to have some knowledge of the political situation in Ireland. Throughout his lifetime, Ireland was part of the United Kingdom and sent its own MPs to the House of Commons in London, where they comprised about one-sixth of the total membership. Irishmen could also stand in other parts of the United Kingdom, as Phineas Finn did. Ireland was also represented in the House of Lords [➤ Peerage]. The Crown was represented by a Lord Lieutenant (Viceroy) in Dublin Castle who was assisted by a Chief Secretary, an MP responsible for the administration of government policy. (Phineas Finn attains this office in *Phineas Redux*.) After 1829, Catholics could vote, be elected to the Commons and hold almost every office. When Trollope went to Ireland, a large 'Repeal' movement, under the leadership of the 'Liberator', Daniel O'Connell, MP (1775–1847), wanted to repeal the Act of Union which in 1801 had united the British and Irish Parliaments. O'Con-

nell – and most other Irishmen in Trollope's lifetime – wanted to preserve the link with the British Crown. This political agitation is reflected in *The Kellys and the O'Kellys*, which opens with the trial of O'Connell and other 'repealers'.

Trollope is more interested in describing the state of Irish society than in giving extensive reports of political debates. He well conveys, for example, the parlous economic condition of agriculture in *The Macdermots of Ballycloran*. Shortly after he finished that novel, the potato famine swept across the island and was particularly horrific in County Cork where Trollope was then living. The famine appeared in the autumn of 1845 and in the next few years the population fell, through death and emigration, from over eight million to about six-and-a-half million. In *Castle Richmond*, Trollope graphically describes the suffering he saw. He always maintained that the great problem before the famine was that there were too many small squires – 'squireens' – pretending to live the life of English gentry. Trollope believed that improved education and a growing respect for work would do more to improve the state of Ireland than any constitutional change. In *Castle Richmond*, in a series of articles he wrote for the *Examiner*, and in *The New Zealander*, he argued that the Famine had ultimately done economic good [Mullen, 207–11]. Trollope also wrote about Ireland in political articles for *Saint Pauls*. His *Palmerston* alludes to Irish topics and contains some recollections of the Famine on Palmerston's Irish estates. When Trollope stood for Parliament in Beverley he advocated the disestablishment of the Church of Ireland.

Few other Englishmen have ever had such a detailed knowledge of Irish life. He once claimed that his postal work had taken him into every parish in the island. Aspects of this emerge in the testimony he gave to various parliamentary committees. He started to write a guidebook to Ireland, but it was never published. He even delved into Irish historical records when he compiled a history of the Irish Post Office. His postal career began in the Irish midlands; then he spent several years in County Cork and he finished with a happy period in Dublin. Surprisingly, Dublin receives little attention in his fiction; for the most part, his Irish novels take place in the countryside and small towns. The counties of Clare, Cork and Galway receive the most consistent attention in his writing.

Trollope's basic attitude towards Ireland was a combination of Liberalism and paternalism. He disliked religious hostility and although he was a member of the Church of Ireland he was always friendly with Catholics, as can be seen in 'Father Giles of Ballymoy' and in his treatment of Father Marty in *An Eye for an Eye*. He felt that Home Rule, a later version of the 'Repeal' movement, would be bad for Ireland. His views on this were well presented through the character of Phineas Finn. In his last year Trollope became deeply pessimistic about Ireland as a result of increasing agitation and terrorism financed from America. He made two trips to Ireland to gather material for his final novel, *The Land-Leaguers*, which reflected his dismay.

Trollope described his Irish experiences with great affection in his *Autobiography*. He often referred to them in his travel books, particularly when meeting Irishmen in America, Australia or elsewhere in the world. His exuberant personality perhaps felt more at ease among Irishmen than among Englishmen: in *North America* he said that he had 'so close an intimacy with Ireland' that he always found more kinship with an Irishman abroad than with an Englishman. He greatly enjoyed Irish music, while 'the dear brogue . . . is always delightful to me' [➤ 'The Turkish Bath']. Trollope frequently used Irish expressions – for instance a persuasive man being able 'to talk the devil out of the liver wing of a turkey' [*The Bertrams*, 21]. At other times he used anecdotes from his Irish days; none of these is more startling than the sudden comparison of a barrister to 'an assassin' he had once known in Tipperary [*Orley Farm*, 75].

Trollope took great care with his Irish dialogue and in *Thackeray* he criticized his friend's Irish dialogue as 'not true to nature'. Trollope generally gives more local colour in his Irish fiction than in other works, for he well knew that the majority of English readers had little knowledge of Ireland [➤ *Is He Popenjoy?*, 3].

Trollope's Irish writings were greatly admired by Irish reviewers and readers in his time and one Irish journal even suggested that he should be sent to the Commons to represent an Irish seat. Escott, his first biographer, felt that Trollope with his vast knowledge of Ireland would have been a great asset to British politics. As the *Dublin Review* said in 1872: 'This Englishman, keenly observant, painstaking, absolutely sincere and unprejudiced . . . writes a story as true to the saddest and heaviest truths of Irish life . . . Mr Trollope had thoroughly mastered' its humour, '... more completely than any other writer'. [➤ Servants.]

Isbister, William (1838?–1916). Trollope knew Isbister as an owner of *Good Words*. When he saw Trollope's manuscript of 'The Telegraph Girl', Isbister asked for an article on the Post Office's new venture in employing women in its telegraph division. Isbister had been a partner of Alexander Strahan since 1859 and when Strahan retired in 1872 the company became known as W. Isbister & Co. Isbister became its sole owner in 1878. His firm published two books by Trollope: *Why Frau Frohmann Raised Her Prices* and *Lord Palmerston*. He serialized *Kept in the Dark* in *Good Words* in 1882. [For the stories and articles published in *Good Words*, ➤ that entry.] In his final years Trollope arranged for Isbister to help his son Henry with a travel book on France. Trollope found his firm respectable and described Isbister as 'a fairly honest fellow but dilatory and vague'.

Is He Popenjoy?. Trollope started writing his thirty-fifth novel on 12 October 1874, a month after finishing *The Prime Minister*. He finished it on 3 May 1875, the day before his ship arrived in Melbourne at the start of his second visit to Australia. He sold the book rights two years later to Chapman & Hall and the serialization rights to Charles Dickens, Jnr, editor of *All the Year Round*. The novel appeared between 13 October 1877 and 13 July 1878 in an expurgated text which removed some of Trollope's alleged vulgarities [➤ below]. Chapman & Hall brought out their three-volume, unexpurgated, edition in April 1878. Trollope received £1,600.

Critics in 1877–8 and later have universally denounced Trollope's choice of title: this was the second and, significantly, the last novel with a title in the form of a question. Some critics, at the time and afterwards, have also found the book 'sordid' and unworthy of its author. The title relates to what is meant to be the main plot. The Marquis of Brotherton is a reprobate who lives in Italy where he produces a son under mysterious circumstances. As heir, the baby bears the courtesy title of Lord Popenjoy. (This silly title is similar to Thackeray's Lady Popinjay or the Honourable Percy Popjoy [➤ Names, Silly].) The birth is investigated by the marquis's brother, Lord George Germain, and by his father-in-law, the Dean of Brotherton. There is no conclusive proof either way regarding the baby's legitimacy. The marquis returns to England, spreads trouble wherever he goes, is knocked down by the dean when he refers to the dean's daughter in derogatory terms because of rumours of an affair, sickens, returns to Italy and dies not long after his infant son. Lord George now becomes Marquis of Brotherton and his own son now becomes the undisputed heir. This plot owes much to the long legal proceedings involved in the Tichborne case. With this story line in mind the novel is similar to others of the 1870s and early 1880s which involve mystery, disputed titles or legacies, and degrees of violence. These include *An Eye for an Eye, Cousin Henry, Dr Wortle's School, Kept in the Dark* and *The Land-Leaguers*.

In some ways the Popenjoy plot is secondary to the conflict between Lord George and his new wife, Mary. Behind this is the manly, robust figure of the Dean of Brotherton, Henry Lovelace, one of Trollope's best-drawn clergymen and one of his most autobiographical characters: he is a keen sportsman, argumentative, ambitious, impulsive, manly, 'worldly' (like Archdeacon Grantly), gifted with no-nonsense common sense and possessed of a fierce temper as well as some unspecified 'advanced' theological views. He is contrasted with the rather played-out Germain family. The debauched marquis is only the epitome of this: his four sisters are all more or less dour, High Church spinsters devoted to good works; the dowager is senile; his brother, Lord George, is a boring, self-righteous and snobbish prig with little to commend him but his good looks and title – 'Birth and culture had given to him a look of intellect greater than he possessed' [1].

The dean is a self-made man whose father worked in a stable. He is far removed from Trollope's other famous dean, Francis Arabin, and his character shows Trollope's understanding of changes that had taken place in the Church of England. It is the dean who presses and pays for the inquiry into the Italian birth. Part of the conflict between the dean and the Germains is that he is wealthy while they are not: his wealth gives him a confidence their breeding cannot match. Their difficulties lie partly in the fact that he is rather liberal, while they are conservatively High Church: 'Even your papa goes [to Church] on Saints' days' [3], retorts the eldest Germain spinster to the dean's daughter.

The conflict of 'new' versus 'old' blood is also seen in relations between the dean's daughter Mary and her husband, Lord George. The novel is, like *He Knew He Was Right, Kept in the Dark, Can You Forgive Her?* and, to a considerable degree, the Palliser series, a study of marriage. Both Lord George and his wife are immature, and she struggles to maintain her own high-spirited personality against both his domineering possessiveness and his oppressive family. This conflict is centred on the couple's house in London where they go for the Season: the house is provided by the dean as Mary loves London Society, while George prefers the quiet of country-house life. It is in London that both succumb to affairs: Mary's is innocent while George's is much less so.

The novel has several sub-plots which provide padding. Among these the most memorable is Trollope's extended and bitter attack on feminists in the person of the two 'lecturers', the German, Baroness Banmann, and the American, Olivia Q. Fleabody, Ph.D. For the latter character's name Trollope may have had in mind that of the American feminist, Elizabeth Peabody, but the two fictional ladies are caricatures of the strong-minded feminists he so disliked. The chapter on the two rivals' speeches at the Rights of Women Institute [17] reminds one in its humour of the chapter devoted to the Negro Soldiers' Orphan Bazaar in *Miss Mackenzie* [27]. His inspiration for the Institute, split into rival camps and torn by jealousies, may be traced to the 1861-2 visit to America, during which he went to Cincinnati to see his mother's famous Bazaar: one of the uses to which it was put after she left was to house a 'college of rights-of-women female medical professors' [*North America*]. Baroness Banmann's sponging off others is also reminiscent of another feminist, Sabrina Dawkins, in 'An Unprotected Female at the Pyramids'.

Trollope introduced many private references into the novel. He sited the Women's College on the Marylebone Road, where he had lived as a young man. He referred to the 'self-sacrificing patriotism of the Post Office' [20] and to the intelligence of letter-carriers [41]. The 'hotel in Suffolk Street' in which Dean Lovelace stayed was Garlant's, where Trollope himself often stayed. When he referred to Mudie [45] he knew that his fame had come through this circulating library. The dean smokes in the Deanery garden, as Trollope did in his own; it was the only place where his wife allowed him to smoke. Captain De Baron, whose dalliance with Lady George Germain was part of her London life, finally got married and grew 'fat, and has taken to playing whist at his club for shilling points' [64]. This is exactly what his creator did.

The passages devoted to cathedral doings are reminiscent of those in Barchester, but these sections are not very developed. The bishop's chaplain, Mr Joseph Groschut, reminds one of Mr Slope in his Evangelical nastiness. Like Mr Slope, he eventually is forced to leave the bishop's employ because of difficulties with a young woman, in this case a farmer's daughter. Like Mr Emilius, he is a Jewish convert. Having warmed to the subject of Evangelicals, Trollope returned to it in the novel's last sentence with an attack on their obsession with Sabbatarianism.

The 'vulgarity' referred to above caused difficulties with Charles Dickens, Jnr, when he serialized the book. Dickens made at least thirty substantive changes to the manuscript. [For a full discussion, see T. C. D., 'Victorian

Editors and Victorian Delicacy', *Notes and Queries*, 2 December 1944.] Some changes related simply to words: he removed 'hitherto unslobbered honesty' [19] in a passage about Lord George Germain, for example. Mainly he removed those words, phrases and sentences that offended current rules regarding sex (kissing, female dimples, adultery and prostitutes), sentences that touched too closely on pregnancy and breast-feeding, and sentences that might annoy religious people. (He removed the sentence, 'Is there not that sin against the Holy Ghost to justify us?' which Trollope put forward as part of man's rationalization for not forgiving someone who had offended him. This occurs in the penultimate chapter [63].)

To include the controversy over breast-feeding [63] was only to keep up with the times. The feminists' attack on the Victorian dislike of women nursing their own babies had been first touched on in *He Knew He Was Right* [81]. While the children in the novel are only babies their existence is vital to the plot, an unusual feature in Trollope's fiction. Likewise little Popenjoy's death, like that of his father later, is one of Trollope's convenient deaths, used to advance the plot. In Mrs Montacute Jones (who would return in *The Duke's Children*) and Lady Sarah Germain, Trollope gives us two of his formidable women, one elderly, the other middle-aged. As in *Lady Anna* and *Marion Fay*, Trollope makes use of his travels in Italy. As in *Lady Anna*, the debauched English peer retires to that country and contracts a disputed marriage.

There are a few classical references: one to Cerberus, the many-headed guard-dog at the entrance to Hades, one to Apollo and one to Argus, the Greek monster with a hundred eyes. There is a standard fox-hunting scene [8], in which there is also a discussion of the question of whether or not clergymen should ride to hounds [➤ also Chapter 10]. There are the usual references to duels [12, 15]. Trollope also uses two of his favourite phrases: 'a good time coming' [64] and 'His lines have certainly fallen ... in pleasant places' [64]. When the Marquis of Brotherton sneers that he will 'do as I please with my own' [22], he is using a notorious phrase Victorians would have immediately recognized: it had originated with the fourth Duke of Newcastle and originally meant he would order his tenants to vote as he instructed or turn them out of their homes. Trollope's reference to the Albert Memorial was still somewhat topical: the Memorial had only been opened to the public on 3 July 1872. The reference to 'a place called Perim' [59] is to the island at the mouth of the Red Sea and is based on his own experience: on his outward journey to Australia, while writing the book, his ship passed the island. He discusses 'the miserable little island' in the second 'letter' written for newspapers back home [➤ *The Tireless Traveler*].

Trollope as usual has much sport with names and in most cases the name relates to the character's chief attribute. There is Baroness Banmann; Mr Grease, the pious editor of *The Brotherton Church*; Mr Battle, the lawyer; Dr Pullbody, the eminent physician; Lord Grassangrains, the breeder of bullocks; Lady Selina Protest, the feminist; and Lord Mountfencer, the riding peer. There is the usual fun with aristocratic titles: Lord Parachute; Lady Florence Fitzflor-ence; Lord Giblet and the De Geese family. There is also Mr Stuffenruff and Messrs Snape and Cashett, more lawyers, Miss Tallowax, and Mr Philogunac Coelebs who marries and is defrauded by Baroness Banmann. He probably derived Coelebs's names from two sources: Philogunac comes from the Greek *philo* (lover of) and *gyne* (woman); Coelebs comes from a novel, *Coelebs in Search of a Wife* (1809) by Hannah More, which he remembered from his youth. Mrs Montacute Jones, who was 'one of the Montacutes of Montacute' adds her maiden name to that of her Welsh husband: Montacute was Trollope's favourite West Country building [➤ Architecture].

When writing his *Autobiography* the manuscript of the novel still lay in his desk and his only comment was that 'the story, as a story, is not I think amiss'. In a footnote he added that since writing this the book had appeared and had met 'with fair success'. Neither it nor *The American Senator* 'encountered that reproach which, in regard to *The Prime Minister*, seemed to tell me that my work as a novelist should be brought to a close. And yet I feel assured that they are very inferior to *The Prime Minister*.' As a novel it contains many of Trollope's recurrent themes or 'sermons': the nature of love and marriage; life in country houses; the rise and decline of families and, especially, the propriety of ambition. This is seen in his defence of the dean's desires for his daughter, desires that in one part of the narration are referred to as 'pagan' [61], the value and role of a landed aristocracy [63] and a declaration of his Liberal politics. 'It is a grand thing to rise in the world. The ambition to do so is the very salt of the earth. It is the parent of all enterprise, and the cause of all improvement. They who know no such ambition are savages and remain savage' [61]. The passage reminds one of his discussion of the Zulus in *South Africa*. His one major criticism of the dean is that he was ashamed of his humble origins: 'the only whitewash against such dirt was to be found in the aggrandisement of his daughter and the nobility of her children' [63].

The novel's first paragraph is a defence of his style of writing with its profusion of background and detail, its necessary length and its use of chronological narration. There is also an attack on novels which begin *in medias res*, although he too would soon violate this rule when writing *Cousin Henry*.

Islington. See *Rachel Ray*.

Italy. Italy played a large role in Trollope's family life and it is frequently mentioned in his writings. Between 1853 and 1881 he visited the country on ten occasions. In his youth he had met Italian radicals through his mother's friendship with General Guglielmo Pepe, the Neapolitan revolutionary. (Trollope borrowed his name for the short story 'The Last Austrian Who Left Venice'.) Trollope's mother and his brother, Tom, settled in Florence in the 1840s and she died there in 1863. The Villino Trollope – which still survives – became the centre of English literary society. Tom, who moved to Rome in the 1870s, wrote widely on Italian history, politics and art for a variety of English and American periodicals. He also wrote a few novels, mainly based on Italian subjects.

Tom Trollope was a firm supporter of the Italian unification movement and was well acquainted with many important Italian politicians. His first wife was fanatically devoted to the Italian cause and was also rabidly anti-clerical. Anthony Trollope, while having a conventional Victorian Liberal's belief in Italian unity, tended to be more moderate. As he once put it, Garibaldi, the hero of radical nationalists, was 'to my thinking, a little too much of a rebel' [Mullen 360, 702]. His most extended comment on Italian politics is in his first letter to the *Liverpool Mercury* in 1875 in which he describes the dangers facing the newly-united Italy [➤ *The Tireless Traveler*].

Three of Trollope's short stories are set in Italy and each deals with an aspect of Italy well known to Victorians. 'The Last Austrian Who Left Venice' is a love story set against the war for Italian unification. 'The Man Who Kept His Money in a Box' is a humorous story featuring Lake Como and demonstrates some of the difficulties of travelling. 'Mrs General Talboys' makes use of his insights into the Anglo-American expatriate community and is a tale of such semi-scandalous characters in Rome. In several novels Trollope made use of his Italian visits. *He Knew He Was Right* contains more Italian scenes than any other novel. It has several chapters set in Florence, the capital of the newly-united Italy in the 1860s, and in the Tuscan countryside which Trollope knew well from travels with his brother. The plots of *Kept in the Dark* and *Ayala's Angel* both make use of meetings among English visitors to Rome, as does the duchess's scheme regarding her daughter's marriage in *The Duke's Children*.

Italy often provides a place where English aristocrats can behave in a secretive and somewhat scandalous way. A marquis in *Is He Popenjoy?* and an earl in *Lady Anna* contract strange marriages with Italians which threaten the orderly succession to English peerages. In *Marion Fay* a young Post Office clerk succeeds to an Italian dukedom as the result of another Anglo-Italian marriage. Trollope evidently took a somewhat critical view of many of the English expatriates in Italy, where Englishmen could live on a fraction of what a similar way of life would have cost at home. Trollope's most memorable portrait of such expatriates is that of the Stanhope family, whose temporary return to Barsetshire causes such havoc in *Barchester Towers*.

There are frequent allusions to Italian travels in his novels: the lakes, especially Lake Como and its surrounding area, seem especial favourites. Not only do the Stanhopes reside there, but Madame Max Goesler spent some of her youth there. The old Duke of Omnium has a villa there and the Hotspurs travel there after some time in Rome in *Sir Harry Hotspur of Humblethwaite* [24]. Plantagenet and Lady Glencora Palliser spend their honeymoon 'amidst the softness of some Italian lake' [*Can You Forgive Her?*, 18]. In *The Last Chronicle of Barset* John Eames makes a hurried visit to Italy in search of Dean Arabin's wife. Trollope recalls several of his own adventures while travelling in Italy in his *Autobiography* and in his *Travelling Sketches*. In *The Bertrams* [9] he is particularly scathing about the way in which many English tourists behave in Italian churches.

For Trollope, Italy was the stage on which Roman history had been enacted, the source of the classical literature which so fascinated him and the home of so many of the great works of art in which he took an informed interest. Italy for Trollope, as for most educated Victorians, was a land with a special place in his affections.

J

James, Henry (1843–1916). James first met Trollope on a transatlantic ship in 1875 and was amazed at his devotion to his daily task of writing. The young novelist complained that Trollope had 'a gross and repulsive face and manner . . . He is the dullest Briton of them all'. Later, after Trollope had befriended him at the Cosmopolitan Club and at a dinner party, he grew to like him. Before their meeting, James had reviewed Trollope's books and had been a severe critic [➤ *The Belton Estate*; *Can You Forgive Her?*]. Trollope was guilty of making his novels too long and, much worse, of making 'authorial intrusions'. But James also praised him, for his depiction of English girls and for his characterization in general. He especially praised *He Knew He Was Right* for its 'conspicuous intensity of the tragical'. [➤ Serialization; 'Three-deckers'.] James's warm tribute to Trollope's 'genius' in the *Century Magazine* (June 1883) remains one of the best assessments of Trollope, in spite of Henry Trollope's disparagement of it as 'lumbering'. Henry James the novelist should not be confused with a close friend of Trollope, Henry James, later Lord James of Hereford (1828–1911), the lawyer and Liberal politician.

[For James's and Trollope's shared interest in transatlantic marriages, ➤ Anglo-American Marriages.]

Jealousy. Jealousy is a frequent source of misery in Trollope's fictional marriages. The worst cases are in *He Knew He Was Right*, in which a husband becomes insane out of jealousy at his wife's innocent friendship with an old family friend, and in *Phineas Redux*, in which another husband is driven mad by jealousy and attempts murder. In *Kept in the Dark* a husband and wife are almost destroyed by jealousy, while in *Is He Popenjoy?* Lord George Germain's unfounded jealousy almost drives his wife from him. Marital jealousy is more of a male vice, but a wife's unjustified jealousy of her husband forms a sub-plot in *Orley Farm*.

Jealousy is quite common between two men who are seeking to marry the same woman. In *Phineas Finn*, in which male jealousy is particularly prevalent, Lord Chiltern fights a duel with Finn because both are in pursuit of the same woman. The same theme occurs in *The Vicar of Bullhampton* (Harry Gilmore and Walter Marrable), *Lady Anna* (Daniel Thwaite and the 'curled darling', Lord Lovel), *Miss Mackenzie* (the Reverend Jeremiah Maguire and Samuel Rubb, along with John Ball) and *The Struggles of Brown, Jones, and Robinson* (George Robinson and the butcher, William Brisket). Once again female jealousy in such circumstances is rarer but in *Phineas Redux* Lady Laura Kennedy's jealous hatred for

Madame Max Goesler when she saves Finn is particularly virulent. Theatrical jealousy over Rachel O'Mahony's success is evident in *The Land-Leaguers*.

Trollope does not seem to have suffered from jealousy in his own marriage. His often misunderstood friendship with Kate Field, or any other 'heart-flutterings' he may have had, were accepted by his wife with the same amused tolerance as that shown by the editor's wife in 'Mary Gresley' over her husband's friendship with a beautiful young writer. Trollope also appears to have had little jealousy of other writers, although he did betray some for Dickens in *The Warden*.

Jewellery. The most important use of jewels in Trollope's fiction is, of course, in *The Eustace Diamonds*, where the plot turns on the ownership and theft of a diamond necklace. However, the most interesting use of jewels occurs in *Barchester Towers* [10] in the famous scene in which La Signora Vesey Neroni arrives at Mrs Proudie's reception wearing a red velvet band across her brow on which is fastened a mosaic brooch with a Cupid on it. To readers it would have seemed appropriate for a woman whose daughter is the 'last of the Neros' to be wearing an antique Roman jewel. Actually Trollope was enjoying a private joke with his wife, who had been given this jewel by his mother when they visited her in Italy. Fanny Trollope in her turn had been given the jewel twenty years earlier by Princess Metternich in Vienna [Mullen, 299]. Trollope used the same jewel in *The Claverings* when Mrs Clavering sends Fanny Burton 'a Cupid in mosaic surrounded by tiny diamonds' [41].

In the novels, jewels often mark important events. When Lord Dumbello discovers that his wife Griselda is not going to leave him, she is given a huge necklace with three rows of emeralds [*The Small House at Allington*, 55]. At the end of the Palliser novels the Duke of Omnium gives his new daughter-in-law a ring with a dozen diamonds that had belonged to his dead wife, Glencora, as a symbol of his acceptance of her [*The Duke's Children*, 72]. In *Phineas Redux* Madame Max Goesler is left a valuable legacy in jewels by the old Duke of Omnium, but she eventually sells them in order to provide a settlement to allow one of the younger Pallisers to marry.

Jews. Although Jews have important roles in several of Trollope's novels, it is difficult to summarize his attitudes towards them. It is easy to assume from reading one or two novels, particularly *The Way We Live Now* or *The Land-Leaguers*, that Trollope was conventionally anti-Semitic. However, there can be no greater mistake than to try to elicit Trollope's views from one or two novels. By that standard *Marion Fay* would prove that he hated Anglican clergymen and *The Small House at Allington* would demonstrate that he had little respect for civil servants. His attitude to Jews was more complex.

Trollope wrote one of the first Victorian novels in which a Christian and a Jew fall in love nine years before George Eliot made this the subject of *Daniel Deronda*. In *Nina Balatka* Trollope shows evident sympathy for the Jewish merchant, although he is careful not to make this man the embodiment of every virtue. Indeed the man appears remarkably similar to young men in Barsetshire except for the fact that he is Jewish and lives in Prague. The novel was inspired by Trollope's visit to the synagogue in Prague, one of the oldest in Europe.

In Trollope's novels, Jews are almost always involved either in finance or in private money-lending. As explained in the entry for *The Way We Live Now*, Trollope is careful to balance the harsh portrayal of the vile Melmotte, whom some believe to be Jewish, with the Jewish banker Ezekiel Breghert: 'He was an honest man,' says Trollope, and there are few of that species in the novel [79]. Dickens, who created the stereotypical Jewish character in Fagin, would have made it clear that Melmotte was a Jew. While Trollope portrays Mrs Melmotte as Jewish, he never says definitely that Melmotte is a Jew. Melmotte is a scoundrel and an outsider; his race and religion are irrelevant. Furthermore, crude anti-Semitic remarks are generally given to stupid characters, such as a silly squire's even sillier wife who proclaims when she hears her daughter wishes to marry the Jewish banker, Breghert: 'It's unnatural ... I'm sure there's something in the Bible about it. You never would read your Bible, or you wouldn't be going to do this' [78]. Trollope does a similar thing in *Rachel Ray* [14–15], where the snide comments about a Jewish parliamentary candidate are made to look ridiculous.

There are numerous money-lenders in Trollope's novels, many of whom are Jewish; most are repulsive figures though often not nearly as bad as the English Christian 'gentlemen' to whom they lend money. *Mr Scarborough's Family* is an excellent and extended example of this. Sometimes

Christian money-lenders are more avaricious. Thus in *Sir Harry Hotspur of Humblethwaite* there is a Jewish solicitor who is involved in lending money; this man, Abraham Hart, speaks with 'a slightly Jewish accent' and Trollope gives several examples such as changing 'w' to 'v', yet the reader surely agrees with young Hotspur that Hart is 'less distasteful' than Captain Stubber, a Christian involved in the same murky business [10]. [➤ Bills.]

Another problem in assessing Trollope's attitude is his use of the word 'Jew'. Trollope's characters frequently worry about their sons or heirs 'going to the Jews' to borrow money. Victorians in this usage did not always mean that the money-lender was literally Jewish in religion or race; it was a slang word for money-lenders. Also, Trollope occasionally used the word to mean someone who 'is anxious to make an unjust and quick profit'. He seemed to be using the word in this way in a private letter complaining about the fee charged by a Sussex surgeon, Robert Cross. Trollope – already in a bit of a rage – says 'he is a Jew – and he must know that I think him so'. One has to be very careful, therefore, when reading Trollope to decide what he – or his characters – actually mean when they say or think the word 'Jew'.

In the Palliser novels Mr Emilius, the clergyman who becomes a murderer, is a Jewish convert from Bohemia. Here Trollope is exercising his well-known detestation of Evangelicals, along with his dislike of fanatical converts in general [➤ Zulus]. [For a similar character, ➤ *Is He Popenjoy?*] Emilius is, after all, exposed by Madame Max Goesler, herself the widow of a Jewish banker. Because Madame Max has mysterious origins many people are convinced she is at least partly Jewish. In *The Land-Leaguers* there is a truly obnoxious American Jewish impresario who has one of Trollope's silliest names, Mahomet M. Moss. He is a caricature, but then so are many other characters in that unpleasant novel.

Trollope's attitude towards Jews was often affected by his loathing for Disraeli. However, Trollope's friend Abraham Hayward – said to be partly Jewish – provided the novelist with much ammunition for attacks on Disraeli. In addition to Hayward, Trollope was friendly with several members of the great Jewish banking family, the Rothschilds. He stayed at their house, Mentmore, and frequently hunted with them.

Trollope in his life seems to have had no great grievance against particular Jews, or Jews in general. Indeed in the introduction to *South Africa* he said, 'I have invariably found Jews to be more liberal than other men.' (By 'liberal' he means generous and fair.) In *The Bertrams*, written while he was in the Holy Land, he frequently praises the beauty of the Jewish women. Thus the best summary one can give of Trollope's attitude towards Jews is this: while at times he was capable of using the odd Jewish stereotype in his writing, he was also one of the first English novelists to portray Jewish characters as real people.

Jilting. In Trollope's fiction, jilting is a frequent occurrence. The most famous example – probably in all Victorian fiction – is Adolphus Crosbie's jilting of Lily Dale in *The Small House at Allington*, but there are numerous others. In *Doctor Thorne* a young man horsewhips a man who jilts his sister [21] and in *Framley Parsonage* the Grantlys fear that their daughter Griselda is about to be jilted by Lord Dumbello. In *The Claverings* Julia Brabazon jilts Harry Clavering, while he is almost led to jilt his fiancée for her. In *The Belton Estate* Clara Amedroz jilts her cousin, Captain Aylmer, and in *The Struggles of Brown, Jones, and Robinson* the butcher, William Brisket, jilts Maryanne Brown for a 'drover's daughter'. In *The Land-Leaguers* an American singer jilts an English nobleman. Trollope once wrote a play called *The Noble Jilt* which was never performed, although he used the plot, which concerned a woman who jilts her too-perfect young man, for *Can You Forgive Her?*

Well into Trollope's lifetime jilting could result in a suit for 'breach of promise', but although this possibility is mentioned it plays no important role in his fiction. In the small circles that normally provide the backdrops for Trollope's fiction, with their numerous interconnections, jilting could darken a life and make the victim the subject of unending gossip and pity. The worst effect of jilting takes place in one short story, 'La Mère Bauche', in which a French girl commits suicide after being jilted. The effects could last for years: it changed the whole course of Lily Dale's life. In *Kept in the Dark* the heroine's marriage is almost destroyed when her husband learns that she had jilted an earlier lover. In *An Old Man's Love* Mr Whittlestaff's life had been made miserable by being jilted years earlier, while Peter Prosper in *Mr Scarborough's Family* was something of a recluse because he had been jilted long ago.

Sometimes a character is unjustly accused of jilting, for instance John Caldigate in the novel named after him. Trollope recounts an amusing story in his *Autobiography* about a woman who came to the Post Office where he worked and claimed that he had jilted her daughter, which he had not done.

'John Bull on the Guadalquivir'. This short story, which makes use of Trollope's travels for the Post Office, was written in the first week of June, 1860. On his way back from Egypt in April 1858 he had a six-day holiday in Spain. In his *Autobiography* he wrote concerning this story that 'the chief incident ... occurred to me and a friend of mine on our way up that river to Seville. We both of us handled the gold ornaments of a man whom we believed to be a bull-fighter, but who turned out to be a duke, – and a duke, too, who could speak English! How gracious he was to us, and yet how thoroughly he covered us with ridicule!' The story was published in *Cassell's Illustrated Family Paper* and was later included in *Tales of All Countries* in 1861. Trollope received £50.

The story, told in the first person, centres on John Pomfret, whose father is a London merchant in partnership with a Spaniard. John travels to Spain to see if Maria Daguilar, daughter of his father's Spanish partner, will marry him. John, still in his hobbledehoyhood, journeys up the Guadalquivir to Seville on a steamer with a friend. The story then follows the incident Trollope recounts in his *Autobiography*. Pomfret is told that an elaborately dressed passenger is a *mayo*, a man who dresses up and spends his time 'hanging about with bull-fighters'. The

two young men mock him and, while examining his gold ornaments, almost pull off a gold pendule which the man then cuts off with his knife. They are slightly embarrassed to learn that he speaks English and offer to pay for the damage. Once in Seville, Pomfret forgets the *mayo* until Maria tells him a story of two gauche Englishmen who mistook the Marquis De Almavivas for a *mayo*. Maria adds, 'They are ignorant of Spanish, and they cannot bring themselves to believe that anyone should be better educated than themselves.' John admits he was one of the two men and at this point the marquis makes his appearance. He forgives the Englishman and gives him the pendule as a memento, which the young man accepts as a souvenir of 'the folly of an Englishman and the courtesy of a Spaniard'. Maria then accepts the young man's offer of marriage.

The story is told in a light-hearted fashion but it is a good insight into English middle-class travel in Europe: 'What a pity that Englishmen should always make so much noise ... They are all just the same as big boys', Maria comments. British boorish behaviour abroad is also treated in 'The Relics of General Chassé', the essay on 'The United Englishmen Who Travel For Fun', and *The Bertrams* [9].

John Caldigate. Trollope's thirty-seventh novel was written between 3 February and 21 July 1877, during which period he also wrote *The Life of Cicero* and travelled to South Africa. He completed the novel aboard ship the day before he arrived at Capetown. The book was first serialized in *Blackwood's Magazine* between April 1878 and June 1879. It was then published in three volumes by Chapman

& Hall in June 1879. Trollope received £1,800 – £600 for the serialization and £1,200 for the rights to the book.

'We poor novelists had not, amongst us, the wit to invent such a grand plot as that,' wrote Trollope to his sister-in-law and fellow novelist, Frances Eleanor Trollope. His reference to the most celebrated legal battle of his time, the Tichborne case, survives in a fragment of a March 1874 letter later quoted by Frances Eleanor [Mullen, 594]. Trollope, as a devoted reader of *The Times*, would have followed the enormous coverage of this long-drawn-out saga in which a man from Australia appeared in England claiming to be the long-lost heir to the Tichborne baronetcy and fortune.

Trollope's younger son, Fred, had gone to Australia in the 1860s. Although there was a constant correspondence between father and son as well as a constant flow of large sums to support Fred's sheep-station, Trollope well knew the difficulties that could beset English families divided by such vast distances. (He sent Fred the issues of *Blackwood's* as *John Caldigate* appeared.) He had himself made two lengthy visits to Australia and had already written a short novel, *Harry Heathcote of Gangoil*, about life there. *John Caldigate*, however, is his most involved attempt to portray the differing social conditions and attitudes between Australia and England. The differences here are at their greatest, because in England Caldigate moves amongst his fellow gentry while in Australia his associates are miners.

John Caldigate is set mainly in Cambridgeshire, a county Trollope knew from his days as the chief Post Office official in eastern England. Trollope stresses the effect of the county's Fens on the characters. The city of Cambridge is used throughout, but there is very little mention of the University even though Caldigate himself pays a visit to Trinity, his old college. Caldigate and his father, the old squire, find it impossible to live with one another [➤ Fathers and Sons]. The old squire is irascible, as so many of Trollope's old squires are, but unlike most of them, Daniel Caldigate is a Radical and something of an intellectual. Trollope no doubt knew that a Radical squire would not be a sympathetic character to most of *Blackwood's* Conservative readers. Young Caldigate begins as a strong Conservative, but eventually comes to share more of his father's views. The squire is opposed to the entail on the family estate, a frequent subject in Trollope's later fiction. When young John comes down from Trinity with little other than debts, the old squire buys out his right of inheritance under the entail, which equips the son to set off for Australia.

The relations between John and his father have some similarity to those between Trollope and his own father which he had recently described in his *Autobiography*. It was never easy in reality or in Trollope's fiction for the heirs to a small landed estate: there was not really enough money to provide them with an independent position and yet there were usually only a limited number of professions open to them [➤ *Mr Scarborough's Family*; *Cousin Henry*]. The old squire, when he had been faced with that position, had taken the unusual course of becoming a writer. When his son failed to become a barrister, there was really little else John could do in England.

Caldigate is like many of Trollope's young men: he is somewhat inclined to flirt and to allow young women to imagine he has serious intentions. Caldigate does this more frequently than most other young men in Trollope's fiction. Unlike such 'hobbledehoys' as John Eames, there is a somewhat sinister side to this aspect of Caldigate. One of his flirtations in England, with Maria Shand, is quite innocent, while another, with his cousin Julia Babington, had been engineered by her mother. However, on the ship he befriends the mysterious Mrs Smith.

Trollope had already sketched the plight of an 'unprotected female' in his short stories, 'An Unprotected Female at the Pyramids' and 'The Journey to Panama'. Euphemia Smith hardly requires protection; indeed, it is Caldigate who really needs protection from her. By going to Australia he has cast off some, but not all, of the Victorian code of manners and the rest of the novel shows what the consequences are. The shipboard scenes are particularly well done and provide a vivid picture of the differences between first- and second-class passengers. Caldigate is in a difficult position: he is travelling in second class yet everyone knows (as they always do in Trollope's novels) that he is 'a gentleman'.

Trollope uses his own visits to Australian mines to give a lively account of life among gold-miners. He had met an old schoolmate of his son at these mines and may well have used him as a model for Caldigate's reactions. Trollope always has a suspicious attitude towards fortunes gained from mining, although this is less obvious in this novel. He stresses that drunkenness is the fatal flaw that can ruin a man's prospects and this is what happens to Caldigate's friend, Dick Shand. Even so, the miners are never 'uncivil' even in their drinking bouts.

Suddenly, after several years, the novel shifts back to England when Caldigate, now successful, returns. This is a most unusual feature in a Trollope novel, but it is very effective as we are left wondering what has happened to the ripening friendship with Mrs Smith, now known as an actress, 'Mademoiselle Cettini'. Like another successful young man returning with a fortune from mining, John Gordon in *An Old Man's Love*, Caldigate has set his heart on one girl: Hester Bolton, the daughter of a prosperous banker. Even their marriage does not reconcile her formidable mother. Mrs Bolton is Trollope's best portrait of a religious fanatic. She is far fiercer than Mrs Proudie in the Barsetshire novels, more narrow-minded than Mrs Winterfield in *The Belton Estate* and more determined to prevent a marriage than Nina's aunt in *Nina Balatka*. Yet just as the Caldigates, father and son, are alike in so many ways, so are the Boltons, mother and daughter. They resemble one another in their ultimate faithfulness to what they believe [➤ Mothers and Daughters].

Once again a sudden reappearance changes the course of the novel: Mrs Smith and her friends arrive in England and, aided by their testimony, Mrs Smith claims that Caldigate had married her. When their attempt at blackmail fails she brings a charge of bigamy against Caldigate and a trial ensues. Agents and investigators were sent all over Australia, as in the Tichborne case. Caldigate weakens his defence by paying money to one of the witnesses, a former partner in his mining ventures, because he is convinced that it is right to recompense the man for some of his losses. This understandably mystifies people; Caldigate is convicted and sent to gaol for two years. However, a postal clerk investigates a suspicious postmark on a vital envelope and his discovery, along with Dick Shand's evidence, proves Caldigate had not married Mrs Smith.

Caldigate's compromising action in appearing to pay the blackmailers grew out of his genuine belief that he was morally, if not legally, obliged to do something. Such an act is in line with other quirky acts of honesty in Trollope's novels: Mr Harding's resignation in *The Warden*, or Madame Max Goesler's rejection of a legacy in *Phineas Redux*. It was also in line with Trollope's own high view of honesty, for instance in repaying a firm of publishers when he found that they had lost money on one of his novels. Even with *John Caldigate* Trollope offered to reduce his agreed payment from Blackwood by one quarter if that would make serialization easier.

Two familiar aspects of Trollope's fiction are also present. Newspapers spread inaccurate reports and lawyers play a large role. It is interesting to see how Trollope brings back a lawyer, Jacky Joram, from *Ralph the Heir*, but by now he has become the more dignified Sir John Joram. In the Australian chapters [8–13] Trollope includes references to things he had admired there and particularly praises the public gardens in Sydney. He seems to be having one of his private jokes when he describes Caldigate stumbling about with a heavy portmanteau, for all Trollope's travel books contain anecdotes of his own adventures with the mounds of luggage with which he travelled.

Of course the main private reference is in the way the Post Office is used. This is the only novel where a postal matter is of prime importance. Usually it provides a source of local colour, introduces an amusing minor character, or is connected with a letter in some way. In *Orley Farm* [41] there is a comment that postmarks were becoming clearer and this improvement becomes vital here when an official is suspicious of the forged postmark on the vital envelope. Samuel Bagwax is the postal clerk who spends hours proving that the postmark on a key piece of evidence is a forgery. (Trollope inserts a footnote apologizing to his friends at the Sydney post office in case they are offended at this.) Trollope admitted to John Blackwood that 'there was a touch of downright love in the depicting of Bagwax. Was I not once a Bagwax myself?' Bagwax is not a portrait of Trollope, but he gives a delightful insight into the world he had left a decade before. Certainly the jealousy aroused by the prospect of Bagwax being sent to Australia on an expenses-paid trip was something Trollope himself had endured in the 1850s.

When Trollope first approached Blackwood, he assured him that the novel would be set in England as his earlier attempts at short continental novels had not proved a profitable venture for the Edinburgh publisher. He wanted the novel to be called 'Mrs John Caldigate'. Blackwood as always was a careful reader and made several worthwhile criticisms. Although he found the story one of 'unflagging interest' he found Caldigate himself – 'the involuntary Don Giovanni' – too cold to arouse sympathy. Trollope agreed that this was a fault and said he would try to add a few softening touches when he got the proofs, but he found this difficult to do. In *Blackwood's Magazine* the novel appeared anonymously. Tom Trollope happened to be reading it while staying with Anthony and was surprised when he heard who the author was.

During the serialization of the novel there was some discussion among the lawyers at one of Trollope's clubs as to whether or not he had made a legal error in having Mrs Smith give evidence at the trial, but Trollope defended himself to Blackwood, saying that he had consulted various friends who were judges and attorneys. Blackwood did not feel that the story was a success and Trollope's reply was characteristic: 'When I am told that I have failed, I never fight the point: one attains a certain average of moderate success, and thanks the gods that the matter is not worse.' However, Blackwood's and Trollope's friend, W. Lucas Collins, told Blackwood he thought *John Caldigate* one of the novelist's best books. Since – unusually – Trollope does not betray the outcome in advance, the suspense is well maintained to the end. When it was published as a book it met with a mixed response from reviewers: some at least felt that Trollope was likely to return to his old popularity.

Jokes. See Private Jokes.

Joram, Jacky. Joram is a barrister who first appears in Trollope's unperformed play, *Did He Steal It?*. In this, an accused man is advised to send for Joram but is warned not to tell him the truth. He next appears in a legal case in *Ralph the Heir* [44]. In *John Caldigate*, Joram's legal career has obviously prospered and he is now Sir John Joram. Here he also tells a client he really does not wish to know about his guilt, to Trollope a cause for censure [40]. Joram, the son of a 'cheesemonger at Gloucester', improves on each of his three appearances. The fact that Trollope could carry this minor character in his memory for about ten years gives a good indication of how real even secondary figures were in his imaginary world. (The name Joram originally derives from 2 Samuel 8:10, in which Joram brings King David vessels of gold, silver and brass. A 'jorum' is the term for a large drinking bowl.)

'Josephine de Montmorenci'. This short story was first published in *Saint Pauls* in December 1869 and later included in *An Editor's Tales*. Like the others in the collection, it is based on Trollope's experience as an editor. In his *Autobiography* Trollope wrote: 'I do not think that there is a single incident in the book which could bring back to anyone concerned the memory of a past event. And yet there is not an incident in it the outline of which was not presented to my mind by the remembrance of some fact ... how I was addressed by a lady with a becoming pseudonym and with much equally becoming audacity.'

Like 'The Spotted Dog', this story begins with a letter from a novelist named Josephine de Montmorenci to Mr Brown, the editor of a magazine, asking him to serialize a three-volume novel she has written. Mr Brown takes up a reference to the publishers who had seen the manuscript, discovers that she is pretty and asks her to call with the manuscript. She writes to say she will not do as he asks and that his letter was cold; she is altogether very high-handed and frank. The editor, who 'loves the rustle of feminine apparel', is intrigued. He then writes 'in earnest' with a request to see the manuscript. He reads it and decides he does not want it, especially its 'feminine metaphysics'. He advises her to publish it as a book and asks to see her. Behind all lies the prospect of a mystery and a beautiful, unmarried woman. A woman arrives but announces she is not Miss de Montmorenci but her sister-in-law, Mrs Puffle. He discovers that her impudent letters were a ruse to get him to act. He hears Mrs Puffle refer to her as 'Polly' and, when he demands to meet Miss de Montmorenci, is told she 'dislikes so very much to talk about her own writings and her own works'. 'Polly' also 'has an idea ... that genius should not show itself publicly'. He learns that Mrs Puffle's husband, Charles, works at the Post Office. He is invited to call and finds a 'little wizened woman', and although she is no older than twenty-five she is crippled by a curvature of the spine. Brown agrees to act as her agent – 'What is a man against a woman in such a matter?' (In real life Trollope did help other writers place their work.) The novel proves a success.

As with 'The Spotted Dog', 'The Adventures of Fred Pickering' and 'Mary Gresley', Trollope uses his story to describe the world of Victorian publishing and to make his point regarding the hazards of writing for a living. Trollope had more than his usual number of private jokes in this story and with Puffle exercised his love of silly names. The most extended joke concerns his friends

George Eliot (Mary Anne Evans) and her companion G. H. Lewes. Like 'George Eliot', Josephine de Montmorenci is a *nom de plume*; like George Eliot, her real name is Maryanne; like her, she uses the nickname 'Polly'. Again like George Eliot, Josephine de Montmorenci filled her novel with 'feminine metaphysics' and disliked talking about her work, especially in public. Finally, like George Eliot, Miss de Montmorenci preferred to live privately, albeit for different reasons. Mrs Puffle's husband smokes cigars, as G. H. Lewes did; his Christian name was Charles and he works in the Post Office, just as did Lewes's son, also named Charles. (It was Trollope who helped to get him the position.)

Trollope had much sport with the question of *noms de plume.* Maryanne Puffle thinks her name would be 'unendurable on a title-page'; de Montmorenci would be better. (This was the name of one of the most ancient French noble families and a member of the family was particularly prominent in French politics in Trollope's youth.) Trollope, as someone who had achieved fame with a surname that had another, somewhat unsavoury meaning, makes a case for Puffle but loses. When arguing, Polly Puffle cites famous *noms de plume* like 'Boz' (Dickens), 'Barry Cornwall' (B. W. Procter), 'Jacob Omnium' (M. J. Higgins) and 'Michael Angelo Titmarsh' (W. M. Thackeray). Procter (or at least his wife), Higgins and 'poor Thackeray' were all friends of Trollope. (Trollope used the name Puffle again in *Mr Scarborough's Family.*)

Journalists. In Trollope's day 'journalist' had two meanings. The first was the older one, defining a man who occasionally wrote for journals and newspapers. Trollope's friend G. H. Lewes was a journalist in this sense, as was Trollope himself with his early articles or 'letters' on Ireland for the *Examiner* and with his essays for the *Pall Mall Gazette* in the 1860s. This type of journalist is seen in the young people who want to write for 'The Panjandrum' and in 'The Adventures of Fred Pickering'. The second meaning was a man who earned his living by writing for a newspaper and it is this type which mainly people Trollope's later fiction. He calls them 'newspapermen'. This group included the 'Bohemian', Quaverdale, who claims to make £500 or £600 a year by writing for the Radical paper *The Coming Hour*, but whose dirty linen undermines his claim to be a gentleman [*Mr Scarborough's Family*, 22]. In *Is He Popenjoy?* it is the slimy Joseph Groschut, the bishop's chaplain, who contributes articles to *The Brotherton Church* in order to attack Dean Lovelace and to advance his own career by praising the bishop. Trollope did not have a very high opinion of either of these men. He described the tragedy of an educated man writing for 'penny dreadfuls' at 45*s.* a week in 'The Spotted Dog'. Tom Towers, a barrister, who writes lead articles for *The Jupiter* is Trollope's best-known journalist; he maintains his genteel status in spite of his somewhat questionable methods. Quintus Slide, whose sensationalist newspaper causes problems for several characters in the Palliser novels, is Trollope's most effective portrait of the newer, late-Victorian journalist. [➤ Editors.]

'The Journey to Panama'. This short story was written in either 1860 or 1861 as a contribution to Emily Faithfull's *Victoria Regia*. The story was published in November 1861 and was included in Trollope's third collection of short stories, *Lotta Schmidt and Other Stories*, in 1867. Trollope, like the other contributors, received no payment. The setting for the story was based on his travels during his 1858–9 Post Office assignment in the West Indies and Central America. Trollope also used the closed world aboard ship in 'John Bull on the Guadalquivir', *The Bertrams* and *John Caldigate*. In a letter of 1867 Trollope discussed how people kept their minds occupied in periods of intense grief: 'It fell to my lot once to have to tell a lady who was going out to be married, (she and I being in the same ship,) – that news had met us that her intended husband was dead. I left her seated on the floor of a small ladies' cabin, & she at once asked to have a large trunk brought to her. In the course of an hour I found her packing & unpacking the trunk, putting the new wedding clothing at the bottom & bringing the old things, now suitable for her use, to the top. And so she employed herself during the entire day.' Trollope used this incident, as well as his meeting with a young Irish governess on her way to Panama to marry a virtual stranger, as the basis for this story. With this background knowledge it is fascinating to see how Trollope made use of two experiences to create a story.

The tale is told by a young widower named Ralph Forrest (the surname Forrest was also used in his novel, *Harry Heathcote of Gangoil*, written in 1873) who is sailing to Panama *en route* for Vancouver aboard the *Serrapiqui*. (Trollope named the ship after the Serapiqui River, which flows between Costa Rica and Nicaragua. He set 'Returning Home', his other story of Central America, on this river.) On board, Forrest meets Emily Viner, a penniless Irish governess who is nearly thirty. She is on her way to Peru to marry a distant cousin who is older than she is, and wealthy. Forrest befriends her as an 'unprotected lady'. When she admits she does not love her intended spouse and does not want to marry him, Forrest advises her to return to England and offers to pay for the journey. She refuses out of pride and out of regard for her fiancé. When they arrive at Aspinwall (Colón) they discover that her cousin has died but has left her enough to live on. Forrest proposes to her but she rejects him out of pride: he knows too much about her and as his wife she could hardly mourn her dead cousin.

In a very touching story Trollope sets forth the plight of unmarried women – most fitting, as the story was written especially for the feminist, Emily Faithfull: 'It is easy to say that a woman should not marry without love, as easy as it is to say that a man should not starve. But there are men who starve, – starve although they work hard.' Few other English writers of the time would have picked an Irishwoman as the heroine of such a story, but this reflects Trollope's affection for Ireland. This tale attacks the emerging Confederate States of America in the reference to the 'palmetto flag', South Carolina's famed banner, and issues a blast at government officials in Central America. His first travel book, *The West Indies and the Spanish Main*, offers some background to other details of the story.

Judges. See Lawyers.

The Jupiter. A newspaper that first occurs in *The Warden* and goes on to feature in several novels. Contemporaries immediately knew that the classical name was being used to score a hit at *The Times.* Jupiter, as king of the gods, used thunderbolts as a way of making his views known. This was therefore a pun on *The Times*'s nickname of 'The Thunderer' and Trollope carried the joke further still by locating the paper at Mount Olympus [*The Warden*, 14]. Trollope's writings in the 1850s and early 1860s are especially full of such classical allusions [➤ *Framley Parsonage*, 23]. In Chapter 14 he also made a timely reference to *The Times*'s power as the 'Vatican of England'. (The Pope had only recently re-established the Catholic hierarchy in England.) The paper was enjoying an unrivalled supremacy in the midst of the Crimean War when Trollope was writing *The Warden*. As Archdeacon Grantly said, 'What the Czar is in Russia, or the mob in America, that the Jupiter is in England' [*The Warden*, 7]. Trollope's worry about *The Times*'s vast power was shared by most informed contemporaries including Queen Victoria and almost all leading politicians. Trollope returned to the position of *The Times* in *The New Zealander*, in which he said, 'One newspaper is "the Press".' Another novelist, the Reverend William Conybeare (1815–57), brought out a novel, *Perversion*, about the same time as *Barchester Towers* in which an all-powerful newspaper, *The Vane*, is featured. *The Times* mildly chastised both novelists for being inaccurate and for 'pandering to a very morbid curiosity'.

The Jupiter went on to play a major

role in *Barchester Towers* through its participation in the debate over filling important clerical positions: the paper sponsored Obadiah Slope for the vacant deanery of Barchester. *The Jupiter* also played a vital political role in *Framley Parsonage*. After *The Small House at Allington* Trollope increasingly portrayed a different type of newspaper, the popular and demagogic press. *The Jupiter* is, however, mentioned in two other novels of the 1850s: *The Struggles of Brown, Jones, and Robinson* and *The Bertrams*.

[➤ Journalists; Towers, Tom.]

K

The Kellys and the O'Kellys. This, Trollope's second novel, was written in 1846–7. Trollope had no desire to have it brought out by the somewhat disreputable publisher of his first novel, *The Macdermots of Ballycloran*, so his mother approached Richard Bentley, who had published several of her books. Trollope insisted that he would only allow the book to be published if he were paid for it and he refused to accept a half-profits arrangement. [➤ Publishers and Publishing.] When Bentley rejected the book, Fanny Trollope went to one of her other publishers, Henry Colburn, who had issued twelve of her novels. Colburn agreed to publish *The Kellys and the O'Kellys* but Trollope was forced to accept a half-profits arrangement. It was published by Colburn in three volumes on 27 June 1848. Although Trollope eventually received £123 19*s.* 5*d.*, he made nothing from the first edition.

Trollope's first two novels are both set in Ireland. However, *The Kellys and the O'Kellys* differs considerably from the first novel, which is a tale of virtually unrelieved misery ending with the hero's execution. His second novel fits more into the pattern of his succeeding books: the young man, or, in this case, young men, eventually marry their true loves. While the action of *The Macdermots of Ballycloran* took place in the decade before Trollope came to Ireland in 1841, *The Kellys and the O'Kellys* is set during his first years there. Although it was written during the height of the dreadful potato famine, Trollope places the novel almost two years before the potato crop failed. Much of the action takes place in Galway and Mayo, the latter being the poorest county in the west of Ireland.

It is rare for Trollope to be precise about dates in his fiction, but here the novel clearly starts in the first two months of 1844 as the opening scene is a trial in Dublin. This was an actual event, and one that was likely still to be in the minds of informed readers when the novel appeared. The trial was of Daniel O'Connell, MP, the leader of the 'Repeal' movement. As the novel makes clear, there was intense interest throughout Ireland in this trial. (The interest was almost as great in England, and *The Times* kept a private ferry in Dublin's harbour so that its correspondent could make a hurried dash to London to be the first with the news of the verdict.) From Trollope's account it sounds as if he himself were present for part of the trial. The novel's action takes place against the background of this trial and its consequences, and we learn in one of the last chapters [38] that O'Connell and most of his associates have been found guilty. (Shortly afterwards

O'Connell was released from prison after a successful appeal to the House of Lords, but he died in 1847.) Trollope argued at the start of the novel – and repeated the observation in other novels – that the Irish greatly enjoyed their grievances against Britain. At almost the same time that Trollope wrote this, the Prime Minister, Sir Robert Peel, was saying the same thing to Queen Victoria.

The plot of *The Kellys and the O'Kellys* has great similarities with the plots of many of the novels Trollope would write in the next three decades. It follows the stories of two young men, Lord Ballindine and Martin Kelly, each in pursuit of an heiress. Neither man is perfect and each acts – like so many of Trollope's later characters – from a mixture of motives. In both cases the better side of their character predominates. Viscount Ballindine is a young peer who has succeeded to an impoverished estate and who must marry in order to secure a fortune. (This peerage in the O'Kelly family was created in 1800, which means it was a reward for promoting that very Act of Union between Ireland and Great Britain that O'Connell was trying to 'repeal'.) Lord Ballindine wants to marry Fanny Wyndham, whose already large fortune has been increased by £80,000 through the death of a rich brother. The viscount's prospects are threatened by the actions of Fanny's guardian, the Earl of Cashel, who wants Fanny to marry his dissipated son Lord Kilcullen, who is deeply in debt. At the end of the novel true love prevails and Kilcullen becomes the first of many characters in Trollope's fiction to flee as an exile to France.

Martin Kelly is a tenant of Lord Ballindine with whom the middle-class Kellys claim a very distant kinship. He too wishes to marry a woman with money, Anty Lynch, and their story is the more important one in the novel. She has inherited half the fortune of the land agent who has cheated the Ballindine estates for decades. Trollope's portrayal of Anty Lynch is the most interesting aspect of the story. Most people regarded her as 'a little weak or so in the upper storey', but Trollope shows her real problem is that she has been 'so little thought of all her life by others' [4]. Both Anty's fortune and her life are threatened by her brother, Barry Lynch, who had been at Eton with Lord Ballindine. He tries to force her into an insane asylum and is even prepared to murder her to get his hands on her money. The Lynch family, like several families in Trollope's Irish novels, is divided in religion: Anty is Catholic while Barry is Protestant. (Phineas Finn would be the most prominent product of such a religiously divided family which was a quite common arrangement in Ireland.) [➤ *An Eye for an Eye*.] She appeals to Martin Kelly for help and he, already planning to marry her for her money, falls in love with her. Soon Barry Lynch, like Lord Kilcullen, flees to Europe.

There are many features of *The Kellys and the O'Kellys* that recur constantly in Trollope's work. The portrait of Earl Cashel [11] shows Trollope's ability even at this early stage to create a character. The fascination with the social role of a clergyman, in this case Mr Armstrong, foreshadows the Barsetshire novels, and others like *The Vicar of Bullhampton* and *The Claverings*. Armstrong emerges as a man anxious to be just and one who pays no heed to Barry Lynch's pathetic appeals to support him as a fellow-Protestant against a 'papist doctor'. [➤ Public Schools.] While Lynch is a complete rogue with no redeeming features, the other rogue, Lord Kilcullen, is allowed by Trollope to have some good characteristics. In the final scene with his outraged father, Kilcullen behaves honourably by promoting Fanny's marriage with Ballindine [33]. (This scene has many parallels with Bertie Stanhope's final talk with his outraged father in *Barchester Towers*.) Certain minor habits, such as referring to a doctor as Galen or giving a servant some variant of the name Richard, begin in this novel. Likewise, those small mistakes that Trollope often makes are evident here: sometimes Mr Armstrong is called Joseph and at other times George.

The Kellys and the O'Kellys also shows how important fox-hunting had already become in Trollope's life and would become in his fiction. This novel has his first hunt: the last would be written thirty-five years later in another Irish novel, *The Land-Leaguers*. The scenes of the fox-hunt which starts at Lord Ballindine's house reveal how closely Trollope had studied Irish speech and how he had already mastered the art of writing dialogue, an achievement that would be much praised by his contemporaries [21–2]. Incidentally, it is a sure sign of his dislike for Barry Lynch that that reprobate turns up at the hunt resplendent in the latest fashionable hunting attire; this is never a good sign in any of Trollope's characters, particularly in a man.

The characters in the novel are constantly moving about Ireland, which reflects the author's own life at the time. His travels for the Post Office gave him many reasons to complain about the state of Irish transport and of most hotels [➤ 'Father Giles of Ballymoy']. The account of the canal boat trip [8] gives an excellent idea not only of the misery of such travel, but also of Trollope's even greater misery at enforced idleness. It was this passion to be busy that would drive him to write forty-seven novels, numerous other books and short stories.

The novel is full of topical allusions beyond those to Daniel O'Connell and the 'Repeal' movement. 'Brian Boru', the name of a racehorse, is taken from the famous High King of Ireland in the tenth century, a name much used in Irish writing. (Thackeray also used it for a racehorse in *Pendennis* a year or two later.) The name of the great Irish temperance reformer, Father Mathew, is mentioned several times. No doubt many contemporaries laughed when reading that Barry Lynch's dishonest attorney had his office in Tuam. To readers of the press this immediately conjured up the rabidly anti-English Archbishop of Tuam, John MacHale. (Trollope attacked him in one of his *Examiner* articles.)

As in *The Macdermots of Ballycloran* Trollope was fascinated by the ways in which religion affected Irish society. In his first novel, a Catholic priest emerges as the real hero; in his second, an Anglican parson takes vigorous action in driving the villain, Barry Lynch, out of Ireland. In the first novel the good priest was contrasted with a younger and more fanatical one. Here Mr Armstrong comes into conflict with another rector, Mr O'Joscelyn, who is a fanatical Protestant and rants about the evils of Catholicism; Trollope makes another topical allusion here, as Lord Jocelyn was one of the leaders of rabid anti-Catholicism at the time. When Mr Armstrong declares, 'I'd sooner by half be a Roman myself, than think so badly of my neighbours,' he is expressing the novelist's own view [38]. Incidentally, Armstrong's trick of borrowing a few parishioners from a neighbouring Catholic priest to impress a visiting Anglican dignitary was not unknown in Ireland. This incident and many others in the novel show how complex the relations between Catholic and Protestant were in Ireland: Trollope was one of the few writers to record this complexity.

Throughout the book, Trollope's love of Ireland and the Irish is quite apparent, but two aspects of the country annoyed him constantly. Too many people were idle – even Mr Armstrong is guilty of this, although a clergyman with a congregation comprising a lady, her daughters and a few policemen would have little to do. Idleness was closely connected to the lack of cleanliness. Trollope believed fully in the Victorian gospel of hard work and cleanliness.

The Kellys and the O'Kellys was not a success. Only 140 of the 375 copies printed were sold. Trollope commented, 'I changed my publisher, but did not change my fortune.' Colburn was probably right when he said that readers 'did not care for Irish novels', particularly when newspapers were already filled with the horrors of the Irish potato famine. The novel did not receive as much praise from reviewers as *The Macdermots of Ballycloran*. Trollope was, however, pleased that on the recommendation of a friend a *Times* reviewer read the book and praised the writer for his sense of reality and

humour. He could recall a reasonably accurate version of the review years later in his *Autobiography*. It is fortunate that he remembered the praise rather than Colburn's stricture: 'It is impossible for me to give any encouragement to you in novel writing.'

Kennedy, Lady Laura. Lady Laura plays a prominent role in *Phineas Finn* and *Phineas Redux*. When the first novel begins she is Lady Laura Standish, sister of Lord Chiltern, and lives with her widowed father, the Earl of Brentford. She is connected to many of the great Whig families in the Palliser novels: she is a niece of the Duchess of St Bungay and a cousin of Barrington Erle. She likes to play a role in political intrigue and determines to advance the career of Erle's protégé, Phineas Finn, with whom she soon falls in love. However, she eventually marries a rich Scotsman, Robert Kennedy, for his money. Since Trollope always believed that it was wrong to marry only for money, she suffers a sad fate; she is forced to go into exile in Dresden to escape her husband, who has become insane. She loses Finn to her rival, Madame Max Goesler. Lady Laura is one of the most tragic figures in Trollope's fiction and he felt she was 'the best character' in the two Finn novels [*Autobiography*].

Kennedy, Robert. Kennedy is an important character in *Phineas Finn* and *Phineas Redux*, and is one of the few Scotsmen to play a major part in Trollope's novels. He was 'a man who had very little temptation to do anything wrong' as he was worth £1,500,000, which would have placed him among the richest men in Britain. This fortune had been built up by his father, a Glaswegian businessman. Kennedy owns a large country seat, Loughlinter, in Perthshire [➤ Scotland]. At the opening of *Phineas Finn* he has been a Liberal MP for about ten years. He sits for a Scottish seat but rarely speaks in the House, although as Chancellor of the Duchy of Lancaster he is a member of the Cabinet. His marriage to Lady Laura Standish [➤ preceding entry] brought him many connections with the powerful Whig families in the Palliser novels. Kennedy's marriage proves an unhappy one as he tries to enforce his gloomy Calvinist ways on his vivacious wife, and she eventually leaves him. Kennedy possesses all the traits Trollope most despises: jealousy, excessive piety, stern Sabbatarianism and meanness. He even tries to prevent his wife from reading novels! In *Phineas Redux* he begins to sink into madness and attempts to murder Finn, whom he suspects as the cause of his wife leaving him, although Finn has earlier saved Kennedy himself from being murdered. Trollope's portrait of Kennedy is one of his most powerful studies of insanity, reminding one of Sir Henry Harcourt in *The Bertrams* and Louis Trevelyan in *He Knew He Was Right*. The *Spectator* rightly thought Kennedy 'a great triumph for Mr Trollope'.

Kensal Green Cemetery. Trollope, like many other enlightened Victorians, supported the idea of cities establishing large public cemeteries as overcrowded churchyards were increasingly hazards to public health. All Souls Cemetery, Kensal Green, opened in 1832, was the first of these in London. Trollope refers to it in *The Struggles of Brown, Jones, and Robinson* [20] and in 'The Panjandrum'. He at-

tended various funerals there, most notably that of Thackeray in 1863. In 1882 Trollope himself was buried there and his grave, with the inscription 'He was a loving husband and a loving father and a true friend', can be found in Square 138. The cemetery is on the Harrow Road along which Trollope as a boy probably passed with his father *en route* to the Inns of Court or to his house in Keppel Street.

Keppel Street. Trollope was born at No. 16, Keppel Street, Russell Square, London in 1815. (His mother had lived with her brother, Henry Milton, at No. 27.) Although he was taken as a baby to a new home in Harrow, the Trollopes appear to have kept their house in Keppel Street for some time. In his autobiographical short story 'Father Giles of Ballymoy', he alludes to 'my own room' at Keppel Street in the paragraph immediately after one in which there is a reference to 'my mother'. The houses in Keppel Street could not, Trollope adds with some exaggeration, 'be called fashionable'. The idea of fashion and pretension were fixed in his mind and recurred in *Lady Anna*, written five years later. Here he describes the rooms of a house in Keppel Street in some detail [20, 42] and again added that 'Keppel Street cannot be called fashionable, and Russell Square is not much affected by the nobility' [20]. His memories of his parents' slightly pretentious style of life had obviously not been forgotten. When his father bought No. 16 the street had only recently been developed (about 1810) on the Duke of Bedford's estate. It was named after Lady Elizabeth Keppel, mother of the fifth and sixth dukes. The houses were popular with lawyers like his father, and prosperous civil servants like his uncle. Trollope's father at one point appears to have owned several houses in the street. In *Orley Farm* the barrister, Thomas Furnival, lived there until his move to Harley Street. Ironically, in 1875 the Irish Nationalist MP, Charles Stewart Parnell, took lodgings at No. 16. The area had become a respectably bohemian quarter and it may be that Parnell was visited by his mistress, Mrs O'Shea, in the Trollopes' old home. [For Trollope's attack on Parnell, ► *The Land-Leaguers*.] Many of the houses were later pulled down to build the University of London's School of Hygiene and Tropical Medicine.

Kept in the Dark. Trollope's forty-fourth novel was written between 18 August and 15 December 1880 and serialized in the monthly, *Good Words*, between May and December 1882, in which latter month Trollope died. The story was then published in two volumes in October 1882 by Chatto & Windus. Trollope received a total of £450.

Kept in the Dark is another novel showing the effects of jealousy in marriage. Cecilia Holt jilts Sir Francis Geraldine in Exeter and later travels to Rome where she becomes engaged to George Western. He tells her of his having been jilted and partly for this reason she does not tell him of her past. She finds it impossible to mention it and the longer she waits the more difficult it becomes. They return to England where they are married and finally her husband learns the truth through Sir Francis Geraldine and Cecilia's exotic friend, Francesca Altifiorla. Western, who like Lord

George Germain in *Is He Popenjoy?* is something of a prig, has no thought of divorce. As his lawyer points out, he could not get one since Cecilia was not guilty of adultery, or what he calls the 'one fault [that] is not pardonable' [14]. Western knows his wife would never even contemplate adultery. He follows the usual course open to unhappy couples in Victorian times and in Trollope's fiction: separation. Western broods on the question and then leaves her, while she returns to Exeter. Eventually a reconciliation takes place. Francesca's attempts to get Sir Francis fail. [► Divorce.]

Cecilia Holt, like Lady Laura Kennedy in *Phineas Redux* and Emily Trevelyan in *He Knew He Was Right*, suffered terribly from her husband's insane jealousy. Yet all three women had – at least by Victorian standards – played some role in bringing about their own tragedies. Cecilia stumbles into her misery not by what she does, but by not speaking up in time. Her fault is one more common in Trollope's young men, like John Eames in *The Small House at Allington*, Henry Jones in *Cousin Henry* or the main character in *John Caldigate*: they do not lie but they do not speak plainly the truth. Many of Trollope's last novels were dominated by the idea of a 'secret'. We can see this in *John Caldigate*, *Cousin Henry*, *Dr Wortle's School*, *The Land-Leaguers* and *Mr Scarborough's Family*. This is certainly true in *Kept in the Dark* and lest the reader forget it, the phrase of the title is repeated constantly throughout the book.

Although no character in this novel would rank among Trollope's most memorable, the two principal women, Cecilia Western and her friend – if that is the right word – Francesca Altifiorla, are interesting characters. This novel also contains more than the usual amount of correspondence, and is a particularly good means of observing how Victorians went about arrangements for dealing with broken marriages. The novel also reveals Trollope's basic attitude towards the woman's role in a marriage by the subtle line he draws between her acceptance of the man's ultimate dominance and her rejection of his tyranny. Another relationship, that between the lady of the house and her servants, is also well described. She is desperate to keep them from knowing of her husband's departure, but as the break becomes open her maid puts aside her normal role and addresses her as a friend, rather than as a trusted servant.

Miss Altifiorla, as her name would imply, is partially of Italian descent and likes to boast of her ancient lineage. Trollope has his usual laugh at this by having a local newspaper report that 'her great grandmother was a Fiasco, and her great-great-grandmother a Disgrazia' [22] [➤ Names, Silly]. She has strange views about marriage, as does another heroine of a novel of the same period, Ayala Dormer in *Ayala's Angel*, but where Ayala is seeking an 'angel of light' Francesca is sceptical about the whole notion of marriage. Francesca slightly resembles a real person, Kate Field. It seems quite likely that Trollope was thinking of her when Francesca contemplates a lecture tour of America to 'those large Western Halls, full of gas and intelligence'[23]. Trollope had never really approved of Kate Field's role as a lecturer [➤ Feminists]. Often Francesca's conversation or her unspoken thoughts have a

touch of the absurd. To take but one example: when she thinks she is going to marry the baronet, she dreams about how good it will be to be within the 'peerage'. Knowledgeable readers would have known that baronets were not peers [15].

The failed love affair between Francesca and Sir Francis Geraldine is the Westerns' marriage in reverse. Cecilia suffers because she is quiet about her previous life; Francesca suffers because she tells everyone, including the newspapers, about her prospects of marrying a baronet. Sir Francis, unusually in Trollope's fiction, is in fact the conventional wicked baronet of Victorian tales.

The novel gives a good picture of the life of the Victorian upper classes who wandered from one place to another. George Western has dabbled in various activities from the House of Commons to membership of various scientific societies, but nothing has really engaged his interest. Western's troubles spring from this lack of work, a lack share by those other jealous husbands, Robert Kennedy and Louis Trevelyan. All three men are therefore able to allow their minds to gnaw at trifles. Sir Francis Geraldine also has no useful work in life and uses his time to cause trouble. As so often in a Trollope novel, idleness is the cause of much misery.

This short novel ranges over more backgrounds than almost any other comparable work of its size by Trollope. (Trollope told a publisher it was 72,500 words long.) Various characters wander about Devonshire, Scotland, London, Berkshire, Italy and Germany. We even hear of places Trollope favoured in his last years, such as Nice and the Swiss mountains. Yet he gives these settings remarkably little local colour – although we are told which is the best hotel in Exeter (The Clarence) and how people can walk by the River Elbe near Dresden. Indeed, the constant contrasting of Italy and Devonshire reminds one of *He Knew He Was Right*. We are given some interesting glimpses of English life in Rome, which Trollope could observe now that his brother Tom had moved there. [➤ 'Mrs General Talboys'.]

Trollope was very fond of Exeter and used it frequently in his novels. However, in this book he actually uses a real clerical figure, the Dean of Exeter. This was an odd lapse as such an important clerical dignitary could well have objected to the use of his position for a fictional character.

This is the first novel Trollope wrote at his new house in the country, at Harting in Sussex, where he had moved after a decade of life in London. Like many of his last novels, large portions of the manuscript are in the handwriting of his niece, Florence Bland, who acted as his amanuensis. Trollope accepted the publisher's demand that strong expressions, mainly variants of damn, 'shall be softened'. He persuaded his old friend Millais, who had illustrated *Framley Parsonage* and some of the other great successes of the 1860s, to contribute one illustration for this novel and that drawing is one of the best in all Trollope's illustrated novels.

The reviews were, of course, affected by the fact that several appeared immediately after Trollope's death. The *Spectator* rightly said that the novel was 'one of the least important' of his works but still found it 'very pleasant'. The *Graphic* believed – somewhat absurdly – that this novel was 'typically characteristic' of Trollope and could stand as 'the text of a criticism' upon his achievements. This review quotes him as saying, 'my real mission is to make young ladies talk' and the review concludes that he did so in this novel.

L

Lady. Trollope once told an audience that the novelist's moral duty was to teach ladies to be women and men to be gentlemen. He meant by this that he wished to broaden the experience and outlook of ladies who, by their training, their demureness and their avoidance of scandal, may not have been exposed to many of life's problems. [➤ Prostitution.] Trollope devoted less time to defining a lady than to defining a gentleman because the preponderance of his female characters are ladies in manners if not always in character. He seldom, therefore, lays down rules for ladylike behaviour, although female characters will tell their women friends when some particular act is not 'ladylike'. In *Is He Popenjoy?* Lord George Germain, admittedly something of a prig, tells his wife, 'A lady should never be in the least loud, nor, for the matter of that, would a gentleman either if he knew what he was about' [19]. In *Mr Scarborough's Family* we know Matilda Thoroughbung is not a lady because of the way in which she rushes into questions of money: she knows her own income down to the last penny [26]. It is interesting that here the servants of her would-be fiancé had 'heard that Miss Thoroughbung was a clever woman, but they did not believe her to be a lady', and they did not like what they had heard [27].

Trollope's most interesting discussion of the subject is in *Miss Mackenzie*, where the heroine, while related to a baronet, also has a brother 'in trade'. She therefore stands on the border between being a lady and not being one. Because she is free to find her own level and to marry either the tradesman or the heir to a baronetcy, she analyses what it means to be a lady: if she marries the heir to the baronetcy she will be a lady. If she marries the tradesman she will not. One lady she knows is Miss Baker for whom, Trollope tells us, 'not to be a lady was to be nothing. It was her weakness, and I may also say her strength. Her ladyhood was of that nature that it took no soil from outer contact.' Even so, Miss Baker 'would have broken her heart rather than marry a man who was not a gentleman. It was not unlady-like to eat cold mutton ... But she would have shuddered had she been called on to eat any mutton with a steel fork ... She would not go out to tea in a street cab, because she was a lady and alone.' Yet of Miss Baker, Miss Mackenzie thought, 'Had she not been so much the lady, she might have been more the woman.' Trollope himself adds, 'No one blames one's washerwoman for not being a lady. No one wishes one's housekeeper to be a lady; and people are dismayed, rather than pleased, when they find that their tailors' wives want to be ladies' [9].

Trollope also discussed a woman's qualification for the status of lady in *The Vicar of Bullhampton*, in which his own liberal views were made clear. He describes Maggie Brattle, the wife of a miller, as a 'modest, pure, high-minded woman, – whom we will not call a lady, because of her position in life, and because she darned stockings in a kitchen. In all other respects she deserved the name' [7]. Many Victorians would not have accepted either statement. In the same novel Trollope discusses the plight of Miss Marrable, undoubtedly a lady, but with little money. She, like Miss Baker, 'never took one of the common street flies, but paid eighteen pence extra to get a brougham from the Dragon' [➤ Carriages]. She insisted that her niece take a maid with her when visiting the vicarage at Bullhampton: 'Miss Marrable had thought that it would, perhaps, not be well for a girl so well-born as Miss Lowther to go out visiting without a maid. She herself very rarely left Loring, because she could not afford it; but when . . . she did go to Weston-super-Mare for a fortnight, she took one of the girls [servants] with her' [9]. (When the Trollopes visited Australia, Rose took a maid with her, largely to help her dress and to arrange her hair. With unmarried girls, maids could also act as a restraining presence.)

The image of an English lady had spread round the world and young women from the colonies or America who think of marrying Englishmen, like Eva Crasweller in *The Fixed Period* [5] or Ophelia Gledd in 'Miss Ophelia Gledd', wonder if they will be accepted as ladies in English society.

American girls at least were prone to be too uncontrolled by their elders, too frank, and too straightforward [➤ Anglo-American Marriages]. (Trollope also discusses the differences in English restraints on unmarried girls, as opposed to restraints in other countries, in *The Vicar of Bullhampton* [14].) For his part, Trollope speculates on this question and writes in 'Miss Ophelia Gledd': 'An Englishman . . . is often at a loss to judge of the "ladyship" of a foreigner, unless he has really lived in foreign cities . . . but I do not know that he is ever so much puzzled in this matter by any nationality as he is by the American . . . the words, and habits, and social carriage, of an American woman, of the best class, too often offend the taste of an Englishman.' While he poses the question, he gives no answer.

[For a comparison of English and foreign women, ➤ Women; for use of the title 'Lady', ➤ Peerage.]

Lady Anna. Trollope's thirtieth novel was written between 25 May and 19 July 1871 and was started on the day after he left for his first trip to Australia. In his *Autobiography* he recalled that the book took him eight weeks to write, with one day missed because of ill-health. He wrote 66 pages a week, each page containing 250 words, and 'every word was counted'. His worksheet has at the top '9 pages a day for 59 days = 531 pages'. The novel began monthly serialization in the *Fortnightly Review* on 1 April 1873 and ended in April 1874. It was also serialized in the *Australasian*, starting in May 1873. It was published in two volumes by Chapman & Hall in May 1874. (Manuscript notes for a story about a tailor may be found in the Trollope family papers in the University of Illinois.) Trollope received £1,200. [➤ Tailors.]

Josephine Murray is an ambitious young woman who marries a man for his title and income. Her husband, Earl Lovel, is a notorious rake who eventually tells her that he has a wife already living in Italy, that she is therefore not his wife, that she is not a countess and that her daughter Anna is illegitimate. She leaves his country house in Cumberland and is sheltered in Keswick by a Radical tailor, Thomas Thwaite. Her husband is charged with bigamy but is found innocent so that she is shown to be his wife and her daughter, Anna, legitimate and therefore entitled to the courtesy title of 'Lady'. In the meantime, unknown to her mother, Anna falls in love with and promises to marry Thwaite's even more Radical son, Daniel. The earl dies and leaves everything to his Italian mistress. The will is contested both by Josephine, now the dowager countess, and by his heir, the new earl. The amount at stake is 'immense'. The new earl's lawyers buy off the Italian mistress with £10,000 and the young peer now battles with the countess for ownership of the estate. The lawyers suggest that Lord Lovel marry Lady Anna and the plot revolves round their frustrated courtship and the tragedy awaiting Josephine when she discovers that her daughter, having gained recognition as an earl's daughter, loves a tailor's son. Lady Anna and her mother move to London. In the end, after many trials for Lady Anna, true love triumphs and her mother gives in. The couple are married and emigrate to Australia, where Daniel Thwaite will not have to live near titled people.

Unusually for Trollope he set the novel in the past, in this case in the 1830s when he himself was a young man. He did this to leave himself room to develop the story as the start of a new series like the Barsetshire and Palliser novels. Trollope never fulfilled the promise of the novel's last sentence, to tell us how the Thwaites fared in Australia.

The novel has two main plots: a love story between two young people – in this case controversial because of the social differences (as in *Marion Fay* and 'The Spotted Dog') and the tragedy of Countess Lovel, who sees her hard-won campaign for social recognition turn to ashes. (A similar fate awaited Julia Brabazon in *The Claverings*.) The book also examines the conflict between the rival claims of tradition and family loyalty versus the self-made world of Victorian liberal expansion, exemplified in Daniel Thwaite. (Fred Neville faced the same dilemma in *An Eye for an Eye*.) This was a constant element in Trollope's thought. There is also violence, when the countess tries to shoot Daniel Thwaite to prevent the marriage. Although the old Earl Lovel is one of Trollope's few totally evil characters, the others are, as usual, a mixture of good and bad. The handsome young earl is something of a 'curled darling'.

Shakespeare's influence on Trollope is nowhere more evident than in this novel. Trollope says in Chapter 26 that in devising the plot he was influenced by *Cymbeline*. When Daniel Thwaite and 'The Keswick Poet' [see below] discuss this same play, Daniel refers to the secret marriage between Imogen and Leonatus Posthumous: 'Imogen was a king's daughter, and married a simple gentleman.' Also Francis, first Viscount Lovell, was a supporter of

Richard III against Henry VII and features in Shakespeare's *Richard III*. In Chapter 45 Lady Anna and Daniel Thwaite discuss their future and Daniel makes two references to Shakespeare's plays (*Henry IV Part 1* and *Hamlet*).

Trollope made good use of the knowledge he had gained in the Post Office in London when describing coaches (which he thoroughly disliked) and London coaching inns. As in so many of his novels, life in a country parsonage plays an important role: in this case it is the parsonage of the young Lord Lovel's uncle. 'The Keswick Poet', who is known as a 'great man' and whom Daniel Thwaite visits, is reminiscent of Wordsworth, who lived in Grasmere from 1799 to 1850. (Trollope's mother and brother Tom had once lived in the Lake District and he had visited them there.) Because Trollope had been criticized for his faulty grasp of legal issues in *Orley Farm*, he asked a lawyer about the law of bigamy before writing this novel. The scene in the court is very well done and Trollope, for once echoing Dickens, attacks the slowness and expense of justice [21]. [➤ Trials.]

Daniel Thwaite's Radicalism is made more offensive when Trollope mentions that Thwaite, like an increasing number of young men in his later novels, does not attend church, thereby hinting at a loss of Christian belief. The story has two of Trollope's forceful women, Aunt Julia Lovel and Josephine Murray, the countess. The countess's plan to take Lady Anna to Europe is similar to that in *Sir Harry Hotspur* and 'The Two Heroines of Plumplington'. Conflicts between children and parents over suitable marriages are common in

Trollope's fiction. Like *Cousin Henry, Orley Farm, Mr Scarborough's Family* and *Is He Popenjoy?*, the novel has a dispute over inheritance.

Trollope wrote in his *Autobiography* of Lady Anna's marriage to Daniel that it was 'my wish of course to justify her in doing so, and to carry my readers along with me in my sympathy with her. But every body found fault with me for marrying her to the tailor. What would they have said if I had allowed her to jilt the tailor and marry the good-looking young lord. How much louder, then, would have been the censure! The book was read, and I was satisfied. If I had not told my story well, there would have been no feeling in favour of the young lord. The horror which was expressed to me at the evil thing I had done, in giving the girl to the tailor, was the strongest testimony I could receive of the merits of the story.'

When a quarter of the story had been serialized he defended his plot to his friend, the novelist Lady Wood. In doing so he showed how he created his plot round a basic idea. She had protested at the prospect of Lady Anna's marriage to the tailor. Trollope replied with some tongue-in-cheek exaggeration: 'Of course the girl has to marry the tailor. It is very dreadful, but there was no other way. The story was originated in my mind by an idea I had as to the doubt which would, (or might) exist in a girls [*sic*] mind as to whether she ought to be true to her troth, or true to her leneage [*sic*], when from early circumstances the one had been given in a manner detrimental to the other – and I determined that in such case she ought to be true all through. To make the discrepancy as great as possible I made the girl an Earls [*sic*] daughter, and the betrothed a tailor. All the horrors had to be invented to bring about a condition in which an Earls [*sic*] daughter could become engaged to a tailor without glaring fault on her side.' He also defended the story to another friend with some playful exaggeration: 'Lady Anna is the best novel I ever wrote! Very much!! Quite far away above all others!!! – A lady ought to marry a tailor – if she chanced to fall in love with such a creature, and to promise him, & take his goodness, when she was not a lady. That is all! Will you deny it?'

The novel is one of the best examples of Trollope's 'divided mind', a mind divided between a Tory devotion to past traditions and a landed nobility and a Liberal passion for 'progress'. There are numerous debates in the novels over these two views, in this case especially those between Thwaite and 'The Keswick Poet' [26] and between Thwaite and Sir William Patterson [47]. The debate is finally won by the forces of change because Thwaite wins Lady Anna.

There are a large number of private jokes and reminiscences: he has the Countess Lovel and Lady Anna change their London address to Keppel Street, his own birthplace. He chose as the young Lord Lovel's Christian name Frederic, the name of his second son who, like Daniel Thwaite, emigrated to Australia. He refers to a baronetcy which 'dated back from James I': the Trollope baronetcy only dated from James I's son, Charles I. When Daniel Thwaite thinks about publishing the banns of his marriage to Lady Anna in Bloomsbury Church, Trollope was re-ferring to the parish church where he was baptized. There is also one of the most moving autobiographical passages in Trollope's writings in which he refers to a 'hard-toiling youth who ... lingers on the pavement of a summer night' to listen to the sounds of music floating down from a first-floor balcony.

While Trollope was writing this novel George Eliot was writing *Middlemarch*, also set in the 1830s, at a time when both authors were young and when, as George Eliot said, it was easier to support reform. Not only was Trollope's novel not a success but it involved him in a correspondence with a 'crack-brained lady' who apparently claimed her family's story had been used. As Trollope wrote to his son, Henry, from South Africa, 'My story was pure fiction. I never make use of stories from private life. But I think she is mad.' [➤ Tichborne Case; Yorkshire.]

'The Lady of Launay'. This short story was requested by the novelist and poet R. W. Buchanan for his new magazine, *Light*, on 2 March 1878. Trollope delivered it sixteen days later. It was the lead story in the *belles-lettres* section of the magazine's first issue on 6 April and continued until 11 May. In 1882 it was included in his fifth and last collection of stories, *Why Frau Frohmann Raised Her Prices*. It was published as a book by Harper & Brothers in New York in June or July 1878. If we assume Buchanan had already fixed on 1 April for the first issue of his new magazine, he gave Trollope little notice. He also wrote that while he did not 'presume to dictate ... we strongly desire a tale with great sexual interest'. Ironically, Buchanan had a reputation for disliking 'decadence' in literature. Trollope received £110 from the magazine.

The story, set in a country estate, Launay, in Somerset, is of love and youthful exuberance versus parental opposition in the form of the 'Lady of Launay', an old, crabbed Evangelical lady, Mrs Miles (she is given no Christian name). Her plan is for her younger son, Philip, to marry someone of 'blue blood' – that is, his distant cousin and not her adopted orphan, Bessy Pryor, the daughter of poor friends. In the end, after Bessy has been exiled to France, love triumphs, and old-fashioned views about class and property inevitably give way to more liberal views (a constant thread in Trollope's works). As one character comments, 'Young people and old people very often will not think alike: but it is the young people who generally have their way.' Other novels and stories in which young love conquers the schemes of powerful elderly women are *Framley Parsonage*, *The Belton Estate*, *Ayala's Angel*, *Lady Anna* and 'Alice Dugdale'. In Trollope's fiction, young love often has to fight against parental authority. [➤ Marriage.] Finally, the story is rich in aphorisms and in Somerset dialect.

Lake District. Trollope used the Lake District as a setting for several novels and one short story. He first became acquainted with the area in the 1840s because his sister Cecilia and, from 1841–4, his mother and brother Tom, lived there. It seems that in 1842 he devoted his first holiday leave after moving to Ireland to a visit there. He also spent part of his honeymoon in the district. Fanny Trollope had built a new house in Cumberland, on three acres overlooking the ruins of Brougham Castle, and Tom planted hundreds of trees in the grounds.

The area made an impression on Trollope and he set some scenes in *The Bertrams* there. In 1861 he used the setting of his mother's house when writing 'The Mistletoe Bough'. The next summer, when he was writing *The Small House at Allington*, he recalled drinking out of the celebrated goblet at Eden Hall in Cumberland, which Longfellow commemorated in his poem 'The Luck of Eden Hall'. In the summer of 1863, when he was beginning *Can You Forgive Her?*, he remembered long and happy walks as a young man along the Lake District's 'mountain tracks' [57]. Four and a half years later, in 1868, he began *Sir Harry Hotspur of Humblethwaite* and used Cumberland, so far removed from London and from the Victorian forces of change, as the perfect setting for an old Tory squire. In *Lady Anna*, begun in May 1871, Trollope again set a novel in Cumberland before transferring the action to London. It is interesting that this novel was set in the 1830s, so that the area was associated in his mind with the past. Perhaps the recollection of his mother's love of Romantic poetry inspired him to paint a scene in *Lady Anna* between the Radical, Daniel Thwaite, and 'The Keswick Poet', a 'great man, a poet'. The character is a little reminiscent of Wordsworth, who lived in Grasmere from 1799 to 1850. In 1879, when finishing *Marion Fay*, he sited Castle Hautboy, the seat of Lord Persiflage, 'near Pooly Bridge, just in the county of Westmorland, on an eminence, giving it a grand prospect over Ulleswater [*sic*], which is generally considered to be one of the Cumberland Lakes' [12].

'La Mère Bauche'. See 'Mère Bauche, La'.

Landed Estates. Landed estates feature in almost all Trollope's novels that are set in England or Ireland and also in a few short stories such as 'The O'Conors of Castle Conor' or 'The Lady of Launay'. Every type of estate occurs in his fiction, from the vast holdings of the Palliser and Hartletop families to the smaller estates of squires such as old Squire Vavasor in *Can You Forgive Her?*, and the even smaller holdings of Irish 'squireens' in *The Macdermots of Ballycloran*. Sometimes these estates provide nothing but a setting for part of the plot, as in *Ayala's Angel*. Usually either the maintenance or inheritance of a landed estate is a conspicuous part of the plot. This became increasingly the case in those novels published in the 1870s, for instance *Sir Harry Hotspur of Humblethwaite*, *Is He Popenjoy?*, *An Eye for an Eye*, *Cousin Henry*, *Mr Scarborough's Family* and *The Land-Leaguers*.

A study of land holdings published in the year after Trollope's death found that there were almost 4,000 individuals who owned estates of at least 2,000 acres that in turn produced an annual income of at least £2,000. These people and their families are the 'landed interest' seen so frequently in Trollope's fiction, although some of his landed families own less: Squire Prosper's estate in *Mr Scarborough's Family* 'did not exceed two thousand a year, an income which fifty years since [in the 1830s] was supposed to be sufficient for the moderate wants of a moderate country gentleman' [3].

The political, economic and social power of this landed interest in Victorian Britain was tremendous. Given the number of landed families, they provided a disproportionate number of MPs, clergymen and officers in the military, something reflected in Trollope's fiction. Trollope took a favourable view of their position, and indeed it is hard to see any other aspect of Victorian society in which he took so 'Tory' a view. He frequently emphasizes the traditional opinion that 'such a property ... does not belong altogether to the owner of it' [*Ralph the Heir*, 28]. All those who lived on it, or whose livelihood was derived from it, were owed a 'debt' by the current owner [*The Vicar of Bullhampton*, 68]. Trollope delighted in showing the way in which tenant farmers or agricultural labourers expressed an almost feudal reverence for the owner, or even more so for his heir [*John Caldigate*, 3]. There are often great celebrations when an heir is born or when he reaches his majority because this secures the estate's continuity for another generation [*Doctor Thorne*, 4]. Some owners devote much thought and effort to improving their estates, while others are too idle to make such an effort. There is a good example of each type in *The Belton Estate*, with the idle old Squire Amedroz and his distant hard-working cousin and heir, Will Belton.

Landed estates came with more obligations and produced less income than money gained from either industry or investments. A character in a novel of the late 1860s estimates that he could get a return of about two and a half per cent by investing in land, while other investments would produce about double that percentage [*Ralph the Heir*, 35]. However, the social prestige of land was virtually unchallenged, hence the great desire of

Archdeacon Grantly to build up a landed estate for his son in *The Last Chronicle of Barset*. Farms on landed estates were normally rented to tenants at agreed rents. These arrangements could last for many years, thereby giving landowners a good idea of just what their estates were worth. It is rare that the owner of an estate makes money from sources other than agriculture, although in *Mr Scarborough's Family* the family's wealth comes from the spread of potteries on their land. Political power often went *with* land, particularly when the way in which men voted was public knowledge. Even a great landowner like the old Duke of Omnium is anxious to increase his land holding in *Framley Parsonage* as a way of extending his political influence. Yet landowners also had numerous obligations. They often had to pay agreed amounts as pensions to dowagers or to provide settlements for daughters. Owners were also severely restricted in what they could do with their land by the terms of an entail. The land they owned often brought with it the duty to appoint clergymen to livings and landowners were expected to contribute large sums to the Church and to local charities [➤ Church of England].

Trollope was himself descended from a landed family and he grew up with the story of his father's losing the inheritance of a landed estate in Hertfordshire [➤ Baronets]. As a young man he saw the world of landed estates from the tenant's side when his father was ruined by being unable to pay the rent on land he rented from Lord Northwick. However, he probably got more of his information about landed estates from his friends in fox-hunting society and from personal observation on his many Post Office trips, especially in the West Country. Although he often portrays incompetent or even corrupt landowners, like Mr Sowerby in *Framley Parsonage*, he had great sympathy with the owners of landed estates and in *Barchester Towers* he expressed the hope: 'May it be long before their number diminishes' [21]. [➤ Country Houses; Entails.]

The Land-Leaguers. This novel, his forty-seventh, was the last Trollope wrote. He began dictating to his niece, Florence Bland, in June 1882 after returning from a trip with her to Ireland to gather material and the manuscript is mainly in Florence's hand. He broke off to return to Ireland and stayed there from 11 August to early September 1882. He began writing again on 2 September. Trollope had completed forty-eight out of a planned sixty chapters by the time of his stroke on 3 November 1882. Henry Trollope used his father's notes to add a very brief statement to explain what would have happened to the main characters. Trollope had first offered the manuscript to George Bentley for £400 for serialization in *Temple Bar*, or £1,100 for the entire copyright, but Bentley declined. He then offered serialization rights to the weekly paper *Life* and agreed, for the first time since writing *Framley Parsonage*, to its starting publication before he had finished the book. It ran from 16 November 1882 to 4 October 1883. The incomplete story was then published in three volumes by Chatto & Windus in October 1883. They had offered £600 but agreed with Henry Trollope to pay £480 for the incomplete manuscript.

The last novel which Trollope wrote was, like the first, about Ireland.

It also rivals *The Macdermots of Bally-cloran* for the designation of his most depressing novel. *The Land-Leaguers* lacks the sparkle and occasional satire one associates with most of his other works. It is filled with violence, hatred, unpleasant characters and cross-grained lovers set against a background of terrorism. He was deeply distressed at the changes that had swept over his beloved Ireland. One should add that his spirits were not helped by his declining health. Had he lived to complete the book, its tone might have been lightened.

It was begun in the month following two momentous events in the increasingly difficult relations between the government and Ireland. The Irish Nationalist leader, Charles Stewart Parnell, had been imprisoned in October 1881 for incendiary speeches. These were in connection with his Land League, which encouraged tenants to refuse to pay rents by employing the 'boycotting' strategy. He was released from gaol on 2 May 1882. On 6 May, terrorists murdered Lord Frederick Cavendish and Thomas Burke in Dublin's Phoenix Park. They had been sent as the new Chief Secretary and Under-Secretary. Few events horrified Victorian England as much as the butchery of these two admirable men. [For Trollope's tribute to Lord Frederick, ➤Chapter 39.] Behind all this was a history of Fenian terrorism dating back to the 1870s and a variety of terrorist acts in England. Many Englishmen unfairly blamed Parnell for the violence.

In Trollope's second novel, *The Kellys and the O'Kellys*, the trial of Daniel O'Connell forms the background. A few years later Trollope said in his *Examiner* articles on Ireland

that 'when there is another O'Connell in Ireland, we may again expect political agitation'. Now nationalists in Ireland had found an effective new leader in Parnell. The great irony is that during the 1870s Parnell had been living in Trollope's childhood home at No. 16, Keppel Street. Also Parnell's mistress, Mrs O'Shea, was the daughter of Trollope's close friend Emma, Lady Wood, whom he had known through fox-hunting in Essex before her death in 1879. Lady Wood had been a novelist and, like Trollope, had been published by Chapman & Hall for whom her husband had been a reader. Trollope had frequently stayed with the Woods. It is not known if Trollope knew any of this about Parnell. However, Trollope may have had information from his close friend and whist partner, W. E. Forster, who had been Chief Secretary until his resignation shortly before the Phoenix Park murders.

The novel has two strands. The first is solely concerned with Ireland and begins when terrorists flood a valuable field of a Protestant landlord, Philip Jones. His ten-year-old son Florian sees the act but is made to keep silent by the terrorists' threats; the child has also become a Catholic and his oath to the terrorists is supported by his priest. Boycotting, intimidation and murder increase, despite the efforts of a police detective, who falls in love with one of Mr Jones's daughters. Finally Florian agrees to tell what he knows but when Jones is taking him to court the boy is shot dead by a terrorist. Finally, after more murders, the tide turns, the boycotting of the Jones family ends and it appears a trial will at last be held.

The book's second strand concerns

two Americans, Gerald O'Mahony and his daughter, Rachel [5]. Gerald is an Irish American and a republican nationalist who has earned his living by lecturing on Irish issues. He is a kindly windbag and with his theoretical knowledge reminds one of Senator Gotobed in *The American Senator*. Rachel is an accomplished opera singer. She falls in love with Jones's elder son, Frank, but leaves for London in search of fame and riches. There she is pursued by her dreadful manager, a Jew named Mahomet M. Moss. Her father is returned as MP for an Irish constituency. Rachel quarrels with Frank, accepts and then rejects the proposal of Lord Castlewell, loses her voice, fends off Moss by stabbing him with a small dagger and is finally reunited with Frank Jones. In due course her father tires of the Commons and applies for the Chiltern Hundreds. In Henry Trollope's 'postscript' we are told that the two couples would have been married and that the murderer of Florian Jones would have been hanged.

The novel was Trollope's contribution to the most debated topic of the 1880s. The whole of one chapter [41] is devoted to 'the political circumstances of the day' and reminds one of the chapter in *The Three Clerks* that was in fact a lecture on the Civil Service. The book is overloaded with moral outrage and marked by an overwhelming sadness. There are similarities to the crimes, trials and executions of terrorists of which people were reading in 1882, and one horrific real murder is actually incorporated into the story [47]. Trollope was furious with Liberal legislation that allowed rents in Ireland to be set not by market forces but by civil servants. He

announces that the book was written to attack the new land law: 'It cannot be denied that the promoters of the Land Laws are weak, and that the disciples of the Land-league are strong. In order that the truth of this may be seen and made apparent, the present story is told' [41]. One assumes Trollope would have eventually broken with the Liberals because of Gladstone's passion for Irish Home Rule.

Several favourite Trollopian themes occur. Three chapters [9–11] are devoted to fox-hunting. When dealing with Catholics he is unusually hostile. There are three priests: one is bad, one neutral, and one good. The most likeable of the three is named Father Giles, recalling the lovable priest in 'Father Giles of Ballymoy'. As in *The Macdermots of Ballycloran*, there are differences between the parish priest and his curates over politics. Trollope balanced this unfavourable view of Catholic priests by denouncing one 'bigoted Protestant' clergyman.

This novel also develops the theme of the Anglo-American relationship, and with it, Anglo-American marriages, in both of which fields Trollope was something of an expert. This is seen not just in Frank Jones's courting of Rachel O'Mahony but in the character of her father, Gerald O'Mahony. Trollope also devotes much attention to the Fenian and Land-Leaguers' dependence on Irish-American money.

This is the only novel in which Trollope developed the character of a child, although a religious conversion at the age of ten is rather questionable. He could have made more of his tragic murder: Dickens would have had his readers weeping aloud. Trollope continued his attack on barristers and Utopian reformers. Mahomet M. Moss is one of Trollope's most stereotyped Jews, although he is not without some redeeming qualities. Unusually, Moss uses the word 'mistress' and the dialogue between him and Rachel O'Mahony is on occasion decidedly improper by Victorian standards. In making Rachel O'Mahony a singer he may have thought of his niece, Beatrice Trollope, who was a well-known amateur singer. He may have garnered details about the worlds of opera and theatre from his friend, the composer Arthur Sullivan.

There are several personal references and private jokes. In what proved to be his last fox-hunting scene, appropriately set in Ireland where he had first ridden to hounds, he gives to the MFH of the Galway Hounds, Tom Daly, a huntsman named Barney Smith. Barney was the Irishman who had for many years been Trollope's own groom [➤ Servants]. Rachel recalls Frank Jones's reading *Paradise Lost* aloud, which she found 'very dull'. Trollope had read the same epic to his wife and niece during the winter of 1881 [➤ Milton, John]. He also has Gerald O'Mahony quote from Henry Taylor's verse play, *Philip van Artevelde* (1834) which Trollope had so admired in his youth. A reference to a Newfoundland dog recalls happy boyhood memories. We are also given a final Trollopian self-portrait when Rachel O'Mahony points out 'a cross-looking old gentleman of sixty, who was scolding a porter violently'. Almost all Trollope's travels saw him involved in arguments with porters.

Since the novel was published after Trollope's death, reviewers tried to treat it kindly. Several observed that it provided excellent sketches of the misery and violence in Ireland at the time. For those, it is still of value. Yet as the *Spectator* said, in spite of 'humorous, easy, clever dialogue' the novel is 'a disappointment'.

'The Last Austrian Who Left Venice'. This short story, written between 8 and 14 December 1866 for publication in *Good Words* in January 1867, was included in Trollope's third collection, *Lotta Schmidt and Other Stories*, published later that same year. Trollope had visited Venice in 1855 and between then and December 1866 he went to Italy five times.

The story is set in the spring and early summer of 1866 in Venice where Captain Hubert von Vincke is a young Austrian officer. (Ironically, had a position in the Post Office not materialized, Trollope himself might well have become an Austrian officer.) He is a friend of Carlo Pepé, a lawyer, and is invited to his home where he meets Carlo's widowed mother and his sister Nina, with whom he falls in love. At the same time Carlo is helping the anti-Austrian forces conspiring to add Venice to the new 'United Kingdom of Italy'. [For Trollope's views on unification ➤ Italy.] When told of the engagement, Carlo, as head of the family, is furious and forbids the marriage. Carlo leaves Venice to fight with Garibaldi and Nina promises that she will not think of marriage until Carlo returns in victory or dies in the effort to secure Italian unity. Within months Austria abandons Venice; Nina, who is now free to marry von Vincke, goes to Verona where she finds her lover in hospital with an arm amputated as a result of the fighting. When Venice is fully integrated into the new kingdom, they are married. They leave for Trieste, still in Austrian hands, to make Captain von Vincke the last Austrian who left Venice.

When writing this story, Trollope not only drew on his first-hand knowledge of Italian life, but on Englishmen's devotion to Italian unification. He used the story – as he did to a lesser degree 'The Man Who Kept His Money in a Box' – to support the cause of Italian unification: in his first sentence he referred to the 'thraldom' in which the Austrian Empire allegedly held Venice, although he agreed he had 'never heard that the Austrians were cruel in what they did'. He had used the same word 'thraldom' about Venice when completing *The Last Chronicle of Barset* [70] a few months earlier.

As so often, he had a private joke when he gave the Italian family the name of Pepé. This was the name of the Italian revolutionary, General Guglielmo Pepe (1783–1855), who had been a friend of his parents in the 1820s. The younger Trollopes had looked forward to the general's visits because he always brought them gifts of oranges and figs.

The Last Chronicle of Barset. This, Trollope's nineteenth novel, is the sixth and final volume in the Barsetshire series and was written between 21 January and 15 September 1866. It was published in thirty-two 6*d.* weekly parts by Smith, Elder between 1 December 1866 and 6 July 1867. It was then published by George Smith in two volumes, the first appearing in March 1867, the second in July. Trollope received £3,000. Trollope, who had failed to persuade Millais to do

the illustrations, was not entirely happy with those by G. H. Thomas and commented: 'Mrs Proudie is not quite my Mrs Proudie.' In fact she looks somewhat like Queen Victoria, for whom Thomas had undertaken several commissions. Trollope made an unsuccessful attempt to dramatize *The Last Chronicle of Barset* as a play, *Did He Steal It?*, but it was rightly rejected by the theatrical manager who had first requested it.

It was almost three years from the time that Trollope completed the fifth Barsetshire novel, *The Small House at Allington*, until he began the final one. In those thirty-five months he wrote seven other novels, including the first in the Palliser series. He was also involved in three important new ventures: launching a new career as a writer of anonymous novels, establishing the *Fortnightly Review* and writing many essays for the *Pall Mall Gazette*. He was, of course, still a senior official in the Post Office. Thus *The Last Chronicle of Barset* is a product of his most hectic and most productive period. He also wrote it during a period of intense political debate about the Second Reform Act, which many people saw as a dangerous 'leap in the dark'.

Politics were becoming very important to Trollope: he was anxious to find a seat in the House of Commons; he was keen to devote more time to political essays; and he was now involved in his new series centred on politics. This is one part of the background to his decision to wind up the Barsetshire series and marks a major shift in his life, symbolized by his resignation from the Post Office the following year, 1867. Not only was Trollope himself changing but early-Victorian

England, and with it the Church of England, was adapting to new times. Doubt was becoming more fashionable and ecclesiastical battles more fierce. All this led to his sad decision to bring Barsetshire to an end.

The action in *The Last Chronicle of Barset* begins about two and a half years after the end of *The Small House at Allington*. It is set in the mid-1860s, certainly no later than 1865 as Mrs Proudie and Archdeacon Grantly have a dispute about the American Civil War. Mrs Proudie makes plain her support for the Northerners, while the archdeacon sees that the Southerners were 'Christian gentlemen' [47]. This is a good illustration of the way in which Trollope was willing to allow his characters their own opinions: normally the archdeacon's views are closer to Trollope's but the author well knew which side his character would choose and it would not be his. The discarded title, 'The Story of a Cheque for Twenty Pounds and of the Mischief Which it Did', gives a hint of the main plot of *The Last Chronicle of Barset*. The novel, like *Cousin Henry*, is unusual in starting *in medias res*. It begins as minor characters discuss the plot: did the impoverished and eccentric Perpetual Curate of Hogglestock, the Reverend Josiah Crawley, steal a cheque for £20, and if not, how did it get into his account? Crawley is driven almost insane and Bishop Proudie tries to force him out of his parish. All ends well as Crawley is cleared and given the living of St Ewold's, worth £350 a year. There are several subsidiary plots, of which the love affair between Crawley's daughter Grace and Archdeacon Grantly's son Henry is the most import-

ant. In addition there is John Eames's renewed offer to Lily Dale; the defeat of Mrs Proudie at the hands of Crawley and her subsequent death; the vulgar world of the Dobbs Broughtons and Van Sievers; and the romantic attachments of the artist Conway Dalrymple. The last two are set in London.

For the main character, Josiah Crawley, Trollope went back to the fourth Barsetshire novel, *Framley Parsonage*. Crawley has several traits in common with the novelist's father. Some of the best analysis of Crawley's near-madness comes from his wife, Mary. Her assessment of her husband [41] bears several parallels with Fanny Trollope's private letters about her husband. Trollope was using not only his own memories of growing up in a disturbed household, but many subsequent years of reflection about his father's sad fate. Trollope's own life for over two decades had been one of expanding prosperity and success, but he never lost that fear of sudden failure and a sympathy for those who, like his own father, had failed despite considerable abilities. The twisted combination of success and failure had marked many of his novels from the late 1850s to the mid-1860s. *The Bertrams* had begun with that curious 'sermon' about the Victorian worship of success. *Framley Parsonage* showed what could happen to a young clergyman whose life had been one easy triumph after another. *The Small House at Allington* had depicted John Eames who, like Trollope himself, had cast off a prolonged 'hobbledehoyhood' to find success and prosperity. Trollope's brooding on his own success and his father's failure produced a sympathetic portrait of the Reverend Josiah

Crawley, a good man soured by a life without luck.

Crawley is always full of envy, but also full of pride in his own intellectual attainments: when he sees his old friend Dean Arabin, he remembers that the wealthy dean knows less Hebrew than the poor perpetual curate. Crawley admits that he suffered from pride and obstinacy and Trollope well understood that the fiercest pride comes after, not before, a fall. At one point Crawley says, 'My poor head suffers so; – so many grievous thoughts distract me, that I am like a child, and know not what I do . . . I am – mad at times' [19]. [➤ Insanity.] His particular misery was, as he explained to a London solicitor, that he had to endure the 'sufferings of poverty' and at the same time 'those feelings of honour to which poverty is seldom subject' [32]. Of course here Trollope is explaining that Crawley was a gentleman by birth, by education, and by his rank as a clergyman. It is not only Crawley who knows this but the poor bricklayers among whom he labours: he is one of the few Barsetshire clergymen whom we see in his parochial work. The grooms at inns immediately know that he is a gentleman and of course the final, unanswerable confirmation comes in that oft-cited and much-admired scene in which the exonerated but still embittered Crawley tells the archdeacon that in the light of the approaching marriage between their children, he wished that both fathers stood 'on more equal grounds'. That unimpeachable authority, the archdeacon, replies: 'We stand on the only perfect level . . . We are both gentlemen' [83]. *The Last Chronicle of Barset*, like the vast majority of Trollope's novels, is always concerned with the question of what it means to be a gentleman.

Trollope's sympathy for Crawley's plight was strengthened because while he was writing the novel he too was involved in ecclesiastical controversy. His *Clergymen of the Church of England* had been subjected to a fierce review by Henry Alford, the Dean of Canterbury, in the new *Contemporary Review* of which Alford was the first editor. Trollope had asked if deans really did much work and, worse, had attacked the great disparity of income among clergymen in which some men earned fortunes and others, like Crawley, pittances. This had set off a controversy in the Church newspaper, *The Guardian*, in which one poor curate wrote in Trollope's defence.

This controversy also makes it seem likely that Trollope must have sought the advice of some knowledgeable clerical friend for details of the complicated procedure used to remove a clergyman from his living. (When he wrote *The Vicar of Bullhampton* two years later he asked a clerical friend for information on another point of Church law.) By making Crawley a perpetual curate, and not a vicar or rector, Trollope symbolized his lowly position. It is also noticeable that Trollope stresses the role of the rural dean, Dr Tempest. The office of rural dean, generally associated with High Church, was revived in the early-Victorian era, particularly in those real West Country dioceses upon which Barsetshire was based. It is therefore in character that the fierce Evangelical, Mrs Proudie, is quite scathing about the rural dean.

The love affair between Major Henry Grantly and Crawley's daughter Grace provides an opportunity for Trollope to discuss the relations between a father and his son. Henry is determined to marry Grace in spite of the scandal clinging to her father's name. By this time he is a widower and has retired from the army, having won the Victoria Cross in India. Major Grantly comes into conflict with his father over his plans. Tensions between fathers and sons were to form an increasing role in Trollope's fiction as his own sons were now approaching maturity. Like the archdeacon, Trollope delighted in building up a goodly inheritance for his two sons. [➤ Fathers and Sons.]

Like a composer writing the last movement of a symphony, Trollope brings back characters from all the previous Barsetshire novels: from *The Warden* comes Mr Harding and the Grantlys; from *Barchester Towers*, the Proudies and the Arabins; from *Doctor Thorne*, Miss Dunstable, now the wife of Dr Thorne; from *Framley Parsonage*, Mark Robarts and Lady Lufton; from *The Small House at Allington*, Lily Dale, John Eames and Adolphus Crosbie. Many other characters appear, including Squire Dale, Frank Gresham, Lady Julia De Guest, and Wilfred Thorne and his sister Monica. The only major characters who do not appear are Mr Slope, although Mrs Proudie remembers him [18], and the Stanhopes. One wonders why Trollope did not take the opportunity of Eames's hurried trip to Italy to give us another glimpse of Madeline Stanhope. Even minor characters who do not reappear are alluded to, such as Sowerby, the villain from *Framley Parsonage*, who is remembered favourably by the archdeacon's gamekeeper. Two important characters had died since *The Small House at Allington*: Earl De

Guest and Lady Alexandrina Crosbie (née De Courcy).

For many readers the frustrated love of Eames – no longer a 'hobbledehoy' – for Lily Dale almost equals Mr Crawley's plight. When *The Last Chronicle of Barset* begins, three years have passed since Crosbie jilted 'dear Lily'. With the death of Crosbie's wife, Lady Alexandrina, he is free to make another proposal to the woman he jilted but still loves. Eames, of course, also remained in love with her. Trollope knew of the widespread demand that he allow Eames to marry his beloved, yet a month before he began writing the novel, he told a young American woman – after whom he claims he had named Lily – that if her namesake married anyone it would be Eames. As 'her literary father' he thought it unlikely that Lily would ever marry.

The subsidiary plots in London centre on Eames but have moved to a higher sphere than those in *The Small House at Allington*. London is viewed through the excited eyes of Lily when she visits the city. There is an even stranger visitor when Crawley comes up to see a lawyer and this forms a parallel to Mr Harding's similar mission in *The Warden*. We learn that this trip cost the hard-pressed Crawley £1 even though he took the cheapest third-class ticket and allowed himself 7s. for a night in an hotel [32]. The solicitor, Toogood, is a cousin of Mrs Crawley and there is also a family connection with Eames. We know we are going to like Toogood when later he denounces one of Trollope's great hates, the fashionable *service à la Russe*, and instead offers Eames a plain meal of mutton and port 'such as you don't get every day in your life' [40].

Toogood is Trollope's most favourable portrait of a solicitor. [➤ Food.]

There are constant echoes of the earlier Barsetshire novels. When Mrs Proudie and the archdeacon have their final dispute, the archdeacon, from his favourite place on the rug, recalls the happy days when clergymen could play whist. Those with good memories may recall a scene in *The Warden* in which the archdeacon and other clergymen indulge in Trollope's favourite card game. In all Mark Robarts's attempts to help Crawley, both are conscious of how the perpetual curate had to admonish the wealthy but wayward vicar in *Framley Parsonage*. When the archdeacon and his wife recall how long it took his father, the bishop, to die, neither mentions what will be remembered by almost any reader of *Barchester Towers*: that this delay kept the son from 'inheriting' his father's mitre. Mr Harding's death has many parallels with that of his friend, Bishop Grantly, in *Barchester Towers* when the warden had prayed, 'Oh that our last moments may be as innocent and peaceful.' Mr Harding's prayerful wish is granted and his death scene is one of Trollope's finest pieces of writing [81]. Perhaps the true test of the real Trollopian is to try to read that chapter with a dry eye. The choice of the mildly archaic phrase 'ever and anon', in 'ever and anon his daughters could see that he was praying', is a perfect touch for our last sight of Trollope's one fictional saint. The archdeacon pays him this tribute: 'He lacked guile, and he feared God – and a man who does both will never go far astray.' The archdeacon now examines his own spiritual state, as he did when his father died. At Mr Harding's funeral, there is a rare reappearance of his devoted old friend Bunce, who had been so prominent in *The Warden*.

In *Barchester Towers* women played a crucial, though often unnoticed role. This is also the case – though perhaps not quite to the same degree – in *The Last Chronicle of Barset*. There are three major occasions when a married couple disagree: the Crawleys debate how he should defend himself; the Grantlys debate how to treat their lovesick son, Henry; the Proudies debate how the diocese should be ruled. When Grace Crawley says, 'Mamma manages generally to have her way at last' [23], she is only making a rare, open expression of what is a frequent occurrence in Trollope's fiction. Mrs Crawley and Mrs Grantly are wise enough to know how to guide their husbands without hectoring them. The advice that these two ladies give always stirs the reader's sympathy, yet both women are always careful not to challenge the formal authority of the husband. Crawley says that his wife is right and he goes to see Toogood and even admits that she would be the better one to go, but he knows that he dare not disregard the Victorian convention that only the man goes into the world to do business. (And, if she went someone should go with her, and this would mean two tickets.) If his wife had openly supplanted him, she would become a 'she wolf' like Mrs Proudie [32]. That lady's final battle with her husband is one of the great moments of *The Last Chronicle* and because she has openly flouted his authority and made a fool of him before another important clergyman, her mistake proves, quite literally, fatal.

In a sense Trollope had reached a

dead end with Mrs Proudie: once her husband had rebelled against her tyranny, what could she do? She has really no other effective exit than to die. Yet even here, faithful to his belief that a character should not be seen as all black, Trollope shows one noble aspect of her character. She had never told her husband of her heart condition although it would surely have been a potent weapon to have used against him. Trollope openly tells his readers that he may have been too harsh in his painting of Mrs Proudie. In the final scene her defences are gone and our sympathy increases when she calls her husband 'Tom' for the only time in the Barsetshire series. Still, we never learn her Christian name. She is always 'Mrs Proudie'. [➤ Names, Use of; Women.]

There has long been an oft-repeated literary anecdote of Trollope's taking the decision to 'kill' Mrs Proudie. The normal version comes from the *Autobiography*. According to this, he was working on the novel at the Athenaeum club and overheard two clergymen muttering about how often Mrs Proudie appeared in his fiction. Announcing who he was, he said: 'As to Mrs Proudie, I will go home and kill her before the week is over.' However, some earlier versions of the story which Trollope told have survived in letters and diaries, and there are strong grounds for arguing that he exaggerated the story. [For a fuller discussion, see Mullen, 458–60.] It is difficult to see how he could write a *last* 'chronicle' without bringing her to a sudden end. Trollope admits he missed Mrs Proudie and that he 'lived much in company with her ghost', but he knew that the domination of a 'would-be priestess' in the Church of England could not be continued, at least not in his century.

The Barsetshire series has three crucial characters who appear from the second novel onwards: Mr Harding, Mrs Proudie and Archdeacon Grantly. Mr Harding and Mrs Proudie are opposites: the one a gentle saint, the other a fierce virago, and they mark the boundaries of the Barsetshire world. Their characters, however, do not develop; one may sometimes see a slightly different aspect, but essentially they remain the same. It is only the third figure, the archdeacon – a man with so many similarities to his creator – who develops, and he does so in this novel. Some of Trollope's most subtle analysis of character emerges in the archdeacon's behaviour in *The Last Chronicle of Barset*. He had already softened considerably from the time of his hectoring of the bedesmen in *The Warden*. We see this softening in the way in which he behaves when discussing with his wife the problem of Henry's obstinacy. The genuine Christianity beneath the archdeacon's 'worldly' bluster also emerges as he realizes that he cannot say his prayers with anger in his heart towards his son. Trollope cleverly makes him more human and less remote by having his wife address him as 'dear' and 'dearest' rather than as 'Archdeacon'. (This, of course, reminds us of Mrs Proudie's final appeal to 'Tom'.) Trollope seems particularly concerned to show every good quality of the archdeacon: we see him fall under the spell of Grace Crawley and, in his parish work, we see his kindness to a gamekeeper and his pastoral concern for the man's sick wife.

As so often, Mr Harding brings out the noble and the religious strain – the unworldly strain – in the archdeacon. When the dying Mr Harding asks him to bestow his living on Crawley, the archdeacon replies by kissing his father-in-law's hand. There is another wonderful touch when Crawley is at last persuaded to put on a new coat and dine at Plumstead. After much memorable banter, the archdeacon finally conquers Crawley by presenting him with a much annotated copy of old Bishop Grantly's sermons. This not only recalls that gentle old man to the reader's memory but allows Trollope to comment delightfully: 'The Archdeacon had hit his bird on both wings' [83]. With that final happy shot, Trollope moves on to his emotional farewell to his 'beloved county'.

There are fewer personal allusions in *The Last Chronicle of Barset* than in most of Trollope's novels. He must have suspected that the Barsetshire series was his best hope for literary immortality and this must have imposed a less facetious manner. Even so, his most loyal readers would have noticed that among the portraits painted by Conway Dalrymple is one of Lady Glencora Palliser, who was already becoming Trollope's favourite heroine. Few could readily understand two private references. The first is about another painting, a version of 'The Three Graces'. This refers to the fact that his wife and her sisters had been called 'The Three Graces' in their Yorkshire home. The second occurs when Lady Julia De Guest asks Eames to get her spectacles at Dollands, where Trollope got his own massive collection of glasses.

The novel met with warm praise, though some critics understandably disliked the sub-plot about the London artist, Conway Dalrymple.

The final words of the novel, 'that this shall be The Last Chronicle of Barset', upset many reviewers. 'The general effect of this announcement,' said the *Spectator*, 'was disconcerting.' One could no longer meet 'almost the best known and most typical ... fellow-countrymen again'. This reviewer had a friend who mourned: 'What am I to do without ever meeting Archdeacon Grantly? He was one of my best and most intimate friends ... Life has lost one of its principal alleviations.' This is a marvellous example of the way in which Trollope's contemporaries viewed his fiction as a virtual dramatized documentary of their own age. In his *Autobiography* Trollope wrote of this final Barsetshire story, 'Taking it as a whole, I regard this as the best novel I have written.' For once Trollope's critical judgement of his own work was right.

La Vendée. See *Vendée, La*.

Lawyers. It is hardly surprising that lawyers are present in the overwhelming majority of Trollope's novels when one remembers the numbers of landowners, the preponderance of the middle classes, the amount of litigation, the incidence of crime and subsequent trials and the many questions over wills, entails and inheritances in his fiction. Lawyers are one of the three most important groups in his fiction, together with doctors and clergymen. All types of lawyers are represented and their morals are as varied as those of the other characters, although hard things are often said about lawyers in general. In *Mr Scarborough's Family* one character gives a solicitor the nickname of 'the Devil', but by doing so Trollope adds, 'she had not intended to signify any defalcation from honesty more than ordinary in lawyers' offices' [33]. As he comments in *Miss Mackenzie*, 'the common repute which we all give to attorneys in general is exactly opposite to that which every man gives to his own attorney' [17]. Lawyers are often attacked because of their alleged reputation for greed: in 'Malachi's Cove', 'though the Camelford attorney took Mally's money, he could do nothing for her'.

Lawyers in Trollope's time, as today, were divided between barristers and solicitors. Trollope's father was a barrister who, after a distinguished start, ruined his career by his irascible temperament and habit of telling solicitors they were 'blockheads'. The young Trollope would have had an opportunity to observe the legal world when he spent some of his summers in his father's dreary chambers in Lincoln's Inn. It is certainly noticeable that a great number of the scenes involving lawyers take place there, often in chambers apparently modelled closely on his father's [➤ *Orley Farm*, 12, and 'The Spotted Dog'].

There are fewer barristers than solicitors in Trollope's writing, but the barristers are often more colourful and more roundly attacked. Frank Greystock was 'intent on mastering the mysteries of some much-complicated legal case . . . in order that he might present it to a jury enveloped in increased mystery' [*The Eustace Diamonds*, 13]. There are bitter attacks on barristers in *Orley Farm*, in which Mr Chaffanbrass is said to be happy because he had managed 'that the truth might be made to look like falsehood . . . If he had done that, he had succeeded in the occupation of his

life' [71]. Trollope's first barrister, Mr Allewinde in *The Macdermots of Ballycloran*, is the model for many that followed. He is a fierce cross-questioner and delights in tearing into witnesses. (The Irish barrister who attempted to undermine Trollope's evidence when he was a prosecution witness in a case of theft [➤ Witnesses] made playful allusions to the character of Allewinde. The experience of that trial gave Trollope great sympathy for any person being cross-questioned and this is evident in almost all the eleven courtroom scenes in his novels.)

Nevertheless, Trollope admired the skill of barristers such as the formidable Chaffanbrass, or the slightly less fearsome Joram. Trollope frequently speculates on the morality of a barrister defending someone he knows to be guilty. In *The Bertrams* he tells us that Sir Henry Harcourt distinguishes himself 'not a little by his success in turning white into black' [12] and later on he refers to the law as 'useful only for assisting mankind to cheat each other' [17]. The longest discussion of this subject is in *The New Zealander*, in which Mr Allewinde reappears with only one 'e' in his name [➤ *Orley Farm*, 56].

In some of the novels Trollope enjoys describing the relations between an elderly lawyer and a younger one in his chambers: this is the case in *Phineas Finn* in which Phineas is in Mr Low's chambers, and there is a similar relationship with another young Irishman in London in *Castle Richmond*. A few of Trollope's barristers have the title of sarjeant, for instance Sarjeant Bluestone in *Lady Anna*. Sarjeants were the highest rank of barristers. Since no more were appointed after 1868, they were becoming a scarce commodity by the time of his later novels. Trollope seemed to delight in depicting lawyers who reached the highest political office: Sir Abraham Haphazard in *The Warden*, Sir Henry Harcourt in *The Bertrams* and Sir Thomas Underwood in *Ralph the Heir* were all Tories who held the office either of Solicitor General or Attorney General, while Sir Gregory Grogram in *Phineas Redux* is a Liberal Solicitor General and Sir William Patterson in *Lady Anna* is a Whig holder of the same office. Judges occur in several novels: in *Orley Farm* (a novel filled with litigation) there is much about the admirable Judge Staveley and his family, while in *John Caldigate* [54] there is a particularly interesting but hostile portrait of a judge contemplating whether or not a sentence is just.

Solicitors – or attorneys as Trollope frequently calls them – are a more varied lot and are generally treated with greater regard. Some are not particularly honest: Finney in *The Warden* is a good example of such a man, and so is Samuel Dockwrath in *Orley Farm*. In 'Mrs Brumby', Messrs Badget and Blister take up Mrs Brumby's fraudulent suit against an editor who is told, 'They'll take up any case ... however hopeless, and work it with superhuman energy, on the mere chance of getting something out of the defendant.' Needless to say the £10 Mrs Brumby got in an out-of-court settlement all went to them. In another short story, the mock-medieval 'The Gentle Euphemia', Trollope has Lord Mountfidget threaten his beloved's father, 'I will set the lawyers at thee, and ruin thee with many costs' – a threat still heard today. There are, however, several solicitors who are

men of great honesty: Thomas Toogood in *The Last Chronicle of Barset* is a superb example, as he is prepared to spend his time and money to secure justice for the irascible Mr Crawley with little hope of either payment or thanks. Mr Grey in *Mr Scarborough's Family* is another solicitor who is an honest man surrounded by dishonesty, and in *Cousin Henry* Nicholas Apjohn's persistence leads to the uncovering of Cousin Henry's duplicity. While some solicitors prepare cases for trials in such novels as *John Caldigate* and *The Three Clerks*, in *Orley Farm* Dockwrath acts more like a private detective. Frequently they are involved in assisting the gentry with their complicated legal and financial affairs, whether in cases connected with wills and entails, (*Mr Scarborough's Family*), or family settlements (*Ralph the Heir*). The loyalty of a firm of old family solicitors is to the family as a whole rather than to any one member of it, and this is perhaps best illustrated by Mr Camperdown in *The Eustace Diamonds*. The firm of Slow and Bideawhile – a superb example of Trollope's use of silly names to describe and poke fun at lawyers – are family solicitors in about half-a-dozen novels, including *The Way We Live Now*.

Solicitors did not rank as high as barristers in society largely because they were usually not university men but were trained through apprenticeship. When the solicitor Mr Finney was invited to Mrs Proudie's reception, his arrival was 'much to the dismay of many who had never met him in a drawing-room before' [10]. In *The Vicar of Bullhampton* Miss Marrable, one of Trollope's redoubtable old Tory spinsters, always 'addressed an attorney by letter as Mister, raising up her eyebrows when appealed to on the matter, and explaining that an attorney is not an esquire' [9]. Josiah Crawley, annoyed at having to ask a solicitor for help, takes comfort in the fact that as a clergyman he has a higher 'rank' than his long-suffering cousin and solicitor, Toogood [*The Last Chronicle of Barset*, 32]. Normally both barristers and solicitors appear in Trollope's fiction to assist or annoy the main characters at critical moments. It is comparatively rare for them to be the main characters or even to appear throughout a novel. Exceptions, other than Phineas Finn, include Sir Thomas Underwood in *Ralph the Heir* and Sir Henry Harcourt in *The Bertrams*, but then the emphasis is generally on their life away from their legal work. In Nicholas Apjohn in *Cousin Henry*, Trollope comes closest to creating a hero who is also a solicitor. While John Grey in *Mr Scarborough's Family* is not a hero, among the major characters he is perhaps the most honourable.

Trollope was frequently attacked for mistakes in legal technicalities. In *Phineas Finn* he asks pity for the 'poor fictionist' who commits errors when describing 'those terrible meshes of the Law' [29]. In an effort to avoid mistakes, he began asking his many lawyer friends at his clubs for help with these problems and in one case, *The Eustace Diamonds*, a barrister friend even wrote one legal opinion for him [25].

The minimum standard fee for a lawyer was 6s. 8d. or one-third of a pound: hence references to a lawyer's 'six-and-eightpences' [➤ Money].

Lectures. Lectures were an important part of nineteenth-century life and in *North America* Trollope devotes a great deal of attention to the way in which they dominated it, particularly in Boston. He regarded them as 'industrious idleness'. However, for famous authors they could be a profitable sideline; among nineteenth-century novelists, Dickens and Thackeray were well known for their lectures or readings. [For Trollope's criticism of Thackeray's lectures, ➤ *Thackeray*, 1, 6.] To Trollope, lectures, like sermons, were often associated with Evangelical crusaders or with earnest proponents of special causes, like Kate Field and her work for women's rights [➤ Feminists]. She was quite successful as a lecturer both in America and in Britain. Lectures occasionally appear in his novels: in *Kept in the Dark* he had America's larger lecture halls in mind when he referred to 'those large Western Halls, full of gas and intelligence' [23]. In *Is He Popenjoy?* he had great sport with the lectures at the Institute for Female Disabilities and with the feminist lecturer, Baroness Banmann, famous for her 'considerable moustache'. In *Orley Farm* various legal luminaries give long lectures to an international congress [17] and in *Framley Parsonage* Harold Smith, MP, gives a lecture in Barchester on Papua and New Guinea, only to have it ruined by Mrs Proudie's noisy interruptions [6].

Trollope's own limited career as a lecturer only began after he had achieved fame through *Framley Parsonage*, and he knew his own limitations. He disliked giving lectures and always feared he would break down before the end. In reply to one invitation he replied, 'to me the labour of preparing a lecture is considerable'. By his standards lectures paid badly: by 1879 he had set his fee at £20 but normally he received a fee of between £10 and £20.

He gave lectures, usually lasting an hour, on issues in which he believed and in order to encourage certain goals, like the advancement of working men through self-education [➤ Working Classes]. He frequently spoke before working-class self-improvement bodies, such as mechanics' institutes, whose committees arranged a variety of lectures and had little money to pay for them. Sometimes he lectured on topics associated with recent trips abroad, such as the Zulus or the Civil War in America. He also jokingly told one correspondent that, when asked to give a lecture, 'I offer to give a radical lecture, or to subscribe £10 – They always take the £10 – saying that the radical lecture is too much for their strength.' Ironically, in 1860 it was he who pushed for a series of lectures for Post Office clerks at St Martin's and got his brother Tom and his friend G. H. Lewes to participate. Trollope himself gave the first lecture on 'The Civil Service as a Profession' in 1861. (He arranged for an abridgement of the lecture to appear in the *Cornhill* and when Rowland Hill protested, he had the entire lecture published, albeit privately.)

We know of nine lectures which Trollope prepared and of these he delivered seven, some more than once. The lecture he delivered more often than any other was that on 'English Prose Fiction as a Rational Amusement', and for this he did a good deal of work: he gave this lecture at least eight times. His first lecture was in 1861; his last, in 1879.

The lectures Trollope delivered, with their place and date of delivery where known, are: 'The Art of Reading' (London, 2 March and 28 November 1876); 'The Civil Service as a Profession' (London, 4 January 1861); 'Higher Education of Women' (1874); 'The Native Races of South Africa', also entitled 'The Zulus and Zululand' or 'The Condition of the Zulu People' (Manchester, 15 November 1878; Nottingham, 23 October 1879; Birmingham, 28 October 1879); 'English Prose Fiction as a Rational Amusement' (Edinburgh, 28 January 1870; Leeds, 17 January 1871; Walsall, 19 January 1871; Stourbridge, 20 January 1871; Melbourne, Australia, 18 December 1871; in addition a letter of April 1870 referred to his giving the lecture four times although one of these may have been on 18 January in Edinburgh); 'Politics as a Study for the Common People' (Leeds, 18 February 1864; Stratford (London), 20 January 1868); 'The Present Condition of the Northern States of the American Union' (30 December 1862; London, 13 January 1863; Bury, 26 January 1864; Leeds, 18 February 1864; Halstead (Essex), 25 February 1864).

One lecture on 'The National Gallery' was never delivered but was published in *St James's Magazine* in September 1861. 'On the Best Means of Extending and Securing an International Law of Copyright' was read out at the 1866 annual meeting of the National Association for the Promotion of Social Science [➤ Boanerges, Lord].

Letters. Letters abound in Trollope's fiction, although as he admitted in one novel, 'It is such an easy mode of writing, and facility is always dangerous' [*Doctor Thorne*, 38]. Almost all the letters he wrote in his novels are entertaining, in contrast to the vast bulk of his own surviving letters, which are brief and businesslike. He never attempted to tell a complete novel in letters because, as he said in a review of a new edition of Richardson's *Clarissa*, it was an outdated and impractical method. The great majority of Trollope's novels contain letters, although there are some that have none or only a few (*The Struggles of Brown, Jones, and Robinson* and *Harry Heathcote of Gangoil*). In one novel, *John Caldigate*, a letter, or more specifically the envelope in which it was sent, turns out to be a vital piece of evidence in releasing an innocent man from gaol. A typical novel, like *Kept in the Dark*, has over a dozen letters although it is one of his shortest works. Certainly Trollope at times overdid the use of letters: *Marion Fay* is a good example of this. They were one of the easiest ways in which an author could provide 'padding' to extend a novel to the length required by the 'three-decker' format. This sometimes meant that a letter was both included and summarized in the narration.

It is important to remember that Trollope lived in the golden age of letter-writing. His own work at the Post Office gave him first-hand knowledge of the importance of letters in English life, an importance difficult to understand today. The introduction of the penny post in 1840 led to a tremendous explosion in letter-writing. Deliveries were so good that two people could, if they lived in large towns or cities, send a letter, get a reply, send a second letter and receive a reply to it – a total of four letters – within a single day for a total cost of 4*d*. (under 2p). One only has to look at the published – let alone the unpublished – correspondence of Victorian luminaries such as Queen Victoria, Newman or Gladstone to see that a

busy and well-educated Victorian with servants to look after the house could read and write several dozen letters a day.

As in most other social matters, the writing, sending and receiving of letters were governed by a widely observed etiquette. A person adhered to the same degree of formality in starting, ending and addressing a letter as in the use of names or in entering or leaving a room. The most formal method – used for almost all condescending letters – was to write in the third person. The best example of this is the short note beginning, 'The Duke of Omnium trusts that Major Poutney will not find it inconvenient to leave Gatherum Castle shortly' [*The Prime Minister*, 27]. Victorians frequently signed their surname as well as their Christian name and this is reflected both in Trollope's practice in his real letters (even to his brother) and in those in his fiction. At times, however, just initials were used: again Trollope followed this practice himself and in *Nina Balatka* he enjoys a private joke in having the Jewish merchant sign himself 'A. T.', just as the novelist did himself. Sometimes initials were used if the letter could be thought in any way compromising [*He Knew He Was Right*, 10]. It was normally considered wrong for a man in writing to a married woman to address her by her first name [*Ralph the Heir*, 53]. It was certainly not unusual for all letters entering a house to be handed to the husband or father, who would – or could – hand them to the addressees. Writing towards the end of his life, Trollope noted the change over the previous fifty to sixty years: girls living at home could by the 1880s send and receive letters at will, without their parents knowing the contents. They were, however, still expected to inform their parents of the correspondence [*Mr Scarborough's Family*, 47]. Trollope offered the wise advice to his readers that they should avoid sending angry letters: write the 'poisoned eloquence' and put it in the drawer [*The Bertrams*, 18]. He did not follow his own advice and frequently his superiors at the Post Office received furious complaints from him made all the more offensive for being put down on paper.

Trollope occasionally liked to have men propose marriage by letter, of which the best-known, and also the best example, is Dr Thorne's proposal to Miss Dunstable [*Framley Parsonage*, 39]. Letters were also useful in allowing Trollope to convey detailed information to the reader, particularly when the letters were from lawyers [*The Eustace Diamonds*, 5]. He often liked to interrupt the text of a letter to give a running commentary on a character's behaviour and at times this can cause confusion, as in *The Kellys and the O'Kellys* [18]. Letters could also cause trouble for a character who might be behaving differently when he is away from home [*An Eye for an Eye*, 2]. Although Trollope did not use letters as much in his short stories, two begin with letters ('The Spotted Dog' and 'Josephine de Montmorenci'). The second of these probably has the highest proportion of letters compared with dialogue and narration of any of Trollope's fiction.

Because of his postal work Trollope often likes to tell the reader when a letter has arrived and whether it was posted in one of his pillar-boxes, and he also likes to settle scores with Sabbatarians by noting that important letters could be delayed if local opinion stopped Sunday deliveries, something that could be done. He also much enjoyed describing the route of a letter until it arrived – if all went well – on someone's breakfast table [*Framley Parsonage*, 5].

Lewes, G. H. (1817–78). Trollope met George Henry Lewes in 1860 at the first of George Smith's *Cornhill* dinners; through him he met George Eliot. Lewes was a self-educated man from a theatrical family who trained to be a physician but gave it up for writing. He studied in Germany and in 1855 published a biography of Goethe. While he tried acting and play-writing, his fame came from his writings on philosophy and science, mainly for journals. He retained a keen interest in the theatre. He was a Radical free-thinker and accepted his wife's liaison with Thornton Hunt, the son of Leigh Hunt. They separated and in 1852 Herbert Spencer introduced him to George Eliot; after 1854 George Eliot and Lewes lived together. (He could not use the 1857 divorce act because he had colluded in his wife's adultery.) Trollope persuaded Lewes to become the first editor of the *Fortnightly Review*. Although he wrote two novels, his most important book was *Problems of Life and Mind*, which began publication in 1873 and finished after his death. Trollope thought highly of Lewes's *Fortnightly* essays on *The Principles of Success in Literature* and urged their republication.

Despite the two men's different outlook their friendship ripened quickly: by the end of 1860 Trollope had asked Lewes for information about a Swiss school for his sons. He also asked him to be one of the lecturers in the series of lectures he was organizing for Post Office clerks, and in 1861 Lewes and Eliot arranged a meeting between Trollope and Carlyle. Trollope helped Lewes's son to get a place in the Post Office and also asked Lewes to write for *Saint Pauls*. They shared an interest in the theatre and in classic French actors and Lewes dedicated a book on them to Trollope. Trollope called on Lewes and Eliot frequently, especially for her famous Sunday afternoon receptions for London's literary set, and supplied Lewes with Cuban cigars. He accepted Eliot's and Lewes's relationship, referred to Eliot as 'your wife' and called them 'Mr and Mrs Lewes'. Trollope made no attempt to understand Lewes's philosophy or scientific knowledge: in the obituary he wrote of Lewes in the *Fortnightly* he said, 'To me personally Lewes was a great philosopher only because I was told so.'

Trollope wrote in his *Autobiography* that Lewes was, '... I think, the acutest critic I know, – and the severest ... His intention to be honest, even when honesty may give pain, has caused him to give pain when honesty has not required it. He is essentially a doubter.' In his obituary tribute Trollope wrote: 'There never was a man so pleasant as he with whom to sit and talk vague literary gossip over a cup of coffee and a cigar.' [➤ 'Josephine de Montmorenci'; Smoking.]

Life. This magazine, the full title of which was *Life: A Weekly Journal of Society, Literature, the Fine Arts and Finance*, was owned and edited by Louis Felbermann and sold for a shilling. The magazine serialized the last novel Trollope wrote, *The Land-Leaguers*, between November 1882 and October 1883. The

magazine also published Trollope's last short story, 'Not If I Know It', in its Christmas issue for 1882.

The Life of Cicero. We know from the work-sheet for *John Caldigate* that Trollope interrupted his writing between 22 February and 12 March 1877 to work on 'Cicero', but this could have meant the two signed articles he prepared for the *Fortnightly* which appeared in April and September 1877. The first, 'Cicero as a Politician', appeared on 1 April 1877; the second, 'Cicero as a Man of Letters' appeared on 1 September. We do know that by 1879 he had written about a quarter of this book. By 26 May 1880 it was finished and he told a friend, 'Oh, the work that I have done. The books I have referred to, and the volumes I have read!' In June he negotiated an agreement with Chapman & Hall (in May he had become one of the three directors of the firm), and the book was published in two volumes in December 1880. Unusually, Trollope was not paid a specific sum for his rights to the book but was given a most generous royalty of 8*s.* 6*d.* (or 35 per cent) on the first 1,200 copies sold, rising to 9*s.* thereafter. He also received £100 from Harpers for unbound sheets for an American edition. It is interesting that in the book Trollope asks if Cicero's dictation to his secretary affected his style because he himself dictated this book to his wife, Rose, and also paid her a charming compliment in it. The manuscript is therefore in her hand.

Trollope's interest in Cicero sprang in the first instance from his devotion to the classics and, in the second, from reading Cicero's works while in Australia in 1875. He was spurred on by recently published books that were critical of the man. Among them were two books by Charles Merivale, who had been so critical of Trollope's rendering of Caesar's *Commentaries*.

According to one acquaintance, this book was the work of which Trollope was most proud [Mullen, 581]. It is interesting that he gave a copy to the Athenaeum club for its library and that he asked his son Henry for a list of any errors he might find. When a review in the *Pall Mall Gazette* criticized his scholarship, Trollope told Henry: 'I do not profess to be a scholar, – but simply one who has read enough of Latin literature, (and have sufficiently understood it,) to be able to tell my story.' There was a savage review in the *Saturday Review* (26 February 1881) and indeed most reviews were unfavourable. His friend, the Reverend W. Lucas Collins, editor of his translation of Caesar's *Commentaries*, wrote to the editor of *Blackwood's Magazine* that: 'I tried to say all the good for it that I *honestly* could [in his review] and in many respects it is a very pleasant book to read, even when one can't quite share Trollope's enthusiastic admiration for St Cicero.' Ironically, Trollope had been staying in Collins's rectory when the book was published.

The book was a labour of love occasioned not just by Trollope's desire to be treated as a serious writer or by his desire to have his classical expertise recognized but by a genuine affection for a man who had in his opinion been slandered by recent writers. Trollope admitted he had no new knowledge but simply a desire to set the record straight: 'I may say with truth that my book has sprung from love of the man, and from a heartfelt admira-

tion of his virtues and his conduct as well as his gifts.' If Gladstone meant to prove that Homer was an honorary member of the Church of England, Trollope wished to establish that 'Cicero was almost a Christian, even before the coming of Christ'. His final chapter, on Cicero's religious beliefs, gives one of the best insights into Trollope's own Christian faith. Trollope was here only continuing an ancient tradition in the Church: Cicero's influence had been very strong among those cultural forces which formed the early Church and he especially influenced St Ambrose, St Jerome and St Augustine.

The difficulty with the book, for those unable to criticize Trollope's scholarship, lay in his desire to make Cicero and his times understandable to Victorians. He referred to Mark Antony as 'one of the greatest rascals the world has known' while a minor politician is 'this dirty fellow'. 'How popular,' he wrote, 'he [Cicero] would have been at the Carlton ... How supreme he would have sat on the Treasury bench ... How delighted would have been the middle-aged Countesses of the time to hold with him mild intellectual flirtations ...' *Punch* had great sport with all this when it published a cartoon showing Trollope placing a top hat on a bust of Cicero.

Trollope used the book to pay tribute to his wife as his 'second self', but he also continued his war with the historian E. A. Freeman over foxhunting. He attacked Freeman for daring to use a quote from Cicero to support his arguments against riding to hounds. While the book made no real contribution to Ciceronian studies it does tell us a great deal about Trollope: it tells of his love of learning, his genuine interest in the classics, his desire to be regarded as a serious writer, if not a scholar, his firm Christian faith and his pride in his own library: 'How impossible it would be for me to repeat this oft-told tale of Cicero's life,' he wrote, 'without a crowd of books within reach of my hand.'

Light (1878). This short-lived weekly magazine was founded in 1878 and edited by the poet and novelist, R. W. Buchanan, now remembered for his article in the *Contemporary Review* (October 1871) attacking the 'fleshly school of poetry', by which he meant Rossetti. In 1878 he asked Trollope for a short story and in March Trollope sent him the manuscript of 'The Lady of Launay'. [For the amusing requirements set by Buchanan, ➤ 'The Lady of Launay'.]

Linda Tressel. Trollope's twenty-first novel was written between 2 June and 10 July 1867 and was serialized in *Blackwood's Magazine* between October 1867 and May 1868. As was usual, his name did not appear. The book contract with Blackwood for this novel was the same as that for *Nina Balatka*, namely that Trollope's name should not appear on the title page of the book version to see if his novels sold without the attraction of his famous name. As it appeared after *Nina Balatka*, the title page read: 'By the author of *Nina Balatka*'. When Blackwood published it as a two-volume novel in May 1868 it was as big a failure as the first book. The publisher then bound the unbound sheets and published it as a one-volume novel with Trollope's name on the title page. Trollope received £450. [➤ Anonymous Novels.]

A few months after *Nina Balatka* finished its serialization Trollope decided to write another anonymous novel with a continental setting, despite the lack of success of the first. For the setting Trollope again turned to his travels and chose an ancient city that appealed to him. *Nina Balatka* had been set in Prague and *Linda Tressel* was to be set in Nuremberg, then part of the Kingdom of Bavaria. Trollope had begun to travel in Germany in the 1860s and eventually he became fond of spending some of his holidays there. He had already set one short story, 'The House of Heine Brothers in Munich', in Bavaria's capital city. When Trollope wrote this novel, 'patient' Bavaria had just been defeated in the Austro-Prussian war of 1866 and it was increasingly coming under the domination of Prussia. Trollope refers to the 'religious idiosyncrasies' of Nuremberg because it was an overwhelmingly Protestant city in a Catholic kingdom. This prepares us for the conflict between religion and love that is the theme of this novel, as it had been of *Nina Balatka*.

Linda Tressel herself is one of the many Trollopian heroines whose life is made miserable by a female relative who is a religious fanatic, Aunt Charlotte [➤ Women]. Nina Balatka suffers from a Catholic aunt in Prague, just as Clara Amedroz suffers from her Evangelical aunt in *The Belton Estate*. Rachel Ray, in the novel named after her, suffers from the Evangelical fanaticism of her sister. The theme would continue into the next decade when Mrs Bolton, a religious zealot in *John Caldigate*, persecutes her own daughter [➤ Mothers and Daughters]. For Trollope, a genuinely religious man, these were all perversions of religion. It particularly annoyed him, as he says in *Linda Tressel*, that some women believed 'the acerbities of religion' should be particularly directed against other, and usually younger, women. (This view was one of his many inheritances from his mother, who had attacked the way in which fundamentalist preachers in America manipulated women.) For Trollope this was a form of the 'crushing' of a personality. The image of crushing occurs constantly throughout this novel.

It is significant that Trollope does not make Aunt Charlotte a Lutheran, the dominant church in Nuremberg, but a Calvinistic Anabaptist. Calvinism was a doctrine Trollope detested and he had encountered it among some English Evangelicals and Irish Presbyterians. By making her part of a rigid minority sect he gave an added acerbity to her views, similar to those held by some of his English Dissenters. His choice of the words 'Calvinistic Anabaptist', as opposed simply to 'Baptist', is interesting. The term 'Anabaptist' was no longer in current English use and Calvinism was a declining force. His choice showed to what a small and old-fashioned sect Aunt Charlotte belonged. Also, Trollope had joined in using the disparaging term Anabaptist almost fifty years earlier in a family ditty making fun of the Trollope children's Baptist nurse [Mullen, 16–17]. Trollope believed that the essence of Calvinism was a denial of human enjoyment, while Catholics, even fanatical ones, were different because 'the force of human nature' brought that Church into line with 'the natural sympathies of mankind' [14]. (The same would apply to some degree here with regard

to Nuremberg's Lutherans.) This contrast is pointed up by making Linda's servant, Techen, a Catholic. For a dedicated reader of Trollope, *Linda Tressel* is one of his most important novels in which to see his religious views, perhaps only exceeded by *The Bertrams*. For Trollope religion could become one of two things: it could be, as it was to him personally, a 'comfort', a word he uses several times in this novel, or it could be what it was to Linda and her aunt, a pitiless tyrant.

The book's plot is a fairly standard Trollopian one and is concerned with marriage. Linda Tressel is an orphan who is raised by her aunt, Charlotte Staubach [➤ Nieces]. She wants Linda to marry the prosperous town clerk, Peter Steinmarc, but he is one of Trollope's middle-aged (he is fifty) bald lovers and Linda is only twenty. Aunt Charlotte, 'though she was now a saint, had been once a woman', and was ashamed to think – albeit for only a short while – the worldly thought that a twenty-year-old girl would not wish to marry a man thirty years her senior. Trollope excels in letting his readers enter into a character's thoughts, and does so here in the form of a question Aunt Charlotte asks herself: 'Was it not fit that the world should be crushed in the bosom of a young girl? and how should it be crushed so effectually as by marrying her to an old man.' (Trollope was in his early fifties when he wrote this, but he was inclined to see his current age as 'elderly'.) Linda is in love with Steinmarc's cousin, Ludovic Valcarm. Aunt Charlotte does not think Ludovic a good choice and she is right, but for the wrong reasons. Linda's love leads to much misery: she elopes with her lover but he is arrested for his revolutionary activities and she returns to be rejected by Steinmarc. In the end, Linda, like Emily Hotspur in *Sir Harry Hotspur of Humblethwaite*, dies of a broken heart – a fitting Victorian conclusion.

Linda and her aunt are very well-drawn characters. Linda has the dark complexion of so many of Trollope's heroines. The aunt has the usual Trollopian mixture: many good qualities overwhelmed by religious fanaticism. The men are less well drawn. Trollope was aware of this and defended himself in an interesting exchange of letters with his publisher, Blackwood, in September 1867. Blackwood had complained – in many ways justly – that young Ludovic is not really a person but a 'myth'. While Trollope agreed that he was a novelist 'who depends more on character than on incident' he went on to justify himself: 'I cannot admit that I am bound always to have a pleasant young man. Pleasant young men are not so common.'

Linda Tressel did not prove a popular success with the reading public. The *Spectator* clearly knew the identity of the author and praised the novel, but it rightly complained that the author did not use the setting of Nuremberg as effectively as he had used Prague in *Nina Balatka*. For most readers the novel was, as Hugh Walpole later put it, 'too lachrymose' and in that sense it was curiously like *The Macdermots of Ballycloran*. It is unlikely that *Linda Tressel* will ever be a favourite among Trollope's novels.

'Lines in pleasant places'. This, one of Trollope's favourite biblical expressions, is normally used in connection with men [*Ralph the Heir*, 14] although it was used for Mrs Dale in *The Small*

House at Allington [3]. Sometimes the negative is used, so that Mr Crawley tries to understand why 'my lines should be cast in such terrible places' [*The Last Chronicle of Barset*, 8]. Likewise, many an English farm labourer's 'lines' had not fallen in pleasant places [*Australia and New Zealand*]. The phrase is from Psalm 16, verse 6, in the Authorized Version: 'The lines are fallen unto me in pleasant places; yea, I have a goodly heritage'. 'Lines' in this sense refer to one's lot in life and have their origin in the marking-out of land boundaries. The psalm is read at Morning Prayer on the third day of the month, but the Prayer Book uses the Coverdale translation: 'The lot is fallen unto me in a fair ground.' Trollope's choice of words may originate in his own reading of the Bible.

Littlebath. See Cheltenham.

Livings. See Church of England.

London. Trollope was the only major Victorian novelist to be born and to die in London. He was characteristically Victorian in the pride he took in London's pre-eminence as the capital of an empire, 'the supreme of power' [*North America*]. Trollope lived in or near London for most of his adult life, except for the years 1841 to 1859 when he was mainly in Ireland – and even then he was frequently in the capital on business for the Post Office. London grew enormously in his lifetime, from a population of about 1,250,000 at the time of his birth to almost 3 million by the 1860s and almost 4 million by the year of his death. He had an extensive knowledge of this rapidly expanding city, which began in his youth when he did a great deal of walking. His last special assignment for the Post Office was in 1866, as temporary Surveyor for North and West London, where he was sent to rearrange deliveries. Even in the 1870s, when he kept a carriage, he normally walked about town.

Yet because Trollope is best known for the Barsetshire novels, he is generally thought of as a novelist of country life. However, London plays a role in about two-thirds of the thirty-six novels he set in England, and eight of the seventeen short stories set entirely in England are set in London. The six short stories in *An Editor's Tales* are all set in London, usually in the poorer neighbourhoods. In this collection 'The Spotted Dog' and 'The Panjandrum' are particularly informative about London, but all six portray London as the place in which successful and unsuccessful writers live. The most perceptive contemporary critic of his achievements as a novelist, R. H. Hutton, saw the importance of London to Trollope's fiction when he wrote: 'In Miss Austen's world, how little you see of London ... In Mr Trollope's novels ... nothing can be done without London' [*Spectator*, 16 December 1882].

London's importance begins with those memorable chapters in *The Warden*, when Mr Harding is forced to spend a day wandering round the capital. There is also much about London in the 1850s in *The New Zealander*. Trollope returned to London later in the same decade with *The Three Clerks* which is mainly set there, and then with *The Struggles of Brown, Jones, and Robinson*, the only novel completely set in the capital. The world of the Palliser novels is a world centred on London. Trollope kept abreast of all the important changes in London: thus in *The Three Clerks* he shows his amazement – and disapproval – at the spread of London: 'It is very difficult nowadays to say where the suburbs of London come to an end' [3]. He described life in these new suburbs in *Marion Fay* (the heroine lives in Paradise Row, Holloway) and in doing so he could well have drawn on his 1866 postal work. In *The Way We Live Now* there is concern that a character could get lost on the Underground, while in *The Claverings* there is criticism of the apparently never-ending growth of railways.

Trollope often enjoys the contrast between city and country life in characters like John Eames who has a foot in both worlds, particularly in *The Last Chronicle of Barset*. Here we can contrast the world of Josiah Crawley with that of Dobbs Broughton, Mrs Van Siever and Conway Dalrymple. We also see London as viewed by Lily Dale when she visits the capital. To simpler country girls in stories like 'Alice Dugdale' or 'The Parson's Daughter of Oxney Colne', and to some degree in the contrast between Adolphus Crosbie and Lily Dale in *The Small House at Allington*, London means a sophistication and urbanity that can be frightening. In the Palliser novels, based on this very sophistication and urbanity, London is the centre of life and the important figures in politics and Society adjourn to their country houses only to continue the life they lead in London. In many of the novels of the 1860s and 1870s, especially *Is He Popenjoy?*, Trollope shows his characters in the midst of the 'Season' with its hectic round of social activities, while the frequent scenes in clubs reflect his own life.

A number of characters in his fiction are suspicious of London and all its works: some, like the elderly baronet in *The Prime Minister*, only come up once a year to see their dentist and tailor, while others rejoice that they live in the Lake District or other areas far from London. A Cambridgeshire squire denounces London as a place of 'feverish idleness, in which one is driven here and there, expecting some gratification which not only never comes, but which never even begins to come', but his fiancée is amazed that a man should 'condemn the very place which most men find the fittest for all their energies' [*Can You Forgive Her?*, 3].

Sometimes London is painted in more sinister colours. It can be the place where young men like George Hotspur, Louis Philippe Scatcherd or Bernard Amedroz are corrupted in *Sir Harry Hotspur of Humblethwaite, Doctor Thorne* and *The Belton Estate* respectively. No Victorian reader would have been surprised to learn that Carry Brattle, rumoured to be a prostitute, had gone to London in *The Vicar of Bullhampton*, and in *Is He Popenjoy?* it is not surprising that the flirtations which almost wreck the Germains' marriage occur in London. [For financial corruption, ► City of London.]

Trollope was alive to London's reputation for crime. The capital was the natural, indeed the only place where he could have set *The Way We Live Now*. In *The Claverings*, when Julia Brabazon returns a cheque to Harry Clavering, she cuts off the signature before posting it, 'whereas Harry Clavering had taken no precaution with it whatever. But then Harry Clavering had not lived two years in London' [2]. London was also the home of much violence. Perhaps his most famous example of violent crime is the attempted garrotting in *Phineas Finn*, but in one article in *Saint Pauls* he refused to be panicked by all the talk of increasing violence in the late 1860s. Not all violence in his fiction occurs in London, but much does. His view remained that expressed in *North America*: 'The battle of life has to be fought in the cities.'

His essay 'A Walk in a Wood' has much of interest on the street noises of Victorian London. The essays republished as *London Tradesmen* give many details about shopping in Trollope's London.

Trollope is commemorated in London by a plaque on his house in Montagu Square and by a memorial in Poets' Corner in Westminster Abbey. His grave is in Kensal Green Cemetery.

The London Review Weekly Journal (1860–69). This magazine was established by the poet and journalist, Charles Mackay. (He was the author of the poem 'Good Time Coming', from which Trollope frequently quotes.) In 1869 the magazine was incorporated into *The Examiner*. Trollope's difficult relations with this weekly magazine began when he offered a short story, 'The Banks of the Jordan', to George Smith for the *Cornhill*. When Smith rejected the manuscript Trollope sold it, with seven others, to the *London Review*, which had previously asked for a novel. The first story, the one rejected by Smith, was published over three weeks, from 5 to 19 January 1861. There was considerable controversy over this story, later re-named 'A Ride across Palestine' and over the second, 'Mrs General Talboys', which the *Cornhill* had also turned down. The *London Review* tried one other story, 'The Parson's Daughter of Oxney Colne', and then asked for Trollope's permission to sell the rights to the remaining five to *Public Opinion*. In these negotiations Trollope acted through Robert Bell, later assistant editor of *Saint Pauls*, who seems to have been something of an agent. [For the controversy surrounding the stories, ➤individual entries.]

London Tradesmen. This collection of eleven articles was written by Trollope and published anonymously in the *Pall Mall Gazette* in the summer of 1880, when he was moving from Montagu Square in London to Harting. By this time the paper had changed its politics and had become Liberal. Its editor was John Morley, whom Trollope had interviewed for the editorship of the *Fortnightly*, and it was probably Morley who commissioned the articles. In this way Trollope renewed his connection with the paper for which he had last written in the late 1860s. In 1927 the collection was edited by Michael Sadleir and published in a limited edition by Elkin Mathews & Marrot in London and Charles Scribner's Sons in New York. The book was reissued in a cheap edition in 1928.

The essays, which are among Trollope's best, with their dates of publication, are: 'The Tailor' (10 July); 'The Chemist' (17 July); 'The Butcher' (24 July); 'The Plumber' (29 July); 'The Horse Dealer' (5 August); 'The Publican' (11 August); 'The Fishmonger' (18 August); 'The Greengrocer' (23 August); 'The Wine Merchant' (26 August); 'The Coal Merchant' (28 August); 'The Haberdasher' (7 September). The essays tell us a great deal about shopping in London, about Trollope's practical sense, about his hatred of modern advertising and his dislike of the newfangled 'departmental' stores that were being introduced from America. It appears that his wife, Rose, liked the new stores.

[➤Horses; *The Struggles of Brown, Jones, and Robinson*; Tailors; Wine.]

Longman (1724–). Of the many publishers with whom Trollope worked, Longman was the most historic. The firm had published many of the great Romantic poets and had led in the establishment of the Whig journal, the *Edinburgh Review*. Trollope worked with William Longman (1813–77) whom he knew through his friend John Merivale. He sent Longman the manuscript of his first Barsetshire novel, *The Precentor* (the title was later changed to *The Warden*) on 8 October 1854. Longman moved quickly and signed a contract sixteen days later. In January 1855 Trollope proposed a sequel, *Barchester Towers*, but as *The Warden*'s sales were so disappointing he turned instead to *The New Zealander*, which Longman rejected. In 1856 Trollope sent *Barchester Towers* to Longman. There was considerable disagreement over vulgarity and much censoring was originally suggested by the firm's reader. In the event Longman proved more accommodating. There was also trouble over money and Trollope demanded, and got, £100 despite Longman's original opposition. (In 1856 Longman paid Macaulay £20,000 for his *History of England*.) The novel was published in 1857 and in the summer of that year Trollope offered Longman two more novels, *The Struggles of Brown, Jones, and Robinson* and *The Three Clerks*.

Longman would not even read the manuscript of the first book. Regarding the second, Trollope insisted on a fee of £200, twice what he had received for *The Warden*. Longman offered £100 and added, 'It is for you to think whether our names on your title-page are not worth more to you than the increased payment.' Trollope did think on it and his reply was to take the manuscript to Bentley, who paid him £250. In his *Autobiography* Trollope had the final word: 'I did think much of Messrs Longman's name, but I liked it best at the bottom of a cheque.' In 1881 he remembered the incident: his real dislike was for the 'half-profits' system whereby publisher and author each took fifty per cent of the profits: 'All was honest with the Longmans. But they did not lay themselves out to make money for me, – but to ensure security for themselves.' When a highly successful novelist, Trollope once again met Longman, through the Alpine Club of which the publisher was vice-president. [➤ Copyright.]

Longroyston. The country home of the Duke of St Bungay is mentioned frequently in the Palliser novels. In *Can You Forgive Her?* it is said to be a remarkably cold building in spite of its innumerable hot pipes [22].

Lord Palmerston. This short biography was written between November 1881 and 1 February 1882. It was commissioned by William Isbister for his 'English Political Leaders' series on 24 August 1881. (The series, which was not a success, was similar to Macmillan's 'English Men of Letters', in which Trollope's *Thackeray* appeared.) It was published in one volume in June 1882,

and was the second in the series. Trollope received £200.

Isbister may well have chosen both his author and his subject through his knowledge of Trollope's longstanding admiration for the Whig prime minister's combination of conservatism and liberalism. Interest in Palmerston's career was revived by the publication in 1878 of the third volume of Sir Theodore Martin's official life of Prince Albert. Martin sided with the Prince and Queen Victoria in the dispute over the royal couple's work in foreign relations when Palmerston was in office. Within days of agreeing to write the book, Trollope was locating a copy of an 1878 pamphlet, *The Crown and the Cabinet: Five Letters on the Biography of the Prince Consort*, by 'Verax' (Henry Dunckley). This was to replace Trollope's own copy which he had lost. His interest in Palmerston had therefore been reflected in his library.

Later that year Trollope told his brother Tom that he did 'not intend writing a "Life of Palmerston", – but a small memoir, such as I did as to Caesar for one series, and as to Thackeray for another, to inform those who wish to know a little by a little easy reading. A few months will do it.' Trollope, true to his Liberal beliefs, disagreed with Tom's advancing Toryism: 'I disagree altogether with your reading of his character – you say Palmerston behaved badly to the Queen – I think that the Queen and Prince Albert, and Baron Stockmar behaved badly to Lord Palmerston.' True to his word, Trollope began his book with a defence of Palmerston against the royal couple. As in his other works of non-fiction, Trollope used the occasion to put forward his own views and the 'memoir' is to some degree an account of his own times.

Occasionally Trollope inserts personal recollections like his being in Washington in 1861 when Britain came near to declaring war against America. He also argued that the government should have paid the Catholic clergy in Ireland: 'Had we paid the priests, as we paid and still pay, the parsons . . . the priests would have worked for the Government. To expect that they should do so under other circumstances is to dream of a Utopia.' He also took the opportunity to write that Lord John Russell was probably the greatest statesman of his lifetime, with the possible exception of Palmerston, something with which few historians would agree. (This view was also expressed in 'The Panjandrum'.)

This is not a good book. The *Athenaeum* was right in calling it 'a sort of Liberal confession of faith' and the *Illustrated London News* wrote that the book was written in 'a sort of familiar, slipshod style, as if he were delivering his private opinion to a friend over a glass of wine'. It told readers little of Palmerston that they did not know already and was really a defence of mid-Victorian Liberalism – not the Liberalism of the 1880s, of Chamberlain, Dissenting industrialists and theoretical rationalists like John Morley. Indeed, between the lines one can sense Trollope's increasing disenchantment with newer Liberalism. If the book shows that Trollope's type of Liberalism had become old-fashioned, it also shows how many of his political views had matured, such as that on Austria. No longer was the empire a 'tyranny' and Franz Joseph a 'tyrant'; the Emperor was now a man who had 'reigned, through many troubles, with

good sense and moderation'. Like his book on Cicero this was a labour of love, a tribute to his hero and to a vanishing age. [➤ Politics.]

Lords, House of. See Parliament.

'Lotta Schmidt'. This short story was written between April and July 1866, while Trollope was also writing *The Last Chronicle of Barset*. In response to a request from Alexander Strahan, Trollope offered to write four stories for the *Argosy* and of these, three were published. (The other two that were published were 'Father Giles of Ballymoy' and 'The Misfortunes of Frederick Pickering'.) This story appeared in the July 1866 issue and was later included in his third collection, *Lotta Schmidt and Other Stories*, published in the following year. Trollope received £60.

This delightful story is set in Austria's capital, Vienna, which Trollope had visited in September–October 1865. While there he had sat in the Volksgarten to hear an orchestra playing the melodies of Johann Strauss (as orchestras still do today) and this story is centred on music and dancing. In the same year in which Trollope was working on this story, Strauss himself was writing the most celebrated of all Viennese waltzes, 'The Blue Danube'. As Trollope finished the story, Austria was suffering a disastrous defeat by Prussia, which may have encouraged Trollope to take a more friendly tone towards the Austrians than he had expressed in 'The Man Who Kept His Money in a Box', 'The Last Austrian Who Left Venice' and *Nina Balatka*.

The plot is a love triangle: a young working-class girl, Lotta Schmidt, is loved by Herr Crippel, who conducts the Volksgarten orchestra. He is one of Trollope's middle-aged lovers – forty-five, a violinist and zither-player, bald and a bad dancer. He has proposed to her on numerous occasions. Her other lover is Fritz Planken, a handsome 'confidential clerk' [bookkeeper] in a Viennese hotel, who is twenty-five, a good dancer and the possessor of a fine head of hair. Herr Crippel is upset to see Planken seated at Lotta's table and puts all his love into a zither solo which wins Lotta's heart.

Trollope reminds readers that in Vienna it is normal for respectable working girls to frequent 'beer-halls' in which they listen to music and dance. Were he to write the same about London women, he added, 'I should be supposed to be speaking of young women as to whom it would be better that I should be silent [prostitutes].' Trollope had seen in Vienna the great mixture of races that marked the city and this is reflected in his description of Lotta herself. Trollope fills the story with references to recent Viennese events including the destruction of the city walls, the construction of the Ringstrasse and the marriage of the Archduchess Maria Theresa to the Duke of Wurttemberg in 1865. The story also contains a small essay on baldness, a matter of some moment to Trollope by the 1860s.

Lotta Schmidt and Other Stories. Trollope's third collection of short stories was published in one volume by Alexander Strahan in August 1867. The stories had been published over a period of six years. The nine stories, with their place and date of publication, are: 'Lotta Schmidt' (*Argosy*, July 1866); 'The Adventures of Fred Pickering' [original title, 'The Misfortunes of Frederick Pickering'] (*Argosy*, September 1866); 'The Two Generals' (*Good Words*, December 1863); 'Father Giles of Ballymoy' (*Argosy*, May 1866); 'Malachi's Cove' (*Good Words*, December 1864); 'The Widow's Mite' (*Good Words*, December 1864); 'The Last Austrian Who Left Venice' (*Good Words*, January 1867); 'Miss Ophelia Gledd' (*A Welcome*, 1863); 'The Journey to Panama' (*Victoria Regia*, 1861). Strahan, who published both *Good Words* and the *Argosy*, proposed issuing the volume in 1867. After Trollope agreed in principle he assumed the title would be *Tales of All Countries*, Third Series. Strahan pressed for a more exciting title and went on to have the collected stories printed as two volumes without consulting Trollope. Trollope was very annoyed at this stretching of the material: 'The pages, as you propose to publish them, are so thin and diluted and contain such a poor rill of type meandering through a desert of margin, as to make me ashamed of putting my name to the book.' In a move characteristic of Trollope he demanded one volume but agreed to a change in the title and insisted on sharing the cost of re-setting the book [➤ Honesty]. For all three collections of his stories Trollope received £1,830, although this does not include payment for the stories when first published.

Love. See Women.

LUFTON FAMILY

The Lufton family is at the centre of *Framley Parsonage* and some of its members return in *The Last Chronicle of Barset*. The family is one of Trollope's admirable possessors of an old English landed estate. The family seat is

Lufton Park in Oxfordshire but family members spend most of their time at their Barsetshire house, Framley Court. The principal members of this fictional family are described below.

Lufton, Lady. Lady Lufton has long been a widow and is a kind and charitable woman, particularly to the Crawleys. She is one of Trollope's redoubtable dowagers and she is a Tory devoted to the High Church cause. As such she is an enemy to the Proudies, and an ally of the Grantlys. Her greatest enemy is the Duke of Omnium whom she despises because she regards him as immoral and a dreadful Whig. Her great fault is her determination to plan other people's lives but on the whole her plans work out well for them. She arranges that her son's boyhood friend, Mark Robarts, should become a clergyman and be given the living of Framley. She even picks out a wife for Robarts and is anxious to do the same for her own son, whose happiness is her greatest concern. Her big mistake is in deciding that Archdeacon Grantly's daughter, Griselda, would make a perfect wife for him. Her opposition to his love for Lucy Robarts provides the difficulty Trollope requires in any love story, in this case in *Framley Parsonage*.

Lufton, (Ludovic) Lord. This basically decent young peer wants to marry Mark Robarts's sister, Lucy, in spite of his mother's opposition. Lufton and Robarts have long been friends and their characters are rather similar. Both get into debt, but this does not become a way of life for them. Lufton is much given to sports such as fox-hunting and fishing. Despite his family's Tory tradition he occasionally 'jeers and sneers at the old county doings'. Lord Lufton prefers to spend time at Framley rather than at Lufton Park.

Lufton, (Lucy) [née Robarts] Lady. Lucy Robarts was one of Trollope's most popular heroines. Lord Lufton fell in love with her when she came to live at her brother's vicarage. Lucy, like so many of his heroines, is a brunette and is one of Trollope's 'brown' girls ; [➤ Women]. She is shy and retiring, particularly in the presence of Lord Lufton or his redoubtable mother, but she is very kind and charitable in helping the Crawleys. In his *Autobiography* Trollope wrote that she was, 'perhaps, the most natural English girl I ever drew'.

Lufton, Justinia. Lord Lufton's sister, Justinia Lufton, was married to Sir George Meredith some years before the beginning of *Framley Parsonage* and is therefore known as Lady Meredith. Her main importance is that her old friend, Fanny Monsell, became the wife of the Reverend Mark Robarts as a result of one of Lady Lufton's plans.

M

The Macdermots of Ballycloran.
Trollope later wrote of this, his first
novel, that he began it in the middle of
September 1843, although the manuscript of his travelling journal implies
he began it between 6 and 30 October
[Mullen, 680]. He finished it in July
1845 and during the time he spent on
the novel he married Rose Heseltine,
moved to Cork and then to Clonmel,
County Tipperary, where he finished
the book. It was published by T. C.
Newby as a 'three-decker' in March
1847. On the title page the author was
called 'Mr A. Trollope'. He eventually received £48. 6s. 9d. but this came
from later editions.

In the autumn of 1843 Trollope was
entertaining his oldest friend, John
Merivale (1815–86), who was visiting
Ireland. Merivale's family were well
acquainted with Trollope's parents
and the two boys were schoolfriends.
Their friendship continued as they
were both beginning careers in
London in the 1830s, Trollope at the
Post Office and Merivale as a barrister.
Merivale's father assessed his son as a
'dreamy imaginative sort of boy –
exorbitantly attached to the reading of
novels'. That was bad enough, but he
was also 'excessively fond' of two companions who like him were known for
'their rambling pursuits and propensities'. (This trio, of which Trollope was
one, is described in Trollope's *Autobiog-*
raphy as 'The Tramp Society'.)
Merivale's twin loves, of fantasy and
of walking, made him the perfect companion for the crucial event in Trollope's life as a writer.

Trollope is not renowned for his
use of local colour or for his descriptions of places in great detail, and in
an article he once wrote he agreed he
had no such ability. However, the
spirit of place could inspire important
events in his career as a novelist. [For
examples, ➤ *Nina Balatka* and *The*
Warden.] Trollope had now been in Ireland just over two years and he was
starting to be seen – for the first time
– as a highly competent official of the
Post Office. His work brought him frequently into contact with the gentry
as often they were the only people in
isolated areas who could answer questions about postal deliveries. As Trollope and Merivale travelled about,
they would have seen a country in fer-
ment. 'The Liberator', Daniel O'Connell, MP, a man who commanded the
loyalty of almost all the Catholics, had
declared that 1843 would be the 'Year of
Repeal'. [➤ *The Kellys and the O'Kellys.*]
The government – of which Trollope
was a highly visible official – was attempting to stop the 'Repeal' agitation and at the same time to conciliate
the Irish.

When walking about, Trollope and
Merivale stumbled across a ruined

manor house and Trollope describes what he saw in the first paragraph of *The Macdermots of Ballycloran*. Parts of his description sound like an Ordnance Survey report, as befits an official who knew the land through inspecting postmen's 'walks' and who was used to working with maps. Several features familiar in his later writings are present in the opening pages. Trollope shows a sympathy for Catholics and makes his gentry family, the Macdermots, Catholics rather than Protestants. His doing so here made a change from the usual run of Irish novels. His refusal to give an exact year for the action of the book by leaving the final digit blank would become his normal practice throughout his fiction. This novel is set sometime in the previous decade, the 1830s, before 1837 but after 'Catholic Emancipation' (1829) which gave Catholics the right to vote and to sit in Parliament.

The matter-of-fact tone at the start is suddenly varied by a little joke about a walk appealing to both the 'brightest' and 'dullest' of men. This is one of the rare occasions on which Trollope uses a flashback to begin a novel. Underneath what we might literally call Trollope's pedestrian account in this opening chapter is the strong vein of Romanticism that was usually hidden beneath his burly, realistic exterior. In his youth, Trollope had seen his family forced to move from one house to another and finally to flee abroad to escape bankruptcy. This gave him an innate feeling for the sufferings of a family like the one he was about to create.

The Macdermots are an example of a class that Trollope believed lay at the heart of Ireland's economic plight:

the small gentry. These 'squireens' did not have the income to keep up their ramshackle houses and their pretensions to gentility. The Macdermots have only a small estate of 600 acres; the rents they obtain are not enough to pay off the debts incurred by the building of their house; and the head of the family, Larry Macdermot, verges on madness as the novel opens. A proud family sinking under debts in an attempt to keep up a certain social standing and a father bordering on insanity were, at least unconsciously, echoes of Trollope's own early years. His own parents had spent an enormous sum building their first house in Harrow, which they could not maintain.

The main character is Larry's son, Thady, who tries valiantly to save the family. He has a younger sister, Euphemia, or Feemy, who is eventually seduced by Myles Ussher, an officer in the Revenue Police. (Trollope gives this character the name of the best-remembered bishop of the Church of Ireland, the seventeenth-century prelate, James Ussher. His *Annales Veteris* is said to be the basis for the dates added to the English Bible in 1701 which proved so important in English religious history.) [➤ Names, Origin of.] Thady kills his sister's lover and, after a dramatic trial, is convicted and hanged. Feemy dies of a broken heart. Round this unhappy story Trollope paints a detailed portrait of Irish rural life and the tensions within it.

Two points that Trollope makes are well worth emphasizing. He saw that education was the best means to improve the condition of Ireland. He describes the clever but despicable squire, Jonas Brown, as one who 'knew that the only means of keeping the

peasantry in their present utterly helpless and dependent state was to deny
them education' [25]. Throughout his
life, whether describing the material
progress of America, standing for Parliament at Beverley or lecturing, Trollope would stress again and again the
importance of education as the best
way to help ordinary people. In this
emphasis on education Trollope was
reflecting one of the great goals of his
age: peaceful change and improvement.

The second point that needs to be
emphasized indicates an area in which
Trollope did not reflect his age. As a
British official in early-Victorian Ireland it was unusual for him to reject
the use of 'paid spies and informers'
to bring criminals and terrorists to justice [11]. In fact, the *Athenaeum* in its
obituary of Trollope would rightly say
that this passage indicated 'the purpose of the book'. Trollope obviously
has no sympathy with the British official, Ussher. All his sympathies in
this book are on the side of the Irish
themselves and more so than in any of
his later Irish novels.

Yet far more startling is the fact that
the real hero of the book is a Catholic
priest, Father John McGrath. Irish
Catholic priests did not normally receive praise from English writers. *The
Times* often used phrases such as 'culti-
vated ruffians' to describe them. 'Culti-
vated' Father John certainly is: educated in France, he is a man of wide
reading, ranging from the Fathers to
the latest Dickens novel. Father John is
the first clerical portrait by the novelist who is the best-known portrayer of
the clergy in English fiction. The Irish
priest does not have many similarities
with the Anglican clergy of Barsetshire although he does resemble Mr

Harding in his simple, pious goodness.
Father John is also remarkably ecumenical. When Thady Macdermot
worries that his sister might marry a
'black Protestant', Father John comments: 'He may be Protestant ... and
yet not "black". I wouldn't have you be
against him for that: that's not the way
to show your religion; it's only nursing
your pride.' Yet as always Trollope
argues that virtues, as well as vices,
have limits, at least in his characters.
There is a limit to the good father's
tolerance and he comforts himself by
saying, 'and sure, mightn't she make a
Catholic of him?' [5].

It is a consistent feature in Trollope's writing about the Irish clergy
that while the parish priest is usually
good, his curate is usually a dirty, disreputable and ignorant bigot. In his
last Irish novel, *The Land-Leaguers*, it
is worse than this. All these unlovely
attributes are present in the curate,
Father Cullen, but it is the portrait of
Father John, the good priest with all
his foibles, that stands out. Trollope
alludes to a contemporary issue by
showing that the tolerant and civilized
Father John was educated in France,
while the narrow-minded Cullen is a
product of the Irish seminary at Maynooth. Debates over a government
grant to Maynooth were part of the
great political discussions taking place
in the months before Trollope began
to write. There are good grounds to
think that Father John and Father
Giles in 'Father Giles of Ballymoy'
were based on the same priest.

The Macdermots is remarkable not
only for the novice novelist's mastery
of the complex structure of Irish
society, but for his mastery of Irish dialogue. This novel has more dialogue
than almost any of his subsequent

books. He did not use Irish speech to raise a laugh or to cause a smile of condescension, something he later accused his friend Thackeray of doing, but to portray real speech. Sometimes he uses colourful phrases such as, 'Take a sup of punch now, Miss Tierney; sure you're fainting away entirely for the want of a dhrop', or 'Ussher's black soul has gone on its long journey this night with more curses on it than there are stones on these shingles.' He even includes words – *salute nostra* – that were unique to the Irish Catholic marriage service [12].

By training his ear to the nuances of Irish dialect Trollope acquired that skill with dialogue that would become one of his most praised characteristics as a novelist. Anyone who has read a variety of Trollope's novels will soon notice a certain cadence in his writing and it is hardly surprising that this cadence is not evident in the early parts of his first novel. However, halfway through *The Macdermots*, in a passage describing Bob Gayner as one of the best riders in County Roscommon, this cadence appears. There are other aspects of his later writing here as well: his method of telling a story as if he were speaking, with all the little interruptions like 'by the by' that give his prose a conversational tone [17]. Another of his traits is already evident: his hatred of a 'mystery'. He lets his readers know what a character's future holds for him, for example when he describes Pat Brady, who eventually betrays Macdermot [11]. There is also the emphasis on the role of the 'gentleman', and some examples of what would be many 'authorial intrusions' – as when he claims precedents to allow him to 'leap over' four months [25].

Trollope worked slowly at the novel. His approaching marriage may well have delayed him and, indeed, he had only completed the first of three volumes before he was married. He even lost the manuscript while he was in the early stages so his new wife was important not only to give him a model for female characters for later books, but also to give him that sense of domestic order in which to write. When he at last finished the work he had the usual problem of the new author: finding a publisher. Fortunately he had the good luck to have a well-known novelist as a mother. In his *Autobiography* Trollope exaggerates both the difficulties he faced in publishing the book and its lack of success. This fits in with the general theme of the *Autobiography*: how hard work overcame the failures of youth. He is less than fair to his mother in her efforts to find a publisher for the novel. What she may have feared was that Anthony might be tempted to give up a promising career in the Post Office to embark on the risky life of an author.

Newby, who published the book, had a shady reputation. He told Fanny Trollope that it was a bad year in which to launch a new novel: an ironic statement, as the same year saw the publication of *Vanity Fair*, *Jane Eyre* and *Wuthering Heights*. All these novels, unlike Trollope's, had a strong and memorable female character. Newby tried to confuse potential readers by listing Mrs Trollope as the author in a few advertisements, while even the title page did not give the author's Christian name. This annoyed the *Observer*: 'Many readers will take them [the three volumes] up under the impression that they are from the pen of

Mrs Trollope though only the production of an unknown Mr Trollope.' The *Spectator*, giving Trollope the first of many favourable reviews, spotted his greatest skill: 'The characters are natural, without much of book exaggeration: they are human in their vices, not mere abstractions of unalloyed folly, villainy, weakness or virtue.'

In *Barchester Towers* [51] Trollope is certainly referring to his own first novel when he comments, 'A late writer, wishing to sustain his interest to the last page, hung his hero at the end of the third volume. The consequence was, that no one would read his novel.' More people appear to have read it when it first came out than he claimed, although it certainly brought him neither fame nor fortune. As he himself said, when commenting years later on the novels of Samuel Richardson: 'The world of readers is averse to be steeped in wretchedness.' [➤ Witnesses.]

Macmillan & Co. (1843–); *Macmillan's Magazine* (1859–1907). This publishing house was founded by two Scottish brothers, Daniel and Alexander Macmillan, in their London bookshop. In 1850 they became a company and prospered throughout the nineteenth century. Among their authors were Charles Kingsley, Thomas Hughes, Lewis Carroll, Mrs Humphry Ward, Thomas Hardy and Henry James. In 1859 the brothers started their own magazine and it just managed to precede the *Cornhill* as the first shilling monthly. Trollope's connection with the firm began in 1869 when he sold it both serial and book rights for *Sir Harry Hotspur of Humblethwaite*. Macmillan in turn sold the book rights to Hurst & Blackett. The Macmillans were canny businessmen: while they paid £750 to Trollope they received £700 from Harpers for the American edition. In 1879 John Morley, editor not only of the *Fortnightly Review* but of Macmillan's 'English Men of Letters' series, asked Trollope to write the volume on Thackeray. That same year Trollope offered *Ayala's Angel* to *Macmillan's Magazine*, but it was rejected. Trollope remained friendly with the Macmillans and was the guest of Alexander Macmillan on the night before his fatal stroke in 1882. A later head of the firm, Harold Macmillan (1894–1986), was one of Trollope's most devoted readers and found his novels a welcome solace during his time as prime minister.

'Malachi's Cove'. This short story was probably written between 6 and 9 September 1864 when Trollope was working on *The Claverings*. The setting is the coast of north Cornwall. The story was written for *Good Words* and was published in December 1864. Trollope had travelled extensively in Cornwall between 1 August and 21 December 1851 and between 11 March 1852 and 29 August 1853 when surveying the West Country and South Wales for the Post Office. This was the first story for *Good Words* after the difficulty over *Rachel Ray*. Trollope included it in his third collection of short stories, *Lotta Schmidt and Other Stories* (1867).

The story is set between Tintagel and Bossiney where Malachi Trenglos and his granddaughter Mahala eke out a living by gathering seaweed and selling it for fertilizer. Although Mahala had attended the parish church in Tintagel for two years, she was something of an 'Ondine' character, 'wild-looking, almost unearthly'.

When farm-workers from a nearby farm came to collect seaweed on 'her' coast Mahala consulted a lawyer, but to no avail. A compromise was reached with the farmer's son, Barty Gunliffe: he would collect seaweed away from the shore where the water was too deep for Mahala. One day, when competing to see who could collect more seaweed, Barty almost drowns in a cove and is saved by Mahala. The Gunliffes accuse her and her grandfather of attempted murder until the injured man calls her name and later thanks her for saving his life. In ending Trollope said, 'I need not, I think, tell the tale any further.' There is a marriage and a happy ending for Mahala's aged grandfather.

It is remarkable, given that Trollope wrote this story at least eleven years after his time in Cornwall, that he remembered the scenery and language so precisely. He also kept the magazine's Evangelical readers in mind. When saying that Mahala had grown up without any regard for Sundays, he inserted a parenthetical comment that 'all days had been, I fear, the same to her'. For two years she had attended parish services because of the influence of her parish priest, even though she had no decent clothes to wear. (When writing *Australia and New Zealand* in 1871–3, Trollope returned to the question of the shabby dress of the rural poor as a factor in their not frequenting church. He contrasted it with Australia, where rural poverty did not exist.) When Mahala rescues Barty, Trollope asks, 'What prayer passed through her mind at that moment ... who can say?' These comments were not out of character for Trollope but if he had written the article for a different journal

they might not have been made. It is interesting that seaweed-gathering is now enjoying a revival due to the growing popularity of the traditional Welsh laver bread which is made from it. Mahala's successors earn from £25 to £40 a hundredweight. 'Malachi's Cove' was made into a film in 1973.

Manliness. Manliness is a central preoccupation in many of Trollope's novels. He believed that a novelist had a duty, particularly to the young, to encourage people to make themselves 'somewhat better' [*The Eustace Diamonds*, 35]. The fictional young men in his novels and the young Victorian men who read them were ever conscious of the need to be both manly and to behave as gentlemen. Many of his young heroes – John Eames, Charley Tudor, Phineas Finn or Harry Clavering in *The Claverings* – are not always manly and therein lie their dilemmas. Trollope also felt a duty to provide gentle instruction to his young female readers in how they could recognize a truly manly man.

Manliness, therefore, has often to be acquired, often painfully, by Trollope's young men. Once acquired it is a great blessing: when the American, Ezekiel Boncassen, attends a reception given by the Duke of Omnium in Carlton Terrace for Boncassen's daughter, soon to marry the duke's heir, he 'bore himself with more ease than any one in the company, having at his command a gift of manliness' [*The Duke's Children*, 74]. The difficulty was to define the gift. Trollope's best discussion is in *Phineas Redux* [68] where he says that no term is 'less understood'. It is not 'a certain outward magnificence of demeanour, a pretended indifference to stings and little torments, a would-be superiority to the bread-and-butter side of life, an unreal assumption of personal grandeur', none of which was 'natural to a man'. Nor is it 'a composure of the eye . . . a reticence as to the little things of life, a certain slowness of speech . . . an indifference to small surroundings . . . [and] personal bravery'. While it is difficult to define the term he does give several 'attributes of manliness', which include being 'faithful to his friends, unsuspicious before the world, gentle with women, loving with children, considerate to his inferiors, kindly with servants . . . frank, of open speech, with springing eager energies'.

The essential ingredient is the lack of affectation. Affectation, 'that endeavour of twopence halfpenny to look as high as threepence', made a man – especially after middle age – ridiculous to Trollope and his contemporaries. Affectation, he continued, is 'nothing deeper than deportment', reminding one of Dickens's Mr Turveydrop in *Bleak House* or Thackeray's frequent assaults upon elderly Regency bucks. Trollope, like his two contemporaries, is not only rejecting the dandyism of the Regency world of his birth but is emphasizing that to be manly one must exercise restraint in one's behaviour and a quiet courage. 'My idea of manliness', says a clergyman to his closest friend, is that 'you should so carry yourself that the eyes of those around you should see nothing of the sorrows within' [*The Vicar of Bullhampton*, 68]. This was not just a sentiment to be inserted into a novel. When his sister Cecilia died he wrote to her husband, John Tilley, one of his closest friends: 'You are not the man to give way to sorrow.' Those

who knew Trollope saw him as possessing the virtue. The *Spectator* said after his death, 'He was, too, not only a man of genius, but a man of energy, ability, and manliness' [20 October 1883]. When William Blackwood was publishing Trollope's *Autobiography* he wrote to Henry Trollope and used the adjective 'manly' when referring to his father.

When portraying the love of a young earl for an older man in *Castle Richmond* he reassures readers that the young man, however infatuated, is still 'manly'. Affectation should not be confused with effeminacy. Affectation, whether in men, manners, prose, furniture or dress was Trollope's real hatred; it was a form of lying [➤ Advertising; Honesty]. This hatred explains why he has such fun with Victoire Jaquêtanàpe in *The Three Clerks* and helps to explain his dislike of the novels of Disraeli. [For the opposite of manliness, ➤ 'Hog in armour'.]

'The Man Who Kept His Money in a Box'. This short story was written by Trollope between 27 January and 1 February 1861 as one of eight stories for the *London Review*. After publishing the first three the magazine sold the remaining five, including this one, to *Public Opinion*, in which it was published on 2 and 9 November 1861. In 1863 Trollope included it in his second collection, *Tales of All Countries*, Second Series. Trollope set the story in Italy at Lake Como, which he visited in September–October 1857 with his wife. Trollope received £50 for the story.

Like many of Trollope's European tales, this one is set in an hotel, in this case Conradi's at Chiavenna on Lake Como. The story is told in the first person by a traveller called Robinson and is about the Greene family who are also staying at the hotel. The father is a prosperous 'City gent' from London, accompanied by his wife and daughter. They are good examples of the slightly vulgar type of British traveller who was increasingly seen on the Continent. Among Greene's luggage are two boxes in which, his wife tells Robinson, she keeps her jewellery and he keeps his money – £350 in gold sovereigns – for fear of Italian brigands who only steal items on one's person, not in one's luggage. (Gangs of brigands were the principal anxiety of Victorian travellers to Italy.) The group travels on to Bellaggio, where they discover the boxes are missing. Searches do not produce them and Robinson begins to fear the Greenes are impostors, especially as they have already borrowed money from him. In the end the missing boxes are found in Robinson's room, having been put there by mistake. Everyone is convinced that Robinson is the thief and he parts from his erstwhile friends and goes on his way.

The story describes how Victorians travelled across the Alps into Italy and how they then made the journey to Lake Como. Robinson – like Trollope himself – enjoyed getting out of the diligence [➤ Carriages] and walking part of the way. Trollope uses the story to include a brief passage showing his support for Italian unification.

Marion Fay. Trollope started writing his forty-third novel on 23 December 1878. He stopped after nine days and only returned to his task on 6 August 1879, after a break in which he wrote *Thackeray* and *Dr Wortle's School*, and

travelled in France, Switzerland and Germany. He completed it on 21 November 1879 and offered it to *Temple Bar* but they rejected it. It was serialized in *The Graphic* in weekly instalments between 3 December 1881 and 3 June 1882. It appeared, also serially, in Australia, in the *Illustrated Sydney News*. Chapman & Hall published it as a three-volume novel in May 1882. There is no complete record of Trollope's receipts but he got at least £550 for the serial rights, an American edition and a cheap edition by Chatto & Windus. The sum includes neither the money from Chapman & Hall nor payment for the Australian serialization. The novel was even translated into Norwegian.

Michael Sadleir, noting how long Trollope took to write this novel, concluded that he 'never "got away" with the book, never had his heart in it. And certainly it reads more perfunctorily than any of his other work'. To Hugh Walpole the book 'is the exact negation of every virtue Trollope possessed'. It is hard to disagree with these views. The plot is based on two proposed marriages between different social classes. Lord Hampstead is the son of the Earl of Kingsbury and both men are political Radicals. The son puts this into practice and falls in love with Marion Fay, whose father is a Quaker and a clerk in the City. However, for the first fourteen chapters the plot centres not on Lord Hampstead and Marion but on his sister, Lady Frances Trafford. She follows her brother's example and is engaged to marry Lord Hampstead's friend, George Roden, a Post Office clerk. The Kingsburys disapprove of both matches but in the end give their approval for Lady Frances once George

Roden discovers he is really an Italian duke. Marion Fay, who declares her love for the young aristocrat but refuses to marry him because of her consumption, dies in one of Trollope's longest 'death scenes'.

To enliven what is a rather tedious novel Trollope has four minor sub-plots. First is the marriage of Lord Hampstead's cousin, Lady Amaldina, the daughter of Lord Persiflage, to Lord Llwddythlw, the colourless heir to the Duke of Merioneth and a man devoted to his political duty, rather like Plantagenet Palliser. The second is the attempt of a presumptuous Post Office clerk, Samuel Crocker, to ingratiate himself with Lord Hampstead and his sister. The third is the discovery that George Roden's mother had married an Italian duke and that George has succeeded to the title: will he accept it and please the snobbish aristocrats or remain true to his radical principles? While the novel ends with him titleless, Trollope tells us that in due course he will use his title, especially as he has been taken out of the Post Office and given a well-paid position in the more prestigious Foreign Office. The fourth involves a scheme to get rid of Lord Hampstead by his stepmother, anxious that her own eldest son should succeed, and by her husband's wicked chaplain, the Reverend Mr Greenwood. Greenwood, a well-drawn character, actually contemplates murder but gives up his plan. [➤ Emilius, The Reverend Joseph for another murderous clergyman.]

The story reads more like a 'silver-fork' novel – those which deal with the lives of the great and wealthy, if not good – or something from the pen of Ouida or Wilkie Collins. (There is even a scene in which Lord Hamp-stead, mourning his lost love at her grave, sees her floating above it smiling, like Giselle in the ballet of that name.) This novel, similar to *Lady Anna* and *The Three Clerks*, is something of a satire on aristocratic snobbery, although Radicals do not come out well. As usual in Trollope, the battle between maintaining exclusive privileges and advancing individual liberty is won by the forces of progress, in this case by George Roden and Marion Fay.

There is the usual attention to fox-hunting: a defence of hunting as against other sports, and a lament for the decline in the sport in which Trollope singles out those men who pay more attention to their 'dandy knick-knacks, and, above all, their flasks' [13]. (The novel was written after Trollope had given up riding to hounds.) As part of his satire on aristocratic snobbishness Trollope has great fun with aristocratic titles and silly names: there is Lord Persiflage, Lady Di Peacock (engaged to Mr Billyboy), Lady Arabella Portroyal, the Ladies Anatolia and Alphonsa, the Earl of Knocknacoppul, and Lord Plunge. He had great sport with Lord Llwddythlw, which in Welsh is meaningless. He did not forget the lower middle classes living in the Fays' and Rodens' street – Paradise Row, Holloway – with the husband-seeking Miss Demijohn. He had almost as much sport with the Row as he had with Park Lane and Castle Hautboy. In his work sheet for the novel Trollope drew a sketch map of the street with the Duchess of Edinburgh pub on the corner.

For the Post Office scenes he drew heavily on his own difficult time in the 1830s, over forty years before. The chapters set in the Post Office are among the best. Some of the exchanges between Crocker and his superior resemble the surviving letters and reprimands exchanged between the young Trollope and his superior, Lieutenant Colonel Maberley. Crocker's superior, Sir Boreas Bodkin, to whom he gives one of his classical nicknames, Aeolus [god of the winds], is based very much on Maberley [7]. [Mullen, 88–91.] Interestingly, Trollope insisted that a Post Office clerk on £170 a year was a gentleman.

When Trollope described Marion Fay's slow decline from consumption he drew on his own painful memories of the early death at eighteen of his sister, Emily. His inspiration for Lord Hampstead's yacht can be traced to the trip he took in John Burns's yacht to Iceland in the summer before he began writing the novel [➤ *How the 'Mastiffs' Went to Iceland*]. However, it does strain the reader's credulity when he tells us that after Marion's death Lord Hampstead plans to buy a new yacht and 'cruise about the face of the world. He would take books with him, and study the peoples and the countries which he visited.'

There are, as always, private references: he refers to the 'well-known' horses, Banker and Buff [13], which were his two favourite mounts. Crocker lived near Mecklenburgh Square: when Trollope was a clerk he got into trouble over a bill with a money-lender 'who lived in a little street near Mecklenburgh Square' [*Autobiography*, 3]. [➤ Bills.] He refers to the Kimberley mines in the 'otherwise uninteresting plains of South Africa' [61]. This was a reference to his 1877–8 trip there as well as to the mines, which he hated. Finally there is a reference to Carlyle when Trollope has Lord Hampstead

quote Teufelsdröckh and the 'memorable epitaph of the partridge-slayer' from Carlyle's *Sartor Resartus* when attacking shooting as a sport [2].

In spite of the melodramatic touches, most English critics gave *Marion Fay* mild praise.

Marriage. Trollope once said that marriage was 'the proper ending for a novel, – the only ending ... which is not discordant' [*Ayala's Angel*, 64]. 'No social question has been so important to us as that of the great bond of matrimony', he said in a lecture on English novels, and certainly his own marriage constantly represented that view. When he announced that 'most marriages are fairly happy', this was certainly true of his own [*Framley Parsonage*, 20]. As he wrote to his friend, G. H. Lewes: 'No pain or misery has as yet come to me since the day I was married; if any man should speak well of the married state, I should do so.' [➤ Rose Trollope for her influence.] The majority of his fictional marriages are happy.

Starting with his second novel, *The Kellys and the O'Kellys*, almost all Trollope's novels are concerned with some aspect of marriage: either the ways in which people went about getting married or the ways in which individual marriages worked. He believed that all young women, or at least those 'healthy in mind and body', should marry because it was 'a woman's one career' at the time. It was, however, almost as important for young men to marry [➤ Bachelors]. Trollope claims in his *Autobiography* that he attempted to write one novel, *Miss Mackenzie*, without any love – and therefore, without marriage – but that he failed as not only did his heroine marry a baronet, but in the novel's last pages two other marriages are in process. This indeed was quite a frequent occurrence in his fiction: when the main characters are at last united in marriage, several minor figures are also set on their way towards the altar.

Love stories, of course, have always been favoured by storytellers, novelists and dramatists. Trollope does show different forms of love, such as that of deep friendship between men or women, or the love between fathers and sons. He was not just conforming to Victorian conventions in his devotion to marriage because in some marginalia in a copy of Bacon's *Essays* he wrote, 'Lust is ever bad, and love ever good. That I take to be a truth as arranged by God.' Yet he also perfectly reflected the ethos of his age by believing that the proper place for sexual love was within marriage. He, of course, knew there were exceptions to this, as exemplified by his friends, Lewes and George Eliot, but he did not believe that fiction was the vehicle for such relationships. Although some men have mistresses and prostitution is alluded to, people in Trollope's novels do not 'live together', at least not in England. It might happen in the colonies or in America where, as one character says, 'there isn't the same sort of prudish sort of life which one is accustomed to in England' [*An Old Man's Love*, 18]. In *John Caldigate* it is implied that Caldigate and Euphemia Smith live together (in Australia), while in *Dr Wortle's School* Mr and Mrs Peacocke did live together (in America) but on the assumption that they were legally married. In *The Belton Estate* Colonel and Mrs Askerton had lived together before marrying, but this was to enable her to escape a cruel husband and had apparently happened in India before the novel began. Even so, in all these cases, suffering, whether deserved or not, did occur.

Trollope's young men usually have some flirtations, mostly with girls of a lower social class than their own, before they actually propose to one of their own class. Young ladies are assumed to be innocent of such experiences although there are exceptions like Lady Glencora Palliser. Trollope believed that Victorian girls were often too sheltered from the realities of life; hence his statement that a purpose of the novel was to 'teach ladies to be women and men to be gentlemen'. By the 1870s he was inclined to show them as more knowledgeable than had been the case with the Barsetshire maidens in earlier decades. This is seen in two novels published in the 1870s: Emily Hotspur, in spite of the fact that she lives a retired life in the Lake District, is aware that her lover has been a 'prodigal' but 'in our rank of life' young men were open to such temptations [*Sir Harry Hotspur of Humblethwaite*, 13]. In *An Eye for an Eye* the innocent heroine gives her love too easily, is seduced and then betrayed by her lover.

Trollope's favourite plot – one repeated time and again in his novels and short stories – portrays the difficult course of true love between a young man and woman. The problems usually stem from the attitude of the young woman's parents and in particular, her mother [➤ Mothers and Daughters]. Occasionally a mother, or other older woman, actively promotes a marriage, as the Duchess of Omnium does before the start of *The Duke's Children*, or Miss Jack in 'Miss Sarah Jack of Spanish Town, Jamaica'. Sometimes young men are too 'faint-hearted' [*The Warden*, 7] and easily discouraged. Sometimes, however, the woman gives in too quickly, thereby making the man think the prize is not as valuable as it really is. This is the fate of Kate O'Hara in *An Eye for an Eye*, or Patience Woolsworthy in 'The Parson's Daughter of Oxney Colne' who is thought to be 'a little too free for feminine excellence'. Occasionally the woman is misled by an idealized vision of a lover, for instance Ayala Dormer in *Ayala's Angel*, or Lady George Germain in *Is He Popenjoy?* Sometimes the girl 'quizzes' her lover and almost loses him, as happens in 'Alice Dugdale'. There are several cases in which the woman persists in her refusal: the most celebrated case is in *The Small House at Allington*, when Lily Dale refuses John Eames's repeated proposals. It could not have been a surprise to Trollope that no event in his fiction caused more comment, and even letters to the author, than Eames's failure. A girl may refuse a man because she has sincere and agonizing doubts about him, as in *Sir Harry Hotspur of Humblethwaite*. Sometimes, as happens with Dorothy Grey in *Mr Scarborough's Family*, a woman whose mother has died becomes something of a *de facto* wife to her father by whose idealized standards suitors are judged and rejected.

Proposals abound in Trollope's fiction; one day in 1867 he came down to breakfast at a friend's house and startled his hosts by announcing, 'I have just been making my twenty-seventh proposal of marriage.' (This was presumably in *Phineas Finn*, his twenty-second novel and one that is full of proposals.) He even used his own proposal in *Doctor Thorne* [7] [Mullen,

132–3]. Frequently young men must make several proposals before they are accepted and it is almost invariably the man who has to make the proposal although the scheming Lady Eustace does violate this rule. Most of Trollope's engagement scenes begin with the man's daring to call the woman by her Christian name and then, after some hesitation, end with a passionate kiss, which Trollope evidently much enjoyed describing. [➤ Names, Use of.] This could cause problems: his publisher objected when a clergyman kisses his betrothed in *Barchester Towers*, even though 'his virgin lips' only touch her cheek.

Sometimes proposals are rejected because there is an objection by the family, particularly when the suitors are not of equal social rank. This can be resolved when the recalcitrant parent finally sees what a good marriage this will be: thus Archdeacon Grantly accepts his son's proposal to Grace Crawley. The parent may have to repeat a son's proposal so that the girl knows he has his parents' approval: this is what happens when Lady Lufton asks her son's beloved to accept him in *Framley Parsonage*. [➤ 'The Lady of Launay'.]

Money is an almost constant difficulty in arranging marriages. In *The Vicar of Bullhampton*, the elderly Miss Marrable pronounces a truth accepted by the middle classes: 'In our position ... marriage cannot be made so common as to be undertaken without foresight for the morrow. A poor gentleman is further removed from marriage than any other man' [30]. Miss Marrable herself can live in relative comfort on £300 a year while her niece would be 'very poor' as a married woman on the same amount [20]. As

Trollope said, this was a greater problem for the middle classes than for those above or below them in status and income [*The Eustace Diamonds*, 76]. The man had to consider whether he could maintain a large family as well as several servants and, in time, have something for his children 'to marry on'. He also had to think how to provide for his family in case of his death. [For the way in which financial provisions were usually made for married couples, ➤ Settlements.] Although Trollope makes his readers aware of the possible difficulties, his consistent advice was that young couples should emulate his example and take the risk of marrying before all their financial worries were resolved. Perhaps no other topic is so often referred to in his novels as this [*The Three Clerks*, 31]. A reviewer of *The Small House at Allington* in the *Saturday Review* in 1864 referred to the love story between Bell Dale and Dr Crofts and criticized Trollope's 'favourite hobby' of advising young people not to pay too much attention to financial considerations. It is not surprising, therefore, that older relatives in Trollope's works often die, or become generous, just in time to allow a marriage to take place [➤ Death]. Legally a woman had virtually no control over her property (at least before 1870) once she was married, although in some cases her second husband might agree that she should manage her own property. Several of Trollope's widows, notably Madame Max Goesler, are shown to be excellent businesswomen, adept at looking after their own financial affairs.

Trollope detested 'mercenary' marriages in which love played no role and only money, social position or a title were considered. That is why the marriages of women like Lady Laura Kennedy, Lady Alexandrina De Courcy, Lady Ongar in *The Claverings* or Adelaide Houghton in *Is He Popenjoy?* are such disasters. The upsets that befall the Pallisers in the early months of their marriage spring from the fact that Lady Glencora had in effect been sold to the Palliser family. However, if a 'mercenary' marriage is wicked and almost always disastrous, Trollope does not preach total disregard of questions of income. His short story 'The Adventures of Fred Pickering' shows the danger of marrying without an adequate income.

Marriages between classes succeed in a surprising number of cases, such as those in 'The Château of Prince Polignac', *Marion Fay*, in which there would have been two successful marriages had Marion Fay not died, and *The Duke's Children* in which a Duke's daughter marries a squire's younger son. The most famous example is, of course, the marriage between an earl's daughter and a Radical tailor in *Lady Anna*. Where such marriages fail, as in 'The Spotted Dog', there are underlying reasons, for instance the hero's 'loud claims for liberty' and rejection of 'the conventional thraldom of the world'.

Trollope's main concern was with marriage among the middle and upper classes, but he touched on working-class marriages in some of his fiction. Perhaps the best insight is in *The Vicar of Bullhampton*, in which he describes the Brattles' way of life. He also touches on such marriages in several short stories: 'The Telegraph Girl', 'The Spotted Dog', 'Mrs Brumby' and 'Catherine Carmichael'.

In 1851 the average age for men to marry was twenty-six although middle-class men tended to be older: Trollope was twenty-nine when he married. Women were usually a few years younger than their husbands. Florence Burton's mother in *The Claverings* admits, 'I think I'd feel ashamed of myself to have a daughter not married, or not in the way to be married afore she's thirty' [4]. In one of Lord George Germain's lectures to his wife he concludes by saying, 'I am older than you.' She pertly replies by pointing out a fact concerning a husband's age that was generally true until recent years: 'Husbands, of course, are older than their wives, but wives generally know what they are about quite as well as their husbands' [*Is He Popenjoy?*, 19]. While the vast majority of marriages in the novels are between the young, there are some marriages between those in their middle years. Trollope's most famous middle-aged marriage is, of course, that between Dr Thorne and Martha Dunstable. The course of true love runs no more smoothly for the middle-aged than for the young: Miss Mackenzie faces numerous difficulties in the novel named after her and in *Mr Scarborough's Family* the comic squire, Peter Prosper, comes totally unstuck in his attempt to marry Matilda Thoroughbung. Sometimes middle-aged lovers defeat much younger men; this happens in 'Lotta Schmidt', *Miss Mackenzie* and 'Miss Ophelia Gledd'. Usually a marriage between a young woman and an older man comes about because of her desire for a title or money, as discussed above. The proposed marriage between the middle-aged William Whittlestaff and Mary Lawrie, one that is based on his genuine love, is put aside by Whittlestaff himself in *An Old Man's Love*. The

sexual passions felt by an older man are described in *Orley Farm* [26] when discussing Mr Furnival's feelings for Lady Mason.

Once a couple agree to marry and overcome any parental or financial difficulties, they must grapple with other problems. First a date has to be set and Trollope often has much fun in showing the disputes that can arise. In one novel he even has the couple select, after much debate, Trollope's own wedding day [*The Bertrams*, 43]. If there is a clergyman in the family that can add further problems as to who should conduct the service and where it should take place [*Mr Scarborough's Family*, 64]. Archdeacon Grantly insists that two marriages of his relatives are held in his church with himself officiating [*Barchester Towers*, 53; *The Last Chronicle of Barset*, 84]. At the first of these Trollope actually quotes part of the Prayer Book service. Generally he does not describe the actual religious service, although in *The Kellys and the O'Kellys* he quotes part of the peculiar service used in Irish Catholic churches. When describing a wedding he usually focuses on one detail such as the lyrical description of 'merry wedding bells' in *The Bertrams* [30].

Victorian propriety would not look kindly on too many allusions to a honeymoon, or to what Dorothy Grey refers to as 'that interior life' of a married couple [*Mr Scarborough's Family*, 52], so normally we are just told that aristocratic couples or couples from landed families go off for several months travelling, usually to the South of France and then on to Italy, while the middle classes go to Cornwall or the Lake District. In Trollope's first novel, *The Macdermots of Ballycloran*, there is open talk of 'wedding beds' and in one of the last, *Mr Scarborough's Family*, the new husband asks if he snores, only to be told, 'Indeed, no! There isn't a sound comes from you. I sometimes look to see if I think you are alive' [64]. But usually things are more subdued: the girl in *Rachel Ray* 'blushes' when her mother mentions the possibility of children in her forthcoming marriage [30]. Pregnancy had to be handled with great tact: it could be camouflaged by the use of a French term like *enceinte* [*The Macdermots of Ballycloran*, 27], by vague allusions to the need to add on to the nursery, or by curious phrases such as 'the fruit of her husband's love' [*The Eustace Diamonds*, 1] or 'Good time coming'. Trollope, like other novelists, had to be careful because he knew that so many of his novels were read aloud in families who might not wish such a subject to be mentioned 'in front of the children'. Adults would understand what Trollope meant in *Is He Popenjoy?* when he described a conversation between the dean's married daughter and the dean: 'Then at last, in a low whisper, hiding her face, she told her father a great secret' [44].

Most Trollope novels end with the happy couple leaving church, ready to embark on married life. Trollope is less interested in the details involved in the course of a marriage. There are exceptions, most notably the Grantlys in the Barsetshire novels and the Pallisers in the series called after them, where Trollope shows the complexities of Victorian marriage. In *He Knew He Was Right* he pays close attention to small details because he is concerned with a husband's domestic tyranny and suspicions. In 'The Adventures of Fred Pickering' he shows a young married couple's struggle against poverty.

Trollope accepted, in theory, that the man must take the lead in marriage and be 'the lord and master'. In *The Belton Estate* he wrote, 'The theory of man and wife – that special theory in accordance with which the wife is to bend herself in loving submission before her husband – is very beautiful; and would be good altogether if it could only be arranged that the husband should be the stronger and the greater of the two...In ordinary marriages the vessel rights itself, and the stronger and the greater takes the lead, whether clothed in petticoat, or in ... trousers' [11]. This happens in the Quiverfuls' marriage in the Barsetshire novels. He never approved of unrestrained male dominance in marriage. 'Fear acknowledges a superior,' he said, but 'love desires an equal' [*The Duke's Children*, 21]. Earlier, in *Orley Farm*, he had warned, regarding a husband's attempts to mould his wife, 'This moulding of a wife had failed with him ... as it always must fail with every man' [54]. When one old woman urges a man to exert total rule over a young wife, Trollope denounces this as contrary to 'the lessons of Jesus Christ' [*An Old Man's Love*, 16]. He delights in showing how Mrs Grantly could cleverly turn her husband, the archdeacon, to follow her wise advice. However, what was horrible to Trollope and to almost all Victorians was the spectacle of a wife domineering over her husband as Mrs Proudie constantly does, and in public [➤ *The Last Chronicle of Barset*]. In his life and writings Trollope fully endorsed the view that both parties in a marriage had their own spheres and thus women almost always arrange the details of entertaining, while men cope with the difficulties of the outside world.

For Trollope the greatest joy of any marriage was 'the long candlelight hours of home and silence' [*Orley Farm*, 21]. Yet he was well aware – partly from his parents' difficult marriage – that marriages could suffer great problems. There are several well-drawn portraits of unhappy marriages: the Kingsburys in *Marion Fay*, the Carmichaels in 'Catherine Carmichael', the Lopezes in *The Prime Minister*, the Furnivals in *Orley Farm*, the Brumbys in 'Mrs Brumby', Lady Anna Lovel's parents in *Lady Anna*, and to a lesser degree, the Proudies. Usually an unhappy marriage is caused by male jealousy and tyranny. Such is Lady Laura Kennedy's plight and also that of Emily Trevelyan in *He Knew He Was Right*. [➤ Divorce.]

Trollope deals rarely with marital infidelity: Maurice Maule in *Phineas Redux* is an unusual example of a married man who maintains 'a long-continued liaison' [21]. The short story 'Mrs General Talboys' features an Irish bohemian who has a wife in Ireland while he lives in Rome where he fathers illegitimate children. It is no wonder that Trollope had trouble with this story, both from his wife and from Thackeray to whom it was sent. The men who maintain mistresses, like George Bertram's father in *The Bertrams* or George Hotspur in *Sir Harry Hotspur of Humblethwaite*, are normally widowed, like Bertram, or are young and unmarried, like Hotspur. While Lady Glencora Palliser in *Can You Forgive Her?* is memorably tempted to abandon her marital vows, she overcomes the temptation and settles down to a relatively happy marriage. The talk of infidelity on the part of Lady George Germain in *Is He Popenjoy?* is all talk.

Trollope's portrayals of Victorian marriage reflect the image that Victorians wished to believe about their society. He knew this was an idealized picture and he therefore sometimes showed marriages that were not happy. When he did so he also showed why they were not happy. Above all, he believed that a prime purpose of the novel was to encourage young people to aspire towards a better life, and for him and his generation this could only be found in marriage. One must not forget that Trollope, alone of the great Victorian novelists, had the great joy of a long and happy married life.

'Mary Gresley'. One of the short stories published in *Saint Pauls*, 'Mary Gresley' appeared in November 1869 and was included in Trollope's fourth collection, *An Editor's Tales* (1870). In his *Autobiography* Trollope wrote: 'I do not think that there is a single incident in the book which could bring back to anyone concerned the memory of a past event. And yet there is not an incident in it the outline of which was not presented to my mind by the remembrance of some fact ... how I was appealed to by the dearest of little women whom here I have called Mary Gresley.'

The story, told in the first person by the editor of a magazine, begins with a very long discussion about the love of older men for younger women and probably tells us a great deal about Trollope's own feeling for Kate Field. Mary Gresley is eighteen, the daughter of a physician in a small town, without money and engaged to a curate on £100 a year. She has always been a 'scribbler' and hopes to bring forward their wedding day by earning money from writing. She is encouraged by a soft-hearted 'man of letters' who has not got the courage to tell her she has no talent. She is upset because her Evangelical fiancé does not approve of novels. He falls ill and has to move to Dorset for his health. She writes two novels before she is eighteen and makes a call on the editor, who warns her of the hazards of writing; but she replies, 'It is so noble!' He weakly agrees to read the manuscript: it is no good and he tells her so. She cites 'Currer Bell' (Charlotte Brontë) as someone who succeeded when young. He cannot avoid her charms and agrees to look at another manuscript. He confesses his infatuation to his wife and she suggests inviting daughter and mother for Christmas dinner. The invitations are repeated regularly.

The editor acts as a sort of agent and sells two stories for twelve guineas. Mary hears her fiancé is dying from consumption, visits him with money from the editor, and promises him to give up novel-writing. Mary and her mother return to their small town; the curate dies and Mary becomes a 'female Scripture reader'. Now the tables are turned and the editor urges her to write: she succeeds with Evangelical tracts and although Trollope admitted 'that mode of religious teaching is most distasteful to us, the literary merit shown . . . was very manifest'. Eventually she marries a missionary, goes to Africa, and dies there.

Like 'The Spotted Dog' and 'The Adventures of Fred Pickering', this story describes the plight of would-be writers in London. It also shows how Trollope found names for his characters: Gresley was the family name of his mother's mother.

The Masonic Magazine (1873–82). Published first as a supplement to the *Freemason*, after the ninth issue the magazine was continued as the *Masonic Monthly*. In 1878 the editor wrote to ask Trollope for a Christmas story and by December he had sent them the manuscript of 'Catherine Carmichael', which was published in the 1878 Christmas issue.

Matching Priory. A country house in Yorkshire in which many scenes in the Palliser novels are set. It is the ancestral seat of the Palliser family and the old Duke of Omnium gives it to his nephew and heir, Plantagenet, when he marries Lady Glencora. The old duke describes it as 'the most comfortable country house I know' [*The Small House at Allington*, 55]. The Pallisers delight in showing guests the statue of Sir Guy Palliser, founder of the family's fortunes, and the ruins of the monastic priory. Lady Glencora is eventually buried at Matching.

Maule, Maurice. A character who occurs only in *Phineas Redux*, especially in Chapter 21, but is the best example in all Trollope's fiction of the way in which Trollope could build up a character through a succession of small details. This portrait of a selfish and idle clubman is well worth careful reading by anyone anxious to understand Trollope's genius.

Melmotte, Augustus. The great and fraudulent financier in *The Way We Live Now*.

'La Mère Bauche'. This is one of five short stories which Trollope wrote in September and October 1859 when he and his wife were travelling in the Pyrenees. This was also the period in which he was writing *Castle Richmond*, which he put aside. This story was one of four Trollope sent to *Harper's New Monthly Magazine* as part of a projected series of twelve. Although they bought the story they did not publish it until 1868; their delay may have been due to the story's ending. It was published for the first time in Britain in his first collection of short stories, *Tales of All Countries*, in 1861. In his *Autobiography* Trollope wrote that the stories included in that collection 'have, most of them, some foundation in such occurrences', that is, in 'true tales of my adventures'. Trollope received $100 (£20).

During their travels the Trollopes had stopped at Vernet-les-Bains and the inn there was used as the focus of the story. It was common for Trollope to use an hotel as the centre of his short stories or novels set on the Continent. The plot, which bears some similarity to 'The Lady of Launay' and *Miss Mackenzie*, concerns the conflict between an autocratic mother's plans for her son's marriage and the son's desire to marry not for money but for love. In this case the girl, Marie Calvert, is an orphan brought up in the inn. La Mère Bauche sends her son, Adolphe, away for a year and urges the girl to marry an older man. Marie finally agrees, but only if Adolphe tells her he no longer loves her. On his return, even though he possesses the Trollopian sign of manhood, a large beard, he gives in to his mother and Marie has to marry the aged Capitaine Campan. After the marriage Marie jumps to her death from a high rock overlooking the baths and in the grotto below Adolphe finds her body.

In Trollope's fiction, young love generally has to fight against parental authority and usually it wins [➤ Marriage]. Tragic endings, especially through suicide, are unusual. *An Eye for an Eye*, written in 1879, also has a tragic ending, though of a different nature. 'La Mère Bauche', like so many of his short stories, shows a remarkable sympathy for the working classes. In many ways this tale reads like Balzac.

MFH. The Master of Fox Hounds, often referred to as 'The Master' or the 'Master of Hounds', was a great figure in Victorian county society. He often came from one of the landed families in the county, but even if he did not, he took high social rank in the district. Lord Chiltern eventually achieves happiness and respectability in the Palliser novels when he becomes an MFH. Trollope delighted in portraying them, from his earliest fictional hunts in *The Kellys and the O'Kellys* until the last hunt he described in *The Land-Leaguers* with 'Black Daly' as MFH. He drew on his own wide experience of fox-hunting in both Ireland and England for his portraits. The best description of 'the greatest man in the county on hunting days' and his activities is to be found in *The American Senator* [9]. Normally Trollope's MFHs are admirable, if authoritarian, men whose only glaring fault is an obsession with hunting. Mr Harkaway in *Mr Scarborough's Family* is unmarried and 'the time which other men gave to their wives and families he bestowed upon his hounds' [28]. Major Tifto, a scoundrel in *The Duke's Children* [6], is an exception to this rule. When two MFHs clash on the field it is a titanic struggle [*Mr Scarborough's Family*, 28–9].

Mildmay, William. Mildmay, the elderly Whig prime minister in *Phineas Finn* [25], also appears in *Phineas Redux* and is frequently referred to in *The Prime Minister*. He is the uncle of Barrington Erle and is related to Lady Laura Kennedy. His career has some parallels with that of the real Whig leader and prime minister, Lord John Russell (1792–1878), for whom Trollope had a somewhat excessive admiration.

Military. Military men seem to abound in Trollope's fiction and many of his novels and short stories are full of captains, majors and colonels. Yet, as so often in Victorian fiction, these turn out to be retired officers still using their titles. They are often disreputable men, for example Major Pountney in *The Prime Minister*, Captain George Hotspur in *Sir Harry Hotspur of Humblethwaite*, Sir Lionel Bertram in *The Bertrams*, Lieutenant Fred Neville in *An Eye for an Eye*, or Captain Mountjoy Scarborough in *Mr Scarborough's Family*. The disreputable men who make up Scarborough's gambling circles in London – Moody and Vignolles – are a major and captain respectively. Sometimes military men are in debt, like Lieutenant Cox in *Ralph the Heir*, or are drunks, like Lieutenant Brumby in 'Mrs Brumby'. In three novels, *Sir Harry Hotspur of Humblethwaite*, *An Eye for an Eye* and *Mr Scarborough's Family*, disreputable retired military men are the 'heroes' of the tales. In some cases a man's title has a somewhat spurious ring: Major Tifto in *The Duke's Children* gained his rank fighting in one of the civil wars that racked Spain in the nineteenth century.

However, not all military men are disreputable. Colonel Jonathan Stubbs

in *Ayala's Angel* is an honourable man and so is Captain Aylmer in *The Belton Estate*, while Captain Yorke Clayton in *The Land-Leaguers* is an officer who is also truly a gentleman. He has carried his title with him, Trollope adds, through 'no fault or no virtue of his own', having once been a volunteer adjutant [15]. Another reputable military man is Major Henry Grantly, VC, who, like Stubbs and Clayton, is the admirable hero of a love story. Captain Bernard Dale in *The Small House at Allington* is dull but virtuous. As always, Trollope balances the good with the bad: the George Hotspurs are offset by the Henry Grantlys. Even so, there are more disreputable than reputable military men in Trollope's fiction.

The actual number of serving officers in Trollope is relatively small and there are very few allusions to their military duties. There are three rare exceptions to this: Major Rossiter in 'Alice Dugdale', Lieutenant Fred Neville in *An Eye for an Eye* and Colonel Stubbs. Even in the case of Stubbs, the officer whose daily life we follow more closely than that of any other serving officer, Trollope still speaks only in vague generalities of his following 'the ordinary pursuits of Aldershot' [31]. His fiction set in other countries has more serving officers. 'The Last Austrian Who Left Venice' concerns a young Austrian officer and 'The Two Generals' is based on the real-life story of two brothers in the American Civil War who fought on opposite sides. When we meet Sir Lionel Bertram in *The Bertrams*, considerable parts of which are set outside England, we learn that he had once been a mercenary officer in Persia.

The fact is that Trollope had very

little knowledge of military matters because, like many Victorians – especially Liberals – he had little interest in or affection for the military. Nevertheless he also had a contempt for pacifists [➤ Utopian]. This is ironic, as the armed forces intruded in his life on various occasions. When a young man living in Brussels his mother had begun to make moves to obtain a commission for him in the Imperial Austrian army, but an opening in the Post Office cut these short. He discussed the military in *The New Zealander*, which is hardly surprising as the book was started during the Crimean War. He devoted a chapter to the army and the Royal Navy and made his views clear in his first sentence: 'Judges and generals, soldiers and policemen are disagreeable necessities in this wicked world' [5]. He returned to military topics in *North America* and admitted: 'I hate military belongings.' [For his views on conscription, ➤ Patriotism.] He had little choice but to devote some of the less impressive parts of that book to military topics as he had arrived in America during the Civil War. Later in the 1860s his elder son, Henry, bought a commission as a cornet in a regiment of mounted yeomanry; at the same time his father was writing *Sir Harry Hotspur of Humblethwaite*, in which George Hotspur's commission was also in a mounted regiment. However, his manuscript notes for *The Way We Live Now*, written in 1873, show that he still needed to ask advice about how the young Sir Felix Carbury sells his commission. The practice of purchasing and therefore of selling commissions had been abolished in 1871.

Naval men are a rare species in Trollope. The most memorable is the retired officer Captain Cuttwater, a stereotyped salty sea-dog in *The Three Clerks*.

[➤ War.]

Milton, John. As a young man in London Trollope read a great deal of poetry and retained this love throughout his life. He had a strong devotion to Milton, a devotion he shared with his mother. He was so annoyed with Dr Johnson's hostile references to Milton in his *Lives of the Poets* that he flung the book out of the window. He tried to instil his love in his nieces by offering them £5 each if they would memorize *Lycidas*. This was his favourite poem and he frequently quoted three lines from it:

Fame is the spur that the clear spirit doth raise
(That last infirmity of noble mind)
To scorn delights, and live laborious days . . .

Indeed, there are more quotes from or references to Milton in Trollope's novels than from any other writer except Shakespeare. In 'The Adventures of Fred Pickering' young Pickering devotes six weeks of futile work to a study of Milton's epic, *Samson Agonistes*. In *The Last Chronicle of Barset* Josiah Crawley knows 'that divine poem', *Lycidas*, by heart and, like young Pickering, is drawn to Samson, the blinded Jewish hero set against the Philistines. Trollope quotes the famous lines, 'Ask for this great deliverer now, and find him/Eyeless in Gaza, at the mill with slaves' [62]. In 1881, the year before his death, he was reading *Paradise Lost* to his family. He owned a bust of Milton which he left to the Athenaeum club, where it still reposes.

Mines. In several of his travel books

Trollope describes his own descent into various types of mines; he felt it was part of his 'duty' to his readers to undertake such visits. These trips also gave him some background for his novels: his Australian experiences gave him details of the goldfields in *John Caldigate*, and his travels for *The West Indies and the Spanish Main* provided background for the Guatamalan mines in *The Prime Minister*. His scathing descriptions of South African mining feature in *South Africa* and in *An Old Man's Love*. In 'Catherine Carmichael', his short story set amidst New Zealand's gold mines, the world of miners is shown not to be corrupt but brutalizing. What he grew to dislike was not so much the mines themselves as the life that sprang up round them. He also had an aversion to sudden riches: those who make instant fortunes are often disreputable characters in his fiction. In *The Three Clerks*, *The Way We Live Now* and *The Prime Minister* dishonest speculators are all concerned with mines. In spite of his general distrust of the effects of fortunes made from mining, he allowed some exceptions. Both John Gordon in *An Old Man's Love* and John Caldigate in the novel of that name return to England with fortunes made from mining, yet remain basically decent men.

Miss Mackenzie. Trollope's sixteenth novel was written between 22 May and 18 August 1864, the year in which he also completed *Can You Forgive Her?* and *The Claverings*. It was published in two volumes by Chapman & Hall on 28 February 1865; like *Rachel Ray*, it was not serialized. Perhaps the difficulties over serializing that novel caused him to decide against serializing another

novel about a woman in an Evangelical setting. Trollope received £1,300, according to his *Autobiography*, or £1,200, according to Sadleir's Bibliography. The extra £100 presumably came from United States and European sales.

In his *Autobiography* Trollope claimed this book was written 'with a desire to prove that a novel may be produced without any love; but even in this attempt it breaks down before the conclusion. In order that I might be strong in my purpose, I took for my heroine a very unattractive old maid who was overwhelmed by money troubles; but even she was in love before the end of the book, and made a romantic marriage with an old man.' Trollope undervalued the novel and was unfair to his creation, Margaret Mackenzie, by exaggerating her disabilities. Neither she nor her fiancé was 'old'. The book is actually a moving portrayal of the plight of a single woman. After reading it, the novelist Sir Edward Bulwer-Lytton (later Lord Lytton) wrote to Trollope: 'I really cannot resist telling you how warmly I admire the conception and execution of the character to which you give that name. It is full of the most delicate beauty.'

Trollope had wanted to call it 'The Modern Griselda' and refers to Margaret Mackenzie as 'our modern Griselda'. [➤ Griselda.] The heroine, Margaret Mackenzie, is thirty-three and for fifteen years has led a loveless life looking after her unmarried brother. When he dies she inherits the fortune he himself had inherited after a bitter legal wrangle with their cousin, Sir John Ball. 'She was neither beautiful nor clever' and had had only one suitor whom her brother had dismissed. Her surviving brother is 'in trade': he sells oilcloths. Once Miss Mackenzie has her £800 a year (defined in *Framley Parsonage* as adequate for 'second-class gentry' and roughly equal to Trollope's Post Office income) she is plagued by unsuitable suitors. She is surrounded by people who patronize her or are jealous of her wealth. She wishes to experience something of life and decides to move to Littlebath. [➤ Cheltenham].

Once in Littlebath Miss Mackenzie has two options: the sinful set who play cards and frequent the assembly rooms or the godly set who follow the Reverend Mr Stumfold and drink tea with his formidable wife. Margaret chooses the safer option, 'the Stumfoldians'. For Stumfold, Trollope drew on aspects of two famous Evangelical parsons, Cheltenham's own Francis Close (whom Trollope detested) and Harrow's J. W. Cunningham (whom Trollope's mother had detested). Margaret Mackenzie, like Eleanor Bold in *Barchester Towers*, is courted by three suitors. The first is her brother's partner, Samuel Rubb, who originally comes to ask for a loan. He is a somewhat vulgar tradesman but is not without redeeming traits. She gives him the money guaranteed by a mortgage on their premises, only to discover the property is already mortgaged. His rival is Stumfold's curate, Jeremiah Maguire, an oleaginous Evangelical described as looking almost like a classical god: he was marked by a 'terrible squint in his right eye which ever disfigured a face that in all other respects was fitted for an Apollo'.

Miss Mackenzie sees through Rubb and is warned by Mrs Stumfold against Maguire. She is invited by her cousins, the Balls, for a visit and while there a third suitor, the baronet's eldest son, John, asks for her hand. She rejects all three. Then her remaining brother dies and she decides to give half her wealth to his widow, when a lawyer tells her that the original bequest to her brother was illegal and the money belongs to the Balls. John Ball renews his proposal – the only one of the trio to do so when she has no money. John, another of Trollope's cautious, bald and middle-aged lovers, agonizes over marrying his cousin because of his mother's violent opposition, but he finally renews his proposal which she accepts. Mr Maguire finally gets a wife and a church in London.

By choosing Littlebath, Trollope can lambast both Evangelicals and the sham, pretentious gentility he and his wife must have found in Cheltenham. Trollope enjoyed describing Mrs Stumfold's tea-party [4] and this has parallels with the play his mother wrote for her children to perform, 'The Righteous Rout', which also attacked an Evangelical tea-party. Trollope's attack on Evangelical-inspired 'do-goodery' occurs in Chapter 27, 'The Negro Soldiers' Orphan Bazaar', in which wealthy ladies sell overpriced goods to raise money for orphans of negro soldiers in the Northern armies in the American Civil War. In his *Autobiography* he remembered that he wrote this chapter 'with a violence which will, I think, convince any reader that such attempts at raising money were at the time very odious to me. I beg to say that since that I have no occasion to alter my opinion.' (This Victorian device for fund-raising originated with the Anti-Corn Law League in the 1840s. It reached its apogee with a bazaar at Covent Garden which led to an aristocratic boycott of the House.) His most concentrated attack on sham gentility occurs in Chapter 8, 'Mrs Tom Mackenzie's Dinner Party'. Here Miss Mackenzie's sister-in-law hires caterers and a butler to serve badly a very bad meal *à la Russe*.

There are the usual private references: apart from placing Miss Mackenzie in the Paragon Buildings, where he and Rose had lived, Trollope refers to young men who prefer beer and skittles to tea with their aunts, just as he had done when his aunt invited him when he first worked in London. The choice of the oilcloth business for the Mackenzie–Rubb partnership may be traced to Trollope's moving into Waltham House in 1859. One of his tasks was to order the latest floor-covering: oilcloth, the forerunner of linoleum. Characters from other novels reappear: Miss Todd and Miss Baker from *The Bertrams*; Lady Glencora Palliser; the Duchess of St Bungay; and Griselda, Lady Hartletop. There are two passages which support the claim that Trollope's writing was, like his mother's, marked by 'vulgarity'. In the first [8] there is a reference to a 'good honest kiss, mouth to mouth'. In the second [9] Miss Mackenzie stands in front of a looking-glass to see if she is 'old' or not, and in doing so she 'pulled her scarf tighter across her bosom, feeling her own form, and then she leaned forward and kissed herself in the glass'.

The novel defends the Sunday post; Trollope points out that if Littlebath had allowed one, Miss Mackenzie would have heard of her brother's fatal illness a day earlier [➤ Sabbatarianism]. There is an attack on anti-Catholicism to correct the prejudices of Mr Maguire. The novel has a

'sermon' about the need for marriage [11]. There are an unusual number of references to Queen Victoria and the Prince and Princess of Wales: by 1864 the controversy over the Queen's retirement from public life was under way and the young couple had only been married a year. There is a reference to dishonesty in public life, in an insurance company of which John Ball is a director [➤ Honesty]. The book is loaded with silly names: the Evangelicals, Mr Frigidy, Mrs Perch (a coachbuilder's wife), Mr Startup, Miss Floss and Mrs Fleebody; the schoolmistress, Mrs Crammer and her sister, Miss Dumpus; the solicitors, Slow and Bideawhile; Madame Colza (colza oil was used for lamps); Mr Grandairs, the pompous hired butler; Mr and Mrs Fuzzybell and Lady Ruff, part of Littlebath's sinful set; the insurance company named Abednego Life and Shadrach Fire (from Daniel 3.12–30 where Shadrach, Meshach and Abednego were the three Jews who would not bow down to Nebuchadnezzar's golden image).

As well as containing some of his most amusing passages, this novel is Trollope's most incisive portrait of the difficulties of unmarried women in Victorian England

'Miss Ophelia Gledd'. A short story apparently written in a rush to meet the deadline set by Emily Faithfull for her book, *A Welcome*. When Trollope wrote to her on 19 February 1863 he was already at work and promised the story by 24 February. The story was donated by Trollope, as he had donated 'The Journey to Panama'. It was later included in his third collection, *Lotta Schmidt and Other Stories*, in 1867.

Trollope's third American short

story is narrated in the first person by Archibald Green, who asks the reader to judge: 'Was Miss Ophelia Gledd a lady' because there was a 'freedom and easiness about her, a readiness to say anything that came into her mind, an absence of all reticence'? She is the 'belle of Boston' and is attractive, even though she has that American 'nasal twang' noted by English writers of the nineteenth century. Her father is an impoverished merchant, her mother a 'nonentity'. Green comes across Ophelia while out sleighing and stops when the sleigh in which she is travelling has an accident. (Trollope had had a sleighing accident in Boston on 8 March 1862.) Green offers to help and they become friends, but then he goes away for a year. On his return he hears that she has two suitors, one American and one English. The English suitor is 'a literary man of some mark, fifteen years her senior, very sedate in his habits, not much given to love-making'. His brother is a baronet. When Green tells the man that everyone is talking about their possible marriage he swears he will take the first ship back to England because he hates to have his private affairs talked about in public. When Green takes Ophelia out sleighing she admits that her goal is to 'make myself an Englishwoman'. She asks Green's advice about marrying her English or her American suitor and he recommends she marry for love. In the end she settles for the Englishman (one of the first of Trollope's Anglo-American marriages) and he ends the story with the question with which he began it: 'Will she or will she not be received in London as a lady?'

This story, as much as any of his novels or stories which feature Amer-ica, examines relations between the two countries and the differences between English and American young women, an aspect of minor differences within a cultural union that fascinated him. His analysis of the differences between the two countries' middle classes is still accurate: English reticence and love of privacy – the 'grandeur of coldness', Ophelia calls it – versus American openness and ease. Some may think the heroine is Trollope's friend Kate Field because she shares so many of her characteristics: she went to 'lectures ... to political debates, and wherever her enterprising heart and inquiring head chose to carry her'. But it was not Trollope's habit to portray friends, but types: undoubtedly his time in Boston, his sleighing accident and his meeting American girls, including Kate Field, gave him the material he needed. Ophelia was one of Trollope's 'brown complexioned' women [➤ Women].

The published correspondence of a Boston woman, Ellen Dwight, who married the brother of an English baron (and baronet), the Honourable Edward Twistleton, shows just how accurate Trollope's portrayal was. Mrs Twistleton (who died a few months before Trollope began his story) liked to recall that the maids at the family's Oxfordshire castle assumed she was a Red Indian and even the family were only won over when they heard that her parents used Crown Derby china in Boston. Twistleton was a minor man of letters and Trollope may well have known him from literary circles or indeed from his postal work in parts of Oxfordshire. [Lady.]

'Miss Sarah Jack of Spanish Town, Jamaica'. This is one of the five stories written when Trollope was on holiday in the French Pyrenees in September–October 1859. The background for the story is derived from his 1858–9 Post Office journey through the West Indies and Central America. During that time he spent a month in Jamaica, as recounted in *The West Indies and the Spanish Main*. This story was first published in *Cassell's Illustrated Family Newspaper* on 3 and 10 November 1860 and was included in his first collection, *Tales of All Countries* (1861). In his *Autobiography* Trollope wrote that the stories included in that collection 'have, most of them, some foundation in such occurrences', that is, in 'true tales of my adventures'. Trollope received £40.

The story is set against the economic decline of Jamaica after the emancipation of the slaves in 1833 and the fall in the price of sugar. (Cassell himself was a well-known opponent of slavery.) This slight tale – one of Trollope's slightest – concerns a young man, Maurice Cumming, who has inherited a run-down coffee and sugar plantation. He is befriended by his maiden aunt, Sarah Jack, one of Trollope's strong-willed women, who lives in Spanish Town. Cumming, hard pressed by his economic problems, is in love with a niece of Miss Jack, Marian Leslie, a flirt, and his courting seems to get nowhere. In the end Marian, who does love him without realizing how deeply, comes to see that love imposes limitations and that flirting is beyond them.

The lesson is essentially Trollopian: a man should not be put off his courting if he is sincere, and secondly, whatever obstacles a man faces he should be forthright in telling a girl he loves her. When he does so, she will see his true value and if she is true, she will accept him. [➤ Marriage.]

'The Mistletoe Bough'. This short story was written sometime between 12 April, when *The Illustrated London News* agreed terms for a Christmas story, and 15 August 1861, when Trollope sent the manuscript to them. The story was published in the Christmas Supplement on 21 December 1861 and was included in his second collection, *Tales of All Countries*, Second Series (1863). The story is set in the Lake District where Trollope's sister Cecilia and her husband, John Tilley, lived; his mother and brother Tom later moved there. The site of his mother's house is used as the location for the story. Trollope received £50.

This love story within a Christmas tale opens with a dispute in the Garrow household over whether mistletoe should be hung during Christmastide: two brothers, Harry and Frank, are for it and one sister, Elizabeth, is against. The boys, who call her a 'Puritan', do not know that her ex-lover, Godfrey Holmes, whose guardian was Mr Garrow, is coming for a visit. Elizabeth is one of Trollope's independently-minded young women who has rejected girlish talk of finding a husband and has resolved 'that in loving her lord she would not worship him, and that in giving her heart she would only so give it as it would be given to a human creature like herself' – hence the breaking-off of her engagement to Holmes. Her fault was a 'reverence for martyrdom in general' – she suffered from 'philo-martyrdom' – and a refusal to accept life, and especially its good things, as it is. She rejects a renewed offer from Holmes and her father accuses her of a 'false feminine pride'. In the end she changes her mind and the mistletoe is hung. [➤ Marriage.]

Trollope enjoys a laugh at excessive Victorian propriety over kissing under the mistletoe. Like many Victorian Christmas stories written after Washington Irving's *Bracebridge Hall* tales, it is set in a large 'establishment', in this case a country house, Thwaite Hall, in Westmorland. There are lots of people and 'the beef and pudding are ponderous'. Trollope has a private joke about excessive work schedules which, in this case, Frank Garrow prepares in order to get through his holiday assignments – to little avail. We also see how he came up with names for his characters: Garrow was the maiden name of Tom Trollope's first wife, Theodosia, and Harry was the name of Trollope's elder son. Trollope's dislike of 'Puritans' (for which read 'Evangelicals') is evident in the comment by Elizabeth Garrow that 'Frank says that I am a Puritan, and pride was the worst of their sins.' He also scores a hit against phrenology. [➤ Spiritualism.]

Mistresses. Although mistresses occur in some of Trollope's fiction, the word 'mistress' is rarely used. He was in fact careful not to use it so as not to upset either Mudie's Circulating Library or people who were reading the novels aloud in a family circle. A man's recourse to a mistress is normally hinted at rather than stated as a fact. Thus when the old roué, Sir Lionel Bertram, retires to Littlebath, readers are told that he had rooms for himself and his servant 'and another smaller establishment in a secluded quiet street' [21]. Again, in *Is He Popenjoy?* Adelaide Houghton says of her husband: 'With whom Mr Houghton

consoles himself I have never taken the trouble to inquire. I hope someone is good-natured to him, poor old soul' [35]. A perceptive reader will at once see that the Marchioness of Hartletop, who is mentioned frequently in both the Barsetshire and Palliser series, has been the mistress of the old Duke of Omnium, but when people talk about her they avoid the word 'mistress' [*Framley Parsonage*, 16].

By the 1870s, the word itself could be used. In *Phineas Redux*, serialized in 1873–4, Madame Max Goesler is aware that her close friendship with the old Duke of Omnium will cause people to think she is his 'mistress' – and she uses the word [30]. As she is half 'foreign' she can use words that sedate English ladies would avoid. In *John Caldigate*, serialized in 1878–9, the word is used several times after Hester Bolton's marriage appears to be destroyed by the bigamy case. Even her fanatically religious mother uses the word 'mistress' as a way to frighten her. In *An Eye for an Eye*, also serialized over 1878–9, Captain Fred Neville, though a reprobate, refuses to trick Kate O'Hara into becoming his mistress, and he too uses the word. The heroine in Trollope's last novel, serialized during 1882–3, is outraged when she is told that all her fellow theatrical people are suggesting that she has become someone's 'mistress' [*The Land-Leaguers*, 27].

Mistresses are seldom allowed to be characters in their own right. In *Can You Forgive Her?*, George Vavasor, a mysterious MP, maintains rooms in London, a place for fox-hunting in Oxfordshire and a third place, 'very closely hidden from the world's eye, which shall be nameless' [12]. In this novel Trollope gives his decided view that, in fiction, 'mystery is a vice' and he therefore allows the mistress to make an appeal for help from Vavasor [71]. A second mistress to appear as a character is Mrs Morton in *Sir Harry Hotspur of Humblethwaite*, serialized in 1870. She is never called George Hotspur's mistress, and she is shown to be a superior person to the man she loved.

Money. Money plays an important role in Trollope's fiction. 'The man who is insensible of the power which money brings with it must be a dolt' [*Lady Anna*, 4]. 'A desire for wealth,' Plantagenet Palliser says, 'is the source of all progress. Civilization comes from what men call greed. Let your mercenary tendencies be combined with honesty and they cannot take you astray' [*Can You Forgive Her?*, 25]. Anthony Trollope was certainly highly sensitive to money, as any reading of his *Autobiography* will show [➤ Chapter 6 in particular]. He did not 'worship' money and he was remarkably generous with what he earned, but he hated the cant that pretends that 'art' has nothing to do with money and that money is not vital to civilized life. He rounded on one witness before the Royal Commission on Copyright who said he would be sorry to hear that writers like Dr Johnson or Dickens had written for money: 'Do you not think,' Trollope replied, 'that an author is in exactly the same category as any other workman, who has it upon his conscience to use his life for doing good work for the world around him and who cannot do that good work unless he is paid for it?' [Mullen, 599]. [For his denunciation of the worship of money, ➤ *The Bertrams*, 44.] In his lecture on the Zulus

he said, 'That love of money, which we observe so often as the parent of all industry, will be so with the Zulu.'

One of the most frequent statements in Trollope's fiction is that a character 'has £— a year'. The income of many upper- and middle-class Victorians – the people who populate his novels – came largely from land or relatively stable investments like government bonds which paid about three per cent a year. In the late novels, by which time Trollope himself was a large investor, characters speak of getting five per cent in safe investments.

Money from land provided the incomes of almost all the clergymen, aristocrats and gentry in his fiction. Their incomes were often governed by legal arrangements such as commuted tithes for clergymen or family settlements for married women and their husbands. The son of a comfortably-off family expected to receive an annual allowance from his father, which would last well into adulthood [➤ Fathers and Sons]. Many Victorians thought that the comfortably middle class comprised those people who paid income tax: when it was introduced it was levied on incomes of about £400 a year and above [➤ *The Three Clerks*].

Trollope has great sport with Plantagenet Palliser's desire to introduce a decimalized currency, something that was fortunately prevented until almost a century after these novels were written. Some readers might find it helpful to know the monetary system of Trollope's time: the pound (£) was divided into twenty shillings (*s.*). A shilling was divided into twelve pence (*d.*) and each penny in turn was divided into two halfpennies, or ha'pence, and four farthings. Characters sometimes use other terms. A guinea (gn.), twenty-one shillings, was frequently used in upper-class speech and was often the measure for fees by professional men. A sovereign was a gold coin equal to a pound, as there were no pound notes. A 'pony' was a slang term, used mainly by gamblers, for £25. A half-crown or half-a-crown was 2s. 6d., or two shillings and sixpence. A florin was a coin worth two shillings. In addition, there was a silver sixpence (6d.) and a silver threepenny coin (3d.). Foreign money is often mentioned in Trollope's fiction. Throughout his lifetime the pound sterling was roughly equal to five American dollars. French currency was more unstable; however, one will not be too far wrong if one assumes that a franc was normally worth slightly less than a shilling.

It is difficult to say exactly what money was worth in relation to prices. By the end of the century prices had, on the whole, come down and the value of money had risen. Probably the highest-paid workmen of the time were the compositors who set the text of books by Trollope and other writers. These men earned about 83s. a week in the mid-Victorian period and some were earning as much as 93s. at the end of Trollope's lifetime. A letter-carrier working under Trollope's direction in East Anglia would receive about 14s. a week, and these were much sought-after jobs. Yet in *Australia and New Zealand* Trollope refers to agricultural labourers and carters getting as little as 11s. a week, but their wages varied. In *The Claverings* an old agricultural worker gets 8s. a week while his daughter gets 6s. However, Larry Twentyman in *The American Senator* pays the labourers on his farm as much as 14s. a week. Thus

almost any unskilled working man earning £1 a week knew that he was definitely doing better than most. A clergyman such as Mark Robarts with his £900 a year had an income equal to more than thirty agricultural labourers working in his parish, and even Mr Crawley with his £130 has an income equal to four or five of his poor parishioners, the brick-makers.

If one compares Trollope's income with most people's it is clear just how well-off he was. He began his Post Office career as a clerk on £90 a year and by the time of his retirement was getting about £900, of which £800 was salary and the rest allowances. This income alone would have raised him to what he calls in one novel 'us second class gentry with our eight hundred a year – there or thereabouts' [*Framley Parsonage*, 17]. His 'thereabouts' at that point was at least double that and within a few years (1863) he calculated his income at £3,496 17s. 7d. By 1869 it had grown to £6,994 18s. 1d. and even though it declined somewhat in the 1870s, he was still a man of considerable wealth. In 1872, the *Spectator* calculated that there were 60,000 British families out of 4,600,000 in what they called the highest or 'comfortable' class, which they defined as those with £800 a year. As a surveyor in the Post Office this was just about Trollope's annual salary and it is the income he most often gives characters in his fiction who are comfortable but not wealthy. Interestingly, he did this in *The Warden* which was written several years before he received that amount as his salary. In the last two decades of his life Trollope's normal annual income was at least five times that amount.

Income, of course, has to be seen in

relation to prices. Trollope paid 3*d*. a day for his *Times* and for 6,000 cigars in 1866 he paid £31 7*s*. 9*d*. To educate his two sons at public school cost him £130 a year for each boy, or about five per cent of his annual income for both sons. Income tax, after a rise during the Crimean War, settled into a rate of a few pence in the pound (the highest from 1860 to 1882 was 10*d*. and the lowest was 2*d*.) We do not know what he paid his servants, but Archdeacon Grantly, a man of comparable wealth, pays his cook £30 a year. Maids, of course, received far less. One short story dashed off in a week could almost pay the wages of his household of servants. [➤ Fox-hunting; Wine.] Although Trollope, unlike most Victorians, preferred to buy rather than rent the houses in which he lived, a good idea of the value of money can be gained from the fact that he has one lawyer renting a substantial house in London in Bloomsbury Square for £120 a year.

Trollope's increasing wealth and his own generosity made a subtle change in the amounts of money mentioned in his fiction. After the 1860s the characters tend to have larger incomes although many moan that they are 'poor' – which is of course a highly relative term. However, there was great pressure for 'respectable people' to keep up appearances and the cost of servants, carriages and education could mount up and overwhelm people with relatively high incomes. The nineteenth century was a time of fairly easy credit and most people settled accounts with tradesmen only quarterly or annually. Thus it was possible to live above one's income, but in Trollope's fiction – as in real life – the day of reckoning did come and that is why so many characters resort to

money-lenders or sign bills. The resort to bills was in part because it was so difficult, especially for younger men, to obtain loans from banks.

Trollope was as increasingly generous with his fictional creations as he was with his own sons and there appears to be an increase of useful aunts or other elderly relatives who kindly expire, leaving a few more hundred a year to various characters. *Phineas Finn* is a good example of this. It is also characteristic of Trollope that he hardly ever sends a character into exile without some small amount of money to provide for basic needs. Probably most of his readers wanted to see people living at a higher level than themselves. Certainly for the type of people about whom Trollope normally wrote – those with money – the Victorian era was truly a golden age. [➤ Doctors; Lawyers.]

Money-lenders. Money-lenders occur frequently in Trollope's fiction and are usually associated with bills and post-obits given to young men in financial trouble. As a young man Trollope had his own miserable experience with a money-lender: a tailor's bill for £12 was passed on to a money-lender near Mecklenburgh Square. (The Square is synonymous in Trollope's fiction with London's money-lenders.) He loaned Trollope a further £4 and in time Trollope came to owe over £200. This story, with its money-lender and his language, was used in *The Three Clerks* [28] and also in *Phineas Finn* [21–2]. The money-lender in *The Three Clerks* is called Jabesh M'Ruen, while in *Can You Forgive Her?* his name is Magruin. They are probably intended to be the same person, as Trollope often forgot the earlier spelling of a character's name. In the latter novel [29–30] he lends £122 10s. to a man already deeply in debt and thus he demands at the end of two months the sum of £500. The money-lender in *Phineas Finn*, Clarkson, is given the same appearance as the real money-lender who pursued Trollope. The title of Chapter 21, 'Do be Punctual', is a phrase used by the money-lender of Trollope's youth. (It is also used in *Can You Forgive Her?* [30].) In *Mr Scarborough's Family* money-lenders play a more important role than in any other novel by precipitating the main plot, and in *John Caldigate* the demands of money-lenders force the hero, after whom the novel is named, to emigrate to Australia.

Often, but not always, money-lenders are Jews although the term 'Jew' can be applied to gentiles. Sometimes the most offensive lenders, men like Captain Stubber in *Sir Harry Hotspur of Humblethwaite*, are not Jewish, while on other occasions Jewish lenders do not have Jewish names. Mr Tyrrwhit in *Mr Scarborough's Family* is called a 'dirty Jew' by the reprobate, Mr Scarborough: this may mean that Tyrrwhit is Jewish or that the term 'Jew' was used to imply a money-grubber [21]. Perhaps Trollope's most important Jewish money-lender is Mr Hart, who appears in two novels: in *Sir Harry Hotspur of Humblethwaite* he is Abraham Hart and in *Mr Scarborough's Family* he is Samuel.

The money-lender who plays, perhaps, the largest role in any novel is Dobbs Broughton in *The Last Chronicle of Barset*. He occupies a higher social rank than most of Trollope's money-lenders and is a partner of two equally discreditable characters, Mrs Van Siever and Augustus Musselboro.

Eventually Broughton commits suicide, an act which to his creator may have been a fitting end for all money-lenders.

Monk, Joshua. The 'most advanced Liberal' MP in the Palliser novels, Monk has quite radical views and is renowned for his honesty and independence. He exercises great influence on Phineas Finn and at the end of the novel of that name they travel to Ireland together. His opposition to voting by secret ballot reflects Trollope's own view. At the end of *The Duke's Children* he becomes prime minister. Some people have assumed that Monk is based on Richard Cobden, the well-known advocate of free trade, who was dead by the time Trollope started to write *Phineas Finn*. Since Trollope was not a great admirer of Cobden [➤ *The Warden*] this is unlikely. Monk springs from a background of commerce, unlike most of his aristocratic colleagues. There actually was a Liberal MP named Monk – C. J. Monk – at the time, and he was well known for advocating a reform close to Trollope's heart: giving civil servants the right to vote. [➤ Parliament; Politics.]

'Most Illustrious Personage.' See 'Illustrious Personage'.

Mothers and Daughters. The relations between a mother and her daughter or daughters formed a recurrent and very important theme in Trollope's fiction. Given the importance of marriage to his novels, the role of a mother was fairly well defined. It was her duty, in which she was sometimes joined by her husband, first to beware of an eligible man's getting near her daughter and then, when one did, to assess her daughter's choice. In 'The Courtship of Susan Bell' her role was compared with that of a shepherdess: 'Could she let this young wolf in among her lamb-fold? He might be a wolf; – who could tell.'

Generally when a mother tries to promote a match her work is in vain: Lady Wanless in 'Alice Dugdale', the Countess Lovel in *Lady Anna*, Mrs Clavering in *The Claverings* and Mrs Mountjoy in *Mr Scarborough's Family* are but four out of scores of mothers who live to see their daughters marry the 'wrong' men. Mrs Mountjoy admits her error: 'But such longings are, I think, wicked, and are seldom realized' [61]. Rarely is the mother's role to encourage a match with a man who is the daughter's choice: one example of this is the Duchess of Omnium, who supports a marriage between her daughter, Lady Mary Palliser, and Francis Tregear in *The Duke's Children*. After the duchess's death it is her husband who opposes the match. Sometimes when a mother works hard for a marriage her work backfires, for instance in the case of Countess Lovel in *Lady Anna* [see below], or Mrs Grantly when she encourages the match between her daughter Griselda and the Marquis of Hartletop: once Griselda is a marchioness she snubs her mother. More normal is Frau Frohmann's reaction when she accepts her daughter's marriage to Fritz Schlessen. She did not do so 'with that ecstasy of joy with which sons-in-law are sometimes welcomed' ['Why Frau Frohmann Raised Her Prices']. As a consequence of the mother's role, disagreement and sometimes bitter fighting between mothers and daughters, and often between mothers and

sons, are a fairly normal part of Trollope's fiction.

While normally the bond between a mother and her daughter, even if they are fighting, is strong, in some novels a woman's motherhood is not that important: Lady Glencora Palliser, later Duchess of Omnium, springs to mind. Sometimes the mother exists but is fairly irrelevant: this is the case in 'Miss Ophelia Gledd'. In others it is too important. In *The Small House at Allington*, Mrs Dale is a woman who has withdrawn from society after her husband's death, so as not to limit her daughters' chances in life. Mrs Ray in *Rachel Ray* is rather similar. [➤ Mourning; Widows.] In *Lady Anna* the mother tries to manipulate her daughter to fulfil her own ambition: Countess Lovel tries to force her daughter to marry a young earl, only to see her marry a Radical tailor.

Sometimes this basic relationship takes on an added dimension as in the case of Mrs Dale, perhaps Trollope's most famous mother. In *The Small House at Allington* she does actually let the 'wolf', in the form of Adolphus Crosbie, into her fold with a tragic result for her daughter Lily. In *An Eye for an Eye* the consequences of letting the wolf into the fold include seduction, murder, a stillbirth and insanity.

Given the importance of this relationship between mother and daughter, there are a surprising number of novels and short stories in which the relationship does not exist. Feemy Macdermot in *The Macdermots of Ballycloran*, Anastasia Bergen in 'Aaron Trow,' Marion Fay in the novel named after her, Mahala Tringlos in 'Malachi's Cove', Maryanne Brown in *The Struggles of Brown, Jones, and Robinson*, the Lady Euphemia in 'The

Gentle Euphemia', Dorothy Grey in *Mr Scarborough's Family*, Clara Amedroz in *The Belton Estate*, Mary Lovelace in *Is He Popenjoy?*, Polly Peppercorn and Emily Greenmantle in 'The Two Heroines of Plumplington', Eva Crasweller in *The Fixed Period*, and the daughters of Philip Jones in *The Land-Leaguers* – all these are without mothers, while not being orphans. In most cases these young women have established close bonds with their fathers.

Stepmothers are fairly rare in Trollope's fiction. Although Grace Crawley becomes stepmother to Major Crawley's daughter, the relationship is not developed. The same is true of Alice Dugdale's stepmother in 'Alice Dugdale'. In 'The Man Who Kept His Money in a Box', the fact that Mrs Greene is Miss Greene's stepmother allows the younger woman to make several telling comments about the elder to a fellow guest. Trollope's most important stepmother is the Marchioness of Kingsbury, who opposes – in vain – the marriage of her stepdaughter to the Post Office clerk, George Roden, in *Marion Fay*.

Mourning. Trollope frequently attacked the excessive Victorian rules about mourning while in private life he followed some of the customs, such as using black borders on his writing-paper after his own mother's death. His own view was something of a pre-Victorian one which he had inherited from her.

The Victorians did not invent rules for mourning but inherited them from the eighteenth century. What they did was to codify them for an expanding middle class and to extend them to working people who often expended large sums or joined 'funeral clubs' to

have a 'proper funeral'. By mid-century, rules regarding funerals and mourning had reached their apogee; by the end of the century they were being relaxed. The degree of mourning depended on the relationship of the deceased: even under the relaxed rules a widow was expected to wear mourning for two years or at least eighteen months, while crêpe was worn only for six months. The widow also wore a white widow's cap under her mourning, but by the end of the century this had gone out of fashion. Widows and ladies in general did not normally go to funerals because of concern for their emotions. (Trollope's widow did not attend his funeral in 1882.) For parents, one was in mourning for one year: crêpe trimmings for six months, plain black clothes for four, and half-mourning for two. (Half-mourning allowed greys but no 'colour'.) Grandparents, uncles and aunts got three months; cousins, one month, and so on. (Relations by marriage were treated as if they were blood relations in the same way in which Victorians often referred to 'in-laws' as 'my sister' or 'my brother', not my 'sister-in-law' or 'brother-in-law'.) In *The Vicar of Bullhampton* Trollope shows how difficult the rules governing mourning could become by having two ladies discuss whether one should go into mourning for a cousin: '"Shall you go into mourning?" she asked; "he was only your second cousin; but people have ideas so different about those things"' [59].

There was special jewellery for women, often made of jet, and while they were not to wear gold for at least twelve months, pearls and diamonds were permitted. There were fewer rules for men simply because the standard Victorian gentleman's dress was already so dull. In *The Last Chronicle of Barset*, Trollope writes of Adolphus Crosbie wearing black studs in mourning for the wife he never loved as an object lesson for his readers in the falseness that rules about mourning could produce. Yet Crosbie's studs or the black clothes Madame Max Goesler wears in *Phineas Redux* [30] immediately allowed people to know they were in mourning. A person in mourning did not go to the theatre or give dinner-parties and so on, and one's writing-paper was edged in black. The black edging was wider for near relations and decreased from the maximum of half an inch (for a husband or wife) to a quarter, to an eighth and lastly to a sixteenth of an inch according to the degree of relationship. Few of Trollope's surviving letters have mourning of more than the minimum.

Trollope's main concern when denouncing mourning was for the effect it had on widows. In his third novel, *La Vendée*, he has one character refer to the widow's 'living sacrifice to a life of desolation from a false regard to her husband's memory' [28]. For her part, Rose Trollope carried on using writing-paper with the narrowest black borders till as late as 1899 but she followed her husband's urging to 'enjoy thoroughly the good things which he has left behind for her use'. This advice had occurred in *The Eustace Diamonds*, in his most powerful assault upon the excesses of Victorian mourning with its 'suttee propensities' and 'hideous forms of clothing' and he rejoiced that women were beginning to abandon suttee in India and the swathes of black in Britain.

MP. See Politics.

'Mrs Brumby'. This is one of the short stories written for *Saint Pauls* and published in May 1870; it was included in Trollope's fourth collection, *An Editor's Tales*, published in the same year. In his *Autobiography* he recalled his time as editor of *Saint Pauls* and remembered how 'a poor weak editor was driven nearly to madness by threatened litigation from a rejected contributor'.

This story is told in the first person, using the editorial 'we', and like 'Mary Gresley', 'The Adventures of Fred Pickering' and 'Josephine de Montmorenci' it describes the world of writers in London and those who try to become writers. Mrs Brumby is the 'most hateful and the most hated' person the editor met in the course of his duties. (Perhaps Trollope had heard from his son Fred that 'brumby' was an Australian term for a wild horse.) She could not write but was determined to 'push her way in London as a woman of literature'. She forces herself on the editor; he is not strong enough to get rid of her and agrees to look at her manuscript. A fortnight passes and she returns, telling the editor, 'You assured me that it would be accepted unless returned within seven days. Of course it will be accepted now.' She has the advantage of a grievance, however unreal: 'The would-be author, who cannot make his way either by intellect or favour, can hardly do better, perhaps, than establish a grievance.'

To get rid of her the editor agrees to read the article at once and finds it 'undeniable twaddle'. When she returns, he tells her it will not do; she demands the name of his solicitors and in a few days they get a letter from Badger and Blister, her solicitors, demanding 25 guineas for Mrs Brumby and £1. 13*s*. 8*d*. costs [➤ Money]. When the editor explains to his solicitor the facts of the case he is reminded that her solicitors will 'take up any case however hopeless, and work it with superhuman energy, on the mere chance of getting something'. The editor is advised to buy her off with £10. The magazine's publishers protest; the editor fears for his position and agrees to go to her address and talk to her husband, in whose name the letter was written. There he finds Lieutenant Brumby, a drunkard who is cowed by his wife. The magazine's solicitor demands that the editor agree to the £10 blackmail and sign a letter apologizing for the delay in reading her manuscript: however unjust, it is better than a lawsuit. The 'moment in which we signed it was perhaps the bitterest we ever knew'. At least Mrs Brumby never got a shilling as the lawyers took it all.

This story is salutary reading for anyone who edits a magazine as Trollope hardly exaggerated the problems, and the absurdities of English libel laws have hardly changed in 120 years. Trollope used the story to comment on the lack of professional outlets or 'ports' for Victorian women: 'Fortunately for us and for the world at large … the port of literature is open to women. It seems to be the only really desirable harbour to which a female captain can steer her vessel with much hope of success.' [➤ Faithfull, Emily; Eliot, George].

Mr Scarborough's Family. Trollope's forty-fifth novel was written between 14 March and 31 October 1881 and serialized in the weekly *All the Year Round*, beginning on 27 May 1882 and ending on 16 June 1883, some six months after his death. It was then published in three volumes by Chatto & Windus in April 1883. Trollope received £1,000, a large enough sum to undermine the argument that in his final years he was in decline as a writer. Half the manuscript is in the hand of his niece, Florence Bland; often a chapter would be started by Trollope, finished by his niece and then corrected by him.

Mr Scarborough's Family is Trollope's last completed three-volume novel and the last one with a multitude of plots, characters and locations; there are ten separate love plots. *An Old Man's Love*, which was his next novel, is a short and uncomplicated work, and his final novel, *The Land-Leaguers*, was never finished. All these – as well as *Lord Palmerston*, the book written immediately after this novel – share one common trait: they are the works of an old man. As he wrote to an American politician only nineteen days before beginning this novel, 'I now am an old man, 66 [actually 65], and shall soon have come to the end of my tether.' He was depressed by the weather and by living in the countryside; his friend George Eliot had died in December 1880 and his niece, his brother Tom's daughter, had died while giving birth when Trollope was halfway through the writing of this book. His depressed mood permeates the novel and is expressed in an aside about the young men of the day: 'for the most part small in stature, well-made little men … wearing close-packed shining little hats … their spoken thoughts seldom rise above a small acrid sharpness. And that in that timeless complaint:

"They respect no one; above all, not their elders"' [22].

Trollope's first biographer, Escott, called this novel 'the most deliberately and elaborately satirical of all Trollope's stories'. How successful a satire it is must depend on individual judgements. There are many other ways in which to see the book. It may be called a novel about entail, about inheritance, or about old age, as three leading characters, Mr Scarborough, Peter Prosper and John Grey, are all either old or prematurely so [57]. It may be called a novel about one of Trollope's favourite themes, honesty. Mr Grey, the honest solicitor, is ultimately defeated by the dishonesty of his client, Mr Scarborough, and retires from the law in disgust. Of his partner, Mr Barry, who takes over, Grey agrees he is honest but 'he does not hate the absolute utter roguery of our own client ... Barry and the rest of them only shake their heads and laugh' [62]. It may be called a novel about the evils of gambling as Mountjoy Scarborough is said to have lost some £100,000 through card-playing – a sum well exceeding £3,000,000 in today's currency. Finally, and with tongue in cheek, the novel could even be said to be about the importance of whist, to which both Mr Scarborough and Mountjoy Scarborough are addicted and through which Mountjoy loses his fortune and, it appears at first, his inheritance.

Trollope had long been concerned with arranging his will so that he could treat both his sons fairly and provide for his wife and Florence Bland [➤ *Cousin Henry*]. Property and inheritance played important roles in his writing, but as he aged they became even more central. In this novel a

clergyman says to his son, 'It is bad waiting for dead men's shoes,' and the son replies, 'And yet it is what everybody does in this world' [24]. Certainly it is what many people do in Trollope's novels, perhaps clergymen most of all. Mr Slope in *Barchester Towers* was only extreme in that he did not wait till the dean was dead before he began to seek support to succeed him, and *An Old Man's Love* would soon show a young curate's chatting away happily about his hopes to succeed his dying vicar. *Mr Scarborough's Family* is unusual only because it features three young men 'waiting for dead men's shoes' to become vacant.

The central plot is a fantastic, not to say improbable, story of twisting and turning by the aged Scarborough. He is not a Christian believer – a 'pagan' to Trollope – and he has a contempt for women's intelligence. He also hates all authority, rules and regulations, but 'of all things he hated most the entail' [1]. (In this he resembles another squire, old Caldigate in *John Caldigate*.) He has two sons: the elder, Mountjoy, is a reprobate captain in the Coldstream Guards [➤ Military], while the younger, Augustus, is a hard-hearted barrister. Mountjoy has signed so many post-obits from 'the Jews' to pay his enormous gambling debts that all the wealth his father has assiduously built up outside of the entail will be lost when he succeeds. Scarborough puts into operation a plan he devised decades earlier when he married his wife twice: he announces, and proves, that Mountjoy was born before his marriage, is illegitimate, and cannot succeed. The post-obits are worthless. Augustus becomes the 'eldest son', but because he is so unsure of his father, he agrees with him to pay the capital borrowed from 'the Jews'. This is his undoing because it shows his distrust of his father and his unfeeling nature. Scarborough becomes disillusioned with Augustus, while Mountjoy, now impoverished, grows in his favour. He reverts to the second option in his plan and proves that the marriage referred to was his second marriage ceremony (to the same woman) and that Mountjoy is not illegitimate.

There are numerous sub-plots. Mountjoy Scarborough is in love with his cousin, Florence Mountjoy. So too is Harry Annesley, the hero of the story, although 'there will be found to be nothing very heroic about him' [3]. His courtship of Florence is the principal love story. While Florence loves Harry, her mother violently opposes the match and takes her off to her uncle's in Belgium – he is Her Majesty's Minister there. Florence is then besieged by two suitors, in addition to Mountjoy and Augustus. Harry is the heir to his uncle, the foolish squire, Peter Prosper. Prosper becomes annoyed with Harry and decides to oust him as heir by himself marrying and begetting an heir. His attempt to marry Matilda Thoroughbung, one of Trollope's fiercely independent spinsters, provides some of Trollope's best comic writing [26–7]. [➤ Names, Silly.] Prosper is frightened off by Miss Thoroughbung and reinstates Harry as his heir, so that Harry can now marry Florence. Finally we follow the difficulties faced by Scarborough's solicitor, John Grey. His relationships with his unmarried daughter Dorothy, as well as with his ne'er-do-well sister and brother-in-law, Captain Patrick Carroll, provide both pathos and humour. (Carroll, with his Irish ways, resembles characters from Thackeray's writings.)

Given that the novel was written by an 'old man' it is not surprising that there are numerous private jokes and personal references drawing on Trollope's own life. Captain Scarborough began his military career as a cornet, the rank purchased by Trollope's son Henry, who also gives his nickname, Harry, to the hero. Mountjoy Scarborough loses enormous sums at whist, Trollope's favourite card game. Florence Mountjoy's Christian name is borrowed from Trollope's niece, and just as the real Florence was Trollope's niece, this Florence is Mr Scarborough's niece. She and her mother take rooms in Cheltenham: Harry Annesley proposes to Florence during a dance in a house in the Paragon buildings where the Trollopes once lived. There is a reference to Brussels as a place where Englishmen could educate their children more cheaply [10], recalling the fact that for a brief time in his youth Trollope was himself an usher at such a school. Monte Carlo, chosen for its gambling by Mountjoy Scarborough when he flees London in disgrace, had been visited by the Trollopes during their Italian trip in the spring of 1881: Trollope refers to this in a first-person 'authorial intrusion' [11]. The Greys live in Fulham: when Trollope was a young Post Office clerk his uncle, Henry Milton, lived there.

When a minor character, Joshua Thoroughbung, is asked how often he hunts, he replies, 'Well, three regular. I do get an odd day with the Essex sometimes' [25]. Trollope is both describing his own hunting habits, at his zenith, and paying a tribute to his own hunt, the Essex. When Thoroughbung agrees with his father's views against cub-hunting, he is echoing Trollope's own views. When Thoroughbung returns from the hunt to be greeted with tea and toast from the hands of his fiancée, he enjoys the same luxury Trollope received from his wife Rose when he returned from a hunt [29]. Peter Prosper's estate is in Hertfordshire, as the estate of Trollope's father's uncle had been. According to family legend he had originally made Trollope's father his heir, as Prosper had made his nephew Harry Annesley, but had cut him off by marrying and begetting an heir himself, as Prosper tried to do. When Augustus Scarborough offers his brother wine, he offers him Léoville [37], Trollope's own favourite claret. Trollope was perhaps enjoying a joke with his friend George Smith when he writes of the gambler, Major Moody, asking for barley water; when told there was none, Moody 'contented himself with sipping Apollinaris' [42]. Part of Smith's fortune came from selling Apollinaris water in the United Kingdom.

Trollope's reading in the dramatists of the seventeenth and eighteenth centuries may well have influenced aspects of the plot, especially Thomas Middleton's *A Trick to Catch the Old One* (1608). There is also some similarity in the two Scarborough brothers to the two Surface brothers in Sheridan's *School for Scandal*. There is a less than flattering picture of journalism when Harry Annesley considers joining his university friend, Quaverdale [22], as a writer. The picture painted has similarities with that in 'The Adventures of Fred Pickering' and, not surprisingly, contains a reference to cobblers in which learning to write is compared with learning how to make a pair of shoes [➤ Newspapers]. It is

typical that Mr Scarborough reads French novels, and that his son, Mountjoy, does not know his Bible: both traits indicate flawed characters in Trollope's fiction.

Trollope's discussion of the relationship between the elderly solicitor, John Grey, and his middle-aged unmarried daughter Dorothy is well analysed and poignantly described [33]. Her position is similar in many ways to that of Ayala Dormer in *Ayala's Angel*, just as Harry Annesley's relationship with his clergyman father, as well as their individual personalities, are reminiscent of those of Harry Clavering and his father in *The Claverings*.

The novel is unusual among Trollope's works in having an 'introduction', by which he meant the first four chapters, and a 'mystery' – something he normally denounced – as to the whereabouts of Mountjoy Scarborough, which lasts from Chapter 4 to Chapter 11. Trollope often claimed that he depended more on character than on plot, but in this novel the plot is in many ways the more important element in the story.

There are numerous echoes of earlier Trollope novels, such as a reference to duelling [24], to the nature of being a lady [26–7] and a gentleman [33], and the familiar use of his favourite phrases like 'God tempers the wind to the shorn lamb' and 'a good time coming'. When Mr Tyrrwhit refers to 'two ponies', he is using a Victorian slang expression for £10 – a 'pony' was five pounds [36]. There is even a possible recollection of an old political enemy with a horse named 'Orange Peel'. Sir Robert Peel had often been called 'Orange Peel' by Irishmen because of his strong Protestant convictions and Trollope would have known the phrase from his time in Ireland.

There are two topical references. The first is to the Land League in Chapter 5, written in the spring of 1881. This refers to the sometimes violent agitation in Ireland against the laws governing land ownership and was written over a year before Trollope began *The Land-Leaguers*. The second reference is when Mr Scarborough talks about his offering 'to keep a school at my own expense, solely on the understanding that what they call dissenters should be allowed to come there'. When he says that the 'School Board has come and made that all right', he was referring to the *ad hoc* education authorities which functioned between 1870 and 1902, in which year county and borough councils became the local authorities responsible for education. The Boards were often inclined towards Dissenters, who in turn often transferred their schools to School Boards.

Reviewers were, of course, kinder in their reviews because the author had died. Although most struggled to find good things to say, both the *Spectator* and the *Saturday Review* – which tended to represent the pro- and anti-Trollope camps – agreed it was a 'failure'. However, many subsequent critics have been more generous.

'Mrs General Talboys'. This short story was written within four days in early November 1860, while Trollope was working on *Orley Farm* after his return from a long visit with his wife to Italy. During this trip Trollope and his brother Tom made a trip to Rome. Trollope had considerable trouble with the story, as he did with 'A Ride across Palestine'. He offered it to

George Smith for the *Cornhill* and told him, 'It shall be among the most inward of my inward things – no one being privy to it but my wife.' Rose Trollope thought it 'ill natured'. Smith had it printed but Thackeray as editor rejected it as indecent, probably because of the reference to a man with illegitimate children. Trollope rejected the charge: for indecency he substituted 'squeamishness' and cited five modern writers who touched on the subject, including Thackeray himself. Trollope then offered the story to the *London Review*, which published it on 2 February 1861, a fortnight after the end of 'The Banks of the Jordan'. [For this, ➤ 'A Ride across Palestine'.] The story was included in Trollope's first collection, *Tales of All Countries*. Trollope received £50.

The story is set in 1859 in a somewhat bohemian Anglo-American colony in Rome. In the group there is one man separated from his wife who has 'comforted himself in his desolation'. It is he who has produced the two offending illegitimate children that Thackeray disliked. Mrs Talboys comes to spend the winter there. She is an enthusiastic woman who had 'no repugnance to impropriety in other women'. While vague about her own Christian beliefs, she is very anti-Catholic and devoted to Italian unification. (With these attributes she may well have resembled Trollope's sister-in-law, Theodosia Trollope.) Mrs Talboys' 'aspirations for freedom ignored all bounds, and, in theory, there were no barriers which she was not willing to demolish'. She flirts first with an American writer, Conrad Mackinnon. After flirting with Mackinnon, Mrs Talboys turns to a young Irish sculptor, Wenceslaus O'Brien, who has left his wife in Ireland and who really loves Mrs Talboys 'in his easy, eager, susceptible Irish way'. When he takes her at her word and asks her to run away with him to Naples she is furious and hits him.

There are good descriptions of Rome and a convincing portrayal of married women's reactions to women who are not-what-they-ought-to-be, and of their husbands' behaviour in such company. One suspects Trollope drew heavily on the expatriate community he saw in Italy. He also includes a passing hit at table-rapping to commune with the dead, an activity favoured by his mother and brother [➤ Spiritualism]. While the story is somewhat 'ill natured' it is also a good study of human behaviour when social restrictions are removed. After writing the story Trollope worried that there 'is not & never has been any real General' Talboys. In the event the name was not one of his silly names and there had been two military Talboys. Luckily for Trollope, one had been beheaded in 1464 while the other had died insane in 1530.

Mudie's Circulating Library. Mudie's exercised an important influence on Trollope's writing. Charles Edward Mudie (1818–90) was a London bookseller and stationer who began lending books in 1842. From this his Library developed and in its heyday it dominated Victorian literature. It allowed tens of thousands among the middle classes, among them Rose Trollope, along with people in the expanding Empire, to obtain books – particularly novels – without having to buy them. It would not be too exaggerated a claim to say that being able to afford Mudie's subscription marked someone as middle class. For one guinea [21s.] a year a subscriber could take out one book or journal at a time but there was no limit on the number he, or more likely, she, could have in the year. Subscribers who paid two guineas were allowed to borrow three volumes.

Mudie, who was cheaper than those rivals who had survived from the eighteenth century, used his powerful influence on publishers to produce three-volume novels with many story lines, sub-plots and 'padding' to reach the prescribed length. (Three-volume novels encouraged people to pay the higher subscription.) Virtually no Victorian ever considered buying the first edition of a novel and almost all copies were bought by Mudie and other lending libraries. This fitted in with the high prices charged and the small numbers printed: 'three-deckers' all sold for 31s. 6d. (£1. 11s. 6d.) or one-and-a-half guineas [➤ Money]. For example, the first edition of *Barchester Towers* numbered 750 copies, of which Mudie bought 200 at less than half the normal price. Once a novel became popular through serialization and lending libraries, cheaper one-volume editions would be published: a one-volume edition of *Barchester Towers* could be bought for 5s. in 1858, for 3s. 6d. in 1866 and for one shilling by 1886.

Because Mudie had a virtual monopoly by the 1860s he could negotiate whatever price he wanted with publishers, usually to their disadvantage: by 1862 he was said to be buying 180,000 books annually, whereas in the 1850s it had stood at 12,000 per year. W. H. Smith was Mudie's closest rival [➤ *The Small House at Allington*]. Although publishers often resented Mudie's power, it did mean that they could form a reasonable idea of how much they might make from a first edition and it allowed them to pay the top rank of novelists – whom Trollope joined in the 1860s – quite high sums.

As a devout Congregationalist, Mudie exercised what might be called a 'morally correct' censorship over what books he selected [➤ Dissenters]. If Mudie rejected a novel, it was virtually impossible for it to succeed. Trollope's career was enormously influenced by Mudie: of forty-seven novels, seventeen were three-deckers. When the reviewer E. S. Dallas reviewed *The Bertrams* in *The Times* he called Trollope 'the most fertile, the most popular, the most successful author – that is to say, of the circulating library sort'. Julian Hawthorne (Nathaniel's son) quipped that Trollope 'was afraid of nobody except God and Mudie'. Trollope probably made more references to Mudie than any other Victorian novelist: in *The Prime Minister*, the elderly barrister Abel Wharton is embarrassed when Ferdinand Lopez sees a yellow label on the book he is reading and knows it must be a novel borrowed from Mudie's; later in the novel, Lopez suspends his wife's subscription to force her to bend to his will; in *The Eustace Diamonds*, Lady Linlithgow complains that Mudie's send her the wrong books; in *Orley Farm*, Mrs Furnival is a subscriber; in *Ayala's Angel*, Ayala's Aunt Dosett does not subscribe, thereby causing distress to her niece; in *The Bertrams*, Mudie himself orders 2,000 copies of George Bertram's *Romance of Scripture*. (This enormous order either showed it was a fabulously popular book or, more likely, that Trollope was having a private

joke.) Eventually Trollope turned against the system created by Mudie but did not know what could replace it. Mudie's loyalty to Trollope continued after his death when he ordered 1,000 copies of the *Autobiography*.

Mudie's domination, which Thomas Carlyle called the 'Mudie Mountain', began to decline in the 1880s. New publishers like Chatto & Windus challenged the system and new lending libraries, such as Boots', offered competition at the lower end of the market. Free public libraries dating from the 1880s also broke the monopoly of distributing books to readers. In 1894, Mudie agreed with W. H. Smith, whose strength lay in cheap editions sold at railway stations, to kill the three-decker by agreeing not to pay more than 4s. per volume of fiction. Mudie's Library survived until 1937.

[➤ Publishers and Publishing.]

Murder. See Violence.

Music. Music provides one of the best examples of the way in which Trollope used his experiences, even limited ones, in his fiction. In his surviving correspondence he refers to the two most moving musical experiences of his life. The first was when, as a young man, he heard the cello played; the second was when he heard his niece Beatrice sing. (She was a highly regarded soprano.) These developed into the two most conspicuous references to music in his fiction. In *The Warden*, Mr Harding gives a moving cello concert and throughout that novel and the rest of the Barsetshire series he often thinks of his cello. In moments of distress he moves his hands as if he were playing it. In the same series Trollope reflects his High

Church views in defending Barchester Cathedral's choral tradition against the onslaught of the Evangelicals, led by Obadiah Slope. Trollope's second musical experience, his niece's singing, found an echo in the character of Rachel O'Mahony, the opera singer in *The Land-Leaguers*, although the reader learns nothing about her operatic roles.

Music also occupies a suitably central role in 'Lotta Schmidt', his short story set in Vienna in which a middle-aged violinist and zither player wins the love of a young shop girl through his playing. Trollope's question in one of his 'authorial intrusions', 'Reader, did you ever hear the zither?' and his account of its 'soft sad wail of delicious woe' shows how much he had been moved by hearing this himself on a recent visit to Austria. There is also a rare and openly personal allusion to his attending a concert – all the more delightful because it was free – with his wife at the casino in Monte Carlo [*Mr Scarborough's Family*, II].

Trollope hardly ever mentions composers: a rare exception occurs early in *The Warden* when he alludes to Henry Purcell and two other composers of English church music [I]. His own involvement with music came through the glee-singing that was so popular among young men in his youth. He belonged to a group called the 'Goose and Glee Club' who delighted in singing although it appears their meetings were not always sedate. (They are mentioned in *The Last Chronicle of Barset* [42].) In *The Three Clerks*, Charley Tudor's fondness for singing popular songs and ballads is almost certainly yet another autobiographical touch by Trollope.

Trollope had a fondness for the poems of Robert Burns and the songs based on them; as N. John Hall points out in his edition of *The New Zealander*, Burns's line 'It's gude to be honest and true' is repeated in several novels, most notably in *Barchester Towers* [46]. [For another use of a popular song and poem, ➤ 'Good Time Coming'.] It is likely that other phrases in Trollope's works echo popular songs, many of which are now forgotten: one good example is in *Framley Parsonage* [II] in which there is a good account of music-making in a country house and a reference to '[I] dreamt that I dwelt in marble halls', from the popular song in Michael Balfe's opera, *The Bohemian Girl* (1843).

Trollope was also quite friendly with Sir Arthur Sullivan, as can be seen in his questioning of that composer during a session of the Royal Commission on Copyright. Trollope is mentioned in one of the songs sung by Colonel Calverley in the Gilbert and Sullivan opera *Patience* (Act I), composed in 1881.

N

Names, Origin of. Unlike some writers Trollope appears to have kept no list of names and the origins of his names are found in a very wide variety of sources. He must have had a good memory for his characters' names as they were frequently re-used. The fact that many of them often have different forms of spelling implies that Trollope relied on his memory rather than on consulting his own published books. Finney (later, Finnie), the Barsetshire solicitor, is a good example, and so is the money-lender M'Ruen, who is first spelt in this way, but reappears in a later novel as Magruin. Trollope thought a good deal about his characters' names and sometimes changed them as he wrote: in *The American Senator* Lawrence Twentyman started life as Launcelot and Kate Masters as Molly (her change of name came after she was described as 'jolly').

Trollope constantly drew on his own family for Christian names: many heroines and female characters are named Fanny, which was his mother's name. Young men are frequently named Fred and Henry (or Harry), the names of his two sons. In the short story 'Mary Gresley', the heroine's full name was the name of his mother's aunt – Gresley had been Fanny Trollope's mother's maiden name. In another short story, 'The Mistletoe Bough', he used the name Garrow, which was the maiden name of Tom Trollope's first wife, Theodosia.

Shakespeare is probably the source for names like the Lovels in *Lady Anna*, the Scroope family in *An Eye for an Eye*, Lord Alfred Percy in *The Fixed Period* and the Hotspurs in *Sir Harry Hotspur of Humblethwaite*. Sometimes one of Trollope's characters resembles Shakespeare's original: Hotspur features in *King Richard the Second* and *King Henry IV Part I* and in the latter he is described as a man 'who is the theme of honour's tongue: amongst a grove the very straightest plant'. This describes Trollope's Sir Harry. 'Percy-cross' for Beverley appears in *Ralph the Heir*. In *The Duke's Children* the peers who attend a party are all drawn from *Romeo and Juliet*.

Trollope uses his classical education for his doctor, Sir Omicron Pie, and for Philogunac Coelebs in *Is He Popenjoy?* but classical gods and goddesses are normally used to describe characters. In *The Warden* his choice of *The Jupiter* for *The Times* was an inspired use of his classical training. Some names, like Theophilus Grantly and Septimus Harding, Undecimus Scott in *The Three Clerks* and Quintus Slide are not so much classical references to the Greek for 'the lover of God' or the Latin for seventh, eleventh or fifth, but a way of naming children inherited from the past. (Ordinal numbering in Latin usually indicated the child's place in the ranking of the children of a family.) Surnames sometimes indicated a character's personality: Mrs Winterfield in *The Belton Estate* and John Neverbend in *The Three Clerks* are, respectively, barren and fanatically rigid.

Biblical names, especially from the Old Testament, were also used. When applied to three Americans, Elias Gotobed, Jonas Spalding, Ezekiel Boncassen, such names were somewhat old-fashioned or perhaps provincial by English standards. (Elias, the Greek form of Elijah, Jonas (or Jonah) and Ezekiel were, of course, Old Testament prophets.) Trollope commented on the 'peculiarity' of the first names, many biblical, of members of Lincoln's Cabinet [*North America*]. Upright working men, for instance Abraham Hall in 'The Telegraph Girl', Jacob Bunce in *Phineas Finn* and *Phineas Redux*, Daniel Thwaite in *Lady Anna* and Jacob Brattle in *The Vicar of Bullhampton*, also had Old Testament names which in those cases confirmed manly uprightness. The name Daniel was used for two Radicals: Daniel Thwaite and Daniel Caldigate in *John Caldigate*, presumably because Daniel had not been afraid to enter the lion's den. In *Miss Mackenzie*, the Old Testament provided the name of an insurance company, Abednego Life and Shadrach Fire (from Daniel 3:12–30, in which Shadrach, Meshach and Abednego were the three Jews who would not bow down to Nebuchadnezzar's golden image). Trollope also used Old Testament names for Evangelical clergymen like Samuel Prong [*Rachel Ray*] and Jeremiah Maguire [*Miss Mackenzie*], perhaps to emphasize a certain hardness of character. On the other hand, the Reverend Josiah Crawley in *The Last Chronicle of Barset* was not an Evangelical but his Old Testament name is perhaps a warning to readers that he will have all the acerbity normally attributed to Old Testament prophets. Trollope took the name of one peer, Lord Boanerges, from the New Testament.

His great knowledge of English literature, especially his intensive reading in seventeenth- and eighteenth-century works, gave him another source. In *The Fixed Period* the citizens of Britannula include Brittlereed, Tallowax, Puddlebrane and Exorses – all redolent of seventeenth-century plays. Their influence is also evident in *The Warden*, in which he caricatured Thomas Carlyle as Dr Pessimist Anticant and Charles Dickens as Mr Popular Sentiment. It is also evident in *The Three Clerks*, in which he caricatured Sir Stafford Northcote as Sir Warwick Deepdene. He got Obadiah Slope's name from Sterne's *Tristram Shandy*. He used Dickens's Mrs Gamp as a midwife in Charley Tudor's manuscript novel 'Crinoline and Macassar', in *The Three Clerks* [22]. This was also her occupation in *Martin Chuzzlewit*. He took Sidonia from Disraeli's novels *Coningsby* and *Tancred* to use in *Barchester Towers* [9]. Trollope had several characters with identical names to Thackeray's characters (►Bunce; *The Claverings*). In *Can You Forgive Her?* he borrowed Thackeray's Lord Cinquebar as a form of tribute. [►*Is He Popenjoy?* for another example of Thackeray's influence.] He used his knowledge of the eighteenth-century theatre for the name of his short story, 'The Panjandrum'.

He sometimes took names from real

figures, such as Fiasco in *The Small House at Allington* or Ussher in *The Macdermots of Ballycloran*. Prominent persons from recent history provided names used in the titles for two of his short stories: 'Relics of General Chassé' and 'The Château of Prince Polignac'. In the second story Trollope named his hero Lacordaire: the French Dominican, Henri Dominique Lacordaire (1802–61), was much in the French news in the 1840s and 1850s as a popular preacher. In *The Fixed Period* Trollope uses the name of a living politician, the Quaker radical and virtual pacifist John Bright, but makes him a great naval hero. His readers would have immediately enjoyed the joke. He did the same with the famous New Zealand prime minister, Julius Vogel, in *John Caldigate*. [➤ Ships.]

His fox-hunting as well as his travels in Britain and abroad also provided him with names. In *The Claverings*, for example, several names are taken from Essex towns; in *Dr Wortle's School*, Lowick, a real place in Northamptonshire, becomes Bowick, while the same novel's Lady Margaret Momson probably owes her name to the Lincolnshire Monsons. Ufford, the site of a house owned by his Lincolnshire relative, Sir John Trollope, inspired the 'Ufford and Rufford' hunt in *The American Senator* and *Ayala's Angel*. Sometimes real places provided names which could be used in other contexts: in *The Vicar of Bullhampton* some of the chapters dealing with the Marrables are set in the Wiltshire town of 'Loring', which is the name of two streets in London which Trollope could well have come across in his Post Office work. In *Orley Farm* the barrister Thomas Furnival owes his name to Furnival's Inn, an inn of court that

was dissolved in 1817. (The name continued in a new building which survived until 1897.) Friends and relations sometimes provided names. In 'Josephine de Montmorenci' he had great sport with the names of his friends George Eliot and G. H. Lewes, and Lewes's son, Charles.

Aristocratic families like the De Courcys or Pallisers often had Norman names. Aristocratic figures are often given impressive Christian names; Augusta was a particular favourite for young ladies. [For the care he took in selecting Lady Alexandrina De Courcy's Christian name, ➤ De Courcy Family.] The most famous Palliser's first name, Plantagenet – which Trollope calls a 'Christian' name – conjures up the dynasty that reigned from 1154 to 1400 – although there is a laugh at his name at the end of the series [*The Duke's Children*, 79]. [For the significance behind Lord Gaberlunzie's title in *The Three Clerks*, ➤ Scotland.] Gentry families had more typically English names such as Dale, Gresham, or Thorne, and Christian names like Thomas, Wilfred, or Monica. Working-class families tended to have names like Brattle, Skulpit, Hopkins or Stringer, with short first names like Job or Sam.

Trollope sometimes makes a private reference in his choice of names: in the short story 'The Last Austrian Who Left Venice', he names the young advocate Carlo Pepé after a friend of his parents, General Guglielmo Pepé. Some of his references would have been easily recognized by Victorians. In *The Struggles of Brown, Jones, and Robinson* he included among the members of the Goose and Gridiron Club 'Old Pan', who was a descendant of the Pancabinets. This was, to Victorians, a rather obvious reference to Lord Palmerston, whose nickname was 'Pam' and who served in numerous Cabinets during a political life which stretched from 1807 to 1865.

American names presented special problems and Trollope sometimes used places for inspiration: thus Lucinda Roanoke in *The Eustace Diamonds* gets her surname from a river in Virginia. Sometimes he seems to have recalled an American name for use in England: Crittenden is a doctor in *The Vicar of Bullhampton* and John Crittenden was a famous senator from Kentucky whom Trollope met when in America. American characters, at least men, are often given a Christian name followed by an initial and a surname: Frederic F. Frew in 'The Widow's Mite' or Hamilton K. Fisker in *The Way We Live Now*. For, as Trollope said when introducing Frew, an American regarded it as 'a point of honour' that everyone should remember his middle initial.

Trollope also used words current at the time of writing for names. He probably got Ayala Dormer's unusual name from a champagne house established in France in 1860 by the son of a Colombian diplomat. In *He Knew He Was Right* he got Wallachia Petrie's name from current events and recent history: in April 1867, the year in which the novel was written, Prince Alexander was deposed as Prince of Roumania, which had been formed eight years before by the union of two provinces, Wallachia and Moldavia.

Names, Silly. Trollope followed the old custom, dating back at least to Shakespeare, popularized in the Restoration theatre and used extensively by Thackeray and Dickens, of giving silly names to various minor characters, partnerships and companies in the novels. Silly names were much rarer in the short stories. Trollope found it impossible not to use silly names even in such serious novels as *The Fixed Period* or *The Land-Leaguers*. In the former there is a visiting cricket side containing Sir Kennington Oval, Lord Marylebone and Sir Lords Longstop, while in the latter there is Mrs Beelzebub and Mr Barytone, opera singers, and a Jew named Mahomet M. Moss.

Lawyers (barristers and solicitors) were often given silly names or names which sometimes describe their alleged attributes, such as Mr Allewinde in *The Macdermots of Ballycloran*, Mr Chaffanbrass, Mr Squercum in *The Way We Live Now*, Mr Gitemthruet in *The Three Clerks* or Sir Abraham Haphazard; solicitors' firms often had silly names that allowed him to criticize them. His most memorable is the firm of Slow and Bideawhile. Names for characters other than lawyers do sometimes describe them, like the dull MP, John Grey and the timid Lord Fawn in the Palliser series.

With aristocratic titles and family names Trollope often had enormous fun, usually when he wanted to expose snobbery: in *Marion Fay* Lady Amaldina Persiflage marries Lord Llwddythlw and in *Ayala's Angel* there is Lord Bordotrade (Board of Trade), whose family name is Traffick. *Is He Popenjoy?* has a host of such titles and in 'Alice Dugdale' there is a Duchess of Ditchwater. In *Can You Forgive Her?* we know that Euphemia and Iphigenia Theodata Palliser are not to be taken seriously: often the daughters of titled families have pretentious names for which Trollope has drawn on his love of the classics or on his knowledge of eighteenth-century literature. One thinks here of the Ladies Amelia and Susanna Germain in *Is He Popenjoy?* or of the Misses Georgiana and Sophia Wanless in 'Alice Dugdale'.

He frequently uses a silly name to describe what the character does or is: John Neverbend, the rigid doctrinaire in *The Fixed Period*; the nasty solicitors, Badger and Blister, in 'Mrs Brumby'; William Brisket, the butcher in *The Struggles of Brown, Jones, and Robinson*; Drs Fillgrave and Rerechild, the less than adequate physicians in the Barsetshire series [➤ Doctors]; the Reverend Mr Quiverful, the father of numerous children; the preacher of platitudes, Mr Comfort [*Rachel Ray*]; Mr Stickatit and Mr Scribble, lawyers in *The Bertrams* and 'The Two Heroines of Plumplington' respectively; Baroness Banmann and Lady Selina Protest, feminists in *Is He Popenjoy?*, and Mrs Bakewell the baker in 'Alice Dugdale'. A hosiery firm is called Legg & Loosefit in *The Struggles of Brown, Jones, and Robinson*, a tailor is Mr Neefit in *Ralph the Heir*, and the farmer who takes Mrs Quiverful into Barchester to meet Mrs Proudie is Farmer Subsoil. Bung and variations thereon, like the Thoroughbungs in *Mr Scarborough's Family*, are frequently used in connection with brewers. In the Palliser novels there is Mr Du Boung a brewer who aspires to a seat in Parliament. In *Rachel Ray* a brewer's family is named Tappitt. [For the significance of Lord Gaberlunzie's title in *The Three Clerks*, ➤ Scotland.]

Sometimes silly names are meant to poke fun at people Trollope disliked, like Olivia Q. Fleabody, Ph.D., the feminist lecturer in *Is He Popenjoy?*. (By giving her a middle initial, normally used only for American men, he is strengthening his attack on feminism.) It is not surprising to find in *Miss Mackenzie* that the hired butler Grandairs serves bad food and does so *à la Russe* [➤ Food]. Occasionally silly names are used for churches: in *Is He Popenjoy?* the High Church ladies of Manor Cross attend their parish church of St Processus, a pun on church processions revived by priests of the Oxford Movement. In *The Way We Live Now* the zealous Catholic priest, Father Barham, asks Melmotte for money to build a new Catholic church to be called St Fabricius. For his joke Trollope turned to Roman history: Gaius Fabricius Luscinus was a consul famous for opposing the growing luxuries of a decadent Rome. Like Father Barham, he was a prophet without a sense of humour or proportion.

Sometimes silly names were based on items with which Victorians were familiar, such as Miss Colza (lamp oil) in *Miss Mackenzie*, Major Fiasco, Sir Gregory Grogram, or the two lovers, Macassar (hair oil) and Lady Crinoline (stiff fabric for women's skirts) in Charley Tudor's novel in *The Three Clerks* [II.7]. His references to Caudle in *The Small House at Allington* refer to Douglas Jerrold's famous *Mrs Caudle's Curtain Lectures* which appeared in *Punch* in 1845 and helped to establish that magazine; Mrs Caudle was the model of a hectoring wife. He turned to Greek for Sir Omicron Pie and Mr Philogunac Coelebs [➤ *Is He Popenjoy?*].

Trollope always had a tendency to overdo silly names. For instance, in *The Three Clerks* he inserts the lawyer 'Gitemthruet' in a chapter otherwise marked by pathos [39]. In *The Fixed Period* the silly names given to the visiting English cricket side undermine the seriousness of the book. Likewise, choosing the name Beeswax for the lawyer-politician in the Palliser series distracts from a character never meant to be seen as silly. His use of silly names did not go without censure, especially by the *Saturday Review*: 'It is a pity Mr Trollope continues that practice of coining stupid names for some of his characters' (review of *Miss Mackenzie*, 4 March 1865).

[➤ Names, Origin of; Names, Use of.]

Names, Use of. 'The use of Christian names is, I think, pleasant and hardly common enough among us', says the Duke of Omnium at the end of *The Duke's Children* when he asks his prospective son-in-law, 'What do they call you at home?' Earlier in the same novel an American girl, the duke's future daughter-in-law, complains that she has never been called by her Christian name since leaving New York.

Some characters are not given Christian names – Mrs Proudie, Mrs Winterfield in *The Belton Estate*, Colonel Marrable in *The Vicar of Bullhampton*, Mr Chaffanbrass – and they tend to be characters who neither invite intimacy nor create affection. Some characters have Christian names that are not used, like Mr Scarborough in *Mr Scarborough's Family* or Mr Whittlestaff in *An Old Man's Love*, and we are meant to assume that age and personality have made them rather remote, if not, as in the case of Mr Scarborough, positively warped.

Throughout Trollope's fiction the use of first names in dialogue between characters provides important clues to their relationships. In this he accurately reflects Victorian usage, which was very formal and which contained set rules as to when one might drop someone's title, including, of course, Mr, Mrs and Miss. In general, men and women never address each other by their Christian names unless they are related or marked by a great difference in age. 'Cousins,' Trollope wrote in *The Vicar of Bullhampton*, 'are Tom, and Jack, and George, and Dick' [14]. A man addressing a young woman by her Christian name is usually a prelude to a proposal and Trollope's young women, or their mothers, usually object to such use. Thus both the daughters and the mother in *Rachel Ray*, as well as the short story set in America on which it is based, 'The Courtship of Susan Bell', are concerned when the young man calls the younger daughter 'Rachel' (or 'Susan').

Sometimes, if a friendship goes back to childhood, a man may continue to address a young woman by her Christian name, as Captain Marrable does with Mary Lowther in *The Vicar of Bullhampton* and Arthur Fletcher with Emily Wharton in *The Prime Minister*. But this may cause problems if the man uses this intimacy as a prelude to proposing marriage, as happens in both these cases. In *The Bertrams* a girl is told by her mother to stop calling a childhood friend by his Christian name when he goes up to Oxford: the boy is now a man and must be addressed as 'Mr'.

Close female friends call one another by their Christian names, so that the Duchess of Omnium calls Madame Max Goesler 'Marie' in the Palliser novels once they have become friends, while Madame Max sometimes calls her 'Lady Glen'. If one of the women has an aristocratic title this can cause further complications, so that Lady Mary Palliser in *The Duke's Children* has to persuade her American friend, Isabel Boncassen, to call her 'Mary'.

Gentlemen rarely address other gentlemen by their first names unless there is a great difference in age between them. While there are occasional exceptions, this usage usually indicates that the man so addressed possesses a certain boyish quality: thus Phineas Finn is often called 'Phineas' by men and even by ladies. Lawrence Twentyman rightly objected to being called 'Larry' in *The American Senator* because 'a man should not have his Christian name used by every Tom and Dick' [1]. It was usual for male friends to address one another by their surnames: when Trollope became a friend of George Smith, 'My Dear Mr Smith' gave way to 'My Dear Smith' in his letters.

Husbands and wives rarely address one another by their first names except when they are alone: even then, Mrs Grantly calls her husband 'Archdeacon' while Mrs Proudie only calls her husband 'Tom' in the emotional scene preceding her death in *The Last Chronicle of Barset* [66]. Slightly vulgar wives will sometimes call their husbands by an initial, thus Mrs Tappitt, the brewer's wife in *Rachel Ray*, calls her husband 'T'.

A wife's Christian name was regarded as a sign of intimacy that had to be guarded to prevent any misunderstanding. It is quite rare for a married lady to be called by her first name by a man not closely related to her. From Trollope's usage in his correspondence we see that he did not refer to the wives of even close friends by their first name. Thus in an exchange of letters with his friend John Blackwood, both men send compliments or give news about 'my wife'. Blackwood reached a slight degree of familiarity by referring to 'Mrs T.' when inviting the Trollopes to visit Edinburgh. Christian names were reserved for family correspondence: Trollope's sister-in-law is called 'Fanny', while a niece is referred to by her nickname, 'Bice' for Beatrice. With an unmarried younger woman the rules were somewhat more relaxed and thus Trollope could write to Kate Field as 'Dear Kate'. (Kate Field was American and the more formal English rules did not always apply.) Had she married, Trollope would have stopped addressing her as 'Kate'. Thus in *Ralph the Heir*, when a squire sends a wedding gift to a girl he had once courted and addresses her by her nickname, he adds that of course he must stop once she is married [53].

Even when the man is a family friend of long standing, and much older, it can cause a problem, as for instance when an old roué continues to call Mrs Trevelyan 'Emily' in *He Knew He Was Right* and this repeated use of her Christian name leads to tragedy. A lady who allowed men to use her Christian name opened herself to criticism. Thus in *The Prime Minister* when Lady Eustace makes a reappearance and a man calls her 'Lizzie', Trollope reminds us of her former reputation by saying that the man little realized 'how many men had called her Lizzie in her time' [54]. For a Victorian reader, no further description of 'Lizzie' was needed.

Servants were addressed in a variety of ways: if young or a maid, by their Christian names; if a cook or housekeeper, by their surname and 'Mrs', whether married or not; if an older male servant, whether in the house or outside, by their surname.

[➤ Names, Origin of; Peerage.]

'Never, Never'. In 1875 Trollope wrote a short self-parody based on his most famous heroine, Lily Dale, and *The Small House at Allington*. The satire, whose full title was *Never, Never, – Never, Never: A Condensed Novel, in Three Volumes, after the Manner of Bret Harte*, was donated to the magazine *Sheets for the Cradle*, and published over three issues in December 1875. This magazine, which only lasted for six issues, was established by Susan Hale to raise funds for the Massachusetts Infant Asylum. Each 'volume' of Trollope's story had three chapters and each chapter was the size of a paragraph. Trollope told the editor, 'As Bret Harte says I have no sense of humour, and won't laugh at mine, I must try to laugh at myself, and make fun of the heroine I have loved best.' Susan Hale was the sister of Edward Everett Hale, a Unitarian minister and member of the Boston literary set whom Trollope had presumably met during his fifth visit to America in 1875. The spoof was re-published in a limited edition in 1971 by Lance Tingay. Another writer who parodied *The Small House at Allington* in Trollope's lifetime was F. D. Planché, who wrote 'The Story of the Small House at Allington. A Three Volume Novel Epitomised'. [For Trollope's spoof of Victorian medievalism, ➤ 'The Gentle Euphemia'.]

Newby & Co. (1843–74). This publishing house was established by Thomas Cautley Newby and died with his retirement. He is, perhaps, the most vilified publisher of the nineteenth century. Mrs Gaskell, in her life of Charlotte Brontë, wrote of him: 'I understand that truth is considered a libel in speaking of such people.' He published three-volume novels for circulating libraries, [➤ Mudie's Circulating Library]. He engaged in shady, if not dishonest, practices: he often insisted on payment by authors before he would publish their works; he placed few advertisements; he did not issue the number of copies agreed. His claim to fame dates from 1847 when he brought out the first novels of Anne and Emily Brontë. That year he also published Trollope's first novel, *The Macdermots of Ballycloran*. Trollope's mother acted as her son's agent and while Trollope did not complain of Newby's dishonesty he did remember that he never received any record of sales for the book. Newby delayed publication, as he did with Emily Brontë's *Wuthering Heights*, and when he finally brought Trollope's book out he listed Frances Trollope as the author in several newspaper advertisements to ensure better sales. His advertising methods were similar to those attacked later by Trollope in *The Struggles of Brown, Jones, and Robinson*. Trollope appears to have borne no ill-will towards Newby.

Newman, John Henry (Cardinal) (1801–90). Trollope first came across Newman in the 1830s when he heard him preach at St Mary the Virgin, the University Church in Oxford of which Newman was then vicar. Trollope may have been visiting his brother Tom, or may have been in Oxford seeking a scholarship. Because of his sympathy with the High Church movement Trollope was friendly towards Newman when he was an Anglican, and, having a sympathetic attitude toward Catholicism, he did not turn against Newman when he became a Catholic. He mentions Newman in several novels, for instance *Barchester Towers* [25]. For his part, the cardinal regarded Trollope as his favourite novelist although he was not uncritical. Newman read *Barchester Towers* in bed and 'burst out laughing, and, when I woke in the middle of the night I began laughing again'. It was not surprising that Newman was attracted to *The Bertrams* [➤ entry for his comments].

Newman – himself a minor novelist – defended the sub-plots in 'three-decker' novels by 'skilful novelists like Trollope' because 'Such a contrivance obliges events to go more slowly – also it gives opportunity for variety and repose.' Only a few days before Trollope suffered his stroke in 1882 he received a letter from Cardinal Newman in which he passed on a treatment that might help Trollope's asthma and praised Trollope's novels. Trollope replied, 'It is when I hear that such men as yourself have been gratified that I feel that I have not worked altogether in vain.'

Newspapers. Newspapers play an important role in Trollope's fiction. They often upset the quiet life of Barsetshire or other provincial places. Men like Septimus Harding in *The Warden*, or later Dr Wortle in *Dr Wortle's School*, are effectively powerless to defend themselves. (Dr Wortle in fact suffers from attacks by two papers.) In the Barsetshire series, the all-powerful *Jupiter* was known by all readers to be *The Times*, which in the mid-Victorian era exercised an influence never equalled by any other newspaper. Mr Slope uses the *Jupiter* to promote his career in *Barchester Towers*. Yet it is rarely appreciated that Trollope's attack on *The Jupiter* was just the start of a persistent campaign against the dangerous power that could be exercised by a powerful press. In *The New Zealander*, his unpublished examination of life in the United Kingdom written between *The Warden* and *Barchester Towers*, he devoted a chapter to 'The Press', which began: 'The most interesting question of the present day in England may perhaps be said to be this. Is public opinion to guide the Press or be guided by it?' Newspapers, he wrote, once guided, then led, but 'now they drive'.

In the Palliser series and in other, later novels Trollope turned his attention to the rapidly growing popular press by attacking the fictional *People's Banner* and its slimy editor, Quintus Slide. In *He Knew He Was Right* Trollope portrays Hugh Stanbury as writing for a Radical penny newspaper, which horrifies his Tory aunt. Stanbury also horrifies young Emily Trevelyan by describing the cynicism that lay behind his Radical paper's reforming zeal. When asked what the *Daily Record* upheld, he answered, 'It upholds the Daily Record. Believe in that and you will surely be saved' [6]. A minor character in *Mr Scarborough's Family* makes the fairly comfortable income of £500 or £600 a year from hack work for another Radical paper, *The Coming Hour*. Trollope also portrayed the world of literary journalism memorably, if not admiringly, in *The Way We Live Now*. The world of struggling journalists is described in 'The Adventures of Fred Pickering' and in two of the short stories in *An Editor's Tales*, 'The Spotted Dog' and 'The Panjandrum'; in the latter we learn of

Trollope's own youthful desire to edit a reforming newspaper.

Not all of Trollope's newspapers are published in London. In *Rachel Ray* the brewer, Mr Bungall, like brewers in real life, establishes the *Baslehurst Gazette and Totnes Chronicle* and is then furious when it attacks his beer. Provincial newspapers often precipitate a rumour into a crisis: two good examples of this occur in *Cousin Henry* and *Dr Wortle's School*. Yet in *Cousin Henry* a newspaper does expose a real injustice.

It is fairly rare for Trollope to mention actual newspapers, although we learn that Phineas Finn reads the *Daily Telegraph* because it is cheaper than *The Times*. The *Morning Post* – the favourite paper of Society – is sometimes mentioned in connection with fashionable marriages [*Ralph the Heir*, 56]. Sporting men often read *Bell's Sporting Life*, particularly in *The Kellys and the O'Kellys*. When characters are travelling on the Continent, they frequently resort to *Galignani's Messenger*, which provided news of home for British travellers; John Eames and Mrs Arabin discover that Mrs Proudie is dead when they read *Galignani's Messenger* at their hotel in Turin [*The Last Chronicle of Barset*, 70].

Religious newspapers, which were published weekly and were often of a high quality, were born and flourished in the Victorian era. They are mentioned in several novels. One Tory squire in *Cousin Henry* reads the distinguished High Church paper, *The Guardian*. Low-church newspapers, which Trollope despised, are attacked through the fictional *Christian Examiner* in *Miss Mackenzie* and the *Brotherton Church* in *Is He Popenjoy?*; in that novel the paper is regarded by the

canons of the cathedral as 'a pestilential little rag'. It attacks Dean Lovelace for fox-hunting and later for his assault on the Marquis of Brotherton. The paper, Trollope tells us, was edited by 'a certain Mr Grease, a very pious man who had long striven, but hitherto in vain, to get orders' [➤ Clergymen]. It opposed the High Church and had as its mission 'to put down popery in the diocese of Brotherton' [10].

In *Doctor Thorne* [3] Trollope made fun of medical newspapers: while the *Lancet*, then a Radical and campaigning paper, and the *Weekly Chirurgeon* supported the good doctor in his selling of medicine and sending out of bills, the *Journal of Medical Science* and the *Scalping Knife* opposed him.

It would be easy to conclude that Trollope despised the press. In point of fact, he much admired sections of the British press and regarded his reading of *The Times* as a daily duty which was vital for keeping up with those current events that had such an important place in his novels. In *North America*, he favourably contrasted the British press with American newspapers, which he – like most British visitors – decidedly did not like.

One of Trollope's earliest attempts to be heard as a serious writer on current affairs was a series of 'letters' on Ireland which he sent to the Liberal newspaper, the *Examiner*, in 1849–50. From 1865 to 1868 Trollope was something of a regular contributor to the *Pall Mall Gazette*, but he disliked the work. Because he was always open to new forms of publication he arranged for another series of 'letters' describing his second trip to Australia and his trip to South Africa to be syndicated in newspapers [➤ *South Africa*;

The Tireless Traveler]. A few years later, in 1879, he had *Cousin Henry* first published through newspaper serialization: this was the first and only time he did this. The novel appeared in two papers, one in England and one in Scotland. Ironically, he had poked fun at novels that were serialized in newspapers twenty-one years earlier in *The Three Clerks* [22]. [➤ Editors.]

New Zealand. Trollope visited New Zealand in 1872 and his visit was described in *Australia and New Zealand*. In 1875 he stopped briefly in the colony on his way home after his second visit to Australia. Trollope had been at Harrow with the Irishman, Robert Godley, who was instrumental in the settlement of the colony. Trollope thoroughly enjoyed his time in New Zealand, despite the fact that his first visit took place during a very bad winter. While he felt very much at home – 'In New Zealand everything is English' – he was worried about the creation of the first English-speaking welfare state. When Trollope met Sir George Bowen, Governor of New Zealand from 1867 to 1872, he suggested that Trollope should write a novel about the recent war with the Maoris but Trollope declined: he said his 'forte was observation and not imagination', although he did think the fate of the Maoris could well be treated in verse. Poetry, however, 'is not my way'. Trollope had a higher regard for the Maoris than for any of the native races – 'savage nations' – he encountered throughout his visits to 'the English world'. He concluded with some sadness that their lack of 'progress' meant that they would 'melt' away. He did use the growth of governmental power in the colony as the basis for Britan-

nula in *The Fixed Period*, and the gold-mining he saw there, as the background for his short story 'Catherine Carmichael'.

The New Zealander. In the midst of the Crimean War, in February 1855, Trollope began an examination of English society in one of those periods when Englishmen fear imminent national collapse, and he wrote *The New Zealander* to describe mid-Victorian society. The manuscript was rejected by Longmans, whose reader wrote: 'If you had not told me that this work was by the author of *The Warden* I could not have believed it. Such a contrast between two works by the same pen was hardly ever before witnessed ... all the good points ... have already been treated of by Mr Carlyle, of whose *Latter-Day* pamphlets this work, *both in style and matter*, is a most feeble imitation.' Trollope worked on the manuscript well into 1856, and rewrote the entire book. Despite this, it was not published in his lifetime and he made no reference to it in his *Autobiography*. After his death it ended up in the collection of the great collector Robert H. Taylor, in Princeton. It was finally brought out in a scholarly edition by Oxford University Press in 1972, edited by N. John Hall. By that time two chapters, on trade and the Civil Service, had disappeared [see below].

This book was Trollope's first extended attempt to establish himself as a serious writer and critic of current affairs [➤ *The Examiner*.] This was an element in his character which lasted until his death. The work was written in a great rush – in some two months – and shared in the national mood of self-doubt which the war's reverses had brought about. Trollope took his title from an article by Macaulay in the *Edinburgh Review* (October 1840) in which he prophesied a day when a New Zealander would stand on the ruins of London Bridge to sketch the ruins of St Paul's. The tone of the book is set out in the motto Trollope chose, 'It's gude to be honest and true' (the same eighteenth-century Scottish song with which Signora Vesey Neroni taunts Mr Slope in *Barchester Towers*), and in the book's first paragraph, in which he asks, 'Is England in her decadence?'

The book as published had thirteen chapters, including an introduction and conclusion. Trollope examined: 'the people and their rulers'; the press; 'law and physic'; the army and navy; the Church of England; the House of Commons; the House of Lords; the Crown; society; literature; art. In writing the book, Trollope was heavily dependent on *The Times*: fretting at his Irish isolation, he had few other sources. The difficulty was that his source was not independent. The paper was, for example, hostile to Prince Albert, and therefore when Trollope used it to discuss the monarchy he was led into blunders. (When he read Sir Theodore Martin's *Life of the Prince Consort* in later years he discovered how wrong he had been, but he also discovered even more reason to dislike the royal couple's treatment of his hero, Lord Palmerston.) When discussing the monarchy his facts were often wrong as was the case when he discussed the House of Lords. Some chapters have hardly any facts and are not so much investigation as opinion: this is true, for example, of that on the Church. From time to time Carlyle's influence is seen in his use of 'thee' and 'thou' when addressing the reader.

As with other 'serious' books, like his *Life of Cicero*, his book on Thackeray or his travel books on America or Australia, this book is better for what it tells us about Trollope than for what it tells us about mid-Victorian England. He invented fictional characters to discuss complex issues: in discussing the Church of England he exercised his love of silly names and placed the Evangelical Mr Everscreech against the intoning Dr Middleage, the High Church lover of medievalism. (When he adopted the same device in *North America* he was severely and justly criticized.) There is a sincere outburst about the condition of the poor and an evident concern for public honesty: this was a perennial theme in his writing and manifested itself in his hatred of advertising, false praise and shady business tactics.

In later years Trollope turned to his unpublished manuscript as a source from which to garner material for later novels. The two chapters on trade and the Civil Service which did not survive in the rewritten version may have been incorporated in, respectively, *The Struggles of Brown, Jones, and Robinson*, which begins with a discussion of commercial trade practices, and *The Three Clerks*, in which he also re-used the name of Everscreech for a clergyman. His answer to the question he posed – how may a nation delay an inevitable decline – remained with him throughout his career: by hard work and honesty, both public and private. Had the book been published it might well have hindered his Post Office career.

[➤ Parliament; Politics; Victoria, Queen.]

Nidderdale, Lord. The eldest son of the Marquis of Auld Reekie, he is an important character in *The Way We Live Now* in which he becomes involved in Melmotte's financial schemes and almost marries his daughter. In the end he marries a daughter of Lord Cantrip. Nidderdale is a cousin of Lady Glencora Palliser and a close friend of her son, Lord Silverbridge, in *The Duke's Children*.

Nieces. Nieces appear in a large number of Trollope's novels and short stories, most often as adopted daughters, thereby reflecting both Victorian practices and his own private life. In the nineteenth century parents were more likely to die during a child's life than today and many families had to take in an orphaned niece or nephew. This sometimes meant that the children had to be separated, as in the case of Rose Trollope's sister's four children.

Trollope and his wife took in three nieces whose mothers had died. The first, Edith Tilley, was a daughter of Trollope's sister Cecilia, who died in 1849. She lived with them for about a year before returning to her father after he remarried. She remained a favourite and was with her uncle when he suffered his fatal stroke. The second was Trollope's brother Tom's daughter, Bice (Beatrice), who lived with them for short periods. The third was Florence Nightingale Bland, a daughter of Rose's sister Isabella, who was an eight-year-old orphan when she came to make her home with the Trollopes in 1863. She became the daughter the Trollopes never had. Once Edith and Florence each received a £5 reward from their uncle for memorizing his favourite Milton

poem, but the headstrong Bice would not remember her lines.

Many Trollopian characters adopt nieces when the girls' mothers die or disappear from the scene. Perhaps the best remembered is in *Doctor Thorne* where the doctor takes in his illegitimate niece, Mary Thorne, whose mother emigrated to start a new life in America [2]. Sir Thomas Underwood adopts his niece, Mary Bonner, in *Ralph the Heir* as does the Reverend Mr Granger in 'The Widow's Mite'. Major Reckenthorpe takes in his wife's niece in 'The Two Generals', while Michel Voss adopts his wife's niece, Marie Bromar, in *The Golden Lion of Granpère*. Sir William Weston, one of Trollope's unattractive baronets, adopts his niece Julia in 'A Ride across Palestine', but with disastrous results. Egbert Dormer's two orphaned daughters are taken in by two aunts, the wealthy Lady Tringle and the 'poor' Mrs Dosett, in *Ayala's Angel*. Mary Crofts is taken in by her uncle, the father of Fred Pickering, in 'The Adventures of Fred Pickering', and in *The Vicar of Bullhampton* Miss Marrable takes in her orphaned niece, Mary Lowther.

Sometimes children were 'farmed out' to relatives. In *Mr Scarborough's Family*, when Amelia Carroll marries her middle-aged curate with five children, she announces, 'The three eldest have to be sent somewhere ... He has got an unmarried sister who can quite afford to do as much as that' [62]. In *Cousin Henry*, Indefer Jones takes in his niece, Isabel Broderick, because her widowed father has remarried and her stepmother prefers her own children. Miss Mackenzie takes in a niece for a while to relieve pressure on a hard-pressed mother: while she does not adopt the girl, she does undertake to pay for her education [*Miss Mackenzie*, 1]. Sometimes, even when not farmed out, nieces could be a burden. Poor Mr Grey in *Mr Scarborough's Family* has no end of problems with his sister's daughters and the generous man ends up promising them £350 each as a marriage settlement although the eldest wheedles £500 out of him. The sum of £500 was often used by Trollope: Miss Mackenzie promises the same amount to her niece should she become incapable of keeping her, that is, should Miss Mackenzie get married. Fortunately she has only one niece to whom the promise applies.

Often a strong relationship develops between the adopted niece and her uncle, as happens with Sir Thomas Underwood, Dr Thorne and Indefer Jones – and as happened with Trollope and Florence Bland. Both in *Ralph the Heir* and in *Cousin Henry* the question of inheritance arises: how can an uncle provide for his niece? In *Cousin Henry* Indefer Jones's action parallels Trollope's when writing that novel.

Sometimes the presence of an adopted niece can cause trouble: Ayala and her sister have difficulties with their aunts. Sir William Weston in 'A Ride across Palestine' crisscrosses the Holy Land to capture his runaway niece. Romance is the normal problem, given the frequency with which cousins marry one another in Trollope's fiction: this happens, for example, in 'The Adventures of Fred Pickering', *The Golden Lion of Granpère* and 'The Two Generals', while in *Ayala's Angel* the son of the Tringle house falls in love with Ayala but to no avail. In *Ralph the Heir* it is when Ralph Newton courts Mary Bonner, the intruding niece, that his first love,

Clarissa Underwood, discovers his unworthiness.

Aunts, like uncles, often face problems with nieces. 'When a girl has a mother, her aunt may be little or nothing to her. But when the mother is gone, if there be an aunt unimpeded with other family duties, then the family duties of the aunt begin – and are sometimes assumed with great vigour' [*The Belton Estate*, 1]. Normally the problems centre on the niece's refusal to marry the man whom the aunt has chosen. This is the problem faced by the overbearing Lady Mountjoy in *Mr Scarborough's Family* when her niece, Florence, refuses to give up Harry Annesley. Miss Stanbury, traceable to Trollope's own cousin Fanny Bent, has difficulties with her niece's refusal to marry the Reverend Thomas Gibson in *He Knew He Was Right*. Miss Marrable is very put out when Mary Lowther falls in love with her cousin and not with Squire Gilmore in *The Vicar of Bullhampton*. Mrs Winterfield uses her deathbed to advance her plan for her niece Clara Amedroz to marry her nephew Captain Aylmer in *The Belton Estate*.

Aunts, as well as uncles, are often very good to their nieces. Sometimes aunts like Miss Jack in 'Miss Sarah Jack of Spanish Town, Jamaica' promote a marriage of which we are meant to approve. Emily Dunstable is fortunate in *The Last Chronicle of Barset* when her aunt, the redoubtable Martha Dunstable, now Mrs Thorne, gives her £20,000 when she marries Bernard Dale. Finally, an aunt can sometimes provide comic relief, as Aunt Greenow does in *Can You Forgive Her?*.

Nina Balatka: The Story of a Maiden of Prague. Trollope's eighteenth

novel was written between 3 November and 31 December 1865 and was first serialized in *Blackwood's Magazine* in seven monthly instalments between July 1866 and January 1867. Blackwood then published it anonymously in two volumes on 1 February 1867. Trollope received £450.

Nina Balatka is the first of three short continental novels that Trollope wrote in the second half of the 1860s. The other two are *Linda Tressel*, set in Germany, and *The Golden Lion of Gran-père*, set in France. Trollope insisted that this novel and *Linda Tressel* should be published anonymously when issued as books to see if they would sell on merit and not because of his name. (Publication in *Blackwood's Magazine* was always anonymous.) [➤ Anonymous Novels.] He also knew that critics were complaining that he was flooding the market with his 'wares'. His problem was that his highly disciplined method of writing so many pages each day, his creativity, the ease with which he could write and the need he felt to write whether his works were published or not drove him to consider this new method. He had been reasonably successful with his short stories, most of them based on life as he had observed it on his travels. Since he found the hardest part of his work as a writer lay in thinking up plots and not in actually writing, he could make more money from producing a few novels based on his travels than from turning out three or four short stories.

After John Blackwood, a shrewd judge, accepted the manuscript he wrote to Trollope that 'the great merit ... seems to me the clearness with which it stands out. There is an individuality about it which will make

anyone who reads it remember it. Whether this is sufficient to make it really popular and stand out ... as the work of an anonymous author is a doubtful point.' Blackwood took no chances and printed a small edition which sold very few copies. Despite this, the novel's serialization and publication in book form began a long and close business relationship and friendship between the two men.

Trollope describes the plot of this novel in his first sentence: 'Nina Balatka was a maiden of Prague, born of Christian parents, and herself a Christian – but she loved a Jew; and this is her story.' This was unusual territory for Trollope, although there are some familiar features: Nina battles against her father, a sick bankrupt, and her family, particularly a highly religious aunt [➤ Women] who urges her to marry her cousin. She finally wins the right to marry the man she wants.

In 1865 Trollope and his wife had visited Prague, which was then part of the Austrian Empire. He found it 'the most picturesque' of all the cities he knew, which by then was a considerable number. He was fascinated by the old quarter, particularly by the Old Synagogue, which claimed to be the oldest in Europe. According to *Murray's Handbook for Austria*, the standard Victorian travel guide, 'The Jews of Prague have preserved more strictly than in most other parts of Europe their ancient manners and customs.' Trollope's romantic side was stirred by old buildings that symbolized a tragic history, or in some cases a tragic end. The sight of a ruined manor house in Ireland had inspired his first novel, *The Macdermots of Ballycloran*. Prague's Old Synagogue sparked his imagination in the same way.

In this short novel Trollope holds the conventional Victorian liberal's attitude towards Austrian rule, by saying 'alas' when mentioning an Austrian barracks. But he also implies sympathy when he sees the vast Hradshin Palace, then the residence of the former emperor, Ferdinand I, who had abdicated in favour of his nephew, Franz Joseph, in 1848. Trollope had a rather complex attitude towards Jews: certainly their portrayal in this novel is different from the Jewish characters in *The Way We Live Now*, written a few years later. The most interesting character in the book is Nina's beloved, Anton Trendellsohn. He is not presented as the embodiment of all virtues, let alone of all vices. He has his good points and his weak ones, much as John Eames or Phineas Finn. This portrayal of Trendellsohn struck the reviewer in the *London Review*: 'In the character of Anton Trendellsohn, the author seeks to vindicate the Hebrew ... He is a human being, neither very good nor very bad, possessed of middle qualities that neither exalt nor degrade.' It is going too far to say that Trollope was trying to 'vindicate the Hebrew': this is to try to intellectualize his work. He was portraying a man, not a race.

Trollope also enjoys one of his private jokes by having Trendellsohn sign his letters 'A. T.' as Trollope frequently signed his own. Beneath the Bohemian costume worn by several characters lurk several old Barsetshire acquaintances. Certainly Nina's religiously fanatic aunt, Sophie Zemenoy, is Mrs Proudie dressed as a Czech Catholic. Following his normal practice, the Catholic priest is treated with respect.

When Trollope commenced writing *Nina Balatka* he followed his usual custom of setting out his schedule at the top of his worksheet: '300 pages at 230 words – 10 weeks at 30 pages a week'. Sometimes even his iron discipline faltered and on Christmas Day he only managed three pages. He drew one of his sketch maps, in this case one showing the location of the famous Charles Bridge, which Nina visits in the course of the novel. This bridge had a few years earlier also inspired Trollope's friend, George Eliot, to write her short story 'The Lifted Veil'. *Nina Balatka* has a great deal of local colour, given the shortness of Trollope's visit, and we are much more conscious of being in Prague than we ever are of being in Wales in *Cousin Henry*, to take another novel set outside England. In his *Autobiography* Trollope wrote that one reason for using so much local colour was to disguise the authorship of his continental novels.

When the novel began to appear in *Blackwood's Magazine* there was a considerable debate in literary circles about the authorship. One of Blackwood's authors, the eccentric Laurence Oliphant, wrote to the publisher, 'I am much questioned as to the authorship ... is it Trollope?' Blackwood replied that the authorship was a secret but he hinted that Disraeli, then leader of the Tory Opposition in the House of Commons, was the author. Others thought the author was Trollope's brother Tom. Trollope's most perceptive and friendly critic, R. H. Hutton of the *Spectator*, announced that 'the "great unknown" is Anthony Trollope'. (The 'Great

Unknown' had been a nickname for Sir Walter Scott.) Hutton in his *Spectator* review explained that he knew it was Trollope as soon as he spotted the novelist's characteristic use of the phrase 'made his way'. Those who know Trollope well will spot other familiar usages: the frequent use of 'picturesque' and the tell-tale habit of calling a doctor 'a son of Galen', to name but two. Hutton was understandably puzzled about Trollope's refusal to use his name, a name that was 'worth a great deal in money value'. (Trollope received £750 less for this novel than he had for *Miss Mackenzie*, also a two-volume novel that was published two years earlier.)

The critics gave it a relatively good reception, but as Blackwood said, 'the book is telling although not selling'. The novel had the advantage of being timely: Prague was much talked about when it was occupied by Prussian troops during the Austro-Prussian war which occurred shortly before *Nina Balatka* began to be serialized in *Blackwood's*; the following year civil restrictions on Jews were ended in the Austrian Empire. Trollope himself thought fairly highly of this novel and in his *Autobiography* rated it higher than *The Eustace Diamonds*. Few would agree with this view. However, as one of the first English novels to treat a Jewish character as a person rather than as a caricature, the book, which appeared nine years before George Eliot's *Daniel Deronda*, should be remembered.

The Noble Jilt. Trollope's first play, which he wrote in 1851, was not printed until 1923 when Michael Sadleir brought out an edition, published by Constable. Trollope's first

three novels had failed in varying degrees and he turned to drama. He had inherited a liking for the theatre from his mother who had taught her children to enact scenes in French from Molière's plays for guests. She also wrote little plays for them: the most amusing to survive is 'The Righteous Rout', a farce that attacks an Evangelical tea-party. (Mrs Stumfold's tea-party in *Miss Mackenzie* [4] must surely have been inspired by this.) She also got her children to analyse Shakespearian characters and scenes.

The Noble Jilt was obviously heavily influenced by Henry Taylor's 1834 blank-verse drama, *Philip van Artevelde*, which had been set in fourteenth-century Bruges. Trollope set his play in the past, in the era when the Low Countries were the main battleground between revolutionary and conservative forces. (His penchant for a French Revolution setting was also a hangover from his most recent novel, *La Vendée*.) The play was partly in blank verse and partly in prose, and centred on a girl who rejects her lover because she is bored with his perfection. Trollope wrote in his *Autobiography*: 'I believe that I did give the best of my intellect to the play, and I must own that when it was completed it pleased me much.' He went over it several times and sent it to George Bartley, one of his mother's theatrical friends and the manager of Covent Garden, then a theatre. He received a crushing rejection, a 'blow in the face'. On re-reading the manuscript in later years Trollope wrote, 'The dialogue, however, I think to be good, and I doubt whether some of the scenes be not the brightest and best work I ever did.' He was still proud of the work when writing to the critic E. S. Dallas in

1868: 'After all old Bartley's criticism, I believe it to be a good play.'

Trollope's work was not wasted: thirteen years later he adapted the plot to a contemporary English setting in *Can You Forgive Her?*, but even here the plot sags somewhat. Some of the characters may be seen as similar to those in the play. He remembered his play ten years after writing *Can You Forgive Her?* when he made one of his private jokes in *The Eustace Diamonds*. Some ladies go to the Haymarket Theatre to see the premier of a new work by 'a very eminent author'. The play's title is *The Noble Jilt* but, Trollope adds, 'The play, as a play, was a failure . . . The critics, on the next morning, were somewhat divided – not only in judgement but as to facts.'

Nonconformists. See Dissenters.

North America. This travel book was written between 16 September 1861, when Trollope was in the United States and Canada, and 27(?) April 1863. It was published in two volumes by Chapman & Hall in May 1862. Trollope received £1,250, £1,000 more than he got from the same firm for his first travel book on the West Indies, published in 1859. He kept the American rights and negotiated an agreement with Lippincott, but Harper & Brothers pirated an edition before Lippincott could bring out his. Some years later, when Trollope was adding up his literary earnings, he came to the figures for this book and wrote in red ink across his record of earnings one word: 'Cheated'. [➤ Copyright.]

In his *Autobiography* Trollope discussed his mother's famous book on America and added, 'I had entertained for many years an ambition to follow her footsteps there, and to write another book.' The outbreak of the Civil War in 1861 was a significant time for a now famous novelist to re-launch his career as a travel writer: his first travel book, *The West Indies*, had been published in 1859 and at the end of that book he announced his desire to write another travel book about 'that people who are our children'. To get permission from the Post Office he went to the Postmaster General after Rowland Hill had opposed his request. He was given leave for nine months on the grounds of previous extraordinary work for the Post Office – his trips abroad. When Hill added a postscript to the PMG's minute granting the leave, noting that it was a 'full equivalent for the special services rendered by me', Trollope demanded that it be removed, and won. He also had a demand that he do some Post Office work while in America countermanded. Nevertheless he praised Hill's 'wise audacity' in pressing for a standard penny post in this book.

His trip to America was the second of five and the longest. He visited all those states that had not seceded, except for California. 'I worked very hard at the task I had assigned myself, and did, I think, see much of the manners and institutions of the people.' He sought advice on points he did not understand about the Constitution and American law. The twenty chapters in Volume 1 and the sixteen in Volume 2 follow his tour, with interruptions to discuss Canada's connection with Britain, an 'apology for the war', the constitution of New York State, the rights of women, education, religion, Congress, the Northern army, the Post Office, hotels, courts, the Federal Constitution and literature. Canada was allotted three of the thirty-six chapters. The book was written as he travelled – the only way in which such a book could be written, he claimed – and has a sense of immediacy.

Trollope's work sheet survives and shows the difficulties he faced. On his first day of writing he only managed 3 pages but by the end of the week this had risen to 30. He now got into his stride and the second week showed 40 pages. There was occasionally some back-sliding and between 25 November and 4 December, when he was being lauded by Boston's literary establishment, he wrote nothing and added, 'Two weeks short. vie vie.' On 27 April he wrote 17 pages, which brought the total to 1,191 and ended the book. He wrote one word, 'over', which might have betrayed a certain weariness.

His first sentence read, 'It has been the ambition of my literary life to write a book about the United States.' Years later, when discussing the book in his *Autobiography*, he was very harsh: 'It contained much information,' he wrote, 'and, with many inaccuracies, was a true book. But it was not well done. It is tedious and confused, and will hardly, I think, be of future value to those who wish to make themselves acquainted with the United States ... [It] was not a good book. I can recommend no one to read it ... as I can do that on the West Indies. It served its purpose at the time, and was well received by the public and by the critics.'

Trollope's judgement was harsh but not inaccurate. His book is unashamedly biased in favour of the North, although not without criticisms, and its author was badly informed about the South. While Trollope disliked the newer, western states, he did see that they would play a decisive role not only in the war but in American development. Two themes dominate the book: the first is the influence of the theory of equality on Americans and the second is, naturally, the war itself. When addressing his American readers he imitated Carlyle's style, as he had done in *The New Zealander* and in the occasional novel: 'O, my friends with thin skin, ye whom I call my cousins and love as brethren, will ye not forgive me the harsh words that I have spoken?' His 'friends' did forgive him and praised the book extensively. It was extremely popular in the Northern states and did much to erase the memory of his mother's work. It does have some good insights into the American character and the most quotable sentence contains an essential key to Anglo-American differences: 'We live in a tea-cup, and they in a washing-tub.'

In Britain the reception was not so enthusiastic. Some reviewers found Trollope's comparison of the break-up of the Union to a divorce in the Jones family trivial and silly. (He had also used fictional characters to explain a complicated situation in *The New Zealander*.) The reviewer for *Blackwood's Magazine* wrote, 'We like his plots better than his travels.' This was a blow as Trollope saw books like this as a way of demonstrating he was not only a novelist but a serious writer and student of current affairs. The book is biased, over-long, diffuse, badly organized and sometimes boring: like many Englishmen who visited America at the time he had a fascination for the constitution of New York State, something few share today. His mother's book, while less well researched, is more enjoyable. The book does, however, tell us a great deal about Trollope the man: his interest in politics and a state system of education, his mixture of conservatism and liberalism, his belief in the future of 'the English world', his love of travel and his almost inexhaustible energy. When Trollope returned to England he was not the same man as when he left; he returned determined to make his mark in the world outside fiction and the Post Office. [For Trollope's views on the United States ➤ America.]

North Britain. See Scotland.

'Not If I Know It'. This short story was written sometime between 2 September and 3 November 1882 for *Life* magazine, which had accepted Trollope's terms on 9 August. It was published in the *Life Christmas Annual* that December, after Trollope's death. Trollope wrote it while working on his last novel, *The Land-Leaguers*.

This Christmas story opens with a quarrel between brothers-in-law on Christmas Eve. Wilfred Horton has asked his brother-in-law, George Wade, to state to the Turco-Egyptian New Waterworks Company that he is worth £10,000, to which Wade replies in anger, 'Not if I know it.' On Christmas Day they go to the parish church where the vicar, Dr Burnaby, preaches on the Prince of Peace. As they take the Sacrament they are moved to forgive each other. George Wade makes the first move and the brothers-in-law are reconciled.

This story, the shortest Trollope wrote, is also one of the most 'religious'. It is based not only on his religious faith but on his knowledge of the Prayer Book. It demonstrates, per-

haps better than anywhere else, his own High Church devotion to the Sacrament. In other Christmas stories, such as 'Christmas Day at Kirkby Cottage' and 'The Two Heroines of Plumplington', the Eucharist or Holy Communion as a sacrament of reconciliation is emphasized but not as strongly as here. 'Then came the Sacrament,' Trollope writes, 'more powerful with its thoughts than its words, and the two men as they left the church were ready in truth to forgive each other – if they only knew how.' Towards the end of the story, after the reconciliation has taken place, George Wade tells his sister and brother-in-law that he wanted 'to make full confession and restitution'. This phrase brings to mind words from the Exhortation that priests were instructed to make when announcing that the Sacrament would be celebrated on the following Sunday: one must 'make restitution and satisfaction ... for all injuries and wrongs' done by you to another before approaching the altar.

Trollope also noted with satisfaction that the sermon was only fifteen minutes long. The phrase 'Not if I know it' was common in Victorian times and indicated a decided refusal to do something. The vicar's surname, Burnaby, had been used thirteen years before in *Ralph the Heir* for the barrister who represents Sir Thomas Underwood during the election.

[➤ Church of England; Religion.]

The Novel. 'We have become a novel-reading people from the Prime Minister down to the last-appointed scullery-maid ... all our other reading put together hardly amounts to what we read in novels,' said Trollope in a lecture in 1870. The Victorian period, arguably starting with Dickens's *The Pickwick Papers* (1836–7), saw an explosion in novels as a truly popular fiction, cheaply available to all classes through part issues, serialization and circulating libraries like Mudie's. It was a national literary culture similar to television in the second half of the twentieth century.

Trollope may be said to have inherited an interest in novels from both parents: his father read eighteenth-century novels to the family and his mother, Fanny, became one of the best-known novelists of the 1830s and 1840s. As a youth he read novels and carefully analysed them, and as a young clerk he often helped his mother deal with publishers. He took the writing and reading of novels seriously and referred to novel-writing as a profession, although he always rated the novelist's calling below that of the poet and in public he usually disparaged his own skills. He was well read in the history not only of the novel but of the theatre [➤ Shakespeare]. He thought of writing a history of fiction from *Robinson Crusoe* to the nineteenth century 'to vindicate that public taste in literature which has created and nourished the profession which I follow'. He was well aware, when writing this in his *Autobiography*, that there still existed a 'prejudice in respect to novels' not so much among puritanical Evangelicals but among intellectuals like Carlyle, which robbed novels of 'that high character which they may claim to have earned by their grace, their honesty, and good teaching'.

The *Autobiography* devotes one chapter to 'novels and the art of writing them' and one to 'English novelists of the present day'. His own view of the novel was most succinctly expressed in Chapter 12: 'A novel should give a picture of common life enlivened by humour and sweetened by pathos.' (By 'common life' he meant, of course, 'everyday life'.) He accepted the tastes of those for whom he wrote and insisted that marriage is 'the proper ending for a novel, the only ending, as this writer takes it to be' [*Ayala's Angel*, 64]. All but three of the novels (*La Vendée*, *Lady Anna* and *The Fixed Period*) and all but two of the short stories ('The Gentle Euphemia' and 'The Panjandrum') were set in or near the time in which they were written. Victorians often correctly described these realistic novels as photographs of their own age.

Trollope accepted the power novelists had attained and insisted it must be used for a noble purpose. In *The New Zealander* he criticized those who only 'wrote up to [pandered to] the popular feeling of the time'. 'A vast proportion of the teaching of the day ... comes from these books' and the fact was that the novelist 'must teach whether he wish to teach or no'. The task was 'to teach lessons of virtue and at the same time make himself a delight to his readers' [*Autobiography*]. He told a Royal Literary Fund meeting that the novelist's moral duty is to 'teach ladies to be women and men to be gentlemen'. The novelist's form of instruction was like a snake in the grass: 'It is the test of a novel writer's art that he conceals his snake-in-the-grass; but the reader may be sure that it is always there' [*Ralph the Heir*, 56]. In his own case, his teaching mission often earned him the label of satirist when he used characters to examine contemporary behaviour and to expose the foibles and hypocrisies he had seen in his extensive travels and work, and in his wide experience of mankind.

In his time he was therefore regarded as a trenchant novelist, not the mere chronicler of a bygone age that some facile people imagine today. Frequent themes include the plight of women with few choices open to them, the nature of a woman's love, marriage, the contest between a conservative desire to retain the old and a progressive demand for the new in which change usually won, difficult relationships between young people and their elders, the problem of honesty in public life, moral dilemmas, and, especially in the later novels, disputes over inheritance and property. Few of his novels do not touch on some controversial topic and he had a constant desire to expose sham and dishonesty in society, the Church, politics and individual behaviour. The novelist must not write 'because he has to tell a story, but because he has a story to tell'. His characters must be true to human nature and his story must not be tedious.

Concerning novelists in general, his 'chief favourite' was Jane Austen. Among other Victorian novelists, Trollope named his friend Thackeray as the greatest. George Eliot was given second place and Charles Dickens, third. Fourth place went to Bulwer-Lytton, later Lord Lytton, after whom came, in descending order: Charles Lever, Charlotte Brontë, Charles Reade, Wilkie Collins, Anne Thackeray, Rhoda Broughton and last and very much least, Benjamin Disraeli.

To Trollope the plot always rated second to the characters and his outlines were not complete to the last incident: the flow of the story sometimes determined events, such as Lady Mason's guilt or innocence in *Orley Farm*. He hated a 'mystery' in a plot and often tells readers how things will turn out, often to the detriment of the novel. One plot was essential: novels, he said, 'not only contain love stories, but they are written for the sake of the love stories. They have other attractions and deal with every phase of life; but the other attractions hang round and depend on the love story.' Novelists needed 'to listen and to observe' the people and incidents round them. Characters must not be caricatures or over-drawn, but realistic mixtures of good and bad, not 'walking on stilts'. He believed that he did his best work when he was able to devote himself totally to his writing, when he could 'imbue myself thoroughly with the characters'. The real work was the planning: 'Forethought is the elbow grease which a novelist ... requires' [*Thackeray*].

Writing was a skill to be mastered and in 'The Adventures of Fred Pickering' a well-known author tells a young aspirant, with some over-statement, that a writer 'must be either a genius or a journeyman'. When he had time to create his plot and characters Trollope was able to 'sit with the pen in my hand, and drive my team before me at as quick a pace as I could'. From his forethought and regular early morning time set aside for writing came his oft-repeated quip about cobbler's wax on the chair seat's being more important than 'inspiration'. From these came his famous work sheets which he used to record his progress, to remind him of the work still to be done and to ensure that he wrote the correct number of words to fit in with the demands of serialization. He disliked talking about his work in public and often dismissed it, thereby earning for himself a reputation among the intelligentsia as lacking seriousness. (His frequent use of humorous names for his characters also sometimes undermined his serious intent.)

A novelist's style, he wrote, must be natural and must come from practice. His was of unadorned, plain English with a penchant for homely metaphors. 'I hold that gentleman to be the best dressed whose dress no one observes. I am not sure but that the same may be said of an author's written language' [*Thackeray*]. He was influenced by the Prayer Book, the Bible, his mother, his need to write precise English in the Post Office and his love of the classics and old English drama. He tried out his dialogue aloud even before dictating novels to his niece or wife. With Disraeli in mind he added, 'A man who thinks much of his words as he writes them will generally leave behind him work that smells of oil.' He often interrupts his narration with 'authorial intrusions' or first-person addresses to the reader, to many people's annoyance.

Between 1847 and his death he wrote forty-seven novels of which one, *The Land-Leaguers*, was left incomplete at his death and one, *An Old Man's Love*, was published posthumously. He wrote: one historical novel, *La Vendée*; one futuristic novel, *The Fixed Period*; one Australian novel, *Harry Heathcote of Gangoil*; one Welsh

novel, *Cousin Henry*; one humorous satire on advertising, *The Struggles of Brown, Jones, and Robinson*; five Irish novels, *The Macdermots of Ballycloran*, *The Kellys and the O'Kellys*, *Castle Richmond*, *An Eye for an Eye* and *The Land-Leaguers*; three 'continental novels', *Nina Balatka*, *Linda Tressel* and *The Golden Lion of Granpère*; six novels in the Barsetshire series and six in the Palliser series. The rest were novels set in contemporary England: *The Three Clerks*, *The Bertrams*, *Orley Farm*, *Rachel Ray*, *Miss Mackenzie*, *The Belton Estate*, *The Claverings*, *He Knew He Was Right*, *The Vicar of Bullhampton*, *Sir Harry Hotspur of Humblethwaite*, *Ralph the Heir*, *The Way We Live Now*, *The American Senator*, *Is He Popenjoy?*, *John Caldigate*, *Dr Wortle's School*, *Ayala's Angel*, *Marion Fay*, *Kept in the Dark* and *Mr Scarborough's Family*. It was Trollope who first created an entire fictional world in Barsetshire and it was he who popularized the idea of a series of novels, all related to another in locations and characters. He thought of writing a third series to follow the Barsetshire and Palliser series. He planned to set it in Australia and wrote the first volume, *Lady Anna*. He then gave up the idea.

[➤ the complete list of Trollope's books on pp. xvi–xviii; Names, Origin of; Names, Use of; 'The Panjandrum'; Private Jokes; Publishers and Publishing; 'Three-deckers'; Vulgarity; 'A Walk in a Wood', and individual novels. *Ralph the Heir* [56] contains many of Trollope's reflections on the novel.]

O

'The O'Conors of Castle Conor, County Mayo'. This short story was written during Trollope's trip to the French Pyrenees in September–October 1859. He set aside work on *Castle Richmond* to work on five stories, including this one; of these he offered this and three others to *Harper's New Monthly Magazine* in New York in which journal it was published in May 1860. It was included in his first collection, *Tales of All Countries*. In his *Autobiography* Trollope wrote of this story and of 'Father Giles of Ballymoy' that 'I will not swear to every detail in these stories, but the main purport of each is true. I could tell many others of the same nature.' Trollope received $100, or £20.

This humorous story is told in the first person with Trollope as the character Archibald Green. Green tells of his first day of riding to hounds and of country life in County Mayo, Ireland, in the 1840s. He is invited to spend the night (for dinner and dancing) by a hunting partner and has his things sent over from the hotel; unfortunately his pumps were left behind. In despair he exchanges his shooting-boots, 'each bearing half a stone of iron in the shape of nails and heel-pieces', for the butler's mismatched pair of shoes, one of which is ill-fitting and down-at-heel. The truth comes out at dinner, the pumps are ordered

and the dancing starts when the shoes arrive. Green stays for three weeks, not one night.

The story is marked by sparkling Irish dialogue, by a genuine love of Ireland and by an enjoyment of the unpretentious, broad and gentle humour of Irishmen. The humour resembles that in Trollope's first novel, *The Macdermots of Ballycloran*. This tale gives a good insight into how Trollope found happiness and acceptance once he took up fox-hunting shortly after coming to Ireland in 1841.

An Old Man's Love. Trollope's forty-sixth novel was written between 20 February and 9 May 1882. The manuscript was found in Trollope's desk after his death, and his son Henry arranged for publication by Blackwood in two volumes in 1884. He assured Blackwood that no one had read it and that his cousin, Florence Bland, to whom Trollope had dictated the story, had forgotten it: a somewhat curious recommendation for a novel. Trollope's estate received £225.

An Old Man's Love should hold a special place in the affections of devoted Trollope readers. It was his last completed novel and the elegiac tone of it seems a far more appropriate farewell than that sad and uncompleted novel, *The Land-Leaguers*. It is a short novel with a simple plot: an older man, William Whittlestaff, adopts a young girl, Mary Lawrie, who is the orphaned daughter of a friend and with whom he falls in love. After much pressure she agrees to marry him, but in the end he gives up his claim so that she can marry her true love, a young man named John Gordon. In the playing out of this plot an observant reader will see many of those little touches that make Trollope such a great novelist.

William Whittlestaff is normally referred to as Mr Whittlestaff, and this Trollopian usage indicates he is not a young man: characters who are normally referred to without their Christian name, or who are given no Christian name, are, or seem, older [➤ Names, Use of]. We would not consider him an 'old man' for when the novel begins he is fifty. Trollope, however, often exaggerated the influence of age and, of course, in the 1880s life expectancy was much less than in the 1990s. In addition, Trollope, who was in his late sixties when he wrote the book, did think that the passing of fifty years combined with Whittlestaff's personality had produced an 'old man'. He is that familiar figure of Victorian legends – though not all that common in Trollope – a man whose whole life has been darkened by being jilted by his beloved. (Another such is Peter Prosper in *Mr Scarborough's Family*.) To add extra touches of pathos, Trollope tells us that Whittlestaff, who 'had been opposed in everything to his father's views', had also failed to get a university fellowship, while his career as a poet had proved yet another disaster [➤ Fathers and Sons]. He sounds remarkably like what Trollope himself could have become if his own life had not turned

out so fortunately. Whittlestaff is, however, redeemed by his deep reading in the classics. Predictably, his devotion is to those authors in whom Trollope himself so delighted, especially Horace, Caesar and Cicero. [➤ Classics.] It is through this reading that Whittlestaff turns from being an embittered man into a serene and placid one.

As so often in Trollope's fiction, when a character appears we are told not only his age, but also his income: in this case, £1,000 a year, which allows him to lead a life of pleasure provided he dispenses with such luxuries as a manservant. This does not mean that Mr Whittlestaff is without servants; indeed, his housekeeper, Mrs Baggett, is not only the most outspoken servant in all Trollope's fiction, but one of the few working-class characters to play a key role throughout a novel. The relationship between Whittlestaff and Mrs Baggett is the most accomplished aspect of this novel. She had been in the service of his parents for years and was especially devoted to the memory of his long-dead mother; a particularly apt touch is the way in which he enjoys hearing his mother's memory extolled by Mrs Baggett, although he never mentions her himself. Mrs Baggett, who is separated from her drunken husband, is understandably perturbed when the orphaned daughter of an old friend is taken into the house, for in many ways she and her employer act, or at least argue, like an elderly married couple

In the novel that Trollope had finished about four months earlier, *Mr Scarborough's Family*, a solicitor comments, 'A man at fifty is supposed to be young enough to marry' [28]. In that novel the fifty-year-old man, Mr Prosper – who looks more like sixty – plans to marry but draws back from it. In *Mr Scarborough's Family* this provides several chapters of rich comedy, but in *An Old Man's Love* a similar story takes on tragic overtones.

Neither Mary herself nor her true love, John Gordon, who returns from seeking his fortune in South African diamond mines, is a particularly interesting character. Trollope used his visit to South Africa in 1877 to provide the background to Kimberley and in his *South Africa* he gives a vivid description of the diamond mines and his own descent into one. When mining appears there are likely to be difficulties, but Gordon is that rare character in Trollope's fiction: a man who is almost unaffected by his time in a mining town save for the fact that he has acquired a delightful fortune. An otherwise unnecessary appearance by another man from Kimberley allows Trollope to show society in this frontier town as similar to that in Australia, shown in *John Caldigate*, or to that in the American West, shown in *Dr Wortle's School*. As one character in *An Old Man's Love* says, in these places 'there isn't the same sort of prudish life which one is accustomed to in England' [18].

The real interest in the novel lies in the way in which Mrs Baggett reacts to the potential marriage of her employer. She knows that when Mary becomes Mrs Whittlestaff she will not need a housekeeper. Even so, she thinks it her 'duty' to badger the girl into accepting a man twice her age. Similar pressure on a young girl took place in *Mr Scarborough's Family* when Lady Mountjoy badgers Florence Mountjoy. (Like so many of Trollope's older women, both Mrs Baggett's and Lady Mountjoy's worst aspects come out when dealing with younger women.) The housekeeper's harangues lead to two important statements that are essential to any understanding of Trollope, not only in this novel but throughout his fiction. The old woman tells the younger that it is her 'duty' to sacrifice herself to a man who has been so good to her and announces that 'people ain't born to have good times of it' [4]. Trollope's comment is that this 'is the greatest lesson we may say which a man or a woman can learn'. In short, we have the oft-repeated Trollopian injunction that one should not moan about one's fate but settle down and work.

For Mrs Baggett this is but a prelude to a further pronouncement about the need for women to accept complete male supremacy. (One might note that Mrs Baggett's own behaviour hardly accords with her theory, but then Trollope always delights in allowing readers to see how seldom practice follows pronouncements.) Whittlestaff ponders Mrs Baggett's view of marriage and at last decides that it is 'damnable' for a man to seek absolute domination or 'gratification'. He concludes by asking: 'Did the lessons of Mrs Baggett run smoothly with those of Jesus Christ?' [16]. The answer is a decided 'no'. *Mr Scarborough's Family* had shown the havoc caused by an amoral 'pagan' and its successor shows an example of Christian resignation by Mr Whittlestaff, as had *The Warden* with Septimus Harding. [➤ 'Not If I Know It', Trollope's last short story, for another example of a direct appeal to Christ's teaching.]

As so often in his post-Barsetshire novels Trollope included a clergyman because he knew that his readers admired his clerical portraits. The Reverend Montagu Blake is the last of that long line of clergymen in Trollope's fiction. Like so many of his predecessors, Blake's lines 'had fallen in pleasant places'. He is a curate with £120 a year – not a bad income for an unmarried priest – but Trollope, generous as ever, provides him with 'as pretty a little parsonage as could be found in England' as well as a 'modest fortune' of his own, producing another £300 a year. Within a few chapters the old vicar expires on the Riviera and young Blake becomes vicar with £250 a year instead of his £120. He is also about to marry the daughter of a prebendary of Winchester who – not surprisingly – comes with £5,000 [➤ Church of England]. Blake, an old Oxford friend of Gordon, is ecstatically in love with his 'Kattie'.

Trollope's clergymen have moved with the times and Blake is a jolly sort of parson who plays cricket. He is even known to follow the hounds in a fox-hunt but only 'by chance'. Thus Trollope's long internal argument as to whether clergymen should hunt, which seemed to have been decided in the negative with Dean Lovelace in *Is He Popenjoy?*, carries on to one final fox-hunting man of the cloth. When someone criticizes the new vicar for not remembering that he is a clergyman, Mr Whittlestaff replies – expressing the sentiments of his creator – 'It will be better for him and for all those about him' that he should always remember that while he is a clergyman he should 'never seem to do so' [17]. At the end of the novel Trollope assures us that Montagu Blake will turn out well.

For the setting of the novel, Trollope did not have to look far. He chose a spot in Hampshire, about fifteen miles across the border from his Sussex home at Harting. The walk that Whittlestaff takes to meditate upon Horace, Mrs Baggett and Christianity seems remarkably similar to the one Trollope used to take near his own home. In calling a local inn 'The Claimant's Arms' Trollope was having a laugh at the Tichborne claimant. (The Tichborne estate was in this area.) As with another recent novel, *Kept in the Dark*, he followed the somewhat odd practice of using real ecclesiastical titles, so we hear of both the Bishop and the Dean of Winchester. One wonders what the real Dean of Winchester would have thought if he had seen himself referred to as an old 'frump'. Perhaps Trollope was sharing a joke with his friend the Rector of Harting, the Reverend H. D. Gordon, who may have been amused to see his own name used for the young lover.

Trollope begins the novel with a private joke about the late delivery of post. His great goal as a postal official had been to get letters on to people's breakfast tables. Trollope probably also used some of the difficulties he was having with a drunken manservant for his portrayal of Mrs Baggett's husband. There is no ground for thinking that Trollope was portraying his own feelings for Kate Field in this novel. (The theme of an older man's love for a young woman is also used in three short stories: 'Mary Gresley', 'Lotta Schmidt' and 'Miss Ophelia Gledd'.)

The fact that the book was published more than a year after Trollope's death meant that reviewers treated it gently, although *The Times* made the good point that Trollope 'needed elbow-room for the effective display of his powers', something the two-volume format did not allow. [For the same view, ➤Newman, John Henry.] While *An Old Man's Love* is neither a great nor an important Trollope novel, it is – like Mr Whittlestaff's Horace – a perfect companion for a summer's day.

Old Women. See Women.

Omnium, Duchess of.
See Palliser Family.

Omnium, Dukes of.
See Palliser Family.

Oriel, The Rev. Caleb. A young and 'very High Church' clergyman who is the Rector of Greshamsbury in *Doctor Thorne.* His wealthy family buys the living of Greshamsbury from Squire Gresham to give him a parish. Trollope's treatment of him is a good example of the way in which he treated High Church clergy: Oriel is basically a good clergyman in spite of a few 'extremist' views due to youthful exuberance. His one great fault is his very 'exalted' view on the celibacy of the clergy. This makes him even more attractive to several young ladies who are in love with him. His good looks and private fortune of £30,000 are added attractions. Trollope delights in portraying Oriel casting off his theories to become engaged to the squire's daughter, Beatrice. Oriel reappears in *The Last Chronicle of Barset* in which he is a rather indecisive member of the Clerical Commission investigating the case of Josiah Crawley. The name Oriel, of course, immediately identi-

fies the young clergyman as High Church as Oriel College, Oxford, was well known as the college of the three leaders of the Oxford Movement: John Keble, Edward Pusey and John Henry Newman [➤Church of England]. Thackeray had also given the name Oriel to a High Church clergyman in *Our Street* (1848) and had also used him in *Pendennis.*

Orley Farm. Trollope's eleventh novel was written between 4 July 1860 and 22 June 1861. It was published first in twenty monthly part issues (between March 1861 and October 1862) by Chapman & Hall, who then published it as a two-volume novel: the first volume appeared in December 1861, the second in September 1862. Trollope received £3,135.

Orley Farm marks an important stage in Trollope's career as a novelist. This was the first time that one of his novels received the supreme accolade of being published in parts. This was the method that had led to Dickens's great fame and in the first paragraph Trollope makes a humorous reference to people asking for the next number of his new novel. [➤Publishers and Publishing.] The first instalment of *Orley Farm* appeared in March 1861, the month before the last chapters of *Framley Parsonage* came out in the *Cornhill Magazine.* That had brought Trollope tremendous acclaim and the payment for *Orley Farm* testified to it. Three years before, Trollope had only received £600 from Chapman & Hall for *Castle Richmond*; now they paid him more than five times that sum.

This was the first novel that Trollope began in his elegant house in Hertfordshire and it is also the first novel that he wrote completely in

England. The large payments, the fame, the country house, his acceptance into London's literary society [➤ Clubs] and his new position in the Post Office gave him the security to look back to some painful days in his early life. The house in *Orley Farm* is therefore based upon the house in Harrow in which Trollope spent part of his youth. He even took Millais to Harrow to allow him to make an accurate drawing of the house. The daughter of another artist who had been taken on a similar tour by Trollope remembered his pointing 'with many chuckles' to the hedge through which he had smuggled his mother's treasures when the bailiffs invaded the farmhouse. It is noteworthy that Trollope began the writing of *Orley Farm* soon after he had written the chapter in *Framley Parsonage* [44] about the misery of seeing bailiffs seizing a family's possessions. Thus Trollope's comment in the penultimate chapter [79] of *Orley Farm* that time lessens suffering had been borne out in his own case.

This is one of Trollope's largest novels with an extensive portrayal of almost every rank in Victorian society, ranging from the elderly baronet Sir Peregrine Orme, Lady Mason's neighbour, down to Mary Snow, the orphaned daughter of a poor engraver. The main plot centres on a will made several decades earlier. Did Lady Mason, the second wife of a wealthy man, forge a codicil to her husband's will which left Orley Farm to his younger, and her only son, Lucius? Mason's elder son, Joseph, a large landholder in Yorkshire, felt that he had been cheated out of this small part of his inheritance by his stepmother. There are numerous sub-plots, too

many no doubt, but the demands of publication by instalments called for that. Many of these plots concern lawyers and the fascinating but repulsive Chaffanbrass: indeed, the law and lawyers are central to the whole novel. 'Mr Anthony Trollope comes to us berobed and bewigged,' said *The Times*. In few other novels are his mixed attitudes to lawyers so evident.

This is pre-eminently a story of respectable, well-to-do people suddenly confronted with possible disgrace. For Lady Mason, the disgrace of her forgery is, as Trollope says, 'the chief interest of our tale'. The two other most memorable characters, her son Lucius and Sir Peregrine, are also caught up in the consequences of her disgrace. Each faces his own misery: Lucius, the loss of his house and income; the elderly baronet, the fact that he cannot now marry the woman he loves because she will bring disgrace to his ancient family. The Furnivals also face humiliation when the wife's silly jealousy of Lady Mason nearly ruins her marriage. *Orley Farm* is in that sense a sombre novel, but unlike Trollope's first novel, *The Macdermots of Ballycloran*, or a more recent work such as *The Bertrams*, the book demonstrates that Trollope as a skilled novelist now knew he must add humour and some scenes of domestic bliss that the Victorians enjoyed. The four chapters describing Christmas in different households – the largest proportion of text that Trollope ever devoted to Christmas in a novel – were no doubt another way to meet the popular market. They appeared in the December 1861 part. One of Trollope's nephews later said that the Christmas food and festivities described in one chapter [22]

were based on Trollope's own celebrations.

These Christmas scenes are at Noningsby, the home of the Staveley
family, and their house also provides
the setting for other pictures of domestic bliss throughout the novel. 'For
those who have managed that things
shall run smoothly ... there is no happier time of life than these long
candlelight hours of home and silence.
No spoken content or uttered satisfaction is necessary' [21]. This is almost
certainly one of his private jokes that
he shared, in this case, with his wife
Rose, for a few sentences later he has
the phrase 'the domestic rose'. The
fact that Trollope himself enjoyed
such a contented domestic life allowed
him to portray middle-class home life
so well. The *National Review*, in its
thirteen-page essay on the novel, said,
'More than a million people habitually read Mr Trollope, and they do so
because the personages in his stories
correspond to something in themselves: the hopes, fears, and regrets are
such as they are accustomed to experience.' Even the *Saturday Review*, often
so hostile to him, wrote that 'He does
the family life of England to perfection. No one has drawn English families better – without exaggeration, and
without any attempt at false comedy.
His gentlemen and ladies are exactly
like real gentlemen and ladies, except,
perhaps, they are a trifle more
entertaining.'

Orley Farm is one of the best of Trollope's novels – indeed, one of the best
of Victorian novels – through which to
see Victorian society and the ideas
that underpinned it. Family, property
and religion were the three essential
pillars that upheld Victorian civilization and they are all present here. We

see a variety of families at home: not
only the main characters mentioned
above, but lesser figures such as the
vulgar Moulders or Joseph Mason and
his mean wife. The experienced
reader of Trollope will immediately
know that we are meant to dislike Mrs
Joseph Mason when, in spite of her
wealth, she serves a guest such a miserable meal [➤ Food].

The finest aspect of the novel is the
portrayal of Lady Mason, a woman
living with a guilty secret about an act
committed out of love for her son, the
only love she had ever known. Her
crime is an attack upon property: she
has unjustly – albeit understandably –
interfered with her husband's property
and taken some of her stepson's inheritance. Wills, inheritance and entails
would come to be a major preoccupation in Trollope's later novels.

Having just finished *Framley Parsonage*, Trollope was anxious to keep the
clergy out of *Orley Farm*, but even
without an abundance of clergymen
the novel has more religious messages
and 'sermons' than almost any other
novel. Particularly notable is an attack
on drunkenness and on atheism, the
latter attack being among the fiercest
writing in all of Trollope's works [➤
Religion]. This occurs when the commercial traveller, Moulder, expresses a
purely materialist view of Christmas
and Trollope denounces 'the modern
philosophy of the Moulders, pigs out
of the sty' [24].

The scenes at the Bull Inn and
characters like Moulder (who works
for the firm of Hubbles and Grease)
sound more like Dickens than Trollope. Perhaps he realized that it would
be wise to take a lesson from the
master of the part issues. Trollope had
a long familiarity with inns from his

work for the Post Office and he had used some of this in *The Three Clerks*. However, *Orley Farm* really takes us inside these hotels with its description of life in the room set apart for commercial travellers. These scenes also allowed Trollope to make use, and better use, of the comic ideas he had used when he began *The Struggles of Brown, Jones, and Robinson* in 1857. It is interesting that he returned to that novel two days after finishing *Orley Farm*. Both were attacks on his old enemy, commercial dishonesty [➤ Honesty].

Among the many sub-plots is a curious one about a young law reformer, Felix Graham, who attends a conference in Birmingham on law reform with a three-hour lecture in German by the celebrated Von Bauhr from Berlin and a short reply from Lord Boanerges. This elderly peer and Lady Mason's barrister, Chaffanbrass, had already appeared in earlier novels: the first in *The Bertrams* and the second, in *The Three Clerks*. In Lord Boanerges, Trollope is clearly having mild fun with the famous legal reformer and habitué of conferences, Lord Brougham. To make the identification absolutely clear to contemporaries Trollope adds the phrase *Vox et praeterea nihil* ('voice and nothing else'), a well-known, though absurd, pun on Brougham's full title of Lord Brougham and Vaux. *Vox et praeterea nihil* also seems an epitaph for the conference. For the conference he drew on the National Association for the Promotion of Social Science, which had Brougham's support. 'To practical Englishmen,' says Trollope, 'most of these international conferences seem to arrive at nothing.' Yet he aims at a balanced view, as always, and at the end of Chapter 17 he concludes: 'A man who strives honestly to do good will generally do good, though seldom perhaps as much as he has himself anticipated.' Thus in *Orley Farm* we have the same divided attitude towards reform – holding up Utopian notions to scorn while endorsing practical measures – that was present a decade earlier in *The Warden* and would mark all his writing. Ironically, five years later Trollope submitted a paper on international copyright for the 1866 meeting of the same association.

Closely connected with this belief in moderate reform, which could come if all men would only 'strive honestly to do good', was Trollope's passionate devotion to work. This novel contains one of his most rhapsodic 'sermons' on it: 'There is no human bliss equal to twelve hours of work with only six hours in which to do it' [49]. While few might agree with this, none could deny that at the rate Trollope was turning out novels in the 1860s, here was that rare preacher who practised what he preached. It is interesting to note that immediately after this sentence he alludes to two of his own early residences: Keppel Street, for the early home of the barrister, Furnival, with its 'small dingy parlour' [10], and the neighbourhood of the Marylebone workhouse where he had rooms as a young Post Office clerk. Personal references abound. When discussing the perils faced by 'gentlemen farmers' he had his own father's tragic experiences upon which to draw [4]. There are also several chapters set in Yorkshire and Trollope could draw upon his wife's recollections for this as she had spent her youth in Rotherham; it is hardly surprising to find a reference to a 'Rotherham Grange'

[28]. When Mrs Furnival wants an excuse for calling at her husband's chambers to have a look at Lady Mason, she says that she 'happened to be in Holborn – at Mudie's for some books' [13] and it was Mudie's Library which did so much to advance Trollope's career.

Two other aspects of the novel are well worth noting: the role of women and the conflict between generations. The 1850s and '60s saw the discussion about women's rights grow rapidly. Four years before Trollope began this novel a woman was refused permission to sit the University of London's examination for the medical diploma, and in 1862, the year in which the part issues of *Orley Farm* stopped, another woman tried in vain to sit for London's matriculation examination. This growing debate is reflected in the novel. Both Lady Staveley and Mrs Furnival present a very conservative view and the latter maintains that 'women ought not to have any spheres'. This opinion is attacked both by her daughter and by young Lucius Mason, who argues that women's minds are 'equal to those of men' and that they 'ought to be able to make for themselves careers as brilliant' [11]. [➤ Feminism.] Throughout the book new ideas and new fashions spring up and cause dissension between older and younger people about important topics such as legal reform, scientific farming and the use of statistics, another Victorian development reflected in movements like Lord Brougham's National Association for the Promotion of Social Science.

Trollope's attack on competitive examinations – 'this hurrying and competitive age' [3] – is a continuation of that in *The Bertrams* and *The Three Clerks* and is a theme to which Trollope returned in other works [➤ Civil Service]. 'Only think what a lift it would give to the education of the country in general,' Trollope continues later on in the same paragraph, 'if any lad from seventeen to twenty-one could go in for a vacant dukedom; and if a goodly inheritance could be made absolutely incompatible with incorrect spelling and doubtful proficiency in rule of three!' One is reminded of the proposal to open the peerage to examination in Gilbert and Sullivan's *Iolanthe*. The denunciation of the Victorian rage for competition and examinations naturally follows from a Trollopian warning that 'fruit that grows ripe the quickest is not the sweetest . . .'. Trollope, himself something of a 'late achiever', returns to this later in the novel [49]. For light relief Trollope includes debates on such topics as the new fashion for iron furniture and a reference to snobbishness based on mealtimes [8] [➤ Food].

Perceptive readers will also note that Dockwrath, like Mr Quiverful, sees the number of his children vary: he has sixteen in the first chapter and fourteen in Chapter 32. In describing Furnival's feelings for Lady Mason [26] Trollope gives a superb insight into a middle-aged man's sexual nature [➤ Marriage]. Interestingly, Trollope sings the praises of clear post-marks [41] seventeen years before one of these plays a crucial role in *John Caldigate*. His odd reference to having known an 'assassin' [75] in Ireland points to his long stay in that country, something to which he would return in the last novel he wrote, *The Land-Leaguers*. There is gentle mockery of zealous young ladies' excessive High Church practices such as Friday fasting and of the re-establishment of convents in the Church of England [58]. Trollope's own reticence in talking about deep religious feeling is seen in his discussion of a conversation between Lady Mason and Mrs Orme [60].

Trollope, who was concerned with the illustrations in his books, was particularly delighted with the forty drawings Millais produced for *Orley Farm*. He believed that they were not only the best of the artist's works, but the finest illustrations for any Victorian fiction. Trollope even takes the unusual step of referring to one of them when he says that the 'idea which the reader will have conceived of her [Lady Mason] as she sat there will have come to him from the skill of the artist, and not from the words of the writer'. He also advises the reader to turn back to an early issue to find this illustration [62]. Millais, who became a close friend of Trollope, seems to have shared his delight in private jokes. The illustration, 'Christmas at Noningsby – Evening' is almost certainly a portrait of the bald Trollope playing the Christmas games he so loved. In a later illustration, 'Sir Peregrine at Mr Round's Office', Millais has placed three tin boxes at the top of the lawyer's bookcase: the one on the left is labelled 'A. Trollope'; in the centre is 'I. [Iosephus] Mason' and to the right is 'V. R.' [Victoria Regina]. Trollope also enjoyed selecting Thomas Furnival's surname: Furnival's Inn was one of the Inns of Court that was dissolved in 1817 [➤ Names, Origin of].

Fifteen years after Trollope's death, Herbert Paul, a well-known historian in the nineteenth century, said that *Orley Farm* had remained Trollope's most popular book with his contemporaries. This is certainly no longer the case. Modern readers can easily be put off by the large number of subplots, the excessive religiosity of Mrs Orme and the rigid notions of honour of her father-in-law, Sir Peregrine Orme. Yet readers who keep their attention firmly on the portrayal of Lady Mason and her dilemma will see that *Orley Farm* is one of Trollope's best novels.

Orphans. Orphans do not occur with much frequency in Trollope's fiction, unlike girls who have lost their mothers [➤ Mothers and Daughters]. Usually the orphans are girls, although Ralph and Gregory Newton had been orphaned before the start of *Ralph the Heir* and in 'The Mistletoe Bough' Godfrey Holmes is apparently an orphan. Perhaps Trollope's most famous orphans are Mary Thorne, who is taken in by her uncle in *Doctor Thorne*, and Mary Lawrie, who is taken in by a friend of her dead father, and who is the heroine of *An Old Man's Love*. Other orphaned girls who are taken into families include Ada Forster in 'The Two Generals', Marie Calvert in 'La Mère Bauche', Marie Bromar in *The Golden Lion of Granpère*, Julia Weston in 'A Ride across Palestine', Nora Field (apparently) in 'The Widow's Mite', Bessy Pryor in 'The Lady of Launay' and Catherine Carmichael in the story of that name. Mary Snow is rescued from her drunken father by Felix Graham in *Orley Farm*. Sometimes the girl's presence causes difficulty for the family which has taken her in because the son of the house falls in love with her, usually against his parents' wishes: this happens in *The Golden Lion of Granpère*, 'The Lady of Launay' and 'La Mère

Bauche', with tragic results in the latter story. In the majority of these cases the orphaned girl is taken in by her uncle. The Trollopes had themselves adopted one niece. [➤ Bland, Florence.].

P

PALLISER FAMILY

The Pallisers receive greater attention than any other family in Trollope's fiction as they dominate most of the six Palliser novels. Some few details of the family history emerge, especially in the first novel in the series, *Can You Forgive Her?* [22]. The family was given the land at Matching in Yorkshire in the fourteenth century by a grateful king who had been given a drink of brandy by Sir Guy Palliser. Here Trollope is probably having a private joke at his own expense, for as a boy he had told a somewhat similar story to explain the origins of his father's family [Mullen, 2]. In succeeding centuries the Pallisers acquired more land and wealth and, eventually, the title of Duke of Omnium. By the time they are first mentioned in the Barsetshire novels they are among the wealthiest peers in the land. (Trollope, of course, is having another schoolboy joke in naming their Barsetshire residence Gatherum Castle; the sham Latin phrase 'omnium gatherum' was often used by Victorians for a miscellaneous gathering. Trollope used the phrase at least once in his private correspondence.) The Palliser men are known for their pride, their Whig politics and their 'ducal silences', a trait Trollope may have taken from several well-known anecdotes in circulation about the Duke of Devonshire's family. The head of the family and heir always have the Christian name Plantagenet, as they received their lands from Plantagenet monarchs. At the end of *The Duke's Children* the duke makes fun of his name. [➤ Peerage.] The principal members of this fictional family are described below.

Palliser, George Plantagenet. The 'old' Duke of Omnium first appears in *Doctor Thorne* and he is also in two other Barsetshire novels, *Framley Parsonage* and *The Small House at Allington*. His wealth is said to be as great as Queen Victoria's. He is unmarried, but 'if report said true, a great debauchee'. The old Marchioness of Hartletop apparently was his mistress for many years. He had succeeded to the title shortly after the Reform Bill of 1832, but while he supports the Whigs, he takes little sustained role in politics. In the Barsetshire novels, in which he is denounced by people like Lady Lufton, he seems quite similar to Thackeray's wicked Marquis of Steyne in *Vanity Fair*. Yet as the old duke is developed in the early Palliser novels, he becomes a much more sympathetic character, particularly in his love for Madame Max Goesler. He dies at Matching, deeply mourned by Madame Max and his nephew's wife, Lady Glencora [*Phineas Redux*, 26]. The old duke is mentioned in more novels than almost any other character in Trollope's fiction.

Palliser, Plantagenet. The 'young' Duke of Omnium first appears as the nephew and heir of the old duke. Because he is only the duke's nephew and not his son, he has no courtesy title. He does not even have the title 'Lord', as he is not the son of a duke [➤ Peerage]. He first appears, at the age of twenty-five, as an MP in *The Small House at Allington* [23], in which he has a most uncharacteristic passion for Griselda Grantly, then Lady Dumbello and the daughter-in-law of his uncle's reputed mistress. When his uncle threatens to cut off his allowance, Palliser gives up this one indiscreet fling of his life. He is well described in this novel as having 'been brought up in a school which delights in tranquillity' and therefore he avoids both the sublime and the ridiculous [55]. His wife, Lady Glencora, can be both sublime and ridiculous at the same time; even so, he deeply loves her. 'Planty Pall', as he is nicknamed, is driven by a deep sense of duty and a veritable passion for politics, particularly for its more abstruse points. Since his pet project is a silly scheme for a decimal currency, he is happiest as Chancellor of the Exchequer. He succeeds as Duke of Omnium in *Phineas Redux* and eventually becomes prime minister in *The Prime Minister*.

Trollope maintained in his *Autobiography* that Palliser is the perfect gentleman and the best argument for an hereditary aristocracy holding political power. He also thought he would be remembered mainly for his portrait of Palliser. Many readers disagree and share the view of Sir Winston Churchill that Palliser is 'a poop' [Mullen, 483]. While Trollope's portrayal of Palliser is marked by great subtlety he only really emerges as a person in the final Palliser novel, *The Duke's Children*, and only after his wife Glencora has died. He is no longer overshadowed by her. In this novel the key to his character is given: 'To endeavour to be just was the study of his life' [7]. Although he does not appear in as many novels as his colourful uncle, no other character in Trollope's fiction receives more detailed attention and analysis from his creator. There are some similarities between Palliser and a real politician, the fifth Duke of Newcastle (1811–64). Trollope felt that this duke, who was in charge of the War Office from December 1852 to June 1854, had been unjustly blamed for disasters in the Crimean War.

[➤ Dickens; *The New Zealander.*]

Palliser, Lady Glencora (Duchess of Omnium). Lady Glencora was Trollope's own favourite among his many female characters and the only one who he expected would be remembered by posterity [*Autobiography*]. She first appears at the end of *The Small House at Allington*, in which her marriage to Plantagenet Palliser, heir to the dukedom of Omnium, is arranged [55]. At this point she is Lady Glencora MacCluskie, the only child of the Marquis of Auld Reekie, 'the Lord of the Isles'. She inherits most of her father's enormous wealth from coal mines and property in Glasgow [➤ Entails; Peerage; Scotland]. She is quite beautiful, short and fair-haired, with round blue eyes. She is charming and enthusiastic, but always indiscreet and impulsive. Her Scottishness is hardly ever apparent. Her relatives are anxious to prevent her marrying Burgo Fitzgerald, a handsome rake whom she loves. This basic plot, outlined in one chapter of *The Small House at Allington*, is developed in *Can You Forgive Her?*. In that novel, even though she has become Plantagenet Palliser's wife, she considers eloping with Burgo.

Lady Glencora is remarkably young when she first appears and is even wealthier than her husband. The story of their stormy marriage is at the centre of the Palliser novels. She is constantly amazed at his great love for her, but her fondness for dabbling in intrigue and politics often annoys him. She reaches the height of glory when he becomes prime minister. Although she dies before the start of *The Duke's Children*, her memory and influence linger. As well as appearing in the Palliser books, she is also in *The American Senator* and briefly in *Miss Mackenzie*, while a portrait of her is exhibited in *The Last Chronicle of Barset*. Trollope's summation of her in his *Autobiography* is excellent: 'She is by no means a perfect lady; but if she be not all over a woman, then I am not able to describe a woman.' She has several children. One daughter, a young Lady Glencora, dies. Her other children, who become important characters in *The Duke's Children*, are listed below.

Palliser, Plantagenet (Earl of Silverbridge). As the eldest son and heir of the 'young' Duke of Omnium, he therefore has the earldom of Silverbridge as a courtesy title [➤ Peerage]. His birth at the end of *Can You Forgive Her?* delights both Plantagenet Palliser and his great-uncle, the old Duke of Omnium. The young boy is brought out by his anxious mother to be dandled in his great-uncle's lap when there is a danger of the old Duke of Omnium making a dangerous marriage [*Phineas Finn*, 44]. He becomes an MP in *The Duke's Children* – temporarily deserting the family's Liberal heritage – and marries the beautiful young American, Isabel Boncassen. [➤ Fathers and Sons; Gambling; Slang.]

Palliser, Lord Gerald. The second son of the 'young' Duke of Omnium, Lord Gerald causes his father distress in *The Duke's Children* when he is sent down from Cambridge. Yet when he is mentioned in *The American Senator* he is about to embark on a diplomatic career. [➤ Diplomats; Fathers and Sons; Slang; Universities.]

Palliser, Lady Mary. The youngest child of the 'young' Duke of Omnium, who also causes her father distress in *The Duke's Children* because she wants to marry Frank Tregear, the son of a small squire and a Tory. (In *Marion Fay*, published two years after *The Duke's Children*, Lady Frances Trafford causes her noble father and stepmother similar problems.) [➤ Gentleman; Marriage.]

Other members of the Palliser family include:

Palliser, Adelaide. The niece of the old Duke of Omnium and a first cousin of Plantagenet Palliser. In spite of her ducal connections, she has little money of her own. Her romance with Gerald Maule in *Phineas Redux* is frustrated because neither has money until Madame Max Goesler provides a solution. Adelaide and her husband return briefly in *The Duke's Children*.

Palliser, Jeffrey. A cousin of Plantagenet Palliser, who would have succeeded to the dukedom if Plantagenet Palliser's son, Lord Silverbridge, had not been born. He provides some entertaining conversation in *Can You Forgive Her?* A brief mention in *The Duke's Children* [1] shows that he has married. [➤ Peerage; 'Poor'; Professions.]

Palliser, Euphemia and Iphigenia Theodata. Two elderly spinster cousins of Plantagenet Palliser who appear in *Can You Forgive Her?* Their silly names, which make use of Trollope's love of the classics, inform us that they are not to be taken too seriously.

Palliser Novels. Trollope's second great series of novels, after the Barsetshire series, consists of: *Can You Forgive Her?*, *Phineas Finn*, *Phineas Redux*, *The Eustace Diamonds*, *The Prime Minister* and *The Duke's Children*. While Trollope did not regard *The Eustace Diamonds* as part of the series, it is generally considered to be so. (This is similar to his view that *The Small House at Allington* was not really part of the Barsetshire series.) The books were written between 1863 and 1876 and published between 1864 and 1880. All of them were either serialized or issued in parts before their publication in book form. The six novels are sometimes called 'the parliamentary novels'. Trollope regarded the development of the main characters in these novels as 'the best work of my life'.

All the novels have multiple plots, but they all depict the world of Victorian high politics and London Society and show how the two were constantly intertwined [➤ Politics for the comment of Sir Winston Churchill]. The Palliser books centre on two main characters: Plantagenet Palliser, who eventually succeeds his uncle as Duke of Omnium, and his wife, Lady Glencora Palliser, who becomes the Duchess of Omnium. Other members of the family play important parts, ranging from the duke and duchess's three children to the old Duke of Omnium. [➤ Palliser Family.] The next most important characters are Phineas Finn, a young Irish MP, and his second wife, Madame Max Goesler. Trollope had thought out the destinies of several of these characters long before he completed their individual histories: in *Phineas Finn* he has someone predict Phineas's personal and political future, although this would take several novels to unfold [31].

The Palliser novels are, in one sense, a history of a marriage. In *Can You Forgive Her?* the marriage of Plantagenet and Glencora Palliser comes under strain when Lady Glencora almost runs off with a handsome adventurer; in *Phineas Finn* and *Phineas Redux* their marriage grows in strength, particularly when Glencora senses a possible threat to her husband's succession to the dukedom; in *The Eustace Diamonds* the Pallisers tend to be seen only as observers and commentators on the main plot; in *The Prime Minister* the duchess achieves her great goal of becoming the leader of Society when her husband becomes prime minister. The duchess dies before the start of *The Duke's Children*, which allows Trollope to concentrate on the duke and his relations with his three children. A dedicated reader can form a better idea of what Trollope was describing in the Palliser marriage by re-reading those parts of the six novels which deal exclusively with the two Pallisers.

The first five novels all have major plots independent of the Palliser family: the first novel has an involved plot about Lady Glencora's cousin, Alice Vavasor, who has to decide which man to marry; *Phineas Finn* and *Phineas Redux* centre on the young Irish MP, Phineas Finn, as he makes his way into Parliament and Society; *The Eustace Diamonds* follows the adventures of Lizzie Eustace, who searches for wealthy husbands and schemes to steal her own jewels; and the most exciting plot in *The Prime Minister* traces the tempestuous marriage of a rich barrister's daughter and a clever speculator even though Trollope thought that the speculator, Lopez, 'and all that has to do with him, to be bad' and only 'a shoe-horn' for the political plot.

The Palliser novels show various ways in which the comfortable and ordered world of the Pallisers and their friends is threatened by upsets from within and without. From within come dangerous forces such as dishonourable aristocrats like Earl Grex, time-serving politicians like Mr Daubeny, and disreputable ladies such as Lizzie Eustace. From without, the Palliser world is threatened by powerful new elements in Victorian society: the slimy journalist, Quintus Slide, the alien speculator, Ferdinand Lopez, and the Radical politician, Turnbull. The enduring strength of the Palliser world is its ability to absorb new people: Phineas Finn, Joshua Monk, Isabel Boncassen. Trollope believed that this 'exquisite combination of conservatism and progress' was England's 'present strength and best security for the future' [*Can You Forgive Her?*, 24].

This is the political message that is constantly conveyed throughout the six novels.

Trollope wrote in his *Autobiography*, when discussing his view of this series, that these novels allowed him a platform for 'the expression of my political and social convictions'. The politics in the Palliser novels normally reflect Trollope's own Liberal beliefs. Yet he manifestly makes an effort to be fair to the Tories (excepting Disraeli) and readers' sympathies are meant to be with the victorious Tory candidates in elections that occur in the last two novels. Some episodes in the novels – particularly the canvassing in *The Duke's Children* [55] or the trial for bribery in *Phineas Redux* [44] – use his own experiences as a Liberal parliamentary candidate for Beverley in 1868. The political debates and events in the earlier Palliser novels have some similarities with events in the real political world of the early 1860s, particularly those discussions on such subjects as the ballot and Irish tenant rights [➤ Ireland; *The Land-Leaguers*]. However, by the time of *Phineas Redux* this is less often the case. The coalition government and the attempt by Daubeny's Tory administration to disestablish the Church of England in *The Prime Minister* have no connection with the real events of the late 1860s or 1870s. Many people have assumed that most of the main characters are based on real politicians, something that Trollope always denied. He gave his best explanation in a letter of 1876 in which he admitted that while 'certain well-known political characters, such as Disraeli and Gladstone, have been taken as models for such fictitious personages as Daubeny and Gresham, it has only been as to their political tenets. There is nothing of personal characteristic here.' His 'Palliser people,' he wrote, 'are pure creations; and (as I think) the best I ever made'. [➤ Grantly Sons.]

The Palliser novels constantly move back and forth between London and the countryside. Unlike the Barsetshire novels, which are clearly based in the West of England, the countryside in the Palliser novels has no strong regional identity. Although many episodes take place in the Palliser country house, Matching in Yorkshire, there is no sense of being in that county. There is, however, a stronger sense of local colour in the Lake District setting for parts of *Can You Forgive Her?* Several of the other characters have country houses in Scotland, and what Victorian Englishmen called 'North Britain' begins here to play a noticeable role in Trollope's fiction. In several of the novels there are scenes on the Continent, whether a duel in Belgium, a visit to the gambling casino in Baden-Baden in Germany, or a sudden meeting of several of the characters at the spa town of Ishl in Austria. (These reflect the increase in Trollope's, and his countrymen's, European travels in the years during which the novels were being written.) A few continentals play important roles in the novels, notably the bigamous Bohemian preacher Mr Emilius and the 'semi-foreign' Madame Max Goesler. American characters also become prominent in the final novel when an American girl marries the heir to the Palliser dukedom. This, like increasing travel, reflects a growing phenomenon in English life.

There are several connections with the Barsetshire novels. Since the Pallisers possess the huge and uncomfort-able Gatherum Castle in Barsetshire, some of the scenes take place in Trollope's 'beloved county'. The Barset town of Silverbridge is the scene of three important election scenes and in the course of the series it passes from being a 'pocket borough' of the Palliser family, which means it always returns a Liberal, to having the freedom to choose its own, in this case, Conservative, MP. Again fiction is reflecting historic change. Some familiar figures from the Barsetshire books also make brief reappearances. Griselda Grantly, Lady Dumbello, who had enjoyed a brief flirtation with Palliser himself in *The Small House at Allington*, appears in the first two novels, and Frank Gresham, the young squire from *Doctor Thorne*, returns in *The Prime Minister* in which he makes a humorous reflection on his youthful and impulsive actions in the earlier novel. The Liberal leader, Mr Gresham, is his kinsman. The old Duke of Omnium is the most prominent figure to grace both series. In addition, two of Trollope's other novels of the 1870s, *The Way We Live Now* and *The American Senator*, provide characters who occur in the last two Palliser books. Trollope also used his formidable barrister Chaffanbrass for a trial in *Phineas Redux*.

Since the Barsetshire novels were so closely identified with clerical characters, Trollope seems determined as far as possible to keep them out of the Palliser series. There is the conspicuous exception of Mr Emilius, but he is hardly the type of clergyman who would have found favour with any Bishop of Barchester. When the clergy do make brief appearances they are rarely developed as characters in their own right, but are only used to make a point, like the rector who denounces 'godless dissenters' in *The Duke's Children* [*55*].

Even more than is usual in Trollope's fiction, there are good and bad examples in almost every group represented in the Palliser series: good aristocrats like Palliser himself and bad ones like Earl Grex; honourable MPs like Finn and wicked ones like George Vavasor; admirable women like Madame Max and contemptible ones like Lizzie Eustace. Each group seems to provide both good and bad examples except journalists, among whom the contemptible figure of Quintus Slide stands virtually alone. Although most of the novels take place in the luxurious and secure settings of the Victorian aristocracy, there is a large amount of violence in the Palliser books. It ranges from murder and attempted murder to duels and robbery [➤ Crime]. Clubs play a prominent role and this is appropriate as Trollope gathered much of his political insight from friends in his various clubs. Foxhunting runs throughout the series and the novels probably contain Trollope's best, and certainly his own favourite, scenes of his beloved sport. Here again there is the contrast of good and bad, with the long portrait of the good MFH in Lord Chiltern set against the disreputable Major Tifto [*The Duke's Children*].

In general, contemporaries did not share Trollope's own enthusiasm for the Palliser series and it is only in recent years that it has become really popular. Readers can usually be divided into those who preferred the Barsetshire series over the Palliser series or vice versa. The Barsetshire novels have more memorable and sympathetic characters, while the Palliser

books have numerous elaborate plots as well as complex characters. Anyone coming to Trollope for the first time would be well advised to read the Barsetshire books first because the Palliser novels require a closer concentration and a more mature taste. If the reader approaches them properly they can be the greatest sustained series of novels in English fiction.

[➤ Aristocracy; Peerage.]

Pall Mall Gazette (1865–1923). This Victorian daily evening newspaper was established by George Smith. Smith, who was a great patron of literature, got his newspaper's title from Thackeray's *Pendennis* in which the 'Pall Mall Gazette' is 'written by gentlemen for gentlemen'. In 1880 Smith gave it to his son-in-law, Henry Yates Thompson, and John Morley became editor. (He had edited the *Fortnightly Review*.) The year after Trollope's death the controversial W. T. Stead was appointed editor. In 1892 it became one of the titles in the Astor stable.

Trollope's connection with the paper began with its first number because Smith drew on writers like himself who were published in the *Cornhill*, which he also owned. Trollope was, as he put it in his *Autobiography*, 'a permanent member of staff' or a regular feature writer from 1865 to 1868 – and wrote, or at least suggested, a variety of topics including political issues, Lord Brougham, a series of 'imaginary meditations', Napoleon III, the Church of England, America, and ladies' bazaars (suggested in 1865, the same year in which *Miss Mackenzie*, which includes such a bazaar, was published). He also wrote book reviews and started a series on London's 'May Meetings' in which he could only get through one essay, after which he had to throw in the assignment. [➤ Zulus.] Smith did not publish all the essays Trollope suggested and among those he turned down was one in 1866 on the inequalities in clerical incomes, a topic about which Trollope cared greatly and about which he suggested numerous articles [➤ Clergymen]. His most important and signed essays were divided into four groups, three of which were published in book form in his lifetime: *Hunting Sketches, Travelling Sketches* and *Clergymen of the Church of England*. The fourth collection, *London Tradesmen*, was published after his death. In 1865 his earnings from the newspaper were £234. 17s. 6d. but by 1868 they had fallen to £7. 17s. 6d. After that, his involvement with the paper ceased until his final years, when he contributed a series of eleven articles on shopping in London [➤ London Tradesmen] as well as an article on moving his library. In his *Autobiography* he admitted that he was 'unfit' for newspaper work. He disliked having his articles edited; he disliked being given subjects about which to write; he disliked being told when to write [11].

In *The Way We Live Now* Trollope based the offices of one of the newspapers in the novel on those of the *Pall Mall Gazette*. The paper was not always loyal to Trollope and attacked his books on the classics, *The Life of Cicero* and *The Commentaries of Caesar*.

'The Panjandrum'. This is one of the short stories written for *Saint Pauls* and published in two parts ('Hope' and 'Despair') in January and February 1870; it is one of Trollope's longest short stories. It was included

in his fourth collection of stories, *An Editor's Tales*, published in the same year. In his *Autobiography* Trollope wrote: 'I do not think that there is a single incident in the book which could bring back to anyone concerned the memory of a past event. And yet there is not an incident in it the outline of which was not presented to my mind by the remembrance of some fact ... how in my own early days there was a struggle over an abortive periodical which was intended to be the best thing ever done.'

This bittersweet story is a brilliant analysis of immature intellectuals setting out to reform the world and of their interminable discussions which produce nothing. It is told in the first person and the narrator is the middle-aged Trollope. It is set at the very end of the 1830s, when the narrator was a young man. It concerns a group of five high-minded young men who want to establish the 'Panjandrum Magazine' as a reforming periodical. They meet at the house of Mrs St Quentin, a lady devoted to 'literary pursuits' who becomes a member of the organizing committee. (Ladies devoted to 'literary pursuits', along with 'men of letters', are generally disliked by Trollope, as professionals always dislike amateurs. They were also attacked in 'Mary Gresley'.) Days are spent in choosing the right name. As with other stories about the world of London writers, Trollope's characters were people who 'were to write and edit our magazine and have it published, not because we were good at writing or editing, but because we had ideas which we wished to promulgate'.

The narrator was to be editor of the journal and describes himself politically as a 'democrat because I was loud against the Corn Laws; and was accused of infidelity when I spoke against the Irish Church Endowments'. While a liberal he was not a radical Chartist because he insists he was against household suffrage, let alone universal male suffrage. However, he did favour annually elected parliaments, a key Chartist proposal. 'We wanted heaven at once.' As usual, Trollope gives the story away by announcing just over halfway through the first part that the magazine was never published. The editor prepares an 'introduction' to be published in the first issue which would set the Thames alight, but his colleagues decide against it. (When Trollope actually did write an 'introduction' to *Saint Pauls* he produced a somewhat muddled affair.) The committee decide to give every member a fortnight to write twenty-one pages for the magazine.

The second part starts with the narrator unable to write a single word about some intellectual topic. He goes for a walk in Regent's Park where he sees a servant woman hurriedly walking with a young girl, perhaps ten or eleven years old. He overtakes them to see what the little girl looks like and hears her say, 'Oh Anne, I do so wonder what he's like!' This fires his imagination and he starts to create a story in which the little girl, transformed into a young woman, becomes his sister whom he only discovers just before he loses her in marriage to his own best friend. In a comment that tells us something of his own creative genius, he writes: 'These wondrous castles in the air never get themselves well built when the mind, with premeditated skill and labour, sets itself to work to build them. It is when they

come uncalled for that they stand erect and strong before the mind's eye.' He returns to his lodgings and writes a 'tale', 'The New Inmate', forgetting the committee's ban on fiction. He is not allowed to read his story to the committee, which then falls apart. As the one Irish member says, 'It isn't so easy, after all, to do this kind of thing.' The narrator went on to publish his story in the first issue of another magazine, *Marble Arch.*

Of the six stories published in *An Editor's Tales* this is the most autobiographical and, for the student of Trollope, the most rewarding. When Trollope was a young man his one surviving sister, Cecilia, had married his friend John Tilley, as in his story. When the narrator parts with his friends from the committee they do so 'under the walls of Marylebone Workhouse'. When Trollope as a young man had lodgings in London he had a room in Northumberland Street (now Luxborough Street) which overlooked Marylebone Workhouse and was near Regent's Park; he must have taken walks there, like the narrator. As always with Trollope, atheists come out badly: of the committee, one was an 'unbeliever'. 'He was generally dirty, unshorn, and, as I thought, disagreeable.' Not surprisingly he was devoted to 'deep thinking, German poetry, and unintelligible speculation generally'. The narrator later heard that he had gone to fight with the Poles in their uprising against Russian rule (presumably the 1863 uprising) and that 'he perished in a Russian prison'. Trollope attacks discrimination against Irishmen when discussing Pat Regan: 'I think the world would have used him better had his name been John Tomkins.' There is a modern ring to his explanation as to why the committee rejected 'The Man's Magazine' as a title for the new magazine. 'We meant the word – man – in the great generic sense; – but the somewhat obtuse outside world would not have so taken it.' [➤ Feminists.]

Trollope's sense of humour comes out in his choice of a title for the magazine: a 'panjandrum' is an imaginary man of great power and importance, at least to himself. The word was invented by Samuel Foote (1720–77), the actor and dramatist famous for his satires, and was included in some nonsense verse. When discussing the problems over choosing a name Trollope remembered the problems he had had in choosing a name for the magazine he was to edit and in which this story was published. There were, finally, two private jokes: when he said his story, 'The New Inmate', helped 'towards the establishment of that excellent periodical', *Marble Arch*, he probably was recalling his own serialization of *Framley Parsonage* which began in the first issue of *Cornhill* in 1860 and which did so much to get that magazine started. Also, Trollope remembered the debate over 'Mrs General Talboys': in November 1860 he had written to Thackeray jokingly that he would publish the story 'in a magazine of my own – it will be called *The Marble Arch*'.

Parliament. Parliament is not only portrayed in the Palliser novels but is woven into much of Trollope's fiction. In his earlier novels it was part of the great world that was synonymous with London and played a relatively small role in the daily life, for example, of Barsetshire. While in many novels and most of the short stories it had little or no place, in later novels Parliament's role tended to become more important and MPs began to appear more frequently. While some characters like Captain Aylmer in *The Belton Estate* or Thomas Furnival in *Orley Farm* are MPs, their work is irrelevant to the plot. Their position is really a device to illustrate their high status in the great world. Occasionally the fact that a character is an MP does affect his life: Lord Llwddythlw in *Marion Fay* has hardly any time to woo Lady Amaldina Hauteville because of his arduous duties in the House of Commons.

From his boyhood Trollope had a great desire to be elected to the Commons and undoubtedly this influenced his writing. In *Can You Forgive Her?* he has an 'authorial intrusion' about the entrance to the House: 'It is the only gate before which I have ever stood filled with envy, – sorrowing to think that my steps might never pass under it' [45]. His failure to win a seat at Beverley was probably the greatest disappointment of his life. He wrote about Parliament from a theoretical viewpoint in *The New Zealander*, referred to it in passing in *Lord Palmerston* and naturally discussed its doings in some of his political articles for *Saint Pauls*.

Although peers abound in his novels, and although his beloved Plantagenet Palliser only became prime minister after he had become Duke of Omnium, Trollope's real concern was always the House of Commons. As with so many other aspects of his fiction he reflected contemporary interests: Victorian newspapers carried page after page of closely printed accounts of speeches in the Commons. Despite the importance of the Lords in the Victorian era, Trollope had remarkably little interest in the Upper House as an institution. Several of the assessments he made about the power of the Lords were incorrect. Nor does he seem to have paid close attention to its work, as can be seen in his references to proxy voting. In the early decades of the nineteenth century, peers could still vote by proxy. Thus in *The Small House at Allington* that busy agriculturalist Earl De Guest, who rarely comes up to London, makes sure that his 'proxy was always in the hand of the leader of his party' [12]. However, Trollope apparently did not notice that the Lords 'discontinued' this practice in 1868 because in the next decade it is denounced in *The American Senator* [29]. In some of his travel books, for instance that on Australia, he compares the House of Lords to colonial legislatures.

Throughout Trollope's lifetime, the number of MPs and constituencies varied: in the year in which he stood for election, 1868, there were 658 MPs sitting for 420 constituencies and of these just over 100 sat for constituencies in Ireland. The number of MPs for each constituency normally varied between one and two, while the largest towns along with several English counties had three. (When Trollope stood for Beverley there were four candidates for two seats.) While most of Trollope's MPs sit for boroughs, it was normally more prestigious to sit for a county, particularly one's own, as Squire Gresham does in *Doctor Thorne*. MPs were not paid and sometimes elections, particularly county elections, could be incredibly costly, as Squire Gresham found to his regret. The Commons normally sat from February to August and usu-

ally met at 4 p.m. although on a few days it might meet earlier, at 2 p.m. There was a two-hour break for dinner between five and seven. On Wednesday nights there was no sitting and this is why many dinner parties in Trollope's novels are arranged for Wednesday night [*Phineas Finn*, 6]. This was also the favourite night for MPs to go to their clubs [*Phineas Redux*, 46]. In 1850 the Commons moved into their new chamber, which replaced the one destroyed by fire in 1834. In Trollope's lifetime two large parties were represented in the Commons: the Liberals, who tended to be the larger party, and the Conservatives; in addition there was increasingly a *de facto* Nationalist Party among Irish MPs [➤ *The Prime Minister*, 12]. Some of the Liberals were still known as Whigs. [➤ St Bungay, Duke of.]

By-elections tended to be more frequent than today: accepting certain offices meant that MPs had to stand for re-election, and elderly MPs were more likely to retire in the middle of a Parliament, thereby causing an election. Seven years could elapse between general elections. When there was one, constituencies still voted on different days. Qualifications for voting varied among constituencies even after the Reform Acts of 1832 and 1867 brought some degree of uniformity. (It was only in 1884 that the United Kingdom got a uniform franchise.) Because certain universities were represented in the Commons (six by the time Trollope stood in 1868), and because the franchise was based on property ownership, some men had more than one vote. Approximately two out of every ten adult males could vote in England (somewhat fewer in Scotland

and Ireland) but after the 1867 Reform Act the number increased to over three out every ten. While Trollope supported widening the franchise, he did not believe in universal suffrage, even for men. He supported the traditional means of voting in which a man called out his choice, although as the century wore on this was often done in a booth or separate room. He strongly opposed voting by secret ballot, something that was only introduced in 1872 [➤ Monk, Joshua]. He himself was one of those civil servants who were not allowed to vote. This was a restriction, largely out of date in his time, inherited from the past as a way to limit the influence of the Crown. He was therefore unable to vote until he resigned from the Post Office. The first election in which he could vote, 1868, was also the one in which he stood as a candidate.

Phineas Finn provides a good example of the different types of seats an MP could represent: his first constituency is a small Irish borough with 307 electors [Phineas Finn, 1]; he is later forced to seek refuge [32] in the 'pocket borough' of a Whig earl whose influence is so great in the borough that no opponent will stand. (While uncontested elections decreased during Trollope's lifetime they were not unusual: in the election in which Trollope stood, of 420 constituencies, 120 were uncontested.) In a later novel, when Finn stands for a large town he has to get the support of coal-miners to gain election [Phineas Redux, 4]. By 1880, when the last of the Palliser novels was appearing, great peers were losing their control over 'pocket boroughs'; this is reflected in The Duke's Children, in which Plantagenet Palliser,

now Duke of Omnium, gives up his control over his local borough.

[➤ Aristocracy; Politics; (for the monarchy); Season, The; Victoria, Queen.]

Parliamentary Novels. See Palliser Novels.

'The Parson's Daughter of Oxney Colne'. This short story was written between 13 and 19 January 1861 when Trollope was working on Orley Farm. The story draws on Trollope's great knowledge of the West Country acquired through his Post Office work there in 1851–3. The story was one of eight he sold to The London Review but after the hostile reception of the first two, 'A Ride across Palestine' and 'Mrs General Talboys', the magazine only published one more, 'The Parson's Daughter of Oxney Colne', on 2 March 1861. It was included in the second collection of his short stories, Tales of All Countries; Second Series (1863). Trollope received £50.

The story, like so many works by Trollope, is set in the West Country, in this case Devon, and centres on Patience Woolsworthy, the headstrong daughter of the incumbent of Oxney Colne. Another resident is Miss Le Smyrger, one of Trollope's strong-willed spinsters with 'a constitution of iron, and an opinion of her own on every subject under the sun'. Miss Le Smyrger was Patience's intimate friend and Patience, although she was unaware of it, was her heir. Miss Le Smyrger's nephew, Captain John Broughton, whose father is a wealthy and important MP, asks Patience to marry him but she puts him off. On their next meeting she accepts him, but after a few days the engagement is ended because of his worries over her lack of sophistication and money as well as her independent spirit, while she worries about his patronizing manner and snobbery. Patience now devotes herself to spinsterly good works in the parish and 'with a large heart she loves many' instead of one.

The story has some features in common with 'The Lady of Launay', also set in the West Country, and the plot is very similar to the story of the engagement between Clara Amedroz and Captain Aylmer in *The Belton Estate*: in that case a girl who is fiercely independent quizzes her beloved and then declares her love too easily. In 'The Parson's Daughter of Oxney Colne' the man regrets his proposal to a woman apparently without a dowry who, after first refusing to say 'yes' then says 'yes' too quickly: the fruit was too easily got. For her part she resents his snobbery and his patronizing manner. The story also contrasts the simple country life with life in London.

Patriotism. Trollope reflected and shared the strong patriotic feelings of his age. These are often best expressed in his short stories, probably because so many of them were written about life outside England or about events with an international aspect. In 'The Widow's Mite' an Englishwoman prepares to marry an American and move to America: 'It was not without a pang that she prepared to give up that nationality, which all its owners rank as the first in the world, and most of those who do not own it, rank, if not as the first, then as the second.' When writing to his American friend, Kate Field, Trollope said, probably with tongue in cheek, 'I was thinking today

that nature intended me for an American rather than an Englishman. I think I should have made a better American.' But he went on to add, 'I hold it higher to be a bad Englishman, as I am, than a good American – as I am not.' (Being in America or writing to Americans obviously set him thinking about his 'Englishness', perhaps because he saw the two countries as being so close.)

In 'Returning Home', a story about English emigrants, he remarked, 'But for a life of daily excitement, there is no life like life in England; and the farther that one goes from England the more stagnant, I think, do the waters of existence become.' He accepted that his view was based on his own success and that for many working-class people, emigration was advisable. This even extended to the cook whom he and his wife Rose took with them to Australia, after she decided to stay there. Sometimes his sentiments may sound strong in a different age, as when he described his own reactions to a large, disorderly crowd of pilgrims in Jerusalem: 'How is it that Englishmen can push themselves anywhere? ... Yet we did', because, he went on, 'a strong smell and dirt' in a foreign crowd are not 'so efficacious in creating awe and obedience in others, as an open brow and traces of soap and water' ['A Ride across Palestine'].

Yet, as on other questions, he had mixed views. He also told Kate Field, regarding military conscription: 'One's country has no right to demand everything. There is much that is higher & better & greater than one's country.' Also, when in America he noticed 'two of our own dear English flags' among the captured banners at the American military academy at West Point. The sight made him 'sick in the stomach and uncomfortable' but it also made him think about how foreigners felt at seeing their flags displayed as trophies in English buildings. A real 'John Bull' of that era would not have thought about others' feelings [*North America*]. He was also highly critical of the boorish behaviour of some 'John Bulls' on the Continent [➤ 'John Bull on the Guadalquivir'; *The Bertrams*]. Trollope's strongest patriotic feelings were for the essential unity of the English-speaking 'race'. He once told the literary critic E. S. Dallas, 'Patriotism is the virtue of a limited & confined sympathy. A truly cosmopolitan feeling is a much grander condition of mind. But you may preach for ever without being able to teach men that they should love all the world as well as their own country.' By describing – as opposed to criticizing – mankind's natural feelings he was, as always, not excluding himself from them.

[➤ Egypt; Emigration; English World; Holy Land.]

Peel, Sir Robert (1788–1850). Robert Peel was subjected to several fierce attacks by Trollope in his novels, which seems extraordinary given the high reputation that Peel enjoyed both in his lifetime and after his death. Peel, Prime Minister in 1834–5 and 1841–6, is most remembered for the repeal of the Corn Laws. In *The Warden*, published nine years after repeal, Trollope launched his first attack. While he does not interrupt the flow of his story to single out the former prime minister, who had died five years before, he clearly means to imply that an opportunistic journalist like Tom Towers would naturally decorate his room with a bust of a politician famed

for 'expediency' [14]. Most readers, even contemporary ones, would not have suspected whom Trollope was really getting at in this statement.

Trollope next attacked Peel in 1858, in *The Three Clerks*. Here he gives the best expression of his views in a lengthy digression. Peel gave a 'great blow' to 'political honesty' by changing his opinions, from opposition to support, on Catholic Emancipation in 1829 and on the Corn Laws in 1845–6. Trollope, as a Liberal, approved these reforms but with his passion for honesty he believed that such a reversal of policy by a politician in office taught ordinary people to look to 'expediency' as the right guide [29]. He thought that Peel should have resigned and let his Liberal opponents carry these reforms. (This is what Peel tried to do at the end of 1845, but the Liberals were unable to form a government.) In addition, Peel was not following his Conservative duty, as Trollope saw it, to resist change. [➤ Catholicism; Politics.] In 1859 *The Bertrams* appeared and a third attack was made in an 'authorial intrusion' that lasted several pages. It is a tirade against Peel's policies and his 'apostasy' [16].

Trollope was perhaps influenced by the fact that his cousin, Sir John Trollope, MP (the current baronet) was prominent among those Tories who refused to vote with Peel in 1846. Several novels in the 1850s make passing references to these Tory MPs: the most notable reference is in *Barchester Towers* [22] in which Wilfred Thorne expresses his admiration for those MPs who resisted 'Peel's apostasy' [➤ also *Phineas Finn*, 26].

A few years later, in *North America*, Trollope began to soften his views about Peel and by the 1870s his fury against the 'bold' Peel was clearly abating, perhaps because it was being replaced by an implacable hatred for another Tory leader, Disraeli [*Phineas Redux*, 5]. (Ironically it was Disraeli who had so savagely attacked Peel in the 1840s.) By the time of *Mr Scarborough's Family*, whose serialization began in 1882, Trollope was referring without comment to a horse called 'Orange Peel', a nickname often given to Peel in Ireland because of his strong Protestant views [24]. In one of his last works, *Lord Palmerston*, he has a *de facto* recantation of his earlier view and refers to Peel as 'a great man' who will 'remain as long as English history is read and understood'. Trollope's treatment of Peel is one of the best proofs that he could change strongly held opinions, albeit rarely. His treatment also shows that his own views had grown more conservative with the passage of time [➤ 'The Panjandrum'].

Peerage. Since peers and their families play such an important role in Trollope's fiction, it is vital to understand the position of what Trollope described as 'the most brilliant nobility in the world' [*The Small House at Allington*, 23]. In 1860 there were 413 peers entitled to vote in the House of Lords. (This does not include 30 bishops and 15 minors.) By 1880 this number had grown to 474 peers. Although the peerage was under constant attack from Radicals, its social prestige was enormous and its political power considerable. Although there were some poor peers and even a few bankrupt ones, the peerage was still virtually synonymous with great wealth. Throughout Trollope's lifetime, numerous new peerages were created

and a few were given to literary figures such as Tennyson and Macaulay. Although Trollope never knew it, he was being considered for a peerage by important figures in the second Gladstone administration, but he was 'condemned as noisy' [Mullen, 644].

Trollope portrays all the ranks of the peerage in his fiction. As he understood the correct usage of titles it helps any reader to understand them as well. Briefly, they may be summarized as follows. The peerage was divided into five ranks in descending order: duke, marquis, earl, viscount and baron. Although there is no difference in law between the ranks, generally speaking for the purposes of Trollope's fiction the higher the rank, the more important and the wealthier the peer.

The real distinction came in the position of peers' children: the daughters of a duke, marquis, or earl had the title 'Lady' before their Christian name. Thus the daughters of Earl De Courcy were called Lady Alexandrina, Lady Amelia, etc. When they married they kept their title unless the husband possessed one of a higher rank. In *The Small House at Allington* Lady Alexandrina De Courcy becomes Lady Alexandrina Crosbie when she marries Mr Adolphus Crosbie. He retains his name as before.

The younger sons of a duke or a marquis had 'Lord' before their Christian names, but they were not peers. Thus the younger son of the Marquis of Brotherton in *Is He Popenjoy?* is Lord George Germain, as Germain was the family surname. When such a man married, his wife was known by her husband's name. Thus when Lord George Germain marries Mary Lovelace, she becomes Lady George Germain.

The daughters of a viscount and baron and the younger sons of earls, viscounts and barons put the title 'Honourable' before their Christian name: a younger son of Earl De Courcy is the Honourable George De Courcy.

The eldest son of a duke, marquis or earl has a 'courtesy title' whereby he uses one of his father's 'lesser' titles. This is by courtesy of the Sovereign and therefore he is not entitled to sit in the House of Lords: in *The Duke's Children*, the Duke of Omnium's son is Lord Silverbridge. In *Is He Popenjoy?* the Marquis of Brotherton's eldest son is called Lord Popenjoy and in the Barsetshire novels the De Courcy heir is known as Lord Porlock. The elder sons of viscounts and barons normally did not have a title other than 'Honourable' before their name. Trollope often has great fun with aristocratic titles and names, perhaps no more so than in *Is He Popenjoy?* [➤ Names, Origin of; Names, Silly.]

Irish peers followed the same rules regarding titles, but not all of Ireland's peers were entitled to sit in the House of Lords; they elected twenty-eight of their number as 'representative peers' to vote in the Lords. The other Irish peers could be elected to the Commons: Lord Palmerston is the best-known example. Many people of the time would have shared Lady Eustace's confusion about Irish peers [*The Eustace Diamonds*, 8]. As Lord Fawn showed her, Irish peers were often anxious to be given a new United Kingdom peerage that would entitle them to sit by right in the Lords. Many Irish peers, for example the Earl of Tulla in *Phineas Finn*, played no role in politics other than in supporting candidates for the Commons.

(Peers do not vote in parliamentary elections because they cannot be represented in a body in which they have a seat by right.)

Knights and baronets were not part of the peerage and their title of 'Sir' only conferred recognition and social prestige. There were no life peers in Trollope's time, although in *The New Zealander* he supported the unsuccessful attempt to create this new type of peer.

Methods of address are always a sign in Trollope's fiction of the way in which people behave and they reflect the social position of the speaker. Once Phineas Finn is accepted into aristocratic society, he addresses the Duke of Omnium by the informal 'Duke' rather than the formal 'Your Grace'. Peers other than dukes, as well as their wives, those with courtesy titles and those with 'Lord' or 'Lady' before their names, including baronets' wives, were addressed formally as 'My Lord', 'Your Lordship', or 'My Lady', 'Your Ladyship'. The less formal form in speech and writing was 'Lord Gerald' or 'Lady Glencora'. Baronets' and knights' wives prefixed their surname with 'Lady'.

Questions of succession to peerages play an important role in two of Trollope's novels, *Lady Anna* and *Is He Popenjoy?*

[➤ Aristocracy; Marriage.]

Phineas Finn, the Irish Member. Trollope's twenty-second novel is the second in the Palliser series. It was written between 17 November 1866 and 15 May 1867. It began serialization in the first issue of *Saint Pauls* and appeared in twenty instalments between October 1867 and May 1869. The book was published in March 1869 in two volumes by Virtue & Co., which also published *Saint Pauls*. Virtue hoped the fame of Trollope's name would help to launch his new monthly. Trollope was at the peak of his fame and earnings as a writer when the book appeared and he received £3,200, the largest amount he had ever been paid for a novel.

Trollope began writing this novel only two days after agreeing to edit *Saint Pauls*. Since he intended politics to be an important part of the new magazine, it seemed sensible that the novel, which was meant to attract readers, should be about the political world. The novel follows Phineas Finn's career, beginning with his election to Parliament for an Irish seat. We watch the handsome young man make his way in the great world of London politics and Society: his involvement first with one woman, Lady Laura Standish (later Kennedy), then with another, Violet Effingham, and finally with a third, the exotic Madame Max Goesler, while all the time he is in love with another; his involvement with the world of aristocrats and the wealthy; his duel with his rival for Violet Effingham's hand; his being offered a place in the government only to lose it on a matter of principle regarding tenant rights in Ireland (the same issue would crop up again in *The Land-Leaguers*) and his return to Ireland. This was an ending Trollope admitted was unplanned and weak.

In his *Autobiography* he goes on to say that it was a mistake to make Finn an Irishman and that he only did so because he fashioned the plot during an Irish holiday after completing *The Last Chronicle of Barset*. There may also be an underlying reason. Trollope had been told by the publisher of his second novel, which like the first had been set in Ireland and which, also like the first, had not been a great success, that English readers 'did not care for Irish novels' [➤ *The Kellys and the O'Kellys*]. Trollope changed tack with *La Vendée* but he was a stubborn man and never gave up his desire to write a successful novel at least based on an Irish character and set in part in Ireland. He had returned to Ireland again in *Castle Richmond*, published in 1860, and would do so again in *An Eye for an Eye* and *The Land-Leaguers*. All these were written after he had established himself as a successful novelist on the basis of non-Irish novels. His editorship of *Saint Pauls* meant that at last he was his own publisher and could do what he wanted.

Between the time that Trollope wrote *Phineas Finn* and its publication, Irish events once again caused great upset in England. While Trollope was writing there were many hopeful signs that Ireland would continue the tremendous progress she had made. However, 'the Fenian outrages', especially a bomb explosion which killed twelve people in London, made a novel centred on an Irish MP less enjoyable to many people. Once again Trollope was undermined by the course of Irish history in his attempt to help Ireland.

One of Trollope's persistent complaints about Ireland in the 1840s had been the lack of a well-established Catholic middle class. When he returned on the brief holiday that gave rise to his plot, he saw how much this middle class had expanded since those years and even during the seven years since he had left. Phineas Finn, who would have been born just about the time that his creator first set foot in Ireland, is a product of this growing

Irish middle class. He is the son of a Protestant mother and a Catholic father, who is a doctor. As was traditional in Ireland the son became a member of the father's church while the daughters joined the mother's, so that Phineas's five sisters were Protestants. (This is a very similar background to that of Edmund Burke in the previous century.)

Trollope was always anxious to explain Ireland to prejudiced English readers, so we are told that Dr Finn's religion 'was not of that bitter kind in which we in England are apt to suppose that all the Irish Roman Catholics indulge'. This is emphasized by young Phineas attending Trinity College, Dublin, the very heart of the Anglo-Irish Protestant 'ascendancy'. Phineas is never a 'stage Irishman' like Captain Patrick Carroll in *Mr Scarborough's Family*. These stereotyped characters – and it was a stereotype with many justifications – were familiar in Victorian fiction, even in the novels of Irishmen like Charles Lever. One gets a trace of such a familiar figure in some of the other Irish characters here, such as Laurence Fitzgibbon, MP, who was closer to the traditional stereotype. Like them, Fitzgibbon was anxious for a government 'job'. Phineas, however, is not concerned to find a comfortable place for himself at the expense of principle.

Phineas is, in many ways, an Irish version of the Reverend Mark Robarts, whose adventures in *Framley Parsonage* had launched the phenomenal success not only of Trollope but of the *Cornhill Magazine*. (Perhaps Trollope hoped that his choice of Millais to provide illustrations would help *Saint Pauls*, much as his work had helped the *Cornhill* when he illustrated

Framley Parsonage.) Both Finn and Robarts are sons of moderately successful doctors in provincial cities and both are men who are lifted to a much higher sphere by their charm, good looks, good luck and friendship with the aristocracy. Today those facts may not be so obvious when we read about Mark Robarts, but they are so when we follow Phineas Finn's rise. That is why Trollope's decision to make him Irish was such a good one. Finn enters into the very centre of the Victorian establishment, but he enters with the perspective of someone who is almost an outsider. For us today, he provides the perfect guide into the curious mixture of politics and High Society that makes up the Palliser novels. Trollope had done something similar in the first novel in the series, *Can You Forgive Her?*, in which Alice Vavasor is virtually dragged into Society.

Finn is a typically Trollopian young man in the mould of John Eames or Charley Tudor. He first appears as a basically decent man, but it takes several adventures and many chapters before he begins to develop any real strength of character. Finn's dalliance with various women while in love with another is reminiscent of the activities of John Eames, Charley Tudor and Harry Clavering [*The Claverings*]. Again like most of Trollope's young men, he begins with little worldly wealth. He is never in want of basic necessities, but his need to maintain his chosen way of life leads him into debt. Like Mark Robarts his problems are increased when he is led into signing a bill for his friend, Laurence Fitzgibbon. However, just as Robarts is saved by Lord Lufton so Finn is saved by Fitzgibbon's sister. While young Eames had been greatly helped by a legacy from an old earl, so Finn is helped by a sudden legacy of the same amount – £3,000 – from an old aunt. [➤ Deaths and Death Scenes.]

Sometimes it is almost possible to forget Finn's Irishness and at one point Madame Max Goesler says to him, 'you English are so peculiar' [44], but then she is half a 'foreigner' and Finn even wonders if she really is one of his 'countrymen'. By that Finn means that he wonders if she is really British, for Irishmen like him were what were later called 'West Britons': they would fight for Ireland's rights but wanted to remain fully within the United Kingdom, where it was possible, though not easy, for them to reach high office. Nor is it often easy to remember that Finn is a Catholic: he makes hardly any references to religion. Just about the only time we are assured that he goes to Mass on a Sunday comes in a later novel, *Phineas Redux*, when he is in gaol awaiting trial for murder. When Finn makes his calls at the Earl of Brentford's house on Sunday we are as likely to hear about his church attendance as we would have heard about John Eames's.

When Trollope started writing *Phineas Finn* British politics were entering a new phase. The death of the aged Lord Palmerston in October 1865 had exacerbated the struggle between those who wanted considerable changes in the Constitution, particularly in extending the franchise, and those who were prepared to concede, at the most, only very moderate alterations. The debates would continue until 1867 when the second Reform Act was passed. He wrote *Phineas Finn* during the Conservative administration of Lord Derby in which Disraeli, whom Trollope despised both as a nov-

elist and as a politician, played the leading role in the Commons. This was the longest period of Tory rule, although admittedly only thirty months, since Trollope had started to write novels. His 'authorial intrusion' that 'Conservative governments in this country are especially prone to die' was true of the 1850s and 1860s, but it also expressed Trollope's hope for the future [5]. All these tensions and frustrations lie behind the writing of *Phineas Finn*.

In the novel one of the debates centres on the question of the ballot. At this time men who had the vote voted by openly naming the candidate or candidates of their choice, although by the late 1860s this was, as often as not, in a room set aside for the purpose. Often their votes were then published in the newspapers or even in local pamphlets. Trollope was firmly opposed to the idea of a secret ballot as he believed that honest Englishmen should never be afraid to express their political views in the open. His attitude on this was quite similar to that put forward by the reformer, Mr Monk, in the novel. Gladstone was also opposed to the idea of a secret ballot although he changed his view after studying the election of 1868. The secret ballot was only introduced in 1872. The ballot is the most conspicuous topic in the novel through which we can see the limits of Trollope's Liberalism. His defence of London policemen during political demonstrations as 'the most forbearing of men' – and there had been trouble in Hyde Park over the Reform Act – is not the opinion of a Radical [25].

Mr Turnbull is Trollope's portrait of a Radical demagogue and when the novel was published in book form, the

Daily Telegraph of 31 March 1869 asserted in a leading article that John Bright had been portrayed in the person of Turnbull. Trollope vigorously denied the charge and particularly resented the insinuation that he had not been 'gentlemanlike'. [For Trollope's views about using real people, ➤ Palliser Novels.] Indeed Trollope had praised Bright in an anonymous article in the previous issue of *Saint Pauls*. If one looks closely at the character of Turnbull, one does see some similarities to Bright, but Trollope specifically says that Turnbull is not a great orator whereas Bright's greatest attribute was his splendid oratory. While Turnbull and Bright share common political beliefs, Turnbull is not Bright. (Trollope would have a joke at Bright's expense, but that was not until fifteen years later in *The Fixed Period*.) Turnbull is a portrait of a Utopian windbag, a political type Trollope had long disliked. Somewhat ironically there is a scene in the novel in which Finn is reading a leading article in the *Daily Telegraph* while thinking 'how little the writer of the article knew about Mr Turnbull' [21]. Finn reads the *Telegraph* for the sake of economy as it was then one-fifth the price of *The Times*. The growing power of newspapers comes in for castigation in this novel. Here Trollope's ire is reserved not for *The Jupiter* but for the newer and more popular newspapers like the *People's Banner* and its demotic editor, Quintus Slide.

As the second of the Palliser novels, *Phineas Finn* introduces characters who reappear in many later volumes. Two of the most memorable and colourful of these are Lady Laura Standish and her brother, Lord Chiltern. Lady Laura is one of Trollope's

most passionate women, although her fierce devotion to her brother may seem somewhat excessive to modern readers. Yet anyone familiar with the diaries and letters of aristocratic girls of that era will know that this was a common thing. They were often so isolated in their youth that their brothers became the source of all their loyalties and interests. Trollope had already shown an example of this in *Can You Forgive Her?* in Kate Vavasor and her brother George. As one of Trollope's most passionate women, Lady Laura is criticized at one point for acting like a man. She is certainly as frank in expressing her desire to have an influence in politics as she is in expressing all her other feelings.

In this novel and its sequel, *Phineas Redux*, Lady Laura finds herself in a situation Trollope was to discuss elsewhere: she married for money and position, not love. Trollope was showing his readers – and here he was thinking particularly of his largest readership, young women – the dangers involved in this. He had already done so with Lady Ongar in *The Claverings* and would do so again with Adelaide Houghton in *Is He Popenjoy?* Lady Laura's reason for selling herself to Robert Kennedy while she really loves Finn may have been the noble motive of helping her brother, but in Trollope's eyes she commits a great sin and therefore she suffers an unhappy fate. In the general sympathy for Lady Laura's plight, one must remember that she does a great wrong not only to herself but to her husband. Kennedy is a well-drawn character and one of the few major characters in Trollope's fiction who is truly Scottish. In *The Last Chronicle of Barset*, Trollope had portrayed in Josiah

Crawley a man who dwelt on the border of insanity; with Kennedy he would show how a man crosses that border. (He used the same theme in the next novel published, *He Knew He Was Right*.) Trollope is also able to use the character of Kennedy to carry on his continuous war against excessive ideas about the proper way to observe the Sabbath.

In Lord Chiltern we meet a man who is not really vicious but headstrong and violent. He is the very antithesis of Plantagenet Palliser. Both come from the inner circle of the Whig aristocracy but whereas Palliser is a man obsessed with work and duty, one who scorns such diversions as foxhunting, Chiltern hates politics and is passionately devoted to riding to hounds. Thus Trollope gives each man one of his own attributes: a love of work and a love of fox-hunting. The latter love allowed Trollope to introduce some of his best hunting scenes in any novel. Finn's adventures in riding Chiltern's horse, Bonebreaker, are said by Escott to be drawn on some of Trollope's own experiences with the Essex Hunt.

The statement that 'women sympathize most effectually with men, as men do with women' could well be taken as the theme of this novel [44]. Phineas wins the sympathy of many women, ranging from Lady Laura to his landlady, Mrs Bunce. Indeed they so sympathize with him that they take the unusual step of often calling him by his first name [➤ Names, Use of]. All the principal women in this novel suffer from the complications that arise from the combination of love and money. Lady Glencora Palliser, as we already know from the first Palliser novel, had been in effect sold to her

husband; we also see how men pursue the young heiress, Violet Effingham. Gradually, as we learn the background of Madame Max Goesler, we see that she also was a young bride married to an elderly and rich man. The only woman who seems free of this complication is the middle-class Mrs Low.

Madame Max Goesler is an extraordinary character and it will repay the reader to watch carefully how Trollope slowly and parsimoniously gives details of her life [40]. It is easy enough to assume that she is Jewish, but what Trollope actually says is that she had married a rich Austrian Jew and that is why she has much property in Vienna to manage. In a later chapter [62] the denigrating remarks about her – 'black-browed . . . a beard on her upper lip . . . a Jewess' – are not part of the narration, but a summary of Lady Glencora's thoughts when she is in a rage at the thought of seeing a duchess's coronet slipping away from her. One should not be misled by the fact that Madame Max manages her own property. While this would have been rare for a Victorian married woman, Madame Max is a widow.

The question of whether or not the Duke of Omnium will marry Madame Max and possibly beget a son and heir, thus depriving his nephew Plantagenet of succeeding to the dukedom (and Glencora of becoming a duchess), had a sad parallel in Trollope's early days. His father was the heir to a comfortable landed estate in Hertfordshire which belonged to his elderly and childless uncle. Suddenly the widowed uncle married and produced a son and the fortunes of the Trollope family received a great setback, one no doubt magnified with many a re-telling. Trollope also included a painful scene from his own past. When the money-lender warns Finn 'Do be punctual' in repaying his debts, Trollope was using the actual words said to him by a money-lender when he was a young postal clerk in debt in the 1830s. No doubt he enjoyed his private joke in dredging up the tale in the novel for which he received his highest payment. Another of Trollope's private references concerns having Finn returned for Loughshane, as this was the name of a person involved in the Mary O'Reilly trial at which Trollope had been badgered as a witness [Mullen, 229–32].

The amount of violence in the novel may surprise some readers who fondly imagine that the mid-Victorian era was a blissful age of peace, and certainly it was for the comfortable clergy and gentry in Barsetshire. In the middle of writing *Phineas Finn*, Trollope joked with John Blackwood that perhaps he ought to put murder in his novels and certainly this novel includes enough violence: a duel, the attempted murder of a Cabinet minister, a riot (to reflect the disturbances in London over the Reform Act), as well as Lord Chiltern's killing of a drunken brute – though admittedly that occurred before the novel begins. By the 1860s duels were something of an anachronism, but they provided a good fictional sub-plot, as did the attempted garrotting of Mr Kennedy as he walked home from the Commons. Garrotting – throwing a cord round the neck of a victim from behind and strangling him to death – had been a tremendous problem in London in 1862–3. Indeed one contemporary historian wrote a few years later that there had been a 'panic' about this and that London had become 'as unsafe . . .

as it had been in the days of Charles the Second'. The streets were deserted at night and men went about armed with sword-sticks and revolvers. In depicting garrotting Trollope was only reflecting what had been a widespread public concern although it had much abated by the time the novel was written. Trollope himself believed, and would argue in *Saint Pauls*, that there was no need for panic about the alleged increase in violence.

The novel has a strange ending when Phineas gives up his political career on a point of principle. Quite characteristically Trollope provides some comfort for him in his Irish exile: 'our poor hero' is offered the place of a Poor Law Inspector in Ireland at £1,000 a year, a very comfortable income, particularly in Ireland. Phineas is thus able, after all his adventures in London Society, to marry the quiet Irish girl, Mary Flood Jones.

Reactions to *Phineas Finn* were quite diverse. As so often happened, critics commented on individual instalments of the novel as they appeared. Thus the *Illustrated London News* noted in November 1868, 'At present Phineas is very low down.' In the same month Trollope was standing for Parliament and his Tory opponents in Beverley circulated a clever ditty against him which had a line saying that if he were elected he would wind up 'bored like his own Mr Phineas Finn'! In his *Autobiography* Trollope makes the rather extraordinary statement that he was satisfied with the book because 'the men who would have lived with Phineas Finn read the book, and the women who would have lived with Lady Laura Standish read it also'. Lady Frederick Cavendish, Gladstone's niece who had married into the

Duke of Devonshire's family, did read it and she disagreed: 'Finished *Phineas Finn*; it has cleverness and some successful characters, but it is a disagreeable, sham sort of book' [➤ *The Land-Leaguers*]. The *Spectator*, however, thought the novel 'contains some of Mr Trollope's best work' though it was not one of his 'very best novels'. In particular they singled out the portrayal of Robert Kennedy, a character often neglected by readers. *Phineas Finn* remains essential reading for anyone who enjoys Trollope for not only does it provide the best introduction to the world of Victorian politics in fiction, but it contains one of the novelist's best female characters in the complex Lady Laura.

Phineas Redux. Trollope's twenty-ninth novel and the fourth in the Palliser series was written between 23 October 1870 and 1 April 1871, although Trollope did not offer it for publication until August 1872. The novel was first serialized in *The Graphic* in twenty-six weekly instalments between 19 July 1873 and 10 January 1874. It was then published by Chapman & Hall in two volumes in December 1873. The editor of *The Graphic* disliked the use of the Latin word for 'brought back' in the title and said most people would assume that it was the character's surname. Trollope was always sensitive about the titles of his novels and disliked having to change them, but in his *Autobiography* he accepted that his choice was in 'bad taste'. He made the rather lame excuse that he could think of no other title. Trollope received £2,500.

No two of Trollope's novels are as closely united as *Phineas Finn* and *Phineas Redux*, as the titles attest. Trollope

maintained that they were, 'in fact, but one novel'. Of course in the list of Palliser novels they are separated by *The Eustace Diamonds*, but Trollope did not consider that book as part of the series. Some readers may prefer to read the two Phineas books in sequence and read *The Eustace Diamonds* later. However, this will cause some slight confusion regarding some of the political events in the novels and also the appearance of the Reverend Mr Emilius. Emilius, who plays a crucial role in *Phineas Redux*, first appears as Lady Eustace's second husband in *The Eustace Diamonds*. Probably the best advice is for readers who have been particularly attracted to the development of the characters of Phineas himself and Lady Laura Kennedy in *Phineas Finn* to proceed straight to *Phineas Redux*. Those who prefer to see the series as a whole should read *The Eustace Diamonds* before *Phineas Redux*.

Almost everything that is said in the entry on *Phineas Finn* has a bearing on its sequel. Apart from Mr Emilius there are few characters of substance who are not in the first novel, while most of the new ones are included in the sub-plot concerning Adelaide Palliser, Plantagenet's cousin. As in the earlier novel the main story follows Phineas Finn's career: his return to the political scene; his election; the renewal of his involvement with Lady Laura Kennedy and her insane husband, Robert; Phineas's trial for a murder he did not commit; and his marriage to Madame Max Goesler. Trollope began *Phineas Redux* just over four years after *Phineas Finn* ceased serialization. Between these two novels several unsettling events occurred in his own life. In 1867 he resigned from the Post Office and began his editorship of *Saint Pauls*, which ended without much regret in 1870; he was defeated in his attempt to enter Parliament for Beverley in 1868; the attempt to launch a new career as an author of anonymous novels had proved a failure; he was about to give up his beloved and elegant home in Hertfordshire to embark on a long trip to Australia to see his younger son. It is hardly surprising that *Phineas Redux* has a darker tone than *Phineas Finn*.

In order to bring Phineas back to the interlocked world of London Society and politics, Trollope had to eliminate his wife. Phineas could hardly exert his attraction – or at least it would not be easy to describe such exertions in a Victorian novel – if he returned to London equipped with a wife. So poor Mary Flood Jones Finn dies in the first chapter. Phineas makes but few references to her afterwards. [For one such, ➤ Chapter 55.] Two years have passed since Phineas retired from politics. According to the *Spectator* of 3 January 1874 there had been a 'rumour of Phineas Finn's return', a comment that gives us an insight into how contemporaries viewed Trollope's serials as chronicles of their own time. Indeed, the same journal commented that readers knew Trollope's characters better than 'ninety-nine hundredths of our own friends'.

In spite of this familiarity, Trollope was faced with one difficulty in the novel: the serialization of *Phineas Finn* had ended in May 1869 and although Trollope wrote the sequel between 1870 and 1871 it did not appear until July 1873, four years after the earlier novel had ended. From time to time, therefore, he has to remind readers of what happened in the earlier novel.

On the whole he manages this fairly skilfully, as when he allows Madame Max to tell Phineas the story of her involved friendship with the old Duke of Omnium. Trollope had increasingly seen himself as a 'chronicler' in the later Barsetshire novels, and in the Palliser series he assumes the guise of an historian although he does not do this with any pomp. When describing the relationship of Madame Max and the old Duke of Omnium he alludes to his role thus: 'The reader, if he has duly studied the history of the age' [17].

For Plantagenet Palliser and his wife Lady Glencora the death of the old duke, about a third of the way through the novel [25], is a crucial moment in the Palliser series, for when the old duke dies Plantagenet becomes Duke of Omnium and, more importantly, Lady Glencora becomes Duchess of Omnium. The old duke's death is described with a tenderness we could hardly have expected when we first met him in the Barsetshire series. The link with that earlier series is emphasized by the presence of two people from it: his doctor, Sir Omicron Pie, and his former mistress, Lady Hartletop [➤ Deaths and Death Scenes]. Although Glencora is now a duchess she remains as impetuous as ever, as she demonstrates in throwing herself into her support for Phineas in the great central drama of the novel, his trial for murder.

The reaction of various characters to Phineas's imprisonment and trial is a crucial part of the whole Palliser series. The account of Lady Laura's visit to Phineas in prison is a particularly fine piece of writing [55]. It contains a good illustration of the nuances of Victorian manners, something emphasized all the more sharply by her sudden departure from them when she flings herself on to Phineas and kisses him. At less passionate moments in this chapter Phineas is obsessed with a problem that had long perplexed Trollope himself: could a lawyer defend a client sincerely if he did not believe him innocent?

In the interval between the two Phineas novels, Trollope had written *He Knew He Was Right*, with its powerful portrayal of a man driven mad by jealousy. This was a help when he returned in *Phineas Redux* to the tragic end of Robert Kennedy. As in the earlier novel, the reader should not allow his sympathy for Lady Laura to hide the fact that she has greatly wronged her husband in their marriage. Most of the charges that he makes against her before shooting at Finn are, in essence, true. When assessing Kennedy's character, Trollope makes an important point which also gives a key to his own character: Kennedy 'died believing, as he had ever believed, that the spirit of evil was stronger than the spirit of good'. Trollope's deepest religious belief was the exact opposite of this and that is why he presents a picture of the Calvinistic Kennedy that is as unsympathetic as those he painted of English Evangelicals with similar views – characters like Mrs Proudie and Mr Slope [➤ Religion]. It is this antipathy to Kennedy's religion, and not his nationality, that causes Trollope's dislike, although it must be admitted that he does have a mild trace of anti-Scottish stereotyping in portraying the Scottish hotel in London [23].

If the comments about the Scots are not really vicious, the portrayal of the Jewish convert clergyman, Joseph Emilius, is. It is hard to believe that the same author could write such a sympathetic portrayal of Bohemian Jews in *Nina Balatka*. In the end Emilius is convicted of bigamy but is not tried for the murder he committed. Perhaps Trollope decided it would be too upsetting to have an Anglican clergyman convicted of murder, although in *Marion Fay*, published eight years later, a clergyman ponders murder but proceeds no further. (Ironically, a few months after he finished writing *Phineas Redux*, a clergyman did murder his wife: this unique Victorian event has been well portrayed in a modern novel, *Watson's Apology*, by Beryl Bainbridge.) Trollope makes one of his small private references in having Emilius take lodgings near the Marylebone workhouse, the neighbourhood in which Trollope himself had lodged in the 1830s.

Trollope used his own experiences at Beverley in writing about the bribery of electors undertaken by Phineas's opponent at Tankerville. Trollope also derived much of the political information and gossip that he used throughout the Palliser novels from his regular visits to the Cosmopolitan Club [➤ Clubs]. This club is portrayed here as the 'Universe' and, like its original, had as its prime purpose conversation among a diverse group of authors, politicians, artists and the occasional royal guest [34]. 'The Prince' in this chapter is the Prince of Wales, the future King Edward VII, who was a member of the Cosmopolitan. The club met in two rooms in Berkeley Square on Wednesday and Sunday nights. Wednesday evening is also the time of the quarrel in *Phineas Redux* [for the choice of Wednesday, ➤ Parliament]. According to Gladstone's secretary, Trollope set the murder of the

President of the Board of Trade, Mr Bonteen, in Lansdowne Passage.

For the trial scene Trollope brought back a lawyer who figured in two of his other great trial scenes: Mr Chaffanbrass. He had appeared for the defence in both *The Three Clerks* and *Orley Farm* when both his clients were guilty of what they were charged. He is even more effective in this novel in which he plays with the witnesses as 'a cat ... with a mouse'. Trollope always had a sympathy with witnesses which dated from his own appearance at a trial in Ireland. Trollope has a private joke in having a novelist, who had observed the quarrel between Phineas and Bonteen at the club, called to give an account. Chaffanbrass has several amusing comments about novels, in particular his charge that English novelists took their plots from French novels. (In this examination Trollope makes an error as he places a murder in the wrong Scott novel: it should be in *Guy Mannering* rather than in *The Antiquary*, and the victim's name is misspelt.)

The political parts of *Phineas Redux* are dominated by the great debate about the disestablishment of the Church of England. Trollope had advocated the disestablishment of its sister Church of Ireland during his campaign for election to Parliament at Beverley and Gladstone's government brought about this controversial measure in 1869 [➤ Ireland]. However, Trollope had a completely opposite point of view about his own Church of England. He was strongly in favour of its continued establishment although, as he admitted in *North America*, he did not normally wish to enter into protracted debate about it. The topic of disestablishment is brought

into *Phineas Redux* because Trollope needed a contentious political topic. An increased suffrage had been enacted in 1867 and the other constitutional issue, the campaign for a secret ballot, had already been used in *Phineas Finn*. Disestablishment in this novel also had another advantage for Trollope, as both a committed Liberal and Anglican. Because it is proposed by a Conservative government it allowed him to show the Tories betraying their ally, the Church, and their traditional cry of 'Church and Throne'. One of Trollope's strongest political views was that, since the days of Peel in the 1840s, two of the Tories' main tricks had been to hold a belief firmly until they threw it over and to take up a reform they had previously vehemently opposed.

Daubeny, the Tory leader who toys with disestablishment, is called 'a political Cagliostro' by one opponent [39] and has often been identified with Disraeli [➤ Disraeli for a consideration of this]. This seems to be one place in Trollope's fiction in which a fictional character has a strong resemblance to a real politician. However, it is only fair to note that Disraeli was himself a sincere Anglican and defender of the Established Church. Yet it was not only the Liberal Trollope who thought it likely that the Tories under Disraeli would abandon the Established Church. Three well-informed Tories, Charles Lever, the novelist and diplomat, Bishop Magee of Peterborough, and even Disraeli's eventual successor, Lord Salisbury, all thought this likely [Mullen, 483]. Thus Trollope's political plot is not as far-fetched as it first seems. Neither Trollope nor Disraeli would have expected that happily the Church of England would still be established a century after their deaths.

Phineas Redux met with a mixed reception. The *Saturday Review* did not like a novel which, it claimed, had 'no plot' and in which almost all the characters were 'on the shady side of thirty'. Perhaps we no longer consider that a handicap for a novel. Certainly *Phineas Redux* remains an essential novel for all who delight in the Palliser series with its rich mixture of politics and high society.

Phrenology. See Spiritualism.

Picnics. Picnics feature in *Can You Forgive Her?* and in *The Bertrams*. In *Can You Forgive Her?* Trollope devotes two chapters [8 and 9] to an elaborate seaside picnic at Yarmouth, complete with tents, music and dancing. Even so, he adds in an aside, it was 'not a happy place for a picnic', a comment written by someone who obviously enjoyed picnics. Trollope had also devised a list of indispensable ingredients: 'Green turf is absolutely an essential. There should be trees, broken ground, small paths, thickets, and hidden recesses. There should, if possible, be rocks, old timber, moss, and brambles ... hills and dales, – on a small scale, and, above all ... running water. There should be no expanse. Jones should not be able to see all Greene's movements' [8]. He probably had in mind the picnics his brother Tom had arranged when Anthony and Rose visited his Italian home. (His brother was famous for his outdoor entertainments and his mother had also been fond of them whether in Italy with Tom or in her younger days in France.) In 'George Walker at Suez' the poor Mr Walker is invited to a luxurious picnic at the 'Well of Moses', only to discover that his host has confused him with another Englishman. In the event he has no better luck than the party at Yarmouth because he, like they, had ignored Trollope's criteria.

Pie, Sir Omicron. Famous London doctor who is often mentioned in the Barsetshire and Palliser novels. In *Barchester Towers* he is summoned to the deathbeds of old Bishop Grantly and of Dr Trefoil, the dean. Sir Omicron charges £20, an enormous sum, for a visit to old Mr Bertram's deathbed [*The Bertrams*, 41]. By the time he attends the dying Duke of Omnium he is a very old man [*Phineas Redux*, 24]. His predictions as to how long patients will survive are almost always wrong. His one sensible suggestion is in telling Mr Gresham to follow the advice of Doctor Thorne, his great rival, and thus Lady Arabella Gresham is unique among Pie's patients in recovering [*Doctor Thorne*, 31]. His name comes from the fifteenth and sixteenth letters of the Greek alphabet, O π. [➤ Classics; Names, Origin of.]

Pillar-box. See Post Office.

'Pitch and not be defiled'. The quotation 'He that toucheth pitch shall be defiled therewith' comes from Ecclesiasticus 13:1. As Ecclesiasticus, a book of the Apocrypha, is not in the Authorized (King James) Version of the Bible Trollope would have heard it at church or as an expression used by those round him. He frequently uses the quote to illustrate one of his principal warnings in those 'sermons' in his fiction directed at young people: to avoid doing evil, avoid those who do evil. As he said in *The Three Clerks*, 'We cannot hear the devil plead, and resist the charm of his eloquence. "To listen is to be lost"'[9].

Politicians. See Politics.

Politics. Politics play almost as important a role in Trollope's works as they did in his life. In the first number of *Saint Pauls* Trollope, as its new editor, wrote that 'of all studies to which men and women can attach themselves . . . the first and foremost' is politics. In the lecture he gave to Post Office clerks on 'The Civil Service' six years earlier, he said: 'I do not much mind what a man's politics are, so that he has got politics . . . I don't love a man with whom I can neither agree nor disagree; who will say that politics are nothing to him. Such a one seems to me to shirk the first of man's duties.' One of the reasons for his dislike of Dickens was that writer's low view of politics about which he was 'marvellously ignorant'.

The Palliser series is based on the close connections between Society in Victorian times and politics, and is centred on the role of a great landed aristocrat in public life. When, at the end of his long life, Sir Winston Churchill came to read some of the Palliser novels, written about the time of his birth, the great statesman was asked what was the principal difference between Trollope's age and the following century. 'They mixed up Society and politics,' he replied. While the world of politics never plays as great a role in the rest of Trollope's fiction as it does in the Palliser novels, the connection between politics and daily life is present in all his novels. It began with his first novel, *The Macder-*

mots of Ballycloran, and only ended with the last, *The Land-Leaguers*: both show how politics affected life in Ireland. Almost all the Barsetshire novels involve politics to some degree: in the first, *The Warden*, political agitation causes Septimus Harding to resign as warden, while a change of government affects the appointment of Bishop Grantly's successor in *Barchester Towers*. In *Framley Parsonage* the Tory, Lady Lufton, detests the old Duke of Omnium not just for his rumoured profligacy but because he is a Whig. In *Lady Anna* the Countess Lovel is horrified not just that her daughter's lover is a tailor but a Radical who does not go to church. The short stories, with the exception of 'The Panjandrum', avoid domestic politics although Frau Frohmann, an Austrian, is rather oddly called a 'Tory' ['Why Frau Frohmann Raised Her Prices'].

Much of Trollope's non-fiction also concerned political topics: his lifelong desire to be regarded as a serious writer naturally led him to political questions from the early years of his writing career. In his first published non-fiction work, his 'letters' on Ireland for the *Examiner*, he answered charges that the government were not doing enough to cope with the Irish famine. In *The New Zealander*, he had chapters on 'The People and Their Rulers', the House of Commons, the House of Lords and the Crown. His travel books all discuss politics in the countries he visited. He was particularly interested in American politics and therefore his *North America* is the most revealing book he wrote about his basic political beliefs: the importance of extending education to all classes and the need for a gradual levelling up within society. He also wrote many political essays, particularly in the 1860s in the *Pall Mall Gazette* and in his own *Saint Pauls*.

Although Trollope's mother became known as a Tory writer, she and his father were for a time 'drawing-room Radicals'. Politics were frequently discussed at home and Trollope from his youth was a Liberal. In his early days he entertained certain Radical views and a great deal of his youthful politics can be discovered in 'The Panjandrum'. By the 1850s, he could be regarded, generally speaking, as a Palmerstonian Liberal [➤ *Lord Palmerston*]. Afterwards he tended to be a strong though not uncritical supporter of Gladstone. In his *Autobiography*, he describes himself as 'an advanced conservative Liberal'. [For the meaning of this Victorian phrase, see Mullen, 477.] In the last year of his life he grew very angry about the decision of Gladstone's government to set aside the rules of a free market regarding land rents in Ireland [➤ *The Land-Leaguers*].

Trollope's attitude towards Conservatives was more complex than that towards Liberals. Part of his view was conditioned by his detestation of two important Tory leaders: Peel and Disraeli. He believed – in an oft-used phrase – that the natural function of the Conservative was to be a brake on the coach of progress [*Phineas Finn*, 35]. Yet he had a respect for the intellect of many Conservatives [*The Eustace Diamonds*, 4]. 'Real Tories', those who opposed change, were 'genuinely English', but were doomed to acquiesce in the constant reforms of the age [*Lady Anna*, 18]. He rightly saw his own century as one in which old, established ways were constantly being overturned and thus the Tory was

forced 'to carry out the purposes of his opponents' ['Why Frau Frohmann Raised Her Prices'].

Trollope's attitude towards liberalism and conservatism only reflected his own make-up, his 'divided mind'. As he wrote in an article in the *Fortnightly Review*, virtually every human being has an inner parliament debating between the old and the new. His friend the Reverend W. L. Collins described Trollope's views in the obituary he wrote of the author: 'On some theoretical points his Liberalism was of the most advanced type ... [but] all his instincts and feelings were conservative.' [For Trollope's attitude towards the Whigs, ➤ St Bungay, Duke of.]

Trollope's extensive knowledge of Westminster politics came from several sources: his own experience as a civil servant who had to deal with ministers and parliamentary committees; his constant study of Parliament through the pages of *The Times*; and friendships with various politicians in his clubs. When he began to write the Palliser novels he was given permission by the Speaker of the House of Commons to have regular entry passes into the gallery to listen to debates.

Trollope, who had a strong sense of fair play and had inherited his father's devotion to justice, was well aware of 'the terrible inequalities' in Victorian society. These are portrayed far more graphically in his Irish rather than in the bulk of his English novels. However, most of his non-fiction works – notably *The New Zealander* – touched on this topic since an important purpose of his travel books was to give information to Britons who wanted to better their condition by emigrating.

Politicians, which in Trollope's day

meant peers as well as MPs, appear constantly in Trollope's writing. Like every other group they are a mixed lot, from the virtuous Joshua Monk in the Palliser novels to the vile Undy Scott in *The Three Clerks*. Trollope believed almost all shared one trait: 'a drunkard or a gambler may be weaned from his ways, but not a politician' [*Phineas Redux*, 13]. He was horrified to find that in the America of Abraham Lincoln, 'the word politician has stunk in men's nostrils' [*North America*]. Even so, he had some sympathy for politicians, whom he compared to soldiers who fight in a narrow valley while historians sit on the high ground criticizing the battle below. Drawing no doubt on his own experience as a civil servant, Trollope had little use for grandiloquent parliamentary orators or those who theorize about Utopian reforms. His ideal of a politician's duty was very high and is best expressed in the Duke of Omnium's advice to his son when that young man has just been returned as an MP. An MP is the 'servant of his country . . . the guardian of your fellow-countrymen, – that they may be safe, that they may be prosperous, that they may be well governed and lightly burdened, – above all that they may be free'. An MP must undertake his duties 'as scrupulously as though you were paid for doing them' [*The Duke's Children*, 15].

[➤ Aristocracy; Honesty; Patriotism; Peerage; Working Class.]

'Poor'. Trollope's use of the word 'poor' can be confusing. Mrs Dale in *The Small House at Allington* is said to be 'poor' though she has an income of about £300 a year, a free house, maids, a large garden and a gardener. Yet Mrs Smith in *John Caldigate* [5] is 'poor, very poor' and she has only enough money to maintain herself in Australia for a few weeks after her ship docks. Jeffrey Palliser in *Can You Forgive Her?* is 'poor' though he has an income of £600 a year, while Miss Marrable, a spinster with £300 a year in *The Vicar of Bullhampton*, is not 'poor' but lives 'decently' with 'very modest means' [9]. In *Can You Forgive Her?* Trollope gave his best short description of what he meant by the word: Jeffrey's income, unlike Miss Marrable's, is not sufficient because he, with £600 a year, has 'a taste for living with people of six thousand a year'. While Trollope often uses the word with regard to the middle or upper classes, he seldom uses it in the normal Victorian sense, meaning the worst paid among working people, those like Lucy Graham on her 18*s.* a week in 'The Telegraph Girl', Catherine Carmichael in the short story of that name or the Brattles who are 'faced with the difficulty of the hardness of their lives' [*The Vicar of Bullhampton*, 5]. Whenever, therefore, a reader meets the word 'poor' in Trollope, the best advice is to pay little attention to it until more information emerges about the character's income. To Trollope it only has meaning when set against the demands of a character's position. [➤ Working Class.]

Porlock, Lord.- See De Courcy Family.

Post-Obits. See Entails.

Post Office. Trollope began his career in the General Post Office on 4 November 1834 with little enthusiasm: 'I did not think it a high calling.' His

Autobiography continues: 'The Post Office at last grew upon me and forced itself into my affections. I became intensely anxious that people should have their letters delivered to them punctually. But my hope to rise had always been built on writing novels, and at last by writing novels I had risen.' He resigned on 31 October 1867, eight years before he had reached the age of retirement. He described his career in his *Autobiography* and he was intensely proud of the innovations and progress made during his thirty-three years there, much of which was due to his work. He included the official letter of praise on his retirement, written by his brother-in-law John Tilley, in his *Autobiography*.

He got his position as a clerk at £90 a year through the intervention of his mother's friend, Mrs Clayton Freeling. Her husband was the son of Sir Francis Freeling, Secretary of the Post Office. Trollope was a clerk at the Post Office headquarters, St Martin-le-Grand, from 1834 to 1841, a period portrayed in *The Three Clerks* and *Marion Fay*. His earliest days, therefore, were in the 'old' Post Office, before Rowland Hill's reforms, the most famous of which was the introduction of the 'penny post'. By 1841 he had advanced to the position of Senior Clerk at £140 per annum and in that year was transferred to Ireland as a Surveyor's Deputy. In 1854 he became Surveyor of Ireland's Northern District and worked in Ireland until 1859.

While there Trollope was sent on three special missions. The first was to the Western District of England (1851–3) to lay out rural postmen's 'walks'. The district included the southern counties of Wales, the Channel Isles and the South-West. While working in Jersey he came up with the idea for 'roadside letter boxes' in the shape of pillars for the collection of letters. These were based on what he had seen in France in the 1830s. He is thus the inventor of the pillar-box [➤ *He Knew He Was Right*]. In 1858 he was sent to Egypt to negotiate a new treaty for deliveries to India and then to the West Indies to examine ways of improving postal deliveries to England.

On 10 January 1860 Trollope officially took up his last position as Surveyor of the Eastern District in England at £700 a year plus expenses, 20s. a day when he was away from his office and £30 a year rental if he used his home as his headquarters, which he did. The Surveyor was the head of Post Office operations in his district. During his career he was asked to undertake temporary assignments in Scotland, Ireland, Yorkshire and London and to appear before Commons committees regarding Post Office matters. After his retirement in 1868, he also undertook a special mission to America to negotiate a new convention regarding mail deliveries between the two countries.

Trollope's career was a distinguished one and his abilities were recognized in the many special missions he was given. He was always keen to improve the lot of postmen and clashed with the Secretary to the Post Office, Sir Rowland Hill, who wanted to reduce their wages. He instituted a course of lectures for clerks at St Martin's and helped to establish a library there; he also donated books, including some by Carlyle. He was scrupulously honest, a hard and efficient worker and a good organizer. He also was a hard fighter for his rights and could be troublesome. As he wrote in his *Autobiography*, 'I was very fond of the department, and when matters came to be considered, I generally had an opinion of my own. I have no doubt that I often made myself very disagreeable. I know that I sometimes tried to do so.' After 1860 his was an anomalous position: his fame and his very large earnings sat uneasily with his surveyor's position. His abrupt manner, as well as his wealth and status in the literary world, made enemies: Rowland Hill intrigued against him while Edmund Yates and Frank Scudamore, who were both figures in London's literary world, were jealous of him.

Trollope felt himself hard used by the Post Office over surveyors' salaries and more especially when his junior, Scudamore, got the post of Assistant Secretary for which he had applied. (Scudamore was later involved in a scandal to which Trollope obliquely referred in his *Autobiography* [15] and more directly in *The Way We Live Now* [50].) He recalled his sense of injustice sixteen years later in his book on Cicero [I. 364]. He was sensitive to the charge that his literary career meant that he had not devoted enough time to his Post Office work. His interest in the Post Office continued into the 1870s as can be seen from his short story on the new telegraph department, 'The Telegraph Girl'.

The effect of his Post Office career on his writing was considerable: he was proud to be a civil servant and always defended the Service against critics like Dickens; his training in writing clear English influenced his style; his need to combine two careers made him a disciplined novelist who thoroughly organized his plots as well as his time for writing; his travels

abroad gave him a knowledge of the world equalled by no other Victorian novelist and were the basis for his career as a short-story writer; his detailed and extensive work in the south-west of England laid the basis for the Barsetshire series and for his knowledge of people and scenery in the countryside and county towns of England. He drew on his Post Office experience to a considerable degree in *John Caldigate*, in which a clerk helps to free an innocent man from gaol by using his Post Office knowledge, and in *Miss Mackenzie*, in which he shows how potentially disastrous would be the ending of a Sunday post as demanded by Evangelicals. He used his experience to a lesser degree to follow the course of a letter in *Framley Parsonage*, to portray a gruff postmistress in *The Small House at Allington* and a one-legged postman in *He Knew He Was Right*. Most of his travel books discuss postal operations in the country he was visiting. In *North America* he praised Rowland Hill and bemoaned the lack of pillar-boxes in America.

[➤ Civil Service; Letters; Lewes, G. H.]

Prayer. In *The New Zealander*, written in the mid-1850s, Trollope wrote, 'A man in his short sojourn here on earth has mainly three things to do; and he should endeavour to do them all well. He has to say his prayers, he has to earn his bread, and he has to amuse himself ... Let a man say his prayers truly and he will say them well, whatever be his special creed' [10]. Given this statement and Trollope's strong Christian faith it may seem surprising that he seldom discusses prayer in his fiction. This was due to his general reticence, a reticence not shared by someone like Dickens, to portray religious practices in fiction. To do so reminded him, as it had his mother, of Evangelicals with their free, easy and excessive talk of religious things. (The one exception was sermons, which he normally only included in order to attack.) Trollope took praying seriously, as he demonstrates in *The Bertrams* [26] when he tells us that 'praying is by no means the easiest work to which a man can set himself. Kneeling is easy; the repetition of the well-known word is easy; the putting on of some solemnity of mind is perhaps not difficult. But to remember what you are asking, why you are asking, of whom you are asking; to feel sure that you want what you do ask, and that this asking is the best way to get it; – that on the whole is not easy.'

In his fiction it is assumed that characters, unless they are outright materialists or atheists, do pray. In *Rachel Ray* [13] we see Luke Rowan, despite the fact that he is a Radical in politics, pray the Lord's Prayer before going to bed at night. When Trollope does show a character praying he seldom intrudes too deeply into that prayer. In *Barchester Towers* there is an exception: Archdeacon Grantly sinks to his knees beside the bed of his dying father, the bishop, when he cannot rid his mind of the thought that only if his father dies quickly will he become the next bishop. Trollope gives us this rare insight to balance his description of the archdeacon as a 'worldly' man [1]. In the novels written in the 1870s one begins to see characters, usually young men, who are not more given to praying than to attending church. In *Mr Scarborough's Family* the fiancée of a young brewer is asked if her lover prays: '"I'm sure he does," said Molly, with confidence more or less well founded' [59].

One form of prayer was particularly disliked by Trollope and that was grace before meals. In *Doctor Thorne* [19] in an extended 'authorial intrusion' he writes that 'such utterances are seldom prayers, seldom can be prayers... Dinner-graces are, probably, the last remaining relic of certain daily [monastic] services which the Church in olden days enjoined ... Let any man ask himself whether, on his own part, they are acts of prayer and thanksgiving – and if not that, what then?' In a later edition of the novel he added a footnote against the word 'services' to justify his argument: 'It is, I know, alleged that graces are said before dinner, because our Saviour uttered a blessing before his last supper. I cannot say that the idea of such analogy is pleasing to me.'

Prayer Book. Trollope was familiar with the Book of Common Prayer through the services he attended as a schoolboy at Harrow and Winchester. At Winchester he attended both the college chapel and the cathedral. As an adult he was a regular attender at church and in Ireland would have heard the same service as in England. In most English parishes Sunday morning service consisted of Morning Prayer and what was called the Ante-Communion, that is, that part of the service of Holy Communion up to and including the Prayer for the Church Militant. He also would have heard Evensong and the Litany. He quotes from or paraphrases the Prayer Book at least fourteen times in his novels: he quotes from the Holy Communion, the Litany, the baptism service and the wedding service. He uses the service of Holy Communion to greatest effect in his Christmas short story, 'Not If I Know It'. Whereas most of his quotations from the Bible are by his characters, nine of the fourteen quotations from the Prayer Book are by Trollope as narrator. The Prayer Book also influenced his style: he liked to use conjunctions – 'and' and especially 'but' – just as Cranmer had done in compiling the book. [➤ Church of England; Religion.]

Prebendary. See Church of England.

The Prime Minister. Trollope's thirty-third novel, the fifth in the Palliser series, was written between 2 April and 15 September 1874. It was published by Chapman & Hall in eight monthly parts between November 1875 and June 1876 at 5s. per part. [➤ Publishers and Publishing.] It was then published in four volumes by Chapman & Hall in May 1876. (George Eliot's *Daniel Deronda* was also published in eight parts and then as a four-volume novel in 1876.) Trollope received £2,500.

In *The Prime Minister*, we reach the high point of the Palliser series when Plantagenet Palliser, who succeeded as Duke of Omnium in *Phineas Redux*, becomes Prime Minister. Perhaps more importantly, his wife is able to play the dominant role in Society that she has long craved. The novel is really made up of two separate stories, each of which has sub-plots, and the two stories are only loosely connected. One is centred on Ferdinand Lopez who marries Emily Wharton, the daughter of a rich barrister. Lopez is

an adventurer and when he appears no one knows much about his background. There are rumours, which most think are true, that he is Portuguese and possibly Jewish. Some think he is a 'grandee of Spain' or an Italian nobleman, while others are content with the general denunciation of him as a 'greasy black foreigner'. Certainly he is stunningly handsome, but as with Burgo Fitzgerald in the first Palliser novel, this is no recommendation to his creator. The different values of an earlier century are revealed when Trollope comments that his teeth, which are 'perfect in form and whiteness', do 'not generally recommend a man to the unconscious judgement' of other men [1].

It is easy to see the portrayal of Lopez as anti-semitic but we are never certain what Lopez is by race, and as far as religion is concerned he says he is a member of the Church of England. Old Mr Wharton's fury at his daughter's choice of a husband leads him to tell Lopez, quite frankly, that he does not approve of him because he is not 'an English gentleman'. Wharton and his cousins in Herefordshire are old-fashioned Tories and like most such, they live in the country, away from London [➤ Landed Estates; Miss Stanbury in *He Knew He Was Right*; Sir Harry Hotspur in *Sir Harry Hotspur of Humblethwaite*; Lady Lufton in the Barsetshire novels]. Their views must not be taken to represent Trollope's own, although he probably shared some of them in a milder form. The real objection to Lopez is that he is an outsider, a man about whom nobody knows anything. One thing that often seems strange to people coming to Trollope's fiction for the first time is the way in which characters so often know essential facts about other characters they have yet to meet. They know where they come from, with whom they are connected, and what they are worth. Yet in this, as in so much else, Trollope was simply representing – with only a mild exaggeration – reality, as anyone who reads widely in Victorian letters and diaries can attest.

The appearance of a Lopez or his predecessor, Melmotte in *The Way We Live Now*, threatened the cosy exclusiveness of the world of the Victorian upper classes, especially in London. Lopez is a much more attractive – and not just physically attractive – character than Melmotte and one does wish that Trollope had given us more of an insight into his past and his real hopes. Lopez's suicide at 'Tenways Junction' (apparently based on Willesden) is one of the most carefully constructed and exciting episodes in all the novels [60].

By normal Trollopian standards, Wharton bears some responsibility for the breakdown of his daughter's marriage as he had refused not only to give his daughter a settlement, but to have any discussion about money with his future son-in-law. The plight of Emily Wharton, once she is married to Lopez, is well drawn and the horrible position of Victorian wives like her is well expressed in Lopez's sneering comment to her father: 'She belongs to me – not to you or herself' [52]. The scenes of the Wharton family in Herefordshire are also well done and the baronet is an excellent example of his type. To those who know Trollope's hatred of pretension, Lopez giving a dinner-party in the *service à la Russe* style is no surprise. An added touch is that having asked a caterer to arrange the meal, Lopez leaves the account for his father-in-law to settle.

The Lopez plot is connected to the second and major plot by the *arriviste*'s sudden popularity with the Duchess of Omnium. This, the Palliser plot, tells the story of the Omnium government and their struggle to survive. The duchess is ever anxious for new 'swans' to add interest to her parties, while for his part the latest 'swan' thinks her favour will gain the duke's support when he stands in a by-election at Silverbridge, a Barsetshire town in which the Pallisers formerly controlled elections. (The by-election is caused because John Grey, 'the worthy man' of *Can You Forgive Her?*, resigns his seat to go on a diplomatic mission to Persia.) However, the duke is furious because he has announced that he no longer intends to exercise any electoral influence in the borough. Here Trollope is, as usual, only reflecting what was happening in the real world: after the 1867 Reform Act enlarged the electorate and the Ballot Act of 1872 did away with open voting, the 'pocket boroughs' of great magnates began to slip from their grasp. (In the same year in which this novel was written, Lord Randolph Churchill had a difficult contest for the Borough of Woodstock, at the very gates of his father's Blenheim Palace.) Elections were fresh in Trollope's mind as he had been busy throughout February 'speechifying and canvassing' (to quote his sister-in-law) in a vain attempt to get his fellow novelist, the Radical Thomas Hughes of *Tom Brown's Schooldays*, re-elected to Parliament.

Disraeli had become prime minister for the second time only six weeks before Trollope started writing the novel. No doubt the great electoral triumph of the Conservatives in 1874 (their first since 1841) greatly annoyed Trollope and contributed to the venom in his portrait of Lopez, an alien adventurer who shares a few characteristics with Disraeli. However, there is no comparison between the real government of Disraeli and the Duke of Omnium's fictional one. The most obvious difference is that while Omnium forms a coalition government, Disraeli was well known for his aphorism, 'England hates coalitions.'

The duke's first trouble in forming his government comes from his own wife, who desires the post of Mistress of the Robes. This was the highest office a lady could hold in the Royal Household and the filling of it was normally a burden to every Victorian prime minister. Years before, Disraeli had written amusingly in *Coningsby* that the difficulties of forming the Royal Household could be as great as those involved in forming a Cabinet. He certainly found it so in reality.

It is fascinating to observe how the relationship between the duke and the duchess develops. The duke, Trollope observes in a most interesting aside, is 'always right in his purpose but generally wrong in his practice' [20]. The duchess often seems to be wrong in both, yet she retains that charming lack of restraint that Trollope normally only allows to American women or to spinsters. She does, however, acquire a special duchess's smile to bestow on inferiors. Her passion for entertaining had no parallel among real Victorian prime ministers' wives other than Lady Palmerston and it is interesting to note that one of Trollope's friends, Abraham Hayward, had

acted as Lady Palmerston's adviser on invitations to her famous receptions. In the last chapter, when the duke has resigned his office, the duchess sums up the difference between them: 'He wouldn't understand what I felt about it; how proud I was that he should be Prime Minister, how anxious that he should be great and noble in his office ...Oh how I did labour for him and how he did scold me ... I was vulgar.' No contemporary reader knew it, but that is the last time the duchess appears as a living person in his novels.

As in the other Palliser novels, familiar names pass in and out of government and drawing-rooms. In the Omnium administration, Phineas Finn becomes Chief Secretary for Ireland and eventually First Lord of the Admiralty. Now the once 'poor' (in the Trollopian sense) Irish MP and his exotic wife, the former Madame Max Goesler, enjoy a cruise on the First Lord's official yacht. (The real yacht had been romantically named *The Enchantress*.) Finn's appointment may seem rather extraordinary but only a few years later Queen Victoria warned Disraeli that admirals might dislike it if 'a man of the Middle Class is placed above them'. That particular man was none other than W. H. Smith, a great power in the world of circulating libraries and railway bookstalls. It was he who was later parodied in Gilbert and Sullivan's *HMS Pinafore*. Finn's denunciation of Irish Home Rule reflects Trollope's own views [12]. When discussing this Trollope makes a curious error in having Finn, a Catholic, say that England does not elect Catholic MPs: Finn himself had sat for English seats and was apparently still doing so. (When Trollope stood for Beverley in 1868, the other Liberal candidate for that two-member constituency was a local Catholic landowner.)

Of all the Palliser novels this one has the closest link with the earlier Barsetshire series. Frank Gresham, who had played such a prominent role in *Doctor Thorne*, reappears in the account of the Silverbridge election when he helps his friend Arthur Fletcher defeat Lopez. There is an amusing aside when Gresham is worried that Lopez and Fletcher may come to blows and Trollope recounts how twenty years ago Frank had thought differently when he horse-whipped another parliamentary candidate who had jilted his sister. It is also appropriate in a novel that has so much in common with *The Way We Live Now* that that novel's Lady Carbury makes a brief appearance.

The Prime Minister illustrates how Trollope kept up with changing fashions: the Whartons search for a 'flat' while the Duke of Omnium, in one of Trollope's private jokes, drinks that popular new beverage, Apollinaris mineral water [➤ Drinks]. We also get intimations of a new topic in British politics when Emily's brother goes off to Germany to study German politics; in an earlier chapter we even hear of Bismarck [20]. Yet in spite of these mild touches *The Prime Minister* is ultimately a conservative novel, because the old order, represented by the Whartons, manages to see off the alien dangers represented by Lopez.

Trollope himself admitted to his favourite correspondent, Mary Holmes, that he had used the Lopez part of the novel as a 'shoehorn' to carry on the story of the Pallisers. He was satisfied with the Palliser story in the novel, but felt that the Lopez side was 'bad'. Many of the critics disagreed and pre-

ferred it to the political part. *The Prime Minister* was still appearing in part issue when Trollope wrote his assessment of the book in his *Autobiography* and discussed what he had been trying to do with his 'perfect gentleman', the Duke of Omnium. Two years later he opened the sealed manuscript and added a note: 'I am obliged to say that as regards the public, *The Prime Minister* was a failure. It was worse spoken of by the Press than any novel I had written.' He admitted that he was 'specially hurt' by the review in the *Spectator*. This was because he wrongly assumed that it had been written by R. H. Hutton, his most perceptive critic. However, it seems to have been written by M. W. Meredith, who denounced the novel for attributing 'to the majority of mankind an inherent vulgarity of thought'. 'Vulgarity' was a frequent charge levelled against Trollope. (The reviewer also said that the duchess's refusal to invite Sir Orlando Drought to dinner was impossible as no prime minister's wife would refuse to invite one of her husband's colleagues. Actually Sir Robert Peel's wife had tried to do just that by declining to invite the Duke of Wellington.) The novel was also criticized for its length and this impression was made all the worse by its part issue and then by its publication in *four* volumes.

There is no doubt that the unfavourable reactions hurt Trollope, because he added a second footnote to his *Autobiography* in which he said the reviews 'seemed to tell me that my work as a novelist should be brought to a close'. Trollope never knew of the comment of another novelist who would create another famous railway suicide in one of his own enormous novels. After reading *The Prime Minister*, Tolstoy wrote: 'Trollope kills me with his excellence.'

Private Jokes. Private jokes and references occur in almost every Trollope work of fiction. Usually only he, his family or his close friends would have recognized them. While hundreds may be identified, no one today can pick up every one. Those that have been identified may, however, be divided into groups, the single largest of which is his choice of names for characters: Frederic and Harry (his two sons), Florence (his niece and amanuensis), and Fanny (his mother) are among those he used most. Indeed in *Mr Scarborough's Family*, his last novel published, there is a niece named Florence. While he does not use his wife's name, Rose, he does refer to her in various ways. In *The Last Chronicle of Barset* there is a reference to a painting, a version of 'The Three Graces'; his wife and her sisters had been called 'The Three Graces' in their Yorkshire home. In *Barchester Towers* and *The Claverings* he refers to a jewel that Fanny Trollope had given to his wife. In *The Small House at Allington* Bell Dale's real name is Isabella, the name of Rose Trollope's sister. In 'The Two Heroines of Plumplington' Mr Greenmantle is, like Rose's father, a banker who lives 'above the shop', who considers himself very much a 'gentleman' and who employs a man whom he wishes to become his son-in-law. (In real life this happened, but not in the short story.) References to sewing are an oblique tribute to his wife's skill with the needle. In *The Eustace Diamonds* a character is married in the Embassy chapel in Paris, just as Trollope's

brother Tom had been. In *He Knew He Was Right* Miss Stanbury's devotion to the arch reactionary, Lord Eldon, reflects Trollope's father's hatred of the Tory Lord Chancellor. There are references to his Irish manservant, Barney Fitzgerald (or Smith) in *An Eye for an Eye* and *The Land-Leaguers*.

There are jokes Trollope shared with his friends: references to George Eliot and G. H. Lewes in 'Josephine de Montmorenci' and to Thackeray as 'that bad man' who attacks mothers-in-law in *The Small House at Allington*. He had George Smith in mind when referring to Apollinaris water, which Smith sold in the United Kingdom, or to gambling losses at Homburg, as Smith had lost money when gambling at that spa [*The Small House at Allington*]. Mountjoy Scarborough loses a fortune at whist in *Mr Scarborough's Family* and Captain De Baron grew fat playing the same game in *Is He Popenjoy?* It was Trollope's favourite card game as it had been his father's and mother's. In *Ayala's Angel* there is a complimentary reference to Cunard's ships: his friend John Burns was eventually head of the company [➤ *How the 'Mastiffs' Went to Iceland*]. The reference to 'our excellent American friend and critic, Mr Hawthorne', who described some English ladies as 'beefy' in *Can You Forgive Her?* [33], is a joke against himself. Trollope carried about with him Nathaniel Hawthorne's comment praising Trollope's novels as 'just as English as a beefsteak'. In *The Way We Live Now* there is something approaching black humour in references to a scandal at the Post Office. This involved his arch-enemy, Frank Scudamore, who was made Assistant Secretary of the Post Office, a position for which Trollope had applied and for which he was better qualified [Mullen, 555–6, 715].

A third and very large group of jokes relates to Trollope himself. When he has young men told by older women that they should go home at night to read good books and drink tea he is remembering advice given him as a young Post Office clerk in London. He was playing a joke on himself when in 'Lotta Schmidt' and elsewhere the bald middle-aged man defeats the 'curled darling' for the love of a young woman. His references to London literary chaps in *Can You Forgive Her?* and 'Miss Ophelia Gledd', to an irate traveller who denounces a railway porter in *The Land-Leaguers*, and to Post Office officials who disturb the peace of a village post office in *The Small House at Allington*, are all to himself. There are frequent humorous references to the Post Office, like that to the 'self-sacrificing patriotism of the Post Office' in *Is He Popenjoy?* [20]. In the same novel, Dean Lovelace smokes in the Deanery garden as Trollope did in his own: it was the only place in which Rose allowed him to smoke. There are jokes based on his favourite breed of dogs, and references to his favourite wine. In *The Eustace Diamonds* he makes a joke about his attempt at writing a play, 'The Noble Jilt'. There are several references to Mudie's Circulating Library, to which he owed his great fame, to Harrow School, which he attended, to his favourite horses, Banker and Buff [*Marion Fay*], and to his own love of John Milton, especially his poem *Lycidas*. When Joshua Thoroughbung comes home from a hunt in *Mr Scarborough's Family* [29] he is greeted with 'a cup of tea and buttered toast' by his fiancée, just as Trollope was greeted by Rose when he got in from a hunt. There are numerous references to pillar-boxes, which Trollope invented, and (in *The Eustace Diamonds*) to the *Fortnightly Review*, which he helped to found. The Irish witness in the trial in *Castle Richmond* [35] is based on his own experience as a witness. In *Cousin Henry* an uncle leaves a niece £4,000 in a will just as Trollope was doing when he wrote the novel. He frequently praises the glory of a man's beard, reflecting his own, and as frequently refers to people living on £800 a year, his own income from the Post Office for many years. In *The Fixed Period* he refers to 'the great Banting', the man who devised a diet which Trollope endured to little effect. In *An Editor's Tales*, a collection of short stories based on his own experiences when editor of *Saint Pauls*, he makes numerous jokes at himself as editor.

On several occasions he refers to buildings or places associated with his own life, like Keppel Street, streets and buildings in 'Littlebath' (Cheltenham), the Marylebone Road or Mecklenburgh Square [➤ Money-lenders] in London. Barristers often have chambers in Lincoln's Inn, in which his father had chambers. In *Can You Forgive Her?* Alice Vavasor is sent to a school in Aix-la-Chapelle, just as Trollope's niece, Florence, was. There are frequent jokes about baronets, especially the snobbishness based on the dates of creation: there were two baronetcies in his family. The short stories 'John Bull on the Guadalquivir', 'Father Giles of Ballymoy' and 'The O'Conors of Castle Conor' are extended jokes against himself. Sometimes jokes are at the expense of his own habits, for instance in 'The

Mistletoe Bough' where he has a joke about work sheets, to which he was addicted. In *The Last Chronicle of Barset* Lady Julia De Guest asks John Eames to get her spectacles at Dolland's, where Trollope got his own massive collection of glasses, and in *John Caldigate* the hero stumbles about with a heavy portmanteau, just as Trollope did when travelling. In his fox-hunting scenes there are references to overweight men, like himself, who ride to hounds badly but with enthusiasm. In *Is He Popenjoy?* the 'hotel in Suffolk Street' where Dean Lovelace stays was Garlant's, where Trollope himself often stayed.

Sometimes illustrations were private jokes: in *Orley Farm* his friend John Everett Millais provided a drawing of Orley Farm which was in fact of Trollope's parents' second house in Harrow. The illustration of Mr Round's office shows boxes containing clients' papers and one is marked 'A. Trollope'. Two others are marked 'I. (Iosephus or Joseph) Mason' and 'V. R. (Victoria Regina])' implying Mr Round was Queen Victoria's solicitor.

[➤ Classics; Names, Origin of; Names, Silly.]

Professions. Trollope often used this term with regard to clergymen and this has led some readers to think he had a low regard for the priest's sacred calling. But Trollope's use was a common sense one: a profession was defined in *The Bertrams* [8] as 'a calling by which a gentleman, not born to the gentleman's allowance of good things, might ingeniously obtain the same by some exercise of his abilities.' Finding a profession was often difficult for Trollope's young men. In *The Claver-*

ings Harry Clavering had to decide between the Church of England and engineering as he knew he would lose his Oxford fellowship by marrying. Having no vocation to the priesthood he chose engineering. The difficulty was greater for those in the upper classes or for heirs to landed estates. In *Mr Scarborough's Family* Peter Prosper gave his nephew, Harry Annesley, an allowance because he was his heir and insisted that the young man 'should follow no profession' [23]. He already had a 'profession' as heir. In *Can You Forgive Her?* Jeffrey Palliser has difficulty managing on £600 a year and, as his cousin Plantagenet Palliser says, 'It is a pity you should do nothing all your life' [25]. The possibilities open to him, other than being, for a while, Plantagenet's heir, were farming, Parliament, the Civil Service, or marriage to a rich woman. The last was the one he most preferred.

Trollope always insisted that writing was a profession as much as the law, medicine, the Civil Service and the Church, although normally only barristers are shown exercising their 'profession'. The nineteenth century saw a burgeoning of this term, its use as a new social category, and an extension of its application. Trollope shared in all this and was very liberal in his use of the term. He had no doubt that engineers were professional men, as were civil servants in the Post Office, as well as those in the more prestigious Foreign Office. Not all his characters shared his liberal views. Miss Marrable in *The Vicar of Bullhampton* had no doubt that the only professions 'intended for gentlemen' were the Church, the law, the army and the navy. As to physicians, the Civil Service and engineers, she was in doubt. Solicitors were most definitely not gentlemen. Her views were becoming quickly out of date as the century progressed [*The Vicar of Bullhampton*, 9].

Proposals. See Marriage.

Prostitutes. Because Trollope meant his novels to reflect Victorian society, because so many of them are set, at least in part, in London, and because so many feature young bachelors, dealing with prostitution was a constant difficulty. The question was one of censorship: novels were often read aloud and the novelists' readership was largely among young women. Prostitution was not a subject that the novelist would lightheartedly touch on as he knew it would risk censorship by the editor, especially if the work were serialized.

Prostitution was rife and London was notorious: estimates for the number of prostitutes in the capital varied wildly in mid-century from 5,000 to 80,000. One researcher estimated that in 1857 there was one prostitute for every eighty-one adult males in London. Procurement was easy because it was not until 1885 that the age of consent for girls was raised from twelve to sixteen. In his own life the subject arose in 1872 when Trollope's elder son Henry announced that he wanted to marry what Trollope's friend G. H. Lewes called a 'woman of the town'. Instead his father sent him to Australia, which cured him.

Trollope first touched on prostitution in his eighth novel, *The Bertrams*, in which he refers to the old roué, Sir Lionel Bertram, as having taken 'another smaller establishment in a secluded quiet street' [21]. This really referred to lodgings for a mistress or 'kept woman' as opposed to one of the prostitutes that one saw on the street. Four years after *The Bertrams* he began writing *Can You Forgive Her?*, in which he first clearly included a prostitute. The 'curled darling', Burgo Fitzgerald, walks down London's Oxford Street after his plan to elope with Lady Glencora Palliser has fallen through. He is accosted by a 'poor wretched girl' who asks for money with which to buy gin. Instead Burgo takes her into a public house and ensures she has a proper meal after which he gives her money for a bed and breakfast. The ruined man who has nothing to look forward to but exile says to the prostitute, 'We are alike then.' It is significant that over the Christmas during which Trollope was writing this novel his American friend William Glenn, a Southern sympathizer and journalist from Maryland who came to England to escape further imprisonment by Lincoln, was staying with the Trollopes. He was shocked at the numbers of prostitutes he had seen when walking along London streets. It was not for nothing that ladies like Rose Trollope used a carriage when in London.

When in 1866 Trollope wrote 'Lotta Schmidt', his short story set in Vienna, he used a beer-hall as background and reminded his readers that in Vienna the sort of young women who went there were respectable working girls. He added that if he were to write about the same young women in London, 'I should be supposed to be speaking of young women as to whom it would be better that I should be silent' – that is, prostitutes. Two years later when writing *The Vicar of Bullhampton* he decided he would not 'be silent'. He tackled the problem head on when villagers in Bullhampton say that Carry Brattle, the miller's run-away daughter, is a prostitute, although the fact is never established. It was the first time he used the actual word [17] and in a preface he warned readers that he would have a girl in his story who was a 'castaway'. He argued that it was right that a novelist who wrote 'for the amusement of the young of both sexes' should include such a character. His aim was to increase compassion: 'Cannot women, who are good, pity the sufferings of the vicious, and do something perhaps to mitigate and shorten them, without contamination from the vice?'

Trollope never apologized for Carry or argued that prostitution was anything but a 'vice'. He accepted that the punishment of social ostracism placed on prostitutes was necessary as a deterrent. However, the punishment was too great if no room for repent-ance and reform were allowed. Even so, Trollope does not trespass against reality: Carry Brattle is brought back from degradation to decency but she is not 'married to a wealthy lover'. While things could never be as they were he wanted to show that there was 'a way out of perdition'. The last sen-tence of his preface reads: 'It may also at last be felt that this misery is worthy of alleviation, as is every misery to which humanity is subject.' In making the prostitute a working-class girl from the country who was seduced and then ended up in London he was reflecting a well-established Victorian myth. More usually prosti-tutes were working-class girls who worked part-time to supplement a family's income or to earn something when unemployed. The work was also seasonal: there were more prostitutes in warmer months and fewer in colder.

In 1869 Trollope continued his new outspokenness in a review in *Saint Pauls* of Dion Boucicault's West End play *Formosa*, which dealt with prosti-tutes. He attacked it because its por-trayal of prostitutes was 'false to human nature, false to London life'. He added, however, 'We do not think that any attempt should be made to conceal the existence of such a class of women from our wives and daughters.' The plight of prostitutes should be neither glorified nor ignored. In 1870 when *Sir Harry Hotspur of Humblethwaite* was published, it is clear that the dissolute George Hotspur has what the late twentieth century calls a 'relationship' with the actress, Mrs Lucy Morton. In his notes Trollope referred to her as 'the woman with whom [George Hotspur] ... is entan-gled – ill used' [Mullen, 183]. While she may not, perhaps, be called his mis-tress, she was definitely not a prosti-tute. On the other hand, one is not supposed to think her a virgin. In *An Eye for an Eye*, begun in the very week in which the French Empire fell, Trol-lope referred to the heir of an ancient earldom's marrrying 'a wretched painted hussy from France' [1]. [➤ Mistresses.]

PROUDIE FAMILY

Members of this fictional family are described below.

Proudie, The Rt Rev. Thomas. Proudie is made Bishop of Barchester at the start of *Barchester Towers*, in succession to old Bishop Grantly. He is nominated by a Liberal govern-ment because he had made himself conspicuous in supporting reform measures and by serving on various committees. Trollope sees him as an example of a new type of bishop: the committee man and administrator as opposed to the older type of bishop, the great local lord, who was more like the bishops of the Middle Ages. (Trollope discussed these changes in the episcopate in his 1865 *Pall Mall Gazette* essay, 'English Bishops, New and Old', later included in his collection *Clergymen of the Church of England*.) Proudie has minor aristocratic connections as the nephew of an Irish baron. His income as bishop has been cut to £5,000 a year by recent legislation. This encourages him to be parsimonious in his entertainments in Barchester, as he is anxious to make a figure in London Society. Bishop Proudie appears in all the Barsetshire novels after *Barchester Towers* and is also alluded to briefly in *The Claverings* [2] and *He Knew He Was Right* [49]. Everyone who encounters the bishop knows that the real power resides in his formidable wife. This, concludes Trollope, undermines his authority: 'He might have been a sufficiently good bishop, had it not been that Mrs Proudie was so much more than a sufficiently good bishop's wife' [*The Last Chronicle of Barset*, 82]. [➤ Church of England.]

Proudie, Mrs. Mrs Proudie is 'a tyrant, a bully, a would-be priestess' [*Autobiography*]. She outranks her husband socially as she is the niece of a Scottish earl. Like the bishop, she appears in all the Barsetshire novels after *Barchester Towers*. She is a dedicated Evangelical and is at first 'guided' by Mr Slope. She makes herself unpopular by her attempts to control everything in the diocese, by her cheapness, by the fact that she spends so much time in London and spends

so little money in Barchester. Although Trollope presents her in a series of outrageous incidents, he was plainly sorry to have to kill her in the final Barsetshire novel. His story that he was spurred on to do so after overhearing two clergymen in the Athenaeum club abuse him for re-using her has been questioned; it is more likely he had decided to kill her when planning the novel [Mullen, 458–9]. In the end, before she dies, he does try to show she has a few good qualities [*The Last Chronicle of Barset*, 56], but her unforgivable sin was not that she ruled her husband but that she did so in public [➤ Marriage]. A few years after Trollope's death, Henry James commented that 'Mrs Proudie has become classical; of all Trollope's characters she is the most referred to.' [➤ *Barchester Towers* for Mrs Proudie's place among domineering Victorian wives.] Although Trollope says that the Proudies have seven or eight children, he only gives some attention to three daughters.

Proudie daughters. The three mentioned are Olivia, Augusta and Netta. Olivia is the eldest and at one time had 'some passages of love' with Mr Slope. All three girls are proud of their aristocratic connections and therefore become jealous of Griselda Grantly's marriage to a peer. Olivia even sends an anonymous letter to Griselda's mother when she thinks her rival's romance has failed [*Framley Parsonage*, 45]. Olivia finally marries a clergyman who is a widower, while one of her sisters also marries a clergyman. Neither husband appears to be a good match.

Public Opinion. Trollope's connection

with this weekly publication dates from December 1860 when he sold the rights to eight short stories to the *London Review*. In the event that magazine only published three because of the controversy which arose. The magazine's manager, William Little, sold the remaining five stories to *Public Opinion*, a magazine of which Trollope had not heard. Publication took place over eight weeks, between 16 November and 28 December 1861. The five stories, in order of publication, were: 'The Man Who Kept His Money in a Box'; 'The House of Heine Brothers in Munich'; 'Returning Home'; 'Aaron Trow'; 'George Walker at Suez'.

Public Schools. Public schools enjoyed a Golden Age in Victorian Britain. Trollope's *Autobiography* presents an unfavourable picture of his own experiences from 1823 to 1834 at two of the ancient schools, Harrow and Winchester. His account was undoubtedly exaggerated, especially with regard to his own unending misery and his reputation as an 'incorrigible dunce', perhaps – unconsciously – to emphasize his subsequent but delayed rise to respectability as a civil servant and to success as a novelist. (The fact that he was not the 'dunce' he proclaimed is seen in his winning a prize at Harrow for an English essay, a fact he does not mention in the *Autobiography*. However, he does mention the fact that he won an important fight, which surely raised his standing among his peers.) A second description of his schooldays at Harrow survives in his analysis of a poem by his mother about Harrow, written when Trollope was in his late teens. In it he comments severely on his schoolmasters [Mullen, 25–6]. A

third source is his article 'Public Schools' in the *Fortnightly Review* of 1865, in which he took a far more traditional view of public schools as 'the backbone of English public and social life'. This needs to be read as a corrective to the *Autobiography* and his teenage criticisms.

Although Trollope had a more extensive experience of two of the most important public schools than any other great Victorian novelist, he gave little detailed attention either to them or to public schools in general in his novels. Young men are almost always introduced into his novels after they have left school and there is only an occasional reference to their schoolboy experiences. The main benefit arising from public schools is the deep bonds of friendship forged at them. Mark Robarts's schooldays at Harrow with young Lord Lufton form the basis of his whole fortune in life. Ironically, such friendships were not experienced by Trollope himself.

Trollope did not engage, at least to any great extent, in the traditional devotion to his own school, or rather schools, at the expense of others. Harrow, it is true, seems to get a goodly portion of manly young chaps such as Lord Lufton and Winchester gets some brainy lads like two of the leading characters in *The Bertrams*, as well as Francis Arabin, the future Dean of Barchester. [➤ under *The Three Clerks* for one use Trollope made of his Winchester days.] Trollope's aristocrats, such as the Pallisers, seem to favour Eton, but so do boys from new wealth such as Tom Tringle in *Ayala's Angel*, and less edifying youths like Louis Scatcherd in *Doctor Thorne*. There is an interesting moment in *The Kellys and the O'Kellys* when the scoundrel, Barry Lynch, attempts to call on an old school loyalty when talking to his fellow Etonian, Lord Ballandine, but this falls on deaf and virtuous ears [35]. The only school for which Trollope had a pronounced dislike was Cheltenham College.

Unlike his father, Trollope did not look down on the newer public schools and sent his two sons to a new, High Church public school, Bradfield. It cost him about £130 a year for each boy there, or about five per cent of his annual income for the two of them.

Despite the 'misery' of his schoolboy life as described in the *Autobiography*, Trollope was much affected by his own public school days. The earliest surviving piece of his writing is the analysis of his mother's poem mentioned above. His schooldays gave him an excellent insight into clerical characters as all his masters were clergymen, and a thorough grounding in the classics which was to last him a lifetime. His schools also played a part in implanting in him a yearning to be regarded as a serious writer and not merely as a novelist. [➤ *The New Zealander*; Travel Books.]

Finally, Trollope's own real unhappiness gave him that genuine sympathy for misfortune which is so conspicuous in his writing. He often liked to insert a little 'sermon' in his novels showing that boys who were remarkable for their success at school did not normally achieve such distinction in later life [*Can You Forgive Her?*, 16]. Maurice Maule, Trollope's finest portrait of an idle and useless man, 'at school had done great things ... one of those show boys of which two or three are generally to be found at our great schools' [*Phineas Redux*, 21].

Publishers and Publishing. The world of Victorian publishing, of books, part issues, magazine and newspaper serialization and circulating libraries, was complex and changed considerably in Trollope's lifetime. [➤ Mudie's Circulating Library.] The greatest changes from the eighteenth century were: an enormous expansion of publishing houses which grew, collapsed and re-grouped with great rapidity; the growth of circulating libraries like Mudie's; the issuing of instalments of novels in monthly or weekly 'part' issues; the serializing of novels in monthly or weekly magazines, and in newspapers, to be published in book form at or near the end of the serialization. These magazines were generally established by publishers or printers like Blackwood, George Smith, Macmillan or Chapman & Hall. The circulating library, by which is mainly meant Mudie's, dominated literature in Trollope's day and authors could only earn large amounts if their novels were serialized. Publishers do not frequently appear in his fiction, but in *The Vicar of Bullhampton* he refers to Messrs Bringémout ('bring 'em out'); and Neversell [68]. [➤ Names, Silly].

Trollope, who was interested in publishing and who was very well informed, was connected with all forms of publishing as his works appeared in book form, part issues, magazine and newspaper serialization and in combinations of all of these. He was published by sixteen different publishers. Chapman & Hall published 32 books; Blackwood, 6; Smith, Elder, 5; while Strahan and Chatto & Windus published 3 each. Colburn, Longman, Virtue, Hurst & Blackett and Isbister published 2 each; Newby, Bentley,

Bradbury, Evans, Tinsley, Sampson Low and Macmillan published 1 each. His publishing career falls into two periods. From his first novel in 1847 to *Castle Richmond* in 1860, all 9 novels were published only as completed books. From *Framley Parsonage* in 1860 to his death, 38 novels were published in five separate forms: 25 were serialized in magazines and then published as books; 6 were published in monthly parts and then as books; 4 appeared only as books; 2 were published in weekly parts and then as books, and 1 was serialized in a weekly newspaper and then published as a book. (His short book, *How the 'Mastiffs' Went to Iceland*, was published privately by Virtue.) [➤ 'Three-deckers'.]

When he offered *The West Indies and the Spanish Main* to Chapman & Hall, he wrote, 'Ah – I wish Providence had made me a publisher.' Providence did make him one when he became a large shareholder and director of Chapman & Hall but he cared little for the work. He also paid for his son Henry to become a partner in that firm. He was friendly with a variety of publishers such as George Smith and John Blackwood and was the most active member of the Royal Commission on Copyright (1876–7) which in effect examined publishing as well as copyright.

Details of publication of individual books and Trollope's business-like manners are discussed under the novels' respective titles and under Honesty. Victorian publishing is discussed in detail in Mullen, Chapter 5.

Puseyite. See Church of England.

Q

Quakers. Trollope particularly disliked Quakers. His first reference appears in *The Warden* [10] in which he includes a passing sneer about a London meeting of 'Quakers and Mr Cobden' to launch an appeal to aid the Russian Tsar (Nicholas I) shortly before Britain went to war against Russia. Within months of writing this he returned to the subject in *The New Zealander*. 'Practical Quakerism can hardly be said to be natural to an Englishman. One might as well attempt to persuade one's bulldog to allow his favourite bone to be taken without resistance from between his jaws, by the semishorn parlour poodle.' In *North America* he wrote that Pennsylvania had 'all those marks which Quakers generally leave behind them' among which he included 'a low character for commercial honesty and a certain flavour of pretentious hypocrisy'. When creating the character of Mrs Crump, who berates the Post Office inspector in *The Small House at Allington*, he drew on his own encounter with the Cornish Quaker sub-postmistress, Betsy Trembath, and remembered his treatment at her hands [21, 60]. In *The Eustace Diamonds* he has Frank Greystock quote 'the Quaker's advice to the old farmer, "Doan't thou marry for munny, but goa where munny is!"' [13]. (Until the middle of the nineteenth century Quakers could only marry Quakers, thereby helping to build up wealthy Quaker families like the Cadburys and Rowntrees.)

His most extensive treatment of Quakers is in *Marion Fay*, in the characters of Marion and her elderly father, Zachary. Here Trollope tried, as always, to be fair and Marion is one of his most noble heroines. As to Zachary, he agreed that the elder Fay 'loved money' but commented that 'he that does not love money must be an idiot', and added, 'He was a stern, hard, just man, of whom it may probably be said that if a world were altogether composed of such, the condition of such a world would be much better than that of the world we know; for generosity is less efficacious towards permanent good than justice, and tender speaking less enduring in its beneficial results than truth' [15]. Trollope also singled out the father's use of 'thee' and 'thou' for special condemnation as 'that touch of hypocrisy'. By the time he wrote this, the use was fast fading and it is not surprising, therefore, that Marion does not use the words.

Quiverful, The Rev. and Mrs. While Mr Quiverful is given no Christian name, his wife's is Letitia. The Quiverfuls appear in three of the Barsetshire novels, *The Warden*, *Barchester Towers* and *The Last Chronicle of Barset*, and

Mrs Quiverful appears alone in *Framley Parsonage*. They are most important in *Barchester Towers* where they are involved in the warfare between Obadiah Slope and Mrs Proudie over the vacancy at Hiram's Hospital caused by the resignation of Septimus Harding. Mr Quiverful is introduced as the Vicar of Puddingdale who survives on £400 a year. He and his wife have fourteen children (although sometimes Trollope gives a different figure). Mr Quiverful is a weak man, 'on the whole a worthy man ... an honest, pains-taking, drudging man', but not 'careful, as another might be who sat on an easier worldly seat, to stand well with those around him ... He could not afford such niceties of conduct ... It must suffice for him to be ordinarily honest'; he therefore ingratiates himself with Slope [*Barchester Towers*, 24]. His reward is, ultimately, the wardenship of Hiram's Hospital. Mr Quiverful also ingratiates himself with Bishop Proudie and is invited to become a member of the bishop's 'commission' to investigate the charges against Josiah Crawley in *The Last*

Chronicle of Barset. In that novel he is described as a man 'whose whole life had been devoted to fighting a cruel world on behalf of his wife and children. That fight he had fought bravely but it had left him no energy for any other business' [54].

Mrs Quiverful is a woman with 'nothing poetic' in her nature, a 'broad heavy woman, not young' who is forced to be the dominant partner in their marriage. She is instrumental in *Barchester Towers* in getting her husband appointed to the wardenship through her intervention with Mrs Proudie but she, too, pays a price. When she briefly appears in *Framley Parsonage* she does so as part of Mrs Proudie's court or, as Trollope aptly describes her, as one of Mrs Proudie's 'ecclesiastical listeners ... a lady who had received favours from her, and was therefore bound to listen attentively to her voice' [45].

The couple's surname is an example of Trollope's occasional use of a name to point to a particular feature, in this case a plenitude of children. [➤ Names, Silly.]

R

Rachel Ray. Trollope's thirteenth novel was written between 3 March and 29 June 1863. After difficulties with the serialization, the novel was published in two volumes by Chapman & Hall in October 1863. *Rachel Ray* caused Trollope more difficulty than almost any of his novels. In the spring of 1862, just after returning from America, he received a letter from Dr Norman Macleod, one of the best-known ministers in the Church of Scotland and editor of *Good Words*, a periodical launched at the same time as the *Cornhill*. Macleod wanted Trollope to write a novel to be serialized in the magazine and asked him to see the magazine's publisher, Alexander Strahan [➤ *Framley Parsonage*].

Good Words was already outselling the *Cornhill* in Scotland and Strahan was anxious to increase its English readership, composed mainly of Evangelicals and Dissenters. Knowing the importance of serialized fiction for any publication, Macleod had written a novel himself for *Good Words* in which a young Scottish sailor, 'Wee Davie', converted his crude shipmates to Evangelical Christianity. Yet both Macleod and Strahan knew that such propaganda would not gain more English readers: they needed to reach Anglican readers. Who better than the novelist already celebrated as the portrayer of Anglican clergymen? Mac-

leod knew Trollope to be 'a Christian worshipper ... an honest believer in Revealed Christian truth'. Trollope and Strahan soon agreed that the writer would provide both short stories and a novel: Strahan offered Trollope £1,000 for the book. For Trollope this was a welcome new market. He could not expect to be constantly published in the *Cornhill* and with his ability to produce novels so quickly he needed new audiences.

Trollope first had to write *The Small House at Allington* for the *Cornhill* but in March 1863 he started work on *Rachel Ray*. Strahan was already busy doing something Trollope detested: placarding London with advertising which proclaimed that *Good Words* would soon boast a new novel 'by the author of *Framley Parsonage*'. This stirred up a controversy with the magazine's main rival in the religious press: *The Record* had long been seen as the principal mouthpiece of English Evangelicals and it was not happy to see a Scottish rival. Uniting Evangelical beliefs with self-interested greed, *The Record* unleashed a barrage of attacks on 'this year's chief sensation-writer for *Good Words*...Anthony Trollope'. They were outraged that such 'trashy tales' could find a home in a Christian publication. Yet another religious publication, *The Patriot*, a Dissenting magazine, joined in the attack on 'Mr Trollope and others of his class' as 'sensation' writers. No doubt these attacks worried Strahan and apparently worried Macleod all the more. When Macleod began to read the early chapters of *Rachel Ray* he decided that it was entirely unsuitable for *Good Words*. In a letter which Trollope describes as 'full of wailing and repentance' Macleod explained that the novel failed to show any 'truly Christian' life. He was also afraid that the '*general impression*' of the novel would annoy Evangelicals and therefore *Good Words* could not serialize it. Trollope saw Strahan, and in a way entirely honourable to both, they agreed terms by which Trollope received £500 and was left free to have the novel published by Chapman & Hall, from whom he received £1,000.

To make fiction acceptable Evangelicals demanded that it be a fictional working-out of a religious truth, as Macleod's nautical tale had been. This was a staitjacket which would not fit Trollope. Indeed, one is amazed that an Evangelical publication would turn to Anthony Trollope for a novel. Perhaps Macleod and Strahan only knew *Framley Parsonage* in which Trollope's hostility towards Evangelicalism is not all that evident. If they had looked at *Barchester Towers* they would have seen how much Trollope had inherited his mother's well-known hatred of Evangelical clergymen.

In one sense Trollope did try to appeal to a different audience. His last few novels had been preoccupied with the 'comfortable classes' [➤ Money]. In *Rachel Ray*, he moved down in society, away from the world of the titled and wealthy. The plot of *Rachel Ray* is quite simple: young Rachel's love for a young man is opposed by two Evangelical bigots, but true love wins in the end. [For its origins, see below.] Rachel's mother is a widow living near 'Baslehurst', a town Trollope placed in his favourite county, Devonshire. Mrs Ray has less than £200 a year, but she manages to maintain a cottage with a maid and a gardener. Rachel, who is almost twenty, is her younger daughter. The elder, Dorothea Prime, is a curate's widow although she is only seven years older than Rachel. Mrs Prime has more money than her mother. The Rays therefore have some similarity with the Dale sisters and their widowed mother in *The Small House at Allington*.

However, anyone who knows Trollope's short stories will see that the obvious parallel is with 'The Courtship of Susan Bell'. That story is set in America where Susan Bell lives with her widowed mother and older sister. Both Mrs Bell and Mrs Ray are the widows of lawyers; both are hard pressed for money; both are rather weak women, dominated by their elder daughters; both are quite religious. There are differences: Mrs Bell takes in lodgers which Mrs Ray avoids, lest it compromise her status as a 'lady'. Both women are afraid when a 'wolf' appears with whom their younger daughter seems to flirt. In America the 'wolf' is an engineer, while in England he is a brewer. Both receive advice from the elder daughter but in America the elder daughter's husband is a live Baptist minister, while in England he is a dead Evangelical curate. But Susan Bell is not thwarted by religious tyranny and, indeed, the Baptist minister is an attractive character. If Trollope had kept those characteristics when he transformed the short story into a much longer novel he might have avoided problems with *Good Words* but he would not have written as good a novel.

The novel is entirely set in Baslehurst and its immediate environs except for a brief trip that Mrs Ray makes into Exeter. There is not one titled person in *Rachel Ray* and only one brief scene at a small country house in the neighbourhood. The novel is centred almost completely on women. Everything is seen through their eyes and the only man to receive much attention is the brewer, Tappitt. The 'hero', Luke Rowan, never really comes alive as a character and Trollope obviously finds it difficult to explain why a 'gentleman' wishes to leave London for a provincial town in which he will become a 'tradesman'. In its portrayal of the customs and daily life of a provincial town, the novel resembles Mrs Gaskell's *Cranford*; but the greatest influence on *Rachel Ray* is Jane Austen. No other Trollope novel so clearly shows his indebtedness to her. Perhaps this is best seen in the wonderful conversation among the three women at Mrs Ray's cottage in the chapter called 'Maternal Eloquence' [15].

The novel has a sub-plot involving Luke's involvement with the local brewery in which he inherits a share. The beer brewed by Bungall and Tappitt is dreadful stuff, sold at 2*d.* a pint, but Luke has ideas to improve it. Setting several scenes in a brewery was also likely to disturb many Evangelical readers whose attitude towards drink was changing by the 1860s. Most of them might not be teetotallers, but there was a growing antipathy towards drink among the type of self-respecting upper-working-class and lower-middle-class people who read

Good Words. For Trollope to make the brewery the source of so much talk and amusement was not a wise step. However, the brewery allows Trollope to introduce the Tappitt family. Mrs Tappitt is one of those slightly vulgar women, like Martha Dunstable, Sally Todd, and Matilda Thoroughbung [*Mr Scarborough's Family*] who was also connected to a brewery. Trollope, like his mother, excelled in the creation of such women.

Since *Barchester Towers*, Trollope delighted in assembling characters at social events: Mrs Proudie's reception, the Ullathorne fête, Mrs Stumfold's tea-party in *Miss Mackenzie* or the party at the Duke of Omnium's castle in *Framley Parsonage.* These events normally occupy more than one chapter and allow Trollope to introduce or develop characters. Mrs Tappitt's ball is the great occasion in *Rachel Ray* and Trollope again shows his ability to keep a sense of movement as the reader is taken about the room, from group to group and from conversation to conversation. Trollope himself had loved dancing in his youth and he clearly enjoyed writing about Mrs Tappitt's ball, even though describing its 'glory' upset the editor of *Good Words.* Strict Evangelicals – like Mrs Prime – would have been horrified enough at Rachel going to a ball, but waltzing was a sin of unimaginable magnitude to many of them.

The strength of the novel lies in that very feature which Macleod feared: the exposure of the bigoted Evangelical's mind. Mrs Proudie and Mr Slope in *Barchester Towers* had both exemplified this part of the Church of England, but their portrayals centre more on their 'worldly' traits of ambition and love of power disguised by cant. *Rachel Ray* shows how Christianity can be perverted into a narrow sect whose main aim is the abolition of all pleasure. The two principal exponents of this are Rachel's sister and her clergyman, Mr Prong. It is essential to remember that these people are members of the Church of England. (Even so well-informed a critic as Hugh Walpole made the mistake of thinking they were Dissenters.)

There are three clergymen in *Rachel Ray*. In Baslehurst, the old parish had been divided by an Act of Parliament and the aged incumbent, Mr Harford, naturally resents that some of his parish (although none of his income) has been given into the care of Mr Prong. Here is a point in which Trollope shows his great knowledge of church politics. When large parishes were divided, the clergyman who kept the original church often resented and looked down upon the new man who had taken some of his parishioners. This can be seen in the unhappy life of the Reverend Patrick Brontë at Haworth: he suffered from being in the same position as Mr Prong.

Trollope, who was no doubt annoyed at *The Record*'s sneers about 'trashy tales', used this novel to repay their compliment. 'The Recordites', as they were known, had established a place to train clergy at Islington, a famous centre for Evangelicals and since 1827 the location for the annual 'Islington Conference'. Trollope, like many people, assumed that there were two essential attributes of an English clergyman: he was a gentleman and he had been at Oxford or Cambridge. [See the attitude towards the Reverend Mr Cruse in *The Bertrams* [9] when it is assumed that he has not been to either university.] The Re-

cordites at Islington challenged both assumptions and Trollope, whose dislike of Evangelicals was partly due to a dislike of the classes from which they were drawn, was delighted to paint a sharp portrait of Mr Prong. Rachel likes to point out that Mr Prong 'had been educated at Islington, and that sometimes he forgot his "h's"' [4]. Her mother agrees and refuses to attend any of Prong's services because he has not come from Oxford or Cambridge. Trollope says quite simply that Prong lacks the one essential attribute of a clergyman: 'He was not a gentleman' [6]. Trollope carried on this war with Islington into another novel in which he attacks the Evangelicals, *Miss Mackenzie*. In that, Mr Frigidy considers becoming a clergyman but worries that he could not pass 'even the initionary gates of Islington' [4]. Sixteen months after he finished writing *Miss Mackenzie* Trollope began publishing his 'Clerical Sketches' in the *Pall Mall Gazette* and wrote that the new theological colleges were producing 'a man less attractive, less urbane, less genial – in one significant word, less of a gentleman' [*Clergymen of the Church of England*]. Perhaps he was making some attempt at being diplomatic towards Macleod when he referred to 'clergymen' of other churches. This is one of the few occasions on which Trollope used the word 'clergymen' for ministers of other denominations.

As so often when portraying Evangelicals like Slope or Prong, Trollope took some pleasure in showing them to be hypocrites. Prong, having preached on the virtues of the simple life, is found at a late breakfast, savouring some shrimp. His proposal to Mrs Prime is couched in the same canting language in which Slope made his to Eleanor Bold in *Barchester Towers* and, again like Slope, Prong is also thinking of her income. He tells Mrs Prime that money is 'dross', but he still wants to get his hands on hers. Mr Comfort, Mrs Ray's elderly vicar, is one of those characters whose name describes his personality. He also preaches platitudes about the vanity of worldly wealth, but he still finds the money to go about in a private carriage. (His daughter's family are the only other 'carriage folk' in the novel.) Mr Comfort has inherited a lot of his wealth because he has been 'blessed with a most surprising number of unmarried uncles and aunts that ever a man had'. Yet his behaviour, like that of the Reverend Henry Clavering in *The Claverings* or the Reverend Mr Annesley in *Mr Scarborough's Family*, only receives mild chastisement from Trollope, for Comfort is clearly a gentleman and in his case is only saying what is expected of him.

For Trollope true religious hypocrisy is an Evangelical vice. If Prong exemplifies that, Mrs Prime has the other great Evangelical fault. 'She had taught herself to believe that cheerfulness was a sin, and that the more she became morose' the closer she got to heaven. She forces her weak mother into an unnatural gloominess. Rachel has the strength to rebel and refuses to attend the frequent 'Dorcas Meetings'. (Dorcas was a figure in the Acts of the Apostles and her name was often used for ladies' sewing circles organized by the churches.) These gatherings were particularly prominent among Dissenters and Evangelicals and ladies would meet to sew clothes for the poor and exchange religious talk and gossip. As so often in Trollope's novels, gossip causes a great many problems and nearly ruins Rachel's happiness. Much of it is spread by spiteful Evangelicals like Miss Pucker and Mr Prong. At the end of the novel, Rachel pointedly asks her mother why 'people who talk most of Christian charity' think evil of others [29].

The way in which Trollope describes the topography of Baslehurst sounds at times like a postal surveyor's report and he even has one of his customary private jokes, this one about the delivery of the post. The sudden and outspoken authorial intrusion about wives remaining loyal to husbands in times of upset and debt is almost certainly a tribute to his mother, who was in the last few months of her life when he wrote this [20].

Rachel Ray received many favourable reviews, but nothing pleased Trollope more than the reaction of his friend George Eliot. He had sent her a copy, perhaps because he knew that she had herself known the narrow world of provincial Evangelicalism and Dissent. She spoke of the 'skill with which you have organized thoroughly natural everyday incidents' and said the book was one of 'those subtleties of art which can hardly be appreciated except by those who have striven after the same result with conscious failure'. The deceptive simplicity of *Rachel Ray* makes it one of the best novels in which to see how Trollope went about his art.

Railways. Railways or railroads – the terms were interchangeable well into the century – played an important role both in Trollope's life and in his fiction; their rise to dominance paralleled his own life. He was fifteen when the first railway opened and by the year in which he published his third novel, 1850, there were almost 7,000 miles of railways. By the mid-1870s, when he used the railways for one of his most dramatic fictional suicides, that total had doubled. By then about three out of every hundred working men were employed by the railways. In his early Irish novels the railways are not important because Ireland only had a few miles of track in the 1840s. (He added a footnote about this in a later edition of *The Kellys and the O'Kellys*.) His only English novel depicting life before the age of railways is *Lady Anna*, but it was not published until 1873–4. In it one gets a good picture of a way of life totally dependent on horse-drawn transport.

Because Trollope was out of England during the years of the great 'railway mania' in the 1840s and 1850s, the effect of trains was perhaps more obvious to him during his visits in the 1850s and on his return in 1859. In *The Three Clerks* (1858) he commented on how the railways had affected London's increasing suburban sprawl [3]. In *The Warden*, his first novel set in England, the growing importance of railways is recognized: they allow characters to make quick journeys to and from London where so much of the action is initiated. With such efficient transport, not only could quiet backwaters like Barchester be connected to London, but metropolitan concerns could quickly influence even the most rural areas. This was particularly the case when trains were combined with the growing power of national newspapers which they distributed throughout the country. When Trollope made his own sketch map of

Barsetshire he carefully marked out two railway routes through it.

His Post Office work gave him a great knowledge of railways. Not only did he use them for official travel, but he had to co-ordinate postal deliveries with railway companies. He saw at first hand what happened to a town if the railways by-passed it and he recalled this when describing Perivale in *The Belton Estate* [7]. From his own family he had knowledge of other aspects of railways: his father-in-law was a railway director and his wife's mother was killed in an early railway accident.

In addition to initiating great social changes the new railways also created huge fortunes. In *Doctor Thorne* the great Scatcherd wealth is built up by Sir Roger Scatcherd from his work as a railway contractor. In *The Way We Live Now* Melmotte and his fellow speculators are involved in a scheme to build a railway, while a railway junction provides a spectacular end for Ferdinand Lopez, yet another speculator, in *The Prime Minister* [60].

Although Trollope never attempted anything like Dickens's rhapsodic description of railway travel in *Dombey and Son*, there are frequent accounts of railway journeys in his novels. His emphasis, however, is always on the way in which people can get to and from stations [➤ Carriages]. There are comparatively few detailed descriptions of characters actually travelling on trains. Among the best are two in *The Small House at Allington*: John Eames's meeting with Crosbie in a railway carriage and their subsequent fight at Paddington station [34] and Crosbie's honeymoon trip to Folkestone with his bored wife [45]. The fashionable Crosbie, on both these occasions, is in a first-class carriage, while Eames is only in first class because he felt compelled to take a seat there after being brought to the station by an earl's servant.

Trollope expected that his readers would understand such terms as 'the 8.22 p.m. down' and 'the 8.45 p.m. up from the north' [*Orley Farm*, 6]. 'Down' denoted a train travelling down from London to the countryside and 'up' a train travelling up to the capital from a station in the provinces. For the timetables of trains, characters frequently consult that essential Victorian reference work, *Bradshaw's Guide*, which Trollope defends against its critics in *He Knew He Was Right* [91]. Indeed, time itself was greatly affected by the railways. In 1852 clocks began to be standardized throughout England: for the first occasion in history it was the same time throughout the kingdom. That may be one reason for the relatively frequent mention of exact times in Trollope's writing, especially as his own life was so closely governed by railway time-tables. The way in which such changes were working through society is illustrated in *Rachel Ray*, when a widow who had been terrified by the speed of trains less than twelve years earlier now complains that they are too slow and that she could have 'walked as fast' [21]. While these changes did cause some, like the Reverend Henry Fitzackerley Chamberlaine, to lament the passing of many of 'the well-bred ceremonies of life, so many of which went out of fashion when the railroads came in' [*The Vicar of Bullhampton*, 24], Trollope had no doubt of their ultimate value as evidence of national advancement.

Many aspects of Victorian rail travel emerge in Trollope's accounts.

Buying tickets, he says in *The Eustace Diamonds*, was one the few times when one had to pay cash and not put the item on one's account. Since there was no food service on trains, Victorians took their own food: the character in *An Old Man's Love* who takes sandwiches and sherry was following Trollope's own practice [20]. He had little use for the food provided at the station buffets: 'The real disgrace of England is the railway sandwich' [*He Knew He Was Right*, 37]. If you wanted to ensure you had privacy in a carriage, you were advised to tip the porter [*The Small House at Allington*, 45]. The ultimate form of privacy was a 'special', when one hired a train for one's own use [*Barchester Towers*, 32].

Of course class was important in train travel, as in everything else. Those like Josiah Crawley, who had to watch every penny, could get a third-class return ticket from Barsetshire to London for 13s. [*The Last Chronicle of Barset*, 32]. Trollope seems to have normally travelled first class: in the 1860s a young American celebrity-seeker leapt on to a moving train to force himself into Trollope's compartment. The porter had pointed out the famous author, seated in a first-class compartment on a 'down train' to Cambridge. Far from being annoyed, Trollope chatted amicably with the man and straightened out affairs with the conductor when it was discovered the tourist had no ticket.

For Trollope as an author the railways provided two important opportunities: a place to write and a place to sell novels. Once when Escott met him on a train going north from London, Trollope first had a long sleep and then took out his pencil and wrote a few chapters of his latest novel. (This is how he began *Framley Parsonage* years before.) The second blessing for a celebrated author was the bookstall in the railway station. One reason Trollope received so much for his novels is that his books were particularly popular with readers who bought the cheap, yellow-back, one-volume edition to read on a train [➤ Mudie's Circulating Library; Publishers and Publishing]. Thus Trollope was having a private joke with the fight between Eames and Crosbie at Paddington station when the combatants fall 'into the yellow shilling-novel depot' of the W. H. Smith bookstall [*The Small House at Allington*, 4].

Trollope was also fascinated with the effect of railways on countries that he visited [➤ 'La Mère Bauche'] and he devoted several pages of *North America* to describing the wonders of American trains, particularly the sleeping-cars. Twice he made the seven-day, 3,000-mile rail crossing of the United States and 'never made a journey with less fatigue' [➤ *The Tireless Traveler*]. For Trollope and his generation, such spectacular feats of engineering symbolized the progress they had seen in their lifetime. This helped to give them that optimistic view of the world so often reflected in Trollope's novels. Railways also provided new expressions for the language [➤ Slang]. Trollope adhered to early-Victorian use and referred to 'The Paddington Station' and 'The Euston Station'. The definite article began to be dropped as the various new stations became part of daily life.

[➤ Hotels; Sabbatarianism.]

Ralph the Heir. Trollope's twenty-sixth novel was written between 4 April and 7 August 1869. The contract, dated 13 April 1869, was with James Virtue, the publisher of *Saint Pauls* of which Trollope was still editor. He paid Trollope £2,520, but he insisted that he should be free to publish the novel other than in the magazine, should he dispose of it. In the event Virtue disposed both of the magazine and of the rights to the new novel by January 1870 to Alexander Strahan, before the serialization had begun. Strahan decided to publish the novel in nineteen monthly parts priced 6*d*. and these appeared between January 1870 and July 1871. Michael Sadleir in his *Trollope: A Bibliography* shows that Strahan took the unsold parts and issued them as a supplement to *Saint Pauls* during the same period, as a way of recouping the large sum he had paid for the manuscript. Strahan then sold the rights for a three-volume novel to Hurst & Blackett, who published it in April 1871. Strahan then brought out a one-volume edition two or perhaps three months later.

Although almost all Trollope's novels draw upon his own experiences for colourful details, *Ralph the Heir* is the only one in which this was obvious to many of his contemporary readers. He used the story of his political defeat as a parliamentary candidate at Beverley in 1868 to provide the most memorable part of the novel. Transforming it into fiction was the only way in which he could relieve his frustration, especially as the book was written in the midst of a frantic period of work, frantic even by Trollope's own staggering standards. Within a few days of starting the novel he was taken 'very ill' and did not write anything for six days – a rare occurrence for him – and his illness may have left him somewhat weak. He also knew he would soon have to give evidence to an official inquiry into bribery by his opponents at that election.

Family matters also weighed on his mind. His younger son, Fred, was about to return to Australia having decided to live there, and Trollope took another four days' break from writing to accompany him to Plymouth where he boarded his ship. Trollope was involved in complicated negotiations to establish his elder son, Henry, as a partner in Chapman & Hall at the huge cost of £10,000. Fred also required a large sum for his Australian venture. Understandably, therefore, money was much on Trollope's mind as he wrote and at the bottom of his worksheet he noted that he would receive £3. 3s. 7½d. per page. (To put this into perspective: a postman who had recently been under Trollope's supervision would have received just about the same sum for a month's work.) Thus the two subjects that weighed on his mind form the most conspicuous features of the novel: an election and the love of a father for his son [➤ Fathers and Sons].

Ralph the Heir is a confusing novel in its construction and it is made all the more so by the fact that the two principal young men have the same name. There are two Ralph Newtons: one is the illegitimate son of a wealthy Hampshire squire, Gregory Newton, while the other is Gregory's nephew, 'Ralph the heir'. (He is heir because of the entail.) To add to the confusion, 'Ralph the heir' has a younger brother, the Rector of Newton Peele, who has the same name as the squire, Gregory. The heir is an idle young man who does little but hunt six days a week. (Trollope normally hunted two or three days a week.) [➤ Fox-hunting.]

The main plot centres on how the squire can avoid the entail. He gets his heir to agree to be bought out so that he can leave the property to his son but is killed while fox-hunting before negotiations are completed. 'Ralph the heir' succeeds and 'Ralph the son' uses the money left in his father's will to buy an estate in Norfolk. The second story-line concerns Sir Thomas Underwood, erstwhile guardian of 'Ralph the heir', who is defeated in an attempt to re-enter Parliament. There are, of course several love plots revolving round the two daughters and one niece of Sir Thomas. Clarissa Underwood is at one time courted by 'Ralph the heir' but is put off by his character and marries the Reverend Gregory Newton instead. While making up his mind about the estate, 'Ralph the heir' courts Polly Neefit, the daughter of a breeches-maker, Thomas Neefit, but she rejects him for the equally absurdly named Ontario Moggs, the son of a prosperous bootmaker. [➤ Names, Silly.] The use of tradesmen's families, like the Neefits and Moggs, shows that Trollope was conscious that the audience of *Saint Pauls* reached into the lower middle classes.

Sir Thomas is the most interesting character in the book: he is a distinguished though gloomy lawyer who was knighted when he was Solicitor-General in a Tory government. (At least he avoids the fate of another Tory ex-Solicitor-General, Sir Henry Harcourt in *The Bertrams*, who commits suicide.) The borough Sir Thomas chooses for his candidature to re-enter Parliament is called 'Percycross' and is clearly modelled on Beverley. In inventing the name Trollope presumably remembered the celebrated fourteenth-century monument to one of the Percy family in Beverley Minster.

The fictional election allowed Trollope the result he had wanted in the real one: in Beverley the Liberals (including Trollope) lost; in Percycross the Liberals defeat the Conservatives, including Sir Thomas. The fictional election resembles the real one in three ways: Sir Thomas, like his creator, hates canvassing for votes; the borough is disenfranchised for gross bribery; the interests of Radical reformers, in the person of Ontario Moggs, are important. (Such influences in Beverley were pointed out in a secret Reform League report.) [Mullen, 514.] Moggs's support for trades unions and strikes was highly topical as the press had been filled with stories about strikes by London tailors and others throughout 1867. (Trollope defended the strikers in an American newspaper interview a few years later.)

The novel also recalls several other aspects of Trollope's own life in a variety of other private jokes or references. Sir Thomas lives in Fulham and often walks from London to his house, just as the young Trollope did when he spent much time there with his uncle, Henry Milton, in the late 1820s. Perhaps it was at Fulham that Uncle Henry laughed at the young Anthony's admission that he wished to stand for Parliament some day. (Trollope usually sent copies of his novels to his uncle's widow.) Another family connection is seen when Trollope says there is 'no prettier' part of England than the area on the Berkshire–Hampshire border round the village of Heckfield. He even alludes to Heckfield church [11, 31]. His grandfather, the Reverend William Milton, had been the vicar of Heckfield. In the chapter set at an exhibition in the Royal Academy, Trollope indicates his own love of visiting galleries (something he again owed to his uncle, Henry Milton) and this allows him to have a gentle private joke at his friend, Millais [49]. [➤ Art.] When 'Ralph the heir' borrows money from Neefit the tailor he is following his creator, who did the same as a youth [➤ Bills].

While Sir Thomas may have shared Trollope's dislike of electioneering, they were poles apart when it came to the writing of books. Sir Thomas has been gathering material for many years for a biography of Sir Francis Bacon, but he never settles into the writing of the book. Trollope's analysis of Sir Thomas's procrastination makes salutary reading for anyone suffering from 'writer's block' [51]. Much of the lawyer's unhappiness and boredom spring from idleness, and the same vice causes the financial and romantic difficulties of 'Ralph the heir'.

While *Ralph the Heir* is a realistic novel it is also Trollope's most reflective since *The Bertrams*. The book contains some of his best deliberations on the importance of slow political change [49] and on how religious belief can save people from despair [51] [➤ Religion]. Trollope's attitude towards the Church of England is well represented in the moving passage in which Gregory Newton wanders round his churchyard [14]. The novel ends with Trollope's best analysis of the way in which a novelist should try to influence 'readers for their good'. The 'preaching' must be administered skilfully, like medicine coated in sugar. This analysis is one of the most important he ever wrote for anyone who wishes to understand Trollope's own view of what he was about in writing novels [56].

Ralph the Heir marks the introduction of a subject that would increasingly feature in Trollope's novels: the problem of entail and how a father should provide for his heirs. We are given a good insight into the way in which his own mind worked when we realize the emotional passage about the delight a father has in preparing an inheritance for his son was written about the time that Fred sailed for Australia [11]. Yet another problem involving family inheritance surfaces when Sir Thomas worries about whether it is right to reduce legacies to his own children so that he would have something to leave an adopted niece [7]. Here Sir Thomas is mirroring the novelist's own concern for his niece, Florence Bland, a concern that would plague him until the writing of *Cousin Henry*. (The problems of entail and inheritance were also tackled in *Mr Scarborough's Family*, *Is He Popenjoy?* and *Sir Harry Hotspur of Humblethwaite*.)

Trollope was unhappy with *Ralph the Heir*: 'one of the worst novels I have written', he noted in his *Autobiography*. Indeed, he felt that it almost justified the view that a novelist over fifty – he turned fifty-four a few days after he started writing – should avoid love scenes. Contemporary critics were kinder about the novel: the *Spectator* particularly praised the portrayal of Neefit, the breeches-maker, while *The Times* thought the election scenes showed Trollope to be the successor to Dickens, who had died recently.

A few years later, while Trollope was on a visit to Australia, he was furious to learn that his friend and fellow novelist, Charles Reade (1814–84), had adapted *Ralph the Heir* for a play called *Shilly-Shally*. The play proved a failure in London, but Trollope refused to speak to Reade for five years, even when they played whist at their club. *Ralph the Heir* has not remained a popular novel; it was tied with *The Land-Leaguers* as the least popular Trollope novel in a survey of Trollope Society members in 1994. It certainly deserves a higher standing than that.

Rattler, Mr. The Liberal whip in the House of Commons [*Phineas Finn*, 6], he appears throughout the Palliser novels. He has the cynical view that MPs will vote for anything to keep their 'places'. [For his opposite number, ➤ Roby, Thomas.]

'Relics of General Chassé'. This short story was written in July 1859 after Trollope's return from his Post Office trip to the West Indies and Central America. It vies with 'The Courtship of Susan Bell' as the first short story he wrote; it was in fact the first published. It is one of two manuscripts he sent to *Harper's New Monthly Magazine* in New York in July 1859. It was published in February 1860 and was later included in his first collection of short stories, *Tales of All Countries*. In his *Autobiography*, Trollope wrote that the stories included in that collection 'have, most of them, some foundation in such occurrences', that is, in 'true tales of my adventures'. Trollope received $100, or £20.

This humorous story describes a visit to the famous General Chassé's apartments in the Citadel in Antwerp and is told in the first person. It features a clergyman, Prebendary Augustus Horne, 'well-fed ... [and] rather inclined to dandyism'. Horne sees a pair of the general's trousers and tries them on. Suddenly five Englishwomen arrive and the prebendary hides. They, with typical Victorian tourist audacity, cut up for souvenirs what they think are Chassé's trousers, actually the prebendary's. The two men get back to their inn when the prebendary gets another pair. The narrator later meets the women and tells them their 'relics' were only the trousers of a fellow English visitor. They take flight and leave their stolen goods behind.

The humour is essentially Victorian: a dignitary of the Church loses his trousers. Trollope drew on his experience of Belgium and its recent history. After Flanders and Brabant revolted against the Dutch an independent kingdom of Belgium was established in 1831, although the Dutch under Baron Chassé held the Citadel of Antwerp from 1830 until December 1832 when a Belgian–French force bombarded the Citadel and forced a surrender. (The general died ten years before the story was written.) For his prebendary, Trollope may have had in mind the Reverend William Drury who was, like all the Drury family, fat. Drury had been a master at Harrow and had fled to Brussels to avoid imprisonment for debt; there he conducted a school for the sons of English exiles in Brussels. He employed Trollope for a short period. [➤ Clergymen.]

Religion. Trollope's religious faith was a manly and straightforward acceptance of orthodox Christianity combined with a Victorian liberal's understanding. He wrote in his *Life of Cicero*, 'Christ came to us, and we do not need another teacher.' He told his friend, G. W. Rusden, 'To my God I can be but true, and if I think myself to have done well I cannot but say so ... And I own that I feel that it is impossible that the Lord should damn me ... I expect ... eternal bliss as the reward of my life here on earth.' To him the Christian religion was a religion that offered comfort in a period when many still emphasized God's judgement. 'Comfort' is a word Trollope uses constantly when writing about religion. [➤ *The Last Chronicle of Barset*, 1.] Comfort came from a forgiving God, a sacramental faith, the beauty of a God-given earth, a natural optimism, the ability to help others. Mr Harding spoke for Trollope when he told his former bedesmen, 'I hope you may live contented, and die trusting in the Lord Jesus Christ, and thankful to Almighty God for the good things He has given you' [*The Warden*, 20].

Trollope's novels do not discuss an individual's private religious life or, normally, religious belief and hence some have concluded that Trollope lacked firm religious belief. What he lacked was the ability glibly to discuss such things in fiction. It is not surprising that he wrote more of religion and of theological debates in his nonfiction. (Two notable fictional exceptions are *The Bertrams* and *Linda Tressel*.) He gives an insight into his own religious debates in *The Bertrams*, in an exchange between George Bertram and Arthur Wilkinson in Chapter 26. He began the novel in the Middle East after touring the Holy Land.

Trollope was the grandson of two Church of England parish priests and was brought up by parents both of whom wrote about religion. The Christian religion was, he once wrote, 'of all things the most important to us'

(*Clergymen of the Church of England*). Religion, however, was not meant to make life miserable or to be prattled about as happened with Evangelicals. While he received little religious instruction at his public schools he frequently attended chapel and grew to know and love both the Bible and the Prayer Book. At Winchester he attended the cathedral's services every Sunday, and even if they were badly read by later Victorian standards, they enriched his religious training. He grew up with a strong love for the Church and a devotion to the old High Church teaching on the sacraments. There may have been some idea of his becoming a clergyman. He was a regular churchgoer throughout his life and, as his last rector wrote, 'a steady communicant'. On his visit to South Africa he could not get to church in time one Sunday, but found 'comfort' in listening to a hymn coming from a church.

Trollope's firm Christian beliefs were tempered by an intellectual liberalism, a large degree of common sense and a Victorian's belief in progress as the will of God. George Eliot once said that Trollope, was 'a Church of England man, clinging to whatever is, *on the whole*, and without fine distinctions, honest, lovely and of good report'. Neither the finer points of dogmatic theology nor the niceties of church order appealed to him. He once wrote, 'Who then shall attempt to exclude from the Church of Christ those who are but professing believers?'

His was not an analytical mind. What mattered was that people should seek 'that Sunday-keeping, church-going, domestic, decent life' [*Ralph the Heir*, 51]. Essential for human society was a shared belief in God and

in the revealed moral order, because belief became by its nature practice: 'I judge a man by his actions with men, much more than by his declarations Godwards.' To him religion and education went hand in hand: he was interested to find greater religious feeling in Australia and greater church attendance among working people there. He traced this to education: 'Teaching produces prosperity; prosperity achieves decent garments, – and decent garments are highly conducive to church-going.' Agnostics he found trying: when he interviewed the agnostic intellectual, John Morley, as editor for the *Fortnightly Review*, he asked abruptly: 'Do you believe in the divinity of our blessed Lord and Saviour Jesus Christ?' Morley was frightfully upset. When Trollope helped to establish the *Fortnightly Review* he insisted that 'nothing should appear denying or questioning the divinity of Christ' although he later admitted that in a Liberal journal this was impractical.

Theologically he was liberal: he welcomed the new 'doubts' regarding biblical texts and a looser adherence to some traditional Church teaching as a corrective balance to the 'deposit of faith' inherited from the past. He read new works like *Essays and Reviews*, supported Bishop Colenso, agreed the new views about eternal punishment and supported the growing disuse of the Athanasian Creed. While he did not dispute the need to accept the great 'mysteries' of the Christian religion – the Incarnation, Trinity, etc. – he insisted that only belief in God was 'essential for forming the conduct of men'. This was, to him, common sense.

His religious views permeate his writings, as he once explained in private: 'To you, if I speak of my own work, I must belittle myself. I must say that it is naught. But if I speak of it to my God, I say, "Thou knowest that it is honest; – that I strove to do good; – that if ever there came to me the choice between success and truth, I stuck to truth."' The last short story he wrote, 'Not If I Know It', culminates at the Christmas Eucharist through which two brothers-in-law are reconciled. In *Sir Harry Hotspur of Humblethwaite* he has one character ask if a 'black sheep' may not be redeemed. 'If it be not so,' Trollope interrupts, 'what is all this doctrine of repentance in which we believe?' [5]. The main influence of his religious beliefs is seen in his characters. Unlike those of Dickens, they were not caricatures of good or evil but products of the Fall of Man, a mixture of good and bad: 'Man is never strong enough to take unmixed delight in good, so we may presume also that he cannot be quite so weak as to find perfect satisfaction in evil' [*The Eustace Diamonds*, 1]. Religion is both the corrective to man's inclination to wrongdoing and the great 'comforter' in his striving to do right. This was often expressed in an old saying he constantly quotes: 'God does temper the wind to the shorn lamb.'

While Trollope wrote much of church life he did not confuse what he called 'things ecclesiastical ... things theological ... [and] things religious' [*The Last Chronicle of Barset*, 34]. He rarely discusses 'things religious'; his concern was for 'things ecclesiastical'. He would write about the Church as an institution – 'things ecclesiastical' – and about clergymen as men because it was a world he knew, but he would not use his writing to preach, as did 'religious' novelists like his sister Ce-

cilia. The novels of the 1870s have more respectable young men who do not go to church than in earlier works, men like young Harry Clavering in *The Claverings*, the two Scarborough sons in *Mr Scarborough's Family* and Daniel Thwaite in *Lady Anna*; they also have more 'fashionable' people who avoid church, for instance those in *The American Senator* [20]. In this Trollope was reflecting changes in English society, but it was a change he did not like.

[➤ Catholicism; Church of England; Dissenters; Grantly Family; Prayer; Sermons.]

Religious Women. See Women.

'Returning Home'. This short story was written between 20 and 26 January 1861 while Trollope was working on *Orley Farm*. It was one of the stories that was sold to *Public Opinion* and it appeared on 30 November; it was reprinted on 7 December 1861. It was included in his second collection of short stories, *Tales of All Countries*, Second Series, published in 1863. Trollope used his travels as settings for stories, in this case his 1859 visit to Costa Rica during his long journey on behalf of the Post Office. A true story similar to this was recounted in *The West Indies and the Spanish Main* [20]. Trollope received £50.

This sentimental story is about the plight of Englishmen who work abroad. Mr and Mrs Arkwright and their baby have been in the city of San José, Costa Rica, for four years and the story is of their doomed attempt to return to England. When they reach the river that will take them to the port whence they can sail for England (Trollope himself had travelled along the tortuous route described in the story), the wife, already weakened, is killed when their canoe overturns. The widowed husband gives up his plan and returns to San José with his child.

In this story Trollope inserted a caveat to his belief in the 'English world' of which he was, elsewhere in his writings, so proud: 'As it is the destiny of our race to spread itself over the wide face of the globe, it is well that there should be something to gild and paint the outward face of that lot which so many are called upon to choose. But for a life of daily excitement, there is no life like life in England; and the farther that one goes from England the more stagnant, I think, do the waters of existence become.' He repeated this view when writing about Australia.

'A Ride across Palestine'. This short story was written in July 1860, the month in which Trollope began *Orley Farm*. Trollope used his travels, in this case his 1858 Post Office trip to Egypt and the Holy Land, for settings for his stories. He first called this story 'The Banks of the Jordan' as one of his 'tales of all countries' which he had started in 1859. He halfheartedly offered it to George Smith for the *Cornhill*. Smith must have expressed an interest as Trollope sent the manuscript and stated that if it were divided into three it must be called 'A Ride across Palestine'. Smith did not altogether like it, wanted it changed – and worse, shortened; he also wanted Trollope to part with the copyright, which the writer needed for a second series of *Tales of All Countries*. Trollope withdrew the article. Part of his refusal to compromise may have been because the story's narrator is something of a

self-portrait. He then included it in the package of tales he sold to the new *London Review* in September 1860 and it was published as 'The Banks of the Jordan' on 5, 12 and 19 January 1861. It was attacked by several readers. The magazine only published two more stories and sold the other five to *Public Opinion*. Trollope received £50. It was included in his second collection of stories, *Tales of All Countries*, Second Series (1863).

The story is told in the first person by Mr Jones whom a young man named Smith approaches in a Jerusalem hotel. He 'looked slight and weak' and slightly effeminate and asks to join Jones in his journey to the Dead Sea, the Jordan River, Jericho and the mountains where Christ is said to have undergone His forty days of temptation. During the trip they come across an Englishman, the uncle from whom Smith is escaping. They journey on to Jaffa, where the uncle confronts Jones, accuses him of eloping with his niece – disguised as 'Mr Smith' – and demands that he marry her. Jones tells the uncle he is already married although he had told 'Mr Smith' he was not, to avoid talking about private matters.

In Trollope's reply to George Smith he referred to the publisher's dislike of the passage in which Jones explains the effects of a Turkish saddle to his new friend by 'taking hold of his leg by the calf to show how the leather would chafe him; but it seemed to me that he did not quite like my interference'. Smith must have disliked even more the passage where the narrator, having bathed in the Jordan River, 'stretched myself out in my weariness . . . my head rested on his legs. Ah, me! one does not take such liberties with new friends in England.' Some readers might well have been upset when the narrator, a married man, admits when he sees 'Mr Smith' as a woman that 'the mistress of my bosom, had she known my thoughts at that one moment, might have had cause for anger'. Most of these criticisms only really make sense when the reader re-reads the story, having discovered that 'Mr Smith' is really a beautiful young woman. These were all examples of what Victorian critics called Trollope's 'vulgarity'.

Others may have disliked Trollope's assertion that in Jerusalem the names of sacred spots were 'bandied to and fro with as little reverence as are the fanciful appellations given by guides to rocks'. If so, they would not have liked the exchange this produces between Smith and Jones: '"For those who would still fain believe, – let them stay at home," said my friend Smith. "For those who cannot divide the wheat from the chaff, let them stay at home," I answered.' Smith could be seen as an agnostic whereas Trollope described 'him' as 'unhappy' with a 'palate out of order'. That the title as published had religious associations – the baptism of Christ by St John took place, of course, in the Jordan – probably did not help to decrease the criticisms. Arabs are denounced wholeheartedly. 'Mr Smith's' uncle is one of Trollope's unpleasant baronets [➤ *The Bertrams*].

Robarts, The Rev. Mark. Robarts is the central character in *Framley Parsonage* and returns in *The Last Chronicle of Barset*. His career is Trollope's best study of what happens when a 'curled darling' suffers his first setback. Because of his schoolboy friendship with young Lord Lufton, Robarts, the son of a doctor in Exeter, is offered the comfortable living of Framley by Lufton's mother, Lady Lufton, who even picks out an admirable wife, Fanny Monsell, for him. Robarts is almost ruined when he loans money and signs a bill for a charming scoundrel who introduces the young clergyman into High Society. Robarts, whose life has been almost nothing but good fortune, is a perfect contrast to his clerical neighbour, Josiah Crawley, whose lines have not fallen in pleasant places. Each in his own way tries to help the other. [➤ Lufton Family for Robarts's sister, Lucy.]

Roby, Thomas. Roby is 'a Conservative gentleman of great fame' who acts as a Tory Whip in several of the Palliser novels [*Phineas Finn*, 6]. He eventually holds several of those offices at the Treasury which were normally held by the Whips. [For his opposite number, ➤ Rattler, Mr.] Thomas Roby's brother, Richard, and his wife, Harriet, are important figures in *The Prime Minister*.

Routledge; *Routledge's Christmas Annual*. In 1836 George Routledge (1812–88) started his publishing business in London. Like so many publishers, he had begun his working life in a provincial bookshop. His firm became famous for its shilling reprints, the 'Railway Library', and for being one of the most successful British pirates of Mrs Stowe's *Uncle Tom's Cabin* [➤ Copyright]. In 1859 there was a reference by Trollope in a letter to his mother about 'that horrid blackguard R.': this probably was a reference to Routledge for issuing one of her novels under a new title, thereby implying it was a new book. Trollope's connection with the firm began in 1867 when Edmund Routledge, one of George's sons, approached him for either a novel or a short story (the context of Trollope's reply does not make the offer clear) for their new magazine, *Broadway*. Trollope turned him down. In 1870 he agreed, after considerable reluctance, to contribute a Christmas story, 'Christmas Day at Kirkby Cottage', to the fifth issue of the *Christmas Annual* in 1870. In 1871 Routledge bought the rights to a one-volume edition of *Can You Forgive Her?* and in the 1870s he did the same with *Phineas Finn*, *Ralph the Heir* and *Phineas Redux*.

Rufford, Lord. Rufford is a central character in *The American Senator* in which he is pursued by the husband-hunting Arabella Trefoil. He is a rich landowner, aged about thirty. He escapes from her and marries Caroline Penge. Like several other characters in *The American Senator*, he returns in *Ayala's Angel*.

Rugs. Rugs or hearth-rugs were symbols of power and position in society, not only to Trollope but to many Victorians, and there was an etiquette which guided their use. At Court only members of the Royal Family were allowed to stand on the hearth-rug and when the Marquis of Kensington Gore stood with another minister on 'a drawing-room rug in Windsor Castle' to discuss the appointment of a new Dean of Barchester, we may be sure the reference is to the carpet – 'a rug' – and not to 'the rug' [*Barchester Towers*, 52]. Until the invention of central heating any position near the fireplace was historically one of pre-

eminence, hence the significance of the rug. (Perhaps the equivalent today is the desk behind which the more important person sits while the lesser stands or sits in front.) When Mr Greenwood goes into the Marquis of Kingsbury's room in *Marion Fay*, he finds the marquis 'standing upon the hearth-rug, by which, as he well knew, it was signified that he was not intended to sit down' [18]. In Trollope's novels, people of importance, or those who think themselves important, stand on hearth-rugs to lecture others. They are normally men. Adolphus Crosbie always occupies the hearth-rug at his club in *The Small House at Allington*, thereby signifying his arrogance. When Harry Clavering and Sir Hugh Clavering argue, Sir Hugh invites him into the breakfast-room to launch his counter-attack. Once there he 'slowly walked up to the rug before the fire, and had there taken his position' [*The Claverings*, 22]. When Archdeacon Grantly first encounters Mr Slope, the archdeacon discovers that while Bishop Proudie sits, his new rival, the power behind the episcopal throne, stands on the rug in the bishop's room in the episcopal palace, 'persuasive and eager, just as the archdeacon used to stand' [5]. Slope's position symbolized his relationship both to the bishop and to the archdeacon. In another meeting, that with Grace Crawley, the archdeacon first takes his place on the hearth-rug before asking her whether she really was engaged to his son. When his kind heart overcomes his worldly arrogance, he leaves the rug and moves close to her [*The Last Chronicle of Barset*, 77]. In the same novel the rug features on two other occasions. The archdeacon, on a rare visit to the Bishop's Palace, naturally gravitates towards his old place of eminence on the rug [47]. When Josiah Crawley calls to be reprimanded by Bishop Proudie the weak bishop leaves his chair and naturally goes to the rug to issue his reprimand, but he can only do so if Crawley remains seated. As he makes his move, Crawley rises, which means the bishop must once again sit down in order to get Crawley to sit down. The pantomime only makes sense when one understands the importance of the rug [18]. When the Dean of Brotherton knocks down the Marquis of Brotherton in *Is He Popenjoy?* the drama is enhanced because the assault takes place on the marquis's own rug, albeit in an hotel room [41]. It should come as no surprise that Trollope himself was well known for 'his usual position on the hearth-rug' at home [Mullen, 565].

Russe, Service à la. See Food.

S

Sabbatarianism. Sabbatarianism, or a strict adherence to the rule that the 'Lord's Day' be set aside for rest and worship, is virtually unique to England and Scotland and those areas settled by them and dates from the Reformation. In England it led to the 'Puritan Sunday'. The revival of a strict observance had been codified in the 1781 Lord's Day Observance Act. Throughout the nineteenth century there were heated debates over the nature of Sunday observances. Trollope certainly believed that Sunday should be a day of worship [➤ Religion] but he also thought it should be used for pleasure and for work, as his own worksheets attest. His novels are full of attacks on Sabbatarians who tried to enforce their own code on others.

The debate over the Sabbatarian vision for England centred in Trollope's fiction on railways and schools. Debates over the Sabbatarians' vision of an England without Sunday trains fill a large part of *Barchester Towers* [5]. The Sabbatarians' opposition to railway travel on Sundays meant there could be no postal deliveries. There was a 'local option' after 1850 whether or not to have Sunday deliveries, and in *Miss Mackenzie* the heroine almost fails to hear in time about the fatal illness of her brother because Evangelical Littlebath has abolished Sunday delivery. (In Cheltenham, the basis for Littlebath, the Evangelical vicar, Close, had tried to do just this.) When some 'special friends' of the postmen, that is, self-appointed do-gooders, suggested to Archdeacon Grantly that his village could do without a Sunday delivery, he simply called them 'numskulls' [*The Last Chronicle of Barset*, 73].

Sabbatarians were also committed to 'Sabbath Schools' which in their beginning were as much concerned with teaching working-class children to read and write as with imparting basic Christian teaching. In *Barchester Towers* Archdeacon Grantly, part of the old High Church movement with which Trollope identified, opposed Sabbath Schools and Sabbatarianism as much as Mrs Proudie and Obadiah Slope campaigned for them. Trollope's dislike of Sabbath Schools probably came as much from the word 'Sabbath' as the fact that these tended to inculcate Evangelical teaching. The Archdeacon's wife did conduct a parish school which did the same work: what he (and apparently Trollope himself) hated was all the organizing and Evangelical talk of 'the Sabbath' and all that went with it. Trollope says of Slope: 'Most active clergymen have their hobby, and Sunday observances are his. Sunday, however, is a word which never pollutes his mouth. It is always "the Sabbath" ... To him the revelation of God appears only in that one law given for Jewish observance. To him the mercies of our Saviour speak in vain . . . To him the New Testament is comparatively of little moment' [4].

The misery of a Sabbatarian Sunday is described in *Phineas Finn* when Lady Laura Kennedy chafes under her Scottish husband's strict rule. '"I won't say that reading a novel on a Sunday is a sin," he said; "but we must at any rate admit that it is a matter on which men disagree, that many of the best of men are against such occupation on Sunday, and that to abstain is to be on the safe side"' [23]. Trollope also liked to portray Sabbatarians as hypocrites, so when Bishop Proudie writes to a clergyman on Sunday night, he dates his letter Monday morning [*The Last Chronicle of Barset*, 17]. Occasionally a Sabbatarian could reform: Lady Rosina De Courcy was a Sabbatarian in *The Small House at Allington* but her fanaticism declines as she ages and by the time she reappears in *The Prime Minister* she is a sympathetic character.

Trollope saw Sabbatarianism as a rejection of one of the central blessings of Christianity – the consolation or 'comfort' it brings: 'Whatever our Sundays be, let them be a comfort to us . . . Unless our day of worship be a comfort, our worship will avail us but little' [*The New Zealander*]. He also disliked the way in which Sabbatarians tried to stop working people from enjoying band concerts or other pleasures on the 'Sabbath'.

Saint Pauls (1867–74). *Saint Pauls* was a magazine started under Trollope's editorship. The printer-publisher James Virtue was anxious to expand his business into the highly competitive field of monthly magazines. His first thought was to re-launch *The Argosy*, (which he printed) because the editor, Alexander Strahan, was considerably in debt to him. To ensure success he asked Trollope to be the editor in the autumn of 1866. He knew the author through the *Fortnightly Review*, which he also printed. He then decided to launch a new magazine with Trollope as editor although Trollope warned him of the risks involved. His hope was that this arrangement would mirror Thackeray's time at the *Cornhill*. He wanted to use Trollope's name in the title, but Trollope refused. He saw the editor's annual salary of £1,000 (Thackeray had received £2,000) as a replacement for his Post Office salary as he wanted to resign without lessening his income. He did so in October 1867, the same month in which the new magazine published its first issue. (He was also paid for those articles and novels he contributed.) Trollope insisted their agreement should last for a minimum of two years.

Trollope saw the magazine as a platform for his Liberal political views [➤ Politics]. Ever since his youth he had been interested in publishing his own magazine as a way to make his mark on political life, and he also knew it would help his chances for a seat in the House of Commons [➤ 'The Panjandrum']. Trollope wanted a title that would reflect his political interests and suggested 'Whitehall Magazine', 'The Monthly Westminster' and 'The Monthly Liberal'. Virtue gave up his demand for the use of Trollope's name and Trollope gave up his demand for a political, if not Liberal, title; they agreed to take the name of a famous London attraction, as had the *Cornhill*, *Temple Bar* and the recently founded *Belgravia*. In the first issue, however, Trollope was still able to give the new magazine a political tone. In his editorial he wrote that 'the good old Liberal cause still needs support'.

The first issue began the serialization of the second Palliser novel, *Phineas Finn*. The magazine also published *Ralph the Heir* as a supplement while it was also being published in part issues. Trollope contributed six of his best short stories, all drawn from his experiences as editor and later published in one volume [➤ *An Editor's Tales*]. He also wrote a variety of articles on contemporary topics, mainly political, and two on fox-hunting: these he later included in another collection, *British Sports and Pastimes*. He liked to encourage self-educated working men and young writers, among whom was Austin Dobson, who later dedicated his first volume of poems to Trollope. He also published works by his brother, Tom, and Tom's second wife, Frances Eleanor. Trollope was not a good editor. After his death the *Spectator* wrote that 'His editing ... was conventional. He did not really know how to use contributors, how to make the most out of them' (27 October 1883).

The magazine was never a serious rival to the *Cornhill* and Trollope admitted that its readers were 'not among the highest class of men and women'. Virtue never got the 25,000 circulation he thought essential: 10,000 seems the largest number achieved despite serializing works by Mrs Oliphant and George MacDonald and publishing articles by G. H. Lewes, Leslie Stephen, Edward Dicey (later editor of the *Observer*) and the Irish novelist Charles Lever. Trollope paid about a quarter of his salary to an assistant and also recruited his wife to read manuscripts and recommend acceptance or rejection. In 1869, Virtue transferred control of the magazine to Strahan and in 1870 Strahan told Trollope he would no longer be wanted as editor; by July 1870 Trollope ceased having any say in the publication and did so with few regrets. Nevertheless in July the magazine published his signed tribute to Charles Dickens. He never really had his heart in *Saint Paul's*: during the first year's publication he was away from London for four months on his Post Office trip to America and also stood for Parliament.

Sampson Low (1819–1914). This publishing house bore the name of its owner who inherited it from his father, a London printer of the same name. From 1837 Low junior became the publisher, and from 1867 the owner, of the *Publisher's Circular*, the publishers' 'bible'. After his retirement in 1875 the firm continued under one of his partners, Edward Marston, and disappeared when Marston died in 1914. Sampson Low published novels by R. D. Blackmore, including *Lorna Doone*, and by Wilkie Collins. It also specialized in re-publishing American books in the United Kingdom and in acting for British authors in America. Trollope became connected with the firm at the start of his career as a short-story writer in the summer of 1859 when it handled the sale of his four short stories to Harpers in New York. The firm acted as Harpers' agent in London. [➤ *Tales of All Countries*, First Series.] It bought the book rights for Trollope's Christmas story, *Harry*

Heathcote of Gangoil, from *The Graphic* and published it as a book in 1874. In that same year Low, who also acted as the London agent of the Boston magazine *Old and New*, negotiated for it to serialize Trollope's novel *The Way We Live Now*. This involved some difficulty as the magazine was distributed in England but the problem was solved when the publication collapsed in May 1875, and with its demise the serialization ended. In 1880 Sampson Low again acted for Trollope in selling sheets of his *Life of Cicero* to Harpers. In 1865 Low announced a new magazine, *The Argosy*, which in time would publish three of Trollope's short stories, but before it appeared Low had transferred it to Alexander Strahan.

The Saturday Review (1855–1938). This Conservative and High Church weekly magazine was a rival to the *Spectator*, and enjoyed a high reputation as a journal of serious criticism of 'politics, literature, science and art', as its sub-title proclaimed. Early contributors included intellectuals like the historian J. R. Green, the law reformer and historian J. F. Stephen, and the Oxford historian E. A. Freeman, with whom Trollope crossed swords over fox-hunting. Despite an 1857 warning against novel-reading 'for mere amusement' it went on to publish works by Thomas Hardy, George Bernard Shaw and Max Beerbohm. The *Review* was very critical of both Dickens and Thackeray although at first it praised Trollope's works, but not uncritically. It criticized his 'authorial intrusions' or what it called his 'conversational' style of writing. It praised *Barchester Towers* and *The Three Clerks*, but took him to task in 1857 for his legal mistakes and for writing too quickly, and

for what it later called, in its review of *The Struggles of Brown, Jones, and Robinson*, his 'extraordinary fertility'. If he could correct these faults 'he has the path clear before him – he can make himself such a name as will not easily be forgotten'. The *Review* saw him as a 'rival' to Thackeray and was enthusiastic over his *West Indies and the Spanish Main*.

Starting with *Framley Parsonage*, however, the *Review* adopted a carping tone while admitting the merits of that novel. The magazine may well have been spurred by jealousy at the tremendous success of the *Cornhill*, in which the novel was being serialized. It could not help but praise *Orley Farm*: Trollope 'does the family life of England to perfection. No one has drawn English families better.' Because the Tory magazine supported the Confederacy in the American Civil War it attacked Trollope's enthusiastic support of the North in his *North America* as 'tedious'. The magazine greatly disliked his re-use of old characters in new novels and must therefore bear some of the blame for his killing of Mrs Proudie. *Miss Mackenzie* was denounced as 'monstrously prosaic' and the magazine continued to attack his novels as dreadfully realistic. The *Review* kept up its attack in 1874 when Trollope wrote to *The Times* to complain about a railway's inefficiency when he was travelling from Switzerland to London. The magazine decided to comment on his letter and accused him of displaying 'more than average . . . ignorance and weakness'. In a second letter to *The Times* he remarked: 'Had I possessed the omniscience of a *Saturday Reviewer* and the Jove-like strength of the editor himself, I could have done nothing.' One of their nastiest comments came in their 1881 review of *Dr Wortle's School*, in which they said the book was 'as happy ... as Mr Trollope usually is when he does not meddle with things too high for him'.

Trollope launched counter-attacks against the magazine, which he obviously read, in several works. In *He Knew He Was Right*, written between November 1867 and June 1868, he has the American feminist Wallachia Petrie tell Caroline Spaulding that when she marries her English aristocrat and has babies she will not be allowed to nurse them. As proof she says, 'You have read what the Saturday Review says. In every other respect the Saturday Review has been the falsest of all false periodicals, but I guess it has been pretty true in what it has said about English women' [81].

Three days after completing this novel he began *The Vicar of Bullhampton*, and here he has two more swipes at the *Review*. When a pompous clergyman visits his nephew he asks to see the *Quarterly Review* and smiles 'blandly' when told it was not taken. 'Then,' adds Trollope, 'he took up the *Saturday Review*, and endeavoured to content himself with that' [27]. Ten chapters later Trollope again refers to the magazine and criticizes it for its views on women and marriage. The *Review*, Trollope says, advocates a 'mock modesty' by which a woman should pretend she is not interested in marriage. This is nonsense, for marriage is natural and, for most women, inevitable. Women who might have been misled by 'word-rebellion here and there' have learned this lesson and now openly talk about it while 'Saturday Reviewers and others blame them for their lack of modesty in doing so,

– most unreasonably, most uselessly, and, as far as the influence of such censors may go, most perniciously' [37]. Two years later Trollope scored another hit in 'The Spotted Dog'. When the editor in the story offers some work to the Cambridge-educated drunkard who is trying to better himself, he examines him on his classical knowledge. He discovers that he has a 'too severe erudition' and comments to himself, 'What a terrible man he would have been could he have got upon the staff of the Saturday Review.' His best riposte came in *Thackeray*, in which he contrasted 'the elephantine tread of *The Saturday*' to 'the precise toe' of its rival, the *Spectator*.

Scatcherd Family. Although the two men in this family only appear in *Doctor Thorne*, the family's fate and fortune affect some of the later Barsetshire novels. Roger Scatcherd began life as a stonemason in Barchester, but killed Dr Thorne's brother Henry after the latter had seduced his sister, Mary. After serving an amazingly short prison term – six months – for manslaughter, he amasses a great fortune as a railway contractor and builder. Here Trollope probably had Sir Samuel Peto (1809–89) in mind. He is referred to as 'Peto the contractor' in *The Three Clerks*, which Trollope finished shortly before starting *Doctor Thorne*. (This was in the chapter he later removed.) Scatcherd becomes an MP and is made a baronet. He is an alcoholic and this weakness is inherited by his wastrel son, Sir Louis Philippe Scatcherd. [For his name, ➤ France.] When both baronets die from their alcoholism, the vast Scatcherd fortune goes to Sir Roger's niece, Mary Thorne, thus greatly affecting the Thorne and Gresham families. Sir Roger's wife, Lady Scatcherd, had married Roger when he was a stonemason and is never comfortable after he has become rich and titled. This kindly woman is devoted to Mary Thorne and reappears in *Framley Parsonage.*

[➤ Prostitution; Railways; Violence.]

Schoolmasters. Schoolmasters do not receive much attention in Trollope's fiction. In one of his earliest surviving writings he noted the relative merits of his Harrow schoolmasters in his copy of his mother's 1834 poem, *Salamagundi*, and decades later in his *Autobiography* he attacked his headmaster at Harrow. For a few unhappy weeks in 1834 Trollope served as an usher, or assistant schoolmaster, at an English school in Belgium. This period is referred to when Julia Ongar slights Harry Clavering by calling him an usher in *The Claverings* [1–2]. It is in *Dr Wortle's School* that Trollope gives his most extensive portrait of a Victorian school. There are several cases of fictional clergymen other than Dr Wortle who, like many real Victorian clergymen, took a few private pupils to supplement their income [*The Bertrams*, 1]. There are some schoolmistresses, apart from those daughters of clergymen who help out in Sunday Schools. Grace Crawley assists at the private school for girls kept by the two Miss Prettymans, but the fact that she is paid a salary is kept quiet as it would lower her rank in society as a potential wife [*The Last Chronicle of Barset*, 6]. In his last years in Sussex, Trollope was quite active as a 'school manager' for his local school in Harting. [➤ Public Schools.]

Scotland. Also known to Victorian Englishmen as North Britain, Scotland played a crucial role in almost every aspect of Victorian life. This is not reflected in Trollope's fiction in which it has little importance. None of his short stories is set there and only a few chapters in his novels have Scottish locations. This is in contrast to Ireland and even to Wales. The reason probably was that Trollope felt he had little extensive knowledge of Scottish life, particularly its religious life. He disliked what he saw of Presbyterianism in Ireland, while the difficulties with a Scottish minister over *Rachel Ray* may also have influenced him. While his Post Office work took him to many places, he was only in Scotland for a comparatively short time to arrange some postal 'walks' in Glasgow in 1858, during which time he was writing *The Bertrams.*

There are several novels, for example *The Eustace Diamonds* and *Phineas Finn*, with Scottish estates to which 'a great many people go . . . in the autumn' [*The Eustace Diamonds*, 32]. Such estates, like Glenbogie in *Ayala's Angel* or Killancodlem in both *Is He Popenjoy?* and *The Duke's Children*, are more prominent in the large novels of his last decade. Scottish characters are comparatively rare: Robert Kennedy is the most important and in his case Trollope for once touches on the effects of Scottish religion. Of course, Lady Glencora Palliser – born Lady Glencora MacCluskie – is Scottish by birth, but this plays virtually no part in her character. Trollope occasionally uses Scots dialect, most notably when the sturdy Andy Gowran confronts his employer, Lady Eustace, in a forthright manner that few English retainers would have attempted [*The Eustace Diamonds*, 26]. [➤ Servants.]

There are, of course, several Scottish characters in England, most of whom are anglicized. In *Phineas Redux* [23] Trollope portrays an hotel in London that caters to Scottish guests. The villain in *The Three Clerks*, the Honourable Undy Scott, is a Scottish aristocrat, but that really plays little part in his villainy. His father, Lord Gaberlunzie, has the rare distinction of being a gentleman who is allowed to speak in Scottish dialect [8]. Gaberlunzie is a good example of Trollope's occasional and deft use of a Scottish word: it means 'a wandering beggar', which is just what Lord Gaberlunzie's son becomes. [➤ Thackeray, W. M.]

Trollope's comparative neglect of Scotland did not spring from any bias against Scotsmen. Several of his close friends, such as his publisher John Blackwood, were Scottish. He enjoyed walking tours of the Highlands and he had a great admiration for the poetry of Robert Burns, whom he often quoted [➤ Music], while he frequently re-read the novels of Sir Walter Scott. In his book on Australia he noted how often Scotsmen prospered in the colonies, while *Miss Mackenzie* shows how a Scottish family fared in England.

The Season. 'The Upper Ten Thousand of this our English world' [*Can You Forgive Her?*, 1] planned their lives round an unchanging calendar which ordained where they should be, or more importantly, should not be, at certain times of the year. Trollope's fashionable characters naturally follow this routine and this is particularly noticeable in novels from the mid-1860s onwards, most of all in the Palliser series. 'The Season' consisted of those months when Society was in London and coincided with the parliamentary year which normally began in early February. It wound down in late July and ended in early August. While the Duke of Omnium's party at his villa, The Horns, did take place as late as 27 July it was a ducal party and was still attended by the 500 most fashionable of the 'Upper Ten Thousand' [*Phineas Finn*, 63–4]. The Season therefore united the worlds of politics and Society and many fateful meetings in Trollope novels take place during those months. [➤ Parliament.]

When MPs and peers assembled for their parliamentary duties, their wives and families also came 'up to town'. People were engaged in an almost constant round of parties, dinners and receptions. In *Can You Forgive Her?* [48] Lady Monk regarded her parties, which begin after Parliament's Easter recess, as her 'special line in life'. There was enormous jealousy about who was invited to the grand occasions; once there, guests battled their way through packed rooms. People were also engaged in those activities, such as riding in 'the Park' (Hyde Park), in which there were particular opportunities for them to see and be seen [*The Last Chronicle of Barset*, 53]. Some of the aristocracy and gentry, particularly those without political duties, did not migrate to town until March or April, while devout fox-hunters would not wish to miss the hunting which went on until March. These regulated migratory patterns of British Society caused much bemusement to outside observers such as Senator Gotobed [*The American Senator*, 19]. One of the best descriptions of life during the Season occurs in *Is He Popenjoy?* [➤ especially Chapter 27].

The Season was also the best time for mothers to hunt for suitable husbands for their daughters, and that is why the De Courcy girls in *The Small House at Allington* or the Longestaffe sisters in *The Way We Live Now* bring such pressure on their fathers to use the family town house during the Season. In *The Vicar of Bullhampton* Lord Trowbridge was 'compelled by circumstances, – the circumstances being the custom of society as pleaded by his two daughters, – to spend the months of May, June, and July at the family mansion in Grosvenor Square' [56]. The Season could be a tiresome duty for both the girl and her parents, as when the Hotspur house in London is opened and Emily Hotspur is taken up to 'town' in order that a husband might be found for her [*Sir Harry Hotspur of Humblethwaite*, 4]. While a fashionable single man, such as Phineas Finn or Maurice Maule in *Phineas Redux*, could enjoy himself for comparatively little money during the Season, it could prove a heavy expense for a man whose wife and daughters wanted to dress in the latest fashion, maintain a carriage and give costly entertainments. According to Trollope, one Somerset squire with an income of £2,000 a year simply could not afford to take his only daughter to London for the Season [*The Belton Estate*, 1]. The Season also provided an opportunity to attend to business in London: thus an elderly Herefordshire baronet came up to town for a week to see his lawyer, his dentist and his tailor [*The Prime Minister*, 13].

Some aristocrats regarded the visit to London during the Season as 'a period of penance'. This is the attitude of the dowager Lady Lufton, who goes up to town because 'all Lady Luftons of whom she had heard . . . had always had their seasons in London'. She goes up in April and stays till June [*Framley Parsonage*, 16]. Those who did not have their own town houses sometimes rented one or took rooms, which is what Archdeacon Grantly and his wife do when their daughter Griselda is looking for a husband [➤ *Can You Forgive Her?*].

People with any pretence to fashion did not like being seen in London in August, after the Season was over, and for someone like Maule it was a miserable period with 'no whist, no society, – it may almost be said no dinner' [*Phineas Redux*, 21]. Thus the Proudies, even before he became a bishop, 'always felt it necessary . . . to retire from London when other great and fashionable people did so' [*Barchester Towers*, 3]. When the Season came to an end, members of Society retired to their country houses, sometimes abroad or increasingly to Scotland. Since Trollope himself spent all his successful career living in or near London, he did not have to follow the schedule with unrelaxed rigidity in his own social life although he knew that his beloved clubs would fill up in the spring and early summer months. He did tend to follow the custom of taking his continental holidays in the late summer and early autumn, after the Season had ended. [➤ See Travels.]

Serialization. Even before one of Trollope's own novels was serialized he writes of Bishop Proudie reading the last number of Dickens's *Little Dorrit* with a glass of hot negus and 'great inward satisfaction' [*Barchester Towers*, 43]. Serialization took three forms: in newspapers, in weekly or monthly magazines, or in weekly or monthly parts. Serializing in newspapers, until the last years of Trollope's life, did not have a good name, as Charley Tudor finds when his novels are published this way. The writer who was serialized in magazines found fame and fortune and reached an enormous audience. In Trollope's later career the part issues, which are associated with Dickens's fame, grew out of favour as magazine serialization increased.

Trollope's first novel to be serialized was his tenth one, *Framley Parsonage*, which appeared in the *Cornhill* in 1860. Before that, all nine of its predecessors had appeared as books; after that, almost all were serialized. Twenty-six novels appeared in periodicals and eight in part issues. Only four novels appeared first as books, and two of these, *Rachel Ray* and *Ayala's Angel*, were meant to be serialized. *An Old Man's Love* appeared as a book, but only after Trollope's death. The only novel written to be published first as a book was *Miss Mackenzie.*

The 26 serialized novels appeared in the following magazines: *Cornhill*, 4; *Fortnightly Review*, 3; *Blackwoods*, 5; *Saint Pauls*, 2; of which one was included as a supplement while also published in monthly parts; *Macmillan's*, 1; *Good Words*, 2; *The Graphic*, 3; *Temple Bar*, *All the Year Round*, 3; *Whitehall*, 1; *Life*, 1. [For titles of serialized novels, ➤ individual magazine entries.]

The effect on Trollope was twofold: on profits and on writing. For *Castle Richmond*, the last novel written before the serialization of *Framley Parsonage*, Trollope was offered £600; for *Framley Parsonage*'s serialization he was given £1,000, and less than three years later *The Small House at Allington* brought in £3,000. A serialized novel had to be constructed in a particular format because readers would read groups of

chapters as they appeared in the magazine. Characters and sub-plots had to keep appearing so that readers would not forget them, and there had to be résumés so that readers would not forget what they had read a week or a month before. Each group of chapters had to end in a way that would bring readers back for a further instalment. The *Athenaeum* referred to the 'landmarks where the story broke off, leaving them hungry and impatient at the month's pause'. [➤ the comment from the *Illustrated London News* in the entry for *Phineas Finn.*]

Magazine editors were more censorious than book publishers [➤ *The Duke's Children*; *Is He Popenjoy?*; *Rachel Ray*], and editors wanted to get as much as they could from a serialization so that novels grew longer and longer. This tied in with the vogue for three-volume novels [➤ 'Three-deckers']. Supporters of the system said it meant that each group of chapters was better constructed. Only once did Trollope fail to produce all the chapters needed to finish serialization. This was in his last novel, *The Land-Leaguers*, unfinished at his death.

[➤ Publishers and Publishing.]

Sermons. In his detestation of sermons Trollope stood apart from the general view of most educated Victorians. He expressed his dislike in many novels and short stories. In *Barchester Towers* he attacks them as collections of 'platitudes, truisms and untruisms' [6] and singled out sermons by young priests, 'Yes, my too self-confident juvenile friend, I do believe in those mysteries, which are so common in your mouth' [6]. He frequently associated sermons with Evangelicals like Mr Slope, whose sermon in the same chapter is Trollope's best-remembered one. In 'The Widow's Mite' he hints at the effect sermonizing may have on the self-esteem of clergymen: 'When a man has a pulpit of his own, why should he trouble himself to argue in any place where counter arguments must be met and sustained?' The maximum length for a sermon should be fifteen minutes: this was a radical proposal in an era when sermons could go on for an hour or more. While Trollope accepted that they could do good, as in his last short story, 'Not If I Know It', he also felt they could do much harm. When visiting America he was shocked at hearing political sermons: 'One is often driven to ask oneself whether the discourse from the pulpit be in its nature political or religious' [*North America*]. His longest sermon occurs in *La Vendée* and in this novel he violated the rule he later adopted against including sermons in his fiction. In his book on Australia he unusually quoted a sermon which advocated the teaching of one's religion, not the damning of others, as a good lesson for those back in the Mother Country. In several places he compared novels to sermons and novelists to preachers: 'But the novelist, if he have a conscience, must preach his sermons with the same purpose as the clergyman, and must have his own system of ethics' [*Autobiography*, 12]. At a speech in Liverpool in 1873 he proclaimed that 'works of the imagination are the sermons of the present day'. His own novels are full of little 'sermons' addressed to readers, especially to young readers and, more especially, to young women. They are usually far more enjoyable, and far shorter, than the pulpit variety. [➤ Novel, The; Religion.]

Servants. Although servants appear in every one of Trollope's forty-seven novels, relatively few are memorable characters. It may seem strange, given his own ability to retain servants for decades, that Trollope rarely treats them as interesting figures in their own right, especially as his readership came from those classes to whom servants were part of daily life. In the decade in which he began to write novels there were about one million servants in Britain. Their normal purpose in his novels is to go about their duties and to provide light relief. They could more easily be characters in their own right in the novels and short stories set in Ireland because there was much greater familiarity between masters and servants there than in England [➤ *Castle Richmond*; *The Land-Leaguers*; 'The O'Conors of Castle Conor'].

In Trollope's novels anyone with the slightest pretension to middle-class status has at least one servant and in this he is presenting an accurate picture of his age. Miss Marrable insisted that her niece, Mary Lowther, have a maid when she visits other people's houses, even though Mary has only £50 a year and Miss Marrable, £300 [*The Vicar of Bullhampton*, 9]. Even Mr Crawley on his meagre income of £130 a year keeps a maid at his vicarage although she is very young and has red arms. Both were signs of poverty that were often found in Trollope's Irish novels. The red arms meant that she, and not a washerwoman, washed the clothes, and her youth meant she was, for her lack of experience, paid little.

Sometimes a servant of great experience breaks through the barriers and becomes a character in his or her own right. Thus when a young wife is estranged from her husband in *Kept in the Dark*, her maid, Mary, says, "'I have known you so long, may I not say a word to you?" ... her mistress jumped up from her seat, took her in her arms, and kissed her' [13]. Sometimes servants can become confidantes: Miss Stanbury confides in her faithful maid Martha in *He Knew He Was Right*. Upper servants, housekeepers for instance, emerge more clearly as people and have not only personalities but also some personal history. The outspoken Mrs Baggett, the housekeeper in *An Old Man's Love*, has the most developed role of any servant in Trollope's fiction. Hopkins the gardener is also outspoken to the Dale family in *The Small House at Allington* and sometimes influences their actions. In *Mr Scarborough's Family* Peter Prosper's butler, Matthew, becomes very chatty with his master but we suspect the approximation to equality did not outlast the crisis over Mr Prosper's failed engagement. The role of an old family servant both in relation to the family and to other servants is well portrayed with Mrs Toff in *Is He Popenjoy?* and with Lady Fitzgerald's maid, Jones — whom everyone else calls Mrs Jones because of her power and considerable savings [*Castle Richmond*, 9]. In *An Eye for an Eye* Mrs Bunce, the housekeeper at Scroope Manor, dominates the household and the old earl. Cooks and housekeepers were normally addressed as 'Mrs', regardless of their marital status.

Trollope sometimes uses servants to mirror their masters or mistresses: thus pretentious people employ French servants as the Melmottes did in *The Way We Live Now*; and the well-named Mr Grandairs is hired by Miss Mackenzie's pretentious sister-in-law in *Miss Mackenzie*. The vulgar Mrs Greenow in *Can You Forgive Her?* gives the name 'Jeanette' to her maid, implying she is French, when they visit Yarmouth. Beginning with his second novel, *The Kellys and the O'Kellys*, Trollope followed a fairly consistent pattern in giving certain names to servants who only make a brief appearance in a novel: Richard for a man or Richards for a maid. The Bunce family provided servants in several novels.

Keeping one's distance from servants who shared the same house was a frequent topic in Victorian writing. Normally the 'upstairs' tried to keep family disputes from the 'downstairs': in *Barchester Towers* Mrs Grantly is quite concerned to keep news of a quarrel between her sister and her husband, the archdeacon, from spreading. In *Kept in the Dark* an overriding concern of the young wife after the breakdown of her marriage, was to keep news of her husband's disappearance from the servants [13]. Servants, however, usually knew what was going on as becomes clear when Plantagenet Palliser expels Major Pountney from Gatherum Castle in *The Prime Minister*, or when Peter Prosper thinks of marrying a woman whom the servants do not think is quite a lady in *Mr Scarborough's Family*. One of the worst fates that could befall a Victorian was to be openly despised by his servants, as happens to Henry Jones in *Cousin Henry*. The difficulties faced especially by the ladies in a family that loses its servants is described in *The Land-Leaguers*. Yet Trollope also understood the growing feeling among working people that they did not wish to become servants, 'from a dislike to be subject at all hours to the will of others' ['The Telegraph Girl'].

Men servants were particularly expensive because they cost more to maintain, because there were fewer of them to go round and because there was a tax of 21s. a year on all men servants over the age of eighteen. A footman, particularly in livery and a wig, was a sign of great social status, and that is why Mrs Proudie is so concerned to have several. 'A little greased flour rubbed in among the hair on a footman's head . . . gives such a tone of high life to the family' [*The Last Chronicle of Barset*, 18]. Apparently Trollope never employed a footman, mindful perhaps of his parents' maintaining a liveried footman even when they had little money. It was quite traditional in Victorian literature and periodicals to make fun of footmen – Thackeray was a master of this – but Trollope rarely does so. However, he does have a footman with the traditional name of 'John' spy on his master in *The Bertrams*. Normally the lower level of servants – maids and grooms – play no real roles in the plots, although Patience Crabstick in *The Eustace Diamonds* does become involved in the theft of the jewels.

We learn much about servants' wages in the novels: the vicar in *The Small House at Allington* pays his cook £16 a year but he does complain that he does not get as good food as Earl De Guest gets from a cook whom he pays £60 a year. Perhaps the best account of servants in a country house occurs in *The Belton Estate* [17] in which a baronet, Sir Anthony Aylmer, although not in 'easy circumstances', keeps up the estate 'in proper English style', that is with a butler, two footmen, a coachman, three gamekeepers, four gardeners and 'sundry inferior men and boys' as well as numerous maids. Ten indoor servants sat down to 'four heavy meals' every day while the Aylmer family had to have 'stingy breakfasts and bad dinners' to afford all this. The great expense of servants was not their relatively small pay, but the amount it cost to feed them: the frugal Mrs Dosett in *Ayala's Angel* [4] decided that a 12lb. shoulder of mutton will feed a middle-class family of three and two servants for two days. (When Trollope bought some tinned Australian beef for his servants they refused to eat it, probably because they feared it meant a lowering of their standards of eating.)

Mark Robarts in *Framley Parsonage* has an income of £900 a year and can maintain a footman, a groom, a gardener, a cook and several maids. In the 1860s Trollope had an annual income which averaged five times this amount. The 1861 census shows that there were five resident servants at his home, Waltham House, and in addition there would have been gardeners and possibly some other non-resident servants. Three of these servants were Irish and had been with the Trollopes some time. He pays tribute to them in *Castle Richmond*: 'Irish servants I have had some in my house for years, and never had one that was faithless, dishonest, or intemperate' [1]. Irish servants might be less regular than English ones but they never refused to perform tasks that were normally done by other servants.

His most important servant was his old groom, Barney (Bernard Smith), who had been with him since his early days in Ireland. As well as looking after Trollope's horses, Barney awakened his master each morning at dawn with a cup of coffee and ensured that

Trollope got to his desk to write his daily quota of pages. For this task Barney was paid an extra £5 a year. [Mullen, 446–7, 710–11.] In his *Autobiography* Trollope says, 'I owe more to him than to any one else for the success I have had.' In *The Land-Leaguers* [9] there is a small tribute to the 'invaluable' huntsman, Barney Smith, which may be taken as a tribute to the man who had helped get Trollope ready for so many hunts.

While Trollope had known relative poverty at some periods of his youth he had never known life without servants. When travelling he missed the 'civility' of the 'well-ordered servant' [*North America*] just as his mother had when she travelled in America thirty years earlier. When he first visited Australia with his wife Rose, he took their cook to ensure that he got his soup. While there the woman left their service, married and became 'quite a lady'. Though no doubt missing his soup, Trollope admired her for seeking to improve her life and said that no woman in her position should stay in England but should go to the colonies to find a better life [*Australia and New Zealand*].

Sometimes the phrase 'board wages' is used in Trollope's novels [*Orley Farm*, 8; *Is He Popenjoy?*, 23]. This was an extra allowance over and above wages that was given to servants to provide for their food when a great house was closed down and meals were not provided. It normally saved the master a considerable sum because if the servants' appetites took them beyond that sum, they had to pay for any extra food. Sometimes parsimonious mistresses used it as a way to save money even when they were in residence.

[➤ Money; Names, Use of.]

Service à la Russe. See Food.

Settlements. Many readers of Trollope's fiction will share the bewilderment of the young American character, Isabel Boncassen: 'I don't know what settlements mean' [*The Duke's Children*, 47]. Almost every Trollope novel that features a marriage in the aristocracy, gentry or upper middle class includes discussions about what the couple would 'live on'. Archdeacon Grantly stood for most well-to-do Victorian fathers when he said he did not want his son, Major Grantly, to live on a 'scratch income' when he married Grace Crawley.

The normal procedure was for a couple's parents to 'settle' or invest a specific amount of capital to produce income from interest or dividends, income which went to the couple: sometimes it was the husband's parents who settled the money on their son but normally it was the wife's parents who settled the money on her. In this case it could be referred to as a 'fortune' or a dowry. If large sums of money were involved, a legal agreement or 'settlement' was drawn up, usually appointing trustees to administer the money. Such settlements were in addition to any outright gift. They guaranteed an income, preserved the parents' capital and protected the woman to a certain degree. Sometimes, when the bride had an income of her own, the settlement was an understanding between her father and her prospective husband. In *Is He Popenjoy?* Dean Lovelace undertakes to rent a house in London at which he expects the couple to live for six months each year during the Season and to give his daughter £300 a year out of which she is to hire a carriage.

His daughter's income passed by law into her husband's hands on marriage [2, 20].

Since rates of interest were so low, large sums were often involved. The settlement would provide enough money for the couple to maintain the status their parents had known and ideally would provide enough income to maintain the large families of the Victorian era. There is an amusing description of the complex negotiations for a settlement between a spinster and her prospective husband in *Mr Scarborough's Family* [26, 27, 43, 44]. Here the lady controlled her own 'fortune' and would only surrender a third of the income to her husband (he had wanted half), while demanding that if she provided the ponies and carriage he had to maintain them.

Settlements could also include arrangements to support the wife if she should become a widow and could specify that if the wife died first, the income was to be 'settled' on the children, and not the husband, as is the case with Alice Vavasor in *Can You Forgive Her?*. Sometimes the mother's money was passed on to her younger children: part of the Duchess of Omnium's fortune eventually goes to her younger children. Trollope knew the importance of settlements from his early life. After his parents fled to Belgium, his mother exclaimed, 'Oh! what a blessed thing is a settlement' [Mullen, 78]. That money helped the family to survive difficult times. Settlements were necessary in an age when 'gentlemen' had such limited areas in which they could earn money and a 'lady' had virtually no way of doing so except by writing. Landed families often had considerable assets but little real income: this could be supplemented by a bride's settlement.

In Trollope's novels, a settlement is normally discussed among those who will pay, as in *The Bertrams* [28], and then arranged by the family solicitors. Difficulties arose when lawyers' arrangements made it impossible for people to get at the money for their own purposes, for instance in *The Kellys and the O'Kellys* when Lord Ballindine's mother hopes to use her new daughter-in-law's settlement to free the estate from debt [39]. One can find several examples of how the system worked in *The Small House at Allington*: Crosbie approaches Squire Dale about what he intends to do for his niece, Lily Dale, because the squire has already agreed to do something in the case of a possible marriage by her sister. In Crosbie's next romance he is approached by Gazebee, the solicitor who manages the business of the De Courcy family, and is forced to agree to difficult terms, the consequences of which appear when the marriage soon collapses. The failure of a marriage could lead to all sorts of legal problems concerning the settlement, as in *Phineas Redux* when Lady Laura Kennedy seeks to regain her £40,000 settlement from her estranged husband.

Sometimes a son approaches his father to ask what could be done for him, only to be disappointed: a selfish and hard-pressed father like Maurice Maule in *The Prime Minister* refuses to do anything when his son wishes to marry a duke's granddaughter. The marriage is called off and only goes ahead when Madame Max Goesler gives the couple money. [➤ Dowagers.]

Sewing. Needlework provides frequent metaphors in Trollope's fiction. His wife Rose was a notable needlewoman who had won a prize for embroidery at the 1851 Exhibition. He shows a knowledge of sewing in his second novel, *The Kellys and the O'Kellys* [26], which is the first one he wrote after his marriage. Allusions to sewing added to the domestic atmosphere that so many readers liked in Trollope's writing. [➤ *The Small House at Allington* for criticism of a mistake in his description of dressmaking; *Sir Harry Hotspur of Humblethwaite*.]

Shakespeare, William. Trollope began reading Shakespeare as a boy. On one school holiday when his mother was in America he spent days in his father's chambers in Lincoln's Inn, and to amuse himself he read Shakespeare 'out of a bi-columned edition ... It was not that I had chosen Shakespeare, but that there was nothing else.' He continued to read him throughout his life and from his own choice. In his fiction he quoted him more than any other writer. As a young clerk in the Post Office he wanted to be a poet and toyed with the idea of writing a dramatic poem about Richard II and Henry IV. As the subject had been 'so perfectly handled by Shakespere [*sic*]' he admitted it would be a 'dangerous job' and gave it up. His surviving notes in his Commonplace Book show he had studied the historical plays in some detail. Among his enormous collection of plays and books on the theatre were forty-seven volumes of the Shakespeare Society's publications, other editions of Shakespeare, concordances and commentaries; eighty-six volumes from Trollope's theatrical collection are now in the Folger Memorial Shakespeare Library in Washington.

He carefully read and extensively annotated (with the dates of annotation) his copies and he was not uncritical, especially of *Henry VI*. His favourite character was Brutus. He praised Shakespeare for being 'definitely beyond his age in discovering the manliness of decency'. He frequently turned to Shakespeare for characters' names, especially in *An Eye for an Eye* and *Sir Harry Hotspur of Humblethwaite*. In three novels he openly admitted that he drew some if not all of his plot from Shakespeare: in *The Struggles of Brown, Jones, and Robinson* he compared Mr Brown's plight with King Lear's; more seriously, in *Lady Anna* he traced his plot to *Cymbeline* [26]; in *He Knew He Was Right* Louis Trevelyan's mental disintegration can be traced to Othello's.

In *Marion Fay* he not only quotes from *Macbeth* but may well have had Lady Macbeth in mind when creating the vindictive Marchioness of Kingsbury [34]. In *The Fixed Period* he quotes the famous lines from *As You Like It* (II.7), 'Second childishness ... sans teeth, sans eyes, sans taste, sans everything', and this lament for old age obviously influenced the writing of this novel. He often quoted Shakespeare in his private correspondence and had a keen interest in the theatre, which he shared with his friend G. H. Lewes. He very much disliked the building of the Shakespeare Memorial Theatre in Stratford as unnecessary.

[➤ Names, Origin of.]

Shilly-Shally. See *Ralph the Heir*.

Ships. Ships figure frequently in Trollope's writing, which is only natural in one who travelled so widely. Many of his travel books give details of ocean voyages, while *How the 'Mastiffs' Went to Iceland* provides an enviable account of the joys of a yacht trip. This trip to Iceland probably gave him the idea of sending Lord Hampstead on a 'cruise about the face of the world' after the death of his beloved [*Marion Fay*, 64]. 'The Journey to Panama' is his best account of life aboard a transatlantic ship and *John Caldigate* is a good description of the lengthy trip to Australia. Both are noteworthy for the depiction of the way in which women were treated on such trips. *The Bertrams* has a very hostile account of the behaviour of Anglo-Indians on a ship returning to England. The dangers of travel by ship become apparent when several characters in *The Claverings* disappear suddenly, and most conveniently, on a fishing trip to Norway. In 'John Bull on the Guadalquivir' Trollope describes taking a steamer up the Guadalquivir river in Spain. Trollope named two ships after controversial contemporary politicians: the SS *Julius Vogel* in *John Caldigate* and HMS *John Bright* in *The Fixed Period*.

In *The Fixed Period*, John Neverbend writes his memoirs aboard ship. Trollope used his own numerous voyages to work and always had the ship's carpenter prepare a desk on which he wrote his daily quota of pages. Thus *Lady Anna* was completely finished on his first trip to Australia, and parts of *The Bertrams* were written both on the Atlantic and the Mediterranean. On one transatlantic voyage the young Henry James was amazed at the way in which Trollope did his daily writing in his cabin. [➤ Travels.]

The Short Story. Trollope began his career as a short-story writer in the summer of 1859 when visiting America for the first time. By then he was already the author of eight novels. While in New York he called at Harper & Brothers to discuss contributing 'tales' to their *Harper's New Monthly Magazine* to take advantage of his travels. After he returned home on 3 July he wrote two stories – probably in July – 'The Courtship of Susan Bell' and 'Relics of General Chassé, which he sent off and for which he was paid $100 (£20) each. He obviously liked the idea of using his travels to generate extra income and suggested to *Harper's* a series of twelve stories which he could then publish in one volume in England.

When he went on a holiday to the Pyrenees that autumn he set aside his work on *Castle Richmond* to devote himself to his new series. Seven weeks later he wrote to Thackeray about publishing these stories in England in his new *Cornhill* magazine, but Thackeray asked him to write a novel instead. He continued writing short stories till within months of his death; in the summer of 1882 he agreed to write ten stories for the magazine *Bow Bells*, for which he would have been paid £70 each. Altogether he wrote 42 short stories for publication in fifteen magazines and two collections: *The Argosy*, 3; *Cassell's Illustrated Family Paper*, 4; *The Fortnightly Review*, 1; *Good Words* (incorporating *Good Cheer*), 8; *The Graphic*, 1; *Harper's New Monthly Magazine*, 4; *The Illustrated London News*, 1; *Life*, 1; *Light*, 1; *The London Review*, 3; *The Masonic Magazine*, 1; *Public Opinion*, 5; *Routledge's Christmas Annual* (1870), 1; *Saint Pauls*, 6; *Victoria Regia*, 1; and *A Welcome*, 1.

Of the stories, 25 were set outside

England: in Belgium, 1; America, 3; Ireland, 2; France, 2; Egypt, 2; the West Indies, 2; Spain, 1; the Holy Land, 1; Italy, 3; Panama, 1; Germany, 1; Austria, 2; New Zealand, 1; France and England, 1, and on the open seas, 1. His fantasy 'The Gentle Euphemia' was set in 'Grandnostrel'. Of the 17 stories set totally in England, 8 were in London, 2 in the West Country and 1 each in Yorkshire, Cornwall, the Lake District, Cheshire, the 'South of England', 'the country' and Barset.

Many of the stories have an autobiographical element because Trollope used incidents from his own experience or because the stories are set in places he had visited, whether in Ireland, France, Italy, the Holy Land, England, the Empire, New Zealand or America. Most, but not all, are or contain love stories which result in marriage, and nine are humorous. Working-class characters play a larger role here than in his novels.

Trollope's attitude towards short stories changed and he grew to find them tiresome. They required too much work. In his negotiations with Donald Macleod over the writing of 'The Two Heroines of Plumplington' in 1882, he wrote that five printed pages of *Good Words* equalled twenty manuscript pages and that writing these twenty pages was 'a week's work'. Even worse was the formulation of plot: he told one publisher, 'The labour is in arranging a plot, rather than in writing the tale.' When another asked for a Christmas story in 1869 and offered a handsome sum, he wrote, 'I must ask you to excuse me ... I would rather be without the work, – as the task of constructing such a story becomes a burden on one, almost as great as is the construction of a prolonged tale [novel].'

He started to charge a minimum fee equal to what he would have earned if he had been working on a novel over the same period. By 1861 he was charging £50; by 1866, £60. In 1878 his minimum reached £100 but by 1882 it had fallen to £70. Sometimes his rate of payment for stories surpassed that for novels: *Cousin Henry*, written in 1878, earned £500 but took six weeks to write; six short stories would have earned £600. (In 1877 he got £175 for 'Why Frau Frohmann Raised Her Prices', the largest fee he ever received for a story, but that is because it was published in four issues, not two as agreed.) If his earnings as a novelist fell by the end of his life to below the pre-1860s peak, his earnings as a short-story writer rose steadily between 1859 and 1882. His Christmas stories fetched more than any other although he disliked writing them. Of 42 stories the sum received is known for 31. Two of these, 'The Journey to Panama' and 'Miss Ophelia Gledd', were written without payment. For the other 29 he received £1,955. When added to the £2,348 he received for his collections the total, £4,313, shows the stories constituted a relatively small percentage of his total writing income.

Of his 42 stories, 37 were published in five collections: *Tales of All Countries*, First Series (1861); *Tales of All Countries*, Second Series (1863); *Lotta Schmidt and Other Stories* (1867); *An Editor's Tales* (1870); *Why Frau Frohmann Raised Her Prices and Other Stories* (1882).

In general terms English short-story writing did not equal that in America or France in the nineteenth century. This was partly due to the serialization of novels which met a demand which elsewhere stories would have satisfied.

Silverbridge, Lord.
See Palliser Family.

Sir Harry Hotspur of Humblethwaite. Trollope's twenty-fifth novel was written between 27 December 1868 and 30 January 1869. The story was first serialized in eight monthly parts in *Macmillan's Magazine* between May and December 1870. It was then published in one volume by Hurst & Blackett in November 1870. Trollope received £750. [➤ Harper & Brothers.]

The novel is set in the Lake District, in Cumberland. Like many later novels, it shows the influence of Shakespeare. When Trollope began writing he called the baronet Brandon: Sir William Brandon is in Shakespeare's *King Richard III* and Charles Brandon, first Duke of Suffolk, is in *King Henry VIII*. He dropped this for Hotspur, a name redolent of medieval history. Like *The Belton Estate* and *An Eye for an Eye* the story begins with the death of an heir to an historic landed estate, in this case Humblethwaite, the home of the baronet, Sir Harry Hotspur. Like so many later novels, this is concerned with property. Sir Harry, an idealized Tory squire, is an unhappy man. On the death of his only son, his second cousin, the reprobate George Hotspur, becomes heir to the baronetcy. Sir Harry has two problems: to find a suitable husband for his only daughter Emily, and to decide whether to leave the property to her, thereby dividing it from the title, or to George. The property has no entail. While loath to divide the two he does so because as an honourable man he cannot leave

his property to his heir, who is a scoundrel. If only Emily could marry George Hotspur his problem would be solved, but as a father he fears for his daughter's happiness. George, no longer in the cavalry, lives in London's 'fast set' [➤ Military]. He cheats at cards; he is in debt; he has a mistress, and, it is later learned, may have to face criminal charges connected with cheating at cards.

George visits Humblethwaite and Emily falls in love with him. He proposes and she accepts. Sir Harry orders George off the property and eventually Sir Harry pays George enough to persuade him to go away. Emily cannot stop loving George, who marries his mistress and descends into drunkenness. Emily goes with her parents to Europe and soon dies of a broken heart in Lugano.

When Trollope began his editorship of *Saint Pauls* he wrote as editor that 'the preaching of the day is done by the novelist'. Nowhere is this more the case than in this 'sermon' on the nature of woman's love and on marriage. Emily 'had confessed her love very boldly to the man who had asked for it; had made her rich present with a free hand, and had grudged nothing in the making of it. But having given it, she understood it to be fixed as the heavens that she could never give the same gift again. It was herself that she had given, and there was no retracting the offering.' When informed of his true character she was unaffected: 'Was not this sort of giving acknowledged by all churches in which the words for "better or for worse" were uttered as part of the marriage vow.'

When writing to Alexander Macmillan, Trollope described the novel as 'a common love story – but one that ends sadly'. In his *Autobiography* he remembered it as 'written on the same plan as *Nina Balatka*', that is, 'telling of some pathetic incident in life rather than the portraiture of a number of living human beings'. In this it is nearer to a modern novel than to a Victorian one. The book, he continued, was 'not, I think, by any means a failure. There is much of pathos in the love of the girl, and of paternal dignity and affection in the father.' George Eliot was not impressed with Emily: 'Men are fond of that sort of dog-like attachment.' Trollope's London has now become a centre of vice and corruption, especially for young men with private incomes like George Hotspur.

The story abounds with current references and private influences: the 'distinguished party in Norfolk' [10] referred to guests of the Prince and Princess of Wales at Sandringham, about whose life there was increasing talk. Like his mother, Trollope preferred homely metaphors and comments on Emily's lack of maturity when judging men: she 'had not yet learned the housewife's trick of passing the web through her fingers, and of finding by the touch whether the fabric were of fine wool, or of shoddy made up with craft to look like wool of the finest' [2]. This obviously originated with his wife Rose, an expert seamstress [➤ Sewing]. As often with Trollope, disreputable men drink gin. (Brandy mixed with curaçao and seltzer water is also a 'bad' drink which George Hotspur consumes in quantity.) When discussing George Hotspur's obtaining and selling his army commission, Trollope used the information recently acquired when his elder son, Henry, got his rank of cornet in a regiment of mounted yeomanry. Also, Trollope's incisive comments on the nature of a parent's love for his child being greater than that of the child for the parent were written when his younger son, Fred, was visiting England after his first visit to Australia and before he left to settle there. Trollope named Emily's rejected suitor Lord Alfred Gresley: Gresley was the name of Fanny Trollope's mother. Trollope also used it in his short story, 'Mary Gresley'.

Readers might wonder why no one denounced George Hotspur for not having 'gainful employment'. Sir Harry never included this among his vices. As a 'gentleman' he would not have been expected to work for a living. The novel also showed the changes in late-Victorian moral standards. Trollope discussed prostitution more openly than in earlier novels but never used the word 'mistress'; and in his notes referred to George's friend as 'the woman with whom [George Hotspur] ... is entangled'. For her part, Emily adopted the 'double standard' as expressed by her mother: 'And then is it not the fact that some little amount of shade in the fleece of male sheep is considered, if not absolutely desirable, at any rate quite pardonable? A male sheep with a fleece as white as that of a ewe-lamb – is he not considered to be, among muttons, somewhat insipid?' [5].

When *The Times* reviewed the book they pointed this out: 'It used to be printed on some French novels, "*La mère en défendra la lecture à sa fille*", and the same might be said of parts of *Sir Harry Hotspur*. But the reading world is not entirely composed of young ladies. This book may do good to many of both sexes more advanced in life.' Finally, the novel raises a theological point about the nature of sin and forgiveness: cannot 'black sheep', even the blackest, be redeemed? 'If it be not so,' Trollope asks, 'what is all this doctrine of repentance in which we believe?' [5].

[➤ French Novels; Names, Origin of; Religion.]

Size of Novels. See 'Three-deckers'.

Slang. In *The Small House at Allington* Lily Dale's sister rebukes her for using a slang word like 'swell' to criticize Adolphus Crosbie and Lily defends her use of it: 'I fancy I do like slang. I think it's awfully jolly to talk about things being jolly' [2]. She remained unrepentant and in *The Last Chronicle of Barset* said that someone had 'skedaddled', to her mother's horror [3]. (Hasty retreats by Northern forces in the American Civil War had popularized this word.) In *Phineas Finn* Violet Effingham used a nautical term to refer to someone as 'A1' [42] and this term occurs often in Trollope's later fiction. In *The Three Clerks* Katie Woodward approves of the hero in Charley Tudor's novel because 'he is so spooney' [22]. Some of Trollope's slang, like Lily's 'swell' and 'skeddadled' and Violet's 'A1', has survived in spoken English while other words and expressions, like Katie's 'spooney' or Count Pateroffs being 'in railroad hurry' [*The Claverings*, 19], have disappeared. Slang occurs throughout Trollope's fiction, mainly in dialogue and generally used by men. Trollope himself said that the novel in which slang is most frequently used is *The Struggles of Brown, Jones, and Robinson.*

A gentleman was not expected to use slang in front of a lady and ladies were not expected to use it at all, but as Trollope admitted in *Is He Popenjoy?*, 'Ladies do sometimes talk slang...' [25]. Lily, Katie and Violet were not alone. Lily not only uses slang but produces something akin to a mixed metaphor in *The Small House at Allington* [3] when she refers to Adolphus Crosbie as 'a duck of an Apollo'. (In Lily's case slang emphasizes how lively she is, which will make her tragedy all the greater.) Some ladies, like Martha Dunstable, stand outside the rule, but her money and age give her freedom. Even so, the biggest offenders are young men like those in the Embassy in Brussels in *Mr Scarborough's Family* [15], and their use of slang is normally disliked and criticized by older people and sometimes by Trollope himself. In *An Eye for an Eye* Lady Scroope has difficulty with Fred Neville's 'jolly as a sandboy', 'right as a trivet' and 'deuced good fellow', but 'she knew that she had to learn to hear things to which she had hitherto not been accustomed' [2]. The Reverend Henry Clavering is confused when his son tells him that a cousin is 'very heavy' on another cousin (meaning he lives off him) in *The Claverings* [10]. (For Harry Clavering, as for most people, there is acceptable slang and unacceptable slang: the former was what he used while the latter was that used by his social inferiors in an engineering office.) Plantagenet Palliser criticizes his wife for using 'the long and the short of it': 'Glencora, I wish you would not use such expressions' [49]. After her death he is even more offended by his elder son, Lord Silverbridge, who uses terms like 'beastly work' and 'bosh'. Palliser, now Duke of Omnium, resolves 'to instruct his son that no gentleman above the age of a schoolboy should allow himself to use such a word in such a sense' [*The Duke's Children*, 56]. His younger son is worse, with terms like 'brute', 'rumpus', 'slap at it', 'craning', 'at one rush', 'tip-top', 'playing high', 'getting one's dander up', 'cut that kind of thing', 'spouting Latin', 'sat upon', 'pitch into', 'brick', 'smash up' and 'setting up his back against' [65].

Slang between men is acceptable, as for instance when Lord Altringham talks to George Hotspur of 'pluck' [*Sir Harry Hotspur of Humblethwaite*, 5]. (When Queen Victoria was explaining to Disraeli why Prince Albert had succumbed to cholera she said, to his amusement, that the Prince had lacked 'what they call pluck'.) In *Marion Fay* Lord Hautboy tells Lord Llwddythlw that 'that's a tidy animal of yours' but Lord Llwddythlw, like Plantagenet Palliser, is none the wiser [39].

Sometimes slang shows class differences: Mr Cockey, the vulgar commercial traveller, offends Squire Harry Gilmore with his slang terms in *The Vicar of Bullhampton*. The young men in the engineering office in *The Claverings* are not quite gentlemen, and refer to Harry Clavering, a Cambridge man, as a 'lad of wax', 'a brick', 'a trump' and 'no small beer', but he was not amused at the compliments [7]. Servants sometimes used slang to the confusion of the serious-minded: Lord De Guest's servant refers to a doctor's 'chaffing' his lordship, thereby making Dr Crofts think he had been slapping the earl's 'hands and feet, and that sort of thing' [*The Small House at Allington*, 20].

Occasionally slang occurs in narration and often has a tongue-in-cheek apology attached. When Trollope says that Mrs Proudie had never 'taken a

licking from anyone', he added, 'if on such an occasion I may be allowed to use a schoolboy's slang' [*The Last Chronicle of Barset*, 34]. In *Doctor Thorne* he wrote that a man 'shut up' and added 'as the slang phrase goes' [5]. But he did not always apologize: when he had Lily describe Crosbie as a 'swell', he added, 'Mr Crosbie was a swell.' He had to be careful, for there were always critics waiting to pounce: in *The Bertrams* [31] he answered their charges: 'If I were to use the word "flabbergasted" as expressing Miss Baker's immediate state of mind, I should draw down on myself the just anger of the critics, in that I had condescended to the use of slang, but what other word will so well express what is meant?'

Slide, Quintus. Slide is a journalist who plays an important role in several Palliser novels. He symbolizes the newer type of journalism that grew up in the 1860s and has a vigorous prose style. When he first appears in *Phineas Finn* [26] he offers to use his paper, the *People's Banner*, to support Phineas Finn, but when Finn rejects him he becomes his bitter enemy. He reappears in *Phineas Redux* in which, as editor of the *People's Banner*, he causes more trouble for Finn. In *The Prime Minister* he directs his fire at the Pallisers after the Duke of Omnium refuses to invite him to Gatherum Castle.

Slope, The Rev. Obadiah. Although he only appears in one novel, *Barchester Towers*, Obadiah Slope is better remembered than any other character whose appearance is limited to just one work. Trollope evidently thought much and carefully about his portrait and there are few chapters in all his writing as venomous as that in which Slope is exhaustively described [4]. Trollope delights in piling on his bad points. It is hardly surprising to note that Slope lacks the manly attribute of a beard. Trollope told Escott that Slope was the 'descendant of my mother's *Vicar of Wexhill*'. This 1837 novel by Fanny Trollope portrayed a scheming and lustful Evangelical clergyman, based in part on a Vicar of Harrow. Anthony, who fully shared his mother's detestation of Evangelicals, created Slope to embody all that he despised in this new type of clergyman. He took the unique course of announcing to his readers that 'we hate' Slope [18] and also lets us know that he got Obadiah's surname from Laurence Sterne's *Tristram Shandy* because, he says, Slope 'is lineally descended from that eminent physician [Dr Slop] who assisted at the birth of Mr T. Shandy'. Trollope tells his readers that, to alter the unfortunate pronunciation, Obadiah added an 'e' to his surname 'as other great men have done'. This is most probably a reference to the Duke of Wellington, whose family had changed the spelling of their surname from Wesley to the more aristocratic Wellesley. The name Obadiah is that of one of the minor Hebrew prophets, and incidentally of the shortest book of the Bible. By this choice, Trollope is emphasizing that Slope draws his inspiration from the Old Testament and not from the New, which speaks of 'the mercies of our Saviour'. (There is also an Obadiah in *Tristram Shandy* and it is he who is sent to summon Dr Slop.) Although Slope disappears from Barsetshire after his defeat by Mrs Proudie at the end of *Barchester Towers* and, unfortu-nately, never returns, other characters in later novels in the series think about him from time to time [*Framley Parsonage*, 40]. Trollope created a somewhat paler version of Slope a few years later in the Reverend Mr Prong in *Rachel Ray*. [➤ Names, Origin of.]

Slow and Bideawhile. See Lawyers; Names, Silly.

The Small House at Allington. Trollope's fifteenth novel, and the fifth in the Barsetshire series, was written between 20 May and 1 September 1862. It was serialized in the *Cornhill* from September 1862 until April 1864 and published in two volumes by Smith, Elder in March 1864. Trollope received £3,000. Millais provided illustrations for the serialization and, with one exception, these were in the published volumes.

Trollope began writing a few days after finishing *North America* and only two months after his return from his second trip to America. He had originally wanted to call the book 'The Two Pearls of Allington', but Smith objected that it might be confused with *The Pearl of Orr's Island*, a novel by Harriet Beecher Stowe then being serialized. The original title was used for an early chapter. Trollope was aware of the growing criticism that he wrote too quickly and that is probably why he did not give Smith the final chapters for several months after he had finished, even though he told the publisher he was always afraid that a manuscript might perish in a fire.

As he had done before, Trollope showed a reluctance to return to Barsetshire. Smith and the *Cornhill* audience had been delighted with *Framley Parsonage*, which had made

Trollope one of the best-paid novelists of the age. He well knew that Smith and his readers had much disliked his failed comic novel, *The Struggles of Brown, Jones, and Robinson*. As far as Trollope himself was concerned, *The Small House at Allington* was not a return to Barsetshire: Allington itself is not in Barsetshire, but in the next county. Few scenes actually occur in Barsetshire, although there is a particularly poignant one in which Adolphus Crosbie sees Mr Harding at Barchester Cathedral [16]. The Grantlys also reappear in their rectory [55], but most of the Barsetshire scenes are set at Courcy Castle, the home of the De Courcys.

The Small House at Allington is really centred on Allington and London, where several male characters are seen at their work or in their social life. London's importance had grown throughout the later Barsetshire novels: here and eventually in *The Last Chronicle of Barset* there is a persistent theme about the different ways in which men behave in London and in the country. Crosbie may be said to represent London and sophistication, while Lily represents country life and simplicity. There is very little of clerical life in the novel: Mr Boyce is just one of the earliest of that line of clergymen whom Trollope inserted in a novel because his publisher and readers wanted at least one.

The Small House at Allington contains three of Trollope's most important characters: Lily Dale, Adolphus Crosbie and John Eames. Although Trollope clearly intended the two Dale sisters to be the heroines of the novel, Lily captured the public imagination far more strongly than her elder sister, Bell. (Trollope may well have

been having one of his private jokes with these names: his wife also had a floral name, Rose, and one of her sisters was named Isabella.) Lily Dale became Trollope's most popular heroine. 'Lilian Dale, dear Lily Dale – for my reader must know that she is to be very dear, and that my story will be nothing to him if he do not love Lily Dale' [2]. The novel revolves round the story of Lily's love for Crosbie and her reactions when he jilts her. Lily Dale is an ideal Victorian heroine: she is, of course, innocent and pure and when once she has given her love, she feels unable ever to give it to another man [► Women]. Years later another writer told Trollope how much he admired Lily and Trollope replied, 'You can have no idea how pleased I am to hear you say that: I am so fond of her myself' [Mullen, 452]. Later, however, he held a contradictory view [► Dale Family].

For many modern readers Crosbie is a more interesting character than Lily for he is the best example of Trollope's view that no character can be completely bad. Crosbie has several good points. He has successfully 'mounted up' in the Civil Service and has a salary of about £700 a year, roughly equal to Trollope's own government salary at the time of writing. For sophisticated readers, Trollope provides one of those hints that Victorian novelists were occasionally allowed when he informs us that Crosbie could not afford 'the comforts of marriage'. This is then followed by: 'But – we will not, however, at the present moment inquire more curiously into the private life . . . of our new friend' [2]. The 'But – ' was enough for the knowing, and one suspects that the troublesome aside could be omitted in any reading aloud of the novel to a family. [➤ Prostitutes.]

Certainly Crawley does evil by jilting Lily, but he tumbles into this by his desire to make his way in Society. His real fault is not so much that he is a snob – like the De Courcys' son-in-law, Gazebee – but that he is a 'coward at heart'. His jilting of Lily Dale is one of the best-known events in Trollope's fiction. In Victorian times such an action was a serious matter and could lead to a 'breach of promise' lawsuit, as any reader of the *Pickwick Papers* will recall. Such events were not confined to fiction: Robert Browning's elderly father fled to Paris to avoid such a suit. Yet Lily's uncle rejects legal action because it would have exposed Lily to publicity – an even worse fate than jilting for most Victorian ladies. A minor Victorian novelist, Amelia Edwards, once asked Trollope, 'Why *did* you let Crosbie jilt Lily Dale?' He replied, 'How could I help it? He *would* do it, confound him!' She said this was an 'earnest' reply and, as she herself knew, once such a character is created, his behaviour is 'governed by the laws of his being as if he were a living and breathing entity'.

Crosbie's behaviour should also be compared with that of other young men in this and other novels. John Eames gives Amelia Roper some encouragement, and he would do so again with another young woman in *The Last Chronicle of Barset*. In *John Caldigate* the central character would allow two young women to believe he was engaged to them, and in *The Claverings* Harry Clavering almost jilts his fiancée after flirting with a former lover. Trollope believed that young men often slid into such deception not through innate wickedness but through cowardice and indecision. In his *Autobiography*, he tells a story of his own youth in which he fled after a girl proposed marriage to him; he was too frightened even to reply to her letters. Matters became worse when her mother appeared in the clerks' room at the Post Office, demanding: 'Anthony Trollope, when are you going to marry my daughter?' He admitted that his hair still stood on end when he wrote about this, forty years later. (By that point there was little hair to stand.) In *The Small House at Allington* Trollope is performing what he regarded as his moral duty by warning young men not to trifle with a girl's affection and reputation. He is also warning young women not to be too hasty in their choice. After all, Lily pledged her love to Crosbie after a very short acquaintance. One should not become so devoted to the 'wounded fawn' as not to see that at least by Victorian standards Lily bore some responsibility for her own fate.

John Eames is the most interesting character in the book from the autobiographical point of view as Trollope drew on his own behaviour as a clerk in the 1830s in creating the character. He had already done this with Charley Tudor. Eames is Trollope's most extended portrait of a 'hobbledehoy' [4], a term that recurs again and again in his fiction. Eames also best displays the gradual process whereby a youth throws off his hobbledehoyhood to become a man.

Since Trollope maintained that *The Small House at Allington* was not really part of the Barsetshire novels, he was reluctant to include it in the collected edition of *The Chronicles of Barsetshire*. Yet one cannot really understand several of the plots in *The Last*

Chronicle of Barset which involve Lily and the two rivals for her affections without having read the earlier novel. This novel also contains several characters from earlier Barsetshire novels, like Mr Harding [16], while Griselda, Lady Dumbello's romantic adventure leads to the brief reappearance of Archdeacon Grantly and his wife Susan. Here Trollope continues the trend noticeable in *Framley Parsonage* in making her more important than her husband. The dreadful De Courcy family is familiar from earlier Barsetshire novels. *The Small House at Allington* can also be considered as a prelude to the Palliser novels, as their two central characters first appear here: Plantagenet Palliser enters Trollope's fiction in the unlikely guise of a passionate figure contemplating adultery [23] and his future wife, Lady Glencora (to whom Trollope became especially devoted), makes her first entrance in one of the final chapters [55]. Her passion for Burgo Fitzgerald would become an important element in the first Palliser novel, *Can You Forgive Her?*

One reason why *The Small House at Allington* was popular with contemporary audiences was the fact that it is a novel of family relationships. All the major characters, except, quite significantly, Crosbie, are seen within their families. Lily's life with her widowed mother and her sister, with the emphasis on daily duties and quiet pleasures, was one well known to many Victorian ladies. Trollope had to be careful with these details and he even received a humorous reproof from one lady, the wife of the famous clergyman John Mason Neale, because, she claimed, Mrs Dale did not order the correct amount of cloth for a dress. The whole Dale family is exceptionally well drawn, particularly the old squire. Trollope liked nothing better than portraying a man with a hard exterior hiding a soft heart – in short, a personality much like his own. The good side of aristocratic family life is shown in the mildly eccentric Earl De Guest and his sister, Lady Julia. The bad side is delightfully revealed in the De Courcys, whose income cannot match their pretensions. We can also observe the complex way in which the Grantlys regard their daughter Griselda once her marriage advances her into a rank far above their own.

Hopkins, the gardener at Allington, receives more attention than virtually any other male servant in Trollope's writing. His relationship with Lily and the old squire gives us a good insight into the complicated way in which Victorians behaved with servants and how both masters and servants each had their own sphere.

The Small House at Allington contains some of Trollope's most effective comic writing. For the scenes set in Eames's boarding-house, as well as the marvellous depiction of civil servants such as Sir Raffle Buffle and Major Fiasco, Trollope drew on his own recollections, although he later used his *Autobiography* to deny rumours which connected Buffle with a real person. There is gentle humour when Lord De Guest falls asleep after dinner, while the satirical scorn flung at the De Courcys' snobbery is reminiscent of Thackeray. Incidentally, Trollope paid tribute to Thackeray and made another of his private jokes in the final chapter in having Lily joke about 'that bad man' who attacks mothers-in-law in his novels – Thackeray was notorious for his frequent and heartfelt attacks on mothers-in-law. When Trollope wrote this his friend was no longer editor of the *Cornhill*, and by the time it appeared Thackeray was dead. One suspects another private reference when Trollope alludes to Earl De Courcy as having lost money by gambling at Homburg, as he had recently joked with George Smith about the publisher's gambling at that German spa town. Among the many private jokes recalling his own earlier life is one met frequently in Trollope's writing, when Eames is advised to spend his evenings with tea and a good book. Trollope's Aunt Milton had urged him to do this when a young man and he liked to repeat the advice in only the slightest of mocking tones.

There are hostile references to newspapers [36, 43] and criticisms of Carlyle, whose *French Revolution* Lily reads only to disagree with his views on Louis XVI [44]. [➤ *La Vendée.*] In the discussion between Lily and Bell on the need for novels to be 'sweet' or 'real', Bell, who advocates realism, gives Trollope's own views [42]. The descriptions of Crosbie and Lady Alexandrina's setting up their house, arranging marriage settlements and arguing about a carriage provide one of Trollope's best depictions of the life of the upper orders in Victorian London. When the marriage breaks down there is no idea of divorce for her or indeed for her mother who is in a similar plight. Mother and daughter retire to Germany, the usual refuge of Trollopian castaways [➤ Exile].

For the character of Mrs Crump, the surly postmistress, Trollope used his decades of experience in inspecting village post offices. Not only did this give him an extensive knowledge of local conditions, but a rare insight – unique among Victorian writers – into independent working women. Mrs Crump has 'a bad temper, but perhaps she has some excuse' as she complains that for looking after the post office she gets 'tuppence farden a day. It don't keep me in shoe-leather' [21]. Here Trollope recalls an actual incident in which he encountered a stubborn Quaker postmistress, Betsy Trembath, in Mousehole while inspecting post offices in Cornwall [Mullen, 243]. At the end of the novel Trollope even introduces a postal inspector who complains that 'this was wrong and that was wrong and everything was wrong' [60]. By resorting to the traditional device of 'low life' characters like the postmistress with her complaints, or Hopkins the gardener with his feuds over manure, the final chapters, in which all three main characters are left unhappy, do not finish on a note of pervading gloom. The novel actually ends with a sardonic reference to Lady Alexandrina's fall from splendour: her ladyship 'is to be seen in the one-horse carriage with her mother at Baden-Baden' [60] [➤ Horses].

The reviews of this novel offer some of the best insights into how Trollope's contemporaries looked at his work. The *Spectator* commented on Trollope's mastery of the way his characters would think. Earl De Guest's first comment to Eames is: 'Have you got into trouble? ... Your poor father used to be in trouble.' This is exactly 'the rough sort of logic of an earl' renowned as a cattle breeder. According to the *Athenaeum* there was as much speculation about Lily Dale and

John Eames as there would have been about any real aristocratic marriage of the day, and reviewers moaned that re-reading the story as a book had a sorrowful aspect as it reminded readers where the monthly episodes had ended, 'leaving them hungry and impatient'. A lesser-known journal, the *Reader*, claimed that 'Mr Trollope's pages have been perused rather as news than as fiction'. It continued with a remarkably accurate prediction: 'Each of his novels is an epitome of contemporary English life; nor is there any other novelist from whom posterity will, on the whole, derive so true and vivid a conception of the actual condition of our society.' 'For the last year,' said the *Reader*, 'Crosbie has been as much a public character as Lord Palmerston' – an amazing statement, given that he was the most popular prime minister of the era [Mullen, 453–4]. The book has continued to be one of Trollope's best-loved novels and well deserves to be. When a prime minister of our own time, John Major, appeared on the BBC's 'Desert Island Discs', he chose it as his favourite book. [➤ Clubs; Rugs; Sport.]

Smith, Elder (1816–1917). This publishing house, like so many in the nineteenth century, was established by a Scotsman, George Smith, in 1816. His partner was Alexander Elder, and soon the firm was doing other business besides publishing, notably as an East India agency. The company prospered under George Smith's son, also named George: it was he who became Trollope's friend. The firm is remembered for accepting the manuscript of *Jane Eyre* from 'Currer Bell' (Charlotte Brontë). The business soared in the

1850s and added Thackeray to its list of authors. In 1860 it launched the *Cornhill* and it was through this magazine that Smith came into contact with Trollope. Smith, Elder were renowned for paying the highest sums of any Victorian publisher. After Smith's death in 1901 the firm declined and in 1917 it was taken over by John Murray. Smith, Elder serialized *Framley Parsonage*, *The Struggles of Brown, Jones, and Robinson*, *The Small House at Allington* and *The Claverings* in the *Cornhill*, and published all but *The Struggles of Brown, Jones, and Robinson* as books. It also published *The Last Chronicle of Barset* in weekly part issues.

Smith, George (1824–1901). Trollope's friendship with Smith came through his offering to write for the new *Cornhill* magazine in 1859. Smith's career began in 1838 when he joined the publishing firm of Smith, Elder, of which his father had been a founding partner. From 1846 he was the head of the firm and under him it prospered. Trollope once wrote that he never 'let anything worth doing slip through his fingers, rated a manuscript's value too high or too low, or ever misjudged the humour of the hour and the taste of the public'. In 1865 he established the *Pall Mall Gazette*, an evening newspaper. His business acumen was legendary: while on his honeymoon he heard about the discovery of gold in Australia and immediately dispatched a supply of revolvers on the assumption that violence followed gold and that men needed to protect their discoveries. He was proved correct. In 1873 he was part of a triumvirate that bought the distribution rights to Apollinaris water, which became a favourite of Queen Victoria. He was a public-minded man and in 1882 began the *Dictionary of National Biography*, one of the Victorians' greatest achievements. He eventually donated the *DNB* to the nation.

Smith's association with Trollope began in 1859 when he persuaded Trollope to put aside *Castle Richmond* and to write 'an English tale, on English life, with a clerical flavour'. From this came *Framley Parsonage*. A friendship developed between the two men: they were both enthusiastic about work and they shared Liberal political views. It was Smith's 'Cornhill Dinners' that first introduced Trollope to London's literary world. The generous Smith gave the Trollopes portraits of Thackeray and of Trollope himself by Samuel Laurence. (The portrait of Trollope is now in the National Portrait Gallery.) Smith also undertook to act as something of an agent for Trollope in buying wine as he was able to get a large discount. In return Trollope passed on some of his Cuban cigars to his friend. They were guests in each other's houses and in *The Prime Minister* Trollope included one of his private jokes by referring to Apollinaris water being served at Windsor Castle [7]. In his *Autobiography* Trollope referred to Smith as 'the spirited proprietor of the *Cornhill*'. Smith's publishing house became one of Trollope's publishers, although the relationship was not without its difficulties [➤ 'Mrs General Talboys'; Publishers and Publishing; 'A Ride across Palestine'; *The Struggles of Brown, Jones, and Robinson*]. When Smith established his daily newspaper, the *Pall Mall Gazette*, Trollope became a frequent contributor in the early years.

After the late 1860s Smith's publishing house did not publish any more Trollope works. Perhaps Smith was annoyed with the 1867 launch of *Saint Pauls* as something of a rival to the *Cornhill*. However, the two men remained friends. In the year after Smith's death, a memorial tablet was placed in the crypt of St Paul's Cathedral in London.

Smoking. Trollope lived at the start of that brief period in history when smoking was respectable. He seems to have started to smoke when he was a young Post Office clerk in London, something he later recalled in 'Josephine de Montmorenci' in which there are many jokes about men who smoke cigars in the Post Office. His devotion to the weed remained fervent throughout his life, even though he suffered from asthma and bronchitis, and it is reflected in his fiction. In the opening paragraphs of his first novel, *The Macdermots of Ballycloran*, he describes how he sat down and smoked a cigar and thought about Irish life. When visiting Cuba in 1859 he made arrangements to import cigars and we know that six years later he received 12,000, many of which were shared with his friends. The next year he bought 6,000 for £31. 7s. 9d. This worked out to a 1¼d. a cigar, a farthing over the amount the carefree Alec Murray spends on his cigars in 'The Telegraph Girl' even though his income is only 12s. a week. By 1873, however, Trollope was spending 8d. per cigar and in a self-pitying mood he moaned that this was too much of an expense and that he was taking up a pipe. A visitor to his house in 1868 described how Trollope devoted one entire wall of his study to 'cupboards or bins . . . filled with cigars'.

By the 1850s smoking had become widespread although an earlier attitude is noted when Mr Harding refuses a cigar [*The Warden*, 16]. While some men, such as Sir Thomas Underwood in *Ralph the Heir*, are allowed to dislike cigar smoke, most men smoked. It was almost exclusively a male weakness: Trollope's mother and wife were not alone in detesting it. An American visitor was amazed that Trollope, like the Dean of Brotherton in *Is He Popenjoy?*, had to go outside to smoke [Mullen, 426–8]. By the time Trollope was living in London in the 1870s he seems to have smoked in his library as he had no garden. Smoking became more widespread and popular as the century wore on: Miss Stanbury, the reactionary spinster in *He Knew He Was Right*, asks her nephew whether all young men now smoke and he replies that they do and he expects young women to take it up soon. Miss Stanbury's anti-tobacco views were considered out-of-date. When a woman in *Rachel Ray* [22] denounces tobacco as 'poison', Trollope meant readers to see this as an absurd prejudice.

Cigarettes in Trollope's fiction are generally smoked by dissolute men like the debauched Marquis of Brotherton in *Is He Popenjoy?* Nor is it surprising that Mr Maule, Trollope's best portrait of an idle man, smokes cigarettes [*Phineas Redux*, 21]. In one case cigarettes symbolize marital domesticity: in *Ayala's Angel* Lord Rufford has given up cards and cigars and 'is allowed two cigarettes a-day' [23]. However, the final novels reflect changing attitudes and young men like Lord Silverbridge are cigarette-smokers. Pipes are normally smoked by radicals like Hugh Stanbury in *He Knew He Was Right*, or by the young men in *John Caldigate*. To the English, Germans were traditionally shown as smoking pipes and they do so in *Orley Farm*. Even worse, by Victorian standards, they smoke them in the presence of ladies [*Linda Tressel*, 5]. A French priest in *The Golden Lion of Granpère* takes snuff. American men were often stereotyped as chewing tobacco and then spitting it on to the floor. In *Dr Wortle's School*, in the chapter set in Chicago, Trollope refers to American men 'chewing a cigar, and covering a circle around him with the results' [v, 9].

Solicitors. See Lawyers.

Somerset. Trollope's work in laying out postal routes in the 1850s gave him a detailed knowledge of Somerset and he used the county as the basis for Barsetshire. In *The Belton Estate*, also set in the county, he complains that 'the prettiness of Somersetshire' was not widely known among his contemporaries. 'The Lady of Launay' is set in Somerset.

South Africa. See *South Africa*.

South Africa. This travel book was written between 23 July 1877 and 2 January 1878. Trollope started it the day after he arrived in Capetown (and two days after finishing *John Caldigate*) and finished it the day before he arrived back in England. The book was published in two volumes by Chapman & Hall in February 1878. It reached a fourth edition after which, in 1879, Trollope brought out an abridged one-volume edition with a new chapter on Zululand. (In October 1879, the year which saw the unpopular Zulu War, he also gave a public lecture on the Zulus.) Trollope received £850. He also received £175 for fifteen travel letters for provincial newspapers through Trubner's press agency.

The book, on what was to become the Union and later the Republic of South Africa, was an example of what the Victorians called 'book-making'. Trollope undertook a long and sometimes arduous journey, without his wife Rose. He undertook the task to complete his plan to write on all parts of 'the English world' [➤ Travel Books]. The American Civil War spurred Trollope to write his American travel book, and the occupation of the Transvaal by Sir Theophilus Shepstone in April 1877 (Trollope called the act 'a typical instance of the beneficent injustice of the British') prompted the desire to visit English colonies in South Africa.

He used one of his son Henry's notebooks on his trip, just as his mother had used some of her sons' notebooks when recording incidents for her American travel book. As when writing his American book, he had difficulty in starting: his first day, 23 July, saw only two pages, but by September he was managing 1,300 words a day. It was, he told Henry, 'hard work' because of the rigours of travel (often by stage-coach), the great heat (96 degrees Fahrenheit in the shade) and the excessive amount of luggage he insisted on taking with him. Also, the topic was a difficult one. Trollope took great pride in the expanding world of English emigrants, as he explained at the start of the book: 'Our Colonies [here including the United States] are the lands in which our cousins, the descendants of our forefathers, are living and still speaking our language.' [➤ English World.]

The colonies in the south of Africa were different because of the racial question. He doubted whether the British position was totally right, doubts he had not had when he was in Australia, Canada or the United States and had had only mildly when he was in New Zealand. His views changed as he travelled and one needs to balance all of them to form a true representation of what he thought. The British view, he felt, stood between the native's and the Boer's: 'The Briton ... knows that he has to get possession of the land and use it ... but he knows also that it is wrong to take what does not belong to him ... As I am myself a Briton I am not a fair critic ... but it does seem to me that he is upon the whole beneficent, though occasionally very unjust.' Against this view was set another: 'South Africa is a land not of white but of black men, and the progress to be most desired is that which will quickest induce the Kafir to put off his savagery and live after the manner of his white brethren.' 'There can be no good done till the two [native and white] stand before the law exactly on the same ground.' As in his other travel books he considered the question of emigration, for like most Victorians he saw emigration as good not just for the world but for Britain. Whereas he had no doubts about recommending Englishmen to go to America, Australia or New Zealand, he had reservations about South Africa. Since most manual work was done by natives, an English emigrant must have above-average intelligence and must be sober.

One cannot say he enjoyed his visit to South Africa as he had enjoyed his visits to the United States and Australia. He preferred Pietermaritzburg above all other places there. While there he was able to hear the famous, or infamous, Bishop Colenso preach; he also visited the Colenso home. He met government officials and native Zulu chiefs and visited libraries and public gardens. He recalled his visit to a diamond mine, a place he loathed, in his last completed novel, *An Old Man's Love* [6]. [➤ Zulus.]

Spain. Spain is the setting for 'John Bull on the Guadalquivir' in which Trollope makes fun of his own rude behaviour during a trip there in 1858. He also praises the manners of well-bred Spaniards. [➤ Travels.] There are several comments about Spanish officials and government in Cuba, which he visited during his 1858–9 Post Office trip to the West Indies and which he described in *The West Indies and the Spanish Main*. Despite the kindness shown him by Spanish officials in Cuba, then a Spanish colony, he believed that what was left of the Spanish Empire 'would go to the wall'. Havana cigars were his favourite. [➤ Smoking; Women (for comparison of Englishwomen with Spanish).]

Spinsters. Spinsters feature in much of Trollope's fiction. The plight of an unmarried Victorian woman could be a difficult one and Trollope had great sympathy for women on their own. When, though, did an unmarried woman become a spinster? In *The Three Clerks* [25] he writes of Lactimel and Ugolina Neverbend: 'There is a distressing habitual humility in many unmarried ladies of an uncertain age, which at the first blush tells the tale against them which they are so painfully anxious to leave untold.' We suspect the two ladies are probably on the far side of thirty. Mrs Burton in *The Claverings* draws the line most definitely at thirty: 'I think I'd feel ashamed of myself to have a daughter not married, or not in the way to be married afore she's thirty' [4]. In *Mr Scarborough's Family* he wrote: 'Report had dealt unkindly with Miss Thoroughbung in the matter of her age. Report always does deal unkindly with unmarried young women who have ceased to be girls. There is an idea that they will wish to make themselves out to be younger than they are, and therefore report makes them older. She had been called forty-five and even fifty. Her exact age ... was forty-two' [26]. (She claims to be thirty-six.)

Trollope usually solved the problem of when spinsterhood begins by introducing his spinsters as already 'settled'. There are exceptions: young women like Lily Dale, or Patience Woolsworthy in 'The Parson's Daughter of Oxney Colne', are in the process of becoming spinsters and devoting themselves to good works for others. In both of these cases they do so only after a disastrous love affair. There are some spinsters, like Margaret Mackenzie in *Miss Mackenzie* or the redoubtable Martha Dunstable in *Doctor Thorne*, who do marry but they are exceptions. Trollope strongly believed that women (like men) should marry: marriage, he wrote in *Mr Scarborough's Family*, 'has to be always thought of, and generally done' by young women [10] but not all of his spinsters long for marriage. Another type of spinster is that particularly Victorian phenomenon, the daughter who devotes her life to looking after 'papa'. His best portrait of such a woman is that of Dolly Grey in *Mr Scarborough's Family* [33].

However, Trollope also delighted in portraying women who survived the period of 'humility', by which he meant, here, their thirties, and who went on to make their own way in life. It is not surprising that if they did not go to the wall they emerged as formidable characters, as what *The Times* called his 'strong-minded spinsters'. One thinks of Monica Thorne, Jemima Stanbury in *He Knew He Was Right*, Dolly Grey in *Mr Scarborough's Family*, Josephine de Montmorenci in the short story named after her, Miss Marrable in *The Vicar of Bullhampton*, Sarah Jack in 'Miss Sarah Jack of Spanish Town, Jamaica', Penelope Le Smyrger in 'The Parson's Daughter of Oxney Colne', Sally Todd in *The Bertrams* and *Miss Mackenzie* or Matilda Thoroughbung in *Mr Scarborough's Family*. Each of these women, even if she plays only a minor role, is a rich character in her own right and all enliven his novels and stories by their independence, humour, common sense, intransigence and occasionally by their opposition to progress. Some, like Sally Todd, Matilda Thoroughbung or Martha Dunstable are slightly 'vulgar' characters.

The number of Trollope's spinsters reflected an aspect of English life in his day: in 1851, eight out of every 100 women in England and Wales above the age of thirty-five were unmarried. By 1881, the year before his death, the number had almost doubled, while the population had only increased by not much more than a third. In his youth Trollope would have known, or known of, two spinsters who were important in his family's life. The first was his mother's cousin Fanny Bent, the inspiration for Jemima Stanbury. The second was Mary Russell Mitford, a playwright and writer now remembered for *Our Village*. He paid tribute to her in *The New Zealander* as the last of his 'painters of home scenes' [10]. [➤ Faithfull, Emily.]

Spiritualism. Throughout the nineteenth century spiritualism was a popular fad, and when Trollope was seriously ill in his mid-twenties his mother summoned two girls who claimed the power to know whether a patient would live or die; they naturally gave a mysterious answer as to the young Trollope's chances [Mullen, III]. Many otherwise intelligent people held seances to 'commune' with the dead. Trollope despised this nonsense and his hatred of it was increased because his mother and many of her friends in Florence became fascinated by it. He believed it undermined her health. Trollope's brother Tom had seances in the Florentine house he shared with his mother but was always sceptical, as befitted a Wykehamist.

In *The New Zealander* Trollope attacked 'men who cannot believe in the mystery of our Saviour's redemption [but who] can believe that spirits from the dead have visited them in a stranger's parlour'. In *The Claverings* he has a laugh at 'those spirit-rapping people' [39]. Nor did Trollope have any use for that other Victorian absurdity, phrenology, whereby someone's character could be divined by the size and location of bumps on his head. This he normally treated with mild ridicule. [➤ 'The Mistletoe Bough'.]

Spooner, Thomas. 'Spooner of Spoon Hall' is a squire in *Phineas Redux* and *The Duke's Children* who is excessively devoted to fox-hunting. Trollope's portrait shows how he could laugh at those who carried his own tastes to absurd lengths. Spooner 'could read and he always looked at the country newspaper; but a book was a thing that he couldn't bear to handle' [*Phineas Redux*, 18]. At one point he wants to marry that 'uncommonly clean-built young woman', Adelaide Palliser.

Sport. For Trollope, sport really meant only one thing: fox-hunting, and this features constantly in his novels. In *Marion Fay*, Lord Hampstead defends hunting against all other sports and especially attacks shooting [2]. This was Trollope's own view. Because of his weak eyesight he was a poor shot and thus it is not surprising that shooting makes only rare appearances in the work of an author who has so many scenes set among rural gentry. [➤ *The Eustace Diamonds* for an exception.] One of the reasons for Trollope's unhappiness at school was that he was not good at sports. A rare echo of a sport – if it can be called that – from this time was his use of badger-baiting as a metaphor for political life [➤ *The Three Clerks*].

Sport was also one way in which his novels kept up with current fashions. Thus within a few years after croquet appeared in England, Lily Dale is playing it in *A Small House at Allington*. Indeed it provides a good opportunity for Lily, 'the queen of the croquet ground', to chat with her 'Apollo' [2]. Perhaps that is why Madame Max Goesler later tells the Duke of Omnium that it is a game made for the young to allow them to flirt. Trollope himself much enjoyed the game.

There are more references to a variety of sports in the later novels, culminating in *The Duke's Children* which provides the largest number. There is an amusing account of a futuristic cricket match, with players like Sir Kennington Oval, in *The Fixed Period* [5]. Archery is another sport that became popular in the Victorian era and it was one considered proper for young ladies ['Alice Dugdale']. In *Marion Fay* and *Is He Popenjoy?* yachting and fishing each have, respectively, a part in the plot. [➤ *How the 'Mastiffs' Went to Iceland*.] In 1868 Trollope edited a collection of essays that had appeared in *Saint Pauls* called *British Sports and Pastimes* in which he wrote the essay on hunting. [➤ *Hunting Sketches*.]

'The Spotted Dog'. One of the short stories written for *Saint Pauls* and published in two parts in March and April 1870, this was included in Trollope's fourth collection of stories, *An Editor's Tales*, published that same year. In his *Autobiography* Trollope wrote of that collection: 'I do not think that there is a single incident . . . which could bring back to anyone concerned the memory of a past event. And yet there is not an incident in it the outline of which was not presented to my mind by the remembrance of some fact . . . how terrible was the tragedy of a poor drunkard, who with infinite learning at his command made one sad final effort to reclaim himself, and perished while he was making it.'

The story is told in the first person using the editorial 'we', and opens when an editor receives a letter from a writer named Julius Mackenzie, who claims to be a public-school boy, Cambridge-educated, agnostic writer for the 'penny dreadfuls' at 45s. a week. He asks for work at 30s. a week for six months to 'rescue myself from the filth of my present position'. The editor should write care of 'The Spotted Dog', a public house in London. The sympathetic editor had recently been asked to find an indexer for a three-volume work of scholarship by a clergyman-scholar who is a friend; the author is prepared to pay £25 for the index. He checks with the landlord of the pub and discovers that Mackenzie's wife is a drunkard, which makes it difficult for him to work at home. The editor therefore arranges with the publican's wife for Mackenzie to work in their quarters. Mackenzie's work is excellent, but he is plagued by his wife's drunkenness and he drinks himself. The author comes to London to see how the work is going and the editor goes to the pub only to discover that the manuscript has been taken away by Mackenzie; he had been drinking again and the publican had ordered him out. Accompanied by the publican, the editor goes to Mackenzie's squalid home, to find him drunk; they also find that Mackenzie's wife has burnt large parts of the manuscript. After the editor has told the author what has happened, the publican's wife comes to tell them that Mackenzie has killed himself.

The sentimental story, reminiscent of Victorian temperance tales, has some very good scenes of London life, fully the equal of Dickens. It explores, as Trollope put it, the difficulty 'of the attempt to befriend a man in middle life by transplanting him from one soil to another'. Trollope argues that being a gentleman has its own restrictions, for good reasons. These are seen in Mackenzie's folly in a marriage to a woman beneath him just 'to take refuge from the conventional thraldom of so-called gentlemen amidst the liberty of the lower orders'. (This question of socially mixed marriages occurs also in *Lady Anna* and *Marion Fay*.) Mackenzie was, in short, too clever by half: 'This was the upshot of his loud claims for liberty from his youth upwards; – liberty as against his father and family; liberty as against his college tutor; liberty as against all pastors, masters, and instructors; liberty as against the conventional thraldom of the world! He was now lying a wretched corpse at the Spotted Dog, with his throat cut from ear to ear.'

It is interesting that Trollope makes the clergyman-scholar who wrote the doomed manuscript a 'dean'. The title, outside Oxford and Cambridge colleges, normally refers to the head of a cathedral chapter but is also used for the Dean of Westminster, the Dean of Windsor and the Dean of Bocking, actually a parish church in Essex where Trollope hunted. Trollope also used the story to discuss the plight of writers in London.

Squires. Squires emerge with a far better reputation than virtually any other group in Trollope's novels. The best contemporary compilation of Victorian landholding was done in the last years of Trollope's life. Its compiler, John Bateman, concluded that there were about 2,500 persons in the United Kingdom who possessed landed estates of at least 3,000 acres, worth at least £3,000 per annum. In addition there were numerous small squires who owned between 1,000 and 3,000 acres. Fictional representations of these few thousand people are seen throughout Trollope's fiction. Unlike the aristocracy, their lives are rooted in their own counties and while they play only a small role in national politics they occupy an important place in county society. They may make fleeting visits to London during the Season for their daughters' sakes, but they are always relieved to return home to their own estates. Sometimes, for instance in the case of Sir Harry Hotspur [*Sir Harry Hotspur of Humblethwaite*], they are baronets, but most squires are untitled.

Squires in Trollope's works are often hard pressed for money either because of their own foolishness, like Mr Gresham in *Framley Parsonage*, or because of laziness, like Mr Amedroz in *The Belton Estate*. This latter novel shows how easily and quickly an estate can decline in value. The poorest squire is probably old Mr Vavasor in *Can You Forgive Her?* who has barely £1,000 a year. However attractive their income sounds at first, one must remember the expenses relating to family and land which they have to meet with a fixed income. In Trollope's books squires who choose a wife from the aristocracy are almost certain to get into financial difficulties because of her expensive tastes. Some squires became wealthy because of urban development or minerals on their land, like Mr Scarborough in *Mr Scarborough's Family*, but Peter Prosper moans in the same novel that his own income of £2,000 a year is no longer an adequate amount to keep up his rank. Trollope liked nothing better than portraying squires like the Greshams or the Thornes, who live on their ancient estates in settled dignity. Not for nothing is Roger Carbury, the Suffolk squire in *The Way We Live Now*,

shown as the embodiment of all that is best in the English character. Nevertheless Trollope still liked to poke fun at pretentious squires and their wives who claimed a more venerable history than they really possessed [*Ralph the Heir*, 56]. He did make one of his great villains, Nathaniel Sowerby in *Framley Parsonage*, a squire of ancient lineage.

[➤ Entails; Farming; Gentry; Money.]

St Bungay, Duke of. The duke is an important political figure throughout the Palliser novels. He is a great friend of Plantagenet Palliser and they serve together in various Liberal Cabinets. St Bungay, who is much older and whose political experience goes back to the early days of the century, is the embodiment of a Whig aristocrat. For such a Whig, politics consisted of moderate reform carried out by a few great families closely interlinked by kinship and marriage. As Trollope puts it, St Bungay holds the Whig view that 'certain great families ... living in a park with deer about it' were the proper guardians of the Constitution. While they were prepared to admit some new men, they wanted to do it slowly [*Phineas Redux*, 40]. St Bungay is really a man from the eighteenth century whose 'patriotism did not disturb his digestion', while to his friend Palliser, a quintessential Victorian, public service is a duty and 'an exacting mistress' [*The Prime Minister*, 72].

Trollope draws some of his best portraits of Palliser, 'our Duke' (of Omnium), by contrasting him with 'the old Duke' (of St Bungay). Trollope often uses his knowledge of recent history when writing about St Bungay. Thus this fictional duke feels that the essence of government is not to enact 'great measures' but to 'carry on the Queen's government'. This was a famous aphorism of the Duke of Wellington [*The Prime Minister*, 72]. Yet, after fifty years of reform, St Bungay comes to the conclusion that the Whigs had only helped 'our worst enemies'. This conclusion mirrors a well-known remark of Lord Melbourne, a Whig prime minister [*The Duke's Children*, 22].

St Bungay's political views and services – though not his personality – have many similarities with the third Marquis of Lansdowne (1780–1863), who served in almost all Whig governments of the first half of the nineteenth century. As *The Times* declared, he was 'the most favourable representative of the English aristocracy', and Trollope would have been reading his obituary at the time he was creating St Bungay.

The duke's family name is Fitz-Howard. His youngest son, Lord James FitzHoward, precedes John Eames as an official in the Income Tax office in *The Small House at Allington* [46] and thus appears in Trollope's fiction before his father.

The Duchess of St Bungay is memorably portrayed as 'a fool' in *Can You Forgive Her?* [22]. To emphasize the family nature of the Whigs, Trollope makes her the aunt of Lady Laura Standish and therefore related to other characters throughout the Palliser series. The St Bungay country house, Longroyston, is said to be remarkably uncomfortable.

Stepchildren. In Trollope's works stepchildren are comparatively rare, but when they do occur problems generally accompany them. In *Orley Farm* Lady Mason's difficulties stem from her acting to help her own son by cheating her stepson. The traditional 'wicked stepmother' appears in *Marion Fay* in the bitter rivalry between the second Marchioness of Kingsbury and her stepchildren and in *The American Senator* in which Mary Masters suffers at the hands of her stepmother when she refuses to marry Larry Twentyman. There is a stepdaughter in 'The Man Who Kept His Money in a Box', which allows her to be more outspoken about her stepmother than would normally be the case with a real mother. In 'Alice Dugdale' it perhaps makes it easier for Alice to be burdened with the raising of her young siblings because her father has produced them by a second marriage.

Whenever possible in the nineteenth century, orphans were sent to be raised by aunts, uncles, or other relatives, thereby making them *de facto* stepchildren. This was the case in Trollope's own life when he and his wife took in her niece. Miss Mackenzie in the novel of that name takes a niece with her to Littlebath as a companion and in *Doctor Thorne* Thomas Thorne takes in his niece, Mary.

Stepfathers. Stepfathers as such play only a small role in Trollope's fiction. One is Francis Arabin who is stepfather to Johnnie Bold in *Barchester Towers*. Usually uncles become *de facto* stepfathers, as in *Ayala's Angel*, *Ralph the Heir* and *Doctor Thorne*. [➤ Nieces; Orphans; Stepchildren.]

Stepmothers. See Mothers and Daughters; Stepchildren.

Strahan, Alexander (1834?–1914). Like so many Victorian publishers, Alexander Strahan was a Scotsman and again like so many others, he started as a bookseller. His greatest achievement was in launching *Good Words*. His involvement in other publishing ventures led to a financial collapse in which he was saved by his printer, James Virtue. In 1882 Strahan's finances were so weakened that he retired from publishing. His connection with Trollope began in 1862 when the Reverend Norman Macleod, editor of *Good Words*, wrote to ask Trollope for a novel. Before he turned in his manuscript, Trollope wrote a Christmas story, 'The Widow's Mite', for the magazine. Altogether Trollope wrote eight stories for *Good Words*, more than for any other single publication. When Trollope finally delivered his promised novel, *Rachel Ray*, both Macleod and Strahan rejected it [➤ *Rachel Ray*]. The dispute did not damage Trollope's friendly relations with either man. In 1866 Strahan again approached Trollope for a novel and more stories, this time for his other magazine, the *Argosy*. Trollope agreed to write four stories, of which three ('Father Giles of Ballymoy', 'Lotta Schmidt' and 'The Misfortunes of Frederick Pickering') appeared. In 1867 Strahan published Trollope's third collection of short stories, *Lotta Schmidt and Other Stories*, and in May 1869, he also published *He Knew He Was Right* in book form. Strahan's business became intertwined with that of James Virtue and in May 1869 Virtue transferred control of *Saint Pauls* to Strahan. Therefore it was Strahan who published *Ralph the Heir* as a supplement to the magazine and simultaneously in monthly part issues. Strahan took over the editorship of *Saint Pauls* when Trollope left.

The Struggles of Brown, Jones, and Robinson: By One of the Firm. Edited by Anthony Trollope. Trollope started this, his twelfth novel, on 27 August 1857, six days after finishing *The Three Clerks*, but put it aside on 7 September; he resumed writing four years later on 24 June 1861, two days after finishing *Orley Farm*, and completed it without interruption on 3 August 1861. Serialization in eight monthly parts in the *Cornhill* began on 1 August 1861 and ended on 1 March 1862. It was published in one volume by Smith, Elder in November 1870. Trollope received £600, which he later said was about the rate he was normally paid for this quantity of fiction.

The bare facts of the book's publication belie its turbulent history. Trollope first proposed it to William Longman on 15 July 1857 for publication 'at Christmas'. After Longman declined it he waited until the summer of 1858 and then offered it to Edward Chapman, also for Christmas. Chapman could either print it under Trollope's name (£150) or anonymously (£120), but Trollope preferred anonymity. Chapman also refused the manuscript because he did not want to publish it without the author's name, yet he was aware of criticism that Trollope was already publishing too much. [➤ Anonymous Novels; *Saturday Review*.] In the summer of 1860 Trollope, now famous because of *Framley Parsonage*, offered the still unfinished book to George Smith. It was published anonymously in the *Cornhill*. Trollope was sensitive about his manuscript and insisted that the magazine should not alter it. Smith agreed, but had he not done so Trollope, displaying something of his father's intransigence, was actually prepared to sever his links with the magazine that was making his fortune.

The serialization was not popular and Smith delayed until 1870 before publishing the story in book form for fear of damaging Trollope's reputation. When he did, Trollope, as always anxious not to mislead readers, insisted the title page should say that it was reprinted from the *Cornhill* of 1862: otherwise people might think it was a different book. Smith agreed, but for obvious commercial reasons he dropped the date. It is hardly surprising that Trollope referred to the novel in his *Autobiography* as 'the hardest bargain I ever sold to a publisher'. He also admitted that in it 'I attempted a style for which I certainly was not qualified, and to which I never had again recourse'. It was meant, he said 'to be funny, was full of slang, and was intended as a satire on the ways of trade. Still I think that there is some good fun in it, but I have heard no one else express such an opinion.'

When Trollope first offered the novel to William Longman, he said: 'It will be intended as a hit at the present system of advertising, but will, of course, be in the guise of a tale. Publisher's advertisements are not reflected on.' This 'satire on the ways of trade' is set in the 1850s and is narrated by George Robinson. The plot is simple: three men combine to set up a new haberdashery in Bishopsgate Street, London, which they call Magenta House. The problem is insufficient capital on which to begin trading which leads, despite an extensive advertising campaign, to shady practices and finally to bankruptcy. Before this happens there are several forays into the world of London tradesmen that remind one of Dickens, and *David Copperfield* is quoted [8]. The narrator, George Robinson, is one of the three partners and is in charge of advertising. He is in love with the fickle Maryanne Brown, daughter of one of his partners; her hand is also sought by William Brisket, a burly butcher in Aldersgate Street [➤ Names, Silly]. The firm crashes when one of their underhand stratagems is exposed. This signals the end and young Robinson loses Maryanne to the butcher, who in turn jilts her for a drover's daughter. Robinson and Brown also discover that Jones has cheated them out of a considerable sum. Robinson, irrepressible as any good advertising man, retains his self-confidence and sets off, like Dick Whittington, to try to make his fortune once again.

This novel, more than any other by Trollope, shows the influence of Thackeray's early works. Trollope even used a characteristic Thackerayean device in pretending that the book was someone else's memoirs that he had 'edited'. In a letter that has only recently come to light, Thackeray told Smith that he found this novel 'very pleasant reading'. Few agreed with that assessment. As Trollope's only effort at sustained humour, the book was not a success; the *Westminster Review* described it as 'a blunder . . . unmitigated rubbish . . . this miserable production'. Their criticism was not that it was not humorous but that the satire was excessive and 'coarse' [➤ Vulgarity]. To the *Illustrated News of the World* it was 'detestable, low, and untrue as ever'. Even so, his reputation was not damaged when the author's identity became known.

This concern for honesty in public

life also permeated *Orley Farm*. In that novel the main plot, Lady Mason's forging of a codicil to her husband's will, is as much about honesty as the sub-plot concerning Mr Moulder and his commercial travelling for Hubbles and Grease. This is not surprising because, as noted earlier, Trollope resumed the writing of this book two days after finishing *Orley Farm*. Advertising and honesty are also discussed later, when writing about the background of Miss Dunstable's wealth. The question of honesty was vital to Trollope throughout his fiction. It was tackled again, later in his career, in *The Way We Live Now*, *Is He Popenjoy?*, *Mr Scarborough's Family* and *The Land-Leaguers*, in his discussions, respectively, about commercial honesty in the City of London, fraud in the succession to a peerage, lying to avoid paying debts and, to him, dishonest government action in setting rents in Ireland. In his final years he wrote about advertising and commercial dishonesty in his essays on London's tradesmen for the *Pall Mall Gazette*.

In this novel Trollope examines his age's worship of success [22] and of excessive competition – 'that beautiful science of the present day, by which every plodding cart-horse is converted into a racer' [5]. This latter theme was more fully developed in *The Bertrams*. By tackling all these serious issues, albeit as satire, he used *The Struggles of Brown, Jones, and Robinson* to express his deeply felt desire to be taken seriously as a critic and commentator of his age. His message was summed up in the last chapter [24]: 'The world of purchasers will have cheap articles, and the world of commerce must supply them. The world of purchasers will

have their ears tickled, and the world of commerce must tickle them.'

There are the usual number of private jokes and references, including one to the 'customary dignity of expression and propriety of demeanour' of the editor (Thackeray) of the *Cornhill*, 'a first class Magazine' [23], and to 'one of Smith and Elder's young men'[1]. 'Brown, Jones, and Robinson' was a common Victorian phrase to indicate ordinary men. Trollope remembered the Goose and Glee Club of his youth in the debating society of which Robinson is a member, the Goose and Gridiron. In the early-Victorian period there were many societies which modelled their serious debates on Parliament. The chapters in which Trollope describes the club's debates [18, 21] are also a spoof of the House of Commons. Members refer to each other as 'the worthy Goose' and include 'old Pan', descended from the Pancabinets and Mr Crowdy – 'There had been no Goose with a bitterer tongue than Crowdy.' 'Old Pan' is a play on Palmerston while Crowdy is almost certainly intended to be Disraeli. Trollope also used silly names for characters, including Miss Polly Twizzle, the hosiery firm of Legg & Loosefit, the firm of Scrimble & Grutts, Miss Biles, and of course the butcher, William Brisket. There are references to Shakespeare in which Mr Brown is compared to King Lear. He uses one or two old words, like 'fardel', and ironically refers to Kensal Green, where he would himself be buried. *The Times* appears once again as *The Jupiter*.

Regarding the choice of 'magenta' as the name of the new shop, Trollope adds that 'This beautiful tint had only then been invented' [4]. The new colour, a reddish purple, was discovered near the time of the Battle of Magenta (4 June 1859) from which it took its name. The battle was between a French force and Austrian troops in the war for Italian unification [➤ Italy]. This would fit in with his dating the novel in 185–.

Despite all the criticisms, Trollope's only full-length effort at sustained comedy is amusing in parts; it is that mild-mannered humour of mid-Victorian Britain, the same humour that filled the pages of *Punch*, and sustained the success of Douglas Jerrold's *Mrs Caudle's Curtain Lectures* and, later, the operettas of Gilbert and Sullivan. Its strictures on advertising are as relevant as when they were published. It is a good portrait of the mid-Victorian explosion in new commercial enterprises. The book was not just a defence of Trollope's own quixotic preference for old-fashioned shopping: small specialized shops versus newer, gaudier and larger stores aiming at an expanding mass market. It was a sincerely felt need to expose a growing corruption in public perception, not just in these gaudy new stores but in the mania for advertising which played on human greed – good value for little money. As George Robinson asks, 'In the first place, did you ever see an advertisement that contained the truth?' [10].

Suicide. In Trollope's fiction it is usually men who commit suicide and they are generally, but not always, bad men. It occurs in: *The Last Chronicle of Barset*, in which the bankrupt drunkard, Dobbs Broughton, kills himself; 'The Spotted Dog', in which the suicide is a pathetic drunk; *The Belton Estate*, in which the debauched brother

of Clara Amedroz kills himself off-stage, in London, thereby making her cousin heir to the estate and creating the framework for the plot; 'La Mère Bauche', in which the suicide is a woman forced to marry a man she does not love and rejected by the man she does; *The Bertrams* in which it is the unpleasant Tory barrister and MP, Sir Henry Harcourt, who shoots himself; *The Way We Live Now*, in which the corrupt financier Melmotte takes poison; and *The Prime Minister*, in which the distraught Ferdinand Lopez throws himself in front of a train in Trollope's most famous suicide. Occasionally a character contemplates suicide, for instance in *Nina Balatka*.

In *The Vicar of Bullhampton* the Reverend Frank Fenwick attacks a friend for considering suicide not because the act would be a sin but because the suicide is 'a coward, and runs away from the burden which he ought to bear gallantly. He throws his load down on the roadside, and does not care who may bear it, or who may suffer because he is too poor a creature to struggle on!' [68]. However, Trollope shared the more compassionate view that was growing in the nineteenth century taken towards those driven to suicide. In 'The Spotted Dog', when the drunk, Mackenzie, has killed himself, the clergyman-scholar whose manuscript has been partly destroyed because of the man, observes: '"The mercy of God is infinite," he said, bowing his head, with closed eyes and folded hands.' Trollope then adds, 'To threaten while the life is in the man is human. To believe in the execution of those threats [of eternal punishment of a suicide] when the life has passed away is almost beyond the power of humanity.' Despite his own firm Christian faith Trollope had a morbid side and this made him aware of suicide. In *Ralph the Heir* he wrote that Christian belief was an antidote to the depression that age brings, the depression that can lead to suicide: 'It is the presence of thoughts such as these that needs the assurance of a heaven to save the thinker from madness or from suicide ... If there be nothing better than this on to the grave ... why should I bear such fardels [burdens].' His own view is given in *Marion Fay*:

'Let the load be ever so heavy, it must be carried' [64].

English law recognized two types of suicide: wilful and that arising from a state of insanity [4 Geo. IV. ch. 52] and this reflected Church teaching. Wilful suicides, according to the 1814 law mentioned here, had to be buried between 9 p.m. and midnight. The law ended the horrible ancient custom of burying wilful suicides at crossroads with a stake driven through the body.

Surveyor. See Post Office.

T

Tailors. There are many tailors in Trollope's fiction. He often made use of their reputation for political Radicalism: this is best exemplified in *Lady Anna*, with Thomas and Daniel Thwaite. Thomas seems to owe something to the famous Francis Place (1771–1854), the 'Radical Tailor of Charing Cross', who lived near the lodgings in Northumberland Street that Trollope took as a young man. Since Trollope's lodgings were kept by a tailor, he may well have heard of Place. In *Phineas Finn* Mr Emilius also has lodgings with a tailor in Northumberland Street. In *The Three Clerks* an unpaid tailor's bill causes Charley Tudor's troubles with money-lenders just as one had caused trouble for the youthful Trollope. In *Doctor Thorne* [17], Augustus Moffat, whose father was a tailor, stands for Parliament in Barchester and his opponents erect symbols of 'tailordom' everywhere. (Trollope probably had in mind the similar treatment of his foe Disraeli when he stood for Parliament and was greeted with old clothes erected on poles, recalling the reputation of Jews as sellers of old clothes.) In *Rachel Ray* the Liberal candidate at Baslehurst is 'the Jew tailor from London' [24]. In *Ralph the Heir* the appropriately named Mr Neefit, the huntsman's outfitter, thinks of 'degenerating into a tailor ... and of compensating his pride by the prospects of great increase to his fortune' – but he manages to save his pride by remaining an outfitter and raising his prices [5]. In *Marion Fay* the Marquis of Kingsbury returns a drunken 'glibmouthed' tailor to Parliament for his pocket borough [1]. In 1880 Trollope included an essay on 'The Tailor' in his *London Tradesmen*. A French tailor is the hero of 'The Château of Prince Polignac'.

In Trollope's own life tailors played a recurring role, from the tailor who was his first London landlord and the cause of so much financial misery. His first appearance in Beverley as a parliamentary candidate was from the balcony of a Liberal tailor. A fashionable tailor was a member of the singing club, the Moray Minstrels, of which Trollope was a member. The president who was being impeached when Trollope paid his third visit to America, Andrew Johnson, had been a tailor: this finds an echo in a novel he wrote in the next year, *Ralph the Heir*, in which Thomas Thwaite 'dreams of a republic in which a tailor might be president or senator' [5].

***Tales of All Countries*, First Series.**
The first collection of Trollope's short stories was published in one volume by Chapman & Hall in November 1861. Of eight stories, the two set in the

West Indies and America were written in the summer of 1859; the five set in Europe and the Middle East were written during travel in the French Pyrenees in September–October 1859 and drew not just on his time in France but on his Irish experiences, the period he spent in Belgium and recent trips to the Middle East, Spain and the West Indies. Of the eight stories, four were sent to *Harper's New Monthly Magazine* in New York. The stories, with their dates of publication, were: 'La Mère Bauche' (1868); 'The O'Conors of Castle Conor' (May 1860); 'The Courtship of Susan Bell' (August 1860), and 'Relics of General Chassé' (February 1860). The other four stories were all published in *Cassell's Illustrated Family Paper* in 1860. These, with the months of publication, were: 'An Unprotected Female at the Pyramids' (6 and 13 October); 'The Château of Prince Polignac' (20 and 27 October); 'Miss Sarah Jack of Spanish Town, Jamaica' (3 and 10 November), and 'John Bull on the Guadalquivir' (17 and 24 November). Trollope received £20 for each story from *Harper's* and £40 from Cassell's. For the book he received £250, a total of £490. He originally offered the stories to Thackeray on 23 October 1859 as part of a proposed series of twelve for the new *Cornhill Magazine*. [➤ also *Framley Parsonage*.]

Tales of All Countries, Second Series. The second collection of Trollope's short stories. They were written in 1860 and 1861 and drew on his experiences in the West Country [➤ Devon] and the Lake District, and on his recent travels in Egypt and the Holy Land, Italy, Germany, Central America and the West Indies. They were first published in three separate magazines and then in one volume by Chapman & Hall in February 1863.

Trollope was approached by the business manager of the *London Review* for a book. Instead he offered them short stories or 'tales'; the first two published in this collection had already been offered to the *Cornhill* and rejected because of 'vulgarity'. The *Review* bought eight at £50 each, published three and then sold the other five on to another London weekly, *Public Opinion*, because of the controversy the first two stories attracted. When the collected stories were published by Chapman, a ninth, a Christmas story, was included. The stories with their places and dates of publication are: 'A Ride across Palestine' (*London Review*, 5, 12 and 19 January 1861, under the title 'The Banks of the Jordan'); 'Mrs General Talboys' (*London Review*, 2 February 1861); 'The Parson's Daughter of Oxney Colne' (*London Review*, 2 March 1861); 'The Man Who Kept His Money in a Box' (*Public Opinion* Literary Supplement, 2 and 9 November 1861); 'The House of Heine Brothers in Munich' (*Public Opinion* Literary Supplement, 16 and 23 November 1861); 'Returning Home' (*Public Opinion* Literary Supplement, 30 November 1861, reprinted 7 December 1861); 'Aaron Trow' (*Public Opinion* Literary Supplement, 14 and 21 December 1861); 'The Mistletoe Bough' (*Illustrated London News* Christmas Supplement, 21 December 1861), and 'George Walker at Suez' (*Public Opinion*, 28 December 1861). Trollope received £400 from the *London Review*, £50 from the *Illustrated London News*, and £250 for the book rights, a total of £700.

'The Telegraph Girl'. Trollope wrote this short story for *Good Words*. In 1876 Trollope told its editor, Donald Macleod, that 'Some weeks since I went to see these young women at work [in the new GPO's London Telegraph Office], and being much struck with them, my imagination went to work and composed a little story about one.' William Isbister, one of the magazine's owners, suggested he should also write an article on the Telegraph Office's employment of women and 'The Young Women at the London Telegraph Office' appeared in *Good Words* in June 1877. As Macleod was about to publish 'Why Frau Frohmann Raised Her Prices' in the same magazine, 'The Telegraph Girl' was saved for the 1877 Christmas issue [➤ *Good Cheer.*] The story was included in Trollope's last collection of short stories, *Why Frau Frohmann Raised Her Prices*, published in 1882. Trollope received £100.

Trollope's 'little story' concerns two single girls in London: Sophy Wilson is flighty; Lucy Graham at the age of twenty-six has been left on her own by the death of her brother with whom she had lived. She has three choices of employment: nursemaid, governess or the new telegraph service which employs women. Lucy is proud, self-reliant, with 'brown' complexion and not anxious to 'get' a husband. (In this she resembles another Lucy – Lucy Robarts in *Framley Parsonage.*) She chooses the Telegraph Office in St-Martin-le-Grand (the same building in which Trollope had once worked) and is paid 18s. a week. She works with 800 other women and shares a 'bed-sit' with Sophy. Sophy is younger, not in the best of health, and is working only until she can get a hus-

band; she sets her cap at Abraham Hall, a thirty-year-old engineer who moves into their lodging house. He is a widower with a two-year-old boy. Then Sophy's health breaks down and the GPO transfers her to Hastings, where she marries a hairdresser. One day Abraham calls in at the Telegraph Office, tells Lucy he has to move out of London to a better position at £4 a week and proposes to her. She accepts him and becomes 'as good a wife as ever blessed a man's household'.

This is one of Trollope's most important short stories, not for any particular artistic merit, but for what it reveals of the writer and his age. It was one of the few occasions on which Trollope set an entire piece of fiction within a working-class environment [➤ 'Catherine Carmichael'; 'Malachi's Cove']. He had earlier refused a request to write a story about factory workers for the good reason that he knew little about 'operatives' [➤ 'The Widow's Mite']. However, his own experiences in the Post Office allowed him to feel some sympathy with the two young women. Although Trollope had not been pleased at the way the Post Office acquired control of the telegraph system a few years earlier [➤ *The Way We Live Now*], his determination to discover the facts about the new department's treatment of its workers says a great deal about his general attitudes.

'The Telegraph Girl' is full of details about the actual expenses of ordinary people's lives – all the more remarkable, given Trollope's own considerable wealth. It also shows that he was, even at this late stage in his career, prepared to accept change, such as the advent of independent working women. The kind way in which the Post Office treated Sophy shows why so many working-class men and then women wanted to work for it.

When writing of Lucy's request for time off to get married, Trollope inserted a private joke, a recollection of his own request for leave to do the same in 1844: 'I remember once when a young man applied to a saturnine pundit who ruled matters in a certain office for leave of absence of a month to get married. "To get married!" said the saturnine pundit. "Poor fellow! But you must have the leave."' When choosing names Trollope, as he normally did, gave the manly working-man whom Lucy marries a first name from the Old Testament and a simple English surname.

There is no better way in which to see the extent of Trollope's coverage of Victorian society than to consider that he wrote this story just after completing *The Duke's Children*, in which an heir to a dukedom loses £70,000 on a racehorse. In 'The Telegraph Girl' the two girls dream about how nice it would be to earn an extra sixpence.

Temple Bar (1860–1906). This shilling monthly was founded in the same year as the *Cornhill* and was one of the most successful Victorian monthlies. It was owned by a variety of publishers and edited first by George Sala and then by Edmund Yates, a fellow Post Office employee and minor writer who was jealous of Trollope. His jealousy was partly based on an offer to Trollope by the magazine's owner in 1861 of the nominal editorship with £1,000 a year for three or five years. He would also be expected to contribute a novel. Yates, already sub-editor, would continue to work under Trollope. Trol-

lope rejected the offer out of hand. The magazine published many of the biggest names in Victorian fiction, including Wilkie Collins, George Gissing, Charles Reade and R. L. Stevenson. Trollope's actual connection began in 1875 when the editor, by then George Bentley, son of Richard Bentley who had published Fanny Trollope's work, asked for a story about 'modern English life'. His plan was to offer them *Is He Popenjoy?* but instead he sent them *The American Senator*, although Bentley was worried lest the title might indicate it was a novel set in America. Trollope was annoyed when Bentley suggested delaying the start of publication but Trollope won his point. In 1882 Trollope offered the magazine the last novel he wrote, *The Land-Leaguers*, but it was declined. Trollope's brother Tom was a frequent contributor to *Temple Bar*, but often complained about the magazine's slowness in paying.

Thackeray. Trollope's book about Thackeray, who had died in 1863, was written between 1 February and 25 March 1879 for Macmillan's 'English Men of Letters' series. This was edited by John Morley, who asked Trollope to write it. The book was published in May 1879 and Trollope received the series' standard fee of £200. (In 1928 Hugh Walpole published his *Anthony Trollope* in the same series.)

Five days after beginning his work Trollope told his friend, John Blackwood, 'I have got the Thackeray in hand and a terrible job I find it. There is absolutely nothing to say, – except washed out criticism. But it had to be done, and no one would do it so lovingly.' When T. H. S. Escott later said that Trollope's book was 'hero-worship with a vengeance', he replied: 'As to dear old Thack the conviction that I am myself correct in my reading of much of his character, and that you are correct also in the reading of much only proves how hard it is to put into words all the nebulous ideas as to another man's identity which go to the formation of a man's judgement.'

Trollope, like all succeeding biographers of Thackeray, knew of his request that no biography be written, and as his friendship with Thackeray only dated from 1859 he was sensitive to criticism from those who had known his hero longer. He solved the first problem by confining the biographical section of his book to the first chapter and by using the succeeding chapters to discuss Thackeray's works. He wrote to men like George Smith for information and asked Thackeray's daughter Anne for names of people to whom he could write for help. Altogether he got information from four old friends of Thackeray. He also sent Anne, herself a well-known novelist, a discreet questionnaire about her father and this survives among Trollope's papers. He struck out certain passages of his manuuscript when criticized. The reclusive poet Edward FitzGerald had been among those he approached, and while he was pleased Trollope was to do the work he criticized the end result: 'Mr Trollope seems to me to have made but an insufficient Account of WMT, though all in gentlemanly good Taste, which one must be thankful for.' [➤ *The Eustace Diamonds.*]

The first, biographical, chapter was the longest; after that there were eight other chapters on various of Thackeray's novels and articles, on his ballads and lectures, and on his 'style and manner of work'. *The Pall Mall Gazette*'s reviewer was among many who were shocked that Trollope, with his usual frank regard for money, told the world exactly how much Thackeray had left his children. (This information he had had from Anne Thackeray.) Trollope added to the annoyance by saying that the money had been 'earned honestly, with the full approval of the world around him'. Sadly the book led to a rupture between Trollope and Anne Thackeray which was not healed until 1882 when they both dined at George Smith's house. She made their reconciliation public in an article written in 1891 and referred to Trollope as 'that kind old friend' whose 'affection' for her father 'never varied' [Mullen, 576–7]. Other friends were irritated because of Trollope's emphasis on Thackeray's indolence. Among Thackeray's admirers who were annoyed was Herman Merivale, who violently attacked the book in his 1891 *Life of W. M. Thackeray*, co-written with Frank Marzials.

As with his book on Cicero Trollope found it difficult to remain aloof from his subject, especially if it was a man he loved dearly. When Hugh Walpole later wrote his book on Trollope, he said of this book: 'One can feel the throb of his affection in every page.' Trollope's book really tells us more about himself than about Thackeray, especially those passages on writing. It is second only to his *Autobiography* for the insights it gives into his own methods and attitudes. As Walpole wrote, 'For anyone who cares for Trollope the man this book is revealing and deserves reading.'

Thackeray, William Makepeace (1811–63). Thackeray was, according to his friend Trollope, 'the first' among Victorian novelists and his *Henry Esmond* was 'the greatest of all English novels'. Trollope's own view on this was thoroughly shared by his wife, Rose. Although Trollope's admiration for Thackeray dated from one of his earliest works, *The Memoirs of Mr C. J. Yellowplush*, which appeared in *Fraser's Magazine* (1837–8), he did not meet him until after he had written in 1859 to ask if he might contribute to the new *Cornhill* magazine which Thackeray was to edit. Thackeray for his part had known Trollope's mother and had much admired *The Three Clerks*. (He would even praise *The Struggles of Brown, Jones, and Robinson*, which was serialized in the *Cornhill*.) He wanted Trollope to write as much as possible for the new magazine[➤ *Framley Parsonage*]. The two novelists became close friends and although the friendship lasted for only four years, Trollope deeply treasured recollections of it after the older novelist's death. As he recalled in his *Autobiography*, Thackeray was 'one of the most tender hearted human beings I ever knew'.

Trollope often paid tribute to Thackeray before their meeting: in *Barchester Towers*, he named a footman, James Fitzplush. After the two men became friends there were several more references and some shared private jokes: in *The Struggles of Brown, Jones, and Robinson*, Trollope referred to the 'customary dignity of expression and propriety of demeanour' of the editor (Thackeray) and to the *Cornhill*, as 'a first class Magazine' [23]. In *The Small House at Allington*, which began serialization in 1862, Lily Dale makes a joking reference to 'what that bad man says in his novels about mothers-in-law' [60] because Thack-

eray was notorious for his hostility to mothers-in-law; but by the time the reference appeared in print, Thackeray was dead. In *Can You Forgive Her?*, which Trollope had begun writing five months before Thackeray's death, he borrowed the name Cinqbars for a minor character, spelling it Cinquebars. The Cinqbars family had been used by Thackeray in numerous works, such as *The Shabby Genteel Story* and *The Book of Snobs*. Trollope, most unusually, inserted a footnote when it appeared in the month after Thackeray's death: 'Ah, my friend, from whom I have borrowed this scion of the nobility! Had he been left with us he would have forgiven me my little theft, and now that he has gone I will not change the name' [16]. In *He Knew He Was Right*, serialized in 1868–9, Trollope again referred to *The Book of Snobs* and added another 'Alas' when referring to the 'great master' who taught us about snobbery [92]. In 1869 Trollope inserted several references to 'poor Thackeray' and to one of his many pseudonyms, Michael Angelo Titmarsh, in 'Josephine de Montmorenci'. Thackeray may have been recalling *The Three Clerks* when he used the name 'Gaberlunzie' for a Scottish castle in *Philip*, although he could have taken it from the same source as Trollope. The two men also used identical names for several characters. [➤ Bunce; *The Claverings*; *Is He Popenjoy?*; Names, Origins of; Scotland.]

Thackeray for his part paid a pleasant compliment to Trollope and his mother in the first of his 'Roundabout Essays' for the *Cornhill*, 'On a Lazy Idle Boy', as well as in two of the later essays. In his last completed novel, *Philip* [14], Thackeray refers to the initials 'A. T.' on a locket and jokingly says it could stand for either Alfred Tennyson (one of Thackeray's oldest friends) or Anthony Trollope. The bald and greying Trollope would have enjoyed the joke all the more because of the added comment that the locket might contain a lock of his 'golden hair'.

Trollope was often seen by contemporaries as a novelist in the Thackeray mould. There are obvious similarities: both men mocked pomposity and pretence, especially among the nobility; both men may be called 'liberal' in their politics, although Thackeray was much more radical; both used satire in their humour; both, while taking the writing of novels seriously, felt there was more to life than writing fiction; both enjoyed London's club life and literary society.

Within a few days of Thackeray's death in December 1863, Trollope wrote a touching tribute to him which appeared in the January 1864 issue of the *Cornhill*. He also wrote an article called 'Novel-Reading' for the January 1879 issue of *Nineteenth Century* which considered the novels of Dickens and Thackeray. In the same year he was delighted to be asked to write the volume on Thackeray in Macmillan's 'English Men of Letters' series [➤ *Thackeray*].

THORNE FAMILY

The Thornes play an important role in the Barsetshire novels. They are an ancient family who are proud of their Anglo-Saxon descent and who look with some disdain on those like the De Courcys who claim Norman ancestry. Members of this fictional family are described below.

Thorne, Wilfred. The head of the family, Wilfred Thorne is an unmarried squire of about fifty when he first appears in *Barchester Towers*. He is an old-fashioned Tory who detests Sir Robert Peel and 'Free Trade'. He has an income of £4,000 a year from Ullathorne, his landed estate. He is something of an expert on the literature of the early eighteenth century, and is inclined to be a dandy. He also appears in *Doctor Thorne, Framley Parsonage* and *The Last Chronicle of Barset*.

Thorne, Monica. The spinster sister of Wilfred Thorne, Monica Thorne is about sixty and 'a living caricature of all his foibles'. She has a romantic view of the Middle Ages and is even more reactionary than her brother, but she is essentially kind and charitable to the poor. She first appears in *Barchester Towers* [22] in which novel she gives the memorable fête champêtre, and she later supports the engagement of the new vicar, Mr Arabin, to Eleanor Bold. She also appears in *Doctor Thorne*, in which Trollope writes of her, 'No kinder heart glowed through all Barsetshire' [47], and in *Framley Parsonage*.

Thorne, Dr Thomas. The second cousin of Wilfred and Monica, Thomas Thorne is the son of a Barchester clergyman. Although the two branches of the family have quarrelled, Dr Thorne is as proud of his descent as are his cousins. He is 'far from perfect' as he is stubborn and moody, but he is also a kind man and a very good doctor. He is often in rivalry with grander doctors in Barchester. In *Doctor Thorne*, in which he is the central character, he lives in Greshamsbury and is the close friend and confidant of the local squire, Francis Gresham. In *Framley Parsonage* Dr Thorne marries the great heiress, Martha Dunstable. He also appears in *The Last Chronicle of Barset*.

Thorne, Mary. The niece of Dr Thomas Thorne, Mary Thorne is the illegitimate daughter of his brother Henry, who had seduced Mary Scatcherd, a straw-bonnet maker in Barchester. Her brother, Roger Scatcherd, killed Henry and after the baby's birth the mother emigrated to America [➤ Women: 'Fallen Women']. Young Mary was adopted by her uncle, Dr Thorne, but kept in ignorance of her birth. Her story provides the main plot in *Doctor Thorne*. Eventually she inherits the Scatcherd fortune and marries Frank Gresham. This marriage also leads to a reconciliation between the two branches of the Thorne family. She also appears in *Framley Parsonage*.

The Three Clerks. Trollope's sixth novel was written between 15 February and 18 August 1857. He first took it to William Longman, who only offered him £100; Trollope wanted £200, or twice what he had got for *Barchester Towers*. He then offered it to Hurst & Blackett but the man he wished to see was out and he refused to leave the manuscript without an offer. From their offices he walked to Richard Bentley's firm. Bentley offered £250 and published the book in three volumes on 30 November 1857. A cheaper one-volume edition at 5s. appeared in January 1859. In this, and in following editions, Chapter 12 of the original Volume 2, called 'The Civil Service', was mercifully dropped. This was really an extended essay giving

Trollope's opinions on the Civil Service as well as an answer to the critics of the profession to which he devoted a large part of his life. The chapter can happily be avoided by anyone reading the novel, save for historians of Victorian government. No other chapter in Trollope's fiction would require so many footnotes to explain all the obscure references to issues of the day, and barbs directed at politicians. Of course the numbering of the other chapters that had originally been in Volumes 2 and 3 had to be changed once they were arranged in the one-volume edition of 1859. Thus in the one-volume edition and in subsequent reprints, until the Trollope Society edition in 1992, Chapter 27, 'Excelsior', is followed by the new Chapter 28, 'Outerman v. Tudor'. Since most readers do not have access to editions which contain the discarded chapter, references throughout this *Companion* are to the revised chapter arrangements. [For the background to this chapter, ➤ Civil Service; *The New Zealander*.]

The Three Clerks has as its action the lives, loves and Civil Service careers of three clerks, Henry (Harry) Norman and his friends Alaric and Charley Tudor, both of whom are cousins. The three clerks fall in love with the three daughters of Mrs Bessie Woodward, a clergyman's widow. Alaric wins a competitive examination for a better place which Harry had wanted and also wins the love of the eldest Woodward daughter, Gertrude, whom Harry had also loved. Alaric becomes friendly with a roguish MP, Undecimus Scott, embezzles money, is sent to gaol and emigrates with his beloved to Australia. Henry succeeds to a landed estate and wins Linda, Mrs Woodward's second daughter, while Charley, a 'hobble-dehoy', has various adventures with money-lenders and barmaids. He is rescued by the love of Katie, the youngest Woodward daughter, who nearly dies from consumption.

The Three Clerks is Trollope's most Dickensian novel, both in its tone and in its setting, which is London and its suburbs, although there is one important trip to the West Country. Two of the most memorable characters, Captain Cuttwater, a rare example of a Trollopian naval figure [➤ Military], and the Honourable Undecimus Scott, MP, sound much more like a Dickens portrayal of a bluff, elderly retired naval officer and a caricature of an upper-class monster. Indeed, Dickens seems constantly on Trollope's mind throughout the novel and no other Trollope work shows how much Dickens exercised the imagination of his age. The second paragraph announces that the author intends this book to be a refutation of Dickens's satirical portrait of the Civil Service in his description of the 'Circumlocution Office' which had appeared in his *Little Dorrit*, published in monthly parts between December 1855 and June 1857. The Circumlocution Office allowed Dickens free rein for his own – and many other people's – view of the bureaucratic incompetence that had caused such misery in the recent Crimean War. Even at the end of the novel, when Trollope makes a long 'authorial intrusion' about punishment, he explains why an educated criminal like Undy Scott deserves a worse fate than Dickens's Bill 'Sikes', as Trollope misspells the surname of the character from *Oliver Twist*. Trollope hardly ever checked references to the spelling or other details of other novelists' characters if he mentions them in his own work. [➤ Thackeray, W. M.]

In his first five novels, the Civil Service or government clerks are scarcely ever mentioned, but by 1857 Trollope had attained the rank of Surveyor in the Post Office and this meant that he had more freedom to express some of his views and make use of his own experiences. But he still had to be careful. Therefore *The Three Clerks* is vague regarding dates, although internal references set it about ten years before it was written. (Most of Trollope's novels are set in the decade in which they are written, hence the replacement by a dash of the last one or two digits.) The reference to a diplomatic dispute about a disreputable merchant called Don Pacifico, Captain Cuttwater's attacks on a Whig government, and the craze for the polka [17] indicate that the novel is set in the late 1840s. However, as early as Chapter 7 some characters are wandering round the Great Exhibition of 1851. Another reason for his vagueness is because he drew on two real events that were more than two decades apart: his own entrance into government work and the famous Northcote–Trevelyan Report on the Civil Service in 1853. If he were to draw upon his own youth, as he obviously did, for the exploits of the three young men and also make the novel relevant to the debates of the late 1850s about Civil Service reform, his story could not be firmly anchored in the world of the 1830s, as *Lady Anna* would be.

The novel's real emphasis is on the two Tudors and 'Charley' clearly is based upon much of his creator's personality and many incidents in his early life. Nevertheless in this novel, with its strong autobiographical elements, Trollope also uses some of his own experiences for the other two clerks: thus Alaric passes some of his youth in Belgium. One of the best-known episodes in the novel, Charley's farcical examination to see if he could become a government clerk [2], is a replica of Trollope's own appointment to the Post Office in 1834. This is 'given accurately', according to Trollope's *Autobiography*. Many other aspects of Trollope's life in the years he spent as a clerk in London (1834–41) pop up throughout the novel. The reference to the Tudors' 'good family connections' as instrumental in getting Alaric his nomination to the Weights and Measures is based on the influence Trollope's mother brought to bear to get Anthony his Post Office position. Charley's problems with debts start with a tailor, as had his creator's when he was Charley's age. The difficulty of living on £90 a year is based on Trollope's own salary. The comparison of Parliament to badger hunts in Hampshire recalls his schooldays at Winchester [32]. An outraged mother coming to the office demanding to know when Charley would marry her daughter actually happened to Trollope [27]. Charley Tudor's fall into the Thames was also based on one of the novelist's youthful escapades.

Although *The Three Clerks* is a novel filled with humour, it is also one in which the novelist is constantly unleashing salvoes against various enemies. Indeed, he attacks more targets in this novel than in any of his books except *The Way We Live Now*. Significantly, both novels deal with financial corruption. Trollope had a passion for

honesty and in the late 1850s he was greatly worried about the possibility that British greatness would rapidly decline because of increasing dishonesty [➤ *The New Zealander*]. The attack upon the financial greed of the City [36] is as great, though not as well remembered, as that levelled fifteen years later in *The Way We Live Now*. Trollope also attacks two prominent people of his age. The extraordinary and absurd onslaught upon the memory of Sir Robert Peel sprang not only from Trollope's Liberal bias, but from his conviction that Peel had taught politicians to change their policies whenever it was convenient to do so in order to retain office. The introduction of the stereotyped Frenchman, Victoire Jaquêtanàpe, allowed the novelist to let off a cannonade at Napoleon III [➤ France]. He even flings a verbal grenade at French passport officers [17].

Another political development of the time greatly disturbed Trollope: the growing demand for competitive examinations as a way of selecting candidates for government posts had led to the 1853 Report on the Civil Service. One might have thought that Trollope's picture of the haphazard way in which Charley wriggles through his entrance examination meant that the novelist was keen to see a better-organized system. However, Trollope's view was that the old way, despite all its admitted faults, allowed 'gentlemen' to be picked, men who would eventually develop into effective civil servants, as Charley does and Trollope himself did. He returned to the question in *The Bertrams*.

The 1853 Report was written by Sir Stafford Northcote, Sir Charles Trevelyan and the Reverend Benjamin

Jowett. All three were already embarked on distinguished careers: Northcote would end up as Tory leader in the Commons; Trevelyan, as a leading civil servant; Jowett, as the famed Master of Balliol College, Oxford. Trollope portrayed them as 'The Three Kings': Sir Stafford Northcote was easily recognized as Sir Warwick Westend; Trevelyan, as Sir Gregory Hardlines; Jowett, as Mr Jobbles. Trollope's satirical portraits are amusing, and Trevelyan at least bore no ill-will. Years later Trollope was told that Trevelyan was jokingly called 'Sir Gregory' in his own family. Yet in many ways the biggest target in *The Three Clerks* remains Dickens. This is no inept parody, tinged with jealousy. Trollope's fury about *Little Dorrit* and the Circumlocution Office was all the greater not only because he knew that he himself was a hard-working civil servant, but because he had been frustrated in an attempt to answer Dickens. (Trollope, with little knowledge of London's literary scene, made the mistake of sending his critical response to the *Athenaeum*, whose editor was a close associate of Dickens.) Trollope greatly resented the way in which the 'popular novelist' with his 'sledge hammer' could belittle the good work of the Civil Service. His anger did not end with *The Three Clerks* for he returned to the theme in an otherwise generous eulogy he wrote after Dickens's death, and even years after that in *John Caldigate*.

Many contemporary readers of the first edition would have seen the chapter on the Civil Service for what it was, an example of what they called 'padding': inserting text to bring a novel up to the obligatory three-volume length. Another example of 'padding' is the chapter 'Crinoline and Macassar' [22] in which Charley reads out one of the dreadful novels he writes for newspapers. [➤ Names, Silly.] Trollope uses this as a way to poke fun at the worst type of popular fiction. One wonders whether Charley's efforts had any precedent in Trollope's own youthful days. If so, no specimens have yet come to light although there is an intriguing reference in a well-informed obituary of Trollope in *The Graphic*: 'It is certain that he published novels before *The Macdermots of Ballycloran* [his first novel].'

The love plots in *The Three Clerks* centre on the three daughters of Mrs Woodward. This kindly widow is happy to entertain her cousin, Henry Norman, and his fellow clerks and much of the novel's action takes place in her house to which the young men happily walk from London. Trollope and his fellow clerk, John Tilley, used to do just this when the widowed Fanny Trollope took a house in Hadley [➤ *The Bertrams*]. Tilley married Trollope's sister Cecilia, who eventually died from consumption. In the novel, Katie Woodward makes a miraculous recovery and lives to marry Charley. Trollope admitted in his *Autobiography* almost twenty years later that tears still came into his eyes when he read the scene in which Katie makes what she thinks is her dying farewell to Charley [42]. Perhaps Trollope drew upon aspects of both his sisters for this portrait; his younger sister, Emily, also died of the disease when Trollope was a young clerk, and his reference to her burial in *The Bertrams* is an emotional passage.

A later phase of Trollope's postal career, his work in the West Country

[➤ Barsetshire], gave him the background to write about Alaric Tudor's fateful trip to inspect the Cornish mine [➤ Hotels]. The account of his fall and eventual redemption by his wife is perfectly Victorian. Trollope reserves his greatest fury – in one of his most outspoken passages [44] – for the aristocratic MP, Undy Scott, who leads the younger man into temptation. Alaric falls because he finds that 'easy is the slope of hell'. This was the title of the chapter that describes his fall and it is a translation of a line from Virgil which was often used by Trollope [29]. [➤ Classics.]

The Three Clerks was the second novel for which Trollope used his new system of preparing a worksheet or schedule of pages. This shows that he worked quite steadily: between 5 and 11 April he averaged twenty-four pages a day, while in the next week his daily average increased to twenty-seven. Sometimes his postal trips interfered with his writing and in one month during which he hardly wrote anything he scrawled across the worksheet: 'Bad foot', although it is not clear why that prevented him from writing. One reason for Trollope's urgency about publication was that he was about to leave for a visit to Italy to see his mother. It was appropriate that Bentley, his mother's old publisher, should have offered him £250. This was hardly a princely sum, but it was a valuable addition to his postal income which was about three times that amount. With such an inducement Trollope was prepared two days later to start on *Doctor Thorne*.

A copy of *The Three Clerks* was soon on its way to Florence, where it was lent to Robert and Elizabeth Barrett Browning. Elizabeth 'was wrung to tears' by the third volume. (Of course the story of Katie's recovery would have particular appeal for her.) She said 'what a thoroughly *man's* book it is' and proved this by commenting that her husband Robert, who rarely finished a novel, was captivated by it. Another celebrated literary figure who claimed not to finish novels, William Thackeray, was also delighted with the book. He later described to Trollope how *The Three Clerks* kept him from taking his after-dinner nap.

The critics also liked the novel, although two criticisms were heard that would be repeated throughout Trollope's career. He was writing too much and he made mistakes, particularly on legal technicalities. (*The Three Clerks* saw the first appearance of Chaffanbrass, Trollope's acerbic barrister.) The *Saturday Review* summed up his literary position well: 'He has the path clear before him – he can make himself such a name as will not easily be forgotten.'

'Three-deckers'. This was a popular term for novels published in three volumes, each volume containing about 300 pages, and selling at a standard price of one-and-a-half guineas [➤ Money]. This form of publishing, which came to dominate Victorian fiction, may be said to have begun in 1818 with Thomas Hope's *Anastasius*. Three years later Sir Walter Scott's *Kenilworth* appeared in three volumes and confirmed the new format. The nickname was probably derived from the three-decker ships of the eighteenth century, although it could also have come from the eighteenth-century pulpit.

Writing three-deckers was the best way for a novelist to earn considerable sums. The system was encouraged by the new circulating libraries which benefited enormously from it and they used their all-powerful influence with publishers to make three-deckers the norm [➤ Mudie's Circulating Library]. The size led to 'padding', over-writing, 'authorial intrusions', repetition and numerous sub-plots in order to make up the number of words required. In addition, the knowledge that the story would be interrupted arbitrarily at the end of the first and second volumes influenced the plot, as did serialization. Trollope, who began writing only after the three-decker system was fully established, commented on it in *Barchester Towers*: 'And who can apportion out and dovetail his incidents, dialogues, characters, and descriptive morsels, so as to fit them all exactly into 930 pages, without either compressing them unnaturally, or extending them artificially at the end of his labour? Do I not myself know that I am at this moment in want of a dozen pages, and that I am sick with cudgelling my brains to find them?' [51].

Of Trollope's 47 novels, 20 were three-deckers, 20 were in two volumes, 6 were in one volume and 1 (*The Prime Minister*) was in four volumes. In Trollope's case serialization was as important a convention as the three-decker format. While many readers, like Cardinal Newman, liked lengthy novels, the format was never without its critics at the time and later. This was largely because of the high price, the close association of the format with circulating libraries and the stylistic demands made on novelists. By the 1860s Trollope, always concerned to give readers and publishers good value for their money, had turned against the format, believing that it

forced fiction into an unnatural mould. By the 1880s publishers increasingly liked cheaper one- and two-volume novels. The increase in the number of novels published meant the circulating libraries had trouble buying all the books their customers wanted. The tide was turning and Trollope adapted himself to it: of the last 10 Trollope novels, published between 1879 and 1884, 5 were three-deckers and 5 were in two volumes. However, the novel Trollope was writing when he died, *The Land-Leaguers*, was designed to fill three volumes. In 1894, both Mudie and W. H. Smith announced they would pay no more than 4*s.* for a volume of fiction: the three-decker was dead.

Three-volume Novel. See 'Three-deckers'.

Tichborne Case. The Tichborne case was the most publicized Victorian lawsuit and it claimed huge coverage in newspapers for two decades. In 1867 a man appeared in Australia claiming to be the long-lost Roger Tichborne, heir to an ancient baronetcy and to large estates in Hampshire. When he returned to England, there was an enormous publicity campaign and eventually a trial (one of the longest in English history) in which he was declared an impostor and sentenced to fourteen years' hard labour. Trollope naturally followed the case and it may well have sparked off the emphasis on the inheritance of estates and titles that became a prominent feature of his writing in the 1870s and early 1880s. Because the case surpassed anything 'we poor novelists' could invent, he was worried that the public's distraction would cause it to stop reading novels. His worries appear in the fragment of a letter that survives only as quoted by his sister-in-law, Frances Eleanor Trollope [➤ *John Caldigate* for a longer extract]. His fear that readers would abandon him to read about Tichborne was exaggerated: the poet Edward FitzGerald, for one, said that he much preferred *The Eustace Diamonds* to the Tichborne case.

Contemporary readers of several novels would have noticed echoes of the Tichborne case. In *John Caldigate* they would have known that many of the details of the search for Caldigate's history while in Australia are similar to those of the search made by 'the Claimant's' friends and foes. Readers of *Lady Anna* would also have recalled the Tichborne case. In *An Old Man's Love* Trollope calls a pub close to the Tichborne estate 'The Claimant's Arms'. In his *Australia and New Zealand* Trollope refers to the support throughout Australia for the claimant, 'that great hero of romance'.

For his part, Trollope did not support him and thought his lawyer, the Irish Radical, Edward Kenealy, 'a beast'. Trollope's view was in general that of educated and propertied people. It may also have influenced his advice to his son Fred to make certain he kept all the information about the births of any male heirs. Trollope could well have been thinking that one of them might some day succeed to the Trollope baronetcy, as indeed one did.

Tilley, Sir John (1813–98). Tilley was Trollope's brother-in-law. They became friends when they were both young clerks at the Post Office in London. Tilley rose faster and farther than Trollope, even though the neurotic Rowland Hill sometimes saw them as co-conspirators and referred to them as 'the brothers'. Tilley eventually succeeded Hill as Secretary, the Civil Service head of the Post Office (1864–80). He and Trollope often went on holiday together even though he did not share Trollope's passion for constant activity, and Tilley was Fred Trollope's godfather. Some aspects of Tilley's life and possibly aspects of his character are present in *The Three Clerks*. Just as Charley Tudor was introduced to Katie Woodward by Harry Norman, Tilley was introduced to Cecilia Trollope by Anthony. While Katie recovered from a nearly fatal illness to marry Charley, Cecilia, whom Tilley married, later died from consumption. After her death, he married Trollope's cousin. The two men remained close friends, though they occasionally had fierce arguments about postal matters. Tilley sometimes proof-read Trollope's novels and acted as agent when his brother-in-law was abroad. Trollope's fatal stroke in 1882 occurred in Tilley's house.

The Times. Despite his attacks on *The Times* as *The Jupiter*, Trollope was a devoted reader of the paper. In *The New Zealander* he said it was 'his duty as an Englishman' to read *The Times*. His 1849 articles for the *Examiner* were in response to articles in *The Times* which had infuriated him by their criticism of government action. [➤ also *The Warden*.] In the 1850s he used the paper to gather information which he used in *The Warden* and *The New Zealander*. For its part the paper did not harbour a grudge against Trollope for his criticisms but in 1859 published an article by E. S. Dallas which included this comment: 'If Mudie were asked who is the greatest of living men, he would without one moment's hesitation say – Mr Anthony Trollope ... Mr Anthony Trollope is, in fact, the most fertile, the most popular, the most successful author – that is to say, of the circulating library sort.' In the following year the paper lavishly praised *The West Indies* in three separate articles. The paper also favourably reviewed many of his novels and supported Trollope against those who said his controversial analysis of Victorian financial life, *The Way We Live Now*, was inaccurate.

Trollope wrote only the occasional letter to *The Times* and on one occasion the obituary of a friend. Rather sadly, at his death the paper, while publishing a laudatory obituary, also published an anonymous article by the then well-known novelist, Mrs Humphry Ward, who felt it was 'rash' to think that Trollope's works would 'long be read'. In fact it is she who is no longer read. *The Times* obituary of Rose Trollope in 1917 was perceptive in acknowledging her crucial importance in his career.

Tinsley Brothers (1858–78); *Tinsley's Magazine* (1867–92). This publishing house, like so many Victorian houses, was founded by London booksellers, in this case by two brothers, Edward and William Tinsley. The firm specialized in producing three-volume novels for the circulating libraries [➤ Mudie's Circulating Library]. In 1862 they gained great fame for publishing the hugely successful novel, *Lady Audley's Secret* by Mary Braddon. The firm also published Hardy's first novel in 1871. In 1867 it founded *Tinsley's Magazine* under the editorship of Edmund Yates, Trollope's foe at the Post Office

[➤ *Temple Bar*]. Trollope's connection with the firm began in 1872 when *Good Words* sold the book publishing rights to *The Golden Lion of Granpère* to the Tinsleys.

The Tireless Traveler. Twenty Letters to the Liverpool Mercury **by Anthony Trollope, 1875.** This compilation was edited by the Trollopian scholar, Bradford Booth, and published by the University of California Press (Berkeley, California, 1941). It included those twenty articles, or 'letters', which in 1874 Trollope undertook to write for Nicholas Trubner's news agency during his second trip to Australia. Trollope received £15 for each letter and would have had £20 for each if eighteen papers had bought the letters. (In the event at least twelve papers bought them.) The most important provincial papers to publish these signed letters were the *Irish Times* and the *Liverpool Mercury*, from which Booth took his text. The letters about Australia are basically a simpler version of his 1873 book with the statistics omitted and the subjects expanded. The letters deal with Australia, New Zealand, Italy, the Suez Canal, Ceylon, Fiji, the South Sea Islands, California and Yosemite, all of which he visited. When he offered the letters to Trubner, he wrote, 'I should endeavour to deal chiefly with the social condition of the people among whom I found myself ... The face of nature generally will of course put itself forward, and what nature under such circumstances produces. But among those products men and women ... will and must be to all readers and to all writers the most interesting.'

Titles, Aristocratic. See Peerage.

Titles, Ecclesiastical. See Church of England.

Todd, Sally. Sally Todd is one of the best examples of Trollope's 'jolly spinster'. He described her as 'fair, fat, and perhaps almost forty'. (Lest some think this 'sexist', he uses almost identical terms – 'fat and over forty' – in an 'authorial intrusion' in *The Bertrams* [28] to describe, not a woman, but himself.) She first appears in *The Bertrams*, in which she entertains her friends with a picnic near Jerusalem [9]. In *Miss Mackenzie* she reappears as part of the sinful set in Littlebath and her card parties annoy the Evangelicals. Michael Sadleir, who had some of his information from Trollope's son Henry, claimed she was based on the Radical writer, Frances Power Cobbe (1822–1904), who wrote in the *Fortnightly Review* and was a friend of Tom Trollope. From what is known of her, the only real resemblance to Sally Todd is her love of travel.

Towers, Tom. Trollope's best-known journalist appears in three of the Barsetshire novels, most memorably in *The Warden* in which he is described as 'a very leading genius ... supposed to have high employment' on *The Jupiter*. Towers is a briefless barrister (as were many Victorian journalists) who exercises great power through his trenchant leading articles demanding 'reform'. In *The Warden*, when he is still in his thirties, he joins his friend John Bold in the attacks on Mr Harding's income; in *Barchester Towers* he tries to help his friend Slope, become Dean of Barchester, and in *Framley Parsonage* he attacks the way in which a young clergyman is given a canonry at Barchester Cathedral.

There is a good specimen of one of his leaders in *Framley Parsonage* [47]. Towers, conscious of the great power he wields, goes about 'striving to look a man, but knowing within his breast that he was a god' [*The Warden*, 14]. Many people assumed that Trollope intended Towers to be a portrait of the most famous editor of *The Times*, J. T. Delane (1817–77). In his *Autobiography* Trollope admitted that *The Jupiter* was obviously *The Times*, but added that when he created Towers he did not know either Delane or anyone else of importance on the newspaper. Some readers have assumed that Towers is the editor, whereas he is only a leading writer, however important. Towers is really intended as a portrait of an all-powerful and dangerous journalist, arrogant in his theoretical understanding of an issue of which he has little real knowledge, who manipulates opinion through the press. His name must be a pun on 'Tom Tower' which dominates Christ Church College, Oxford. Later, Trollope saw an even greater threat in journalists like Quintus Slide. [➤ Peel, Sir Robert.]

Transport. See Carriages; Horses; Railways; Ships; Walking.

Travel Books. Trollope wrote five travel books along with a series of essays on travellers which he then brought out as a book, *Travelling Sketches*. He wrote a series of 'letters' describing his trip round the world on his second visit to Australia and this was published as a book many decades after his death [➤ *The Tireless Traveler*]. He wrote a second series of letters during his visit to South Africa. His mother had started the 'family line' of writing with her first book, *Domestic*

Manners of the Americans (1832), and Anthony wanted to emulate her example of using travel books as a way of financing his passion for travel. His first travel book was *The West Indies and the Spanish Main*, published in one volume in 1859. Next came *North America*, in two volumes in 1862. Eleven years later he published *Australia and New Zealand* in two volumes, and five years after that, in 1878, *South Africa*, again in two volumes. All four were published by Chapman & Hall. His desire to be taken as a serious non-fiction writer made him overload the last three with 'blue book' statistics and constitutional, legal and historical information. In 1878 he wrote his fifth travel book, *How the 'Mastiffs' Went to Iceland*, which was printed privately in one volume.

As he put it, he wrote *currente calamo pedibusque simul currentibus* ('with a racing pen and, at the same time, racing feet'). This may not have been the best way to produce a book of information, he agreed, but his aim was to give 'to the eye of the reader, and to his ear, that which the eye of the writer has seen and his ear heard' [*Autobiography*]. Sometimes, as with his book on America, he accepted that he could write with too great a haste and say things he would later regret. This style could also lead to inconsistencies as there could be different opinions in different parts of a book. However, it does give the reader a sense of immediacy which a more polished treatment would have lost. His three travel books on America, Australia and South Africa had a moral purpose: to describe how 'England's children' were re-making the world and to offer advice to any other Englishmen who might wish to join them [➤ Emigration;

English World]. Because he put so much of himself into these travel books, they also contain some of the best insights into his mind, character and opinions; this is valuable in helping readers better to understand his novels.

Travelling Sketches. The *Sketches* were written between January and, at the latest, early September 1865. Like Trollope's 'Hunting Sketches', they were part of his arrangement with George Smith for publication in his *Pall Mall Gazette*. They were published between 3 August and 6 September 1865 and then re-published under the same title in one volume by Chapman & Hall in February 1866. There is no record of what Trollope earned as the payments were included under 'sundries' in his *Autobiography*; but we do know he received £234. 17s. 6d. for his 1865 contributions to the *Gazette*.

The eight sketches, with their dates of publication, are: 'The Family that Goes Abroad Because It's the Thing to Do' (3 August); 'The Man Who Travels Alone' (7 August); 'The Unprotected Female Tourist' (10 August); 'The United Englishmen Who Travel for Fun' (14 August); 'The Art Tourist' (22 August); 'The Tourist in Search of Knowledge' (29 August); 'The Alpine Club Man' (2 September), and 'Tourists Who Don't Like their Travels' (6 September).

When Trollope wrote these sketches he was one of the most, if not the most, well-travelled writer in England and in these sketches – as in many of his short stories – he used his observations of his fellow countrymen abroad to good effect. He had dined with the Alpine Club but had not joined because, as he said, 'time and flesh' were against him: he was forty-seven at the time. The lover of art who travels abroad was very similar to Trollope himself, noted for 'that laborious perseverance which distinguishes the true Briton as much in his amusement as in his work' ['The Art Tourist'].

Many of the sketches have similar themes to those developed in the short stories: 'The Family that Goes Abroad Because It's the Thing to Do' is similar to 'The Man Who Kept His Money in a Box'; 'The Man Who Travels Alone', to 'George Walker at Suez'; 'The Unprotected Female Tourist', to 'An Unprotected Female at the Pyramids'; and 'The United Englishmen Who Travel for Fun', to 'John Bull on the Guadalquivir'. [➤ Travels.]

Travels. Trollope was probably the most travelled writer in the nineteenth century and had seen more of the world, and of England, than any other major novelist. The *Spectator* wrote in 1873 that he aspired 'to be a greater traveller than Marco Polo'. In his insatiable appetite for movement, as in so many things, he took after his mother, Frances. He was notorious for his sense of adventure and energy when travelling: 'All holiday-making is hard work, but holiday-making with nothing to do is the hardest work of all' [*The Small House at Allington*, 46]. His wife Rose was prepared to join him on most of his travels but when doing so she always insisted she have one night out of four in an hotel bed. He also was known for taking an excessive amount of luggage, which he frequently had to shed, and for taking his own bath. Brandy was another requisite.

Between 1834 and 1882 Trollope visited or lived in the following places:

Belgium, the Netherlands, Ireland, Scotland, Wales, Italy, France, Switzerland, Germany, Canada, the United States, Hawaii, the West Indies, Central America, Cuba, Bermuda, South Africa, Australia, New Zealand, Ceylon, Spain, Gibraltar, Egypt, the Holy Land, Malta, Iceland and the Austrian Empire. His travels began in April 1834 when he was nineteen and his family fled to Belgium; he lived there until the autumn of that year when he returned to London. In 1841 he left London for Ireland where he lived in a variety of locations until 1859, when he moved to England. He returned to Ireland in 1865, 1866, 1873, 1878, and twice in 1882.

In the early 1840s he visited his mother who was then living in the Lake District and in 1851–2 he travelled extensively in the south-west of England, the Channel Isles and Wales. In 1858 he went on Post Office business to Scotland and the North of England and he returned to Scotland in 1865. Through Post Office work, family connections and hunting he knew East Anglia. This summary does not include brief holidays in various parts of Great Britain, for instance one to the Isle of Wight.

In 1853 he had his first extensive holiday abroad, in Italy, where he visited his mother and his brother Tom. It was the first of ten visits between 1853 and 1881. Generous Civil Service holidays meant he and his wife could have long trips in Europe almost every year: between 1856 and 1874 they visited France, Switzerland, Germany and the Austrian Empire, in addition to Italy. In the late 1860s and 1870s they seem to have preferred Switzerland, and sometimes Germany and France, to Italy. He paid at least six visits to

Switzerland as he, and even more, Rose, liked mountain scenery. After his death she frequently stayed in the Tyrol. In 1862 he also visited Holland and wrote an article about it for the *Cornhill*.

The Post Office sent Trollope on several trips abroad: in 1858 he was sent to Egypt and took the opportunity to visit the Holy Land, Malta, Gibraltar and Spain; in 1858–9 he was sent to the West Indies and Central America and returned via the United States. In 1868 he went to the United States on a postal mission.

In his private capacity he visited America four times: in 1859, 1861–2, 1872 and 1875. The 1859, 1872 and 1875 visits were *en route* to England. He visited Australia and New Zealand in 1871–2 and Australia again in 1875, taking in Ceylon during that journey. In 1877 he made his last major trip abroad, to South Africa.

Trollope made enormous use of his travels in his novels, short stories and articles for newspapers and drew on almost every place he visited. He very much disliked the 'John Bull Englishman', who pushed his way through foreign countries 'with his eye to his Murray [handbook]' [*The Bertrams*, 9]. He published five travel books. In his early days in Ireland he had approached John Murray, editor of the famous *Handbooks* on foreign travel, for a book on Ireland, but got nowhere. In 1860 George Smith suggested a book on India, but this came to nothing. His first two novels were set in Ireland, while the third was set in revolutionary France. The first novel to make use of his travels outside the United Kingdom was *The Bertrams* (1859) and many of his novels included trips, or sometimes exile, abroad. How-

ever, he believed that the day of the travel novel, for which his mother was famous, had passed [➤ *Can You Forgive Her?*]. He set four novels outside the United Kingdom: *Nina Balatka* in Bohemia; *Linda Tressel* in Germany; *Harry Heathcote of Gangoil* in Australia, and *The Golden Lion of Granpère* in France.

Of his forty-two short stories, twenty-two were set totally or in part outside the United Kingdom: 'The Château of Prince Polignac'; 'George Walker at Suez'; 'John Bull on the Guadalquivir'; 'The Journey to Panama'; 'The Man Who Kept His Money in a Box'; 'A Ride across Palestine'; 'Returning Home'; 'Miss Sarah Jack of Spanish Town, Jamaica'; 'Relics of General Chassé'; 'The Courtship of Susan Bell'; 'La Mère Bauche'; 'An Unprotected Female at the Pyramids'; 'Mrs General Talboys'; 'Aaron Trow'; 'The House of Heine Brothers in Munich'; 'The Two Generals'; 'Miss Ophelia Gledd'; 'Lotta Schmidt'; 'The Last Austrian Who Left Venice'; 'Christmas at Thompson Hall' (in part); 'Why Frau Frohmann Raised Her Prices'; and 'Catherine Carmichael'. When he first started writing short stories they were to be 'tales' based solely on his foreign travels.

[➤ Devonshire; English World; Harper & Brothers; *The Tireless Traveler*.]

Trials. Court-room trials or hearings figure in *The Macdermots of Ballycloran*; *The Kellys and the O'Kellys*; *The Three Clerks*; *Orley Farm*; *The Vicar of Bullhampton*; *The Eustace Diamonds*; *Phineas Redux*; *Lady Anna*; *John Caldigate*; *The Land-Leaguers*; and *The Last Chronicle of Barset*. In addition there is a hearing into bribery after the election at Percycross in *Ralph the Heir*, and in *Is He*

Popenjoy? and *Cousin Henry* trials or hearings are scheduled but do not take place. In *Doctor Thorne* there is a trial 'off-stage' and in *Mr Scarborough's Family* and *Is He Popenjoy?* trials are in the offing but do not occur. In *The Last Chronicle of Barset* Bishop Proudie sets up his own 'commission' to inquire into the charges against Josiah Crawley. The trial which begins Trollope's second novel, *The Kellys and the O'Kellys*, is based on the real trial of the Irish leader, Daniel O'Connell, and his son for conspiracy.

In *Lady Anna* there are two trials. The first concerns a criminal charge of bigamy against Lord Lovel, of which he is acquitted. The second is a civil suit between Lord Lovel's heir and his widow over the estate, which the widow and her daughter, Lady Anna, win. In *Phineas Redux* there are also two trials, the first for parliamentary bribery [44] and the second for murder [61ff.] There is also a hearing for bribery in *Ralph the Heir* [44], which Trollope based on his own experiences in Beverley. As well as famous trials for murder, like that of Phineas Finn, there are trials or hearings concerning bribery of parliamentary electors, bigamy, corruption, forgery, theft, conspiracy and embezzlement.

Trollope had been criticized for his lack of understanding of the law, so for the trial for bigamy in *John Caldigate* he asked lawyers and judges for advice regarding the law in this field, just as he had asked for advice on the legal points regarding inheritance for *The Eustace Diamonds*.

[➤ Chaffanbrass; Lawyers; Violence; Witnesses.]

TROLLOPE FAMILY
The Trollope family greatly influ-

enced Trollope's career in numerous ways. The Trollopes were descended from a long line of Lincolnshire baronets. Influential members of the family are given below. [➤ Baronets.]

Trollope, Thomas Anthony (1774–1835). The grandson of the fourth Trollope baronet was Trollope's father. He was a man whose irascible temper, bad luck and ill-health led to a series of failures both as a barrister and as a gentleman farmer. He was the son of a country vicar and was educated at Winchester and New College, Oxford. He expected to inherit the estate of his uncle, a Hertfordshire squire, but his uncle unexpectedly produced an heir. Events similar to this occur or are threatened in many of his son's novels, such as *Ralph the Heir*, *The Eustace Diamonds*, and *Mr Scarborough's Family* in which a Hertfordshire squire threatens to deprive a nephew of his expected inheritance. The elder Trollope was the author of a legal text and an uncompleted reference work, the *Encyclopaedia Ecclesiastica*, which probably gave young Anthony some of his knowledge of ecclesiastical terms.

He influenced his son's writing in several other ways: he gave him a love of the classics; he taught him how to write clear prose; he instilled in him a horror of idleness. Thomas Anthony fled abroad to escape his debts and died in Bruges. Trollope often reflected on his father's fate and this gave him his sympathy for those who had bad luck [➤ *An Autobiography*]. Although Trollope disapproved of a novelist portraying his own father in fiction [➤ Dickens], echoes of his father's personality are almost certainly to be found in the Reverend Josiah Crawley.

In 1809, Thomas Anthony married Frances Milton.

Trollope, Frances Milton (1779–1863). Frances Milton married Thomas Anthony Trollope, Anthony Trollope's father, in 1809. The date of Frances's birth is 1779, not 1780 as is normally given in reference works. Frances, or Fanny as she was known, was the daughter of a clergyman, although her family was not quite the social equal of her husband's. [For her father, the Reverend William Milton, ➤ *Ralph the Heir*.] After years of contented marriage, she seemed to grow tired of her husband's increasingly moody temper and found an opportunity to go to America in 1827 accompanied by some of her children, but not by Anthony and Tom. After several frustrating years there she returned a Tory, having left England as a 'drawing-room Radical', and published her first book, *Domestic Manners of the Americans* (1832). She is still remembered for this classic piece of travel writing with its penetrating though sarcastic tone. Having discovered that she could make money by her pen, she settled down to a steady schedule of writing and for almost two decades turned out a constant stream of novels and travel books. She became one of the best-known and most popular novelists of the early nineteenth century. Her name was of considerable assistance in Anthony's early career [➤ *The Macdermots of Ballycloran*]. Even as late as the 1870s, when he visited New Zealand, he was described as the son of Mrs Trollope. In *Rachel Ray*, written when she was in her last months, Trollope inserted an 'authorial intrusion' about a wife remaining loyal to her husband in time of trouble. It was a fitting tribute to his own mother [20].

She was the greatest influence on Anthony's career and there are many similarities in their writings. Both used their travels to provide settings for novels as well as material for travel books. Their novels often portray – as she put it – 'the clergy of England, their matronly wives and highly educated daughters'. Both emphasize the role of women and the influence of religion on manners. Both detested and ridiculed Evangelicals. Both use homely metaphors and have a common-sense, matter-of-fact approach to life. Both were realistic writers and thus both were often accused of being 'vulgar'. Above all, Trollope learned from his mother that the only way he could produce such an extraordinary number of books and enjoy a prosperous life was to harness his creative genius to a rigorous schedule, to rise at dawn and settle down to the serious business of writing, heedless of any elevated theories. She spent her last fifteen years in a comfortable villa in Florence, living with her son Tom. She is buried in the Protestant Cemetery in that city. [➤ Italy; Names, Origin of.]

Trollope, Rose Heseltine (1820–1917). Rose Heseltine married Anthony Trollope in 1844. She was a strong and resilient character, able to stand up to his exuberance. Her father, Edward Heseltine (1779?–1855), was the manager of a bank in Yorkshire as well as a railway director [➤ Dissenters; 'The Two Heroines of Plumplington']. In the 1850s, shortly after he retired, the bank accused him of embezzling funds, and he fled to France. For many years little was known about Rose Trollope, but all that has now been discovered shows her to have been a tremendous influence on her husband's writing [Mullen, 143–9]. Although Trollope says little about their marriage in his *Autobiography*, he alone of the great Victorian novelists enjoyed a long and contented married life, which made him the supreme chronicler of English domestic life. Rose was the only person allowed to read and comment on his writing before it went to the publisher. She often prepared copies of the earlier novels, a task in which she was eventually succeeded by her niece, Florence Bland, who virtually became their adopted daughter. Rose herself was interested in fiction and one of her tasks was to keep her husband informed of developments among other novelists. They both agreed that Thackeray was the greatest novelist of the time. However, Rose could be forthright when she disagreed with Anthony and once told him that a title was 'claptrap'. [➤ 'Mrs General Talboys'.] After Anthony's death she spent much time with her niece, often in Austria, and at one point tried to write short stories. In 1897 she was given a royal pension by Queen Victoria. She spent her last years with her son Henry at his home in Minchinhampton, where she is buried in the parish churchyard. Nathaniel Hawthorne's son Julian carefully observed the two Trollopes in the 1870s and concluded, 'His wife is his books.' [➤ *Life of Cicero*; Sewing.]

Trollope, Henry Merivale (1846–1926). Henry ('Harry') was Trollope's elder son. He was sent to schools in Ireland and then to the new High Church public school, Bradfield, but not on to university. His father encouraged him to follow the 'family line' and bought him a partnership in Chapman & Hall. Harry eventually took to writing, particularly on French literature, and years after his father's death brought out an impressive biography of Molière. He edited his father's *Autobiography*. His one novel, *My Own Love Story* (1887), is a pale and lifeless imitation of his father's works.

Harry, whose name was used for many of his father's young heroes, was a serious and somewhat dilatory man – perhaps this was only to be expected as the son of such an energetic and powerful father. Nevertheless the affection between the two of them was remarkably strong, as can be seen from Trollope's moving letters to him in the last years of his life. His short connection with the military was used by his father. In addition, Trollope's love for both his sons is reflected in several of his later novels, such as *Cousin Henry, Ralph the Heir*, and *Mr Scarborough's Family* where inheritance and a man's provision for his heirs is a major theme.

[➤ Military; Names, Origin of; Slang; Wine; Women: 'Fallen Women'.]

Trollope, Frederic James Anthony (1847–1910). Frederic ('Fred') was Trollope's younger son. His education mirrored that of his elder brother Henry, but Fred was less intellectual and more active than his brother. In 1865 he went to Australia and a few years later settled there permanently. His father provided a small fortune to back Fred's sheep station. His struggles are recounted in *Harry Heathcote of Gangoil*, which was based on him. Trollope's first visit to Australia in 1871–2 resulted in his travel book *Australia and New Zealand*, and his second visit, this time without Rose, in a series of newspaper articles [➤ *The Tireless Traveler*]. Fred provided the name for many of Trollope's heroes and one of his descendants eventually succeeded to the Trollope baronetcy. In 1982 Professor P. D. Edwards published *Anthony Trollope's Son in Australia: The Life and Letters of F. J. A. Trollope (1847–1910)*, which included twenty-six letters written to family members in England. [➤ Names, Origin of.]

Trollope, Thomas Adolphus (1810–92). Thomas ('Tom'; often called by his contemporaries 'T. A.' or 'T. Adolphus Trollope') was Anthony's eldest brother and the only other Trollope son to survive the family curse of consumption. He became a writer of travel books, histories and novels, as well as a huge number of articles for English and American journals. Most of these were on Italian themes as he spent much of his life in Florence and Rome. In his own time he was well known for a multi-volume history of Florence. Anthony felt that his brother was too learned to write entertaining novels. Although he and Anthony were not devoted to one another at school, they became very close in their mature years and constantly assisted one another in their writing. Tom provided the plot for *Doctor Thorne*, while Anthony often helped him in finding publishers and editors to take his work. His elegant homes, first in Florence and then in Rome, provided the focus for many of Anthony's continental travels. Frances Trollope spent her last years in his Florentine home. [➤ Spiritualism.] Tom Trollope was for years the best-known English writer in Florence and at the centre of the English literary scene; he often assisted authors when they visited the city. He was a close friend of both Dickens and George Eliot, whom he helped with *Romola*. His rambling though delightful memoirs, *What I Remember*, provide several interesting insights into his younger brother's life and character. He was something of a free-thinker; as he aged he became more politically conservative than his brother. He returned in his last years to England, where he died.

Trollope, Theodosia Garrow (1825–65). Theodosia was Thomas Adolphus Trollope's first wife and was a poet devoted to the cause of Italian unity, a fact which is honoured by a plaque on their home, the Villino Trollope, in the Piazza dell' Indipendenza in Florence. She came of a mixed English, Jewish and Indian background. Anthony seems to have found some of her radical and extremely anti-clerical views trying. He used her family name in one short story, 'The Mistletoe Bough'. Her daughter, Beatrice Trollope (1853–81), was a headstrong though highly talented girl who fascinated her Uncle Anthony.

[➤ Italy; Nieces.]

Trollope, Frances Eleanor Ternan (1835–1913). Frances Eleanor was Thomas Adolphus Trollope's second wife and was selected by Anthony to be a governess for his motherless niece, Beatrice; she then married the widowed Tom. Frances Eleanor soon became a novelist. Anthony was very fond of her and helped promote her writings as well as publishing some in *Saint Pauls*. After both Trollope brothers were dead, she wrote a biography of their mother with help from Anthony's widow, Rose, and this is another important source for Trollope's early life. Frances Eleanor was the sister of Ellen Ternan, who was Dickens's companion and possibly his mistress.

Anthony Trollope had two other brothers who died young, **Arthur** (1812–24) and **Henry** (1811–34). Two sisters both succumbed to consumption. The burial of the younger, **Emily** (1818–36), is recalled in a beautiful and emotional passage in *The Bertrams* [30]. The older, (1816–49), Cecilia, produced one High Church novel, *Chollerton*, before her early death. She married Trollope's close friend, John Tilley. Aspects of both sisters and their illnesses seem to have been used in *The Three Clerks*, and Cecilia's High Church devotions are also put to use in Trollope's description of various young ladies [➤ *Doctor Thorne*, 32].

Tudor, Charley. Charley is the 'hero' of *The Three Clerks*, in which he is a Civil Service clerk in the 'Internal Navigation Office'. His traits and many of his activities in this novel are based on the young hobbledehoy Trollope as drawn by his middle-aged creator in 1857. He is Trollope's most autobiographical character. While he almost comes to grief through association with money-lenders and unsuitable friends, especially the barmaid Norah Geraghty at the Cat and Whistle, he eventually rights himself and marries the angelic Katie Woodward. He also writes novels.

'The Turkish Bath'. This short story was first published in *Saint Pauls* magazine in October 1869. It was reprinted in his fourth collection of short stories, *An Editor's Tales*, in the following year. In his *Autobiography* Trollope

wrote: 'I do not think that there is a single incident ... which could bring back to anyone concerned the memory of a past event. And yet there is not an incident in it the outline of which was not presented to my mind by the remembrance of some fact: — how an ingenious gentleman got into conversation with me, I not knowing that he knew me to be an editor, and pressed his little article on my notice.'

This humorous story, which takes place in the Turkish baths that used to be in Jermyn Street, London, is told tongue-in-cheek, using the editorial 'we', and is clearly autobiographical. The narrator is approached by an Irishman who engages him in conversation, gives him a cheap cigar and then traps him into agreeing to consider an article; the man had known all along that he was the editor of a magazine. The scene now switches to the editor's office when the Irishman, Michael Molloy, calls. Molloy treats him to a hard-luck story; the editor is charmed and offers to lend him a pound, which he refuses. The offered manuscript turns out to be rubbish. Molloy returns twice with other manuscripts. The editor visits his lodgings to find he has been hoaxed by a man who was only mad, not bad. [➤ Insanity.] The warning to editors is clear: 'The butter-boat of benevolence was in our hand, and we proceeded to pour out its contents freely. It is a vessel which an editor should lock up carefully; and, should he lose the key, he will not be the worse for the loss.'

The story has many Trollopian aphorisms about the world of writers and shows his ability at self-mockery.

Turnbull, Mr. Turnbull is a Radical politician in the Palliser novels. His most important role is in *Phineas Finn* [18], in which his activities lead to a riot. He also reappears in *Phineas Redux* and briefly in *The Prime Minister*. Trollope strongly denied in a letter to the *Daily Telegraph* that Turnbull was based on John Bright (1811–89). The political opinions of the real politician and the fictional creation were similar, but Turnbull lacks Bright's most famous attribute, his gift for political oratory. [➤ Utopian.]

Twentyman, Lawrence. Twentyman is Trollope's happiest portrayal of a jolly gentleman farmer and fox-hunter. He is a principal character in *The American Senator* and returns briefly in *Ayala's Angel*. He had been educated at Cheltenham College, which allowed Trollope to launch another attack on an old foe, Cheltenham. He disliked being called 'Larry'.

[➤ Fox-hunting; Gentlemen; Names, Silly; Names, Use of.]

'The Two Generals'. This short story was written between the end of October and 8 November 1863 while Trollope was working on *Can You Forgive Her?* This was nineteen months after his second visit to America (24 August 1861 to 25 March 1862). The story was first published in the December 1863 issue of *Good Words* as a Christmas story and was included in his third collection of short stories, *Lotta Schmidt and Other Stories*, in 1867.

The story is set in Kentucky, which Trollope visited in 1862, and is based on Senator John Crittenden of Kentucky who tried to effect a compromise to avoid war. His two sons each rose to the rank of Major General, George in the Confederate and Thomas in the Union army. Trollope met Senator Crittenden in Washington, but thought his compromise, while 'honourable', was 'moonshine'. When mentioning this in *North America*, Trollope also alludes to the way in which the war was affecting the Crittenden family. The actual details of the battles have nothing to do with the real careers of the Crittenden brothers.

The story centres on Major Reckenthorpe (Crittenden) and begins in the Reckenthorpes' town house in Frankfort, the capital of Kentucky, at Christmas, 1860. The major's two sons take opposing sides and their vehemence horrifies the orphaned niece who lives with the family and who is betrothed to the elder son, Tom. The younger brother, Frank, an officer in the US army, also loves the girl, Ada Forster. Tom leaves the house as both his father and brother oppose secession.

The narrative jumps to Christmas 1861 when Tom secretly returns to see Ada, fulfilling a promise made between them when he left. Frank also comes but leaves rather than meet his brother. Tom, who gains glory in the Confederate army, seems to be patterned on J. E. B. Stuart and his daring cavalry raids. He promises to be there at Christmas 1862. The two men meet on the battlefield and each lowers his pistol. Despite this Tom is still wounded and then captured. His leg is amputated; he is exchanged for a US prisoner and he returns on Christmas Day 1862 to Frankfort, where his father has already died. Ada, in spite of her pro-Northern views, marries the wounded Confederate general. Trollope ends with an emotional appeal to his largely pro-Northern audience: 'The carnage of their battles [is] terrible to us when we think of them; but may it not be that the beneficent power of Heaven, which they acknowledge as we do, is thus cleansing their land from that stain of slavery, to abolish which no human power seemed to be sufficient?'

Trollope's anti-Confederate bias was evident in two other short stories of that time, 'The Widow's Mite' and 'The Journey to Panama'. Nevertheless he did admit here that the 'South have fought the best'. The device of dividing a Christmas story on the basis of three separate Christmas Days was used again in 'Catherine Carmichael'.

'The Two Heroines of Plumplington'. This is Trollope's only short story set in Barsetshire. He first proposed it to *Good Words* in May 1882 and delivered the manuscript at the end of the following month. It was published in their Christmas number *Good Cheer* that year but was not included in the fifth collection of his short stories, *Why Frau Frohmann Raised Her Prices*. The story was also published as a novel in America by Harper & Brothers, probably before it appeared in *Good Cheer*. Trollope received 100 guineas (£105).

Trollope had told an American admirer in 1881 that he remained disinclined to return to Barset. However, this story allowed Trollope to allude to familiar names such as the Greshams, the Duke of Omnium and Gatherum Castle, as well as to the dispute over Hiram's Hospital.

This humorous story is set in Plumplington, the second town of Barsetshire, in the weeks before Christmas. It concerns two young girls who are friends. In both cases their fathers reject their choice of fiancés. Emily Greenmantle is the daughter and heir of Mr Greenmantle, the pompous manager of one of the town's three banks. He wants Emily to marry Harry Gresham of the Greshams of Greshamsbury but she fancies Philip Hughes, a cashier in the bank earning £4 4s. 6d. a week. The second young girl is Polly Peppercorn, only daughter of Mr Hickory Peppercorn, a well-off official at the local brewery; she is in love with Jack Hollycombe, who works for a corn-factor in Barchester for 40s. a week. Polly resolves to 'go down' in the world by dressing plainly so that she will be at Jack's social level and can marry him. For her part, Emily follows a more genteel course and stops eating. When Mr Peppercorn sees Mr Greenmantle and says they are both in the same boat, Greenmantle's hauteur is offended; although Peppercorn has money, he is still 'in trade' and not a gentleman. Greenmantle plans to take Emily to the Continent for six months and when he learns that Peppercorn is planning to do the same thing he is mortified. This kills the idea. Mr Peppercorn begins to yield; Emily takes to her bed and her father gives in. The girls' supporter all along has been their vicar, Dr Freeborn, whose belief is that 'everybody ought to be happy just because he told them to be so'. He invites the Peppercorns and Greenmantles together with Hughes and Hollycombe to Christmas Day dinner and toasts the two girls as 'the two heroines of Plumplington'.

Trollope drew part of the setting from his wife's own background: she, like Emily, had been brought up above a bank in which her father was the manager. Like Greenmantle, Rose Trollope's father, Edward Heseltine, considered himself very much of a gentleman. Rose's sister, Isabella, married the head cashier of the bank [➤ Bland, Florence]. This is one of Trollope's best stories for observing Victorian attitudes to class, epitomized in the tilting between Greenmantle and Peppercorn, in the contrast between Polly Peppercorn and Emily Greenmantle, and in the discussions about the nature and role of a 'gentleman'.

When Polly Peppercorn refers to Ida Pfeiffer, 'the great traveller', she is referring to a real person: the Viennese-born Ida Pfeiffer (1797–1858) was perhaps the nineteenth century's most famous and intrepid woman traveller and made two journeys round the world. Dr Freeborn's use of the phrase 'a bad time coming' is a reversal of one of Trollope's favourite phrases, 'a good time coming'.

[➤ Church of England (for Trollope's references to the Christmas Eucharist); Food (for Mr Greenmantle's dining habits); Names, Silly.]

U

Uncles. See Nieces.

Universities. Universities played virtually no role in Trollope's own life and only a marginal one in his fiction. While his brothers, Tom and Henry, were at Oxford and Cambridge respectively, his several attempts to gain a place at either university were unsuccessful. Later, when writing *Thackeray*, he concluded that Thackeray's 'studies there [Cambridge] were not very serviceable to him', and in his novels a few characters attack universities as places where young men waste their time studying a 'sort of lingo [that] was spoken ... six hundred years before Christ' [*The Claverings*, 8].

Although universities are often mentioned as places where characters meet, Trollope rarely sets scenes there. *The Bertrams* – arguably his most 'intellectual' novel – is the only one in which university friendships and ideas, particularly about theological topics, form a constant theme throughout the novel. *Barchester Towers* [14, 20, 34] shows the life of an Oxford college as well as the role of Oxford itself in public, especially in Church, life. This is done through Dr Gwynne, Master of Lazarus College, the Reverend Tom Staple and the Reverend Francis Arabin. In this novel Trollope also shows that he was following the current controversy in *The Times*

about university reform [11, 34]. Cambridge is the setting for *John Caldigate*, but the emphasis here is on the town not the university.

Sometimes Trollope refers to a character holding a fellowship at an Oxford or Cambridge college while not being resident there or doing any teaching. Harry Clavering in *The Claverings* is one example. [➤ *Clergymen of the Church of England* for article on Fellows.] Until the completion in 1881 of changes begun in 1877, it was normally the case that Fellows were clergymen, or would become clergymen. Men could be elected to college fellowships, normally after an examination, without being required to reside or to teach. Teaching was normally done by 'tutors', men like Tom Staple [*Barchester Towers*, 34]. If the Fellow was not a clergyman he was normally expected to take Holy Orders in the Church of England within a specified period, and if he did not, he lost the fellowship. If he did take Orders he had to remain celibate, and if he married he also lost the fellowship. He could also lose it if he inherited a landed estate with an income larger than the value of his fellowship, or if he took one of his college's livings that could not be held with a fellowship. In the Reverend Francis Arabin's case he took the living of St Ewold's and even though it was not a college living he was allowed to keep his fellowship – until, that is, he married Eleanor Bold.

In Trollope's fiction several young men get into trouble at university and are sent down, notably Lord Gerald Palliser in *The Duke's Children*. In 'Alice Dugdale' a baronet makes continual allusions to his own Oxford college, Christ Church, as opposed to his acquaintance's less prestigious one.

A fairly large number of characters have studied at foreign universities, particularly in Germany, and these include Lucius Mason in *Orley Farm*, Ferdinand Lopez in *The Prime Minister* and Bertie Stanhope in *Barchester Towers*. In all three cases it increases their isolation within English society. While in *North America* Trollope criticized Harvard for not producing as many scholars as Oxford or Cambridge; he also argued that American universities produced better results among the mass of their undergraduates. He remembered another American college he had visited, Washington University in Missouri, in *Dr Wortle's School*.

'An Unprotected Female at the Pyramids'. This short story was written during September and October 1859 when Trollope visited the French Pyrenees. It was published in *Cassell's Illustrated Family Newspaper* on 6 and 13 October 1860 and was included in his first collection of short stories, *Tales of All Countries* (1861). Trollope received £40.

In Cairo an English family, the Damers, are joined by a Frenchman, an American, Mr Jefferson Ingram – 'who was comprising all countries and all nations in one grand tour, as American gentlemen so often do', and by an Englishwoman travelling alone,

Miss Sabrina Dawkins. They set out on a trip down the Nile to the Pyramids. The party encounters mishaps; the young American falls in love with Miss Damer; the difficulties of travel are treated with sardonic humour; and Miss Dawkins tries unsuccessfully to join the Damers as they continue down the Nile.

The story is made up of examples of the English paterfamilias, effete Frenchmen, beautiful young women (Miss Damer), hapless middle-class wives and 'unprotected' or independent women. Trollope treats his young American with respect, although he does have him lecture on the glories of the American Constitution. He also followed custom in using 'Jefferson' as a firstname for American men: Trollope's mother used it in her 1836 anti-slavery novel, *Jonathan Jefferson Whitlaw* and Dickens did the same in *Martin Chuzzlewit*. Trollope's dislike for the lone Englishwoman, Miss Dawkins, is obvious, although it is not so much because she is independent but because she is strident, gushing and spiteful when crossed [➤ *Travelling Sketches*]. Her independence does not preclude her trying to 'sponge' off others. As usual with Trollope, the French do not come out very well: the English and the American struggle manfully to the top of the pyramid while the Frenchman is virtually carried. The Egyptians fare even worse. The engagement between Miss Damer and the American is the first of several Anglo-American marriages in Trollope's fiction.

Utopian. When used by Trollope 'Utopian' is usually an adjective of contempt for those who advocate radical change according to preconceived theoretical notions which are at war with human nature. This is only to be expected from a man whose childhood had been blighted by his mother's sudden enthusiasm to visit a Utopian colony in America. In his *Australia and New Zealand* Trollope maintained that Utopian politicians tried to get away from despotism but ended up creating only more despotism; he specifically denounced the role of Edward Wakefield in the early colonization of Australia. He had a similar contempt for American Abolitionists, whom he sneeringly calls 'the philanthropists', who held out ideas of 'Utopian bliss' if slavery were abolished overnight [*North America*]. This dislike of Utopian ideas also lies behind his opposition to competitive examination as the sole means of judging a young man's qualifications [*The Three Clerks*, *The Bertrams*].

Utopianism is also denounced in his fiction, generally through theoretical reformers like Miss Lactimel Neverbend in *The Three Clerks*, her namesake John Neverbend in *The Fixed Period* and Gerald O'Mahony in *The Land-Leaguers*. His ridicule of women like Baroness Banmann and Olivia Q. Fleabody, Ph.D. in *Is He Popenjoy?*, or Wallachia Petrie in *He Knew He Was Right*, is because their feminism is another example of Utopian unreality. *The Warden* shows how an idealistic reformer like John Bold causes havoc not only for a man he respects, but even for the poor he is trying to help.

In *La Vendée* [22] Trollope singles out Robespierre as an example of a man who begins with Utopian ideals only to end up by slaughtering those who disagreed with him. Two novels written near the end of his life had sustained attacks on Utopian theorists. The first was *The Fixed Period*, which is a novel whose purpose is to attack the consequences of Utopian advocates of euthanasia. The second is *The Land-Leaguers*, in which Trollope attacks those Americans like Gerald O'Mahony who have theoretical views about Irish 'independence' – and who give support and money to Irish terrorists – without any knowledge of Irish life.

For Trollope, however, Utopianism was not just a political heresy. One of the basic themes in his fiction is that young people must give up some of the abstract notions in which they delight and accept the realities of life. Young men, like Fred in 'The Adventures of Fred Pickering' with his visions of being a great author, and young women, like Ayala Dormer in *Ayala's Angel* with her dreams of a perfect man, only achieve happiness when they leave the imaginary world in which they have been hopelessly wandering. Having said this, Trollope does not deny that theoretical ideals of reform do good. His best defence of this view is in *Orley Farm*: 'Such efforts,' he concludes, 'are seldom absolutely wasted' [17]. [➤ *Lord Palmerston*.]

V

La Vendée: An Historical Romance.
Trollope's third novel was written during 1848–9 and was published in three volumes by Henry Colburn in June 1850. Trollope received £20 as an advance against royalties. This was the first money he ever received from his writing as the monies received for his first two novels came from later editions.

La Vendée, set in the midst of the French Revolution, is Trollope's one historical novel. It also has the widest chronological spread of any of his novels, covering almost twenty-five years. His first two Irish novels had not been successful and he was evidently at a loss as to how to continue his writing career. In 1848 Ireland saw a brief and somewhat farcical uprising led by his fellow Harrovian, Smith O'Brien. (When Trollope remembered this in his last novel, *The Land-Leaguers* [41], he rightly said that it produced nothing but O'Brien's own banishment.) Yet as Trollope carefully read *The Times* throughout 1848, he saw stories of other revolutions throughout Europe, some more successful than O'Brien's. For Trollope, many of the fallen princes and politicians who stumbled ashore in England were literally 'household names' as they had entertained his mother or received her at their courts and had then gone on to feature in her travel books on Paris and Vienna.

These revolutionary events caused Trollope to look back to that earlier revolution, the last act of which had closed at Waterloo only a few weeks after his birth. His choice of topic also reflected the great interest felt in the French Revolution by educated people of his generation who had been born into the shadow it cast across the world. Carlyle had brought out *The French Revolution* in the previous decade and Dickens would publish *A Tale of Two Cities* ten years after *La Vendée*. Even today, as could be seen at the time of the bicentenary in 1989, the Revolution understandably is not regarded as a glorious event by many people in France's Vendée region.

La Vendée opens with the fall of the French monarchy in August 1792 and deals with real events and real historical figures. In the west of France, in the province of Brittany and the surrounding regions, there were mass uprisings of peasants against the revolutionaries of Paris. Led by the local gentry and aristocracy, including Henri de Larochejaquelin (Trollope's spelling), and with the enthusiastic support of the clergy, the peasant armies posed a serious threat to the Revolution. The peasants were particularly outraged by the attacks on the Church. It was a fierce war and the revolutionaries engaged in wholesale massacres of priests, nuns and peasants, as well as aristocrats, as they successfully put down the revolt. Set amid the comings and goings of armies are several love stories, among which is that of the fictional Agatha de Larochejaquelin, Henri's sister, who is loved by two men, one an aristocrat, Adolphe Denot, who joins the republicans and tries to kidnap her, and the other, Jacques Cathelineau. Cathelineau, a real historical figure [see below], was a charismatic leader of the peasants. Ironically he fights for a world which denied him the freedom to marry his beloved. (Trollope would later return to the theme of marriage between different social classes in *Lady Anna* and *Marion Fay*.) Cathelineau's death ends Agatha's dilemma.

Trollope was much influenced by the *Memoirs of the Marquise de La Rochejaquelin*, which had been immensely popular in England since Sir Walter Scott's translation in 1816. In the preface to the novel, Trollope said he had made 'very general use' of these 'delightful' memoirs and he had a copy of the book in his library. From it he took details such as the peasants' fervid devotion to a captured cannon they called 'Marie Jeanne'. (This can now be seen in the Musée des Invalides in Paris.) Madame de La Rochejaquelin (1772–1857) appears in the novel as Madame de Lescure, as she married Louis de La Rochejaquelin after the death of her first husband in 1793. (Her second husband was killed during the Vendée's final struggle against Napoleon, which is briefly described in the novel's conclusion.) Trollope was also indebted to the ten-volume *History of the French Revolution* by Sir Archibald Alison. This provided him with a highly detailed chronicle of events. Disraeli portrayed Alison, a strong Scottish Tory, as 'Mr Wordy' in one of his novels. (Trollope also expressed a debt to Lamartine's *Histoire des Girondins* which took a different view of the Revolution. Lamartine was the dominant figure in the Republic that replaced Louis Philippe in 1848.) Trollope could draw on his mother's recollections for details about the Revolution, details that she had obtained during her lengthy visits to the Liberal Marquis de Lafayette in the 1820s. She preserved a long account of these talks in which Lafayette had greatly praised the good intentions of King Louis XVI.

The dependence on the La Rochejaquelin *Memoirs* and on Alison partly explains why *La Vendée* has such a strongly conservative and royalist tone, at variance with that striving for balance and recognition of mixed motives so evident in Trollope's other writings. The *Examiner* criticized the novel for its 'ultra-royalist bias, real or affected'. There is some justice in this for the novel is full of royalist language, including references to the 'murder of the Queen' and 'the tyranny of the democrats' (a phrase heard again in *The Warden* when Archdeacon Grantly uses it to describe America). Yet Trollope's understanding portrait of Marie Antoinette [23] has similarities to the picture painted by most of her recent biographers.

Trollope ends the final chapter by asking how long it will be before the republic – the form of government in France when he was writing – is replaced by a second restoration, and answers, 'Surely before the expiration of half a century since the return of Louis [1815], France will congratulate herself on another restoration' [34]. When the novel was reissued in a cheap one-volume edition in 1875 – sixty years after that Restoration – Trollope added a footnote to modify, but not to abandon, his original view. This was written when France was once again a republic but when a restoration was still possible: 'France must again wait till the legitimate heir of the old family [Bourbons] shall be willing to reign as a *constitutional* sovereign.' [Italics added.]

Trollope's basic hostility towards the Revolution appears most clearly in his assessment of Robespierre [22], who embodied the Utopian approach that Trollope always distrusted. Such theoretical notions, he argued, usually led to 'the lowest abyss of crime and misery'. The overthrow of Louis Philippe shortly before he began writing may also have given Trollope a temporary push towards the right. Years later in *North America* he would write that the only fallen ruler for whom he ever had sympathy was that 'poor citizen King of the French'. Another, underlying reason behind the tone of this book was his sympathetic attitude towards the Catholic religion, already evident in his two Irish novels.

The difficulty he faced was not simply an over-dependence on his sources but a lack of knowledge about the region in which the novel is set. This is one of the many weaknesses of the book. It was mitigated to some degree because he had a ready source on which to draw: his brother Tom had written two detailed travel accounts of western France and it seems almost certain that Trollope used these. Tom, for instance, writes about 'the noble-hearted Larochejaquelin', a view echoed by his younger brother.

Although a few of the characters, notably Agatha and Denot, were 'the offspring of the author's brain', to quote the preface, some of the most notable characters were historical. The most obvious one is Jacques Cathelineau (1759–93). The real man was a carter, but Trollope changes him into a postillion. This is probably because Trollope's only real chance of studying the French 'lower orders' had been in observing the postillions on a hurried coach trip to Paris in the 1830s. His observations were not detailed enough to allow him to make any real difference in the dialogue between aristocrats and peasants and this makes for a certain flatness. He would again make use of continental locations for three of his shorter novels and several short stories. As in *La Vendée*, they would give greater prominence to working-class characters. [➤ Anonymous Novels; Short Story, The.] Later he also used the difficulties of a woman being pursued by two or more lovers in a wide variety of novels and short stories. This book conformed to his view that novels should end with marriages. He also discussed what constitutes a gentleman [12], a question he would frequently bring up in his fiction.

Religion plays a larger role than in virtually any of his other works because it was the religious policy of the Parisian revolutionaries which drove the Breton peasants to revolt [71]. Trollope was able to use his knowledge of Irish Catholicism to demonstrate the devotion of simple country people to their priests and their traditional beliefs. While his brother Tom took the normal Protestant view that the French priests were 'blind leaders of the blind', Trollope portrays Father

Jerome, a leader in the revolt, as an intelligent and devout priest, much as he had portrayed Father John in *The Macdermots of Ballycloran* and would portray other Catholic priests. This is not to say that he is uncritical: the priest is definitely shown using 'superstition to forward his own views'. *La Vendée* is also notable for having more extracts from sermons than all Trollope's other novels put together.

La Vendée has never received much attention. When Trollope looked at it before writing his *Autobiography*, he admitted that he had known nothing of the area about which he wrote but insisted that the story was 'not dull'. In the 1920s, Hugh Walpole, who later became a distinguished historical novelist, praised the novel, and pointed to the completely fictional character of Adolphe Denot as an example of the way in which Trollope could allow a character to reveal himself in words and action. Walpole's judgement has found few supporters and *La Vendée* remains as it has always been, one of the least read of Trollope's works.

The Vicar of Bullhampton. Trollope's twenty-fourth novel was started on 15 June 1868, in Washington, DC on his third American trip, and was finished on 1 November that year. The novel was commissioned by E. S. Dallas, editor of *Once a Week*, for serialization. The publishers, Bradbury, Evans, offered Trollope £2,800 for serialization and book rights but reduced it by £300 when the text was slightly shorter than agreed. They then asked if they could serialize it not in *Once a Week* but in another magazine they published, the *Gentleman's Magazine*. The reason was a delay in printing the English translation of Victor Hugo's *L'Homme qui rit*, which would mean that they would simultaneously have two novels, one ending, one beginning, and there was not enough room. The potential overlap occurred because the French publication had not been concluded in time; this was due to Hugo's incessant alterations to the manuscript. Trollope was furious at Hugo's unprofessional behaviour – 'this sententious French Radical', he called him in his *Autobiography* – and refused. The publishers then decided to drop serialization and to revert to an old-fashioned part issue. There were eleven issues between July 1869 and May 1870. In April 1870 they published a one-volume edition. In 1879 Trollope gave permission for a French translation.

The novel is set in the village of 'Bullhampton', which Trollope sited in Wiltshire, and the action has three separate strands. The vicar, Frank Fenwick, is involved in all three plots. Indeed, one of the book's great attractions is that the love story is only one-third of the novel and does not dominate it. The first plot, which opens the novel, is the tangled story of Mary Lowther's love life. She is a guest of the vicar and his wife and they press her to marry the squire, Harry Gilmore. She eventually agrees to do so although she does not love him, and makes the condition that if she does meet a man she loves she may renounce the engagement. When she returns to live with her aunt, Miss Marrable, she falls in love with her cousin, Captain Marrable, and renounces Gilmore to marry him. However, their engagement is broken off because he has no money and she therefore, under yet more pressure, renews her engagement to Gilmore.

When her cousin becomes *de facto* heir to a baronetcy and a landed estate he renews his offer. She accepts and once again renounces Gilmore, who is heartbroken and leaves for a tour of Europe.

The second plot centres on the Brattle family who run the village mill. Sam, who helps his father, associates with bad men who murder a farmer in the village. He is accused of murder, but is supported by the vicar and is eventually cleared. Sam's sister Carry, who had been seduced, lives in London; rumour has it she is a prostitute. Unusually, the word 'prostitute' is actually used [17] and her seducer is one of the two men eventually tried for the murder. She returns home and is eventually forgiven by her stern father.

The third story line centres on the vicar's relations with the local peer, Lord Trowbridge. This aristocrat, who is quite stupid, grows to despise Fenwick and goes so far as to tell someone that 'the Vicar of Bullhampton was ✳✳✳' in connection with Carry Brattle: the three asterisks may be taken to read 'whoremonger' or 'client' [47]. To spite Fenwick he befriends the local Primitive Methodist minister and builds him a chapel just opposite the vicar's gate. It turns out, however, that the land on which it is built is not his to give but glebe land (belonging to vicars of Bullhampton) and, through pressure of Trowbridge's heir, Lord St George, the chapel is pulled down and the peer and Fenwick are reconciled.

The novel was controversial because it dealt with a 'fallen woman'. For only the second time Trollope, who knew that young ladies made up the largest part of any novelist's readership, added a preface to defend himself in advance for discussing the subject: 'Cannot women, who are good, pity the sufferings of the vicious, and do something perhaps to mitigate and shorten them, without contamination from the vice?' He reminded readers that 'no fault among us is punished so heavily as that fault'. He included the preface in his *Autobiography*. The other preface had been for *La Vendée*.

It may surprise readers that Trollope accepts that the best solution for Carry's rehabilitation lay in her being sent to a 'reformatory', sometimes called a 'penitentiary'. These institutions, which numbered well above a hundred when Trollope wrote, were set up by religious bodies. Here 'fallen women' were taught a trade or skill and given a renewed sense of personal dignity, so vital to Victorians. Although by this time the penitentiaries had lost much of their prison-like atmosphere, the reputation remained and made them offensive to men like the vicar. Frank Fenwick is too 'tender', and this is a fault as Trollope says in an 'authorial intrusion': 'The crooked places of the world, if they are to be made straight at all, must be made straight after a sterner and a juster fashion' [40]. It is interesting that at the novel's end Carry has been accepted back into the family, but readers are told nothing about her future and are reminded that shame still hung round the family. As he said in the preface, 'I have not married her to a wealthy lover ... things could not be with her as they would have been had she not fallen.' To write otherwise would not have been true to nature.

The novel is held together by Frank Fenwick. He is Gilmore's closest friend; he befriends both Sam and Carry Brattle and it is he who feuds with Lord Trowbridge. Fenwick is more involved with his parochial duties than any other clergyman in Trollope's fiction. He is Trollope's ideal, but never idealized, clergyman whose ministry was marked by an 'abstinence from reproof' because he was more concerned with God's love than with His righteousness [7]. God, Fenwick tells his wife, must not be measured 'with a foot-rule' [14]. Trollope makes his identification clear when he comments on Carry Brattle's rejection by her sister-in-law: 'What this woman had been saying to him [the vicar] was only what the world had said to her, – the world that knows so much better how to treat an erring sinner than did Our Saviour when on earth' [41]. Trollope's own High Church inclinations are seen in his references to Passion Week and Holy Week, terms abhorred by Evangelicals and Low Churchmen [➤ Church of England]. Many of Fenwick's virtues as well as his vices are akin to his creator's. Trollope reminds his readers that one reason for Fenwick's support of Carry when all the world is against her is that she is very beautiful: all motives are mixed. Trollope cannot forbear to give some advice to clergymen reading his novel when he has the vicar tell his wife, ' "People know what is good for them to do, well enough, without being dictated to by a clergyman!" He had repeated the words to himself and to his wife a dozen times, and talked of having them put up in big red letters over the fire-place in his own study' [63].

The Vicar of Bullhampton also tackles two aspects of the problems facing women: the first is obviously the plight of Carry Brattle by a world which, then, had severe punishments for women who 'fell'. The second aspect is seen in Mary Lowther. She is virtually forced into marriage, not just by the pressure of the Fenwicks and the fervour of Harry Gilmore, but by the lack of any alternative future to marriage. 'When a girl asks herself that question, – what shall she do with her life? it is so natural that she should answer it by saying that she will get married ... It is a woman's one career – let women rebel against the edict as they may' [37]. The novel is often said to have one 'message', that concerning the plight of fallen women, but there is another, given at the end: Mary Lowther's troubles arose because 'for a while, she allowed herself to believe that it would be right for her to marry a man whom she did not love' [71].

The novel also contains Trollope's most extended discussion about Dissent, something he clearly greatly disliked. While his portrayal of the Primitive Methodist minister, Mr Puddleham, is not vicious, neither is it flattering. The man is shown to be uneducated, a sycophant and unforgiving – it is he, not the vicar, who condemns Carry Brattle on hearsay. Trollope saw Dissent as a social more than a religious phenomenon and disliked what he saw [35, 43, 60]. In a private letter written to collect information about the plot [see below] he referred to the Methodist chapel as 'a very hideous tabernacle and sickly Salem': his public and private views were the same. Despite his obvious knowledge of rural Dissent he made mistakes, referring, for example, to the village's Methodists as having 'elders'. Also, one minor character starts as a Baptist only to become later a Wesleyan Methodist [Dissenters.]

There are several well-drawn minor

characters: Mary's maiden aunt, Sarah Marrable, is one of Trollope's strong-willed Tory spinsters who survive on £300 a year. Gilmore's uncle, Canon Henry Fitzackerley Chamberlaine, is introduced to enhance the novel's clerical flavour, so loved by Trollope's readers. He is superbly depicted by Trollope [24]. There is another of Trollope's baronets in the person of Sir Gregory Marrable, 'a very quiet man' [13] with an income of £3,000 a year. His son, Gregory, is a reclusive and sickly scholar with a 'new theory about Stonehenge' [13]. His character bears some resemblance to Trollope's father, who devoted his later years to a mammoth encyclopedia of the Church. His convenient death – like those in *The Claverings* – makes Captain Marrable the *de facto* heir to Sir Gregory and allows his marriage with Mary Lowther to take place.

It is unusual in Trollope's novels to have so much of the action set among the working classes in the form of the Brattles and the smarmy Methodist minister, Puddleham. Generally the short stories give more attention to working people. The poverty that is never far away from the Brattles was real enough: in *The New Zealander* Trollope had noted that agricultural wages in Wiltshire were among the lowest in the kingdom. In describing Jacob Brattle, the head of the family, Trollope introduced one of the few unbelievers in his fiction. Of Brattle, Trollope wrote, 'There was a stubborn strength in the infidelity of this old Pagan which was utterly impervious to any adjuration... That which he saw and knew and felt, he would believe; but he would believe nothing else' [63]. The novel also contains one of Trollope's most beautiful passages on

close friendship between men, in this case the vicar and Harry Gilmore [62].

The novel is also unusual in giving slightly more attention to children, in this case the vicar's [2]. They serve to heighten the happy home life that Mary Lowther is missing by not marrying. The novel has some similarities to *Mr Scarborough's Family*, *Cousin Henry*, *Sir Harry Hotspur of Humblethwaite* and *Is He Popenjoy?* in Sir Gregory Marrable's worries about the Marrable inheritance.

There are several private references and jokes. Harry Gilmore, like Trollope, was at Harrow. Trollope jokes about his practice of giving potted family histories when describing the Marrable family; when he brings the family tree to its last subject he adds, 'after him the confused reader shall be introduced to no more of the Marrable family' [13]. There are attacks on excessive mourning, when Mary Lowther and the vicar's wife debate going into mourning for a second cousin [59], and on suicide [68]. The phrase 'do what he likes with his own' is referred to by a barrister [42] and used by Lord Trowbridge [43]. Victorians would have recognized it as a notorious phrase used by the Duke of Newcastle in the 1840s to justify evicting tenants who did not vote as he wanted. When Trollope says that Miss Marrable preferred eighteenth-century literature to Dickens, who 'manufactured a kind of life that never had existed, and never could exist', he was expressing his own view [9]. Another literary reference to the *Saturday Review*, allowed Trollope to settle a score with that magazine [27, 37]. The reference to the 'Alabama claims' [47] is to the legal dispute between Great Britain and the United States just starting as Trollope wrote. He would have heard much of it while in America. The United States sued Britain for damage done to them by Confederate ships built in Britain during the recent Civil War. Among these was the CSS *Alabama*. An international tribunal found in America's favour in 1872 and Britain had to pay £3,100,000. The Captain Boodle at Walter Marrable's 'military club' in London [33] is presumably the same Boodle who befriends Archie Clavering in *The Claverings* and appears in *Phineas Redux* [➤ Military]. Trollope's reference to the unscrupulous publishers, Bringémout and Neversell, who publish 'a pretty volume in green and gold on the half-profit system' for the vicar gave him an opportunity to attack the system whereby publisher and writer shared any profit [68]. [➤ Names, Silly; Publishers and Publishing.] The system worked to the advantage of the publisher and was hated by Trollope. His first two novels were published on this basis and he, like Fenwick, earned nothing.

To avoid criticism by lawyers, as had happened over *Orley Farm* and elsewhere, Trollope wrote to a clerical acquaintance concerning glebe land: he needed to know where ecclesiastical title deeds and maps of glebe lands were kept. While the vicar eventually became content to let the offending Methodist chapel stay where it was, the vicar's wife – and apparently Trollope himself – felt it had to go.

Reviews generally were not favourable, although *The Times* was not shocked by the Carry Brattle story and found the novel 'safe reading ... for old ladies and young ladies' [3 June 1870]. The *Saturday Review* enjoyed pointing out an error: Mr Puddleham quotes the Church of England Catechism, which he would never have read, thinking it was the Bible. Not surprisingly that magazine found the novel 'third-rate' but did like the portrayal of Jacob Brattle and added, 'Mr Trollope's third-rate is more readable than most novelists' best' [4 May 1870]. For once Trollope could agree with at least part of the magazine's criticism. When remembering the book in his *Autobiography*, he wrote, 'As regards all the Brattles, the story is, I think, well told. The characters are true, and the scenes at the mill are in keeping with human nature. For the rest of the book I have little to say. It is not very bad, and it certainly is not very good. As I have myself forgotten what the heroine [Mary Lowther] does and says ... I cannot expect that anyone else should remember her. But I have forgotten nothing that was done or said by any of the Brattles' [18]. As usual he was unnecessarily harsh in his verdict on his own work.

Victoria Press. See Faithfull, Emily.

Victoria, Queen (1819–1901; reigned 1837–1901). Trollope had a genuine respect for his Queen, but did not like some of the grandiloquent adulation bestowed on her. This is best seen in the public banquet in *Rachel Ray*. The 'middle-class Englishman' stands for the Loyal Toast and Trollope analyses his attitude towards the Queen, 'whom he reveres and loves by reason of his nature as an Englishman, but against whose fulsome praises as repeated to him *ad nauseam* in the chairman's speech his very soul unconsciously revolts' [27]. His attitude towards the Queen came from a wholehearted belief in constitutional monarchy. His was an early, not a late, nineteenth-century view. In *North America* he praised constitutional monarchy as the best guarantor for 'individual freedom to all who live under it', but in *Doctor Thorne* he mocked too 'servile' a devotion to 'the very nail-parings of royalty' as the sign of a democrat and something that was destructive of constitutional monarchy.

He made two serious attempts to discuss the British monarchy, if not the Queen herself. The first was in *The New Zealander*, in which he greatly underestimated her political and ecclesiastical importance in his chapter on 'The Crown'. The second was an article, 'On Sovereignty', published in the first issue of *Saint Pauls* (October 1867). This was a theoretical comparison of England's constitutional monarchy with America and France and he avoided personal criticism of Victoria by reverting to the old custom of referring to the monarch as 'the king'. He took Palmerston's side in his disputes with the Queen and believed she had behaved 'badly' to his hero: this is seen in his 'memoir' of the former prime minister, *Lord Palmerston*. Like most people he disliked her 'withdrawal' from the ceremonial duties of the monarchy after the Prince Consort's death. Given his dislike of excessive Victorian mourning this is hardly surprising. When Trollope was presented at Court before his 1868 Post Office trip to America he was presented to the Prince of Wales, who stood in for the Queen. Trollope disliked Disraeli's influence on the Queen.

The Court is referred to in *The Kellys and the O'Kellys* and *Barchester Towers*, and in *Marion Fay* we are led to believe that the Queen – on another occasion 'a very high quarter indeed' – favours George Roden's taking his Italian dukedom. Trollope's most personal comment comes in *Miss Mackenzie* when he discusses Victoria's isolated position. Most of his references to the Queen are in his Palliser novels. He does not attempt to portray her and normally refers to her indirectly in terms like 'a most illustrious personage'. In *Phineas Finn* he made one of his silliest errors when he wrote that in the midst of a Cabinet crisis the Queen 'telegraphed to Germany for advice' [9]. By then the highly experienced Queen in fact wired Germany to give advice to her daughter, who had married the heir to the Prussian Crown, not to ask for it. Victoria's political role was also referred to in *Phineas Redux* and *The Duke's Children*. For her part the Queen preferred George Eliot and Mrs Oliphant as novelists. When she read *Barchester Towers* to Prince Albert she thought it did not have 'enough romance' [➤ *Barchester Towers*].

Trollope and his sovereign shared many views. Like Trollope she saw nothing wrong in postal deliveries on Sundays; like him she disliked seeing barristers defending those they knew to be guilty; like him she supported the work of Emily Faithfull; like him she retained a somewhat romantic attitude towards duelling, and like him she was genuinely distressed at the trend towards self-indulgence which she saw in Society in the 1870s. This was a theme he expounded in *The Way We Live Now*, *Sir Harry Hotspur of Humblethwaite* and *Mr Scarborough's Family*. Fifteen years after Trollope's death she agreed a Civil List pension for his widow, Rose.

Victoria Regia: A Volume of Original Contributions in Poetry and Prose. This collection was edited by the poet Adelaide A. Procter, and appeared in November 1861. Like *A Welcome*, it was published by Emily Faithfull and printed by her recently established Victoria Press. It was dedicated to Queen Victoria – hence the title – and was something of a manifesto for Emily Faithfull's crusade to expand the opportunities open to women. (Adelaide Procter was herself interested in social questions concerning women.) Besides Trollope, who contributed 'The Journey to Panama', other contributors included friends of his such as Mrs Oliphant, Henry Reeve, Sir Henry Taylor, Thackeray, the American poet James Russell Lowell, and Tom and Theodosia Trollope. Tennyson and Matthew Arnold were also contributors. All the contributors gave their works *gratis*.

Violence. Those who have read only the Barsetshire novels would be surprised at the amount of violence in Trollope's novels. To those who lived through it the nineteenth century seemed a violent one and things appeared to be getting worse, with rioting, Irish terrorism and garrotting on the increase. For self-defence, gentlemen like Robert Kennedy [*Phineas Redux*] carried revolvers while others carried swords disguised as walking-sticks. In *The Land-Leaguers* Rachel O'Mahony always conceals a small dagger on her person, and in *Lady Anna* Countess Lovel has her own pistol. In the first issue of *Saint Pauls* (January 1868) Trollope wrote an article on 'The Uncontrolled Ruffianism of London'. He refused to panic at the reported crime wave and wrote, 'We decline to recognize any necessity for altering our usual mode of living.' For a man who wrote of life round him it is not surprising that violence is a frequent ingredient, although usually the development of the main story line does not depend on it. It is essential, however, in turning the plot in *Phineas Redux, An Eye for an Eye* and *The Fixed Period*. There are murders in *The Macdermots of Ballycloran, Doctor Thorne, The Vicar of Bullhampton, Phineas Redux, An Eye for an Eye* and *The Land-Leaguers*. There are attempted murders in *The Kellys and the O'Kellys, Can You Forgive Her?, Phineas Finn* (when Phineas saves Kennedy from garrotters), *Phineas Redux, Lady Anna, The Fixed Period* and *The Land-Leaguers*, and in 'Aaron Trow' an escaped convict is killed. Murder is seriously contemplated in *Marion Fay* and threatened in 'Aaron Trow' and *Dr Wortle's School*. Seductions occur in *The Macdermots of Ballycloran, Doctor Thorne, The Vicar of Bullhampton* and *An Eye for an Eye*, and there is an attempted seduction in *The Way We Live Now*. There is an execution in *The Macdermots of Ballycloran*. There is a case of arson in *Harry Heathcote of Gangoil*. There are wholesale murders in *La Vendée* and terrorism in *The Land-Leaguers*. Assaults occur in *Can You Forgive Her?, The Small House at Allington, The Struggles of Brown, Jones, and Robinson, Phineas Finn, The Way We Live Now, The Prime Minister, Doctor Thorne, Dr Wortle's School, Mr Scarborough's Family*, and *Is He Popenjoy?* in which it is doubly shocking because a clergyman, and a cathedral dean at that, knocks a marquis into the fireplace. There are suicides in *The Bertrams*, 'The Spotted Dog', *The Belton Estate, The Way We Live Now*, 'La Mère

Bauche', and *The Prime Minister*, and an attempted suicide in *Nina Balatka*. There is a riot in *The American Senator* and a near riot in 'Father Giles of Bally-moy'. There is a duel in *Phineas Finn* and a kidnapping in *He Knew He Was Right*. A horse is nobbled in The *Duke's Children*. [➤ War.]

Virtue, James Sprent (1829–92). In 1855 Virtue became manager of the London branch of the publishing house established by his father, George. The firm became famous for the quality of its art works, especially for its magazine, the *Art Journal*. James Virtue was in charge of this until his death. In 1866, he decided to enter the highly competitive world of monthly periodicals and his first thought was to buy *The Argosy*, but then decided in 1867 to launch a new magazine, eventually called *Saint Pauls*, with Trollope as its editor. When this proved an economic failure Virtue returned to the safer world of publishing illustrated books. He published the book edition of *Phineas Finn* and privately printed Trollope's *How the 'Mastiffs' Went to Iceland* (1878). He was also the printer for Chapman & Hall. Virtue has another claim to fame: he was partly behind the famous 1873 'Spy' cartoon of Trollope. He invited Trollope to his home along with the cartoonist, Leslie Ward ('Spy'), who took the opportunity to sketch the novelist. Trollope was furious.

Vulgarity. That he was 'vulgar' was a criticism often levelled against Trollope, as it had been against his mother, Fanny. The *Saturday Review* often accused him of 'vulgar characters' and 'vulgar incidents'. 'Vulgar' was an epithet that Victorians flung at anything

they disliked, much as 'racism' or 'sexism' are sometimes used today. The *Spectator*, for example, heavily criticized *The Prime Minister* and said that it was marked by a 'vulgarity of thought' and concluded that not only Lopez but Lady Glencora Palliser and even the Duke of Omnium were all 'vulgar' [22 July 1876]. The wife of the British Ambassador in Rome, when she met Trollope, found him 'rather vulgar, like his books, but interesting' [➤ Diplomats]. Those who brought the charge meant a variety of things. To some it was too vivid a description of physical characteristics or acts while to others it meant characters they disliked. Longmans, for example, forced him to change 'fat stomach' to 'deep chest' in *Barchester Towers* and also disliked his having a clergyman kiss a woman to whom he was not yet married. George Smith disliked the short story, 'A Ride across Palestine', in which Trollope has a character explain the effects of a Turkish saddle to his new friend by 'taking hold of his leg by the calf to show how the leather would chafe him; but it seemed to me that he did not quite like my interference'. (The new friend was actually a woman in disguise.) Smith must have disliked even more the passage in which the narrator, having bathed in the Jordan River, 'stretched myself out in my weariness . . . my head rested on his legs. Ah, me! one does not take such liberties with new friends in England.'

Trollope's mention of 'bosoms' or 'busts' would also have been considered 'vulgar' by some Victorians. In *Doctor Thorne*, when writing of Lady Arabella Gresham's refusal to suckle her baby son, he commented on her sort of woman: 'Nature gives them bosoms for show, but not for use. So Lady Arabella had a wet-nurse' [2]. In *Miss Mackenzie* Trollope describes a spinster who stands in front of a mirror. She pulled 'her scarf tighter across her bosom, feeling her own form, and then she leaned forward and kissed herself in the glass [9]. In *The Claverings* he refers to a woman's 'majestic bust' [47] and in *The Bertrams* he described Jewish women in the Holy Land as 'glorious specimens of feminine creation. They were somewhat too bold . . . with their naked shoulders and bosoms nearly bare' [9].

Kissing and feminine lips caused problems even after his disagreement with Longmans. In *The Vicar of Bullhampton* there are lips which, sadly, no man 'would think to ravage in boisterous play' [1]. In his last, complete novel, he wrote that 'Her lips, alas! were too thin for true female beauty, and lacked that round and luscious fullness which seems in many a girl's face to declare the purpose for which they were made' [*An Old Man's Love*, 31]. Another 'vulgarity' that often occurs is a reference to a 'good honest kiss, mouth to mouth' [*Miss Mackenzie*, 13]. Any mention of prostitutes also laid him open to criticism.

The fact that some characters occasionally curse while others use antiquated phrases or references could cause trouble. In *The American Senator* one character refers to 'a knot of self-anxious people who think they possess among them all the bowels of the world' [73] and others refer to the old song, 'Captain Bold of Halifax', which concerns seduction and suicide. Characters, too can be 'vulgar', that is, with few manners, like Samuel Rubb in *Miss Mackenzie*, Mr Moulder, the commercial traveller for Hubbles & Grease in *Orley Farm*, Aunt Greenow with her new money in *Can You Forgive Her?*, and the world represented in *The Struggles of Brown, Jones, and Robinson*. The *Saturday Review* and other magazines particularly disliked the people in this book, as well as those portrayed in *Miss Mackenzie*.

Editors who serialized novels in their magazines often censored 'vulgar' passages [➤ *Is He Popenjoy?*]. Trollope compromised when he had to, but in the book he was writing when he died, *The Land-Leaguers*, the scenes featuring Rachel O'Mahony and the theatrical world centred on her agent, Mahomet M. Moss, are decidedly racy in speech and some of the characters have very questionable histories.

W

Wales. Wales plays a small role in Trollope's fiction. His first visit to the Principality was in 1852 when he was setting out 'walks' for the Post Office. His time there did not impress him, although this may have been due to bad weather. He told one friend, 'I could wish you nothing worse than a residence in South Wales for the rest of your life.' He did not set any of those short stories based on his travels there, and he did not use Wales for a novel until *Cousin Henry* (1879) and that novel is not marked by any particular sense of place. The influence of his fictional return to Wales may have stayed with him when he started *Marion Fay*, fifteen days after he finished *Cousin Henry*; there he had one character, Lord Llwddythlw, heir to the Duke of Merioneth [➤ Names, Silly].

'A Walk in a Wood'. Trollope wrote this essay for the series 'Half-Hours in the Fresh Air' in *Good Words*. When William Isbister, one of the magazine's owners, decided it did not fit into the series he suggested re-naming it. Trollope offered, 'How we write our books' and added, 'It must not be more personal than that.' Isbister preferred the original title and published it in September 1879.

The essay is one of the best analyses not only of the novelist's art but of Trollope's own work. In it he describes how he devised plots while walking: for Trollope, physical exertion, whether walking, working or riding to hounds, was essential to his creative, as well as to his emotional and physical well-being. As a boy he had built 'castles in the air' but he had done so while trudging the muddy lanes of Harrow. Great forests, whether in Switzerland, South Africa, Australia, California or 'England, dear England', were his chosen places but he preferred Germany's Black Forest above any other, for its peace and quiet: 'Gradually as I walk or stop, as I seat myself on a bank, or lean against a tree, perhaps as I hurry on waving my stick above my head till with my quick motion the sweat-drops come out upon my brow, the scene forms itself for me. I see, or fancy that I see, what will be fitting, what will be true, how far virtue may be made to go without walking upon stilts [➤ Dickens], what wickedness may do without breaking the link which binds it to humanity, how low ignorance may grovel, how high knowledge may soar, what the writer may teach without repelling by severity, how he may amuse without descending to buffoonery . . .'

Insights into his creative genius are also to be found in 'The Adventures of Fred Pickering' and 'The Panjandrum'. [➤ Novel, The.]

Walking. Walking played a large role both in Trollope's own creative life and in his fiction. Like his brother Tom, he had a passion for long walks. When in Wales on Post Office business in 1852 he walked twenty-four miles one day. Those who watched him said he then set out at a stride of six miles an hour [Mullen, 247]. Throughout his adult life he found walking therapeutic. On one occasion he and Tom walked from Harrow to London to visit Vauxhall Gardens, a return journey of thirty miles. As a young man working in London he walked the capital's streets. He was a member of the Tramp Society in which three friends explored the Home Counties on foot and sometimes walked as far as Southampton. When working in Ireland, a walk with a friend led him to the ruins of a country house which inspired his first novel, *The Macdermots of Ballycloran*. When his work took him to the southwest of England he spent many days walking round villages. This gave him an unsurpassed knowledge of country life, while an evening's walk round Salisbury gave him the idea for *The Warden*. Walking alone, preferably in a wood, continued to be the best place for his creative ideas to come to life, as he explained in his essay 'A Walk in a Wood'. In later years he was also a member of the Gaiter Club, which undertook walking tours in Scotland, wore gaiters and had an annual dinner. Other members included Norman Macleod and the Scottish industrialist, John Burns.

Trollope's characters, at least his male ones, often seem capable of arduous feats of walking: Josiah Crawley insists on walking almost all the thirty-mile return journey to Barchester when summoned by the bishop. Trollope added that such a feat demanded 'great physical exertion' but also wrote that it was 'a practicable distance' [*The Last Chronicle of Barset*, 17]. In *The Claverings* Mr Saul walks six miles twice a week to take services in a chapel near the village. Trollope, with tongue in cheek, calls this a 'pleasing occupation' more because of the times of the walks than because of the distance: the first was before breakfast and the second was after dinner [2]. But both these clergymen are eccentric and long walks may be a sign of eccentricity, poverty or both. On the other hand, an aversion to walking is generally associated with moral depravity: the debauched Marquis of Brotherton hates walking in *Is He Popenjoy?* [41]. In *The Vicar of Bullhampton* young Sam Brattle walked seventeen miles with 'no sign of fatigue' because he had no choice. When asked by his father how he had come, he used what must have been an old pun: 'By the marrow-bone [Marylebone] stage, as don't pay no tolls; how else?' [69]. (Foot passengers did not normally pay tolls on bridges.)

Victorians were famed for being great walkers because, until the development of cheap systems of public transport in the expanding towns, they had little alternative unless they had money for a cab (in towns), owned a private vehicle or had access to one. [➤ Carriages.] In smaller towns and in the countryside walking remained the principal means of getting about for most people: a man, if he had the money, could hire a horse or a gig, as Frank Fenwick did for a return trip of about twenty-four miles in *The Vicar of Bullhampton* [39]. When faced with a return journey of eight miles on a hot

August day to see Mrs Proudie, Mrs Quiverful despaired of the 'terrible task' and asked Farmer Subsoil to take her in his cart [*Barchester Towers*, 25]. In *Rachel Ray* almost all the characters, male and female, walk between the town and Mrs Ray's country cottage, but the distance is only a mile and a half. Women, whom Trollope assumed to be the bulk of his readership, are much less involved in long walks although some take walks in the country: in *The Claverings* Fanny Clavering is proposed to by Mr Saul during a walk but, as in *Rachel Ray*, it is only one and a half miles in length.

Trollope argued that gentlemen, because of their fondness for sports, were usually capable of greater endurance in walking than working men [*John Caldigate*, 11]. The walk that George Vavasor takes in the Lake District in *Can You Forgive Her?* is based on one that Trollope and his brother took in their youth. In that novel Trollope asks, 'What are five miles of a walk to a young man, even though the rain be falling and the ways be dirty? what, though they may come after some other ten that he has already traversed on his feet?' [57].

The walks undertaken by a lady in London are quite as limited in Trollope's fiction as they were in reality. Trollope once moaned that his wife would walk for miles in the Swiss mountains, but would not walk a mile in London where she preferred to be taken about in a carriage. The reasons for this were complex: ladies in towns used carriages or hired cabs, especially when shopping, not just to maintain their ladylike demeanour but to avoid walking along streets paved with prostitutes. Ladies could also go 'walking' as a form of exercise but in prescribed places, normally parks. Sometimes this could lead to problems: in *Is He Popenjoy?* Mrs Adelaide Houghton flirts with Lord George Germain during a walk in London's Kensington Gardens and in *Ayala's Angel* some of the difficult love-making undertaken by the Dormer sisters was done through walks.

War. Trollope was born a few weeks before the end of the Napoleonic Wars and in his lifetime Britain fought only one major war, the Crimean War, which he supported. [➤ *The New Zealander*; *Lord Palmerston*.] Some of his travel books mention smaller colonial wars, but he rejected an idea from the Governor-General of New Zealand that he should write a novel about the Maori wars. The only war he saw at first hand was the American Civil War, when he twice crossed the border from Washington into the Confederacy. He did not see any fighting and the experience only confirmed his dislike for the military. War plays a very small role in his fiction. His historical novel, *La Vendée*, is dominated by battles in the French Revolution. 'The Last Austrian Who Left Venice' is set against the fighting between Austria and forces fighting for a united Italy. 'The Two Generals' is set in the American Civil War. War is also the background to 'Relics of General Chassé' and 'The Widow's Mite': the first is the war of 1830–32 to free modern Belgium from Dutch control while the second is, again, the American Civil War. Next to the French revolutionary wars, this war receives the most attention of any in his writing. [➤ *North America*.] European wars rarely enter into his fiction other than as background for characters:

Major Tifto, for example, was involved in the third Carlist war in Spain (1872–6) [*The Duke's Children*, 6], while Plomacy, the steward of the Thornes in *Barchester Towers* had been involved in an attempt to rescue Queen Marie Antoinette from the horrors of the French Revolution.

The Warden. Trollope's fourth novel and the first book in the Barsetshire series, was written between 29 July 1853 and the autumn of 1854. (Trollope gives the wrong date for completion in his *Autobiography*. His son Henry said in a letter of 15 October 1883 to Blackwoods that this mistake was 'probably' made by his father.) William Longman, whom Trollope had met through his friend John Merivale, and to whom Trollope sent the manuscript, suggested he should change the original title, 'The Precentor', and he agreed. The book was published by Longman, Brown, Green, and Longmans early in 1855. By the end of the first six months they had sold 388 copies and given away thirty-eight. Trollope received £9. 8s. 8d. although he eventually received more money in later years.

Trollope's first three novels had not been successful and he paused for some time before embarking on a fourth. In the early 1850s he was asked by the Post Office to lay out routes in the south-west of England and in May 1852 he came to Salisbury. In his *Autobiography* he describes how, 'whilst wandering there on a midsummer evening round the purlieus of the cathedral I conceived the story of *The Warden*, – from whence came that series of novels of which Barchester, with its bishops, deans and archdeacon, was the central site'. Yet it was some time before he actually started writing as

he was constantly on the move. He later told Escott, his first biographer, that he was fascinated by the letters in *The Times* from clergymen and tried to imagine their lives. He had ample opportunity during this period to do just this because his work required him to visit many clerical homes and to talk to many clergymen. [➤ Barsetshire Novels.] Among the places he visited was 'the sweet close' of Hereford where a cousin was a canon [➤ *Cousin Henry*]. He actually started writing in the small town of Tenbury on the Worcestershire–Shropshire border.

The Warden has as its theme the reactions of an unworldly clergyman under public attack for the large income he derives as warden of Hiram's Hospital, a medieval almshouse. (The Warden is also the precentor, or priest responsible for music, in Barchester Cathedral: hence the original title.) In the early 1850s there were three great disputes about the administration of charities by the clergy in Winchester, Dulwich and Rochester and all three are mentioned in *The Warden*. Radicals and Dissenters pointed out that a few privileged and well-connected clergymen of the Church of England could make use of vastly increased rents from land left for charitable purposes. Trollope was fascinated with both the Radical attacks on the Church and the strong defence put forward by many of the clergy. *The Warden* demonstrates better than any of his other novels Trollope's divided mind when it came to great political or ecclesiastical questions. He was torn between his belief in liberal 'progress' and his genuine veneration for old institutions. He also believed that 'a loving tenderness with which admitted abuses are endured' was a national trait.

When Trollope was a schoolboy at Winchester, he constantly saw the Holy Cross almshouses, founded in 1136. Although he knew other almshouses from his travels, Winchester's were the ones he knew best and they most influenced his portrayal of Hiram's Hospital. He was also well informed about the attacks on the Master of Holy Cross, the Reverend Francis North, who was also the fifth Earl of Guilford. This made him a doubly tempting target for Radicals. As Master he was accused of taking huge profits from the increased value of the Hospital's lands. The catalogue of Trollope's library shows that he possessed many pamphlets attacking such abuses, including the best known, *The Extraordinary Black Book* [Mullen, 693–4]. He makes his indebtedness clear in *The Warden* [2] when we learn that Archdeacon Grantly has written a pamphlet, under the *nom de plume* of 'Sacerdos', to defend the Earl of Guilford, which Trollope continually misspells as Guildford, in 'the well-known case of The Hospital of St Cross'.

The Warden, the Reverend Septimus Harding, is Trollope's best-loved character and the central figure of the whole Barsetshire series. He is faced with a dilemma when a young Barchester doctor, John Bold, unleashes a campaign of which the target is Hiram's Hospital. Bold and his supporters contend that the Warden is receiving too much money – £800 a year – for too little work. (£800 is close to the income Trollope would later receive as his official salary when he became a Surveyor.) Bold is opposed by the most powerful clergyman in the diocese, Archdeacon Grantly, who

exercises most of the power of his elderly father, the bishop. For Mr Harding there are many additional difficulties: his younger daughter, Eleanor, seems likely to marry Bold but his elder daughter, Susan, is already married to the archdeacon. Eleanor and Bold provide the love story that Trollope and Victorians generally considered essential in novels. All these family complications add interest and humour to the plot, but the main attention is always on the struggle going on within the Warden's conscience. With uncharacteristic brevity, Henry James aptly summed up the book: 'It is simply the story of an old man's conscience.'

Bold's case is soon taken up by *The Jupiter*, the powerful newspaper that dominated public life. Everybody knew that the author intended *The Jupiter* to mean *The Times*. This was a topical allusion, for Trollope was writing in the midst of the Crimean War (1854–6) and the novel was published before the war had ended. *The Times* played a role in that war that has never been equalled by any other newspaper in history. Not only did it virtually invent war reporting with its famous correspondent, W. H. Russell, but its thundering leaders made and unmade governments. ('Billy' Russell eventually became a close friend of Trollope, but Trollope was not uncritical of him.) [➤ *Autobiography.*] Queen Victoria and almost all politicians were alarmed at this despotic power and most of them made statements which were echoed by the archdeacon: 'What the Tsar is in Russia, or the mob in America, that *The Jupiter* is in England.' Trollope had long had a grievance against *The Times* because of its coverage of the Irish Famine.

This explains the reference to 'the cabins of Connaught' in Chapter 14. [➤ The *Examiner*; Ireland.]

Trollope's satire on *The Times* is fairly effective and it was the first of many assaults upon the way newspapers could intrude into and destroy a man's life. This theme would recur in many later novels. *The Times* waited until its review of *Barchester Towers* to issue a mild rebuke to the presumptuous novelist. Many people assumed that Trollope intended Tom Towers, *The Jupiter*'s principal writer, to be a portrait of the famous editor, J. T. Delane, but Trollope always denied this.

If the satire on *The Times* was quite successful and has retained its force, three other attempts at satire were failures. In describing the archdeacon's three sons, Trollope poked fun at the three most prominent bishops of the time [➤ Grantly Sons]. There were also extended attacks on the two biggest names in the literary world: Dickens (Mr Popular Sentiment) and Carlyle (Dr Pessimist Anticant). Not only is Trollope's satire heavy-handed, but it sounds like an unsuccessful author attacking those who have achieved fame. However, these are only minor flaws in an otherwise splendid novel. Trollope had at last, after three comparative failures, found the right subject when he invented Barsetshire.

There are several features worthy of note in this novel. For the first time we see the importance of London, even to a provincial city like Barchester. The chapters set in London, particularly when Mr Harding wanders round Westminster Abbey or sees Sir Abraham Haphazard, are among Trollope's finest. We can also see how accurate Trollope was on small points: Mr Harding visits a 'cigar-divan' in the Strand and pays 1s. for a cup of coffee and a cigar [➤ Smoking]. Peter Cunningham's *Handbook* for London, published three years before, advises visitors that this is the best place to have coffee in London and gives the same price as that paid by the Warden [16]. Of course the account of the chop house was based on Trollope's own days as a clerk in London. When he shows the archdeacon playing whist, and playing for money, Trollope is telling us that the old High Church clergyman is unmoved by the new Evangelical campaign against gambling and even cards: that storm would only hit Barchester with the arrival of the Proudies in *Barchester Towers* [➤ *The Last Chronicle of Barset*].

One sees a deft hand in the portrayal of the relationship between the Warden and the Hospital's twelve bedesmen (eight of whom are named), most particularly the head bedesman, Bunce. The unvarying ritual in which Bunce always refuses a third glass of port is a marvellous insight into the deferential manners of the time. If the picture of Sir Abraham Haphazard shows a touch of Trollope's Liberal bias, the affectionate portrayal of the deferential devotion that Bunce has for Mr Harding reveals Trollope's conservative instincts.

The Warden contains more topical allusions and references to living people than any other Trollope novel, particularly if one considers its length. Numerous politicians of the day are mentioned in passing. Generally speaking, Liberal politicians such as Lord John Russell or Lord Palmerston appear in a mildly favourable light while Conservative politicians like Peel and Disraeli receive the opposite treatment. Trollope's real ire is reserved for Radicals such as the two MPs, Sir Benjamin Hall and Edward Horsman. They are presented in such a way as to provoke a smile of bemused contempt from most contemporaries who would have known their reputation for outrageous language in their attacks on the Church of England [Mullen, 274]. Contemporaries would also have had a laugh about Sir Abraham Haphazard's 'Convent Custody Bill', the 107th clause of which 'ordered the bodily searching of nuns for Jesuitical symbols by aged clergymen' [16]. Every well-informed reader knew this was an allusion to the perpetual efforts of C. Newdigate Newdegate, a real Tory MP and a fanatical Protestant, to introduce government inspectors into Catholic convents. Incidentally this is an excellent example of the way in which Trollope normally contrived to make all such attacks upon Catholicism or High Church Anglicanism quite ludicrous. Although the same chapter contains a gentle laugh at ladies who have gilt crosses on their Prayer Books, High Church foibles are never as menacing as the sinister activities of their critics [► Trollope, Cecilia].

Nor were real artists forgotten: when Trollope mentions that Tom Towers's room was decorated with a bust of Peel by 'Power', he was not just identifying the Tory politician with an opportunistic journalist but was giving publicity to the American sculptor Hiram Powers, a friend of his mother, Fanny. Another artist, John Everett Millais, appears in an unfavourable light. In his use of *The Warden* to level blasts at various contemporary events and groups that annoyed him he included the Pre-Raphaelite movement, which he felt was inclined towards an unrealistic portrayal of life [14]. Within a few years, however, Millais would become one of his closest friends. By the time of the later Barsetshire novels, Trollope had become a figure in the London literary world and also had become acquainted with many politicians. *The Warden* is, in this sense only, a book by a man who was not yet part of the great world: he was still a provincial portraying provincials.

The Warden met with a favourable reception from most reviewers although many could not decide whether the author supported Church reform or not. The answer was simple: Trollope supported reform but disliked reformers. Longmans' reader had thought that the book would have a strong appeal to 'low Churchmen and dissenters'. This absurd view has not been shared by anyone else. Far more accurate was the opinion of a clergyman well known for his books on cricket, who advised his publishers, Longmans, that they now had an author who was 'breaking new ground': 'let your new author stick to that; so will he add to your wealth and, if he have staying power, build up his own fame'. Trollope certainly had 'staying power' and *The Warden* did begin his 'fame'. As he said in his *Autobiography*, all his friends now knew that he was an author. As well as the £9. 8s. 8d. he received in 1855, he had another cheque for £10. 15s. 8d. in 1856. This total, £20. 4s. 4d., was not a vast amount of money for a novel: 'stone-breaking would have done better,' he noted.

Yet Trollope had found his subject and was now free to develop it. *The*

Warden is not only a promise of better to come, but is a considerable achievement in its own right. Strangely, many modern critics never rate *The Warden* as highly as it deserves. It is a marvellous novel and one that repays frequent re-reading. There is no better book with which to introduce anyone to the joys of Anthony Trollope.

[➤ Bold, Mary; Chadwick, John; Music; Religion.]

The Way We Live Now. Trollope started his thirty-second novel on 1 May 1873. He stopped writing on 1 June 1873 to devote that month to *Harry Heathcote of Gangoil*, resumed writing on 3 July and finished on 22 December 1873. During the second fortnight in August he and his wife were in Ireland. The novel was first published by Chapman & Hall in twenty monthly parts, at 1*s.* each, between February 1874 and September 1875. They published the novel in two volumes in June 1875. Trollope received £3,000.

In a letter to Richard Bentley, who had published so many of the Trollope family works, Tom Trollope wrote from Rome: 'My brother['s] ... "Way we live now" was a charming book to us exiles from our country – so very consolatory! Upon my life you must have become a delightful set of people ... at least if there is truth in Anthony's picture.' While *The Way We Live Now* annoyed many of Trollope's contemporaries, it has been greatly praised in recent decades as a searing portrait of Victorian materialism, a portrait that contains a great deal of truth.

The novel's main action centres on Augustus Melmotte who arrives in London from nowhere to establish a great financial empire, to earn a place in Society and to get a seat in the House of Commons. (Ferdinand Lopez would follow a very similar course in *The Prime Minister*, which Trollope began writing four months after finishing this book.) The novel follows Melmotte's rise to power and Society's sycophancy towards him. He turns his hand to forgery to keep his empire alive but fails and finally commits suicide. The love plot is provided through his daughter, Marie, who is courted by many fortune-seekers, is jilted by the one she chooses and who then marries an American speculator.

There is no other Trollope novel that requires more knowledge of the immediate background of his life at the time of writing. He began the novel in the week after his fifty-eighth birthday. The previous few months had been among the most unsettling of his life – certainly the most unsettling since he had begun writing. In December 1872 he and Rose returned to England after a nineteen-month trip to Australia to see their younger son, Frederic. For the first time since 1859, Trollope was without a house. They had let their much-loved home at Waltham Cross before going to Australia and eventually sold it with a loss of money. For the first time in thirty years Trollope was living in London, and the search for a permanent home naturally brought the subject of money much to the fore. Even when he found a new house in Montagu Square – which provided a name for one of the main characters in the novel – he had to spend £1,700 to furnish it.

He had come back in a depressed mood. He wondered if he would ever see Fred again and was unhappy with what he found when he returned. His elder son, Henry, was planning to marry 'a woman of the town'. Trollope acted promptly, even by his standards: within days Henry was on his way for a long visit to Fred. As Trollope worked to complete his *Australia and New Zealand*, he became increasingly convinced that those distant colonies were producing 'a very much better life than we have here'. On board the ship to Australia, Trollope had written *Lady Anna*, a novel set in the 1830s against the background of liberal and radical ideals, many of which Trollope had himself shared. Yet as he settled into London life, he clearly felt that many ideals were being swamped by the rising power of the financial world centred in the City of London.

Trollope had long had a deep belief in the importance of honesty and it had been a recurrent theme in his novels, particularly those written in the 1850s. Now everywhere he looked he seemed to see dishonesty, greed and corruption. On his way back from Australia he had passed through America, then in the midst of an era of great commercial speculation and dishonesty: Mark Twain and C. D. Warner portrayed this in their novel *The Gilded Age* (1873). Trollope evidently was not pleased with his hurried trip through the American West and his annoyance is present throughout *The Way We Live Now*. One of the many speculators in the book 'had sprung out of some California gully' [35]. There are also several references to Salt Lake City, which Trollope visited. It seems highly likely that he would have met the son of his old friend Lord Stanley of Alderley, who had gone there after several prominent Englishmen had been lured into a fraudulent speculation about the Emma silver mine – a fraud promoted by the American Minister in London. Some Americans, with long experience of life in England and Europe, were horrified by some of their countrymen who were pouring into London. It is worth noting that Trollope invited Kate Field to dinner in July, when he was in the course of writing this novel, and she probably mentioned that her recent book attacked 'the "shoddy" ... nouveaux riches' coming to Europe with their 'frequently ill gotten fortunes'.

Trollope was not alone in his fears that increasing speculation and dishonesty were destroying the moral fibre of the upper classes. *The Times* had been denouncing the changes in English society and it was one subject on which both Queen Victoria and Mr Gladstone were in agreement. Only two weeks before Trollope signed the contract for this novel, the monarch and the prime minister discussed contemporary society. She said aristocratic young men were becoming 'ignorant, luxurious, and self-indulgent' while the women were 'fast, frivolous, and imprudent'. She blamed much of this on the French example. Gladstone agreed and added that the 'plutocracy' was becoming too powerful and it was producing 'a bastard aristocracy and [real] aristocracy shows too much disposition, in Parliament especially, to join hands with this bastard and it was also corrupting the Clubs'. This sounds exactly like a summary of *The Way We Live Now*. (The Queen, Trollope, and the editor of *The Times* were all in their fifties while Gladstone was already in his sixties – just the right age to bemoan declining standards.)

The Queen's reference to France was appropriate. Napoleon III had suffered a catastrophic defeat in 1870 which many people, including Trollope, saw as the result of the financial corruption and other immoralities for which Imperial Paris had been renowned. There are several hints that Melmotte was also involved with Austrian financiers. Not only had Austria suffered a series of military defeats in the 1850s and 1860s, but in 1873 the Vienna stock-market collapsed, thereby destroying numerous banks and speculators. These events would have added to a growing awareness of corruption, a feeling of general unease.

Trollope's notes for *The Way We Live Now* have survived in the Bodleian Library, Oxford and show that the focus of the novel changed as he thought about it. Anyone who has read the novel will immediately think of one character: Augustus Melmotte, the great speculator. Yet in Trollope's original working list of characters he is not listed except as the father of Marie. Trollope added a few details to the notes to give himself some background on where Melmotte's house was located and on his past: 'Melmotte has been in prison in Hamburg.' The 'fact' people seem to recall from the book is that Melmotte is a Jew and many assert that the novel has a strongly anti-Semitic tone. Actually, Melmotte is described as 'the great French swindler' in the notes and in the novel itself his origins are kept mysterious. It is not explicitly said that he is Jewish. (Trollope did the same thing with that highly admirable character Madame Max Goesler in the Palliser novels, and with Lopez in *The Prime Minister*.)

The important point about Melmotte is that he is an 'alien': someone who threatens the stability of British society from without, not only through his own wickedness but by acting as a magnet for all that is evil. Madame Melmotte, his much-abused and stupid wife, is Jewish and so is Melmotte's associate, Cohenlupe. Yet as so often in Trollope's fiction, when a group produces a nasty character it also produces one who is the exact opposite. Thus Ezekiel Breghert, a London banker who nearly marries into the Longestaffes, a gentry family, is definitely Jewish and, Trollope tells us, 'He was an honest man' [79]. There are few of that species in this novel. To bring home his point, Trollope has one ignorant member of the Longestaffe family misquote the Bible in a crude attack upon Breghert. Disraeli, whom Trollope detested, was on the verge of becoming prime minister while Trollope was writing his novel and this probably contributed to some of the bitterness so evident in his description of Melmotte's career as a Conservative MP. To make his views perfectly clear, Trollope refers to the Conservative leader assisting Melmotte when he takes his seat in the Commons.

Trollope originally thought of the book as the 'Carbury novel' because it opens with the efforts of the dowager Lady Carbury, the widow of a baronet, to gain much-needed money through her writing. He planned to make her 'the chief character'. She and her two children, the despicable young baronet Sir Felix and the delightful Henrietta, provide several of the many love plots. Through Lady Carbury, Trollope developed aspects of the world of writers that he had dealt with in some of his short stories. She is dishonest, though not despicable, in the way in which she tries to persuade editors to 'puff' her book. In Trollope's notes for her he describes her as 'thoroughly unprincipled from want of knowledge of honesty' and in this she resembles Mrs Brumby, the chief character in the short story written three years earlier and named after her. It has recently been suggested that Trollope intended Lady Carbury as a portrait of Mrs Oliphant, but his notes give no trace of this and it seems highly unlikely.

We can also get some indication about the way in which he worked from other sections of Trollope's notes. The young roué, Sir Felix Carbury, had 'sold out' of the army, that is, he had sold his commission as an officer. Trollope knew little of military life, so he notes, 'enquire about this'. (The practice had been abolished in 1871.) For another world, that of editors, Trollope did not need to ask for information. Alfred Booker, editor of the *Literary Chronicle*, was based on a real figure, Alfred Shand, and the offices of another editor in the novel, Nicholas Broune, were based on the offices of the *Pall Mall Gazette*, which Trollope knew well [➤ Newspapers].

Trollope's notes also show that the two clerics in the book were based on real people. The tolerant Bishop Yeld was based on a recent Archbishop of Canterbury, 'old [Charles] Longley', who had died in 1868. Bishop Yeld seems to be one of those clerical characters inserted in Trollope's novels because he knew his readers expected one. Since his first novel, *The Macdermots of Ballycloran*, Catholic priests had been better treated than virtually any other group in his fiction. That is not the case here with Father Barham. It is not easy to see the reason for including Barham in *The Way We Live Now*, it may be because Trollope needed to vent his spleen on paper. Barham leaves an unpleasant feeling because he is based on a real character: in the notes he is described as 'Pervert. Waltham Priest.' (Interestingly, Trollope normally avoided the word 'pervert'. This was a term used by both High Churchmen and Evangelicals in retaliation for the equally inappropriate Catholic term 'convert', for those who left the Church of England for the Catholic Church [➤ *The Land-Leaguers*, 1].) Trollope had in mind Father George Bampfield, who had 'perverted' from the Church of England to become a zealous Catholic priest near the novelist's house [Mullen 560–61].

When a Catholic friend, Mary Holmes, objected to the portrait of Father Barham, Trollope replied and his letter provides one of the best insights into his own personality: 'The parish priest I knew myself, & loved, & opened my house to him, and fed him when he was fearfully, horribly, hungry from sheer want, – and he was a gentleman at all points; but I could not go on with him, not because he was intent on converting me, for which I did not care; but because he would say nasty things of my religion which could only be answered by nasty things as to his, which I could not say to any guest, or to any sincere Christian. But yet he was a man who will certainly go to heaven, if a mortal may presume to say so much of any man.' Trollope appears to have had Bampfield in mind in an earlier novel, *The Golden Lion of Granpère*, when he was praising a French priest for not having the fanatical zeal to convert all whom he met. A second reason for including Barham is because Trollope saw his 'unbearable' behaviour as yet another sign of the times: an abandonment of good manners in the interests of a rabid pursuit of a doctrinaire creed. Barham has also become an 'alien' from his own family by his fanatical attempts to convert them [16].

The 'hero' of the novel is the Suffolk squire, Roger Carbury, an example of the old-fashioned Tory Trollope liked so much. He expresses the central message of the book when he says that Melmotte would be 'too insignificant for you and me to talk of, were it not that his position is a sign of the degeneracy of the age'. He adds that 'they who do set the example go to his feasts'. The greatest feast – and one of the most memorable parts of the book – is Melmotte's reception for the visiting Emperor of China, for which all members of Society are frantic for invitations.

For this banquet Trollope drew on a real event which occurred six weeks after he began the novel when a real eastern despot, the Shah of Persia, visited England. A ball was given for the Shah by Albert Grant, MP, a fraudulent speculator who had many similarities with Melmotte. Born in Dublin of German-Jewish descent, Albert Gottheimer eventually acquired the title of Baron from the King of Italy. Baron Grant was heavily involved in the American silver mine company in Utah, mentioned earlier. Eventually his bankruptcy ruined thousands of small investors.

Trollope may have taken some characteristics of Grant for Melmotte, although Grant's financial disasters occurred after the novel was written. In recent years attention has turned from the attempt to find a progenitor of Melmotte to commenting on the remarkable parallels with a latter-day version. The mysterious death and financial collapse of Robert Maxwell in 1992 led to numerous articles showing his many similarities with Melmotte. There is, perhaps, no better example of how Trollope's superb insights into human nature remain valid more than a century after his death. However, we must remember that Trollope had long been suspicious of City speculators and of any get-rich-quick scheme. (This partly explains his dislike of mines.)

Trollope also had an opportunity to observe City financiers because, at the time he started to write *The Way We Live Now*, he began hunting with Baron Ferdinand de Rothschild, whose great hospitality extended to many 'City gents'. 'The baron' began to figure regularly in references to foxhunting in Trollope's later novels. Trollope liked Rothschild and Melmotte's character was in no way based on any of the baron's family; but he may well have studied some of the other City men at the hunt, and we know he always kept a notebook with him while he rode.

Trollope's attack on speculators was timely because 1872 marked the first time that the number of joint stock companies began to climb above a thousand: in the 1860s such companies had accounted for less than half that total. The nature of British enterprise was changing from the smaller, family firm to the larger, more impersonal company.

It was not only with Father Barham that Trollope settled a private 'grievance', to use one of his favourite words. In the account of Marie Melmotte's frustrated elopement [50], there is a reference to 'the gentlemen who spent all the public money without authority' when acquiring the private telegraph business for the Post Office. Two of Trollope's rivals in the Post Office, the minor novelist Edmund Yates, and another writer, Frank Scudamore, were involved in this malpractice, which sullied the high reputation hitherto enjoyed by the Post Office. It also forced the resignation of two of Trollope's old schoolmates from the Cabinet and nearly brought down the Gladstone government. This occurred as Trollope was writing his novel and was yet another sign of declining standards.

When Trollope was asked to write in Ferdinand de Rothschild's guest book a few weeks before he began *The Way We Live Now*, he composed a piece of doggerel in which he said that a short satire 'ill-natured sharp and sour' was beyond his power. No one could call *The Way We Live Now* short, but when it was published many, including his own brother, found it sharp and sour. However, *The Times*, which provided so much of the background information for it, was forthright in its praise of a book which was 'a likeness of the face which society wears to-day'. Yet Trollope's assessment in his *Autobiography* is true: he overdid the dark colours when he took 'the whip of the satirist' in his hands, as he had done in his other exposé of financial corruption, *The Struggles of Brown, Jones, and Robinson*. *The Way We Live Now* remains a great book, but it is not a good 'Trollopian' novel as it lacks that balance and fundamental optimism that marks his more characteristic works.

[➤ Clubs; Hotels; *The Three Clerks*.]

A Welcome: Original Contributions in Poetry and Prose. The welcome here is to Princess Alexandra of Denmark on the occasion of her wedding in March 1863 to the Prince of Wales, later King Edward VII. The collection was published by Emily Faithfull in March 1863. The format was patterned on that of Adelaide Procter's earlier *Victoria Regia*, to which Trollope had also contributed and which Emily Faithfull had also published. He contributed, without charge, 'Miss Ophelia Gledd'.

West Indies. See *The West Indies and the Spanish Main*.

The West Indies and the Spanish Main. Trollope's first travel book was written between 25 January and June 1859 while he was touring the West Indies and Central America for the Post Office. He left London on 16 November 1858 and returned on 3 July 1859. While he was in Jamaica he offered the book to Edward Chapman, and his brother Tom signed the agreement in his absence. The book was published by Chapman & Hall in one volume in October 1859. Trollope received £250.

Trollope wrote in his *Autobiography* that he regarded this as 'the best book that has come from my pen. It is short, and, I think I may venture to say, amusing, useful, and true.' It was, he said, his most 'readable' travel book. He began it aboard ship on his way from Jamaica to Cuba and the book opens with a description of his journey. There was no preparation and no notes. This may not have been the best way to write a book of information, he said, but his task was to give 'to the eye of the reader, and to his ear, that which the eye of the writer has seen and his ear heard'. Because of this one finds different opinions in different parts of the book.

Once in Central America Trollope had as little time for local officials of those nations that had broken away from Spain as he had for the Spanish colony of Cuba. In Costa Rica he descended a volcano and insisted on going further down than his friend, the diplomat Sir William Ouseley. He crossed from the Atlantic to the Pacific on a mule and then went on the Serapiqui River to the great lake of Nicaragua. He returned to England via Bermuda and New York, where he called in at Harpers to offer them rights to his book. He even had time for a short visit to Niagara Falls and Canada before returning to Ireland via Liverpool. At the end of his first travel book, Trollope announced that he hoped to write another about 'our children' in the United States [➤ *North America*].

Trollope's attitude to the places he saw was a mixed one. He visited a variety of islands but wrote most about Bermuda and Jamaica. In the latter he was delighted with the countryside, especially with Blue Mountain to whose top he climbed in order to see the sunrise (in fact the weather made this impossible). He was not as delighted with the people, whom he closely observed. He was speaking of the island when he wrote, 'There is nothing so melancholy as a country in its decadence, unless it be a people in their decadence' ['Miss Sarah Jack of Spanish Town, Jamaica']. He readily admits that the hot, humid weather, combined with the weariness of continual travel, did not help his temper. While late-twentieth-century tourists delight in 'unspoiled' societies, Victorians like Trollope found such places

'triste'. His devotion to work as the way to advance humanity was the basis for his criticism of the people's listlessness: 'These people are a servile race, fitted by nature for the hardest physical work...He *is* a man; and if you will, my brother; but he is the very idlest brother with which a hard-working workman was ever cursed.' The reference to brotherhood was a jibe at the English abolitionists' emblem, designed by Wedgwood, showing a kneeling black slave in chains with the motto 'Am I not a man and a brother?' running round the edge.

In Bermuda he was just as depressed but not as hostile: 'One cannot but feel it sad to see people neglecting the good things which are under their feet...there seemed to be no energy, no idea of going a-head.' His criticism was not based on race, because he admits that the black man '*is* a man; and if you will, my brother', but on the lack of a desire for progress. Part of the listlessness was, of course, due to Britain's adoption of free trade, which ruined the islands' economies, and to the economically unsettling results of the abolition of slavery twenty-five years before his visit. Trollope was always opposed to slavery, but he was not happy with most of the results of emancipation.

His vision of the islands' future was one in which the mixed races would come to dominate and displace the English. While in Jamaica he felt a limited black franchise could work but by the time he had left the Caribbean for Central America he had changed his view. Throughout the book he is at war with 'philanthropists' who believed that emancipation would immediately solve every problem

[➤ Utopian]. He had a special dislike for Harriet Beecher Stowe, author of *Uncle Tom's Cabin*, and for the 'Duchess'. This was the Duchess of Sutherland who was Mrs Stowe's fawning hostess during her 1853 visit to London. (In this he agreed with the views of both Dickens and Thackeray, and his duchess may be compared to Dickens's Mrs Jellaby in *Bleak House* and Thackeray's Lady Sheepshanks in *Vanity Fair*.) Not surprisingly, Thomas Carlyle, the great hater of 'do-gooders', thoroughly liked the book. When he and Trollope met later they got on well; obviously Carlyle had never read *The Warden*. Trollope was also praised in the High Church, Tory magazine, the *Saturday Review*, as well as in the *Spectator*. However, Robert Browning, who later became his friend, told his wife that the book 'exceeds in slovenliness any clever man's production within my experience'.

Of greater importance to Trollope was the reaction of *The Times*: they printed three news articles praising the book. These were probably written by Mowbray Morris, the paper's manager and brother-in-law of the editor, John Delane. Morris was the son of an English planter in the West Indies and, like Trollope, had no time for London's 'philanthropists'. In his *Autobiography* Trollope remembered that 'by that criticism I was much raised in my position as an author'. With this book Trollope had finally won that recognition as a serious writer on serious matters, something for which he always longed. In 1860 there was an American edition by Harpers; by 1869 the book had had six editions in England. There was also an immediate benefit: 'I at once went to Chapman & Hall and success-fully demanded £600 for my next novel.' (For his last novel, *The Bertrams*, he had only received £400.)

He used his transatlantic journey and his time in the West Indies and Central America in four short stories: 'Miss Sarah Jack of Spanish Town, Jamaica'; 'Aaron Trow'; 'Returning Home'; 'The Journey to Panama'.

[➤ Post Office; Travels..]

Whist. A popular card game in Trollope's time, whist occurs in many of the novels, particularly the later ones. It receives most attention in *Mr Scarborough's Family* as the game through which Mountjoy Scarborough loses a fortune. In *Is He Popenjoy?* Trollope makes a private joke when he says that the once jaunty Captain De Baron has married, put on weight and 'has taken to playing whist at his club before dinner for shilling points' [64].

Trollope had inherited his devotion to the game from both his parents, particularly his father. During the 1870s, when he lived in London, Trollope played whist at the Garrick Club most afternoons. There is a print showing him at a whist table with the well-known politician, W. E. Forster, and the well-informed political essayist, Abraham Hayward. It is likely that he got many helpful details for the Palliser novels during these whist games [Mullen, 487–8, 588–9]. Trollope also wrote an amusing and anonymous article, 'Whist at our Club', for *Blackwood's Magazine* (May 1877). In this he referred to the game as the 'delight' that 'makes easy the passage to the grave'. In his *Australia and New Zealand* he admitted that for him 'whist is a jealous mistress'. Nevertheless he criticized men like Maurice Maule in *Phineas Redux* [21] who devoted virtually their whole lives to the game. Far worse were those who used gambling at cards to win money, such as Lord Percival in *The Duke's Children*. In *Mr Scarborough's Family* he shows that the game was not confined to old men: Mountjoy Scarborough, who almost loses his inheritance because of gambling at whist, is a young man. In *The Prime Minister* [40, 72] Trollope employs terms from whist when he describes the fate of two characters.

Other card games are sometimes played, such as Pope Joan [*The Last Chronicle of Barset*, 17] and bezique [*Ralph the Heir*, 55]. One of the many reasons why Trollope disliked Evangelicals was their frequent denunciation of card games as a 'sin'. This is nicely illustrated in the Barsetshire novels. In *The Warden* [6], Archdeacon Grantly and three other clergymen play merrily at whist and even quote Scripture facetiously to describe a move. However, in *The Last Chronicle of Barset* [47] Mrs Proudie is horrified to hear that whist was once played in the episcopal palace, and Mrs Grantly admits that public attitudes have changed towards things like card games, with gambling, in a bishop's palace. What was once acceptable is no longer so. The contrast between these two episodes and the opinions expressed are good examples of how Trollope reflected carefully on his characters' behaviour and also of how he rounded off the final novel in the Barsetshire series with constant references to the earlier volumes.

Whitehall Review. Trollope's connection with the magazine dates from 1878 when he sold Chapman & Hall the rights to *An Eye for an Eye*. They then sold the serialization rights to the magazine, in which the story appeared between August 1878 and February 1879.

'Why Frau Frohmann Raised Her Prices'. Trollope wrote this short story in 1876 for Norman Macleod, the editor of *Good Words*. He wrote it to be published in two parts and for his setting used the Tyrol in Austria, which he and his wife Rose had visited several times. In the event the story was 'stretched', as Trollope put it, over four issues: February to May 1877. In 1882, it was included in his fifth collection of short stories, *Why Frau Frohmann Raised Her Prices and Other Stories*. When discussing the re-publication with his publisher, William Isbister, Trollope remarked that it 'is a good story, though I say it who ought not'. Trollope benefited from the 'stretching' because he got £175 for the story. His surviving records show that this was the largest amount he ever received for a short story.

Frau Frohmann is the landlady of the Peacock Inn near Innsbruck. A debate is taking place on the need to raise charges as the inn is losing money: Frau Frohmann, her son Peter and her parish priest, who is one of her two advisers, are opposed; the Frau's solicitor, Fritz Schlessen, and her daughter Amalia are in favour. (It was quite a regular feature for Trollope to include a priest in continental works set in hotels, for example in 'La Mère Bauche' and *The Golden Lion of Granpère*). As a staunch 'Tory' Frau Frohmann is opposed to change, but likes to provide the best. The landlady refuses either to raise her charges or to reduce the quality of her 'establishment'. This is partly due to pride and partly to a dislike of the idea of charging tourists more and villagers less. Amalia, who is in love with Fritz Schlessen, fears that her mother will not be able to afford her dowry. The Frau forces her suppliers to lower their costs but this angers her neighbours. Her employees and suppliers begin to leave. The inn's reputation starts to decline. Finally Frau Frohmann agrees to increase her charges. As a result Amalia and Fritz are married.

The story opens with a little essay on one of Trollope's favourite themes, the conflict between a 'Tory' (traditionalist) opposition to change and a liberal presumption of it. Although an Austrian Catholic, Frau Frohmann is an embodiment of 'Tory' values to Trollope: a hatred of change; a love of paternal power to be used to benefit others; a distrust of education; a belief in fair dealing. In the end she yields, as Tories always do. The story may be read as a parable of the nineteenth century: conservative, old, Catholic and unchanging versus liberal, new, Protestant and progressive. It is the (presumably) Protestant English guest, Mr Cartwright (in many ways a self-portrait of Trollope), who brings the world of change, the English world, into her Austrian inn. It is he who tries in vain to make her understand the relationship of gold and silver to inflationary forces.

This story also develops another Trollopian theme: the opposition of a strong-willed woman to change and, for a time, to her daughter's marriage. He attacked anti-Popery in a magazine largely read by people from an anti-Catholic tradition, when he referred to Frau Frohmann, already established as a thoroughly 'good' woman as 'no better than a Papist'. After Trollope's death, his widow Rose and her niece spent much time in Tyrolean hotels where they could have full board for less than six shillings a day.

Why Frau Frohmann Raised Her Prices and Other Stories. Trollope's fifth and last collection of short stories was published in one volume by William Isbister in December 1882. The five stories were originally published between 1876 and 1878. The contents, with the dates and places of original publication, are: 'Christmas at Thompson Hall' (*Graphic*, Christmas issue, 1876); 'The Telegraph Girl' (*Good Cheer*, Christmas, 1877); 'Why Frau Frohmann Raised Her Prices' (*Good Words*, February–May 1877); 'The Lady of Launay' (*Light*, Belles Lettres section, 6 April–11 May 1878); 'Alice Dugdale' (*Good Cheer*, 1878). Trollope thought 'Frau Frohmann . . .' the best of the five stories. He received £150 for the book but would already have been paid for individual stories. [➤ Christmas Stories.]

Widows. Widows play a considerable part in Trollope's fiction, beginning with Mrs Mary Kelly in *The Kellys and the O'Kellys*. Perhaps his most famous is *The Small House at Allington*'s Mrs Mary Dale who, like her forerunner Mrs Bell in 'The Courtship of Susan Bell', jealously guards her daughters from the 'wolves' who try to court them. In *Rachel Ray*, Mrs Ray is an English version of the American Mrs Bell. All three women are widows who subjugate their own lives to the good of their daughters. So too does Mrs Woodward in *The Three Clerks*, Signora Pepé in 'The Last Austrian Who Left Venice' and Mrs O'Hara in *An Eye for an Eye*. Sometimes widows are pitiable creatures surrounded by overbearing daughters, like the dowager Marchioness of Brotherton in *Is He Popenjoy?* Not all widows are so self-effacing: Madame Max Goesler, Madeline Neroni (if she is a widow) in *Barchester Towers* and Arabella Greenow in *Can You Forgive Her?* might be called 'merry widows'. In 'The Château of Prince Polignac' Frances Thompson, a widow, presents an example of English common-sense to her ardent French lover. Sometimes widowhood is the punishment meted out to women who marry for money or position: this is the plight of Lady Ongar in *The Claverings*, Lady Laura Kennedy and Lady Eustace.

In the nineteenth century there was a widely held prejudice that widows should not re-marry and few of Trollope's widows violate this custom. Exceptions include Eleanor Bold, Lady Eustace, Madame Max Goesler, Lady Harcourt in *The Bertrams* and Emily Lopez in *The Prime Minister*. Such marriages are usually quiet affairs or 'off-stage', and in the case of Emily Lopez and Lady Harcourt they are rewards from their creator because they have suffered enough with their first husbands. When marriage is a possibility it often is because the widow in question has money, like Eleanor Bold, Madame Max Goesler or Lady Eustace, and is therefore pursued by fortune-hunters. Some widows are alluring and dangerous to know, for instance Winifred Hurtle in *The Way We Live Now*, while others, like Mrs Ray, suffer because they come under the domination of religious zealots like the Evangelicals Trollope so disliked Sometimes widows act as fairy-godmothers in bestowing wealth to allow marriages otherwise impossible,

as Madame Max Goesler does. Sometimes they become autocratic women who dominate much or all of a story or novel: Mrs Winterfield in *The Belton Estate*; Mrs Miles in 'The Lady of Launay'; the Countess Lovel in *Lady Anna*; Mrs O'Hara in *An Eye for an Eye*, Madame Bauche in 'La Mère Bauche'; Lady Lufton in *Framley Parsonage*; Frau Frohmann in 'Why Frau Frohmann Raised Her Prices'; and Lady Mason in *Orley Farm*.

Trollope had great sympathy for widows and felt that the view which required them to live a life of constant mourning was wrong and cruel. Prolonged withdrawal from life was unnatural, as he wrote in *Barchester Towers*: 'How much kinder is God to us than we are willing to be to ourselves! . . . How seldom does such grief endure! How blessed is the goodness which forbids it to do so!' [2]. The hypocrisy such a situation can create is shown through Lady Ongar in *The Claverings*. The short story 'The Widow's Mite' in fact has nothing to do with widowhood.

Widowers feature less frequently in Trollope's fiction. However, both his first novel and the novel he was writing when he died featured widowers: Larry Macdermot in *The Macdermots of Ballycloran* and Philip Jones in *The Land-Leaguers*. His widowers, like his widows, come in all types, from the saintly Septimus Harding in *The Warden* to the notorious John Scarborough in *Mr Scarborough's Family*. In *The Duke's Children*, *Ralph the Heir*, *Orley Farm* and *Mr Scarborough's Family*, widowers play central roles. Sometimes they are rather played-out men, like Bernard Amedroz in *The Belton Estate*, Philip Jones in *The Land-Leaguers*, Zachary Fay in *Marion Fay* and Mr

Brown in *The Struggles of Brown, Jones, and Robinson*. Occasionally widowers are known or suspected of having led lives less than chaste in their widowhood, men like Sir Lionel Bertram in *The Bertrams*. Seldom are they lovers: three exceptions are John Ball in *Miss Mackenzie*, Maurice Maule, who tries his hand with Madame Max Goesler in *Phineas Redux*, and Sir Peregrine, who loves Lady Mason. When a widower re-marries he normally comes with a large number of children: John Ball has nine, while in *Mr Scarborough's Family* the Reverend Mr Matterson has five and £150 a year. It is rare for husbands to become widowers in the course of a novel or short story. Notable exceptions are the Duke of Omnium in *The Duke's Children* and Bishop Proudie in *The Last Chronicle of Barset*. Two comic widowers appear in 'The Two Heroines of Plumplington'.

'The Widow's Mite'. This short story was written between 1 and 8 December 1862. Trollope was approached by Alexander Strahan for a Christmas story for *Good Words*, to be published in January 1863. The editor, the Reverend Norman Macleod, suggested as a title 'Out of Work', to tie in with the 'cotton famine': the cotton essential for Lancashire's mills was not being imported from America due to her Civil War, and much suffering and unemployment resulted. Various appeals were launched to help the sufferers. Trollope, who knew the limits of his own skills, rejected the suggested setting because it would mean a story told by a mill operative and Trollope wrote, 'I do not think I could manage this. But the line of the story shall be of the same nature – if possible.' [➤ Working Class.] The title comes from

St Mark 12:41–44. The story was later re-published in his third collection of short stories, *Lotta Schmidt and Other Stories*. Trollope received £100.

The story is set during a weekend in 1862 in a parsonage in rural Cheshire, near the distressed manufacturing areas. The vicar and his family discuss the nature of charity and the suffering allegedly involved in the Gospel story; they also work tirelessly to help the distressed workers and do without to give to the poor. Living with them is the vicar's wife's niece, Nora Field, who is to marry an American, Frederic Franklin Frew, who supports the North while the vicar favours the South. The family discuss the widow with her two mites (one farthing) and Nora agonizes about spending so much on her trousseau ('very nearly twenty pounds altogether'). Her desire for a personal sacrifice is opposed by almost all her family and her fiancé but she carries her point. After her wedding Nora doubts if her action was what she meant it to be, because there was no real suffering: 'It is not easy to be a widow with two mites.'

The discussion of Anglo-American marriages brings to light the difficulties facing an English bride. The story also illustrates Trollope's keen patriotism and his support of the Northern cause in the American Civil War, also to be seen in *Dr Wortle's School*, 'The Journey to Panama' and 'The Two Generals'.

Wills. Wills occur with some frequency in Trollope's novels. The most memorable are in *Mr Scarborough's Family*, *Sir Harry Hotspur of Humblethwaite*, *Orley Farm* and *Cousin Henry*, in which Trollope actually used part of his own will [➤ Bland, Florence].

There is much speculation among relatives about the wills of wealthy people like Mrs Winterfield in *The Belton Estate* or old Mr Bertram in *The Bertrams*. Wills also provided a way in which Trollope could allow a favourite character, for instance John Eames or Phineas Finn, to come into money through a legacy. However, some people were strangely unhappy when they inherited a great deal in a will: both Madame Max Goesler and Lady Laura Kennedy were in this position in *Phineas Redux*. There could also be considerable legal wrangling about the terms of a will, as in *The Eustace Diamonds*.

[➤ Deaths and Death Scenes; Entails.]

Wilson, Legge. A scholarly Cabinet minister who appears in most of the Palliser novels as well as in *The Way We Live Now*.

Wine. Wine was one of Trollope's great pleasures. He often used it in his fiction to point to a character's personality: it sometimes indicates either meanness or pretension. It is hardly surprising that Mrs Proudie serves 'curates and country vicars' cheap Marsala at 20*s.* a dozen at her grand reception [*Barchester Towers*, 10], or that another hostess combines meanness and pretension by trying to make a bottle of champagne do among too many guests [*Miss Mackenzie*, 8].

Men are often particularly proud of the port they serve their guests [*The Claverings*, 8] and clergymen seem to have a particular devotion to it. They cite its vintage with a reverence as great as that given to Scripture [*The Last Chronicle of Barset*, 22]. Trollope's own favourite wine was a claret,

Château Léoville 1864, which, he informed readers, 'I regard as the most divine of nectars' [*Ayala's Angel*, 5]. He paid 72*s.* for a case and on one occasion laid down twenty-four cases, mainly as a present for his son Henry. Trollope liked to buy wine at a discount, which some of his publishers – George Smith, for instance – could arrange. He predicted a good future for Australian wines in his *Australia and New Zealand*. He was critical about aspects of the wine trade in one of his articles for the *Pall Mall Gazette*.

[➤ 'Alice Dugdale'; Drinks; Food; 'Gladstone Wine'; *London Tradesmen*.]

Witnesses. Trollope generally showed great sympathy towards witnesses in trials because he believed they were badly treated: they were people 'entitled to the greatest respect' [*Orley Farm*, 75]. It might appear that his oft-stated view came from his own experience in 1849 when he was a witness in a case in which a popular postmistress was accused by him of stealing money from the Post Office [Mullen, 229–32]. However, he had earlier expressed sympathy for an 'unfortunate' witness in *The Macdermots of Ballycloran* [28], and his account of the way in which a man was treated in a cross-examination by a rough barrister was actually quoted against him when he appeared in the court in 1849. Witnesses are often treated harshly in his court-room scenes, particularly by the fearsome barrister Chaffanbrass. In at least one case, that of Carry Brattle's torture at the hands of a 'burly barrister' in *The Vicar of Bullhampton* [69], the barrister's badgering backfires. Such mistreatment of witnesses was one factor in Trollope's low regard for lawyers. The most amusing, though not particularly sympathetic, portrayal of a witness is in *Phineas Redux*, in which Chaffanbrass destroys the testimony of Lord Fawn and engages in a literary dialogue with the novelist, Mr Bouncer.

Wives. See Marriage.

Women. The range of women in Trollope's fiction extends from that child of nature, Mahala Tringlos in 'Malachi's Cove', to the haughty Society figure, Griselda, Marchioness of Hartletop; from the saintly Marion Fay in the novel named after her to the malicious Sophie Gordeloup in *The Claverings*; from the exotic Signora Madeline Neroni in *Barchester Towers* to the humdrum Florence Burton in *The Claverings*; from the overbearing Mrs Proudie to the humble Fanny Brattle in *The Vicar of Bullhampton*; from the redoubtable Martha Dunstable to the forgettable Mary Horton in 'Not If I Know It'; from the fiendish Mrs Brumby in the short story of that name to the ill-used Anty Lynch in *The Kellys and the O'Kellys*.

Trollope was himself the son of a fascinating woman and many of his most important characteristics may be traced to her. He was happily married to a woman with a personality strong enough and stable enough to stand up to his own exuberance and he had a *de facto* daughter in his niece, Florence Bland. He was part of the inner circle of his century's most esteemed female novelist, George Eliot. He knew that the bulk of his readership was female and he bore this in mind when writing. He was genuinely concerned with the changing status of women that the nineteenth century was effecting and was prepared to help

in expanding the opportunities open to women of all classes. He encouraged women writers [see below]; advocated greater educational opportunities for women [➤ Lectures]; worked in an organization, the Post Office, that employed women; helped women like Emily Faithfull; continuously denounced what he saw as excessive rules about mourning and widowhood because they cut women off from active life; and took part in a campaign to limit the hours of work of women shop-workers [➤ Working Class].

He admitted in 'Alice Dugdale' that 'though turned the hill of middle life', he had 'still an eye for female charms'. When Mr Jones is asked in 'A Ride across Palestine' if he dislikes women, his reply reflects much of his creator's views: 'No, by Jove! I am never really happy unless one is near me, – or more than one ... But I always like those best who are most helpless.' His portrayal of spinsters and of strong-minded women shows that Mr Jones's reference to 'helpless' women did not reflect the totality of his creator's view. His infatuation with Kate Field – a far from 'helpless' woman – influenced hiis short story, 'Mary Gresley'.

It was Trollope's high regard for women that led to his defence of 'chivalry' as a 'spirit [that] has taught men to endure in order that women may be at their ease; and has generally taught women to accept the ease bestowed on them with grace and thankfulness' [*North America*]. This high regard underlay his frequent 'sermons' advising young women or 'girls' to be careful about quizzing their lovers too much ['Alice Dugdale'], about being too flirtatious ['Miss Sarah Jack of Spanish Town, Jamaica'], about preferring an idealized lover to real men despite their foibles [*Ayala's Angel*], about agreeing to a proposal too quickly as Florence Burton did in *The Claverings*, or about fancying a false martyrdom – 'philomartyrdom' as Trollope called it – in 'The Mistletoe Bough'. His novels also emphasized that men were seldom heroic and that what a woman should look for was manliness above all things.

In choosing a husband Trollope warned young women against following the course of Mary Scatcherd [*Doctor Thorne*] or Kate O'Hara [*An Eye for an Eye*] and yielding to a man's sexual entreaties before marriage. On the other hand, a woman's strength lay within herself, not in triumphing over men. When talking of Lily Dale he referred to 'that sense of security which women should receive from an unconscious dependence on their own mingled purity and weakness' [*The Small House at Allington*, 6]. He attacked Mrs Proudie, not because she was naturally stronger than her husband but because she exercised her strength in public.

In his works women are often at their hardest with other women, for example in *Rachel Ray* or *An Old Man's Love*. One of the reasons he so disliked Evangelicals was that he felt they talked down to women. While he disliked feminism as a Utopian theory, he helped women he knew to get ahead and urged society to expand the opportunities open to women. Many of his women lament having no choice but marriage [*The Bertrams*, 10] and he described the plight of such women in numerous novels, and with great sympathy in his short story, 'The Journey to Panama'. While acting on their behalf in this way and while accepting that 'in intellectual capacity' women were equal to men, he always argued

that 'The necessity of the supremacy of man is as certain to me as the eternity of the soul. There are other matters on which one fights as on subjects which are in doubt, – universal suffrage, ballot, public education, and the like – but not, as I think, on these two.' While he felt that marriage was the natural state for women even more than for men, he also had a great sympathy for unmarried women [➤ Spinsters]. His description of the habits, speech, thoughts and dress of young women was praised in his own time as unequalled. [➤ Girls; Mothers and Daughters.]

Trollope's language reflected his attitudes towards women. In 'The Panjandrum', probably written in 1869, he described the debates of a committee choosing a title for a new magazine. They thought of calling it 'The Man's Magazine' but someone points out that this might mean it 'was not adapted for the perusal of females'. Trollope adds, 'We meant the word "man" in the great generic sense; – but the somewhat obtuse outside world would not have so taken it.' However, in the same decade in which this story was written, he began making more frequent use of 'men and women' rather than the more traditional 'men'.

In his descriptions of the hundreds of women who people his fiction certain characteristics and types, and certain themes, emerge. These will be mentioned alphabetically.

Autocratic or strong-minded women. Trollope's fiction is filled with strong-minded women who are usually either middle-aged or elderly. Often they are spinsters but just as often they are mothers, like Mrs Sarah Mountjoy in *Mr Scarborough's Family*, Lady Ball in

Miss Mackenzie or Lady Aylmer in *The Belton Estate.* Sometimes they are women who are forced to be the breadwinner, like the nasty Mrs Brumby in the short story named after her. On other occasions they are women like Martha Dunstable with a 'fortune' that gives them an independence unusual in the Victorian age.

Beauty. Any reading of Trollope's prose shows that he was greatly attracted by female beauty. Those women, like Madeline Neroni in *Barchester Towers,* whose beauty is perfect tend to be dangerous. The same is true with men like Burgo Fitzgerald. Usually his beautiful women have at least one flaw, however slight, to make them more human. In *The Bertrams* he refused to describe his heroine, Adela Gauntlet: 'Let each reader make what he will of her ... and endow her with any amount of divine beauty'[41]. It was an experiment he did not quickly repeat because he manifestly enjoyed describing beautiful women. He loved to describe a woman's hair and attacked those who wore false hair or wigs, like Lady Ongar in *The Claverings.* He wrote pages on women's teeth, lips, eyes, noses, complexions, voices, walks, heights, bosoms, feet and hands. He described the shape of their dresses and the materials that were used to make them with great care, although in 'The Château of Prince Polignac' he said some very hard things about English dress design when compared with French.

Breast-feeding. Trollope entered the unending debate over breast-feeding in 1858 with the publication of *Doctor Thorne,* in which he sneered at Lady Arabella Gresham (née De Courcy) for not doing so. 'Nature gives them

bosoms for show, but not for use'[2]. He returned to the subject in *He Knew He Was Right* [81] and was attacked for vulgarity.

Brown complexion. When discussing a girl's complexion, Trollope frequently calls her 'brown'. Fanny Brattle in *The Vicar of Bullhampton,* Alice Dugdale in the short story of that name, Lucy Graham in 'The Telegraph Girl', Ophelia Gledd in the short story named after her and Lucy Robarts in *Framley Parsonage* spring to mind. By 'brown' he means a complexion that is not pale or 'ladylike'. 'Brown' usually also signifies a darker hair colour. For Trollope, a darker complexion and dark hair were signs of good health and, normally, of stronger character.

Comparisons with other nations. Because of Trollope's extensive travels he was better equipped than any other Victorian writer to compare English women, their personalities and upbringing, with women from other nations and parts of the United Kingdom or the 'English world'. He analyses Victorian customs regarding the upbringing of girls, and compares it with stricter rules in Europe and more relaxed rules in America. He liked to contrast English and American women. [➤ Anglo-American Marriages, as well as the various works listed under America.] He contrasted English women with Arabic, in *The Bertrams;* with Australian, in *Harry Heathcote of Gangoil* and *John Caldigate;* with Austrian, in 'Lotta Schmidt' and 'Why Frau Frohmann Raised Her Prices'; with Czech, in *Nina Balatka;* with French, in 'La Mère Bauche', *The Claverings* and *The Golden Lion of Granpère;* with German, in 'The House of Heine Brothers in Munich' and *Linda*

Tressel; with Irish, in *The Macdermots of Ballycloran*, *The Kellys and the O'Kellys*, 'The O'Conors of Castle Conor', 'Father Giles of Ballymoy', *Castle Richmond*, *Phineas Finn*, *An Eye for an Eye* and *The Land-Leaguers*; with Italian, in 'The Last Austrian Who Left Venice' and *Is He Popenjoy?*; with New Zealand, in *The Fixed Period* (in the form of Britannulists) and 'Catherine Carmichael'; with Spanish, in 'John Bull on the Guadalquivir'; with Jewish, in *The Way We Live Now* and *The Bertrams*; with Welsh, in *Cousin Henry*; with West Indian settlers, in 'Aaron Trow' and 'Miss Sarah Jack of Spanish Town, Jamaica'.

'Double standards'.   Trollope makes discreet allusions to mistresses maintained by several of his male characters, but Victorian readers would have been horrified if his women had been permitted lovers. The closest he gets to this is Lady Glencora Palliser's near elopement with Burgo Fitzgerald in *Can You Forgive Her?* Trollope's young women evidently accept this double standard, although they rarely actually say so. However, a young lady in *Sir Harry Hotspur of Humblethwaite* states that young men are different. On her view, Trollope comments: 'And then is it not the fact that some little amount of shade in the fleece of male sheep is considered, if not absolutely desirable, at any rate quite pardonable?'[5].

'Fallen women'. Trollope first included the plight of a young woman who had been seduced in the character of Feemy Macdermot in his first novel, *The Macdermots of Ballycloran*. He next treated the subject in *Doctor Thorne* (1858) with Mary Scatcherd. She was more fortunate than Feemy and survived the birth of her child. Despite

her fall, Trollope wrote that 'she should, in a distant land, be the worthy wife of a good husband, and the happy mother of many children'[2]. He returned to the topic in *The Vicar of Bullhampton* with Carry Brattle, and in *An Eye for an Eye* with Kate O'Hara. His 'sermon' was threefold: 'respectable' women should concern themselves with those who had 'fallen' in order to help them; while social ostracism was necessary to prevent others from 'falling', unending punishment was too severe for the 'crime' committed; and some women who had 'fallen' were shown to be capable of leading perfectly respectable and worthwhile lives. It is interesting that all four women were seduced. In this same vein Trollope urged compassion for Mrs Askerton in *The Belton Estate*. She had run away from a cruel husband to live with another man who married her when her husband died [➤ Divorce].

Love. Trollope had no doubt that the nature of a woman's love differed inherently from that of a man's. In *Is He Popenjoy?* Trollope tells his reader that it is part of a woman's loving nature to forgive: 'Then, and not till then, he is her equal; and equality is necessary for comfortable love' [32]. In *Mr Scarborough's Family*, Florence Mountjoy tells her lover, Harry Annesley, 'A man's heart can be changed, but not a woman's. His love is but one thing among many' [61]. To the assertion that a man 'can love but one woman' Trollope answers in an 'authorial intrusion', 'So you say, and are so convinced, but no conviction was ever more false ... A man, though he may love many, should be devoted only to one' [*The Claverings*, 28]. Lily Dale cannot bring herself to accept the love offered by John Eames because she had given her own to Adolphus Crosbie. In *Sir Harry Hotspur of Humblethwaite*, Emily Hotspur goes with her parents to Europe to die of a broken heart because she accepts that she can never marry her debauched cousin. George Eliot rather acidly commented, 'Men are fond of that sort of dog-like attachment.' But this is not always the case and Trollope allows some female, as well as male, exceptions: when Clara Amedroz jilts Captain Aylmer in *The Belton Estate* she is quite capable of transferring her love to her cousin, Will Belton. When Trollope tried to write a sympathetic portrait of a spinster without a love story he gave up the task as impossible [➤ *Miss Mackenzie*].

Old Women. Most of the old women in Trollope's fiction are fascinating characters, for instance Miss Marrable in *The Vicar of Bullhampton*, or Sarah Jack in the short story named after her, or Monica Thorne in the Barsetshire novels. They have weathered the storms of life and come out the stronger, or at least the more interesting. Generally they tend to be spinsters but can as easily be widows [➤ Dowagers]. Sometimes, however, their age has embittered them and enables them to do much harm to younger people, especially younger women. In *Miss Mackenzie* Lady Ball tries to browbeat Margaret Mackenzie into marrying her son and Trollope comments, 'It is astonishing the harm that an old woman may do when she goes well to work and when she believes she can prevail by means of her own peculiar eloquence' [7].

Religious women. While Trollope's most famous religious woman remains Mrs Proudie, his fiction is filled with women who are zealous for religion. Occasionally, as with the unmarried sisters of Lord George Germain, they are High Church, but usually they are Evangelicals, like Letty Fitzgerald in *Castle Richmond*. Often his female zealots are at their nastiest with other, sometimes younger, women. One thinks here of Rachel's sister in *Rachel Ray*, Mrs Winterfield in *The Belton Estate* and Mrs Stumfold in *Miss Mackenzie*. [➤ Religion.]

Working women. See Working Class.

Writers. While the portraits he paints of novelists – Lady Carbury, for example, in *The Way We Live Now*, or Mrs Brumby in the short story of that name – are far from flattering, Trollope was keen to advance the careers of women writers. In 'Mrs Brumby' he wrote of the few opportunities open to women: 'Fortunately for us and for the world at large ... the port of literature is open to women. It seems to be the only really desirable harbour to which a female captain can steer her vessel with much hope of success.' Some of his best short stories concern women who write, or try to write, stories like 'Mary Gresley' or 'Josephine de Montmorenci'. [➤ Eliot, George; Writers.]

Work. Work to Trollope was part of the natural order, the basis of civilization and a moral virtue. In *The New Zealander* he refers to 'labour' as 'the great necessity of our lives' and this was true of his own after he had got over his hobbledehoy days in London. Once he arrived in Ireland, he developed a tremendous capacity for hard work which lasted until his death. He was very single-minded, worked quickly and passionately, and had a love of order. His brother Tom wrote of him: 'Work to him was a necessity and a satisfaction. He used often to say he envied me the capacity for being idle.' Trollope had little tolerance for anyone who did not work, whether they were former slaves in the West Indies, minor 'squireens' in Ireland, Society's 'curled darlings' or Zulu warriors. His male characters, unless retired, tend to work if truly noble, although if part of the landed classes they do not have to work for a living. In a lecture on the Zulus he said, 'The natural, I may say, the only happy condition of a man is to work for his living.' As a good Victorian he felt that work was the basis for a nation's and an empire's greatness. When visiting South Africa he wrote: 'Who can doubt but that work is the great civilizer of the world – work and the growing desire for those good things which work only will bring.'

Workhouse. The Victorian workhouse dated from the 1834 Poor Law and quickly got a reputation for harshness and misery as a place to which the destitute poor, the sick and the elderly were sent to live in prison-like austerity. (Trollope's mother was one of the first to attack them in her novel, *Jessie Phillips: a Tale of the Present Day*.) In *The Claverings* Sophie Gordeloup, who has a low opinion of English life, points to a workhouse as that 'black building' and calls it 'Little England' as part of her attack on 'this accursed country'. Trollope did not refute her charges in defence of the building that 'fronts so gloomily upon Mount Street' [46]. In *Australia and New Zealand* Trollope spoke favourably of the

'Benevolent Asylums' in Melbourne in contrast with English workhouses.

In Trollope's life his dislike was enhanced by personal experience. In the mid-1830s, when Trollope was a Post Office clerk in London, he had lodgings on Northumberland Street, off the Marylebone Road and opposite the Marylebone workhouse in which about 1,500 impoverished people, mainly worn-out servants, lived. For him the Marylebone Workhouse became a symbol of poverty and degradation that he never forgot. In *Orley Farm* he recalled 'dirty lodgings . . . somewhere near the Marylebone workhouse' [49] and in *Phineas Redux* Mrs and Miss Meager live opposite 'the deadest part of the dead wall of the Marylebone workhouse' [56]. Almost thirty years after he lived opposite the workhouse he referred to it in his short story, 'The Panjandrum', but by then the bitterness seemed to have disappeared and there is no denunciation.

Working Class. Working-class characters do not play a large role in Trollope's novels, although they do figure more often in his short stories. His attitude was summed up when an editor suggested he write a story with the title 'Out of Work' about the thousands of mill-hands in Lancashire who were laid off because of the lack of cotton from America [➤ 'The Widow's Mite']. He said he could not write such a short story.

If he did not feel competent to depict industrial working-class life he did feel more at home with rural society [➤ *The New Zealander*]. He gave his most considered attention to working people in the story of Sam and Carry Brattle in *The Vicar of Bull-*

hampton and showed that he could handle such characters. He never patronized or glorified them, and he wrote in this novel: 'Among the rich there is that difficulty of the needle's eye; among the poor there is the difficulty of the hardness of their lives' [5]. His portrait of all the members of the Brattle family, especially of the old miller and his wife, 'one of those loving, patient, self-denying, almost heavenly human beings', neither patronizes nor glorifies.

In *The Warden* the bedesmen are all old working men and are shown to be rather gullible, while Bunce, their leader, is a noble character. In *The Last Chronicle of Barset* he describes with great sensitivity the plight of the poor brick-makers in Josiah Crawley's parish. Normally, however, working people are servants or farm labourers, and his Irish novels are peopled with working men. Several of his short stories are almost totally concerned with the plight of working people and some in particular with working women. 'The Telegraph Girl' shows the limited range of opportunities open to a young working-class girl on her own. 'Malachi's Cove' deals with the struggle for existence of a young woman on the Cornish coast. 'Catherine Carmichael' tells the story of a gold-miner's daughter in New Zealand, forced into a marriage because she has no other choice open to her. 'Lotta Schmidt' describes the much happier fate of a working woman in Vienna.

The depths of urban poverty and degradation, and the role played by drunkenness, are described in 'The Spotted Dog', and 'The Adventures of Fred Pickering' tells the sad story of an ambitious young man from the provinces who fails to succeed as a writer in London.

Writers. Writers appear in a variety of guises in Trollope's novels and short stories. Among the first to appear are Dickens and Carlyle, whom Trollope attacked in *The Warden*. In *The Bertrams* George Bertram publishes a controversial theological work but never becomes a writer in the proper sense. There are amusing portrayals of two pretentious poetesses, 'the American Browning' in *He Knew He Was Right* and Ugolina Neverbend in *The Three Clerks*. The latter also deals with Charley Tudor's work as a novelist. In *Phineas Redux* another novelist, Mr Bouncer, is forced into a weak defence of novelists when he is a witness at a murder trial [61]. Writers, however, can be intimidating and one duchess is 'rather afraid' of Mrs Conway Sparkes, 'a literary lady', in *Can You Forgive Her?* [23].

Lady Carbury, one of the central characters in *The Way We Live Now*, is a popular author, whose main skill lies in manipulating reviewers to 'puff' her ill-researched books. In *Mr Scarborough's Family* Mr Quaverdale takes to writing to earn a living because he has quarrelled with his father and lost an income; in *John Caldigate* old Mr Caldigate lived by his writing until he inherited an estate. There are clergymen who dabble in writing, like the Vicar of Bullhampton who 'did a little in the way of light literature on social subjects' in the novel named after him [68], and of course Mr Harding in *The Warden* spent a great deal of his income in subsidising his book of church music. Sir Thomas Underwood in *Ralph the Heir* is a superb example of a man who finds innumerable excuses to avoid starting a book he wants to write. In 'Mrs General Talboys' the slightly bohemian group of Englishmen and Americans who live in Rome include one writer, the American 'literary lion' Conrad Mackinnon, who in several ways resembles Trollope himself. In 'Miss Ophelia Gledd' the Englishman who wins Ophelia for his wife is 'a literary man of some mark'.

Trollope, who spent a great deal of his time working for a charity, the Royal Literary Fund, that helped writers and who was generous in privately helping authors, was well aware that few achieved the prosperity which he himself knew. He depicted the less appealing side of writing in 'The Adventures of Fred Pickering' and in six stories he published in *Saint Pauls* in 1869–70. These were later republished as *An Editor's Tales*. The importance of writing to women who wished to, or had to, earn their own living is discussed in 'Mrs Brumby', 'Josephine de Montmorenci' and 'Mary Gresley'. The *Autobiography* and *Thackeray* also contain many reflections on writers and the art of writing. He argued in his *Commentaries of Caesar* that because of the demand for long books and the requirements of serialization, Victorian writers 'rarely give ourselves time for condensation'.

[➤ *Autobiography*; Copyright; Editors; Journalists; Newspapers; *The New Zealander*; Novel, The; 'Three-deckers'; Women (for women writers).]

Y

Yorkshire. Yorkshire is the location for those scenes in the Palliser novels set at Matching. There are also scenes in Yorkshire in *Orley Farm*, *The Belton Estate* [17], and *Lady Anna* with its descriptions of the Wharfedale countryside round Bolton Abbey [15]. 'Christmas Day at Kirkby Cottage' is also set in Yorkshire. Since the election at Percycross in *Ralph the Heir* is based on Trollope's own unhappy experiences as a parliamentary candidate at Beverley, that novel has a connection with the East Riding. There is a good example of Yorkshire dialect in *The Bertrams* when one of the characters visits a lonely country house on the borders of Yorkshire and Westmorland. In *Orley Farm* Mr Kantwise refers to the county's legendary care in monetary matters when speaking of Mrs Mason, in whose 'persevering sharpness she beats all that I ever met with, even in Yorkshire' [9].

Trollope had a personal connection with the county because his wife Rose and his niece Florence Bland were from the West Riding: this may provide the basis for the dialogue in *The Bertrams* [43] and *Ralph the Heir* [20], and explain the occasional use of words in narration, such as 'shandy' to describe a girl in *An Old Man's Love* [6]. Dialect dictionaries say this term was Yorkshire dialect in the nineteenth century. Rose's background may also explain a statement in 'Miss Ophelia Gledd' that 'at different periods of my life I have learned to love an Irish brogue and a northern burr'.

Z

Zulus. Trollope's connection with the Zulus began in 1865 when he wrote an article about a meeting of the London Society for Promoting Christianity Amongst the Jews for the *Pall Mall Gazette.* This was supposed to be one of a series of articles on London's 'May Meetings' or annual gatherings of various religious and charitable bodies, widely covered by newspapers. He wrote under the guise of a visiting Zulu convert to honour the controversial Bishop Colenso, the great friend of the Zulus and translator of the Bible into their language. The guise also gave him a common-sense viewpoint from which to continue his long war against Evangelicals as this was an Evangelical society. He hated the experience and in his article an Evangelical clergyman is seen patronizing women by refusing to discuss theological doubts before them. To this the Zulu reporter says, 'Now, Mr Editor, let me tell you that Zulu women would not stand such a treatment as that. In what we believe and what we don't believe our women go along with us.' The article also shows Trollope's distaste for the way in which this Evangelical group made a public display of its Jewish converts.

When he visited South Africa in 1877 he met several Zulu chiefs who donned trousers for the occasion. Trollope had a higher hope for the Zulus than for other natives because of the attitudes he encountered: 'That love of money which we observe so often is the parent of all industry will be so with the Zulu.' Meeting Zulus affected his views towards South Africa, with its black majority. He wanted equality for them before the law and knew that 'the progress to be most desired is that which will quickest induce the Kafir to put off his savagery and live after the manner of his white brethren'. On his return to England he gave at least three lectures on the Zulus.

[➤ Colenso, Rt Rev. John William; Imperialism; Lectures; Religion; *South Africa*; Work.]